JAPAN'S NEW ORDER IN EAST ASIA

ITS RISE AND FALL
1937–45

JAPAN'S NEW ORDER IN EAST ASIA

ITS RISE AND FALL
1937-45

BY

F. C. JONES

M.A. (Bristol); PH.D. (Harvard)
Reader in History, University of Bristol

Issued under the joint auspices of the
Royal Institute of International Affairs
and the Institute of Pacific Relations

OXFORD UNIVERSITY PRESS

LONDON NEW YORK TORONTO

1954

Oxford University Press, Amen House, London E.C.4

GLASGOW NEW YORK TORONTO MELBOURNE WELLINGTON
BOMBAY CALCUTTA MADRAS KARACHI CAPE TOWN IBADAN

Geoffrey Cumberlege, Publisher to the University

————

PRINTED IN GREAT BRITAIN

PREFACE

THIS book recounts Japan's attempt to secure the hegemony of Eastern Asia, and her ultimate catastrophic failure. The documentary materials for the fateful years, 1937–45, are at present incomplete. It is in particular regrettable that no Foreign Office archives are available, apart from what will appear, up to September 1939, in forthcoming volumes of the *Documents on British Foreign Policy 1919–1939*. No doubt, as the issues involved are far from dead, it is in the national interest that it should be so and the historian cannot complain, even though it means that for evidence of British policy he must depend largely upon American or Japanese sources. There is little original material from China or from the Soviet Union, or, under existing circumstances, likely to be. One curious result of this is that the vanquished can tell their story more fully than the conquerors, in consequence of the war crimes trials and the enforced opening of the German and Japanese archives, or of what remained of them after air raids and deliberate burnings.

One principal source consists of the vast mass of material accumulated in the course of the sittings of the International Military Tribunal for the Far East. I have used the complete collection in the Treasure Room of the Harvard Law Library at Langdell Hall. This material, in mimeographed form, includes the Record of the Proceedings of the Court; the numerous Exhibits of the Prosecution and the Defence; the majority Judgment; the partially dissenting opinions of the French and Netherlands Members of the Tribunal and the completely dissenting Judgment of the Indian Member. It in addition includes the preliminary interrogations, which are important, both because they were made before the trials opened and the accused had the aid of counsel and also because they extended to persons who were not subsequently brought to trial. There are, in addition, a number of documents, prepared either by the prosecution or the defence, which were rejected as evidence in Court, not because the material in them was untrustworthy, but because they were held to be irrelevant to the particular point at issue. For example, Japanese consular reports on Communist activities in China were rejected as evidence in defence, because these were held not to justify the Japanese attack upon China.

The *Saionji–Harada Memoirs*, which were begun in 1929 and continued down to Prince Saionji's death in the autumn of 1940, deserve a word of explanation. Prince Saionji, the last of the Genro, or Elder Statesmen, entrusted his secretary and confidant, Baron Kumao Harada, with the task of compiling periodic reports on current political, military, and diplomatic events. Harada enlisted the aid of Viscountess Konoye, Prince Konoye's sister-in-law. As she explained to the IMTFE, Harada would at varying times dictate to her what he had learned from talks with various personages, she would take down what he said in shorthand and then render it into Japanese. It would afterwards be taken to Saionji who occasionally made corrections in it, either of what he had said himself, or of something he believed had been wrongly rendered. Then Viscountess Konoye would re-write it accordingly. No doubt in this process something would get lost or garbled; also Harada picked up a good deal of gossip and rumour. Thus the *Memoirs* can be used only with caution, but they are, as they were meant to be, a useful check on evidence from military sources or from others close to the Army. Excerpts from the *Memoirs* are scattered through the Record, but the full *Memoirs* are together in Nos. 56 and 57 of the bound volumes of the Exhibits.

I am deeply indebted to the Rockefeller Foundation, Division of Humanities, for a grant for research in the United States during 1950–1, and to the Fulbright Organization for a trans-Atlantic travel grant. I am glad, too, to take this opportunity of thanking Mr. Pulling, Director of the Law Library of Harvard, and his assistants in the Treasure Room, for permission to work there and for their aid in using the mass of IMTFE materials. I am equally grateful to Mr. W. L. Holland, for putting the resources of the I.P.R. Library in New York at my disposal; to Dr. Edwin Beal, Jr., head of the Japanese section of the Division of Orientalia, Library of Congress, and to Mr. Cecil Hobbs, of the South Asia Section; to Professor Claude Buss, of Stanford University, and to the officials of the Hoover Library; as also to Mr. C. C. Brett, of the University of Washington, who allowed me to see his unpublished thesis on 'Japanese Rule in Malaya, 1942–45'.

Sir Robert Craigie was kind enough to read the chapters dealing with the period 1937 to the outbreak of the Pacific War and to make many valuable suggestions and criticisms, for which I am very grateful to him. I have also to thank Miss H. Oliver, of Chatham House, for checking and consolidating the numerous references to meet the requirements of the Oxford University Press.

For the opinions expressed, particularly in the concluding chapter, I am alone responsible.

F. C. JONES

BRISTOL
September 1953

CONTENTS

ABBREVIATIONS
USED IN FOOTNOTES AND TEXT

(After the first full citation, all publications are referred to in an abbreviated form. Those not included in this list may be found in the Bibliography)

CSM   *Christian Science Monitor.*

Churchill, *Second World War*, i–v   W. S. Churchill, *The Second World War*, vols. i–v (London, Cassell, 1948–52).

Ciano, *Diary*   Galeazzo Ciano, *Diario 1939* (–1943), 4th ed. (Milan, Rizzoli, 1947), trs. as *Ciano's Diary 1939–43*, ed. Malcolm Muggeridge (London, Heinemann, 1947).

D Brit. FP   *Documents on British Foreign Policy, 1919–39*, ed. E. L. Woodward and R. Butler, 3rd series, vols. i–iv, 1938–9 (London, 1949–51).

FEQ   *Far Eastern Quarterly.*

D Ger. FP   *Documents on German Foreign Policy, 1918–45, from the Archives of the German Foreign Ministry*, published jointly by the US Dept. of State and the British Foreign Office, Series D (1937–45).

GFM   German Foreign Ministry.

Goebbels Diaries   Josef Goebbels, *The Goebbels Diaries*, trs. and ed. by L. P. Lochner (London, Hamilton, 1948).

Hull, *Memoirs*, i, ii   *The Memoirs of Cordell Hull*, 2 vols. (London, Hodder & Stoughton, 1948).

IMTFE   International Military Tribunal, Far East, Tokyo, 1946–8: *Record of Proceedings, Exhibits, Judgment, Dissenting Judgments, Preliminary Interrogations, Miscellaneous Documents* (in mimeographed form).

IMT Nuremberg   *Trial of the Major War Criminals before the International Military Tribunal*, Nuremberg, 1945–6. Proceedings and Documents in evidence. 42 vols. (Nuremberg, 1947–9).

JFM   Japanese Foreign Ministry.

Japan 1931–41   US Dept. of State, *Foreign Relations of the United States: Japan, 1931–41*, 2 vols. (Washington, 1946).

Konoye Memoirs   In US Congress, Joint Committee on the Investigation of the Pearl Harbor Attack, *Hearings*, pt. 20 (Washington, 1946).

Korean Aid Hearings US House of Representatives, Committee on Foreign Affairs, *Korean Aid Hearings*, 81st Congress, 1st session, June 8–23, 1949 (Washington, 1949).

NCA   *Nazi Conspiracy and Aggression* (A collection of documentary evidence and guide materials prepared by the American and British prosecuting staffs for . . . the International Military Tribunal at Nürnberg). 8 vols. with 'Opinion and Judgment' and supplements A and B. (Washington, 1946–7).

Nazi-Soviet Relations US Dept. of State, *Nazi-Soviet Relations, 1939–41: Documents from the Archives of the German Foreign Office*, ed. R. J. Sontag and J. S. Beddie (Washington, 1948).

NYT   *New York Times.*

Pearl Harbor Attack US Congress, Joint Committee on the Investigation of the Pearl Harbor Attack, *Hearings,* 39 pts. (Washington, 1946).

Pearl Harbor Attack: Report of Joint Committee (This report was issued separately from the above).

RIIA, *Documents* *Documents on International Affairs* (London, Oxford University Press for Royal Institute of International Affairs, 1929–; in progress).

RIIA, *Survey* *Survey of International Affairs* (London, Oxford University Press for Royal Institute of International Affairs, 1925–; in progress).

Saionji–Harada Memoirs (These memoirs are included in the IMTFE *Exhibits*).

SCAP, *Political Reorientation of Japan* Supreme Commander for the Allied Powers, Government Section, *The Political Reorientation of Japan, September 1945 to September 1948* (Washington, 1950; the Appendices are bound separately).

Statement of de Weerd: Statement of Klaas A. de Weerd, IMTFE, *Exhibit* 1351 (see p. 371, n. 2).

Surrender of Italy, Germany and Japan U.S. Senate, *Surrender of Italy, Germany and Japan, World War II: instruments of surrender, public papers and addresses of the President and of the Supreme Commanders . . . October 4, 1945* (Washington, 1946; Senate document no. 93).

USSBS   United States Strategic Bombing Survey.

USOSS   United States Office of Strategic Services, Research and Analysis Branch.

Weizsäcker, *Memoirs* Ernst von Weizsäcker, *Memoirs,* trs. by John Andrews (London, Gollancz, 1951).

Welles, *Seven Decisions* Sumner Welles, *Seven Decisions that Shaped History* (New York, Harper, 1950); Eng. edition: *Seven Major Decisions* (London, Hamilton, 1951).

NOTE

British Parliamentary Debates (Hansard) are cited in the form suggested in the bound volumes of the official records, 'H C Deb.' (Commons) and 'H L Deb.' (Lords). All Commons Debates are those of the fifth series.

CHAPTER I

Japan Challenges the Old Order

IN 1937 the nations of the West still retained that political, military, and economic predominance which they had built up in Asia during the nineteenth century. India, Ceylon, Burma, and Malaya were British possessions, and the Indian Ocean was a British lake. India was the keystone of the edifice of British power in this region. In this respect Britain's ability to raise armies in India was even more important than her financial and commercial stake there, in an age when the British Commonwealth was faced by hostile forces in Europe, the Middle East, and the Far East. While the Indian Army was kept at moderate size in peacetime, in both world wars large forces were raised and employed mainly in the defence of the British position in the Middle East.[1]

Most of South East Asia was divided between the colonial empires of Great Britain, the Netherlands, France, the United States, and Portugal. Their possession of these vast territories, rich in such vital raw materials as tin and rubber, was an important factor in the economies of Britain, the Netherlands and, to a lesser degree, of France, in assisting them to redress their adverse balance of trade with the United States. Even Siam, the one independent political entity in this region, was, in financial and economic matters, largely dependent upon the British Empire, despite the growing importance of Japan in some aspects of Siamese foreign trade and the pro-Japanese leanings of certain members of the largely military oligarchy which had ruled Siam since 1932.

While the colonial Powers derived important advantages from their dependent areas, they all provided two benefits of which the value to all classes of the population are apt to be overlooked or taken for granted, until they have disappeared. The Western colonial Powers maintained peace and order through the media of normally small and relatively inexpensive defence and police

---

[1] During 1914–18 the Government of India recruited on a voluntary basis over a million men, combatant and non-combatant. Some 1·2 million served overseas, chiefly in the Middle East (*Cambridge History of India*, vi. 401). During 1939–45 2·25 million troops were raised in India, and were of vital importance in the Middle Eastern and the Burmese campaigns (*Indian and Pakistan Year Book*, 1949, p. 175).

establishments. Each of them ruled over a congeries of peoples who differed in antecedents, in religion, and in the stage of social and cultural development. In general, making allowance for variations, they maintained an equitable balance between these through the instrumentality of honest and efficient administrations.

The special rights and privileges of the Western Powers in China, which comprised certain leased territories; foreign-administered Concessions and Settlements in the treaty ports, foreign navigational rights in coastal and inland waters, and foreign extraterritorial jurisdiction, gave China a status sometimes stigmatized as semi-colonial. The Kuomintang régime had succeeded in removing or modifying some of these servitudes and had not lost sight of its objective of securing the eventual relinquishment of them all. But the split between the Chinese Communists and the Kuomintang, with consequent civil war, combined with the rising Japanese menace to make the Chinese National Government increasingly dependent upon the goodwill of the Western Powers. Consequently the 'rights recovery movement' lost something of its immediacy after 1931.

In general, therefore, the Western position in China and in South East Asia, while obviously menaced by the rising tide of nationalism in those regions, appeared unlikely to be vitally impaired by it in the immediate future. The Communist threat, too, seemed less crucial than in the stormy years which followed the end of the First World War. This was in part because of the débâcle of Communism in China in 1927–8, in part because of Comintern 'united front' policies, in face of the danger to the USSR from a militant Germany and Japan.

The imminent challenge to the 'Old Order in Eastern Asia' arose from the resurgence of militarism and expansionism in Japan. There was a marked dichotomy in Japan's relation to Asia, which in large measure accounted for the recurring internal conflicts and compromises over foreign policy up to Pearl Harbour. On the one hand Japan was an imperial Power with a colonial empire of her own and a participant in the special rights of the Treaty Powers in China. Thus she was a member of the 'club' of privileged nations in the Far East. Japan had won this position with the support and approval of Great Britain and the United States at the time when she was embattled against Imperial Russia. The older generation of her statesmen looked back with regret to the days of the Anglo-Japanese Alliance, which had been in a sense a formal recognition of Japan's status as the one non-Occidental Great Power. Furthermore, the insular position of Japan combined with the strong national consciousness of her people and the officially fostered belief in the divine origins and unique excellence of her imperial polity to set her apart from the rest of Asia, and to imbue her people with a conviction of their innate superiority to other Asiatics.

On the other hand, the Japanese *are* Asiatics, conscious of their cultural indebtedness to the Asiatic mainland peoples, the Chinese in particular, their attitude to whom was in consequence a curious mixture of arrogance and deference. Japan, too, had been subjected to the treaty port and extraterritorial system, from which she had emancipated herself only after thirty years of diplomatic struggle. Her assiduous copying of the West, especially in military and industrial technique, had been stimulated in the main by fears of invasion and conquest by one or more of the Western Powers. In later years she had been at one with the rest of Asia in her demand for the recognition of racial equality and in her resentment at the barriers to Asiatic immigration imposed by the United States and the British dominions.

Since 1920 this sense of kinship with the rest of East Asia had been strengthened by the abrogation of the Anglo-Japanese Alliance, by the American Immigration Act of 1924, and through the gradually deepening rift between Japan and her former allies and friends. In the early thirties this trend was greatly accentuated by the great depression and its aftermath of increasing trade barriers, by the Manchurian controversy, with consequent Japanese withdrawal from the League of Nations, and by the breakdown of the Washington Conference agreements of 1921–2. All these events increased the Japanese sense of isolation and insecurity, conscious as they were of the great inferiority of their economic resources to those of the United States, the British Commonwealth, and the USSR.

But Japan could not easily emerge as the champion of Asiatic freedom and independence. Her victory over Russia in 1904–5 had sent a thrill of anticipation throughout the Asiatic continent and had greatly stimulated nationalist movements in India, China, and in Asia generally. But her record of continental expansion since that time had caused her to be largely regarded, not as the leader and light of Asia, but as the latest and worst of the imperialist Powers. This was especially true of China, and Japan in consequence had cause to apprehend danger for herself should the rising sense of national feeling in that vast country ever bring about effective political unity and military strength. Therefore Japan could not rely on Asiatic goodwill to ensure her the markets and raw materials which she needed to free herself from her economic dependence upon the United States and the British Commonwealth. Only if the Japanese underwent a radical change of heart, abandoned their dreams of hegemony over East Asia and progressively relinquished the fruits of former conquests might they be accepted as leaders of Asiatic emancipation. But, with few exceptions, this was more than a proud and emotional people could contemplate. What the Japanese really wanted was the consent of the Western Maritime Powers to their hegemony in East Asia, and only when it was clear that this would not be forthcoming did the pan-Asiatic note become at all dominant.[1]

The quarrel among the expansionist groups in Japan over foreign policy, therefore, was one of means rather than of ends, of expediency, not of morality. In the crucial year 1941 it became a contest between those who would throw down the gage of battle to the United States rather than abandon their Chinese conquests and those who in the last resort were prepared to adopt a policy of *reculer pour mieux sauter*, as had been done in 1895. It was this latter group who, when defeat became apparent, worked to secure surrender rather than national suicide and who were successful in preserving the imperial institution from the wreck.

But the quarrel was none the less real, the more so because it was inextricably connected with the internal struggle for prestige and power. The main element in this struggle was the effort of the Army to regain for itself that pre-eminence in the shaping of national policy which it had enjoyed, especially during the period 1894–1918, and which it had appeared to be losing during the nineteen-twenties. Then there had occurred one of those short-lived enthusiasms for the latest foreign fashions which occasionally

[1] This came out, amusingly enough, even in Japanese propaganda to Asiatic peoples during the war. Thus, for example, an editorial in the *Shonan Times* of 25 Feb. 1942 declared that although Japan had contributed much to the success of the Allied cause during the First World War, afterwards she found herself opposed by Great Britain and the United States 'and it was then that Nippon realized that her own advancement lay in collaboration and co-operation with the countries of East Asia and not with the Anglo-American combination.'

sweep Japan. The defeat of the Central Powers in 1918 was popularly regarded in Japan, as elsewhere, as a victory for democracy and for internationalism. The failure of the Siberian expedition and the check to Japan's continental ambitions administered at the Washington Conference were other factors which combined to dim the prestige of the Army and to expose it to neglect and even to insult. General Araki in February 1946 gave his interrogators a graphic description of the state of affairs which prevailed when he was a divisional commander. The Army, he said, lacked modern machine-guns and had no tanks, aircraft, gas masks, or wireless equipment; in these respects it had fallen behind European armies. In such limited manœuvres as were possible the soldiers practised with paper models of aeroplanes stuck on bamboo poles and rattled sticks to imitate machine-guns. Their clothing was shabby and they sometimes carried out bayonet exercises barefooted to save their boots. Their food and fuel were scanty and their barracks often infested with vermin. The officers were in little better plight and they found it almost impossible to live on their meagre salaries. People looked down on the soldiers and sometimes abused them when riding on the crowded tram-cars saying that the spurs on their boots were a nuisance.[1] This portrayal, by a man awaiting trial for his part in promoting the expansionist 'young officers' movement, may be overdrawn in details, but is essentially borne out from other sources.[2]

Since the defeat of Japan her Army and especially the Army officers have been denounced, both in the West and by Japanese civilians anxious to cultivate the good graces of the victors, as a crew of irresponsible fanatics who led their country to ruin. This view has the merit of simplicity, but contributes little to a real

[1] Araki, 'The Domestic and Foreign Situation and the Movements of Young Officers since the End of World War I until the Showa Era', IMTFE, *Defence Document* 674.

[2] 'It was adding insult to injury when the public began to look down upon the army as a superfluous, if not a parasitical, element of society in a peaceful world. The best brains of the nation went to the universities and turned to careers in business and industry, while the military and naval academies were barely able to fill their quotas. It became impossible for them to attract the cream of the nation's crop into the military profession. Times were such that even young women showed preference in matrimony for civilians, and particularly those in a business or industry with a future. In the mid-twenties the prestige of the military had reached the lowest point, for officers on active service preferred to don mufti when off duty rather than to be conspicuous in their uniforms to become the object of pity or silent ridicule' (By permission from Chitose Yanaga, *Japan since Perry* (New York, McGraw Hill, 1949), pp. 508-9).

understanding of why the Army officers felt and acted as they did. Now (in 1952) it appears that the time is not far off when Japan will again have an Army. It may be well, therefore, to try and grasp the outlook of men who, ruthless as they were towards their opponents at home and abroad, were prodigal of their own lives in what they conceived to be a righteous cause.

In so far as the Japanese officer was patriotic, devoted to his profession, ready in peacetime to serve his country for a pittance compared with the rewards obtainable in a business career, and to lay down his life for her in time of war, he but exhibited the qualities expected by all countries of their officer class. It is therefore absurd to condemn in the Japanese officer traits which are honoured in those of one's own country and still more absurd to applaud or condemn them according to which side Japan happens to be on in a war.

Nor was the Japanese officer unique in regarding peace as but an interlude between wars in the perpetual struggle for power among the nations and in cursing the folly of Governments which starved the Army in time of peace only to rue it bitterly when war came. Across the water he saw that Japan had two vast countries as neighbours, one of them, Soviet Russia, inimical to everybody and slowly recovering her giant's strength; the other, China, still weak and wracked by civil wars, but endeavouring, by trade boycott and other means, to wrest from Japan the position, especially in Manchuria, which his forebears had secured at the cost of much blood and sacrifice. His remedy for this was what most soldiers would have recommended in the circumstances.

He was even more bitter over what appeared to him to be the disastrous trend of social and economic developments at home. During the nineteen-twenties power seemed to be passing from the former predominantly military oligarchy to party politicians dependent upon a majority in the Diet. But the two major parties, the Seiyukai and the Minseito, had very close and often scandalous connexions with the great business houses—the Mitsui, Mitsubishi, Sumitomo, and Yasuda, who between them dominated most of Japanese industry and commerce. Japan consequently seemed to be developing into an urbanized plutocracy, to the detriment of the agrarian community. This was anathema to the younger generation of Japanese officers, who were in the main drawn from the ranks of the smaller landowners, and the men under them predominantly from the peasantry. They felt that the cities exercised an unfair predominance over the economic life of the countryside and that urban financial and industrial groups rigged both taxes and prices against the agriculturalist. Furthermore no relief in this matter could be looked for from Tokyo where, so the average Japanese officer felt, there existed an unholy alliance between the Zaibatsu, the court officials, and even some of his own seniors, to depress and despise the farmers.

He was equally antipathetic to the social and intellectual consequences of urbanization. He feared that the concept of the Japanese nation as one vast family united in common loyalty and devotion to the Emperor was breaking down in the face of growing inequalities of fortune and giving place to what he considered pernicious Western doctrines of individualism and of class strife. The old simplicity and refinement was passing and manners and morals declining before these corrosive foreign influences. Unless these insidious dangers were met and overcome, the achievements of the Meiji era would be undermined and Japan, torn by faction, be again in peril from abroad.

In these strictures upon the evils of the times, the Japanese officer would have found many sympathizers among his compeers in other countries passing through the stresses and strains of the post-war era. Like them, too, he tended to attach overmuch importance to surface phenomena and to underestimate the strength of the cohesive forces in society, especially the depth of patriotic feeling. But, swayed as he was by his fears and prejudices, he had some reason for apprehending that the unchecked play of discordant opinions might have fatally decisive consequences to a highly emotional people with a heritage of centuries of internal strife.

Indeed, the Japanese officer himself was to a marked degree a product of these feudal influences. He was brought up in fanatical loyalty and obedience to the imperial dynasty, the symbol of unity and stability. But, despite the injunction in the Emperor Meiji's Rescript to the Army to regard an order from a superior as equivalent to an order from the Emperor himself, there was a latent tendency for the officers to regard themselves, like the feudal vassals, as a body of equals under the Throne, so that the junior officer, while obedient to his superior in strictly military matters, was inclined to consider himself entitled to an independent voice in questions affecting the national welfare. Hence the phenomenon, so difficult to understand by peoples with armies of a longer professional tradition and more detached from politics, of the 'young officer' in Japan, obedient to the death on the battlefield, yet ready at times to turn his sword against his superiors in some political or doctrinal quarrel. Hence also the tendency, very marked in the Japanese-occupied regions, for jealousies and rivalries to grow up between the headquarters of different Japanese armies and for each to pursue its own semi-independent policy.

But it was in his attitude to the civil authorities that the Japanese officer exhibited the most striking contrast to his fellow in countries where the military had long been subordinate to the civil rule. In Japan the tradition had been the opposite for over a thousand years, and, in consequence, the Army regarded itself as the rightful arbiter of the national policy and as certainly entitled to the final voice in all matters which affected the national security. The organization of a national conscript army and the establishment of a Constitution made little difference in this respect. The operational plans of the armed forces and the execution of those plans in time of war belonged to the function of supreme command, which was exercised by the Emperor upon the advice of his chiefs of the General Staff, who were solely responsible to him, had the right of direct access to him, and were independent of the Cabinet. This practice, although not written into the Constitution of 1889, was accepted by its framers and had never hitherto been questioned.[1] In time of war Imperial Headquarters were established; these consisted of the General Staffs of the Army and the Navy. Such liaison as there was between them and the Cabinet was provided by the two Service Ministries, and, in particular, by the Directors of the Military and the Naval Affairs Bureaux within the War and the Navy Ministries. These officers came to have an importance in the framing of policy out of all proportion to their nominal position, a recurrent phenomenon in Japanese history.

By Article 12 of the Constitution, the Emperor also determined the peacetime strength of the armed forces. But he did nothing without advice and the Constitution was silent as to whose advice he should take in this matter. The services, however, had a powerful weapon at their disposal in this respect through the

[1] T. Takeuchi, *War and Diplomacy in the Japanese Empire* (New York, Doubleday, Doran, 1935), pp. 14–15.

practice whereby only generals and admirals on the active list could be selected to head the Ministry of War and that of the Navy. This custom, although not set forth in the Constitution, was nevertheless approved by Prince Ito as necessary to preserve the prerogatives of the supreme command, and to keep the armed forces clear of the vicissitudes of party politics.[1] It was legalized by Imperial Ordinance in 1900, thanks to the efforts of Field-Marshal Yamagata.[2] Since officers on active service were under military discipline they could be prevented from accepting office or forced to resign after they had done so. But this was a weapon to use sparingly, since otherwise it would make civil government impossible and provoke antipathy to the services. The Army received a lesson in this respect in 1913 when, after having brought about the downfall of the Saionji Ministry, it was compelled to accede to an alteration of the active service rule to permit the selection of retired officers if necessary.[3] These, especially if they had contracted any political or business affiliations, could not be so effectively controlled. Although in fact the Service Ministers continued to be drawn from the active list, it is significant that there was no more Cabinet wrecking by this means until 1936 when the Army succeeded in getting the Service Ministries once more restricted by Imperial Ordinance to officers on the active list.[4]

Normally the Army did not push matters to such extremes and the defence estimates were arrived at by discussion and compromise between the military and the civilian elements in the Government. In the period 1918–30 the latter seemed to be gaining the ascendancy, thanks to the prevalent pacifist sentiment and to the growing strength of the political parties. In 1922 and again in 1925 the Army was forced to consent to retrenchment programmes which reduced its peacetime strength by four divisions.[5] At the same time financial provision for the modernization of its equipment was postponed. In 1930 the Japanese standing Army totalled some 250,000 men, organized into 17 divisions and 4 independent brigades.[6] This was by no means an unduly large force in view of Japan's position in Korea, Formosa, and the

[1] ibid. p. 29 n.
[2] Yanaga, *Japan Since Perry*, p. 121.
[3] ibid. p. 525. A quarrel between Army and Navy leaders facilitated this change (Takeuchi, *War and Diplomacy*, pp. 14–15).
[4] Yanaga, *Japan Since Perry*, pp. 525–6.
[5] M. D. Kennedy, *The Problem of Japan* (London, Nisbet, 1935), pp. 61–62.
[6] IMTFE, *Record*, p. 9074.

Kwantung Leased Territory. Added to these responsibilities were the uncertain situation in China and the recrudescence of Soviet military power in the Far East. This last was exhibited by the swift and successful Russian military intervention in northern Manchuria in 1929, an action which, while in one way not unwelcome to Japan, also aroused disquiet in the minds of her Army chiefs.[1] In May 1931 the 'Big Three' of the Army, the War Minister, the Chief of the General Staff, and the Inspector-General of Military Education, declared that no further reductions in military expenditure were possible and emphasized the need for modernizing much of the Army's equipment.[2]

The uncompromising stand of the Army chiefs was a sign that they were not prepared to submit tamely to the sort of thing that the Navy had undergone in the previous year. At that time Mr. Hamaguchi, the Premier and leader of the Minseito Party, had upheld the London Naval Treaty, in which the Japanese Government had accepted a lower ratio of cruiser strength than that declared by the Naval General Staff to be essential to the national security. With the backing of the last surviving elder statesman, Prince Saionji and of the Court officials, the Premier had been unshaken by the resignation of the Chief of the Naval Staff and had secured the ratification of the Treaty by the Privy Council. At the same time he had avoided as far as possible the delicate question of the extent of the prerogative of supreme command, so as not to provoke the Army, which otherwise could not interfere openly in a purely naval question. But in press and periodical articles Professor Minobe and other jurists were more outspoken in declaring that the power to decide the strength of the armed forces was a matter for Cabinet decision and that the advice of the military and naval authorities was not binding upon it.[3] Professor Minobe also held the view that the Emperor exercised the functions of supreme command by virtue of his position as Commander-in-Chief, as distinct from that of Head of the State. As the latter was the superior position, that implied the complete subordination of the military to the civil authority. This is in accordance with theory and practice in Western constitutional States, but it was not the intention of the framers of the Japanese Constitution, nor, as has been seen, was it in line with Japanese traditions. To the Japanese

---

[1] Kennedy, *Problem of Japan*, pp. 78–79.
[2] Takeuchi, *War and Diplomacy*, p. 343.   [3] ibid. pp. 283–336.

officer it appeared as a baneful revolutionary concept which, if accepted, would jeopardize his career by placing him at the mercy of party politicians, who were already demanding further sweeping reductions in military expenditure in view of the prevalent industrial and commercial crisis. Japan would then become outwardly a parliamentary democracy, but in reality a plutocratic oligarchy, to the detriment of the soldier and the farmer, and the further enrichment of the financier, the industrialist, and the merchant.

In their virulent opposition to any such development the new generation of Japanese officers found allies from forces both old and new in the national experience. The strength of traditional authoritarian ideas remained very great outside of the major cities and expressed itself in demands for the preservation of Kodo, 'the Imperial Way', an adaptation of the Chinese Confucian concept of 'Wang Tao' or the 'royal road'. The essence of this was the concept of a benevolent autocrat ruling over a loyal and obedient people. To this in Japan was added the idea of the blood kinship of the whole Japanese people, conceived as one great family, of which the divinely founded Imperial House was the head. Such beliefs had been carefully fostered by the founders of the Meiji Restoration as a means of preserving and solidifying national unity, and inculcated through the national educational system and the cult of State Shinto. They had by these means hoped to preserve the traditional patterns of Japanese society, while at the same time bringing about the essential modernization in her industrial and commercial structure. But the growth of large-scale industry, with its concomitant of urban expansion, inevitably vitiated this attempted synthesis, and appeared to threaten the breakdown of social cohesion and to herald the rise of class division and conflict.

How could this be prevented? The Japanese officer himself was as a rule too inarticulate to do more than repeat the maxims on which he had been reared and to denounce the dangerous trends of the era. He therefore drew inspiration from civilian theorists for any kind of reasoned alternative. The younger infantry officers were profoundly influenced by the theories of Ikki Kita, Seikyo Gondo, and Kosaburo Tachibana. These were at one in asserting that agriculture was the foundation of Japanese society and industry but a parasitic growth upon it. Kita, in his *Outline for the Reconstruction of Japan*, which first appeared in 1919, advocated a measure of State and municipal land ownership, together with limitations on private fortunes and private estates.[1] Gondo and Tachibana were opposed to the government of the rural areas through a bureaucracy directed from Tokyo. They wanted a decentralized administration, and the development of local autonomous communities of small owner-farmers, organized on a co-operative basis. They wished to call a halt to the growth of factory industry and large cities, and to return to a predominantly agrarian economy, with local small industry and handicrafts. In this way, they thought, Japan could avoid the ills which were afflicting Western society and they were fierce in their denunciation of the Zaibatsu and their allies, the party politicians.[2] They hoped to cure the ills of the rural community through a reduction of tax burdens, and of tenant farming through the abolition of absentee landlordism. For the solution of over-population they looked to colonial expansion, especially in Manchuria.

These doctrines gave the Japanese officer what he was looking for, a theoretical justification of his opposition to the forces which he felt were undermining all that he believed in and threatening his own livelihood. They thus obtained a wide prevalence, especially among the junior officers. But the impracticality of any return to pre-Meiji conditions if Japan were to provide for her growing population and to develop an effective war potential was not lost among the senior ranks of the Army, and especially among the staff officers, who formed, in Japan as elsewhere, always something of a separate caste.

Among these, as also among a section of the bureaucracy, the intellectuals, and even some of the politicians, totalitarian ideas from Europe began to make headway. The influence of Italian Fascism and, later, of the Nazi movement in Germany, resulted in the appearance of Fascist groups in Japan, though the shifting character of Japanese political movements and the lack of any outstanding leader, combined with the growing dominance of the Army over politics to prevent any repetition in Japan of the course of events in Italy and Germany, where the soldiers normally stood aloof from politics.

All these different parties and groups, however, from old-

---

[1] Yanaga, *Japan Since Perry*, p. 500.
[2] The Aikyojuku, or 'Native Land Loving School' founded in 1931 by Tachibana, was concerned in the assassination of Mr. Inukai in 1932 (ibid. pp. 500–1).

established societies such as the Genyosha of Mitsuru Toyama; the Black Dragon Society of Ryuhei Uchida, to the movements launched by Kita, Gondo, and Tachibana, and the pro-Fascist parties of Kenzo Adachi, and (later) of Seigo Nakano, met on common ground in their advocacy of overseas expansion for Japan. Just as inequalities of wealth were to be redressed at home, so abroad there was to be an 'equitable distribution' of the resources of the world in which Japan, as a 'have not' nation, would benefit. Since it was unlikely that the more fortunate countries would yield any of their holdings through peaceful negotiation, force of arms was necessary. All such themes were grist to the Army's mill.

There is also to be considered the effect of Communism, which exercised a dual influence. The Japanese Communist Party, founded in 1922, never had a very large membership, and was broken up and driven underground by the police, especially after the enactment in 1925 of the Peace Preservation Law. But the influence of Communist ideas and Communist literature went far beyond the confines of the party. While their attacks upon the imperial institution, their advocacy of world proletarian revolution, and their connexion with Moscow caused the Communists to be regarded with abhorrence by the vast majority of Japanese, their denunciation of capitalism and advocacy of State control of the means of production evoked a more sympathetic response in many quarters. The Japanese Army and the rightist societies, too, like the Kuomintang in China, learned something from Communist methods of organization and of propaganda. Furthermore, the practical results of Communism, as portrayed in Soviet Russia, the erection of an authoritarian State structure, the repression of all conflicting ideas, and the inculcation of a militaristic spirit among its followers were not very far removed from the 'national policy' advocated by a section of the Army and some of its rightist civilian auxiliaries. It was thus no accident that a good many of those who had been Communists or near-Communists in the twenties emerged as supporters of the Army in the next decade. Indeed, Prince Konoye, in 1945, told the Emperor that he believed that the course of events since 1931 had been planned by the Communists.[1] This view, like all 'conspiracy' theories, was an

---

[1] In a conversation with the Emperor on 14 February 1945 Konoye expressed alarm at the possibility of a Communist revolution in Japan if the war was not soon ended. He said that a majority of the younger officers seemed to think that the existing form of the Japanese Government was compatible with Com-

over-simplification, and took no account of the complexities of domestic politics in Japan and of the part which is always played by opportunism, in domestic as in foreign affairs.

Communist activities in Japan had also another effect, in frightening the Court party, the bureaucracy, and the Zaibatsu. These were consequently weakened in their opposition to the policies of the Army and some of them, at least, were ready to play along with the military after 1931, as the least of the two evils. This furthered the plans of that section of the Army, who, as will be seen, did not wish to eliminate the industrialists, but to reduce them to a position of subordination, as servants of the military.

The Japanese military scene was akin to the political in being characterized by the appearance of numerous groups and cliques, usually centring around some personality and constantly coalescing or dividing. Generalizations and the drawing of hard and fast lines of division are therefore more than usually deceptive. But it is possible to discern two main schools of thought in the Army. The younger field service officers, mostly drawn from rural localities, were apt to be disciples of Gondo and Tachibana. They were eager to overthrow the capitalistic régime and ready to use violence and terrorism in doing it. They were known as the Kodoha, or Imperial Way group, but, perhaps on account of their hostility to any kind of centralized administration, they were without any effective form of organization.[1] They constituted rather a great ground swell of discontent within the Army, which was, however, always liable to heave up in a storm of blood and terror. Closely associated with them were the civilian terrorist organizations, like the Ketsumeidan, or Blood Brotherhood League. In the senior ranks of the Army they had leaders, or at least sympathizers, in Generals Araki and Mazaki.

The other main faction in the Army became known as the Toseiha, or Control Group. This was made up of officers of more senior grade, especially members of the General Staff, who realized the futility of attempting any return to a primitive decentralized society. Their aim was to preserve and to control the existing

munism and that the Communists were encouraging this idea. 'I have now come to seriously doubt whether the whole series of events from the Manchurian Incident to the present war have not been what they [the Communists] have purposefully planned' (USSBS, *Japan's Struggle to End the War*, 1 July 1946 (Washington, USGPO), p. 21).

[1] Araki, 'Domestic and Foreign Situation'. Also evidence of Saburo Suganami, a former member of the Kodoha (IMTFE, *Defence Document* 2568).

bureaucratic administration, to merge the political parties into a single-party system which they would dominate, and to render the industrialists and the Court officials subordinate to their will. These aims they planned to achieve by a process of gradual pressure rather than by a violent coup d'état.[1] But they were, for a while, tolerant of the terrorist methods of the Kodoha and its civilian associates, because these resulted in the death of some of their foremost opponents and in the cowing of the remainder.

In the domestic sphere the two groups worked in comparative harmony during 1931–5. These years were marked by a constant series of plots and attempted coups d'état which kept the opponents of the military in continual apprehension. In the early months of 1932 Mr. Inouye, an ex-Finance Minister and the Chairman of the Election Committee of the Minseito, and Baron Dan, the Chairman of the Board of Directors of the Mitsui Company, were both murdered by members of the Aikyojuku. Hard upon this came the 15 May affair, in which the capital was terrorized by a group of naval, military, and civilian extremists and the Premier, Mr. Inukai, was assassinated. This affair was utilized by the Army chiefs to bring party government to an end. They warned the Genro, Prince Saionji, that another party administration would infallibly produce fresh acts of violence and he in consequence secured the appointment as Premier of Admiral Saito, with a predominantly non-party Cabinet. General Araki, regarded as the leader of the Kodoha, retained his position as Minister of War. The Saito administration upheld the action of the Kwantung Army in Manchuria, by formally recognizing Manchukuo on 15 September 1932 and by withdrawing Japan from the League of Nations in March of the following year, after the condemnation of Japan by the League of Nations. The succeeding administration of Admiral Okada yielded to the Army in attacking the imperial universities at Kyoto and Tokyo and compelling them to dismiss professors of liberal views. Professor Minobe, in particular, was assailed for his thesis that the Emperor was an organ of the State and not above it and was compelled to resign from the House of Peers in the autumn of 1935. Thus the 'Control Group' was steadily moving towards its objectives. It had, *inter alia*, in 1933

[1] The members of the Control Group included Generals Minami, Matsui. Itagaki, Tojo, Tatekawa, Watanabe, and Nagata (Yanaga, *Japan Since Perry*, p. 510 n.).

secured the adoption of the long-desired programme of modernization of the Army's equipment.

But by 1935 the Kodoha apparently came to realize that they
were being made the tools of the Toseiha.[1] In January 1934
General Araki had been replaced as War Minister by General
Hayashi, who came to share the views of the Toseiha. The
Kodoha bitterly resented this and two of their members, while
under suspension for complicity in an alleged plot to assassinate
members of the Government, came out with a pamphlet in which
they made public the cleavage between the two factions in the
Army.[2] The Toseiha answered this by the removal, in the following July, of General Mazaki from his post of Inspector-General
of Military Education. This step was engineered by General
Nagata, Director of the Military Affairs Bureau, who was regarded
as the 'brains' of the Toseiha. He followed this up by systema-
tically transferring other members of the Kodoha to remote
posts in Japan and the colonies. But, on 12 August 1935, one of
these, Lieut.-Colonel Aizawa, who had been ordered to Formosa,
came to Tokyo and murdered Nagata.[3] Aizawa was arrested and
put on trial, but while this was still dragging on, accompanied by
much denunciation of the plutocracy and Court aristocracy by his
defence counsel, the military *émeute* of 26 February 1936 occurred.
Some 1,400 troops of the First Division, in which there were
numerous adherents of the Kodoha and which had been ordered
to Manchuria, rose in revolt and seized a part of the capital. They
besieged the residence of the Premier, but he escaped death.[4] The
Finance Minister, Mr. Takahashi, the Lord Keeper of the Privy Seal,
Admiral Saito, and the Inspector-General of Military Education,
General Watanabe, were less fortunate and were all killed. Strong
military and naval forces were concentrated against the mutineers

[1] In July 1933 occurred the affair of the Shimpeitai or 'God-sent Troops', a
group led by Tatsuo Amano, leader of the Patriotic Workers' Society. He
planned to assassinate the Cabinet and the party leaders, but the plot was detected
on the eve of its execution. The plotters were not brought to trial until 1937
and the case dragged on until 1941 when all were acquitted (Yanaga, *Japan
Since Perry*, p. 505). It seems as though some of these conspiracies were never
intended to be carried out, but were organized with the knowledge of the Toseiha
to frighten their civilian opponents.
[2] They also declared that the suppressed plot was a fabrication of the Toseiha.
The case against them was dropped for lack of evidence, but they were dismissed
from the service for writing the pamphlet (ibid. pp. 512–13).
[3] ibid. pp. 513–15.
[4] His brother-in-law, who resembled him, was killed in mistake for him (ibid.
p. 517).

and, on 29 February, they were persuaded to surrender, in obedience to an imperial command. Their leaders were brought to trial, and in the following July thirteen army officers and four civilians were executed.

The February 1936 affair resulted in the destruction of the Kodoha as an organized group and the firm establishment of Toseiha control over the policy of the Army. It also furthered something of a rapprochement between the Army leaders and their civilian opponents. The Zaibatsu, in particular, while still nervous of the ultimate plans of the Army for controls over industry, were partly reconciled to its expansionist policies, because of the obstacles to peaceful economic expansion caused by the world-wide trade depression and its aftermath, the tariffs and quotas on Japanese exports imposed by various foreign countries. Rearmament also gave opportunities of employment and profit. So did the far-reaching schemes of industrial development fostered by the Army in Manchukuo, despite the state-socialist régime which the Kwantung Army had initiated there. The Toseiha, for their part, realized that they could not get along without utilizing the skill and experience of the great industrial concerns in building up the Japanese war potential. They profited, too, by the rivalries between the older industrial countries and the newer or 'Shin-Zaibatsu', in whom they found ready allies.[1] They had still to face the covert opposition of the Court aristocracy and of the political parties, but these steadily lost ground. During the Hirota Cabinet, which followed that of Okada, the Army succeeded, as has been seen, in restoring in full vigour the active service qualification for Service Ministers and, in February 1937, utilized it to prevent the appointment as Premier of General Ugaki, who had consented to a reduction in the size of the Army in 1925, and who was regarded as having undesirable political connexions. The Army leaders, however, while concerned to restore what they held to be the due and proper predominance of the military in the national counsels, desired to respect the forms of the Constitution and to avoid an overt military dictatorship. Furthermore, few generals possessed

---

[1] Prominent among these was Yoshisuke Aikawa, the founder of Nissan. He said that one of the considerations which induced him to accept the invitation of the Kwantung Army in 1936 to head the Manchurian Heavy Industry Company was the difficulty in Japan of building up an independent vertical combine because of the older Zaibatsu interests. (Preliminary interrogation of Y. Aikawa in Sugamo Prison, 28 January 1946, IMTFE.)

sufficient political experience and acumen to head an administration, as was revealed by the ineptitude of Hirota's successor, General Hayashi.[1] Thus the Army could no more dispense with the political leaders than it could with the Zaibatsu. In May 1937, however, it thought that it had secured a Premier with whom it could work in harmony and who at the same time commanded the necessary prestige and confidence to maintain a stable administration. This was Prince Fumimaro Konoye, who, as a scion of one of the oldest noble families and a distant relative of the Emperor, was acceptable to the Court and to business circles, and was at the same time an associate of some of the Toseiha clique.[2]

Meanwhile the Army was engaged in the consolidation of its position on the continent. During 1931–3 the Kwantung Army, with the benevolent goodwill of its superiors in Tokyo, had wrested Manchuria and Jehol from Chinese control and had organized the puppet State of Manchukuo. This was Japan's first challenge to the existing order, and its success increased the prestige of the Army at home and emboldened it to further ventures abroad. On this latter point, however, there were divisions of opinion within the Army. The Kodoha group were of the opinion that Japan should concentrate all her energies upon the exploitation of Manchurian resources, so as to build up that country as a 'continental war base' in the event of a conflict with the USSR, to promote Japanese agrarian settlement therein, and in general to erect in Manchuria the kind of political and economic order which they held up as the ideal at home. But these were huge undertakings and the leaders of the Kodoha evidently considered, not unreasonably, that Japan had bitten off as much as she could chew for a good while to come. They were consequently averse to any further immediate expansion.[3]

The Toseiha group, while equally intent upon the exploitation of Manchuria, was more affected by that general tendency of empire-builders to go a step further in order to protect what has already been won. The Chinese National Government, engaged in war with the Communists and other dissidents, and disappointed

---

[1] The Hirota Cabinet fell in February 1937, after a revolt in the Diet against the Army's demands for greatly increased military expenditure and for the establishment of a 'quasi-war-time economy'.

[2] Saionji had recommended Konoye as Premier in March 1936, but he had at that time declined, ostensibly for reasons of health.

[3] T. Kase, *Eclipse of the Rising Sun* (London, Cape, 1951), pp. 34–35; Yanaga, *Japan Since Perry*, p. 567.

in their hopes of foreign aid, had been compelled to agree to the Tangku Truce on 31 May 1933. This action, brought about by the pro-Japanese group in the National Government, headed by Wang Ching-wei, provoked an outburst of popular wrath in China and more rebellions.[1] It therefore appeared both propitious and advisable to the Toseiha to work for the establishment of a buffer autonomous régime in North China, from which the influence of Nanking and any possible menace to Manchukuo from that quarter would be excluded.

They also considered that a good opportunity existed for penetrating Inner Mongolia, and, if possible, undermining Soviet influence in Outer Mongolia, with the object of establishing another Japanese-controlled corridor between China and the USSR, and so preventing any effective collaboration between these two Powers. The USSR had not overtly resented the Japanese occupation of Manchuria; it had on two occasions, in 1931 and 1933, made overtures for the conclusion of a Soviet-Japanese non-aggression pact, and had initiated the negotiations which led to the sale of the Chinese Eastern Railway to Manchukuo in 1935. But the Japanese regarded this conciliatory disposition as arising from the need to gain time for the USSR to recover from the debilitating effects of the revolutionary years and to build up its armed strength and economic potential in Siberia. When that had been accomplished they expected the USSR to challenge Japan in Manchuria unless Japan had in the meantime secured an advantageous strategic position.[2]

Apart from these general considerations of policy there were the rivalries and jealousies of the local Japanese armies on the continent. The Kwantung Army had done well for itself by its conquest and domination of Manchukuo; it was now looking for fresh opportunities. The Japanese North China garrison, stationed in the Peiping–Tientsin area by virtue of the Boxer Protocol of 1901, wanted its share of glory and profit, and was ready to emulate in North China the exploits of the Kwantung Army in Manchuria.

[1] Wang Ching-wei had returned from Europe and resumed his post of President of the Executive Yuan in March 1933.
[2] On 23 March 1936 Itagaki, then Chief of Staff of the Kwantung Army, told Arita, Foreign Minister in the Hirota Cabinet, that if Outer Mongolia could be brought in with Japan and Manchukuo, Soviet territory in the Far East would be in a very dangerous condition and it was possible that the influence of the Soviet Union in the Far East might be removed without fighting (IMTFE, *Judgment*, p. 670).

It busied itself during 1934–5 with collecting data on the political and economic situation in North China, with plans for the seizure of the area in case of war, and with schemes for the erection of a State there which would be *de facto* independent of Nanking.[1]

For a while things seemed to be going the Japanese way. The Kwantung Army established close relations with Prince Teh, the leader of a group of Mongol chieftains who were anxious to secure Inner Mongolian independence of Nanking because of their well-founded fears of Chinese colonization and political domination. In June 1935 the Japanese took advantage of an alleged insult to some of their officers in Chahar to secure, by the Chin–Doihara Agreement, the withdrawal of Chinese troops from that Province and the dissolution of the Kuomintang organizations therein. This was followed by the organization of a Mongolian secessionist régime in northern Chahar, which also claimed sovereignty over the neighbouring provinces of Suiyuan and Ninghsia.

In the same month an agreement between General Ho Ying-chin, then Chairman of the Peiping Military Council, and General Umezu, Chief of Staff of the Japanese Army in North China, provided for the withdrawal of Chinese Central Government troops and of organs of the Kuomintang from the Province of Hopei. This was followed by the abolition, under Japanese pressure, of the Peiping Political Council, and, in September, by a public declaration on the part of General Tada, Commander of the Japanese forces in North China, in favour of a new political régime there, which should be independent of Nanking. But, despite threats, intrigues, and blandishments Tada failed to evoke any concrete response from Chinese political and military figures in the north. These had little love for Nanking, but even less for the Japanese, and were inclined, so far as they could, to balance between the two. Moreover, in view of the rising anti-Japanese sentiment among the Chinese people in general, no one wished to court denunciation as a traitor. Only in the demilitarized zone established by the Tangku Truce were the Japanese able to sponsor the so-called East Hopei anti-Communist Government, headed by Yin Ju-keng. But, to obviate a possible further Japanese coup d'état, the Chinese National Government, on 11 December

---

[1] T. K. Koo, 'Some Economic Documents Relating to the Genesis of the Japanese-sponsored régime in North China', *FEQ*, Nov. 1946, pp. 65–76; IMTFE, *Record*, pp. 3475–80.

1935, agreed to the establishment of the Hopei–Chahar Political Council, under the headship of General Sung Cheh-yuan. But he too, while endeavouring to avoid a frontal clash with the Japanese, proved to be no puppet of theirs.

Meanwhile the Government in Tokyo had been endeavouring to persuade Generalissimo Chiang Kai-shek to agree to an accord which would have lined up China as a satellite ally of Japan. The first sign of this came with the famous Amau statement of 17 April 1934, in which the Foreign Ministry spokesman claimed that Japan had sole responsibility for the preservation of peace in the Far East and that she opposed any efforts on the part of China to seek foreign assistance in order to resist Japan, and any technical, financial or military assistance by a third party or parties to China. Unfavourable foreign repercussions caused Hirota, then Foreign Minister, to declare that Amau had spoken without official sanction, but, although he was said to have been reprimanded, he was not removed from his post.[1]

During the summer and autumn of the following year general proposals for a Sino-Japanese accord were worked out in discussions between the Foreign Ministry, the service chiefs, and Japanese foreign service officials in China. These proposals took shape as the Hirota 'Three Principles'—by which China was to repress anti-Japanese activities, to accept the situation in Manchuria, and to co-operate with Japan against Communism. The plan was formally adopted by the Inner Cabinet on 4 October. It envisaged a general treaty of friendship between Japan and China, to be followed by an agreement on matters of detail.[2] The 'Three Principles' were revealed to the Chinese Ambassador, Chiang Tso-pin, on the eve of his departure to attend the Fifth National Congress of the Kuomintang. On 21 November the Japanese Ambassador, Ariyoshi, reported that he had raised the matter with Generalissimo Chiang Kai-shek. According to Ariyoshi, Chiang had said that he was by no means anti-Japanese and that he was

---

[1] According to the evidence of Kazue Kuwashima, Director of the Bureau of Asiatic Affairs in the Foreign Ministry at this time, the Japanese Foreign Ministry was alarmed at the activities of M. Monnet, a member of the League Secretariat, who was thought to be planning a scheme of international financial and economic aid for China from which Japan would be excluded. Consequently the Foreign Ministry sent instructions to its representatives in China to frighten him off, if possible. Amau got hold of these instructions and incorporated them in his statement; for which he was reprimanded by Hirota (IMTFE, *Record*, pp. 29484–7). [2] ibid. pp. 29621–31.

sincerely hoping for friendly relations between China and Japan. He expressed agreement with the three principles, but warned Ariyoshi about the situation in North China and indicated that if anything happened there it would render impossible discussions upon the three principles.[1] It was apparently as a result of this that Hirota, on 21 January 1936, told the Diet that the Chinese Government had agreed to work with Japan in accordance with the three principles. This was promptly refuted by Nanking, where the pro-Japanese elements had suffered a blow through the attempted assassination and consequent retirement of Wang Ching-wei. During 1936 all Hirota's efforts to secure a definite acceptance of the three principles failed and the negotiations were brought to an end by the Suiyuan affair in November. This was an invasion of that Province by the forces under Prince Teh, with the encouragement and barely concealed assistance of the Kwantung Army. But the invaders were completely defeated by the Suiyuan provincial forces, led by General Fu Tso-yi. This resulted in a severe blow to Japanese prestige among the Mongols and at the same time it greatly stimulated the popular movement in China for resistance to Japan. It was closely followed by the Sian affair in December, when the Chinese Generalissimo was kidnapped by the forces of Chang Hsueh-liang and released only through the intervention of the Chinese Communist leaders, who saw in this an admirable opportunity to convert Chiang to their policy of a united front against Japan. Whether or not they reached any definite agreement with him at that time, the Sian affair was followed by a halt in the long conflict between the Chinese Communists and the Kuomintang and by negotiations for a settlement between the two parties.[2] This was viewed with growing alarm by the Japanese, although the intransigent policy of their military leaders in China had been an important factor in bringing it about.

By the end of 1936 the Japanese found themselves increasingly isolated, faced by a marked stiffening of attitude on the part of the Chinese, and by a worsening of their relations alike with the

---

[1] ibid. p. 29635.

[2] Miura, the Japanese Consul-General at Hankow, reported to Tokyo that he had information from one of his agents that the whole Sian affair had been planned on the instructions of the Third International and that Chiang Kai-shek, in an interview with Chou En-lai, had agreed to a change of policy and to combined resistance to Japan. Miura to Hayashi, 21 February 1937. This and subsequent telegrams from Miura are among the rejected defence documents of the IMTFE.

Western Powers and with the Soviet Union. The Amau *démarche* may have had some effect in preventing the formation of any joint financial assistance to China under the aegis of the League, but it did not stop individual aid in the form of loans for railway construction by Great Britain, Germany, France, and Belgium, or the dispatch of military advisers and the sale of war equipment to China by Germany and Italy. The Japanese military were especially irked by British advice and assistance in the Chinese monetary reform of November 1935 which, if successful in establishing a stable currency, would greatly enhance the prestige and power of the Central Government throughout the country.[1] The example of what had taken place in Manchukuo had taught the Western Powers that Japanese-sponsored régimes resulted in the creation of industrial and commercial monopolies which effectually nullified the principle of equal opportunity. They had given *de facto* acquiescence to this process in Manchuria, but they were not prepared to be so complaisant at the prospect of its extention to the rest of China.

Meanwhile the Japanese Navy had added fuel to the fires of discord. It had always chafed under the inferior ratio assigned to it by the Washington and London Naval Limitation Treaties. It now contended that the increased radius of warships and aircraft were offsetting the advantages Japan had gained by the arrangements in the Washington Treaty of 1922 for the non-fortification of certain insular possessions in the Pacific. In conversations held in London in the autumn of 1934 the Japanese demanded a common upper limit of tonnage, within which each country could build the types of war vessel it felt to be necessary for its security. When this thesis was rejected by the British and American Governments Japan, on 29 December 1934, as she was entitled to do, gave notice of her denunciation of the Washington Treaty, to become effective at the end of 1936.[2] In December 1935, in accordance with the provisions of the Treaty of 1930, a further Naval Conference assembled in London, but when their demand for parity was refused the Japanese on 15 January 1936 walked out of the Conference.[3] Japan's action was answered by greatly increased naval appropriations on the part of both the United States and Great Britain.

[1] For the Leith-Ross mission and Chinese monetary reforms see Sir J. T. Pratt, *War and Politics in China* (London, Cape, 1943), pp. 235–6, and RIIA, *Survey, 1935*, i. 308–11, 322–4, 404–6. [2] See ibid. *1936*, pp. 63–76.
[3] The Foreign Ministry would have been willing to compromise on the matter, but this time the Navy stood firm (Kase, *Eclipse of the Rising Sun*, p. 32).

During 1936 relations grew tense between Japan and the USSR. In March the conclusion of a Pact of Mutual Assistance between the USSR and its satellite, the Mongolian People's Republic, came as a challenge to the Kwantung Army's ambitions for a Japanese-directed pan-Mongol State. Discussions for a regulation of boundary questions between Manchukuo and the USSR also came to nothing.[1] The growing strength of the Soviet Union in the Far East, reflected in its more confident diplomacy, combined with the failure of Japan's schemes in North China and western Inner Mongolia, aroused alarm in Tokyo.

Japan was thus isolated and confronted by a number of increasingly hostile Powers. Her General Staff consequently pricked up their ears when, in the autumn of 1935, they received a telegram from General Oshima, the Japanese military attaché in Berlin, to say that Ribbentrop had asked him to ascertain their views on the conclusion of a German-Japanese agreement to afford no help to the Soviet Union should either be involved in war with that Power. The Japanese Vice-Chief of Staff, General Sugiyama, responded by dispatching one of his subordinates, Tadaichi Wakamatsu, to Germany to find out what influence Ribbentrop had and to sound the German Army on the matter. Wakamatsu was in Germany during November and December 1935, and had interviews with Ribbentrop and with General von Blomberg, the German Minister of Defence. They agreed on the idea of a separate German-Japanese Anti-Comintern agreement.[2]

But, according to Kensuke Horinouchi, who was at this time Vice-Minister of Foreign Affairs, the Japanese Foreign Ministry objected to the conclusion of a pact with Germany alone. It believed that, in view of their alarm and resentment at the proceedings of the Third International in Moscow during the previous summer, Great Britain and other Western European Powers might be willing to conclude Anti-Comintern agreements. The Army was averse to an approach to Britain, but the Foreign Ministry said that it would not agree to negotiations with Germany alone. The Army gave way and the newly appointed Ambassador to Great Britain, Shigeru Yoshida, was instructed to sound the British Government. Ribbentrop was informed of this and proved

---

[1] According to K. Kameyama, who was Secretary of Embassy in Moscow at the time, the discussions went on during April–November 1936, but no agreement could be reached (IMTFE, *Record*, pp. 35419–21).

[2] Evidence of Tadaichi Wakamatsu (IMTFE, *Record*, pp. 33700–4).

agreeable, since he was about to become Ambassador to Great Britain and was full of ideas for an Anglo-German understanding. But the British Government were cool to the proposal and Ribbentrop's activities in Great Britain did not improve matters.[1]

Tokyo also approached the Netherlands and discussions took place in October 1936 between the Japanese chargé d'affaires and the Netherlands Foreign Minister. The Netherlands Government apparently showed some willingness to consider an arrangement for an exchange of information on Communist activities in Asia, which were causing unrest in the Netherlands East Indies. But they drew back sharply upon the conclusion of the German-Japanese Pact, fearing involvement in a German-Soviet clash.[2]

The German-Japanese Anti-Comintern Pact, concluded on 25 November 1936, consisted of a public declaration of three articles, by the first of which the two Powers agreed to exchange information on the activities of the Comintern and to collaborate in preventive measures. They agreed in the second to 'jointly invite third States whose internal peace is threatened by the subversive activities of the Communist International to adopt defensive measures in the spirit of this agreement or to take part in the present agreement.' By the third article the Pact was to run for five years with provision for renewal.[3]

The public declaration was accompanied by a secret addendum, also composed of three articles. The first of these provided that, should either of the signatories become the object of an unprovoked attack or an unprovoked threat of attack by the USSR, the other would do nothing which would have the effect of relieving the position of the USSR, while both would consult on the measures to be taken for the safeguard of their common interests. By the second article the two contracting Powers declared that, except by mutual consent, they would not conclude any political treaties with the Soviet Union which were not conformable to the spirit of the secret agreement, while this was in force. By the third article the secret agreement became operative at the same time as the public one and for the same period of five years.[4]

[1] Evidence of Horinouchi, IMTFE, *Defence Document* (reject).
[2] Annual Report of the Official Business for the Year 1936, Bureau of European-Asiatic Affairs, Foreign Ministry, Tokyo (IMTFE, *Defence Document* (reject)).
[3] RIIA, *Documents, 1936*, pp. 297–9.
[4] De Witt C. Poole, 'Light on Nazi Foreign Policy', *Foreign Affairs*, October 1946, pp. 136–8; IMTFE, *Record*, pp. 5936–8. Shigenori Togo, who at this

This did not constitute a definite military alliance even of a defensive character, although it laid the foundations for one, and was intended as such by its framers, the Japanese General Staff on the one hand and the Ribbentrop Bureau on the other. Horinouchi told the Tokyo Tribunal that it was not at first intended to keep these additional articles secret and that this was done at the request of the Japanese Government which was nervous of possible Soviet reactions.[1] It seems, however, that Moscow did learn the contents of the secret pact.[2] At all events, the Soviet Government refused to accept the official Japanese explanation that the Anti-Comintern Pact was not directed against the USSR, but only against the Third International for which Moscow had disclaimed responsibility. The Soviet Government retaliated by breaking off the negotiations for a new Fisheries Treaty with Japan.

The United States, Great Britain, and France, suspecting that there was more to the (publicized) Pact than met the eye, also disapproved. In Japan itself, opposition in the Diet developed because of the prejudicial effect on Japan's important fishery concessions in Soviet waters and, while this did not prevent the ratification of the Pact, it was a factor in the downfall of the Hirota Cabinet. In Germany the regular Foreign Ministry officials headed by the Foreign Minister, von Neurath, disapproved of the Pact and, as will be seen, refused to consider it as in any way committing Germany to support of Japanese policy in China.[3]

The Anti-Comintern Pact was regarded as the beginning of a German-Japanese line-up, not only against the Soviet Union, but also against the Western Democracies. This impression was strengthened, after the war, by the discovery that, on 11 August 1936, the Japanese Inner Cabinet had adopted the 'Basic Principles of National Policy', originally framed by the two Service Ministries. These were: (1) Japan must strive to correct the aggressive policies of the great Powers and to realize the spirit of the Imperial Way by a consistent policy of overseas expansion. (2) Japan must complete her defensive armament to secure the position of her

time was Director of the Euro-Asiatic Bureau of the Foreign Ministry claimed at his trial that he got the phraseology of the public pact modified and the word 'unprovoked' introduced into the final version of Article I of the secret pact (ibid. p. 35646). [1] Evidence of Horinouchi (loc. cit.).
[2] Yanaga says that Soviet agents at The Hague intercepted and decoded the telegrams passing between Oshima and Tokyo (*Japan Since Perry*, p. 570).
[3] Ernst von Weizsäcker, *Memoirs*, trs. by John Andrews (London, Gollancz, 1951), p. 116.

Empire as the stabilizing power in East Asia. (3) Japan should strive to eradicate the menace of the USSR in the north in order to stabilize Japan–Manchukuo national defence and to promote sound economic development. Japan should also be prepared against Britain and the United States, and attempt to bring about economic development by close collaboration between Japan, Manchukuo, and China. However, in achieving these objects Japan should pay due attention to friendly relations with other Powers. (4) To further her plan to promote social and economic development in the South Seas, and, without rousing other Powers, Japan should attempt to extend her strength by moderate and peaceful means. Thus, with the establishment of Manchukuo, Japan might expect full development of her national resources and her national defence.[1]

This document, however, did not embody any new departure in Japanese policy; indeed the curious mixture of belligerent threat and friendly sentiment indicates that it was one of the many compromises between the views of the armed services and those of the Foreign Ministry. Running through it, too, there may be detected an undertone of appeal. Japan would fight, if she must, to preserve her continental gains, and to secure the hegemony of East Asia which she considered as her right, but she still had hopes that the Western Powers would peacefully acquiesce in this. She was well aware of her immeasurable inferiority in economic resources to the United States, the British Commonwealth, and the Soviet Union, and, while she was endeavouring to rectify this through aggrandizement on the Asiatic continent, she was at heart nervous of the unfavourable reactions which she had herself provoked.

There is some evidence that this applied even to the Army. A Japanese General Staff appreciation of the world situation, made in the spring of 1937, considered that a general war in Europe was coming, although it was not likely in the immediate future. When it came Japan should keep out of it and go on building up her national strength, making special efforts to improve the efficiency and the equipment of her Army. In view of the increasing power of the Soviet Union in the Far East and of the growing national feeling in China, the Japanese forces stationed on the continent should be circumspect and do their best to avoid trouble. In June

[1] IMFTE, *Judgment*, pp. 119–24.

1937 Lieut.-Colonel Okamoto was sent to North China to impress this policy upon the Japanese garrison forces there.[1]

This, however, was not the view of the Kwantung Army. They felt that, in view of the growing strength of the Chinese National Government and the increasing evidence that a Kuomintang-Communist united front against Japan was in the making, Japan might be faced in the future with a Sino-Soviet coalition. General Tojo, who on 1 March 1937 had succeeded General Itagaki as Chief of Staff of the Kwantung Army, on 9 June 1937 sent a telegram to the General Staff in Tokyo warning them of this possibility and suggesting that Japan should first of all strike a blow against Nanking.[2] No doubt the extension to the Far East of the purge of military and civil officials in the USSR, which seemed to preclude any possibility of immediate Soviet intervention, encouraged Tojo and his colleagues in this view. Tojo's advice did not find favour with the War Minister or the Chief of the General Staff, but there were evidently many in the lower echelons of the Army, both at home and abroad, who thought as he did, and herein lay the danger.

Furthermore, the Army was not willing to abandon its cherished idea of establishing buffer autonomous States between Manchukuo and China and between China and the USSR. In March 1937 Mr. Naotake Sato, the Foreign Minister in the Hayashi Cabinet, told the Diet that he intended to resume the discussions for a general Sino-Japanese accord which had lapsed the previous December, but this time on a basis of equality. But it subsequently became evident that the Army had no intention of abandoning its claim that North China should be regarded as a 'special area', or of abandoning the puppet administrations in North Chahar and East Hopei. Indeed to consent to this, or to any modification of the Chin–Doihara or Ho–Umezu Agreements, would have been an admission of defeat and would have reacted adversely against the Army's position both abroad and at home.

The Chinese Government, for their part, insisted that respect for Chinese territorial and administrative integrity must be the prelude to any negotiations for a general understanding, and backed by the increasingly confident and bellicose public mood, they showed a more determined spirit in dealing with the 'smug-

[1] Evidence of General Torashiro Kawabe (IMFTE, *Record*, pp. 21974–80).
[2] ibid. pp. 31673–5; *Judgment*, pp. 169–70.

gling' problem, and with officials of dubious loyalty in the north.[1] In these circumstances little resulted from the Sato overture.[2] Neither Tokyo nor Nanking was looking for war in the summer of 1937, but both Governments were being impelled towards it by forces which neither could adequately control.

[1] See RIIA, *Survey, 1936*, pp. 911–13 and *1937*, l. 170–8.
[2] Sato had at the same time made overtures to Great Britain for an accord on China, on general economic policy and on financial questions. The moving spirit in this was apparently Shigenori Togo, then Director of the European-American Bureau of the Gaimusho. He hoped to see an Anglo-Japanese agreement on China, a prospect which aroused apprehension in Nanking. But apparently Yoshida gave warning, when instructed to open negotiations in London, that general declarations by Tokyo of respect for foreign (third party) interests in China would not be sufficient, and requested wider powers. Hardly had the *pourparlers* started when the Lukouchiao affair and its repercussions caused their suspension (IMTFE, *Record*, pp. 35413–14).

CHAPTER II

The Sino-Japanese Conflict
July 1937 to January 1938

AT the opening of July 1937 the Japanese garrison Army in the Peiping–Tientsin area consisted of about 7,000 men, made up of two infantry regiments, with artillery and tank units.[1] It was commanded by General Tashiro, but he had been stricken with a mortal illness, and, while still nominally in charge, was incapable of active direction at the time of the Lukouchiao incident.[2] His successor, General Katsuki, did not arrive until some days later. The Chief of Staff was General Gun Hashimoto; the head of the Army's Intelligence Section was Lieut.-General Takachi Wachi; the head of the Special Section was Colonel Takuro Matsui; while Major-General Shozo Kawabe was in command of the brigade of infantry. When the clash occurred at Lukouchiao Kawabe was at Shanhaikuan, attending the inspection of the second infantry regiment. Part of the first regiment was on manœuvres in Tungchow, leaving only one company in Peiping itself, and one battalion, under the command of an officer called Ichiki, at Fengtai.[3]

The Chinese forces in Hopei and Chahar consisted of the Twenty-Ninth Army, under the command of General Sung Cheh-yuan, Chairman of the Hopei–Chahar Political Council. He, however, had been absent since the beginning of May 1937, when he had gone to his country home 'to sweep the tombs of his ancestors', a time-honoured Chinese device for being out of the way when trouble appears likely. The second in command was General Chin Teh-chun, who was concurrently the Mayor of Peiping. The Chinese Thirty-Seventh Division, commanded by General Feng Chih-an, was stationed in the environs of this city, while the Thirty-Eighth Division, under General Chang Tzu-chung, who was also Mayor of Tientsin, was in and around that

---

[1] The figure of approximately 7,000 was given by General Hashimoto (IMTFE, *Record*, p. 20612).
[2] General Tashiro had been ill for some time but was not entirely incapacitated until two or three days before the Lukouchiao clash. He died about a week later and his funeral took place in the Japanese Concession in Tientsin on 16 July. (Evidence of Hashimoto, ibid. p. 20637.) His successor was Lieut.-General Kiyoshi Katsuki.   [3] Evidence of Kawabe, ibid. pp. 20521–2.

city. Of the two remaining divisions, one was in southern Hopei and the other in Chahar; neither came immediately into the picture.[1]

The disposition of both armies goes to show that neither had planned to attack the other at this time. Relations between the senior officers on both sides continued to be outwardly friendly but antagonism was growing between the junior ranks and between the soldiers.[2] The Chinese troops were increasingly affected by the rising tide of the anti-Japanese propaganda, while the repeated warnings from the military authorities in Tokyo to the officers of the Japanese force in North China against starting any trouble is in itself indicative that they had reason to fear that this would happen.[3]

Through their occupation of Fengtai, for which they had extracted Chinese consent in the previous September, the Japanese were established on the Peiping to Tientsin railway, a few miles south of Peiping. From Fengtai a short transverse line ran westwards to join the Peiping–Hankow railway near Lukouchiao, or Marco Polo Bridge, across the Yunting River. Close by, on the east bank, is the small walled town of Wanping and, below the west bank, the town and station of Changhsintien. The Chinese had a regiment here with a battalion at Lukouchiao and Wanping.[4] According to the Chinese district magistrate, Wang Lung-chai, the Japanese, with the connivance of the Director of the Peiping–Liaoning railway, Chen Chueh-sun, had carried out a survey of some 6,000 mou (about 1,000 acres) of land between Fengtai and Lukouchiao, where they wanted to build a barracks and an airfield. But the local Chinese owners were unwilling to sell or to lease their land, despite Japanese cajolery and pressure. One form of the latter appears to have been to hold frequent manœuvres in the area—Wang said that the Japanese had done this six times since his assumption of office in the autumn of 1936. He had summoned the local landowners to meet him, had urged them to stand firm, and had taken sworn statements from them that they had no wish

---

[1] 'A Factual Account of the July 7th Incident', by General Chin Teh-chun, 23 July 1946 (IMTFE, *Exhibit*, 198).

[2] Evidence of General Shozo Kawabe (IMTFE, *Record*, p. 20523). Hashimoto testified that Sung Cheh-yuan came alone and unguarded to the funeral of Tashiro on 16 July and wept over the loss of a friend (ibid. p. 20619).

[3] Kawabe said that when he was appointed to his brigade command in 1936 he was told by the Chief of the Military Operations Section of the General Staff, Major-General Kanji Ishihara, that 'the Central Authorities have no intention of fighting a war with China. You will please keep this in mind in the line of duty' (evidence of Kawabe, ibid. p. 20525).

[4] Chin Teh-chun (IMTFE, *Exhibit*, 198).

to sell. Consequently, when the Japanese complained that the Chinese authorities were preventing their purchase of land, these statements were produced in refutation.[1] The Japanese, according to General Chin Teh-chun, had furthermore demanded that the Chinese forces should be withdrawn from Wanping and Changhsintien, but without success.[2]

There was thus a good deal of background to the Lukouchiao affray. Had the Japanese been able to get control of Lukouchiao and Wanping, they would have been astride the Peiping–Hankow line, as well as the Peiping–Tientsin line at Fengtai, and so well placed to cut off Peiping from the south whenever they chose to do so. A clash between their troops and those of the Chinese in the Lukouchiao area would afford them an excellent opportunity of reviving their demand for the withdrawal of the Chinese forces.

On the night of 7 July General Chin Teh-chun was informed by the Commissioner of Foreign Affairs of the Hopei–Chahar Council that Colonel Matsui had complained that a company of Japanese soldiers on night manœuvres near Lukouchiao had been fired upon, that one Japanese soldier was missing, and that they wanted to enter Wanping in search of him. General Chin rejected this demand and told the local Chinese commander at Changhsintien to hold Wanping against any Japanese attack but not to fire first. Chin also summoned Wang Lung-chai to Peiping to assist in the discussions with Matsui. Chin and Wang stood firm against letting Japanese troops into Wanping and it was agreed that there should be a Sino-Japanese investigation on the spot. Meanwhile the Ichiki battalion had arrived at Lukouchiao from Fengtai, while the Chinese commander at Changhsintien in response to Chin's warning had come with another Chinese battalion to Lukouchiao. On 8 July after the Japanese investigator, Lieut.-Colonel Morita, had again unsuccessfully tried to persuade Wang to let Japanese troops into Wanping, fresh fighting broke out.[3]

On the early morning of 8 July General Shozo Kawabe, at Shanhaikuan, got a telephone report of the affair at Lukouchiao. Kawabe got back to Fengtai in the afternoon, where he received a message from General Hashimoto to say that the policy of the

[1] Affidavit of Wang Len-chai (the name is probably Wang Lung-chai; IMTFE, *Record*, pp. 3317-27).
[2] Chin Teh-chun (IMTFE, *Exhibit*, 198).
[3] Evidence of Chin Teh-chun (ibid.) and of Wang Len-chai (IMTFE, *Record*, pp. 3321-3).

Army was to achieve a solution on the spot. The regimental commander, Colonel Mutaguchi, had ordered the Ichiki battalion to remain where they were, pending the investigation, but as they reported that they were being fired at by the Chinese troops in Wanping, Kawabe told them to fire back if this went on. When Morita arrived at Lukouchiao he found the Japanese battalion about to attack and reprimanded them for this. They referred to Kawabe's order and, as more firing came from Wanping, Morita let them attack on the morning of 9 July.[1] But the assault met with stiff resistance and the Japanese got rather the worst of the conflict.[2] Meanwhile on the evening of 8 July the General Staff in Tokyo sent a telegram to the headquarters of the Army in North China, instructing it to exercise prudence and not to extend the hostilities. The next day a second telegraphic instruction warned Hashimoto not to raise any political matters with the Chinese local authorities, but to secure an apology from them; a promise to punish those responsible for the firing on the Japanese at Lukouchiao; the withdrawal of Chinese troops from that area and their replacement by a detachment of Paoantui, or Peace Preservation militia; and a guarantee to exercise strict control over anti-Japanese elements.[3] Hashimoto said that he himself went to Peiping with these conditions.[4] The Chinese appear at first to have been unwilling to accept them all although agreeable to a mutual withdrawal of forces to their positions as of 7 July.[5] However, on the evening of 11 July they consented.[6]

[1] Evidence of Kawabe (ibid. pp. 20524–34). Hashimoto also referred to his telephone call to Kawabe to stop the fighting (ibid. p. 20263).

[2] Evidence of Wang Len-chai (ibid. p. 3323).

[3] Evidence of General Torashiro Kawabe, then section Chief in the General Staff. He said that he helped to prepare the telegrams (ibid. pp. 21982–3). Both telegrams were certified as being among the documents burned at the end of the Pacific War (ibid. pp. 20793–4).

[4] ibid. p. 20623.

[5] This would appear from statements to the Tribunal by both Hashimoto and Wachi that there was an agreement on 9 July, and by Wang Lung-chai that he heard of this on the morning of 10 July (ibid. pp. 20623, 20580, 2406, 3323).

[6] General Sugiyama, the War Minister, in a public statement on 27 July 1937 reviewing the course of events, declared that on the morning of 11 July the Chinese had rejected the Japanese terms, but then they heard of the Japanese decision to send reinforcements and agreed to all the demands at 8 p.m. of that evening. (RIIA, *Documents, 1937*, pp. 654–8). General Torashiro Kawabe also declared that the report of an agreement reached Tokyo on the evening of 11 July (IMTFE, *Record*, p. 21986).
That the terms did include the withdrawal of Chinese troops from Lukouchiao and Wanping and their replacement by Paoantui was admitted by Chin Tehchun in cross-examination (ibid. pp. 2450–1). Wang Lung-chai, in his statement,

On 11 July it was officially announced in Nanking that a Sino-Japanese Agreement had been concluded in Peiping for the cessation of hostilities and the withdrawal of the troops of both sides. But already the Japanese Government had taken the fateful decision to send reinforcements to North China. It appears that shortly after they had dispatched their warning to Hashimoto the Japanese General Staff received a report that four Chinese Central Government divisions, with air support, were moving towards the Honan–Hopei border, and that the local Chinese forces in Hopei were preparing for war. The General Staff therefore decided, on the evening of 10 July, to dispatch strong units from the Kwantung Army and from the Japanese Garrison Army in Korea to reinforce their North China Army and, in addition, to prepare to send three divisions from Japan itself.[1] On 11 July the War Minister, General Sugiyama, demanded that the Cabinet endorse this decision.[2] Prince Konoye objected, since he feared that such a move would precipitate large-scale hostilities. Sugiyama denied that the Army had any such sinister intent but insisted that the reinforcements must be sent in order to avert disaster to the Japanese troops and to Japanese civilian residents in North China. Konoye was not convinced, but he found his Cabinet divided on the issue and he feared that if he persisted in his refusal, the War Minister would resign and a political crisis occur. So he gave way and it was agreed, and publicly announced, that reinforcements were to be sent.[3] Then, after the decision, came the news of the Peiping Agreement. Upon this, the Army agreed to halt the dispatch of the home divisions,

said that when the Paoantui, who numbered some 300, came to take over in Wanping, the Japanese declared that there were too many and that they did not need to have any machine guns. So only half the number were allowed past the Japanese lines. Furthermore, the Japanese left some of their own troops posted in the neighbourhood (ibid. pp. 3323–7).

[1] Affidavit of Shinichi Tanaka, who was at this time a section chief in the War Ministry (ibid. pp. 20676–8), and of Torashiro Kawabe (ibid. p. 21986). Shinrokuro Hidaka, Counsellor of the Japanese Embassy in Nanking, deposed that when on 11 July he queried the Chinese Foreign Minister about reports of Chinese troop movements, the latter did not deny them (ibid. p. 29903). General Chin Teh-chun declared that he considered the agreement in Peiping to be only a Japanese pretext to gain time and that he ordered the Chinese division in south Hopei to proceed to Peiping (*Exhibit*, 198).

[2] Evidence of K. Horinouchi, then Vice-Minister of Foreign Affairs (ibid. 3260; *Record*, p. 29688).

[3] *Saionji–Harada Memoirs*, 14 July 1937. According to Harada, Sugiyama had said that it was necessary to send a large force in order to smash the opposition and settle the matter in a short time. Konoye was backed in his opposition by the Foreign Minister (Hirota) and the Navy Minister (Yonai), but some of the others, especially the Home Minister (Baba) leaned to the Army view.

but not the forces from Manchuria and Korea.[1] From 12 July onwards these began to pour into North China.[2] On the night of 13 July it was agreed between the General Staff and the War Ministry that the Peiping arrangement should be accepted, but that if the terms were not carried out or if the Chinese Central Government interfered Japan should take 'resolute steps'.[3] Three days later, as hostilities had reopened around Lukouchiao, and reports of Central Government troop movements continued, Tokyo instructed the Tientsin headquarters to demand that General Sung should sign the settlement of 11 July and apologize in person; that he should dismiss General Feng Chih-an, and should complete the execution of the agreement by 19 July.[4]

But it was already evident that the Chinese Central Government did not intend to be excluded from the negotiations. On 10 July they had demanded that the Japanese troops should be withdrawn to their original positions and had reserved their legal claims to compensation for the Lukouchiao affair. The following day Hidaka, on instructions from Tokyo, informed the Chinese Foreign Ministry that the Japanese Government desired to bring about a local settlement and asked Nanking to do nothing to obstruct this. The Chinese Foreign Minister replied that Japan should send no reinforcements to North China and that any local settlement would need the confirmation of the Central Government. On 16 July the Chinese Government demanded that the Japanese reinforcements should be withdrawn, and that the troops responsible for the original affray should retire from the Lukouchiao region. They furthermore again reserved their right to claim compensation. The next day Hidaka, in accordance with instructions from Tokyo, called upon the Chinese Government not to obstruct the execution of the agreement reached in Peiping, and to refrain from all provocative speeches and actions.[5] Meanwhile, on the previous day the Chinese Government had appealed to the signatories of the Nine-Power Treaty of Washington and to others with interests in the Far East. They denounced Japan's actions as a violation of her Treaty obligations and asserted that they were

[1] Affidavit of Tanaka (IMTFE, *Record*, p. 20678) and of Torashiro Kawabe (ibid. p. 21987).
[2] They included two brigades, one mechanized, from the Kwantung Army as well as air units, and a division from Korea (*Record*, pp. 20629, 21986).
[3] Evidence of Tanaka (ibid. pp. 20680-1), and of Torashiro Kawabe (ibid. p. 21990).   [4] Evidence of Kawabe (ibid. pp. 21991-2).
[5] Affidavit of Hidaka (ibid. pp. 29902-6).

'bound to control closely the basis of settlement, since it is a well-known tactic of the Japanese military to promote disruption in North China by insisting upon overawing the local authorities.'[1] They also, according to Hidaka, delayed a reply to the Japanese note of 17 July until they had discussed it with the Ambassadors at Nanking of Great Britain and the United States.[2] On 19 July the Chinese Foreign Minister replied that Chinese troop movements were in self-defence in view of Japan's action in dispatching fresh forces to Hopei. He suggested that both sides agree to stop further troop movements and to withdraw the forces already sent. He reiterated that any local settlement needed the confirmation of the Central Government.[3]

On the same day Chiang Kai-shek, in a speech to officials and educationalists at Kuling, declared that the Japanese had engineered the Lukouchiao affair as a means to achieve their objectives in North China and that if the Chinese Government gave way to them, Peiping would soon become a second Mukden, and there would be no end to their demands. While China still desired peace, any settlement must at the minimum uphold Chinese territorial and sovereign rights, and should not entail any alteration in the status of the Hopei–Chahar Political Council, any removal of local officials, or any restrictions on the dispositions of the Twenty-Ninth Army.[4]

Outwardly, matters seemed to be at an impasse, but in the next few days the two sides came near to a definitive settlement. On 18 July General Sung Cheh-yuan went to Tientsin, proffered an apology to General Katsuki for the Lukouchiao affair, and agreed to the arrangements reached in Peiping. This was followed by a partial withdrawal of the Chinese forces.[5] Hidaka had talks with Kao Tsung-wu, the head of the Asiatic Department of the Chinese Foreign Ministry, and with General Chang Chun, the Governor of Szechuan, a friend and confidant of the Generalissimo. Hidaka and Chang Chun reached an understanding that when the settlement in Peiping was carried out, the Japanese Government would

---

[1] RIIA, *Documents, 1937*, p. 654.   [2] IMTFE, *Record*, p. 29906.
[3] ibid. In their statement of 30 August to the League of Nations the Chinese Government declared that they had at this time also offered to settle the dispute by negotiation, through third party mediation, or by any pacific means (RIIA, *Documents, 1937*, p. 671). Hidaka did not mention this.
[4] RIIA, *Survey, 1937*, i. 187–8.
[5] Evidence of Hashimoto and of Torashiro Kawabe (IMTFE, *Record*, pp. 20625–6, 2994).

publicly announce their intention of withdrawing their reinforcements from North China. In fact the Central Chinese Government troops were first to begin to go back to their bases; this was to be immediately followed by the withdrawal of the Japanese troops. Hidaka thought peace was ensured and Konoye was also optimistic.[1]

But then there came a sudden and rapid turn for the worse in North China. On 22 July General Hsiung Pin, the Vice-Chief of the Chinese General Staff, had arrived in Peiping, and the Japanese suspected that the real object of his visit was to encourage the Twenty-Ninth Army not to carry out the agreement.[2] Meanwhile General Wachi had gone to Tokyo to put the viewpoint of the Japanese North China Army. It seems fairly evident that he and his colleagues resented the orders sent them and wanted to deal the Chinese a crushing blow.[3] They soon had an excuse to do so. On 25 July a Japanese force sent to Langfang, on the Tientsin–Peiping railway about midway between the two cities, came into conflict with Chinese troops stationed there; each side accusing the other of beginning the fighting. This was shortly followed by a fight between Japanese troops sent to reinforce their Legation Guards in Peiping and Chinese forces guarding the south-west gate of the city. Renewed conflict also broke out at Wanping. On 26 July General Katsuki sent an ultimatum to the Chinese demanding that their troops at Lukouchiao and Wanping should retire by noon of the following day and that the whole of the Thirty-Seventh Division should leave the area around Peiping on 28 July and retreat across the Yungting River, prior to being sent to Paoting. If this were not done the Japanese Army would take any action which it might deem appropriate.[4] The Japanese General Staff in Tokyo had given permission for this ultimatum, but warned the North

---

[1] ibid.; also *Saionji–Harada Memoirs*, 19 July 1937.

[2] But General Chin Teh-chun, questioned on this point by the Japanese defence counsel, denied that the Vice-Chief's visit had resulted in a more belligerent attitude on the part of the Chinese troops (IMTFE, *Record*, p. 2449).

[3] From Wachi's own affidavit it appears that he complained that the Chinese had forbidden Japanese troops to use the Peiping–Tientsin railway, and spoke of 'other indignities'. He described himself as 'submitting to complete humiliation and inconvenience', in accordance with the orders from Tokyo (ibid. p. 20582). According to the *Saionji–Harada Memoirs* he objected very strongly to the decision taken by the Government. The Japanese Army in North China were said to be annoyed about reinforcements coming from home; it had wanted to settle the matter on its own. Wachi returned to Tientsin on 28 July, after the Langfang and Peiping clashes.

[4] Affidavit of Hashimoto (IMTFE, *Record*, pp. 20631–2).

China Army not to go beyond the line of the Yungting River.[1] They also decided to mobilize the three divisions of the Japanese home Army which they had originally intended to dispatch to China, but which they had halted upon receiving the news of the Peiping Agreement.[2] At midnight on 27 July Colonel Matsui informed General Sung that, in view of the Peiping affair and of non-compliance with the Japanese demands, the Japanese intended to attack. The next day the Chinese troops around Peiping, including the division from south Hopei, were attacked and defeated by the Japanese. General Sung Cheh-yuan, finding his position untenable, left for Paoting in the night of 28 July, accompanied by General Chin Teh-chun.[3] In the course of the following days the Japanese, after severe fighting in Tientsin and at Tungchow, where they had to cope with a revolt of their own puppet forces under Yin Su-keng, made themselves masters of the whole Peiping–Tientsin region. So ended all hopes of an immediate pacification and both China and Japan began to prepare for general hostilities.[4]

It is just possible that the Japanese Government might have been emboldened to take a firmer line with the recalcitrants, at home and abroad, if they had been faced with united opposition on the part of foreign Powers to a Sino-Japanese conflict, but this was not forthcoming. At the end of May 1937 the British Prime Minister, Neville Chamberlain, had sounded the American Secretary of State, Cordell Hull, on the possibility of an Anglo-American-Japanese agreement on the Far East. He hoped by this to preserve peace in that region and to avert the danger of Great Britain

---

[1] ibid.; also Torashiro Kawabe (ibid. pp. 21995–6).

[2] Kawabe (ibid. pp. 21995–6); also affidavit of Tanaka (ibid. p. 26684).

[3] According to Chin Teh-chun, the Generalissimo had sent repeated telegrams to Sung to go to Paoting and direct operations from there (*Exhibit*, 198).

[4] In commenting upon these unhappy developments Prince Konoye declared: 'The results of my efforts to ascertain the policy of the military towards China revealed that at least as far as the leaders were concerned their policy was not fundamentally different from that of the Government. Consequently I came to the conclusion not that the Government lacked the power to check the military, but that the military leaders themselves were unable to command the whole Army' (Extract from 'Efforts for Peace' by Konoye; in IMTFE (rejected), *Defence Documents*). Shortly after Lukouchiao, Konoye wished to send two of his intimates, Miyazaki and Akiyama, on a special peace mission to Nanking, but they were arrested on suspicion of espionage by the Kempeitai (Japanese Military Security Police) and held for a week (ibid.). Konoye told Sugiyama of his intention and thought that he was responsible for the arrest of the envoys, but the War Minister declared that the Kempeitai had done it on their own account and were defiant about it (*Saionji–Harada Memoirs*, 12 Aug. 1937).

becoming involved in war in Europe and in the Far East simultaneously.[1] But the proposal found no favour in Washington. Hull replied on 1 June in a memorandum which referred to the traditional policy of the United States 'not to enter into those types of agreement which constitute or which suggest alliance'. He indicated that the American Government preferred consultation, followed by parallel action, to any kind of joint action, and he added a scarcely veiled warning against any Anglo-Japanese accord which deviated from the Nine-Power Treaty of Washington. On the other hand, he declined to state in advance what the United States would do in the event of aggression in the Far East.[2] Chamberlain was probably not much disappointed by this answer; as early as June 1934 he had noted, prophetically enough, that 'we ought to know by this time that USA will give us no undertaking to resist by force any action by Japan, short of an attack on Hawaii or Honolulu.'[3] But he was too acutely conscious of the peril to Great Britain of a two-front war to accept Hull's dictum that her Government should make no accord with Tokyo. The Anglo-Japanese discussions for the time being continued and, after the outbreak of Sino-Japanese hostilities, the British Government strove to prevent their extension and to bring about a settlement.

Both London and Washington urged restraint upon Tokyo and Nanking, but the British Government were ready to go further than this. They appear to have proffered their good offices to Tokyo, as early as 15 July, but Hirota at that time replied that his Government had not given up hopes of a local settlement.[4] Hull, however, had rejected a Chinese appeal, on 12 July, for American mediation, and four days later he issued a statement of general principles of policy to which he requested all Governments to adhere. This they all did; the Japanese Government, however, remarked that 'the objectives of those principles will only be attained, in their application to the Far Eastern situation, by a full recognition and practical consideration of the actual particular

---

[1] *The Memoirs of Cordell Hull* (London, Hodder & Stoughton; New York, Macmillan, 1948), i. 531. In the autumn of 1934 Chamberlain had noted: 'if we had to contemplate the division of our forces so as to protect our Far Eastern interests while prosecuting a war in Europe, then it must be evident that not only India, Hong-Kong, and Australasia would be in dire peril, but that we ourselves would stand in far greater danger of destruction by a fully-armed and organised Germany' (Keith Feiling, *The Life of Neville Chamberlain* (London, Macmillan, 1946), p. 234).
[2] Hull, *Memoirs*, i. 532–3.   [3] Feiling, *Chamberlain*, p. 253.
[4] Evidence of Horinouchi (IMTFE, *Record*, p. 29690).

circumstances of that region'.[1] This left things as they had been
before.

On 20 July the British Government asked the United States to
join with Great Britain and France in a joint recommendation to
the Japanese and Chinese Governments to suspend all further
troop movements. This would be followed by Anglo-American
proposals for a settlement of the Sino-Japanese conflict.[2] On 21
July Hull declined this proposal for joint mediation. His reasons,
as given in his *Memoirs*, were that he believed that such a move
would only serve to stiffen the backs of the Japanese military, that
there was no intention on the part of either Great Britain or of the
United States to support such a démarche by the threat or use of
force, and that any suggestion of joint action with Great Britain
would arouse a clamour on the part of isolationist elements in the
United States.[3] So a chance to put out the Far Eastern conflagra-
tion before it spread beyond control was lost. No doubt if the
joint intervention had been made it would have aroused resentment
in Japan, especially if the proposed peace terms had appeared to
favour the Chinese contentions. But, if the Western Powers were
not prepared for serious trouble with Japan, she was not herself
ready for war, and would not be for some years. The Army had
only just secured the adoption of its long-term programmes for
armaments expansion and the Japanese General Staff were concerned at the prospect of a general war with China, the more so as
they could not be absolutely sure that the USSR might not intervene.[4] The Japanese naval staff, too, would almost certainly have

---

[1] Hull, *Memoirs*, i. 535–6.   [2] ibid. p. 538.
[3] ibid. pp. 538–9. Hull says he also considered that, if any joint action was
taken at all, 'it should be by all the nations having an interest in the Far East, or,
better still, by all the peaceful nations of the world.' As will be seen, the British
Government did approach Germany and Italy, but without success.
[4] According to the evidence of Shinichi Tanaka, the Japanese General Staff
in July 1937 estimated Soviet strength in the Far East at 28 infantry divisions,
6 mechanized brigades, and 4½ cavalry divisions. This compared with a peacetime strength of 17 divisions and a wartime one of 30 divisions for Japan. The
General Staff therefore reckoned that they could employ at the outside only 15
divisions in China and for these they had only eight months' supply of ammunition. Consequently, if there were a protracted war with China, serious difficulties would arise, and any outside intervention would create a very critical
situation for Japan. Tanaka said he was present when the General Staff made
this appreciation (IMTFE, *Record*, pp. 20671–3). At the same time, in view of
the purges in the USSR and the readiness she had shown to settle pacifically a
frontier clash on the Amur in June, the General Staff did not believe that she was
ready to intervene. On 12 July Baron Harada was told by the Lord Keeper of
the Privy Seal, Kurahei Yuasa, that Prince Kanin, Chief of the General Staff,
had been asked by the Emperor what would happen if the USSR intervened.

taken a stronger line against involvement in China if this had looked like provoking a clash with Great Britain and the United States.

Nor could Japan at this juncture expect any assistance from her anti-Comintern partner. The German Foreign Ministry viewed the prospect of a Sino-Japanese conflict with alarm, not only because of the disastrous effect it would have upon the large and profitable German commerce with China but also because they feared that it would weaken Japan *vis-à-vis* the USSR.[1] They knew from the reports of Trautmann, the German Ambassador in Nanking, that the Chinese were in a confident and belligerent mood and were prepared to answer any Japanese attack on the north by launching general war.[2] Consequently the German Foreign Ministry had sharply rejected the Japanese claim for their support on the basis of the Anti-Comintern Pact,[3] and had taken the first opportunity to declare German neutrality in any Far Eastern conflict.[4] They were not, however, at this time, pre-

Kanin replied that the Army thought that she would not start anything. The Emperor was said to have replied 'But if they do', and Kanin to have answered, 'nothing can be done' (*Saionji–Harada Memoirs*, 14 July 1937). Presumably Kanin meant that nothing could be done in China. It is evident that there was a division of opinion in the Japanese Army between those who thought that Chinese resistance could be quickly crushed and Nanking brought to terms and those who doubted this and did not want to take the risk. A joint démarche by foreign Powers *might* have swung the balance in favour of the latter.

[1] 'We are following developments with great concern and earnestly desire an early peaceful settlement of the incident for the sake of our economic interests in the Far East and ... in view of our anti-Comintern policy. A military show-down between China and Japan would benefit the Soviet Government, which has an interest in engaging Japan elsewhere and weakening her by military operations'. (GFM to various German Diplomatic Missions, 20 July 1937, *D Ger.FP*, series D, i. 733–4.)

[2] Trautmann on 21 July quoted General von Falkenhausen, head of the German military advisers in China, as saying that Chiang Kai-shek was prepared for 'a military showdown' rather than sacrifice vital Chinese interests, for capitulation 'would lead to personal attacks on him and to serious internal political conflicts'. The war would be waged everywhere and the Chinese felt militarily secure on the northern front and in Shanghai. Falkenhausen considered that the Japanese would have no chance of victory unless they used their entire army, that the morale of the Chinese Army was good, and that in the air the combatants were about equal (Trautmann to GFM, 21 July 1937, ibid. p. 736). Falkenhausen overrated the Chinese Army; his estimate may have been a factor in deciding Chiang to fight. But he was right in his prediction that the war would turn into a death struggle and that Japan's victory was not a foregone conclusion.

[3] Weizsäcker, *Memoirs*, p. 116. Baron von Weizsäcker was at this time the head of the Political Department of the German Foreign Ministry. On 28 July he told Dirksen, the German Ambassador in Tokyo, that Japanese action in China was contrary to the Anti-Comintern Pact because it would drive China into the arms of Russia, and that Germany did not welcome Japanese radio propaganda in German describing their actions in China as a war against Communism (*D Ger.FP*, series D, i. 742–3).

[4] On 20 July; GFM to Missions Abroad, ibid. pp. 733–4.

pared to join in any joint démarche, or separately to offer their
good offices, which they knew that Japan would resent.[1] But they
had counselled restraint in both Tokyo and Nanking and there is
no reason to suppose that they were not sincere in this.[2] They wanted
to keep on good terms with both Japan and China, but, as the
future was to reveal, the outbreak of general hostilities between
these Powers would force Germany to make a choice between them.
The Italian Government, whose interests in China were small, were
inclined to curry favour with Japan, though they, too, declared
that they had recommended a pacific solution in the Far East.[3]
The outbreak of large-scale hostilities in North China made a
general Sino-Japanese conflict practically certain, in view of the
prevalent mood in Nanking. The Japanese Government, however,
were still hoping to effect a settlement. The proposed terms were
worked out in discussions between high-ranking officials of the
General Staff, and the War, Navy, and Foreign Ministries at the
end of July and approved by the Japanese Inner Cabinet on 7
August.[4] Hirota then sent a special emissary named Funatsu to
Shanghai to get into touch with Kao Tsung-wu. However, before
Kao, who was in Nanking, and Funatsu could meet, the Japanese
Ambassador to China, Kawagoe, who had been in North China and
Manchuria, returned to Shanghai on 7 August and took over the
negotiations.[5] On 8 August Hirota telegraphed Kawagoe the
terms which had been agreed upon in Tokyo. These were for
a 'demilitarized' zone in Hopei, to extend to the Yungting River
and to embrace, therefore, the entire Peiping–Tientsin area.[6] All

---

[1] On 24 July a British *aide-mémoire* to Berlin said that the British Foreign
Secretary had on 21 July requested the Japanese Ambassador to urge on his
Government the greatest possible restraint, and had warned him not to under-
rate Chinese determination to resist. Mr. Eden had also spoken with Dr. H. H.
Kung, the Chinese Vice-Premier and Minister of Finance (who was then in
London). Kung had said that he knew that the German Government were
anxious for peace and had agreed with Eden on the desirability of Anglo-
German co-operation. But Weizsäcker replied to the British chargé d'affaires
that Germany had tendered her good offices to neither of the parties, 'nor would
we do so, for we had no political interests in the Far East' (ibid. pp. 738–9).

[2] Weizsäcker's memo. of conversation with the Japanese Counsellor of
Embassy, 22 July 1937 (ibid. p. 737).

[3] ibid.; also von Hassell (Rome) telegram to Berlin, 21 July 1937 (ibid. p. 735).

[4] IMTFE, *Exhibit* 3735; also evidence of Horinouchi (*Record*, pp. 29692–4)
and of Tanaka (ibid. p. 20697). The Inner Cabinet meeting consisted normally
of the Premier, Foreign Minister, and the two Service Ministers; if necessary the
Home or the Finance Minister would be included.

[5] Horinouchi, loc. cit.

[6] Hirota to Kawagoe, 8 Aug. 1937. Kawagoe was given some latitude in the
matter of the precise boundary of the demilitarized zone, but was warned that

Chinese troops were to leave this zone and be replaced by Paoantui. Furthermore all Central Government troops were to evacuate Hopei. When this had been done the Japanese forces in North China would be reduced to the number which had obtained prior to Lukouchiao. The Hopei–Chahar and East Hopei régimes would be abolished, so would the provisions of the Tangku Truce, subject to certain safeguards, and also the Ho–Umezu and Chin–Doihara Agreements. The Chinese Central Government would then be free to administer the North, on the understanding that the principal officials it appointed should be men 'fitted for the attainment of Sino-Japanese reconciliation'.[1]

Along with these proposals went a plan for the overall adjustment of Sino-Japanese relations which Kawagoe could propose at the same time or keep until later as he thought best. This plan embodied Hirota's 'Three Principles': Chinese recognition, or at all events tacit acceptance, of Manchukuo; a Sino-Japanese anti-Comintern pact, with special reference to the proposed demilitarized zone; and suppression of anti-Japanese agitation throughout China. In return Japan would cease to undermine the authority of Nanking in Inner Mongolia and Suiyuan, would co-operate in the abolition of the 'special trade'—i.e. smuggling—in Hopei, and would, if the Chinese wished it, abrogate the Shanghai Truce Agreement of 1932.[2] Kawagoe was warned that only a few of the highest ranking officers in the General Staff and the War Ministry knew of these proposed terms for fear of opposition in the Army if they leaked out prematurely. He was instructed to keep them secret from the Japanese military and naval attachés.[3] He was told that it was also important to reach an agreement with the Chinese before 20 August, because by that date the three divisions to be sent from Japan to China would have finished their concentration.[4] The *modus operandi* was for Kawagoe to contact Kao and informally suggest a settlement on the lines indicated, and then it was hoped in

its purpose was 'to include the strategically important hills on the right bank of the Yungting and the Huai Rivers and all-important points such as Tientsin and Taku' (Hirota's no. 171, same date, IMTFE, *Record*, pp. 29938–42).
  [1] ibid.
  [2] ibid. pp. 29943–4. There were also to be provisions for economic collaboration between Japan and China. 'In disposing of the Incident we expect to see the creation of such conditions in Central China and South China as to be suitable for the continuous promotion and development of trade between Japan and China' (Japanese Cabinet decision of 7 Aug., IMTFE, *Exhibit* 3735).
  [3] Hirota to Kawagoe, telegrams of 7 and 8 Aug. 1937.
  [4] IMTFE, *Record*, pp. 2926–7, 29946.

Tokyo that the Chinese Government would take the initiative in publicly proposing negotiations.[1]

Kao Tsung-wu did come to Shanghai and meet Kawagoe. On being apprised of the terms Kao replied, according to Hidaka, that he thought they might be acceptable although there would be some points of difference. He promised to lay the proposals before his Government and return to Shanghai with their answer. But then came the outbreak of fighting at Shanghai and the discussions were not resumed.[2]

Hirota considered that both the Chinese and the foreign Powers ought to be pleasantly surprised at the generosity of the proffered terms.[3] But as they were victor's terms it was unlikely that Chiang Kai-shek could or would have accepted them. Like Konoye, he was walking on eggs in the matter. If he had asked for peace and accepted a demilitarized zone in the north—in the sense that Chinese troops should evacuate it, while a Japanese garrison remained under the terms of the Boxer Protocol—he would have been faced with revolt on the part of sections of the Kuomintang, as well as from without the party. He, personally, would no doubt have preferred an arrangement, but, especially after his experience in the Sian coup, he was not going to risk an internal upheaval, as he had indicated to von Falkenhausen. According to General Chennault, Chiang on 6 August had decided to fight Japan, and his German-trained troops were already on the move towards Shanghai.[4]

Japan, in common with the other Treaty Powers, maintained a force at Shanghai for the protection of her nationals and interests in that great commercial and maritime centre. This force was the Naval Landing Party, which normally consisted of some 2,000

[1] Hirota to Kawagoe, telegram no. 169, 8 Aug. 1937 (ibid. p. 29935).
[2] Hidaka said that the meeting was 'on or about 10 August' (ibid. p. 29924).
[3] 'The broad-minded policy of our government will be beyond the expectation of the Chinese themselves and is worthy of winning the respect of the whole world for the fair and disinterested attitude of our Empire' (Hirota's no. 169 to Kawagoe, ibid. p. 29937).
[4] C. L. Chennault, *Way of a Fighter* (New York, Putnam, 1949), pp. 41–42. Chennault had just been appointed as Director of the Chinese air fighter squadrons. He says that he and the Generalissimo's political adviser, W. H. Donald, were present at the Conferences of Chinese military leaders at the Nanking Military Academy. Chiang wanted to gain time, but leaders of all groups came in to demand a stand (ibid.). The Kao–Kawagoe conversation is referred to in the *Saionji–Harada Memoirs*, 20 Aug. 1937. Hirota said he wanted Kawagoe to fly to Nanking and try to continue the peace discussions, even after the outbreak at Shanghai, but Kawagoe did not go.

men. It held the Hongkew and Yangtzepoo areas of the International Settlement and an external defence area in north Hongkew. After the Sino-Japanese hostilities in this area in 1932, an armistice Agreement was reached on 5 May of that year, which provided that the Chinese troops should remain in their existing positions—about 20 kilometres from Shanghai—'pending later arrangements upon the re-establishment of normal conditions.'[1] The Japanese had in mind a conference of the Treaty Powers which should establish a permanent neutralized zone around Shanghai, but this never took place.[2] The Chinese Government established a special Peace Preservation Corps, equipped with small arms, to police the zone. The head of this force was originally the Chinese Mayor of the Municipality of Greater Shanghai, but in April 1936 its command was transferred to an army officer, General Yang Hu.

The Agreement of 5 May also provided for the establishment of a Joint Commission, to be composed of Chinese and Japanese representatives and also those of the participating 'friendly Powers', to ensure the execution of the armistice arrangements. This body, however, had not met since 1932. In June 1937 the Japanese Consul-General, Suemasa Okamoto, with the approval of the Commander of the Naval Landing Party, called a meeting of the Commission, in order to protest against the rebuilding of the Woosung forts and the construction of field fortifications in the demilitarized zone.[3] At the meeting on 23 June Okamoto formulated his charges. The Chinese Mayor, O. K. Yui, replied that Woosung was outside the scope of the armistice Agreement, which statement Okamoto contested. Yui also asserted that the Chinese were not expressly precluded by the Agreement of 1932 from constructing defences within the zone. The consular representatives of third Powers decided that 'they were not in a position to express an opinion on the conflicting interpretations of the Chinese and Japanese delegations.'[4] They did, however, suggest that, without prejudice to his case, the Chinese representative might make a voluntary declaration on the numbers of the Peace Preservation Corps and the extent of the fortifications. Yui replied

[1] F. C. Jones, *Shanghai and Tientsin* (London, Oxford University Press for RIIA, 1940), p. 55.
[2] For subsequent diplomatic exchanges see ibid. pp. 57–58.
[3] Okamoto had become Consul-General at Shanghai in the previous May (affidavit of Okamoto, IMTFE, *Record*, p. 21152).
[4] Minutes of the Joint Commission Meeting, June 1937 (*Exhibit* 2517).

that he could not do this without the permission of his Government, but said that the Chinese authorities harboured no hostile intentions in what they were doing.[1] On or about 15 July, he invited Okamoto, together with the Japanese military and naval attachés, to a social gathering. At this Yui said that he did not want a repetition of the 1932 affair, that he would do all in his power to avoid this, and that he hoped the Japanese would co-operate with him to preserve peace in Shanghai. Okamoto replied that he had instructions from Tokyo to avoid trouble and that he trusted that the Chinese authorities would keep control over anti-Japanese terrorist organizations.[2] But tension grew after the outbreak of large-scale hostilities in North China, especially when the Japanese authorities ordered the evacuation of their nationals from the Yangtze outposts and their concentration in Shanghai. Apparently on 8 August the Chinese Government made an oral representation to the Ambassadors of the Powers in Nanking. They declared while they themselves had no intention of attacking the Japanese forces in Shanghai, the situation would be entirely altered if the Japanese there launched an attack, or if they were reinforced.[3] Also on 8 August the British Ambassador made representations to Hidaka on the necessity of keeping the peace in and around Shanghai.[4]

At about the same time Chennault, then at Nanchang, got a message from Madame Chiang Kai-shek to go to Shanghai and warn the American Consulate that the Japanese were going to attack. He returned from Shanghai on 10 August and *en route* his train was stopped, its passengers put out, and the train loaded with Chinese troops bound for Shanghai.[5]

Did the Japanese intend an attack at Shanghai? The minutes of the Japanese Inner Cabinet Conference of 7 August said that the principal areas for using land forces were Hopei–Chahar and Shanghai.[6] This the International Tribunal at Tokyo considered proof of hostile intent. It does not, however, show beyond question that the Japanese meant to send troops in any case, an interpretation which would make nonsense of the rest of the proceedings. These were concerned with the peace terms Kawagoe was to offer. It

[1] ibid.
[2] Affidavit of Okamoto (*Record*, p. 21160).
[3] RIIA, *Survey, 1937*, i. 209.
[4] Affidavit of Hidaka (IMTFE, *Record*, p. 29909).
[5] Chennault, *Way of a Fighter*, pp. 43–44.   [6] IMTFE, *Exhibit* 2517.

may perhaps be read in conjunction with a General Staff decision of 27 July to send two home divisions to North China and to keep two more in reserve, earmarked for the protection of Japanese residents in Tsingtao and Shanghai.[1] The Japanese Navy did send reinforcements to Shanghai, which Tokyo later justified on the ground of the reports they had received of Chinese troop movements into the demilitarized zone[2]—reports which Chennault's evidence tends to bear out.

On 9 August a Japanese naval lieutenant, Oyama, and a seaman, Saito, were shot by Chinese soldiers in Monument Road, near the Hungjao aerodrome, on the south-west outskirts of Shanghai. The Chinese version of this affair was that the two Japanese had tried to enter the aerodrome, and had killed a Chinese sentry who tried to stop them before being themselves killed. The Japanese naval authorities denied the attempted entry and said, both at the time and later, that Oyama was, by agreement with the Shanghai Defence Committee, in charge of a small Japanese detachment guarding Japanese nationals in the western external roads area, and that the Chinese had shot their own sentry to cover up a wanton murder.[3] This affair increased the mutual ill feeling, but otherwise did not have any marked effect on the course of events.

On 11 August Okamoto protested to Yui about the reinforcement of the Paoantui in the demilitarized zone. The Chinese Mayor responded that Japan was to blame for sending naval reinforcements; he nevertheless agreed to do all he could to preserve the peace.[4] But there was now little either he or Okamoto could do; affairs were passing from civilian to military control on both sides.[5] On 12 August the Chinese Eighty-Seventh and Eighty-

[1] Evidence of Torashiro Kawabe (*Record*, p. 21996).
[2] Jones, *Shanghai and Tientsin*, p. 59. The Naval Landing Party was reinforced by 300 sailors from Japanese warships which collected at Shanghai from the Yangtze, and by a further 1,000 from a squadron of 15 ships which arrived from Japan on 11 August. (Affidavit of Admiral Isamu Takeda, Senior Staff Officer of the Naval Landing Party, IMTFE, *Record*, pp. 21250–1.)
[3] Jones, *Shanghai and Tientsin*, p. 59. Takeda told the International Tribunal that, whereas Oyama was unarmed and the seaman Saito had only a revolver, an autopsy held at Chenyu in the presence of Chinese and Japanese medical officers showed that the dead Chinese had been killed by a rifle bullet. He also said that the Chinese senior adjutant had apologized for the affair. This was in the course of his cross-examination. (IMTFE, *Record*, pp. 21273, 21277.)
[4] Affidavit of Okamoto (ibid. pp. 2166–7).
[5] Okamoto said that when one of his subordinates telephoned Yui on the morning of 12 August the Mayor was found to be at his home in the French Concession. When reached he declared that he was not going to his office as he could do nothing when the situation got bad like this (ibid. p. 21168).

Eighth Divisions poured into the area adjacent to the Japanese Naval Landing Party's positions. So, on the same day, Okamoto called another meeting of the Joint Commission and protested against the Chinese troop movements. The Chinese Mayor again replied that these were justifiable measures of self-defence in view of the arrival of Japanese naval reinforcements. He furthermore contended that the Japanese themselves had invalidated the armistice Agreement of 1932 by their action in 1936 when they had stationed a force at Paitzuchiao, in the neutralized zone. Yui further objected to any measures being taken by the Joint Commission as such, though he said he would welcome suggestions by the neutral members acting in their capacity as Consuls-General.[1] The Italian Consul-General proposed that part of the Japanese sector might be taken over by the defence forces of third Powers, and Okamoto agreed.[2] But this was felt to be a matter for the commanders of the defence forces to decide and nothing immediate came of it.[3] When, on 18 August, the British Government proposed that both combatants should withdraw their forces and leave all civilian residents to be protected by the forces of neutral Powers, Japan rejected this offer, declaring that she was responsible for the safety of her nationals.[4]

Meanwhile on 11 August the American, British, French, German, and Italian Ambassadors had urged on China and Japan the co-operation of all parties in maintaining peace at Shanghai. Hidaka said that he reported this to Tokyo and got a reply on 12 August to say that the Japanese Government were acquiescent, provided China observed the Agreement of 1932.[5] On the same day Hidaka received a message from Okamoto to ask that he persuade the Chinese Government to withdraw all their forces from the vicinity of the International Settlement. He took this up with the Chinese Vice-Minister of Foreign Affairs on that afternoon, and, on the next day, 13 August, after further instructions from Tokyo, with the Chinese Foreign Minister. But, according to Hidaka,

[1] Minutes of Meeting of the Joint Commission, 12 Aug. 1937 (*Exhibit* 2516). Paitzuchiao, the Eight Character Bridge, was about half a mile beyond the defence line. Yui said he had made representations to the Japanese at the time of their action, but had not lodged a formal protest as this would have disturbed the then friendly relations (ibid.).   [2] ibid.

[3] This would have upset the pre-arranged defence arrangements and, in view of the temper of both sides, might have involved neutral forces in the fighting.

[4] So Hirota told the Diet on 5 September (RIIA, *Documents, 1937*, pp. 662–3)

[5] Evidence of Hidaka (IMTFE, *Record*, p. 29910).

Dr. Wang Chung-hui also contested the continuing validity of the 1932 Agreement.[1] On the same day, 13 August, fighting began between the Chinese and Japanese forces at Shanghai.[2] On 14 August an attempt by Chinese aircraft to bomb the Japanese cruiser, *Izumo*, caused heavy loss of civilian life in the International Settlement.[3] On 15 August the Japanese Government decided to send army units to Shanghai and appointed General Iwane Matsui, who had been in retirement since 1935, to command them.[4] They also issued a public statement in which they declared that 'drastic measures' were necessary 'to chastise the lawless Chinese troops and to impress upon the National Government the necessity for reconsideration of its attitude toward Japan.' They asserted that they had no territorial designs upon China and that they would respect the rights and interests of foreign Powers.[5]

China and Japan were now at war, in all but name. One immediate result of this was the conclusion on 21 August 1937 of a Sino-Soviet Non-Aggression Pact. The negotiations for this had been going on for a considerable time prior to the Lukouchiao affair, but the Chinese had hitherto held off, for fear of antagonizing other Powers. By the first article of the Pact the USSR and China pledged themselves to make no attack on the other, either individually, or in concert with other Powers. The second article provided that neither signatory would assist in any manner any aggressor against the other. The third article excepted from the operation of the Pact any pre-existing rights and obligations arising out of treaties already concluded by either side.[6]

On 30 August the Chinese Government were at pains to explain to Berlin that they had been compelled to conclude the Pact 'to eliminate the possibility of conflict with Soviet Russia in order to secure her [China's] rear for the defence against the Japanese

---

[1] ibid. p. 29911.

[2] Each side, as usual, blamed the other for the outbreak. Takeda said that at 1 p.m. on 13 August the Commander of the Naval Landing Party warned his officers not to fight unless attacked. He claimed that the Chinese had already begun firing and that at 4 p.m. they opened an artillery bombardment. The Japanese, who were outnumbered by at least ten to one, were nearly overwhelmed on 16 August. (Affidavit of Takeda, ibid. pp. 21256–7.)

[3] Chennault says that the Chinese aircraft disobeyed his orders not to fly over the Settlement (Chennault, *Way of a Fighter*, p. 45).

[4] The first troops sent were the 3rd Division and the 11th Division, less one brigade. Matsui wanted five divisions at the start in view of the reported numbers of the Chinese. Reinforcements were sent piecemeal and his strength did not reach five divisions until October (evidence of Matsui, IMTFE, *Exhibit* 3498).

[5] RIIA, *Documents, 1937*, pp. 659–60.　　　　　[6] ibid. pp. 664–5.

attack.'[1] They added that the Pact was not an alliance and that there were no secret clauses.

Nor would it make any change in the domestic policy of the Chinese Government whose recent release of Chinese Communist leaders had not been at the behest of Moscow, and had been done only to bring about the greatest possible internal unity. The Chinese Government were anxious to continue their friendly relations with Germany and hoped that she would maintain her neutrality in the Sino-Japanese hostilities.[2] In reply the Chinese Ambassador was told that the news of the Pact had been received with surprise and with serious misgivings in Germany, especially as the Pact contained no non-intervention clause.[3]

On 12 September the Chinese Government formally appealed to the League of Nations against Japan. The Council of the League referred the matter to the Far Eastern Advisory Committee, which detailed a sub-committee to investigate, and this body produced two reports. The first report, after reviewing the course of events in the Far East, found that Japanese military operations against China were 'out of all proportion to the incident that occasioned the conflict', that they could be justified 'neither on the basis of existing legal instruments nor on that of the right of self-defence' and were 'in contravention of Japan's obligations under the Nine-Power Treaty of the 6th February, 1922, and under the Pact of Paris of the 27th August, 1928.'[4] The second report recommended that the League of Nations should invite those of its members who were signatories of the Nine-Power Treaty together with other States with interests in the Far East, to confer on the situation. These reports were adopted by the Advisory Committee on 5 October and by the League Assembly on the following day.[5]

The proposal to convene the Washington Treaty Powers was obviously intended to bring in the United States. Two Great Powers, Germany and Japan, had withdrawn from the League; a third, Italy, was on the point of doing the same; as against that, the USSR had joined it and was now, along with China, urging that

[1] Memo. by Dr. Gaus (head of the Legal Department, GFM), 30 Aug. 1937 (*D Ger.FP*, series D, ii. 756). [2] ibid. pp. 756–7.
[3] ibid. p. 757. On 8 September, at the time of registering the Pact with the League of Nations, the Chinese delegation at Geneva issued a statement to point out that Article 6 of the Sino-Soviet Treaty of 1924, which forbade either signatory to support revolutionaries or to spread propaganda in the territory of the other, remained valid (RIIA, *Survey, 1937*, i. 297).
[4] ibid. pp. 281–3. [5] ibid. pp. 283–4.

some concrete action be taken against Japan, but Russian motives and capabilities were alike suspect. Great Britain and France, who were faced with the growing power and ambitions of Germany and Italy, and with the tense situation arising out of the Spanish conflict, could not risk involvement in the Far East without assurances of American support. The Department of State had sent an observer to the proceedings of the League sub-committee in the person of the American Minister to Switzerland, and had taken parallel action with the League in condemning Japanese bombing of Chinese cities.[1] On 6 October it expressed agreement with the findings of the League Assembly.[2] Even greater interest and hopes were aroused by President Roosevelt's speech at Chicago on 5 October in which he compared the 'epidemic of world lawlessness' to an 'epidemic of physical disease', in the case of which 'the community approves, and joins in, a quarantine of the patients'.[3] This evidently implied some form of collective sanctions and made everybody prick up their ears.[4]

But the hopes of China and the League as well as the apprehensions of Japan were soon quelled. Roosevelt had in fact himself inserted the 'quarantine clause' into the speech prepared for him by the Department of State.[5] The prepared portion was couched in more cautious phraseology. In the United States the suggestion of sanctions provoked a storm of adverse comment within and without Congress, and Roosevelt, like the adroit politician he was, promptly drew back and tried to explain away his unfortunate language.[6] The episode served only to reveal to

[1] Hull, *Memoirs*, i. 543. [2] ibid. p. 544.
[3] RIIA, *Survey, 1937*, i. 274.
[4] Roosevelt had been meditating upon the 'quarantine' idea which was apparently to take the form of some sort of naval blockade, since the early summer of 1937 (Sumner Welles, *Seven Decisions that Shaped History* (New York, Harper, 1950), p. 8).
[5] Hull, *Memoirs*, i. 544–5. Hull considered Roosevelt's action disastrous: 'As I saw it, this had the effect of setting back for at least six months our constant educational campaign, intended to create and strengthen public opinion toward international cooperation' (ibid. p. 545). The speech provoked adverse reactions in Japan, Italy, and Germany. The German Ambassador in Washington, Dr. Dieckhoff, on 15 October told Berlin that the 'quarantine' threat originated with the President. He pointed out that the threat was directed principally against Japan, to some degree also against Italy, but scarcely against Germany, and that German press reactions had been needlessly violent (*D Ger.FP*, series D, i. 639–41).
[6] In a radio broadcast on 12 October Roosevelt declared: 'The purpose of this conference will be to seek by agreement a solution of the present situation in China. In efforts to find that solution, it is our purpose to cooperate with the other signatories to this Treaty, including China and Japan' (Hull, *Memoirs*, i. 551).

the world that American opinion remained overwhelmingly hostile
to any action which might involve the United States in conflict,
whether in Europe or in Asia. The British Government on 6
October informed Washington that they approved the holding
of a conference; in reply the American Government expressed
concurrence and suggested Brussels as the venue.[1] The Belgian
Government agreed to be the host and on 16 October sent out
invitations to all the Powers who had originally or subsequently
adhered to the Washington Treaty.[2] It was stated that the purpose
of the conference was 'to examine the situation in the Far East and
to study peaceable means of hastening the end of the regrettable
conflict which prevails there.'[3] This by implication ruled out any
form of pressure. The British Government stated, both publicly
and privately, that they were prepared to go as far, but no farther
than, the United States did.[4] The French Government were not
prepared to do anything unless they had the solid support of
Great Britain and the United States, including a joint guarantee
of the defence of Indo-China.[5] Hull, who expressed resentment at
any idea that the United States should take the lead, made it
clear both before and during the Brussels Conference that the
United States was not prepared for any kind of pressure on Japan.[6]
The British Government repudiated any suggestion that they
were trying to throw the main burden upon the United States, but
Hull remained suspicious.[7]

Nor was there much chance of the Conference achieving its
professed object of furthering peace between China and Japan.
Even before the invitations to the Conference went out, the
Japanese had made it plain that they would not attend. The
Japanese Vice-Minister for Foreign Affairs told the German
Ambassador that this was because the Conference was being con-

---

[1] ibid. i. 550.
[2] ibid.   [3] ibid.
[4] The British Foreign Secretary, Mr. Eden, on 19 October told Washington
there were three possible courses:—to do nothing; to express moral condemnation of Japan; or to aid China and to bring economic pressure on Japan. He
did not specifically advocate the third course, and he pointed out the risks of
war which this would entail. He concluded that 'sanctions would have to be
preceded by mutual assurances of military support and guarantees of the territorial integrity of other nations.' The Department of State replied that 'consideration of sanctions did not arise in a conference whose objective was to find
a solution of the conflict by agreement' (ibid. pp. 550–1).
[5] ibid. p. 552; Herbert Feis, *The Road to Pearl Harbor* (Princeton University
Press, 1950), p. 15.
[6] Hull, *Memoirs*, i. 551.   [7] ibid. pp. 552–5.

vened on the basis of the League of Nations resolution condemning Japan.[1] But Japanese objections ran deeper than that;
the Washington Conference and the Nine-Power Treaty were a
bitter memory to them, and they regarded the Brussels Conference
as another attempted line-up of the Powers against them. Efforts
to persuade them that this was not the case had no effect. According to the *Saionji–Harada Memoirs*, the British Ambassador, Sir
Robert Craigie, told Hirota that there would be no coercion of
Japan and that the Conference would endeavour to find some third
Power to mediate in the Sino-Japanese conflict. Hirota replied
that Japan preferred direct negotiations but would welcome
secret mediation by Great Britain or the United States.[2] On 21
October, however, Hirota told the German Ambassador that

Japan was opposed on principle to the idea of such comprehensive
conferences, because they were detrimental to the settlement of the
conflict. The Japanese were at all times prepared for direct negotiations
with China, and would also welcome it if a power friendly to China,
such as Germany or Italy, should persuade the Nanking Government
to seek a settlement.[3]

On 27 October Japan formally refused the invitation to the Conference.[4]

Japan had also asked Germany and Italy to refuse.[5] Italy,
however, who was both a member of the League and a co-signa-
tory of the Washington Treaty, found it difficult to do so, and
instead arranged with Tokyo to be present as an expounder and
champion of the Japanese viewpoint.[6] Germany was in a different
position. She was neither a member of the League nor a signatory
of the Washington Treaty; she could therefore decline with a good
grace.[7] On the other hand, she had her commercial interests in
China to consider and the Chinese Government wanted her to

---

[1] GFM memo. 13 Oct. 1937; GFM to Trautmann, same date (*D Ger.FP*,
series D, i. 764–5). Hull says he was told on 22 October by a member of the
Japanese Embassy that Japan would not accept 'because her Army in South
China (i.e. Shanghai) jealous of the triumphs of her army in North China, had
to win a compelling victory of its own' (*Memoirs*, i. 551). But this factor did not
prevent a Japanese peace offer to China, as will be seen; in fact neither Government nor Army wanted to go to Brussels.

[2] *Saionji–Harada Memoirs*, 25 Oct. 1937.

[3] Dirksen to GFM, 21 Oct. 1937 (*D Ger.FP*, series D, i. 770).

[4] RIIA, *Survey, 1937*, i. 285.

[5] Dirksen's no. 331 (*D Ger.FP*, series D, i. 769).

[6] ibid. Germany suggested that Italy should attend (memo. by von Neurath,
14 Oct. 1937, ibid. p. 766).   [7] ibid.

accept the invitation to Brussels.[1] Trautmann, too, advised acceptance,[2] but, in view of Japan's attitude, the German Government decided otherwise. On 27 October Hitler told von Neurath that if Germany received an invitation, she should refuse it.[3]

The Brussels Conference convened on 3 November. The Belgian Foreign Minister declared that

The present Conference must not consider itself as a sort of international tribunal before which Japan should be summoned to appear and explain her actions in conditions incompatible with her dignity and honour. What we want is to accomplish a work of conciliation and peace without bias and without passion, taking into account all the legitimate interests which are present.[4]

The American, British, and French delegates spoke in generally similar vein.[5] The Soviet and the Chinese delegates protested against the lack of discrimination between China and Japan; *per contra* the Italian delegate suggested that all the Conference could hope to achieve was to try to bring the two belligerents into direct contact with each other—which, in the circumstances, meant advising China to ask Japan for terms.[6]

A second invitation was dispatched to Tokyo, in which stress was laid upon the conciliatory objects of the Conference and which asked Japan at the least to send representatives to exchange views, within the framework of the Nine-Power Treaty, with those of a subcommittee of the Powers.[7] But the Japanese remained adamant. On 12 November the Japanese Government, in a Note of rejection, reiterated their former stand that their actions in China were taken in self-defence and so were outside the scope of the Nine-Power Treaty, and that since Japan had been wrongly accused of violating the Treaty she could not in honour attend a Conference summoned under its terms.[8]

The Chinese delegate then raised the question of aid to China and economic sanctions against Japan, but received no support.[9]

[1] Memo. by von Neurath, 15 Oct. 1937 (ibid. pp. 766–7). Neurath reminded the Chinese Ambassador that in 1926 China herself had expressed opposition to Germany becoming a signatory of the Nine-Power Treaty (ibid.).
[2] Trautmann to GFM, 16 Oct. 1937 (ibid. p. 767).
[3] 'In my report to the Führer today I broached, among other things, the subject of participation in the Brussels Conference. The Führer decided that, if an invitation comes, we should decline' (memo. by von Neurath, 27 Oct. 1937, ibid. p. 772).
[4] Quoted in RIIA, *Survey, 1937*, i. 287.   [5] ibid.
[6] ibid. pp. 287–8.   [7] ibid. p. 288.
[8] ibid. pp. 288–9.   [9] ibid. p. 289.

Great Britain and France would make no move without a lead from the United States, but the latter, in view of the state of American public opinion, could do nothing and resented any suggestion that she should take the initiative.[1] The Soviet Union was equally careful not to propose any concrete measures against Japan, while the Scandinavian countries were concerned only to keep out of trouble.[2] Consequently the only action taken was the drafting of a declaration which rejected the Japanese view that the matter should be left to direct settlement between the combatants and held that, if Japan persisted in her refusal to co-operate, the States represented at Brussels should consider what was to be their common attitude.[3] This manifesto was adopted on 15 November.[4] It was rather worse than useless since it served only to irritate Japan without affording any concrete help to China. On 24 November the Conference adjourned *sine die*, 'in order to allow time for the participating Governments to exchange views and further explore all peaceful methods by which a just settlement of the dispute may be attained consistent with the principles of the Nine-Power Treaty and in conformity with the objectives of that Treaty.'[5]

The Brussels Conference was worse than a fiasco, it was a disaster. It completely discredited the concept of collective action and it contributed to the ruin of such chance as existed in 1937 of restoring peace between Japan and China. For, on the one hand, by arousing alarm and anger in Japan, it helped to frustrate the unofficial overtures which were being made, especially by Great Britain, to induce Japan to offer China moderate terms of peace.[6] On the other hand, by buoying up the Chinese Government with false hopes, it was a factor in their refusal in early November even to discuss the terms, which, as will be seen, Japan *did* offer them at that time. When, a month later, they *were* prepared to consider

[1] Hull on 17 November instructed the American delegate 'to do what you can to counteract what I am convinced is a general effort on the part of some of the states represented at Brussels to put the entire responsibility for action in the present situation upon this Government, in spite of their own unwillingness, made apparent to us repeatedly in private, to take definite action' (*Memoirs*, i. 555).   [2] Feis, *Road to Pearl Harbor*, p. 15.
[3] RIIA, *Survey, 1937*, i. 290.
[4] ibid. p. 289. Italy dissented and Norway, Sweden, and Denmark abstained from voting.   [5] Quoted ibid. p. 291.
[6] 'As regards Japan, the Conference left the situation rather more rigid than before and lessened the prospects of friendly mediation' (Sir Robert Craigie, *Behind the Japanese Mask* (London, Hutchinson, 1946), p. 51).

these, it was too late; the Japanese Army, elated with victory, had forced the Tokyo Government to demand much more. Ironically enough, if the hint given by the Italian delegate had been taken and China advised to make peace, peace might have been made.

In Japan discussions between officials of the Foreign Ministry and of the War and Navy Ministries resulted in an agreement to seek the mediation of a third Power and also upon the terms to be offered China. These terms were ratified at a conference of the Japanese Inner Cabinet on 1 October.[1] The proposals in respect of North China were generally similar to those communicated by Kawagoe to Kao Tsung-wu in the previous August—the evacuation of Chinese troops from a zone extending to Kalgan and the Yungting River, the abolition of the Hopei–Chahar and East Hopei régimes, and the restoration of Chinese authority in the north, with the proviso that the chief officials should be advocates of Sino-Japanese co-operation. One new feature was the requirement that China should recognize the Inner Mongolian régime headed by Prince Teh. There was also to be another demilitarized area in and around Shanghai. From this all foreign forces, except warships, were to be withdrawn, and all Chinese forces, apart from police who were to co-operate with the International Settlement police in the preservation of order.[2]

These terms were communicated unofficially by Hirota to Craigie with the intent that they should be conveyed to the Chinese Government.[3] This was done, but the terms found no favour in Nanking. According to the *Saionji–Harada Memoirs* Craigie told Hirota that Chiang Kai-shek had bitterly disapproved the proposal for a demilitarized zone. The British Ambassador suggested that this servitude might be subject to a time limit.[4] These unofficial and exploratory talks went on during October and November, with Craigie attempting to tone down the Japanese demands.[5]

---

[1] Evidence of Horinouchi (IMTFE, *Record*, p. 29696).

[2] Outline of Policy of 1 Oct. 1937 (IMTFE, *Exhibit* 3262).

[3] Evidence of Horinouchi (*Record*, pp. 29740–2). Horinouchi said that he was present at some of the talks with Craigie and that Hirota told him what had happened at others. Hirota himself did not testify.

[4] *Saionji–Harada Memoirs*, 8 Oct. 1937.

[5] Craigie says that the withdrawal of Japanese troops to the positions occupied before the Lukouchiao affair was at one time seriously considered. 'But, as usual, the military extremists succeeded in blocking any reasonable proposals and the utmost they would contemplate was withdrawal by stages.' So . . . 'the proposals which finally emerged from the discussions were not such as would interest the Chinese National Government' (*Behind the Japanese Mask*, pp. 50–51).

But Japanese opinion, especially in the Army, was hardening against any official British mediation or good offices, and in favour of utilizing Germany in this respect.[1] At the same time the German Foreign Ministry was coming round to the idea of offering its good offices in the hope of extricating Germany from the awkward position in which she was placed.

This dilemma arose first because of the large contracts for arms and military equipment which the Chinese Government had placed with German firms before the outbreak of the Sino-Japanese hostilities. Germany acquired much needed foreign exchange through these sales and also some valuable strategic materials, including tin and wolfram.[2] At the outset of the conflict Japan demanded that all German arms deliveries to China be halted including those for which China had already contracted.[3] The German Government, in view of their proclamation of neutrality, agreed to make no fresh deliveries of arms, but were nevertheless understandably loath to cancel existing contracts.[4] Sharp words passed between Tokyo and Berlin on this subject, the Japanese even threatening to seize the arms shipments *en route* to China.[5]

The second difficulty arose through the presence in China of thirty ex-officers of the Reichswehr, who were employed as military advisers by the Chinese Government and who had done sterling work in the training of Chiang Kai-shek's Army. These officers had come out to China mostly between the years 1929 and 1934; they had individual contracts with the Chinese Government and they did not constitute an official German military mission. Some of them, indeed, were very far from being enthusiastic supporters of the Nazi régime. But the good work they had done increased German prestige and influence in China and to recall them would not only be an affront to China, but might result in Russian officers coming to fill their places. This was the very last thing that the German Government wanted to see.[6] But the Japanese Government raised this issue also, and were not calmed by assurances from

---

[1] Evidence of Horinouchi (IMTFE, *Record*, p. 29699).
[2] As at 17 August 1937 German armament firms were working on orders totalling 223 million Reichsmarks (memo. of GFM, 15 June 1938, *D Ger.FP*, series D, i. 876).
[3] Memo. by Weizsäcker, 22 July 1937 (ibid. pp. 737–8).
[4] GFM to Dirksen, 28 July 1937 (ibid. p. 743).
[5] Memo. by Weizsäcker, 28 July 1937 (ibid. p. 745).
[6] GFM to Dirksen, 28 July 1937 (ibid. p. 743).

Berlin that the German advisers had been warned not to take part in active operations, and that their work was confined to the training of Chinese troops and did not include staff work.[1]

As has been remarked, the German Foreign Ministry officials, while keeping clear of the League of Nations and the Brussels Conference, disapproved of Japan's onslaught upon China. Hence they were disinclined to yield to her importunities about the arms shipments and the advisers. But Hitler's 'unofficial' Foreign Minister, Ribbentrop, had early convinced himself that Japan would win a swift victory and was wholeheartedly upon her side. Also Oshima appears to have held out to him the bait of special economic privileges in China for Germany if she aided Japan to win the victory.[2] In face of these conflicting counsels Hitler himself pursued a vacillating policy. On 16 August, after a discussion of Far Eastern affairs with the War Minister and the Foreign Minister at Nuremburg, he told von Neurath that 'he adhered in principle, to the idea of co-operating with Japan, but that, in the present conflict between China and Japan, Germany must remain neutral.' He ordered that deliveries of military materials already contracted for by China should be continued 'camouflaged as much as possible, of course.' Further Chinese orders for military equipment should 'as far as possible' not be accepted.[3] But on 18 October General Goering who, as Commissioner for the Four-Year Economic Plan, had taken over HAPRO, the German concern organized to barter arms to China in return for raw materials, issued orders to stop all arms deliveries to China. Goering told General Keitel that the Japanese had threatened to withdraw from the Anti-Comintern Pact 'if support of the Chinese by Germany was continued in its present form' and that 'the Führer had decided that an unequivocal

---

[1] '... the policy of keeping our military advisers away from the theatre of war is becoming illusory.... The planning of Chinese operations by them is becoming more obvious' (Dirksen to GFM, 23 Aug. 1937, ibid. p. 755). Foreign press reports that Falkenhausen and other advisers were active on the Shanghai front, although denied by Trautmann, caused fresh trouble (Dirksen's no. 280, 21 Sept. 1937, and Trautmann's reply of 28 Sept. 1937, ibid. pp. 759 and 761–2). Dirksen in his memoirs says that members of the mission *did* direct Chinese operations around Shanghai and that Japanese officers nicknamed the hostilities 'the German War' (Herbert von Dirksen, *Moscow, Tokyo, London* (London, Hutchinson, 1951), p. 191).

[2] 'Contrary to all rumours that have been spread, especially in Nuremberg, that the Japanese had bogged down ... I still have the clear impression and the inner conviction that the Japanese troops will win a decisive victory over China in the not too distant future' (Memo. for the Führer by Ribbentrop, 19 Sept. 1937, *D Ger.FP*, series D, i. 758–9).

[3] Memo. by Neurath, 17 Aug. 1937 (ibid. p. 750).

attitude was to be adopted toward Japan.'[1] Keitel protested that it would not be feasible to stop all deliveries, some of which had already been paid for. The German Minister of War, Marshal von Blomberg, agreed and, backed by the Foreign Ministry, got the decision changed and the deliveries resumed.[2]

In view, however, of the pro-Japanese leanings of Hitler's Nazi entourage, it was clear that if the conflict continued, Germany would finally come down on the side of Japan. On the other hand all parties in Berlin could agree that an end to the Sino-Japanese struggle would be a vast relief to Germany from both the economic and the political standpoints. Dirksen, as early as 23 August, had suggested that when both sides had begun to feel the strain of war and the Chinese in particular were ready to make some concessions, Germany might offer her mediation.[3] He thought that the German military advisers might be used to prepare the way for this by warning Chiang Kai-shek not to prolong the struggle until China was bled white.[4] Hirota's overture of 21 October appeared to provide the awaited opportunity. So, on 22 October, Trautmann was instructed to tell the Chinese Government that Germany would probably decline any invitation to the Brussels Conference, on the ground that it would be futile without Japanese attendance. He was to say that Germany considered 'direct negotiations more promising for the present and would, if the occasion arose, be prepared to serve as a channel of communication.'[5] Trautmann carried out this instruction in an interview with the Chinese Vice-Minister of Foreign Affairs on 29 October. The Vice-Minister replied that the Marshal (Chiang Kai-shek) would first like to know what the Japanese conditions were. Trautmann, therefore, requested Berlin for more definite information on the Japanese attitude before he went to a scheduled meeting with Chiang Kai-shek.[6] Meanwhile on 28 October the Japanese Government had again

---

[1] Memo. by von der Heyden-Rynsch, 19 Oct. 1937 (ibid. pp. 768–9).
[2] ibid. Also further memo. of 22 Oct. 1937 (ibid. p. 772).
[3] Dirksen's no. 228 of 23 Aug. 1937 (ibid. p. 755).
[4] ibid. Dirksen and Ott, the German military attaché, were agreed upon this (*Moscow, Tokyo, London*, p. 89).
[5] GFM to Trautmann, 22 Oct. 1937 (*D Ger.FP*, series D, i. 771).
[6] Trautmann to GFM, 29 Oct. 1937. Trautmann had got an outline of the Japanese terms from General Ott, the German military attaché in Tokyo, who had come to Shanghai; Ott thought that either Trautmann or Falkenhausen might convey them to Chiang Kai-shek. Ott said that he undertook this mission at the request of Tada, the Vice-Chief of the Japanese General Staff (Interrogation of Ott, 20 Feb. 1946, IMTFE; Trautmann's no. 272 of 31 Oct. 1937, *D Ger.FP*, series D, i. 777).

asked Germany to use her influence to get China to initiate peace talks.[1] In reply the German Foreign Ministry asked Dirksen if he thought that the Japanese were really sincere in their professed desire for negotiations and instructed him to tell them that Germany was not prepared to exercise pressure on China.[2] Trautmann was informed of this and warned that Germany was not contemplating mediation, but wished in the first instance only to be a 'letter-carrier'.[3]

Dirksen on 3 November reported that Hirota that day had told him of the Japanese terms. These were in general accord with the decisions of the Inner Cabinet Conference of 1 October. Hirota had emphatically declared that if China refused to consider them, 'he would carry the war to the point of the total defeat of China and then exact far more difficult terms.'[4] Dirksen considered that the Japanese Government were sincere, both in wishing to make peace on these terms, and in their resolve to carry the war on to the bitter end if Nanking did not accept. He judged the terms to be acceptable and again suggested that the German military advisers in China be utilized to persuade Chiang Kai-shek to agree to negotiate.[5] So von Neurath instructed Trautmann to convey the terms to Chiang, adding that they 'seem acceptable to us as the basis for the opening of negotiations.'[6]

On 5 November Trautmann carried out this instruction. Chiang Kai-shek replied that 'he could not accept any Japanese demands

---

[1] Dirksen's no. 336, 28 Oct. 1937 (ibid. p. 773).
[2] 'Please tell the Japanese that in our opinion we have done everything possible since the outbreak of the conflict to exert a friendly influence on China, and we consider a more far-reaching pointed move premature' (GFM to Dirksen, 30 Oct. 1937, ibid. p. 775).
[3] GFM to Trautmann, 30 Oct. 1937 (ibid. p. 776).
[4] The terms were: 'I. Inner Mongolia would establish an autonomous government corresponding to the status of Outer Mongolia under international law. II. In North China a demilitarized zone would be created along the Manchukuo border to a point south of the Peiping–Tientsin Line.' Hirota said that 'the whole administration of North China would be left to the Nanking Government if peace were to be concluded at once.' If not, and the Japanese established a new administration, they would expect it to continue when peace was concluded later. He also indicated that the pre-conflict negotiations for mineral concessions would have to be concluded satisfactorily. 'III. Shanghai. Creation of a demilitarized zone which was to be larger than the present one. Control by an international police. No other changes. IV. Cessation of Anti-Japanese policy. ... V. A common fight against Bolshevism. According to information received from the Chinese Ambassador here, this would be compatible with the Sino-Russian Nonaggression Pact, provided that there is no secret agreement. VI. Reduction of customs duties on Japanese goods. VII. The rights of aliens shall be respected' (Dirksen's no. 345, 3 Nov. 1937, ibid. pp. 778–9).
[5] ibid.
[6] GFM to Dirksen, 3 Nov. 1937.

so long as the Japanese were not prepared to restore the *status quo ante*.'[1] He added confidentially 'that the Chinese Government would be swept out by the tide of public opinion if he agreed to these demands. There would be a revolution in China.'[2] He furthermore said, no doubt with the idea of influencing Germany to exert a moderating influence on Japan, that if the war continued and the Japanese succeeded in overthrowing his Government, the Communists would get the upper hand in China and *they* would never capitulate. Chiang also declared that it was 'impossible for him to take official cognizance of the Japanese demands because China was now the concern of the powers at the Brussels Conference, and they had the intention, for their part, to work for peace, on the basis of the Washington Treaty.'[3] Trautmann reported to Berlin that he had heard from other sources that the Chinese Government were hoping for Anglo-American mediation.[4]

While there was considerable truth in Chiang's contention that he would be faced by an internal upheaval if he accepted the Japanese terms, his refusal even to discuss them and his demand for the restoration of the *status quo ante* undoubtedly arose from his hope of some form of Anglo-American intervention in China's favour.[5] Otherwise since, according to what he told Trautmann, he knew that China had no chance of victory,[6] he would probably have agreed to discuss the Japanese proposals, as he was prepared to do a month later. But in the meantime the military situation changed disastrously for China. On the very day of Chiang's rejection of the terms a fresh Japanese army, under General

---

[1] Trautmann to GFM, 5 Nov. 1937 (ibid. p. 780).   [2] ibid.
[3] ibid. pp. 780–1.   [4] ibid. p. 781.
[5] Hirota was still pretending to Craigie that Japan would welcome British mediation. Apparently on 5 November Craigie saw Hirota privately, having possibly got wind of the Japanese approach to Germany, and asked whether British good offices were still acceptable, in view of the dislike for Britain manifested in some Japanese circles. Hirota replied 'England is still the most suitable country, haven't we been holding preliminary conversations with you for some time.' He added that German or Italian mediation would not do at all (*Saionji–Harada Memoirs*, 5 Nov. 1937). Horinouchi, who testified in defence of Hirota before the International Military Tribunal, was confronted with this evidence of double-dealing, and made an evasive reply (IMTFE, *Record*, pp. 29790–1). According to Horinouchi the British Government suggested joint mediation by Great Britain, Germany, and the United States, but this was disliked by both the Japanese Army and the German Government (ibid. p. 29699). Hull says that on 18 November the British Government proposed a combined offer of good offices by Great Britain and the United States to both contestants. But Hull declined on the ground that it might involve the transmission of terms to China which were inconsistent with the provisions of the Nine-Power Treaty (*Memoirs*, i. 555).   [6] *D Ger.FP*, i. 780.

Yanagawa, began landing in Hangchow Bay.[1] This force soon menaced the rear of the Chinese defence line near Shanghai, which they had held so stubbornly and compelled a general retreat of the Chinese forces, which in the third week of November degenerated into something like a rout. By the end of November Nanking itself was in danger and the best Chinese armies had suffered grievously in men and munitions. At the same time the complete failure of the Brussels Conference showed how false had been the hopes of any foreign aid. Meanwhile the Germans had continued to urge the Chinese to agree to direct negotiations with Japan. Dirksen once more proposed that the military advisers be used to represent the gravity of the military situation to Chiang and to point out the disastrous consequences to China of prolonged war.[2] This, at Trautmann's request, Falkenhausen did.[3] In mid-November Hirota told Dirksen that

Japan expected the initiation of peace negotiations within a short time, with Germany participating. In spite of the recent military successes of the Japanese, the previously transmitted Japanese demands would not be made more severe on the main points; in particular autonomy in North China would still not be demanded.[4]

Trautmann was instructed by Berlin to bring this to the knowledge of the Chinese Government, which he did.[5] In Berlin von Neurath urged on the Chinese Ambassador the wisdom of concluding peace as soon as possible.[6]

At the beginning of December the Chinese Government came round to this view. According to Wang Ching-wei's memoirs Chiang Kai-shek on 2 December held discussions in Nanking with his leading generals and they all advised him to make peace.[7] At 5 p.m. of the same day he had an interview with Trautmann. He asked him if the Japanese terms remained the same, to which Trautmann replied in the affirmative. The Generalissimo then said that China would accept the terms as a basis of discussion; that Chinese sovereignty and administrative control over North China must not be violated; that Germany should act as mediator

[1] Evidence of Matsui (IMTFE, *Record*).
[2] Dirksen to GFM, 8 Nov. 1937 (*D Ger.FP*, series D, i. 783).
[3] Trautmann to GFM, 9 Nov. 1937 (ibid. p. 784).
[4] This is included in a GFM record of the conversations communicated to the Tokyo Embassy on 4 December (ibid. pp. 794–5).   [5] ibid. p. 796.
[6] Memo. by von Neurath, 1 Dec. 1937 (ibid. p. 787).
[7] J. T. C. Liu, 'German Mediation in the Sino-Japanese War, 1937–8' *FEQ*, February 1949, p. 161.

from the beginning, and that agreements between China and
third Powers should be excluded from the negotiations.[1] Trautmann replied that Germany would not participate directly in the
negotiations, but would rather do what she could behind the scenes
to help China.[2] In further conversation Chiang showed himself
amenable to the appointment of an official friendly to Japan as
head of the North China administration, said that the question of
Inner Mongolia could be negotiated with Japan, and did not
dispute Trautmann's suggestion that an Anti-Comintern Pact with
Japan would not conflict with the Sino-Soviet Non-Aggression
Pact.[3] He and Trautmann agreed that once Japan and China had
consented to open negotiations, Hitler might publicly appeal to
both Governments to conclude an armistice.[4] From Tokyo
Dirksen reported that the Japanese General Staff wanted peace.
They were alarmed at the expansion of the area of military operations and at the increase in war expenditure. But they were 'hesitant at present in regard to peace overtures by Japan, in view of the
radical opposition and the striving on the part of some army groups
to eliminate Chiang Kai-shek completely.'[5] They were therefore
hoping that Hitler would persuade Chiang Kai-shek to make an
overture for peace to which Japan would then respond.[6] That the
senior officers of the General Staff wanted peace at this time and
were prepared to accept moderate terms is borne out from several
Japanese sources.[7] The Vice-Chief, and real head, of the General
Staff, General Tada, took the view that Japan, like Bismarck after
Sadowa, should concede generous terms to her beaten foe and thus

[1] Trautmann to GFM, 3 Dec. 1937 (*D Ger.FP*, series D, i. 787-9).
[2] ibid. p. 788.   [3] ibid.
[4] ibid. Chiang urgently asked that the Japanese Government keep the preliminary negotiations and especially the peace terms a secret. Trautmann told
Berlin that if this were not done Chiang might have to go 'and the Government
will fall into the hands of the pro-Russian group' (ibid. p. 789).
[5] Dirksen to GFM, 3 Dec. 1937 (ibid. p. 790).
[6] ibid. p. 790. In a further telegram of the same date Dirksen said that
'military circles' had in mind those [terms] of November 3, with the reservations
that Chiang Kai-shek must resign himself to a possible reconstruction of the
State and that it has in the meantime become necessary to prolong the stay of
the Japanese garrison' (ibid. p. 792).
[7] Marquis Koichi Kido, who had become Minister of Education in the Konoye
Cabinet on 17 October 1937, declared that Generals Honjo, Ishihara, and Itagaki
were among those who wanted the China Incident settled as soon as possible
(IMTFE, *Exhibit* 3340). Konoye also vouches for Ishihara, who was chief of
the Operations Division of the General Staff, Itagaki, and Tada. Sugiyama
leaned to the extremists. Umezu, the Vice-Minister of War, appears to have
been more moderate and there was already a move to replace him by Tojo
(*Exhibit* 3300).

facilitate a reconciliation. This would leave Japan free to face the USSR, of whose growing strength in the Far East the General Staff were afraid, and against whom their armaments programme was principally directed. It appears that the establishment of Imperial Headquarters on 20 November was intended to control the recalcitrant Japanese armies in China, who were flushed with victory and booty and who wanted to overthrow the Nanking Government completely and set up régimes run by themselves, after the pattern of Manchukuo.[1]

But these extreme views were not confined to the Army, they existed also in the Cabinet, where they were advocated most vigorously by the stormy petrel of Japanese politics, Admiral Suetsugu, now the Home Minister.[2] General public opinion in Japan, too, inflamed by the heavy losses at Shanghai and excited by the Japanese victories, made the position of the moderates difficult and dangerous. Konoye, as usual, was in a state of indecision and thinking of resignation; he had made an attempt to resuscitate the Kodoha faction, but had only got into hot water as a result.[3] Both he and Hirota were now inclined to wait till Nanking fell and then put forward harsher terms. This was the line of least resistance and, after the Brussels episode, they had no fear of foreign intervention.

Consequently, when on 7 December Dirksen informed Hirota that the Chinese were ready to discuss the Japanese peace terms, Hirota replied that he doubted 'whether it would still be possible to negotiate on the basis, drawn up a month ago, that is before the great Japanese military successes', and that he would have to consult the Army and the Navy.[4] When Dirksen reminded him that as late as mid-November he had declared that the terms remained the same, Hirota 'replied that the last few weeks had brought about a different situation; the Field Army had become more exacting in its demands.'[5] He also asserted that the peace proposal of 2 November had dealt with main points only. These required further definition, 'thus, for instance Japan naturally demanded other concessions in North China in addition to those for minerals.'[6]

[1] *Saionji–Harada Memoirs*, 10 Nov. 1937.
[2] ibid. 10 Dec. 1937, 8 Jan. 1937.
[3] Konoye Memoirs, in *Pearl Harbor Attack*, pt. 20; *Saionji–Harada Memoirs*, 9 and 13 Oct. 1937. Saionji was among those who opposed this move.
[4] Dirksen to GFM, 7 Dec. 1937 (*D Ger.FP*, series D, i. 799).
[5] ibid.
[6] ibid.

Neurath was taken aback at this news,[1] but he nevertheless decided that German good offices should continue although he instructed Dirksen to intimate to the Japanese that Germany could not go on transmitting to China terms 'which Japan herself within a very short time might say needed broadening.'[2]

At this time Nanking had not been taken, although its fall was imminent and actually occurred a week later. It was evidently believed in Japan that the loss of the capital would be followed by military defections from Chiang Kai-shek and so by the collapse of his administration. Thus the conflict of opinion which occurred in Japan was not so much between the advocates of moderate peace terms and those of more severe ones, as between those who still wished to offer terms, albeit harder ones than those of 2 November, and those who urged that no terms be offered Chiang, so that after his expected collapse Japan would have a free hand in setting up new administrations of her own devising. Apparently on 12 December Konoye thought that the advocates of this extreme course had got their way and declared that he would resign, but Harada and Kido persuaded him against this.[3] In the event, the extremists were for the time being partly checked;[4] at a Liaison Conference on 20 December it was decided to offer fresh terms to Chiang Kai-shek.[5] On 22 December Hirota communicated these to Dirksen. They comprised four 'basic conditions'. China was to 'abandon her pro-Communist as well as anti-Japanese and anti-Manchukuo policy and cooperate with Japan and Manchukuo in carrying out their anti-Communist policy.' She was to agree to the establishment of 'demilitarized zones and special régimes in areas where necessary.' Agreements for 'close economic cooperation' were to be concluded between Japan, China, and Manchukuo. Finally, China was to 'pay Japan the required indemnity.' Hirota declared that China must signify her readiness to accept these terms in their entirety by about the end of the year, otherwise Japan 'would be forced to treat the present situation from an entirely different point of view from that maintained hitherto.'[6]

In reply to Dirksen's inquiries as to just what these general stipu-

[1] Neurath to Dirksen, 10 Dec. 1937 (ibid. pp. 800–1).
[2] ibid.   [3] *Saionji–Harada Memoirs*, 12 Dec. 1937.
[4] The *Panay* and *Ladybird* incidents on 12 December, which threatened serious complications with the United States and Great Britain, may have had a sobering effect. See Ch. V below.
[5] Evidence of Horinouchi (IMTFE, *Record*, pp. 29701–2).
[6] Dirksen to GFM, 22 Dec. 1937 (*D Ger.FP*, series D, i. 802–3).

lations involved Hirota gave him some details, 'which' he said 'were very secret and under no circumstances intended for the Chinese.' The first condition meant Chinese recognition of Manchukuo. It was also 'very desirable, though not required' that China should join the Anti-Comintern Pact and terminate the Sino-Soviet Non-Aggression Pact. The second condition included demilitarized zones in North China and the Yangtze Valley. A special régime was contemplated only for Inner Mongolia, but the administration of North China, while it would remain under Chinese sovereignty, 'must have extensive powers and not be dependent upon the Government.' The third condition implied agreements on tariffs and general trade.[1]

When Dirksen protested that these terms went far beyond those previously given him and that their acceptance by the Chinese Government was extremely improbable, 'Hirota answered that the changed military situation and the pressure of public opinion had not allowed any other formulation.'[2] Dirksen informed Berlin that the terms were a compromise which had emerged from severe conflicts within the Government. The Army had wanted to make Chiang Kai-shek acknowledge that he was guilty of the war, before informing him of the terms, but had failed in this; there had also been a demand for even more severe conditions. The present ones had been decided upon by the Cabinet and approved by the Emperor, they therefore constituted a binding Japanese State document. He added that he had heard confidentially that a considerable part of the Cabinet, 'under the pressure of the Field Army and industry', considered the terms too mild and hoped that

---

[1] ibid., pp. 803–4. Hirota also declared that hostilities must continue until the conclusion of the peace treaty (ibid. p. 803).

[2] ibid. p. 804. Hirota told Dirksen that the Italian Ambassador had asked for information about the German-Japanese conversations so that Italy could join Germany in 'mediating the conflict' (Dirksen's no. 411 of 23 Dec. 1937, ibid. p. 804). The German Government had hitherto denied that they were mediating between Japan and China, which was technically correct, as they were not proposing terms, but only using their good offices to bring the two parties together. They did not want the Italians in on the conversations, because Italy's openly pro-Japanese attitude was bitterly resented by China (memoranda by Weizsäcker, 24 Nov. 1937, ibid. p. 786, and 8 Dec. 1937, ibid. p. 800). On 29 November Italy recognized Manchukuo. She had been pressing Germany to join her in this, and the Japanese had been dropping hints to the same effect, but Germany was not yet ready to do so (memo. by Neurath, 22 Nov. 1937, ibid. pp. 785–6). On 24 December Neurath said that the Italians would be informed in general terms, but since there was so far no mediation, German-Italian co-operation need not be considered (Neurath to Dirksen, 24 Dec. 1937, ibid. pp. 808–9).

they would be rejected by China 'in order to make it possible to carry through the war of annihilation against Chiang Kai-shek.'[1]

The German Government, as well they might, had serious doubts whether or not to transmit these terms to China, but finally decided to do so, while carefully refraining from expressing any opinion upon them.[2] When, on 26 December, Trautmann informed H. H. Kung of the Japanese conditions, Kung was filled with consternation and declared that nobody could accept such demands.[3] He also indirectly intimated to Germany that China would continue resistance to the last and would throw herself into the arms of the Soviet Union.[4] This, the one card that China could play, caused the German Government to urge moderation upon Tokyo. Dirksen on 30 December succeeded in getting Hirota to agree to the unofficial transmission to the Chinese of the secret details which he had communicated on 22 December; Hirota at this time revealed some additional ones.[5] The Germans also prevailed upon the Japanese to extend their time-limit; they pointed out to Tokyo the delays involved through the roundabout methods of contact.[6] They furthermore got them to agree to stop the hostilities once the negotiations had begun and provided that the Chinese gave a guarantee to carry out the peace terms.[7]

Trautmann unofficially communicated to Nanking the details he had been given by Hirota, but this could not be done in a form which was binding upon the Japanese Government.[8] The Chinese Government, now in Hankow, held conferences with military and political officials from all over the country and wavered between acceptance and refusal. On 3 January 1938 Chiang Kai-shek made a desperate appeal to Roosevelt for help, but none was forthcoming.[9]

---

[1] ibid. p. 804.
[2] GFM to Dirksen, 24 Dec. 1937 (ibid. p. 808).
[3] Trautmann to GFM, 26 Dec. 1937 (ibid. p. 809). Chiang Kai-shek himself was ill. Madame Chiang was present at the meeting with Kung.
[4] Trautmann to GFM, 27 Dec. 1937 (ibid. p. 810).
[5] These were: That there were to be three demilitarized zones—Inner Mongolia, North China, and a part of the occupied territory in the vicinity of Shanghai. Shanghai outside the International Settlement was to have a 'special régime'. The indemnity was to include partial reimbursement of the cost of the war, compensation for destroyed Japanese property, and payment of the occupation expenses. (Dirksen to GFM, 30 Dec. 1937, ibid. p. 812.)
[6] GFM to Dirksen (ibid. pp. 808-9).
[7] Dirksen's no. 427, ibid. p. 812 and n.
[8] Hirota had stipulated this (ibid.).
[9] 'As Mr. Roosevelt realized, we could not make specific promises of direct aid. The reply informed Chiang Kai-shek that we were doing everything we could to bring about peace' (Hull, *Memoirs*, i. 566-7). Hirota on 14 January told

While the Chinese were still trying to make up their minds, the conflict within the Japanese Cabinet and the Army was continuing. Fresh conferences between civilian and service chiefs resulted in another compromise decision on 10 January, which was ratified at an Imperial Conference on the following day.[1] This decided that negotiations should be opened with China on conditions which were specified in an attached Annex. These were in general the same as the ones communicated to Dirksen, but it was now stipulated that Japanese troops were to be stationed in certain districts of North China, Inner Mongolia, and Central China for as long as might be necessary. Should China agree to the terms and really carry them out, Japan would be prepared to withdraw her troops, give up the demilitarized zones and the 'special administrations', and also to consider the rendition of her Concessions in China and the surrender of her extraterritorial rights. If the Chinese Government were to refuse the terms, they were to be completely overthrown and a new régime set up in their place.[2]

On 12 January Trautmann, who had been apprised of the ominous developments in Tokyo, warned the Chinese Government that they should delay no longer in replying.[3] Accordingly on 13 January the Chinese Foreign Minister replied that 'after due consideration we have found that the altered terms are rather too broad in scope. The Chinese Government desires therefore to be apprized of the nature and content of the newly submitted conditions in order to make a careful examination and reach a definite decision.'[4]

When on 14 January this reply was conveyed to Hirota, who had already warned Dirksen that a Chinese reply that they were considering the terms would not be sufficient, he was very annoyed. He declared that the reply was plain subterfuge and that the Chinese had been given all the particulars they needed to answer yes or no.[5]

Dirksen that 'the Chinese attempt to win American support for the peace negotiations had failed. Roosevelt had declined to intervene in any way' (Dirksen to GFM, 14 Jan. 1938, *D Ger.FP*, series D, i. 816).

[1] The real business was always transacted at the Liaison Conferences between representatives of the Supreme Command and of the Government. The Imperial Conference simply ratified the decision already made. The Emperor presided but usually he said nothing. This was the case on 11 January 1938 (IMTFE, *Exhibit* 3264).

[2] ibid.   [3] *D Ger.FP*, series D, i. 814–15.

[4] Trautmann's no. 22 (ibid. p. 815).

[5] Dirksen to GFM, 14 Jan. 1938 (ibid. p. 816). It appears that the Japanese General Staff had also transmitted particulars through Ott and the German advisers (*Saionji–Harada Memoirs*, 19 Jan. 1938). Ott, however, did not mention this in his interrogation.

Dirksen endeavoured to mollify him by pointing out that the Chinese Government knew *officially* only of the four basic conditions. The additional details had been communicated to them, at the Japanese request, only in a very vague form. Dirksen suggested that these might now be made official.[1]

But, on the same day, a further Liaison Conference decided, despite the opposition of General Staff representatives, to end the peace efforts. A statement was framed which embodied the decision to withdraw recognition from the Chinese Central Government, to cease dealing with them, and to rely upon 'the establishment and growth of a new Chinese régime', with which Japan would co-operate for the adjustment of Sino-Japanese relations and 'the building up of a rejuvenated China'.[2] On 15 January H. H. Kung made an oral statement to Trautmann for transmission to Tokyo, in which he said that China really wanted peace with Japan and was not being merely evasive in asking for further details of the content of the basic conditions.[3] But this came too late. Before it could be transmitted to the Tokyo Government, Hirota, on the morning of 16 January, gave Dirksen the declaration which had been drawn up two days before, together with a Note for transmission to Hankow. This, after thanking Germany for her good offices, declared:

We cannot but conclude that the attitude of procrastination on the part of the Chinese Government reveals no intention to sue for peace by accepting in their entirety the basic conditions for peace negociations, which I had previously made known. Therefore the Imperial Government had now decided to abandon the present negociations for peace . . . and to deal with the present affair from an entirely new standpoint.[4]

Dirksen expressed his regret at this hasty decision and warned Hirota that Japan would incur world condemnation for breaking off the peace overtures. He furthermore told Hirota that a continuation of the war would have unfavourable effects on the relations between Germany and Japan. It would worsen Anglo-Japanese relations, which Germany considered undesirable; it would lead to the bolshevization of China; and it would weaken

---

[1] Dirksen to GFM, 14 Jan. 1938 (*D Ger.FP*, series D, i. 816).
[2] Evidence of Horinouchi (IMTFE, *Record*, pp. 29842-3).
[3] Trautmann to GFM, 15 Jan. 1938 (*D Ger.FP*, series D, i. 817).
[4] Dirksen to GFM, 16 Jan. 1938 (ibid. pp. 819–20). Dirksen says that the Chinese statement was being decoded when Hirota's message came through (*Moscow, Tokyo, London*, p. 191).

Japan, as against the USSR.[1] Hirota replied that strict instructions had been issued to the armed forces to avoid any further incidents with Great Britain, with whom relations would not be allowed to deteriorate, that Chiang Kai-shek was coming more and more under Communist influence anyway; and that the war would not be protracted.[2] He could hardly have been more wrong on all points.

The Japanese Government were soon bitterly to regret this disastrous decision, which spelt years of bloodshed and suffering to both China and Japan. It was not entirely the fault of the Army, for although large sections of that service, both at home and in China, were intoxicated by an apparently decisive victory; the same was true of many of the civilians. As to Konoye, assuming his sincerity in desiring peace, his failure to make a firm stand in support of the policy of the General Staff revealed his utter unfitness for leadership in a time of crisis. Finally, it is interesting to notice that this is one of several episodes which show Germany and Japan not as firm partners in policy, but as very much at cross-purposes.

[1] Dirksen to GFM, 17 Jan. 1938 (*D Ger.FP*, series D, i. 821).
[2] ibid. Hirota also declared that Japan did not for the time being intend to declare war or to attack Canton or Hainan Island. On 17 January the German Foreign Office instructed Trautmann to convey the Japanese reply to the Chinese Government and to say that Germany regarded her role as letter-carrier ended for the time being (GFM to Trautmann, 17 Jan. 1938, ibid. p. 820). Hirota had asked German consent to his revealing that Germany had played this role. The German Government decided to issue a press communiqué themselves, after first showing it to the Chinese and Japanese Governments (ibid.). This they did on 19 January 1938. Japan had on 16 January published her decision no longer to deal with the Chinese Central Government, and two days later each side recalled its ambassador (RIIA, *Survey, 1937*, i. 246–7).

CHAPTER III

Japan, Germany, and the New Order in East Asia

AT the time the Japanese Government issued their statement of 16 January 1938, the establishment of local pro-Japanese régimes in occupied China had already made marked progress. The Kwantung Army, which in the autumn of 1937 had overrun the provinces of Chahar and Suiyuan, sponsored a meeting at Kweihua of representatives of the Mongol tribes. These in October proceeded to establish a Federated Autonomous Government for Inner Mongolia with Prince Yun as nominal head, and Prince Teh, for long the prime agent of Inner Mongol separatism, as the real head. This régime adopted a national flag of its own and harked back to the great days of Genghis Khan by dating its State documents from his era.[1] The Inner Mongolian régime was intended as a permanent *de facto* independent State; had peace been concluded with the National Government of China their nominal sovereignty over the region might have been admitted, as in the case of Outer Mongolia, which, indeed, the Japanese cited as a precedent for their action.[2]

In North China the Japanese Army established a joint Peace Maintenance Commission for the Peiping–Tientsin area, staffed by Chinese politicians of pre-Kuomintang vintage. Similar Commissions were organized in other occupied regions in the North, and these established connexions with the Peiping–Tientsin body.[3] These moves were to some degree dictated by the necessity of having some sort of an administration to preserve order in the conquered regions. They were, too, sanctioned by the Japanese Inner Cabinet decisions of 7 August and 1 October 1937, though only as temporary wartime measures.[4] As has been seen the Japanese Government, up to December 1937, were willing to restore the political and administrative authority of Nanking over North China as part of a general peace settlement.[5]

[1] RIIA, *Survey, 1937*, i. 249–50.
[2] Dirksen to GFM, 3 Nov. 1937 (*D Ger.FP*, series D, i. 778).
[3] RIIA, *Survey, 1937*, i. 247–8.
[4] See above, pp. 42–43, 56.   [5] See above, p. 62.

The Japanese Army in North China, now under the command of General Terauchi, with Major-General Kita as head of the Special Service Section, had other ideas. They were jealous of the Kwantung Army's proceedings in Inner Mongolia and were eager to set up an autonomous régime of their own. This they hoped would become the nucleus of a new Government, centred in the North, to replace that of Chiang Kai-shek. As a sop to northern Chinese pride and dislike of rule from the south, they had already, in October, decreed that the city of Peiping should revert to its time-honoured appellation of Peking.[1] They then proceeded to attempt to recruit Chinese officials of some standing for their intended régime. The man they would most have liked to have secured as its head was Marshal Wu Pei-fu, who in the nineteen-twenties had been a leading warlord and politician, and who, though in retirement since the rise of the Kuomintang, was still considered the head of the Chihli political group. But he at this time remained deaf to Japanese overtures. Failing him, General Kita fixed upon Wang Keh-min, who had been an outstanding banker and financier and had served as acting head of the former Peiping Political Council, which had preceded the Hopei–Chahar Council. Wang was at this time living in Hong Kong, and Kita dispatched emissaries there to persuade him to come to Peking and be installed as leader of the proposed Government. These persuasions were eventually successful; Wang on 24 November came to Shanghai and thence on 6 December went to Fukuoka, in Japan. Here he came to terms with the Japanese and proceeded to Peking.[2] On 14 December a 'Provisional Government of the Chinese Republic' was set up in this city, with Wang as Chairman of the Executive Commission. This was followed, on 24 December, by the formation of the Hsin Min Hui, or 'New People's Party', whose professed objects were to promote Sino-Japanese friendship and to combat Communism. This was endowed with a profession of faith, in the form of the Hsin Min Chui or 'New People's Principles', as a counter to the San Min Chui of the Kuomintang.

The Japanese Inner Cabinet had, on 24 December, ratified the action of the North China Army, with a proviso that the Peking régime might be abandoned if the peace offer to Chiang Kai-shek

---

[1] RIIA, *Survey, 1937*, i. 248. Peking (Peiching) means 'Northern capital'. In 1928 the Kuomintang had established the national capital at Nanking and renamed Peking Peiping (Northern Peace).
[2] IMTFE, *Exhibit* 463.

matured.[1] Two days after the decision to abandon the peace discussions, Konoye told the press that it was possible that the Chinese National Government might change their policy and agree to compromise with the Peking Provisional Government. He added: 'We do not consider that the Peking Government must become the Central Government of China, but probably they will form a nucleus in which other similar régimes will be incorporated.'[2] In Peking Major-General Kita made it clear that he expected the North China régime to develop into a new national government for all China.[3]

This, for a variety of reasons, did not occur. First and foremost was the 'localism' of the various Japanese armies in China. This arose from the rather haphazard and piecemeal conduct of the war. There was as yet no Japanese Commander-in-Chief of all the forces in China and no overall plan of operations. Control from Tokyo was hampered by quarrels between the Vice-Chief of the General Staff, who was worried about the munitions shortage which developed during the Shanghai operations as well as about over-extension in China; and the War Minister, who held that the hesitations and delays in dispatching a force adequate to strike a decisive blow was causing the undue prolongation of the affair. Consequently the field commanders were often left without clear directives. After the fall of Nanking the Imperial Headquarters decided to reduce the forces in China from sixteen to ten divisions; then, when after all, the Chinese Government did not yield, this had to be reversed and fresh operations decided upon.[4]

This wavering policy at home increased the innate tendency of Japanese local armies to go their own way, especially in political matters. Their tenacity in this was partly a matter of prestige, partly one of pecuniary gain, for Japanese officers in China, like the Spartans abroad, soon yielded to the opportunities of peculation which their control of a puppet régime made possible. Hence Kita's ambitions were regarded sourly both by the Kwantung Army and by the Japanese Army in Central China, which was planning to establish a régime of its own choosing in that area and which objected to emissaries from the North trying to recruit Chinese from the Shanghai area.[5] In December 1937 the Ta Tao

[1] IMTFE, *Record*, pp. 29817–30.
[2] RIIA, *Documents, 1938*, i. 341.   [3] RIIA, *Survey, 1937*, i. 253.
[4] Evidence of Torashiro Kawabe (IMTFE, *Record*, pp. 21998–9), and of Shinichi Tanaka (ibid. pp. 20687–701).   [5] ibid. p. 5298.

administration had been set up for the Greater Shanghai Municipality. General Matsui had endeavoured to follow this up by the
erection of a pro-Japanese régime for the Shanghai–Nanking area,
but his overtures to various Chinese ex-officials met with no
response. They feared for their lives if they came out openly on
the Japanese side in view of the strength of Chinese Nationalist
organizations which could still operate from the shelter of the
foreign-administered areas of Shanghai and they were also watching to see whether peace might not yet be made with Chiang
Kai-shek.[1]   Also the most time-serving Chinese politician might
hesitate to associate himself with General Matsui, who was held
responsible for the orgy of massacre and rape by the Japanese
troops in Nanking. In the spring of 1938, after Matsui's recall and
the arrival of General Shunroka Hata as Commander-in-Chief
of the Central China Army, matters made more progress. A
number of ex-officials, members of the former Anfu political group,
were persuaded to take office in the 'Reformed Government of the
Republic of China', which was set up in Nanking on 28 March
1938. The nominal head of this was Liang Hung-chih, and the
moving spirits behind it were Major-General Harada and Colonel
Kusumoto of the Special Service Section of the Central China
Army, and also Colonel Kagesa, a 'China expert' of the General
Staff.[2] The new régime professed not to be a rival of the Peking
Provisional Government and declared its intention of amalgamat-
ing with that body so soon as conditions should permit. But no
such amalgamation took place, even after the battle of Suchow in
May 1938 drove Chiang Kai-shek's forces from the intervening
territory. The only measure of co-ordination achieved was the
establishment, in the following September, of a joint council of
representatives of the two régimes under the presidency of Wang
Keh-min.[3] This but thinly concealed the rivalries and jealousies
of the Japanese administration-builders and of their Chinese
auxiliaries.

These, however, might have been overcome had the Japanese
Government been united in a determination to set up a rival
Government to that of Chiang Kai-shek. But they remained
divided upon Chinese policy; even after the apparently irrevocable
decision of 16 January, a strong body of military and civilian

[1] ibid. pp. 5304–6.
[2] ibid. pp. 5308–11.   [3] ibid. pp. 3589–90.

opinion continued to work for a direct settlement with the Chinese
National Government. They knew that there was a group within
the Kuomintang, headed by Wang Ching-wei, which was striving
to bring about such an accord. Wang's attitude derived partly
from the personal rivalry of himself and his wife to the dominant
Chiang–Soong 'dynasty', partly from his pro-Nazi and anti-
Communist affiliations. Chiang Kai-shek himself, while he still
hoped for outside assistance and was unwilling to risk his position
and prestige by accepting the Japanese demands *in toto*, would
apparently not have been averse to a compromise. He saw clearly
enough that the continued loss of territory by the Kuomintang, in
so far as it did not tell in favour of the Japanese, was resulting
in the spread of Chinese Communist influence in the rural areas,
and he was under no illusion on what that would mean for himself and his party if it went on unchecked. So he was not averse
to a compromise.

This possibility seemed furthered by military and political
events in the spring and summer of 1938. The Chinese armies,
profiting by the halt in Japanese operations after the fall of Nanking,
had recovered their morale. In early April 1938 they succeeded in
inflicting a severe reverse upon a part of the Japanese North China
Army in a battle at Taierchwang, in southern Shantung. The
disconcerted Japanese had to send back the divisions they had
withdrawn from China.[1] They then engaged in a great encircling
manœuvre against the Chinese forces around Suchow, an important junction on the Lunghai and the Peking–Nanking railways.
But the Japanese failed to bring off the Tannenberg for which
they had hoped; the Chinese Army was badly mauled, but the
bulk of it escaped. The Japanese pursued them westwards across
Honan; to save themselves and to prevent the development of a
Japanese advance upon Hankow from the north, the Chinese on
13 June blew a gap in the Yellow River dyke near Chengchow,
which diverted that great river into the old south-easterly course
over which it had flowed until 1853. The consequences were
catastrophic to the Chinese peasantry in the region, but the military
objective was achieved.

The Japanese then began a direct advance upon Hankow by way

---

[1] Gist of talks by Colonel Kenryo Sato, Chief of Army Press Section, to
Conference of Police Bureau Chiefs, at Home Office, 25 and 29 August 1938.
Sato said the reservist divisions had been sent home but had to be recalled for
the Suchow operation (ibid. pp. 3635–6).

of the Yangtze, but this was a course fraught with formidable geographical and climatic difficulties. Before it had got well under way, the crisis in Soviet-Japanese relations, caused by the Changku-feng affair, appeared to presage war between Japan and the Soviet Union and caused a temporary suspension of the operations against Hankow.[1] Meanwhile on 26 May General Ugaki had suc-ceeded Hirota as Foreign Minister in the Konoye Cabinet. He had a reputation as a moderate and the consequent dislike of him by a section of Army opinion had cost him the Premiership in 1937. His appointment as Foreign Minister seems to have been a last attempt by Konoye to secure a policy of moderation at home and abroad.[2] Ugaki, in 1948, declared that, as a condition of taking office, he had secured from Konoye a promise that the Japanese Government statement of 16 January 1938, against further dealings with the Chinese National Government, should be annulled when circumstances permitted. He further said that, upon assuming his duties, he had found unofficial peace overtures going on via Hong Kong, and these he had continued.[3] One Japanese emissary in this was General Takaji Wachi, who in March 1938 had been seconded for duty with the General Staff, who gave him the task of contacting the Chinese Government. Wachi went to Hong Kong in June 1938, and got in touch with Hankow through a Chinese inter-mediary called Hsia Chen-ying. According to Wachi the terms proposed were that the question of the recognition of Manchukuo should be left over, that Chiang Kai-shek should retire temporarily, that the members of the existing pro-Japanese régimes should be absorbed into the Chinese National Government, and that Japan would demand no annexations or economic monopolies. Wachi

---

[1] For the Changkufeng incident see below, pp. 180–1. Hata's Central China Army was reinforced by seven divisions, as well as by an army of four divisions and a cavalry brigade under Prince Higashikuni. But the Changkufeng affair caused the Kwantung Army to delay the dispatch of aircraft which it had promised for the Nankow operation (evidence of General Masakazu Kawabe, who was Hata's Chief of Staff in 1938, IMTFE, *Record*, pp. 21701–5).

[2] Saionji was opposed to the appointment; he thought—in the event rightly —that if Ugaki failed as Foreign Minister, he would spoil his chances of becoming Premier in the future, which was what Saionji wanted (*Saionji-Harada Memoirs*, 26 May 1938).

[3] Evidence of Ugaki (IMTFE, *Record*, pp. 38811–17). The prosecution confronted him with a document entitled 'Ugaki's Report to the Emperor', 21 September 1938. This, *inter alia*, referred to Japan's policy of bringing about the destruction of the Chiang régime. Ugaki replied that this was a draft report prepared for his consideration by the East Asiatic Bureau of the Foreign Ministry. They did not know of the under-cover negotiations and the opinions in the draft were *not* what he actually told the Emperor (ibid.).

returned to Tokyo about the end of August and was given authority by the War Minister, General Itagaki, and by the Vice-Chief of the General Staff, Tada, to negotiate on these terms. He returned to Hong Kong in September to resume the overture, but the fall of Hankow brought it to an end.[1]

Whether or not as the result of Wachi's activities Chiang Kai-shek sent Kao Tsung-wu on a secret mission to Tokyo, where he arrived around the end of June.[2] Apparently the proposals he brought were that Chiang was willing to accord *de facto* recognition of Manchukuo and an autonomous Inner Mongolia, and to adopt an anti-Communist policy. But he was not prepared to accept demilitarized zones or the stationing of Japanese troops in China, or to give an indemnity. He was also ready to retire from public life following an agreement on these lines.[3]

But the course of events told against Ugaki. There was from the first strong opposition to any direct dealings with Chiang Kai-shek. This was increased when the diplomatic settlement of the Changkufeng incident in mid-August left the Japanese Army free to concentrate upon the Hankow campaign. There was thus a disposition in Tokyo to await the result of the attack.[4] By the end of September Hata had stormed his way to within eighty miles of the city, of which the fall could not be long delayed. In consequence those who insisted upon the overthrow of the Chiang Government gained the upper hand and at the same time renewed with greater insistence their demand that a special governmental organ for the direction of Japanese policy in China should be established in Tokyo. This was intended to exclude the Foreign Ministry from control of such policy and Ugaki, faced with this demand and lacking support from Konoye in resistance to it, resigned on 29 September.[5] Konoye

---

[1] Affidavit of General Takaji Wachi (ibid. pp. 20584–6).

[2] Harada said Konoye told him of Kao's arrival on 30 June 1938 (*Saionji–Harada Memoirs*, 4 July 1938). See also evidence of Colonel (later General) Yoshiaki Kagesa, who was the General Staff's contact man with Kao (IMTFE, *Record*, p. 23478). He put Kao's visit to Tokyo in the spring of 1938, but he was speaking from memory and the *Saionji–Harada Memoirs* are probably more reliable as to date.

[3] This was what Kenryo Sato told the police chiefs he had heard were the terms an emissary of Chiang had recently brought (ibid. pp. 3638–9).

[4] ibid. p. 3639. According to the *Saionji–Harada Memoirs* (28 Aug. 1937) the British Ambassador in China transmitted a peace overture from Chiang in late August. The terms were said to be very advantageous to Japan, but Konoye decided to wait awhile. Saionji was very disappointed at Konoye's attitude (ibid. 7 Sept. 1938).

[5] ibid. 16 Sept., 1 Oct. 1938. Apparently both the War and Navy Ministers opposed Ugaki on this matter (ibid. 4 Oct. 1938).

took over the Ministry of Foreign Affairs for a month, during which he agreed with the Army Chiefs that the proposed Asia Development Board should take over China policy, with the exception of matters affecting Japanese relations with third Powers, which were to remain under the jurisdiction of the Foreign Ministry. Having thus given the Army the substance of what it wanted, Konoye turned over the Foreign Ministry to Mr. Hachiro Arita, who believed in the division of the world into Power blocs, each headed by a leader State.[1]

The downfall of Ugaki and the defeat of the moderate groups in Japan coincided with the crisis in Europe and the Munich Agreement. This was followed, in mid-October, by the dispatch of a Japanese expeditionary force against Canton.[2] This force, after a rapid advance, which met with no effective opposition, seized the great city on 21 October. By this achievement they blocked the main avenue of foreign supplies to China, via Hong Kong and the railway to Canton and Hankow. Four days later Hata's victorious armies entered Hankow, from which the Chinese Government had previously withdrawn to Chungking.

These victories, combined with the German diplomatic triumph in Europe, emboldened Tokyo to come out openly in favour of a New Order in East Asia, which in fact meant Japanese hegemony in that region. In a radio broadcast of 3 November Konoye asserted that the Chiang Kai-shek Government had been reduced to a local régime, that Japan possessed sufficient reserve force to ward off any outside intervention, and that the key to China's fate was in Japanese hands. He then defined Japanese aims, as 'not the conquest of China, but co-operation with her.' It was, he asserted, 'a historical necessity that the three great neighbour nations— China, Manchukuo, and Japan—while fully retaining their sovereign independence, should stand closely united in their common duty of safeguarding East Asia.' Konoye denounced the Chinese Government for not having cared whether China was 'left a prey to Communism or relegated to a minor colonial status' and asserted that it was 'undisputed history' that China had been 'a victim of the rivalry between the Powers whose imperialistic ambitions have constantly imperilled her tranquillity and indepen-

---

[1] Craigie, *Behind the Japanese Mask*, pp. 61–63.
[2] The decision to attack Canton had been taken on 7 September, 1938 (*Saionji–Harada Memoirs*, 7 Sept. 1938).

dence.' Japan realized the need of 'fundamentally rectifying' such a state of affairs and was 'eager to see a new order established in East Asia—a new structure of peace based on true justice.' He declared that the National Government of China might participate in this task if it were prepared to 'repudiate its past policy, remould its personnel, and offer to join in the task as a thoroughly rejuvenated régime.'[1] On the same day the Japanese Government as a whole issued a similar statement of objectives, although in shorter form, in which they declared that the establishment of a New Order in East Asia was 'the immutable policy and determination of Japan.'[2]

The actual terms Japan intended to exact were revealed by Arita in a report to the Privy Council on 29 November. These were the recognition of Manchukuo by China, the conclusion of a Sino-Japanese military alliance against the Comintern, in furtherance of which Japanese troops would be stationed in Inner Mongolia and North China, and China would contribute to the upkeep of these forces. Japan would exercise the right of supervision over Chinese land and water communications and would co-operate in the 'improvement and adjustment' of the Chinese military and police forces. Special zones of 'close Sino-Japanese collaboration' were to be established in North China, in the Yangtze basin, and in certain islands along the south China coast. Japan was to control the exploitation of raw materials needed for 'national defence' especially in Inner Mongolia and North China. The Chinese currency, tariff, and the maritime customs service were to be reorganized to promote trade between Japan, Manchukuo, and China.[3]

These terms, which resemble the famous Japanese Twenty-one Demands upon China in 1915, would have reduced China to the position of a vassal State. Something, at least, of the Japanese intent appears to have become known in Chungking. According to Kagesa, in the late autumn of 1938, Kao Sung-wu and Mei Ssu-ping came to Shanghai with tentative peace proposals. Kagesa and Colonel Imai, also of the Japanese General Staff, took these to Tokyo and were sent back with amended terms.[4] They arranged with the Chinese emissaries that Wang Ching-wei should seek to convert the Chinese Government to acceptance of these terms, or,

---

[1] RIIA, *Documents, 1938*, i. 348–9.   [2] ibid. pp. 350–1.
[3] IMTFE, *Record*, pp. 3590–7.
[4] Evidence of Kagesa (IMTFE, *Record*, pp. 23979–80).

if he failed in this, should escape from China and bring over as many
of his following as he could. Konoye, for his part, was to issue a
public statement of peace terms at a pre-arranged moment.[1]
Wang failed to persuade either the Generalissimo or the powerful
civil and military leaders of the Kuomintang right-wing groups and
on 18 December fled from Chungking to Kunming and thence to
Hanoi in French Indo-China.

On 22 December Konoye publicly announced Japan's basic
terms of peace. These were that China should recognize Manchukuo, should conclude an Anti-Comintern Pact with Japan,
similar to the extant one between Japan, Germany, and Italy,
should agree to the stationing of Japanese troops at specified points
in China for the duration of the Pact, and should concur in the
designation of Inner Mongolia as a special anti-Communist area.
In the economic field China was to recognize the freedom of residence and trade on the part of Japanese subjects in the interior of
China and was to extend to Japan facilities for the development
of Chinese natural resources, especially in the regions of North
China and Inner Mongolia. Japan in return would annex no
territory and demand no indemnity for the expense of her military
operations. She would respect Chinese sovereignty and would
give 'positive consideration' to the questions of the abolition of
extraterritoriality and the rendition of foreign Concessions and
Settlements.[2]

But Chiang Kai-shek stood firm against any yielding to Japan.
In a speech of 26 December he denounced the New Order proclaimed in Tokyo as 'a term for the overthrow of international
order in East Asia, and the enslavement of China as the means
whereby Japan may dominate the Pacific and proceed to dis-
member other States of the world.' He said that since what Japan
really desired was domination over all China and the utilization
of all her territory and resources for Japanese ends, it was easy,
but meaningless, for Konoye to deny that Japan desired to annex
any particular part of China, or to talk about the rendition of the

---

[1] Kagesa refers only to the plan for Wang's escape from Chungking (ibid.).
But, according to Harada, Konoye told him on 9 December that Wang was to
issue a statement in Chungking in response to one by Konoye, but that a
telegram had come from Wang saying that Chiang Kai-shek, who had been in
Kunming, had returned to Chungking and this made it difficult for Wang to
play his part. Konoye commented that this was the second time the matter had
been prolonged and that perhaps Wang was deceiving him (*Saionji–Harada
Memoirs*, 10 Dec. 1938).   [2] RIIA, *Documents, 1938*, i. 353–4.

Concessions. He declared that the Konoye terms were 'many times more comprehensive and virulent' than were Hirota's three principles. 'If we could not accept Hirota's "three principles" at the commencement of hostilities, how could the enemy entertain the hope that China might now accept these degrading terms?'[1] Chiang urged his compatriots to continue the struggle and hinted that foreign assistance would eventually be forthcoming for China.[2]

Chiang undoubtedly realized that the Chinese forces alone could not hope to defeat and expel the Japanese invaders, though they might wear them down and by continued resistance bring Japan to abandon in large measure her far-reaching designs. But this would be a contest of endurance, in which the Kuomintang, badly shaken by the loss of its richest territories and the major portion of its revenues, could well prove the loser. However, the deepening world crisis seemed to afford the possibility of a quicker solution. Germany had now aligned herself, along with Italy, in favour of the Japanese cause in the Far East, and Chiang may well have known something of the movement in Berlin and Tokyo for a closer association of the three 'have-not' Powers. At the end of 1938 it appeared possible that, in the event of a world conflict, these three would be ranged against Great Britain, France, and probably the Soviet Union, with the United States as a sympathizer—and perhaps an ultimate ally—of the latter group. Victory for this combination would mean the freeing of China.

Wang Ching-wei, *per contra*, with his German associations, believed in the victory of the Axis. He may have imagined that Germany, were she victorious in Europe, would be less acquiescent in Japanese ambitions in the Far East, a possibility which, as will be seen, was in 1940 very present in Japanese minds. But the bulk of the Kuomintang stood with Chiang, and while some of Wang's immediate clique followed him in his defection, they did not include any of the really outstanding figures in the Kuomintang right-wing groups, nor, even more important, any of the generals.

In April 1939 Wang, with the aid of Kagesa, left Hanoi and came to Shanghai, where with his following he conducted an agitation for peace, playing especially upon the anti-Communist and anti-Western notes, which Tokyo had sounded in the previous year.[3] In June 1939 Wang went to Tokyo, where he had discus-

[1] ibid. pp. 335–8. [2] ibid. p. 340.
[3] Evidence of Kagesa (IMTFE, *Record*, pp. 23983–6).

sions with Baron Hiranuma, the new Premier, and with General Itagaki, who had continued as War Minister, on the establishment of a new Central Government with himself at the head.[1] Wang wanted this to replace the existing pro-Japanese régimes, but this encountered objections from the officers who had sponsored them. Hiranuma and Itagaki in general supported Wang and a compromise was reached whereby Wang's proposed régime should absorb the existing 'reformed Government', whose members he would take in, but not the North China administration, which would remain *de facto* separate.[2] But the Wang Government remained in suspended animation during 1939 in part because his 'orthodox Kuomintang' was looked upon with suspicion by a section of Japanese Army opinion; in part because undercover peace overtures to Chungking were still going on.[3]

There were other reasons for the relative pause in both military and political activities in China on the part of the Japanese during 1939. Primarily this was because Japan, like China, was waiting on the development of the general international situation.

Despite very formidable spatial and topographical obstacles the Japanese armies could have penetrated farther into China with the object of conquering the great and rich province of Szechuan, the heart of Free China. But, even had they succeeded in doing so, there was no absolute guarantee that Chiang Kai-shek would come to terms; he might still have bidden defiance from the even more remote areas of north-western China. Furthermore such an advance would have greatly accentuated the already considerable problems of communication and supply with which the Japanese were grappling and would have given fresh opportunities to the Chinese guerrillas. These were weighty objections to a policy of further territorial conquest and occupation.

Furthermore such a policy would have entailed a great increase

[1] ibid. p. 23900.
[2] ibid. pp. 23993–6.
[3] ibid. p. 30318 (evidence of Itagaki). Apart from overtures to Chungking, the Japanese were still endeavouring to get Wu Pei-fu to join them in the hope that he might bring about the military defection from Chungking which Wang Ching-wei had failed to accomplish. In July 1938 Konoye had sent emissaries to contact Wu and Tang Shao-yi, a veteran ex-official, but the assassination of Tang by pro-Chungking terrrorists interrupted these plans (evidence of Itagaki, ibid.). But the inducements to Wu continued; in June 1939 the China Affairs Board set aside $ 10 million out of Maritime Customs funds to finance the setting up of Wu as head of a new central Chinese Government (IMTFE, *Exhibit* 3743). But Wu did not take the bait and his death in February 1940 put an end to Japanese hopes of using him.

in the armed strength which Japan was employing in China. This in itself would not have placed too great a strain upon Japanese military and economic resources, about which a good many misconceptions were prevalent in China and in the West. Japan's casualties had been considerable but had been much more than replaced by the annual increment of men of military age in a rapidly increasing population of over 70 million. She had, too, employed a large proportion of older second-line troops in the China fighting, and had retained the cream of her forces in the homeland and in Manchuria. In her transition from a peacetime to a full war economy, Japan was encountering difficulties in the form of shortages of skilled labour and of bottlenecks in production, especially of machine tools. Consequently her actual military expenditures tended to lag behind the bond issues sanctioned by the Diet. But these difficulties would not have precluded an increase in her military effort against the ill-equipped Chinese, an effort which would have called for only a moderate expenditure of munitions. Japan's national debt was rising rapidly, but it was all internal debt and was offset by an expansion in her national income under the stimulus of war production and full employment of labour. The Japanese people were getting somewhat weary of the endless 'China Incident' and were irritated at shortages of consumer goods, in particular of clothing and footwear, but increased taxation and savings were holding inflationary tendencies in check and there was no serious popular unrest. Japan's foreign exchange reserves for the purchase of raw materials were running low, but she had accumulated large stocks. Japan in 1939 resembled a country engaged in a wearisome colonial war, rather than one exerting all its strength and utilizing all its resources against an adversary of equal power.

But the Japanese General Staff was preparing for such a war, the prospective enemy being the USSR. In 1936 they had formulated a 'National Defence Plan', which consisted of a five-year programme for the expansion of armaments industries and six-year programme of expansion and re-equipment of the armed forces.[1] Closely connected with this was the five-year plan for the development of industry in Manchuria, also devised in 1936.[2] All these

[1] So General Kenryo Sato declared in a speech on Army Day, 11 March 1942 (IMTFE, *Judgment*, pp. 176–9).
[2] Jones, *Manchuria Since 1931*, p. 147.

plans went into operation in 1937. The China conflict affected these schemes in two different ways. The state of *de facto* war made it difficult for the industrialists to resist the Army pressure for controls over industry, and also enabled it to extract huge budgetary appropriations for military purposes, the bulk of which was expended on general military preparations and not on the war in China.[1] But the China war, the armaments expansion, and the industrial expansion schemes at home and in Manchuria together represented a severe strain on the Japanese economy. The Manchurian plans were especially hampered because the controversy between Japan and the Western Powers precluded any possibility of foreign, especially American, capital investment in Manchukuo.[2] There were thus strong economic and financial reasons against any further large-scale operations in China.

There were equally potent military and political ones. The Army planners were aiming at being ready for war by, at the latest, 1942. They would then be in a position to match the industrial and military development of the Soviet Union in the Far East. This was also about the time when they expected general war in Europe to begin.[3] But, in the meantime, they were not ready for war and they were nervous about possible Soviet intervention on the side of China. To extend themselves still further by a plunge into the vast spaces of western China might tempt Stalin to strike, despite his domestic and European preoccupations.

In July 1939 the Chief of Staff of the Japanese Army in Central China sent an appreciation of the situation to the Vice-Minister of War in Tokyo. In this he said that the Chinese Army had lost its offensive power and could not recuperate. There was therefore no need for the Japanese Army to undertake fresh large-scale operations to conquer new areas. It should confine itself to maintaining peace and order in the occupied areas, to crushing any attempted counter-attacks, and to bombing strategic points in the interior, so as to promote terror and the rise of anti-war feeling

---

[1] Sato said that in general 40 per cent. of the budgetary appropriations were spent in the China Incident and 60 per cent. on armaments expansion (IMTFE, *Judgment*, pp. 206–7).

[2] Interrogation of Aikawa, 28 Jan. 1946 (IMTFE).

[3] Evidence of Kawabe on General Staff appreciation of world situation in 1937 (IMTFE, *Record*, pp. 21974–5). Hitler in November 1937 told his generals that Germany must strike not later than 1943–5 (Hossbach Memorandum in *D Ger.FP*, series D, i. 29–39). But it does not appear that the Japanese knew anything about this.

among the Chinese populace. He anticipated that this, together with the efforts of Wang Ching-wei, might bring about the collapse of the Chiang régime by the beginning of 1940.[1] In that event he considered that the Chinese Communists would not be strong enough to constitute a new threat; they would, he thought, remove to the north-west and seek closer ties with the USSR after the fashion of Outer Mongolia.[2] This was a revealing opinion, in view of Japanese propaganda which represented Communism as a major threat in China.

These were the tactics the Japanese did pursue after 1938. They undertook local offensives for particular objects, such as the scattering of Chinese troop concentrations, or the cutting off of supply routes to Chungking, and they carried out mass bombings of Chungking and of other cities in Free China to a degree which shocked a world not yet hardened to this form of warfare. For the rest, they devoted themselves to mopping-up expeditions against the guerrilla forces which infested large interior areas of occupied China and hampered the movement of food and raw materials to the cities. To ensure co-ordination among their armies in China they established, in September 1939, a General Headquarters, China Expeditionary Force, with General Nishio as the first Commander-in-Chief.[3]

Meanwhile, on 16 December 1938, an Imperial Ordinance had established the Koain, or Asia Development Board, generally called the China Affairs Board, to control political, administrative, and economic policy in China. The Japanese Premier was *ex-officio* President, with the Ministers of War, Marine, Foreign Affairs, and Finance as Vice-Presidents.[4] But their functions were nominal; real power was vested in the Director-General and the head of the Political Affairs section. Both were military men; General Yanagawa was the first Director-General, and General Teiichi Suzuki the first head of the Political Affairs section.[5] The Board established branches in the chief cities of occupied China

---

[1] IMTFE, *Record*, pp. 3663–8.   [2] ibid. pp. 3668–70.
[3] Evidence of Itagaki (ibid. p. 30318).
[4] Imperial Ordinance no. 768, Regulations Governing the Organization of the China Affairs Board, 16 Dec. 1938 (IMTFE, *Exhibit* 453).
[5] Evidence of Shigenori Togo (IMTFE, *Record*, pp. 35747–8); of Genshichi Oikawa (ibid. p. 4768); of Teiichi Suzuki (ibid. p. 35174). The Central Office in Tokyo had four sections, Political, Economic, Cultural, and Technical. Oikawa was originally director of the Political Section of the Shanghai branch; in April 1941 he replaced Suzuki as Director of the Political Section of the Central Office (ibid. pp. 4760–1).

and worked in close liaison with the Special Service sections of the Japanese forces and with the Japanese-sponsored administrations. One of the Board's main tasks was the supervision of the distribution and sale of opium, the proceeds from which, especially in the first five years of the China conflict, were a major source of revenue for the Japanese-sponsored régimes, especially that in Inner Mongolia.[1] It was also a source of 'secret service' funds for the Japanese Army. Tojo, when Premier, used these for subsidizing candidates whom he favoured for election to the Diet.[2]

The Economic Section of the China Affairs Board was charged with the supervision of Japanese financial and economic activities in China, in particular those of the two semi-official 'policy' companies, established in November 1938. These were the North China Development Company, with a capital of 350 million yen, and the Central China Development Company, with a capital of 100 million yen. Half of the initial capital was to be furnished by the Japanese Government which also guaranteed dividends to private investors. These were holding companies, intended to invest in, but not directly to control, subsidiary enterprises, with the object of fostering the production of strategic raw materials and their export to Japan. The North China Company invested chiefly in communications, electric-power concerns, coal and iron mines; the Central China Company in transport and public utilities. The results were far from spectacular in the first years of the China Incident and the companies were never profitable concerns.[3]

Effective economic exploitation of Chinese resources could hardly be expected under wartime conditions, and this constituted another reason for endeavouring to bring Chungking to accept peace on the Konoye terms. This would be materially facilitated if foreign Powers could be induced to abandon their support of Chungking and to accept the New Order. Then Chiang Kai-shek, deprived of the moral fillip and, in some degree, material aid which he derived from foreign sources, and despairing of more active aid, might yield, or, if he did not, a substantial part of his following might desert him and come into Wang Ching-wei's camp. These calculations were by no means erroneous; the alarm and despon-

---

[1] Evidence of Oikawa (ibid. pp. 4763–5); and of Mei Ssu-ping (ibid. pp. 4910–11).
[2] Mei Ssu-ping (ibid. p. 4913); Yanaga, *Japan Since Perry*, p. 605.
[3] Evidence of Okinori Kaya, President of the North China Development Co., 1941–5 (IMTFE, *Record*, pp. 30642–7).

dency manifested in Chungking at any sign of an accommodation between Japan and Great Britain or any other major Power showed how much store was set on continued foreign diplomatic support.

The Japanese proposed to bring the Powers to heel by two methods. The first was to bring pressure to bear upon them through threatening to liquidate their holdings in China, especially in the foreign-administered Concessions and Settlements: Great Britain, who had the largest Western stake in China, and who was faced by the German menace in Europe, was singled out as the particular target for this attack.[1] The second was to conclude a closer accord with the Axis Powers in Europe, especially with Germany. This could be used as a kind of diplomatic blackmail to induce Great Britain and France, as Arita put it, either to co-operate with Japan in China, or at least 'to stand idly by'.[2] The threat of a two-front war would also, it was anticipated, remove any danger of Soviet intervention. Thus increasingly the China issue tended to shift from the military to the diplomatic arena.

Here, during 1938, Japan had scored a notable success. Germany had hitherto resisted Japanese pressure upon her to recognize Manchukuo, to stop all deliveries of arms and munitions to China, and to recall the German military advisers. On 26 January 1938 Dirksen, in a lengthy political report to the German Foreign Ministry, recommended that these steps be taken. He assumed that Japan would be victorious and that China 'insofar as it does not rely upon Britain and America' would 'drift farther and farther into the Russian orbit.' Therefore the German advisers should be withdrawn both because they might be held responsible for the Chinese defeats and thus German prestige be lowered, and also because they might be expected to collaborate with Soviet Russian military and air personnel in China, which, in Dirksen's view, was impossible. The recognition of Manchukuo and the suspension of arms deliveries to China were necessary to avoid estranging Japan who was already annoyed at the delay in effecting these measures. Dirksen further suggested that Germany should concentrate her political and economic activities in North China and endeavour to

---

[1] The Chief of Staff of the Japanese Central China Army declared in July 1939 that Great Britain should be threatened with the loss of all her interests in China and that the International Settlement in Shanghai should be 'cleaned up' immediately (IMTFE, *Record*, pp. 3671–3).

[2] Arita's Report to the Privy Council, 29 Nov. 1938 (ibid. pp. 3597–9).

establish a close liaison with the Japanese civil and military authorities there.[1]

Dirksen's report, sent by mail, did not reach Berlin until 17 February,[2] by which time the decision to recognize Manchukuo had already been taken. For on 4 February Ribbentrop had replaced Neurath as Foreign Minister. This cleared the way for the adoption of the pro-Japanese policy for which Ribbentrop had been pressing and to which he had converted Hitler. On 5 February Dirksen telegraphed that Hirota had again asked for the suspension of German arms deliveries to China and for German recognition of Manchukuo.[3] Trautmann on 12 February was warned that the latter step was 'probably imminent';[4] he made urgent representations against it, in which he pointed out the ill-feeling which it would arouse in China and the consequent adverse effects on German commerce there.[5] But on 17 February Hitler decided on recognition of Manchukuo[6] and on 20 February he publicly announced this decision in the course of a speech to the Reichstag when he justified it as 'sober respect for actual facts.'[7] Moreover, while he declared that German neutrality would continue and professed hopes for peace between China and Japan, he made it clear that he had accepted the Japanese plea that they were fighting Bolshevism in China, which hitherto the German Foreign Ministry had refused to countenance.[8]

The Japanese Government were duly gratified,[9] and the Chinese bitterly affronted, although, in the hope of avoiding further blows from Berlin, they limited themselves to a protest and tried to calm the excited Chinese press comment.[10] But nevertheless worse was to come. Trautmann, who on 2 March had received a copy of Dirksen's report of 26 January, on 8 March dispatched to Berlin an extensive refutation of it. In this he denied Dirksen's assumptions that Japan was bound to be the victor and that China would

---

[1] *D Ger.FP*, series D, i. 826–31.   [2] ibid. p. 826.
[3] ibid. p. 832.   [4] ibid. p. 833 n.
[5] Trautmann's nos. 71 and 72 to GFM, 14 Feb. 1938 (ibid. pp. 833–5). No. 72 referred to 'the quasi-monopolistic preferential position that was recently offered us again in Kwangsi' (ibid. p. 834). This is interesting as an indication that the Chinese Government, in desperation, were ready to infringe Article 3 of the Nine-Power Treaty of 1922, in which they had agreed not to accord preferential rights to any foreign Power.   [6] ibid. p. 839.
[7] GFM to Trautmann, 21 Feb. 1938 (ibid. pp. 938–40).
[8] ibid. p. 840.
[9] Memo. of GFM, 24 Feb. 1938 (ibid. p. 841).
[10] Memo. by German State Secretary, 24 Feb. 1938 (ibid. pp. 843–4).

become a satellite of the USSR. He declared that the Japanese Army had lost a chance of a rapid seizure of Hankow; instead they had spent four weeks in plundering and burning Nanking.[1] His estimate of China's military chances were over-optimistic, but he rightly prophesied that 'even if the Japanese troops triumphed in a military sense, it is nevertheless possible that Japan might not be able to end the war in a "political" sense so simply as she had thought'. He declared (though incorrectly) that the recent mission of Sun Fo to Moscow had proved a complete failure; he had not been received by Stalin. He added that the Russians were doing very little more than were other States to help China, while the Chinese Government were exercising a close watch on Communist activities.[2]

Trautmann further said that the best commentary upon the proposed economic liaison with the Japanese in North China was 'the efforts of the Japanese to monopolize the exports of North China and to take them away from foreign firms, including German firms. Any Japanese régime in China will shut the door to foreign trade, all official Japanese assurances to the contrary.'[3]

As Dirksen leaned to the Japanese side, so did Trautmann to the Chinese, but his analysis of the situation was much nearer the truth than that of his colleague in Tokyo, and was shared by the German business community in China, who, in common with the English and American communities, had suffered much from the Japanese military operations.[4] But Trautmann's advice went unheeded in Berlin where Ribbentrop was pursuing the mirage of German preferential rights in a Japanese-dominated China and of a military alliance with Japan against Great Britain.[5] For these he and his master, Hitler, whom he had converted to his views, were ready to sacrifice the goodwill and the valuable commercial position which Germany had built up in China since 1921.

[1] ibid. pp. 844–6. On 16 February Trautmann had forwarded an account of a German eyewitness of the Japanese excesses in Nanking, who said: 'It seems like mockery to see this bestial machinery appearing as champion of anti-Communism and outwardly stand up loudly for the renovation and liberation of China; whereas only naked Communism and the uprise of all evil and inferior elements can flourish in its tracks' (IMTFE, *Record*, p. 4397).
[2] *D Ger.FP*, pp. 847–8.   [3] ibid. p. 849.
[4] Trautmann, on 14 January 1938, had sent to Berlin a report from John Rabe, who had been Chairman of the International Refugee Committee in Nanking. Rabe said that 40 out of 60 houses belonging to German nationals had been plundered; 4 had been burned (IMTFE, *Exhibit* 329).
[5] Weizsäcker records how on Easter Sunday 1938 Ribbentrop poured out to him his plans for an alliance with Japan against England (*Memoirs*, pp. 126–7).

On 28 April Goering issued instructions that all exports of war materials to China were to be prohibited immediately, irrespective of the date of conclusion of the delivery contracts.[1] The prohibition went into force on 3 May. At the same time an oral instruction intimated that the prohibition was to be interpreted narrowly, and confined to such goods as were clearly for military use.[2] Even so, the loss to the German armaments industry was considerable; added to the direct loss was the reluctance of other foreign countries to place orders with German armament firms in face of this example of breach of contract.[3] On 9 May Chiang Kai-shek protested to Trautmann against this decision. He said that even Italy had not stopped the delivery of supplies which had already been ordered and had only recently sent tanks and aircraft to China. He hinted at economic concessions to Germany if she would hold to her previous policy. Trautmann warned Berlin that 'we are risking all our constructive work in China since the war and perhaps in the future if we now act abruptly in regard to the question of the military advisers and the deliveries of war matériel.'[4]

Trautmann had already been advised that the German Government desired the military advisers to leave China.[5] Falkenhausen replied through Trautmann on 29 April. He said that if the advisers broke their contracts they would be liable for damages and would not be paid their return passages. This would mean that they would be stranded in China unless the German Government assumed the costs. Furthermore, it would spell ruin for many of them since no equivalent position could be offered them in Germany. He himself had told Chiang Kai-shek, in response to the Generalissimo's inquiry after Hitler's speech of 20 February, that he would honour his contract. So far he had not informed the other advisers that Berlin wanted them to throw up their positions.[6]

Ribbentrop, who at the beginning of May had told Tokyo that the advisers would be withdrawn,[7] replied on 13 May that the

[1] Memo. by Wiehl, 28 April 1938 (*D Ger.FP*, series D, i. 856).
[2] GFM memo. based on information from the Economic Ministry, 15 June 1938 (ibid. p. 875).   [3] ibid. p. 876.
[4] Trautmann to GFM, 9 May 1938 (ibid. p. 860).
[5] On 22 April, so it appears from Trautmann's no. 197 of 29 April enclosing Falkenhausen's reply (ibid. p. 856).   [6] ibid. pp. 856–7.
[7] Dirksen had been recalled and replaced as Ambassador in Japan by Ott, formerly the military attaché. On 5 May Hirota expressed his appreciation of the German decision (memo. by Ott, 5 May 1938, ibid. pp. 858–9).

advisers must leave as soon as possible. Trautmann was to ask the Chinese Government to release them from their contracts; the German Government would pay their return fares and also compensate them for their loss of further salary.[1] Trautmann, who had met Ott in Shanghai, reported on 15 May that he and Ott were agreed that a gradual withdrawal of the advisers would be preferable.[2] Ribbentrop on 17 May replied sharply that this was out of the question; it was the Führer's order that the advisers were to leave at once. If the Chinese Government made difficulties about terminating the contracts, Trautmann was to intimate that this would lead to his recall. The advisers themselves were to be told that any failure to comply with instructions would have serious consequences.[3]

The Chinese Government were informed of the German Government's desire on 21 May.[4] Chiang Kai-shek was very reluctant to let the advisers go, because of the loss of prestige that this would mean to him at such a critical moment. He asked that at any rate a few of them might remain and apparently also that Falkenhausen might be appointed military attaché to the German Embassy.[5] On 13 June Ribbentrop replied that this was out of the question and that the advisers must all return. Further opposition on the part of Chiang would result in the immediate recall of Trautmann.[6] Chiang, however, insisted upon retaining some of the advisers for a while.[7] Ribbentrop then on 20 June dispatched an ultimatum for presentation to the Chinese Government. This said that if by 23 June the Chinese Government had not consented to the immediate departure of the advisers and guaranteed that it would be carried out, Trautmann was to hand over to a chargé and leave China. He was to warn the Chinese that complete severance of diplomatic relations would follow. The advisers themselves were to leave China as soon as possible; if necessary against the will of the Chinese Government. Any who disobeyed would lose their German citizenship and have their property in Germany confiscated. This they were to be told 'in no uncertain terms'.[8]

[1] Ribbentrop to Trautmann, 13 May 1938 (ibid. pp. 861–2).
[2] ibid. p. 862 n.   [3] ibid. p. 862.
[4] Trautmann, to GFM, 21 May 1938 (ibid. p. 872).
[5] ibid. p. 872 n.
[6] Ribbentrop to Trautmann, 13 June 1938 (ibid. p. 872).
[7] Trautmann to GFM, 14 June 1938 (ibid. pp. 873–4).
[8] Ribbentrop to Trautmann, 20 June 1938 (ibid. p. 878).

The Chinese Government on 23 June replied that they would waive their legal rights in the matter, would terminate the contracts of the advisers, and would permit them to leave China. But they intended to give five or six advisers instructions to remain in China temporarily in order to wind up their affairs. Behind this, as Trautmann reported, lay Chiang's obstinacy in the face of threats and also his wish to keep in China those of the advisers who had special knowledge of the fortifications on the Yangtze covering Hankow.[1] He evidently suspected that if these returned to Germany pressure would be put on them to reveal what they knew for transmission to Japan. Ribbentrop replied on 24 June to order the execution of the ultimatum. Trautmann was to leave and the chargé d'affaires was to see that the advisers went.[2] In face of this the Chinese gave way and it was agreed that the advisers should leave Hankow on 5 July.[3]

While Ribbentrop was thus bullying the Chinese Government and the hapless military advisers, he was already beginning to discover the truth of Trautmann's remark in the previous March on the inadvisability of giving Japan something for nothing.[4] In November 1937 a Japanese economic mission had arrived in Germany, where it remained until the following April. It was headed by a retired naval officer, Admiral Takuo Godo, who had been Minister of Commerce and Industry in the Hayashi Cabinet and who had business connexions in Japan. It was not a governmental mission and was not authorized to enter into any commercial negotiations. Its task was to sound out the possibilities of German-Japanese economic and technical collaboration in Manchukuo and North China. Mushakoji, who was Japanese Ambassador when Godo arrived, apparently did not mind his having preliminary talks with German officials. Godo had interviews with Neurath, Ribbentrop, and Goering, among others. Either directly or through Oshima Godo gave Ribbentrop the notion that Japan would be ready to grant Germany 'parity' of treatment with herself in occupied China on economic matters to the exclusion of third Powers.[5]

---

[1] Trautmann to GFM, 23 June 1938 (ibid. pp. 881–2).
[2] Ribbentrop to Trautmann, 24 June 1938 (ibid. pp. 883–4).
[3] GFM to German Consulate-General, Hong Kong, 29 June 1938 (ibid. p. 884).
[4] Trautmann's report of 8 March 1938 (ibid. p. 848).
[5] Evidence of Godo (IMTFE, *Record*, pp. 37081–100); of Shudo (Japanese commercial attaché, Berlin, Feb. 1937–Dec. 1938, ibid. pp. 35442–5). Shudo

At the end of 1937 Mushakoji was succeeded as Ambassador by Shigenori Togo. Although he had been educated in Germany and was married to a German woman, Togo had no sympathy for the Nazis.[1] He was one of the few Japanese statesmen who were in favour of a Russian-Japanese accord; he had long wanted the Moscow Embassy, which he had been promised, and was disappointed when Hirota sent him to Germany instead.[2] Upon arrival in Berlin he was annoyed to find that Godo had been trying his hand at economic negotiations. On 23 February 1938 Ribbentrop told Togo that he had already told 'the Japanese Gentlemen' that in case of co-operation in China he expected Germany to have complete equality with the Japanese in business transactions in China. Togo replied that he alone was authorized to conduct economic negotiations, that this matter was not included in his instructions, and that Godo had no official standing.[3] In further conversations Togo rejected the German claim for economic parity with Japan in China, but Ribbentrop insisted upon at any rate a preferential position over third Powers and demanded that Tokyo be apprised of this request.[4] This Togo perforce did, but at the same time he advised his Government to reject the demand, on the ground that it would be a breach of Japan's treaty obligations to foreign Powers should she promise Germany anything more than most-favoured-nation treatment.[5] However, the Japanese Government in reply authorized Togo to promise that German economic interests in China would be given preference over those of third Powers. Togo told the Tokyo Tribunal that he narrowed down this instruction before presenting it in the form of a *Pro Memoria*.[6] As

said that Godo had discussed the question of German-Japanese economic relations in China with Oshima or with Kojima, the naval attaché. Godo denied this, and so did Kojima (ibid. p. 37057), but they were not very convincing.

[1] Evidence of Kurt Meissner (ibid. pp. 35460–3).
[2] Evidence of Togo (ibid. pp. 35634–5).
[3] ibid. pp. 35655–6. The German memorandum of the conversation on 23 February refers to Togo's protest about Godo. It says that Togo promised to transmit to his Government the German desire for economic parity with Japan in China (*D Ger.FP*, series D, i. 842).
[4] Memo. by Ribbentrop, 8 April 1938 (ibid. pp. 851–2).
[5] Evidence of Togo (IMTFE, *Record*, p. 35656) and of Shudo (ibid. p. 35444).
[6] ibid. pp. 35656–7. The *Pro Memoria* was dated 20 May 1938. It said: '(a) The Japanese Government will in the future not only not give Germany the subordinate position of a third power in regard to her economic activities in North China, but will favorably consider German interests where possible in individual cases in which proposals may in future be made by Germany. It should, however, be mentioned that this benevolent treatment could not, of course, be in the nature of precluding cooperation with third powers. (b) The Japanese

presented, it promised only 'benevolent treatment' to German economic activities in North China, and equality of treatment with Japan only to German foreign trade in China, and that subject to limitations.

There then followed some months of acrimonious discussions between Togo and the German Foreign Ministry. Ribbentrop, in a conversation with Togo on 20 May, pointed out bitterly that all Germany had got in return for her services to Japan was worse treatment than Japan had accorded to other countries. This was exemplified by Japan's attitude in the release of foreign exchange for payment of goods and interference with German trade in North China. Germany had got less response than even the United States and Great Britain had received in the matter of claims for war damage to properties in China.[1] Togo replied that Goering had already written to Oshima to assess the losses resulting from the stoppage of war materials to China at 150 million Reichsmarks. The Japanese Ambassador unkindly remarked that 'not until this claim for losses was presented did the Japanese realize how enormous the German deliveries of war matériel to China must have been thus far.' Ribbentrop retorted that the figure included the estimated losses, from fresh contracts, which China would have made but for the interdict. He furthermore insisted upon a definite concession of the preferential position in occupied China which he claimed Japan had repeatedly promised Germany.[2] But Togo stubbornly resisted the inclusion of the phrase 'preferential treatment' in the proposed agreement.[3] Ribbentrop, who realized that Togo was personally opposed to conceding the German demands, then approached Oshima on the matter. Oshima agreed with Ribbentrop that preferential treatment should be

Government is of the opinion that German foreign trade in the Chinese market should basically be on the same footing as that of the Japanese, and therefore it will do its best to have both countries enjoy the same treatment with respect to customs in China, and to see that, in addition, in case of the application of any special import or export regulation, German interests will be respected and considered as favourably as possible. However, it should be emphasized that it will be necessary to safeguard any special position of Japan resulting, for instance, from the necessity of preserving the monetary system in North China, which is inseparably connected with the Japanese monetary system' (*D Ger.FP*, series D, i. 866–7).

[1] Memo. of conversation between Ribbentrop and Togo, 20 May 1938 (ibid. p. 867).

[2] ibid. pp. 867–8.

[3] Memo. by Wiehl (Director of the Economic Division, GFM), 3 June 1938 (ibid. p. 871).

granted and that the agreement should take the form of an official exchange of Notes, which Togo also wished to avoid.[1]

But Togo continued to resist and was evidently backed up by Ugaki, who, as the Germans suspected, was trying to arrive at an accord with Great Britain on financial and economic matters in China.[2] On 29 June Togo submitted a revised *Pro Memoria*. In this the Japanese Government promised to regard Germany's economic activities in China 'with special favor' and to 'grant her at least the most favorable treatment enjoyed by third powers (Manchukuo excepted).' They agreed that German foreign trade in China should basically be on the same footing as that of Japan, and, in any particular cases where this was impossible in practice they promised to grant 'at least the most favourable treatment accorded other powers (Japan and Manchukuo excepted).'[3] Togo told Ribbentrop that 'the Japanese Government could, unfortunately, not guarantee Germany, by treaty, preferential treatment, over all other powers', though he endeavoured to persuade the German Foreign Minister that this would be done in practice. Ribbentrop was not convinced and replied that he was dissatisfied with the formula proposed in the *Pro Memoria*.[4] On 5 July he told Oshima this and the latter promised to contact the Japanese General Staff on the matter.[5] At the end of July the Japanese proposal of 29 June was definitely rejected.[6] Wiehl told Togo that German diplomatic and consular reports from China showed that all foreign trade in North China, German included, 'was being ruthlessly eliminated in favor of the Japanese', and he cited particulars of this. He especially complained of 'the complete exclusion of Germany, since the Japanese occupation, from two fields in which we have for many years held a dominant position, namely in deliveries of railroad equipment and in electric power.'[7] Wiehl added that Ott, who had come to Berlin for consultation, had been briefed on the matter and, upon his return to his post, would raise it directly with the Japanese Government.[8] On 9 August Wiehl sent official instructions to the German Embassy

---

[1] Memo. of conversation between Ribbentrop and Oshima, 17 June 1938 (ibid. p. 876).   [2] Craigie, *Behind the Japanese Mask*, p. 61.
[3] *D Ger.FP*, series D, i. 886–7.
[4] Memo. by Ribbentrop, 29 June 1938 (ibid. pp. 884–5).
[5] ibid. p. 887.
[6] Memo. of conversation between Wiehl and Togo, 27 July 1938 (ibid. p. 890).
[7] ibid., also Enclosure pp. 892–4.   [8] ibid. p. 891.

in Tokyo to raise the matter with the Japanese Foreign Minister. He remarked that

according to confidential reports . . . it seems that Japan has promised Britain that she will not grant any country a preferential position. Whether, under these circumstances, we shall win our demand for a written assurance of the 'more favorable position' appears doubtful. . . . The observations of our Missions in China do not justify us, accordingly, in expecting that the *de facto* preferential position promised us by the Japanese even remotely corresponds to the *status quo ante*. Thus far we have not been able to discover any signs of consideration corresponding to the sacrifices that Germany has made to advance Japanese interests in China.[1]

Wiehl's forebodings were amply justified. Even after the fall of Ugaki in September 1938 and the replacement in October of Togo by the more pliant Oshima as Japanese Ambassador in Berlin, the Germans got no satisfaction. On 17 November Ott reported that he had made an urgent protest to Arita about the claims of German concerns on account of damage to their property in China and also about the hampering of German business activities in occupied China through Japanese restrictions and monopolistic practices. He had presented Arita with a list of 126 claims for damages, which had hitherto gone unheeded by the Japanese, despite previous verbal remonstrances. He had, furthermore, complained that the Japanese Government had promised favourable consideration of British complaints about damage to and interference with British economic interests in China, provided Great Britain changed her attitude in the China conflict in favour of Japan. But, said Ott, such consideration was denied to Germany, despite the fact that she had of her own volition come down on the Japanese side. Ott reported that he had repeated the demand for a written promise of preferential treatment for German industry and commerce in occupied China. But he had found Arita hesitant and evasive. He declared that he would take the matter up with General Yanagawa, the Director of the China Affairs Board.[2]

But Ott's efforts were evidently of no avail, although he seems to have reported optimistically to Berlin. On 21 December Wiehl had an interview with Oshima in which he reiterated the now familiar lament that Germany, despite all the support which she had accorded to Japan in the China Conflict, was being treated

[1] ibid. p. 895.   [2] Ott to GFM (ibid. iv. 690–1).

no better, indeed if anything, worse, than Powers like Great Britain and the United States, who were opposing Japan's policy and aiding China.[1] Oshima replied that he personally agreed, but that there was opposition in Japanese economic circles to conceding a preferential position to Germany. He also made the usual Japanese excuse that restrictions on German trade were owing to military necessity. He added that there was irritation in Japanese military circles in China because Chinese troops had been found equipped with German weapons.[2]

Apart from the reluctance of Japanese military and economic circles in China to share any part of the booty, it seems clear that the Japanese Government did not want to court British and American hostility by openly violating the principle of equality of opportunity, which, subject to the special needs of Japanese 'national defence', they still professed to observe. Furthermore they still hoped, by a mixture of blandishment and menace, to bring the American and British Governments to acquiesce in the New Order. Germany had already done so and had burned her boats so far as China was concerned; hence, as Trautmann had warned would be the case, Japan had no further need to court German favours.[3] This situation continued until June of 1940, when the Japanese Government, alarmed at what a Germany, apparently victorious in Europe, might elect to do in the Far

---

[1] IMTFE, *Record*, pp. 37900–1; *D Ger.FP*, series D, iv. 694–5. Wiehl said that he had information from Tokyo that the Japanese Government were willing to accept the German demands (*D Ger.FP*, iv. 694–5). Ott told the Tokyo Tribunal in 1947, when appearing as a defence witness for Shiratori, that whenever he reported to Ribbentrop anything which did not accord with the latter's preconceived opinions, Ott encountered 'distrust and suspicion'. So he tended to stress the opinions of people like Shiratori and Oshima, whom Ribbentrop had met or heard of. This gave Berlin an exaggerated idea of their importance (*Record*, pp. 34900–2). Ott could not afford to arouse suspicion in Nazi circles. He had been an aide to General Kurt von Schleicher, who was killed by the Nazis in June 1934. The head of the OKW, General Keitel, would have given Ott a military command, but Hitler suggested him for the Japanese Embassy, probably because he did not altogether trust him. (See Keitel to Ribbentrop, 17 March 1938, *D Ger.FP*, series D, i. 851).

[2] IMTFE, *Record*, p. 37901; *D Ger.FP*, series D, iv. 695.

[3] 'From the report of the Embassy in Tokyo, it appears that Japan has thus far been in a predicament which has prevented her from clearly expressing her dissatisfaction with Germany, because she needed Germany as her only support in the world. I believe that we ourselves are releasing Japan from this predicament if we simply grant her demands one after another without asking anything in return, only to keep her in a good mood. With our help she could emerge from her isolation and adjust her relations with England and Russia. Japan would then, from the standpoint of realistic policy, have even less interest in us than heretofore' (Trautmann's report of 8 March 1938, ibid. i. 848).

East, began to show more signs of co-operation. Wiehl at that time sourly commented that Japanese thanks came pretty late and that the sacrifices which Germany had made in stopping supplies of war materials to China and so depriving herself of important Chinese raw materials, had hitherto got no recognition from Japan.[1]

Such were the results of Ribbentrop's diplomacy. He had destroyed the goodwill which Germany had built up in China since the Sino-German treaty of 1921 without obtaining any tangible return for this sacrifice. He had added a fresh cause of estrangement between Germany and the United States through his support of Japanese policy in China, despite the warnings of the German Ambassador in Washington on that score.[2] The growing antagonism between Great Britain and Germany, while of course in the main created by German policy in Europe, was increased by the German attitude to the Far Eastern situation.[3] All these adverse consequences were incurred, without any compensations either in the economic sphere or, as will be seen, in the political one.

[1] Memo. by Wiehl, 19 June 1940 (IMTFE, *Record*, p. 6166).
[2] 'Since Germany maintains, or seems to maintain, close contact with Italy and Japan, and since for many other reasons she is not liked . . . she is lumped together . . . with the other two "aggressor nations"' (Dieckhoff to GFM, 7 Dec. 1937, *D Ger.FP*, series D, i. 655).
[3] 'Ronald then said that what the British wanted most of all was Anglo-German cooperation in the Far East. The Foreign Secretary was particularly interested in this, but unfortunately we would not consent to it' (memo. by von Selzam—of the German Embassy, London—of his conversation with Mr. N. B. Ronald, Deputy Head of Far Eastern Dept., Foreign Office, on 10 January 1939, ibid. iv. 382).

CHAPTER IV

The Triple Alliance Negotiations of 1938–9

THE German-Japanese Anti-Comintern Pact of 25 November 1936 was ostensibly directed against the Comintern, as distinct from the USSR. The secret agreement, which accompanied that Pact, provided for consultation in the event of a threatened or an actual attack by the USSR upon either partner, but committed them to no more than that and thus fell short of being a definite military alliance.[1] There is evidence from German and Italian sources that the Japanese General Staff, in the winter of 1936 and again in the spring and autumn of 1937, made proposals to Blomberg and Keitel for more definite military arrangements, but met with an unfavourable response.[2]

Shortly before the conclusion of the German-Japanese Pact discussions were begun between the Italian and the Japanese Governments on the possibility of a similar Italo-Japanese pact.[3] But Hirota was cautious; he feared that the conclusion of such an agreement would have an adverse effect upon Anglo-Japanese relations, which he hoped to improve. At the same time he did not want to alienate Italy, so on 18 November 1936 he authorized the closing of the Japanese legation in Abyssinia, thus according *de facto* recognition to the 'Roman Empire', while at the same time the Manchukuo Government approved the opening of an Italian Consulate-General in Mukden, which meant *de facto* recognition of Manchukuo by Italy. Hirota also sent a letter to Count Ciano, the Italian Foreign Minister, in which he expressed the Japanese desire to strengthen their friendship with Italy, but did not refer to a definite agreement.[4] He instructed Hotta, who in May 1937

---

[1] See above, p. 25.
[2] Report by Keitel, 8 July 1937 (Political Intelligence Dept., Foreign Office, Document Section, GAP/C No. 73); also M. Toscano, *Le Origini del patto d'acciaio* (Florence, Sansoni, 1948), pp. 3–4.
[3] According to the statement of Horinouchi, prepared for the defence of Hirota, but not used, the initiative came from Ciano (IMTFE, (reject) *Defence Document*). Ciano (*L'Europa verso la catastrofe*, pp. 121–2) says the overture came from Tokyo. But his account of the negotiations given on 20 October to Hassell and Raumer rather bears out Horinouchi (Hassell to GFM, *D Ger.FP*, series D, i. 16).   [4] ibid.

succeeded Sugimura as Ambassador to Rome, to mark time with Italy in view of a possible Anglo-Japanese rapprochement.[1]

The outbreak of the China conflict spoiled any immediate hopes of this, and made Italian support more necessary to Japan, so, at the end of July, Hotta was told to go ahead with negotiations for a pact.[2] This would have been a separate Italo-Japanese agreement.[3] On 8 September 1937 Dirksen reported that Hirota had told him that the negotiations for an Italo-Japanese pact were progressing well, but that 'Mussolini had proposed in addition the conclusion of a political agreement providing for benevolent neutrality in case of war, as well as for mutual consultation. Hirota had misgivings about entering into such an agreement for fear that Italy thereby wished to commit Japan against England.' Dirksen added that he had got the impression from conversation with members of the Italian Embassy that Italy hoped by this means to obtain a freer hand in the Mediterranean.[4] It was perhaps as a means of avoiding such commitments that on 22 September the Japanese Ambassador in Berlin sounded the German Foreign Minister on the possibility of a tripartite Anti-Comintern Pact.[5] Neurath replied that 'we did not desire such an agreement. We already had the Anti-Comintern Pact with Japan. We had also made agreements with Italy, as he knew. It was now for Rome and Tokyo to decide whether they wished to make similar direct agreements.'[6]

This remained the view of the German Foreign Ministry as late as 19 October, and the Japanese Government appear to have acquiesced.[7] German objections to Italian adhesion to the Anti-Comintern Pact were probably owing to the reluctance of Berlin to reveal the secret articles to Rome. A separate Italo-Japanese Anti-Comintern Pact was on the point of signature, when the situation was changed by the intervention of Ribbentrop, who announced his intention of proceeding to Rome to secure the adhesion of Italy to the German-Japanese Pact, in the form of an

---

[1] Statement of Horinouchi (p. 99, n. 3 above).   [2] ibid.

[3] Ciano (*L'Europa*, pp. 199–202) says that the Japanese proposed a public Anti-Comintern Pact with an accompanying secret agreement for technical collaboration and 'benevolent' neutrality, should one of the signatories become involved in war with a third Power. Horinouchi declared that it was the Italians who wanted this, whereas Tokyo preferred an Anti-Comintern Pact, as with Germany but without secret articles.

[4] Dirksen to GFM (*D Ger.FP*, series D, i. 757).

[5] Memo. by Neurath, 22 Sept. 1937 (ibid. p. 760).

[6] ibid.

[7] GFM to German Embassy in Italy (ibid. p. 15).

original signatory of that instrument.[1] Ciano was ill pleased at this; he declared that he had no objection in principle, but preferred a new agreement altogether to a mere accessory protocol. He also asked to be informed of the content of the secret articles. Raumer, Ribbentrop's agent, denied that there were any, but Ciano replied that 'he had learned from various sources including even German sources, of the existence of secret agreements.'[2] Ribbentrop, however, appears to have overcome these objections by urging that the adhesion of Italy to the Anti-Comintern Pact would be but the prelude to the formation of a definite tripartite military alliance in preparation for the inevitable conflict with the Western Powers.[3] Accordingly on 6 November 1937 the protocol providing for the accession of Italy to the German-Japanese Anti-Comintern Pact was signed in Rome by Ribbentrop, Ciano, and Hotta, the Japanese Ambassador. Italy was not informed of the contents of the secret articles and did not become a party to them.[4]

The Italo-Japanese conversations on the possibility of a bilateral pact of consultation, technical collaboration, and benevolent neutrality had made little progress because the Japanese Government were unwilling to go beyond verbal assurances on either neutrality or consultation.[5] At the end of November 1937 the Japanese Ambassador expressed his Government's appreciation of the stand taken by the Italian representative at the Brussels Conference and said that the negotiations for a pact of military consultation might shortly be resumed.[6] But nothing further occurred, and by the opening of 1938 Mussolini and Ciano became cool towards Japan. Mussolini was annoyed that Japan had sought German good offices in her peace overture to China, without even informing Italy. On 4 January he told Hassell that Admiral Suetsugu's speech 'made brutally clear the real Japanese aims which were directed against all white peoples.'[7] In early April 1938, when the Italian military attaché in Tokyo received an overture from the Japanese General Staff, Ciano instructed Auriti, the Italian Ambassador, that he was not prepared to negotiate with the Japanese military behind the back of the Japanese Government.[8]

---

[1] Evidence of Horinouchi (IMTFE, (reject) *Defence Document*); Hassell (Rome) to GFM, 20 Oct. 1937 (*D Ger.FP*, series D, i. 16).   [2] ibid. p. 17.
[3] Toscano, *Patto d'acciaio*, p. 7, n.   [4] Evidence of Horinouchi.
[5] Toscano, *Patto d'acciaio*, p. 4, n.   [6] ibid. p. 8, n.
[7] Hassell to GFM, 5 Jan. 1938 (*D Ger.FP*, series D, i. 169). For Suetsugu's remarks see RIIA, *Documents, 1938*, i. 340-1.
[8] Toscano, *Patto d'acciaio*, p. 4, n.

They then turned to sound Germany, with very different results. In June 1938 Oshima received word from the Japanese General Staff that it would be desirable to strengthen German-Japanese co-operation against the Soviet Union.[1] At the beginning of July discussions began between Oshima and Ribbentrop. The latter, in a telegram of 26 April 1939 to Ott, declared that Oshima had begun by saying that the Japanese Army believed the time had come to conclude a general defensive alliance between Germany, Italy, and Japan and had outlined the terms of such an instrument.[2] Oshima in 1946 told the Tokyo Tribunal that he had only raised the subject of a pact of consultation in the event of an attack by the USSR.[3] This, however, is hardly credible in view of the existence of the secret protocol to the Anti-Comintern Pact, which already provided for such consultation. It may have been Oshima who laid stress on an alliance against the USSR and Ribbentrop who insisted upon a pact of more general application. Tokyo certainly got the impression that this had come from Germany.[4]

Oshima declared that he warned Ribbentrop that Tokyo was unlikely to agree to a pact of general application and would be prepared to act only against the USSR, but that Ribbentrop urged him to sound the Japanese General Staff on the matter, which he did, and received its sanction to continue the conversations.[5] At this time Russo-Japanese relations were at a critical stage; Japanese protests about Soviet aid to China had been rebuffed, while on 11 July fighting began at Changkufeng between Soviet and Japanese forces. This strengthened the long-standing desire of the Japanese Army for an alliance with Germany against the USSR, even if a price had to be paid in the form of commitments against other Powers as well.

The exploratory conversations between Ribbentrop and Oshima had been kept secret from the Japanese Ambassador in Berlin, Shigenori Togo, who was known to be hostile to the idea of closer ties between Japan and Nazi Germany.[6] In the second half of

---

[1] Evidence of Oshima (IMTFE, *Record*, pp. 6050–1).
[2] ibid. pp. 6098–6102.
[3] ibid. pp. 6051–2.
[4] On 9 August Konoye told Kido that, having previously consulted with Hitler, Ribbentrop had made an important proposal to Oshima. Kasahara had just returned from Berlin with the details (Kido's Diary for 9 Aug. 1938, ibid. p. 16226).   [5] Evidence of Oshima (ibid. p. 6052).
[6] On 21 June Konoye told Harada that Godo had been complaining of

July Oshima informed Major-General Yukio Kasahara, a staff officer who had been seconded to Berlin, ostensibly for language study, with a view to his eventually becoming military attaché there.[1] Oshima sent Kasahara as special courier to Japan with the German proposals for a treaty—this method of communication was employed to prevent any possibility of leakage. Kasahara travelled by air to Singapore and thence by sea to Japan, where he arrived at the beginning of August.[2]

Kasahara laid Ribbentrop's proposals before the Army General Staff. So far, it should be observed, the stage of formal negotiations between the two Governments had not been reached. The Japanese Army General Staff had, through Oshima, sounded Ribbentrop on the possibility of a military pact against the Soviet Union; Ribbentrop was now sounding the General Staff to get its reactions to a pact of more general application. The draft proposal brought by Kasahara consisted of three articles; of which the first provided for consultation between the signatories in the event of any of them becoming involved in diplomatic difficulties with a third State or States; the second for political and diplomatic support in the case of a threat; and the third, and most important, for military assistance in the event of an attack by a third Power or Powers.[3]

The Army leaders took a generally favourable view of the project. They saw in the proposed pact an insurance in the event of war with the USSR, and also a means by which China might be induced to come to peace terms with Japan and the Western Democracies frightened into the abandonment of the limited support which they were according Chungking. So they informed the Foreign Minister, who in turn laid the matter before the Inner Cabinet.[4]

Togo's attitude in the economic negotiations and that Itagaki, the War Minister, had asked Ugaki to remove him. The General Staff wanted Oshima as Ambassador in Berlin. But Ugaki was unwilling and this had caused strained relations between the Foreign Minister and the War Minister (*Saionji–Harada Memoirs*, 27 June 1938).   [1] Evidence of Kasahara (IMTFE, *Record*, p. 35434).
    [2] Evidence of Oshima (ibid. pp. 6055–6) and of Kasahara (ibid. p. 33718).
    [3] Ribbentrop to Ott, 26 April 1939 (ibid. pp. 6098–6100). 'The German proposal was to the effect that political support would be given in case Japan, Germany, or Italy were threatened by a third Power, while military assistance would be given in case they were attacked' (evidence of Kasahara, ibid., pp. 33718–19).
    'The essence of this proposal is to reinforce the relationship between Germany and Japan and contains three clauses. The third clause provides that in case one nation is attacked by a third country the other will render military aid' (Kido's Diary, 9 Aug. 1938, ibid. p. 16226).
    [4] Evidence of Oshima, 26 Nov. 1947 (IMTFE, *Record*, p. 33998).

Ugaki's action, which appears to have taken place on or about 8 August, resulted in discussions in the Japanese Inner Cabinet which lasted until the end of the month.[1] The Premier was dubious about the effect the proposed pact might have upon Japan's relations with Great Britain and the United States, but at the same time was ready to clutch at any hope of ending the China war. The Navy Minister, Admiral Yonai, was prompt to oppose any obligations which might involve Japan in conflict with the British and American Navies.

On 29 August the Vice-Ministers of War and of the Navy sent a telegram to Oshima and to Kojima, the naval attaché. This said that the Army and the Navy were in agreement with the purport of the draft brought by Kasahara, subject to a number of changes, that they wanted to conclude the treaty quickly and that they hoped that the German Government would soon submit a formal plan. The telegram also listed some of the modifications wanted, though these were set out more fully in another telegraphic instruction of the same date from the War Ministry to Oshima.[2]

Taking the two instructions together, the changes required were these: First, a preamble making it clear that the treaty was an extension of the existing Anti-Comintern Pact, and that the Soviet Union, and not Great Britain or the United States, was the chief prospective enemy.[3] In the second place, the support to be given in

[1] ibid. pp. 33998–9. On 9 August, when Konoye told Kido of the German proposal, he said that the Navy objected to the third article and that the situation was serious. He agreed with Kido that Japan ought to be careful about adopting any policy which might arouse the hostility of Great Britain and the United States (IMTFE, *Record*, pp. 26226–7, 30586). Toshio Shiratori, in his affidavit, stated that he went to see Konoye in August 1938, having learned that the Premier had recommended him to Ugaki for the Rome Embassy. Konoye told him of the negotiations for an Axis Pact. 'He said that he was not enamoured of the idea himself, but that inasmuch as direct negotiation with Chiang Kai-shek had so far proved almost useless, some other diplomatic means had to be sought to quickly dispose of the China mess. In his opinion a friendly intervention by England and America was the greatest desideratum, but nothing short of a possible alignment of Japan with the Axis would cause them to modify the anti-Japanese attitude they had maintained ever since the Manchurian imbroglio. I [Shiratori] concluded from all he told me that at the moment it was not so much the actual rapprochement with Germany and Italy that he really desired as the effect such a gesture on Japan's part would have on England and America in regard to their China policy' (ibid. pp. 35032–3).

[2] *Saionji–Harada Memoirs*, 15 June 1939. At that time Konoye told Harada that he had been looking at the telegrams sent by the War Ministry and that he thought that these two telegrams of 29 August had been the cause of all the trouble. Harada said that he got hold of them secretly from Captain Takagi, and he gives the texts of them in the Memoirs.

[3] 'The Preamble Draft is that the Treaty is an extension of the existing Anti-Comintern Pact and is a plan which makes clear the intent that the Soviet

the event of a menace or threat of war was to be limited to economic aid. Finally, Article 3, which provided for military assistance, was to be redrafted so as to operate only in the event of an unprovoked attack and, even in that event, Japan wanted to limit her *immediate* obligation to consultation with her allies on what assistance could be given.[1] It was explained that the object of this was to prevent Japan from becoming involved in a purely European quarrel against her will. Oshima was also told that Tokyo would like to have a secret protocol to the treaty, this protocol to set forth in detail just what Japan's obligations would be to her allies in the matter of military assistance. Meanwhile, around the middle of August, Sakaya, the First Secretary of the Japanese Embassy in Berlin, who had got to know of the Ribbentrop–Oshima talks and of Kasahara's mission to Tokyo, informed Togo. The latter cabled to Tokyo to advise that the *pourparlers* be dropped; he urged that Japan would not be able to settle the China Affair by such means and might well find herself involved in a European war. Togo got a reply at the end of August which told him of the decision to continue the conversations. He dispatched a second remonstrance, but in answer received a telegram from Ugaki who demanded his consent to be transferred to the Moscow Embassy. Togo demurred, but a second and more peremptory cable left him no choice but to concur. He received his appointment as Ambassador to Moscow on 15 October and left on 27 October, when Oshima took over as Ambassador.[2]

Kasahara was told, by Major-General Machijiri, of the Army General Staff, of the decision reached by the Inner Cabinet and was sent back to give Oshima a verbal account of it. Leaving Tokyo at the beginning of September, Kasahara arrived in Berlin around the 20th of that month, and explained the situation to Oshima, who subsequently told him that he had 'communicated the Japanese decision to the German side.'[3]

From the foregoing chronology of events it may be inferred that by the time of the Munich Conference Ribbentrop had been

Union is the chief target; care was taken so as not to give the impression from the wording that England and the United States are the chief enemies. The Text Plan Obligation of Military Aid in Article 3 is not instantaneous or unconditional. In order to nullify the danger of becoming involved *in a purely European problem against our will, a conference* before we enter with military aid is the principle' (ibid.). The words in italics are missing from the record of Oshima's rendering of the second telegram (IMTFE, *Record*, pp. 34116–19).

[1] *Saionji–Harada Memoirs*, 15 June 1939.
[2] Evidence of Sakaya (IMTFE, *Record*, pp. 35454–5) and of Togo (ibid. pp. 35659–60). [3] Evidence of Kasahara (ibid. pp. 33718–19).

informed of the Japanese Government's response to his overture
in July and that the draft of a tripartite agreement which he gave
Ciano at Munich on 29 September was an attempt to meet the
Japanese reservations.[1] The draft opened with a preamble on
the need to defend the 'common ideological interests' of the three
Powers against the threat caused by the development of Comintern
activities in Asia and Europe since the conclusion of the (tripartite)
Anti-Comintern Pact. There followed three articles which provided
for consultation in the event of a signatory being involved in
diplomatic difficulties; full diplomatic and political assistance in
the event of a threat from a third State or States; and military
assistance and aid in the event of an unprovoked attack. This
was to be a public agreement. Upon its signature, commissions
were to be appointed by the signatory Governments to work out
the details of the assistance—political, economic, or military—to
be given under the articles in each case that might arise, taking
into account the geographical situation of each country.[2] Their
findings were to be embodied in a supplementary agreement—by
inference secret.

In Berlin Oshima continued discussions with Ribbentrop and
with Gaus, the head of the Treaty Department of the German
Foreign Ministry. The upshot was that a draft treaty was officially
communicated to Oshima, now Ambassador, and was sent by him
to Tokyo, where it was received early in November.[3] This was
the first German *formal* proposal to Japan for an alliance. It is,
curiously enough, not mentioned by Ribbentrop in his summary of
the negotiations sent to Ott on 26 April 1939, and while there are
frequent references to it in the testimonies of Oshima and Itagaki,
they do not give its text. It is *possible*, however, that the draft pact
which Ciano says he received from the Japanese naval and military
attachés in Rome on 27 October was a copy of that given to Oshima
by the German Foreign Ministry.[4] The draft received by Ciano
was in regular treaty form, but otherwise was generally similar to
the 'Munich draft' of 29 September. It contained, however, two

[1] Toscano, *Patto d'acciaio*, p. 19. Ribbentrop, in his conversation with Ciano
in Rome on 28 October, referred to an initial version of the proposed treaty
having been given to Italy at Munich (*D Ger.FP*, series D, iv. 516).
[2] Toscano, *Patto d'acciaio*, pp. 19–20.
[3] Evidence of Oshima (IMTFE, *Record*, pp. 33995–6) and of Itagaki (ibid.
p. 30308).
[4] Toscano, *Patto d'acciaio*, p. 24. Ciano also got the revised draft from
Ribbentrop on 29 October (*D Ger.FP*, series D, iv. 516).

additional articles: (4) which stipulated that, in the event of war occurring under the stipulations of Article 3, the signatories should make no separate armistice or peace; and (5) by which the treaty was to run for an initial ten years, and, unless denounced a year before the date of expiring, for an additional five years. Furthermore the supplementary agreement making provision for Commissions to formulate the terms and conditions of assistance was now termed 'a secret additional protocol'.[1]

In Tokyo Ugaki had resigned on 26 September, and Konoye, after retaining the portfolio of Foreign Affairs himself for a month, had selected Hachiro Arita as the new incumbent. The German proposal was first laid before the Inner Cabinet on 11 November.[2] Itagaki, in his testimony before the International Military Tribunal, declared that he had pressed for a speedy conclusion of the tripartite pact. He had hoped that if this followed soon after the fall of Hankow, it would make the Chungking Government despair of foreign aid and so induce them to conclude peace with Japan. But internal disagreements in the Japanese Cabinet prevented Itagaki's hopes from being realized. It may be well, at this point, to consider the nature of these disagreements, both within Japanese governing circles and between Japan and her prospective allies.

There was general agreement in Tokyo on a military alliance directed against the USSR. Togo, who since 1932 had pleaded in favour of a Soviet-Japanese rapprochement, was a voice crying in the wilderness at this time. But fervent dissension arose over the question of Japan incurring any sort of commitments to war against the Democracies. Those in favour of this urged that it could be utilized to induce the democratic Powers to abandon their hostility to Japan's policy in China and so to compel Chungking to come to terms. This argument evidently had weight with Konoye and Arita, as well as with Itagaki. But there were strong countervailing arguments. It was becoming evident that the German and Italian dictators intended to continue their policy of aggrandizement in Europe, even if it involved them in war with Great Britain and France. But it was also becoming clear that the Washington Government were primarily concerned to prevent a Nazi-Fascist domination of Europe, and it was already possible that in this matter interventionist might come to outweigh isolationist feeling

[1] Toscano, *Patto d'acciaio*, pp. 24–26.
[2] Evidence of Itagaki (IMTFE, *Record*, p. 30308).

in the United States. Then, should Japan have incurred military commitments to Germany and Italy, she would be faced by the two most powerful navies in the world; and how much aid could the German and Italian fleets afford her? She would almost certainly find herself cut off from her main sources of vital raw materials and foodstuffs, and as yet she was obtaining very little of these from the occupied areas of China, including Manchuria.

This was a consideration which counted for much with the Japanese Navy and one which in the next year was given added weight by the return to Pacific waters of the bulk of the United States fleet under instructions of 10 April 1939. The senior officers of the Japanese Navy were, as a whole, firmly opposed to any general pact with the Axis, and they proved strong enough, in conjunction with other opposing elements, to prevent the conclusion of any such pact despite the pressure from Army leaders in its favour.[1] This split between the Japanese armed services was to have decisive consequences, both in the prelude to the general war and upon that war itself.

The opponents of a pact of general application demanded as a safeguard the exchange of a secret written guarantee at the time of its signature which should absolve Japan from the obligations of Article 3 of the pact, except in the case of Soviet Russia. This the German and Italian Governments were not prepared to accept to the extent of releasing Japan from all commitments in respect of the Democracies, although, as will be seen, they were ready to go a long way in meeting the Japanese desires. It was over the form and nature of the proposed secret understanding that the main battle was waged, both diplomatically and internally in Tokyo.

In mid-November Oshima received a telegram from Arita who said that there was agreement on the idea of concluding a treaty which would help Japan to terminate the China Incident, would strengthen her military position *vis-à-vis* the USSR, and would improve her general diplomatic position. Arita added, however, that the Government were studying the actual wording of the treaty.[2] Shortly afterwards another telegram came from Arita to

---

[1] In 1945 Admiral Osamu Nagano testified to the consistent opposition of the Navy to an Axis pact involving war with Great Britain and the United States (USSBS, *Interrogations of Japanese Officials*, vol. ii, 1946, pp. 352–6). Admiral Nomura said much the same (ibid. pp. 384–5). The Navy was not, however, without its pro-Axis representatives. The Tripartite Pact of September 1940 was concluded in different circumstances and with a different objective.

[2] Evidence of Usami. He arrived in Berlin on 11 November as Counsellor of

say that there seemed to be a misunderstanding about the object of the treaty, i.e. on the question of its application to countries other than the USSR. Oshima asked that he should be cabled further details about this but he received 'no clear answer'.[1]

The hold-up in Tokyo was due to the fact that the Konoye Government was tottering to its fall. It was undergoing a crisis over both foreign and domestic issues. In addition to the rift over the proposed pact with Germany and Italy, there was a quarrel between the advocates of direct negotiations with Chiang Kai-shek and those opposed to such a course; the Army itself was split on this issue.[2] In the field of domestic politics a conflict was going on between the pro-totalitarian groups in Japan and those who wished to preserve the existing policy. Both advocates and opponents of a single-party system and of something resembling a National-Socialist régime were to be found in the armed services, the bureaucracy, and the Cabinet. The totalitarians were strongest among the Army officers, but were less prominent in the Navy; they enjoyed a considerable representation in the bureaucracy, but there were few of them in Court circles or among the Zaibatsu. In the Konoye Cabinet the most vehement advocate of a single-party system was the Home Minister, the turbulent Admiral Suetsugu, 'a great admiral and a great Fascist', as he had been sarcastically termed by a Diet critic at the time of the serio-comic episode in Tokyo known as 'the march on Rome without Mussolini'.[3] On the other side stood Mr. Seihin Ikeda, the Minister of Finance, who was a firm opponent of totalitarianism in politics and in business. Prince Konoye's own record is equivocal; perhaps the best judgement on him is that he was at heart opposed to totalitarian methods at home and to a line-up with the Nazi-Fascist Powers abroad, but that he was a man of weak and irresolute character, prone to take the line of least resistance, to procrastinate as long as possible, and to lay down the burden of office when evasion would no longer serve him. He had been wanting to resign for some months, but

Embassy (IMTFE, *Record*, pp. 33730–44). Also of Oshima (ibid. pp. 6055–8). He mentioned a fourth point in Arita's telegram—that Japan would get technological and economic assistance from Germany.

[1] This is according to the testimony of Usami. Oshima does not mention the second telegram, but says he waited for a long time and in December sent another telegram to the Foreign Ministry 'asking why I did not receive an answer' (evidence of Oshima). But he was always rather shaky on the sequence of events, and Usami is perhaps a better authority on this.

[2] Kido's Diary, 7 Sept. 1938 (IMTFE, *Record*, pp. 16230–1).

[3] This occurred on 17 Feb. 1938.

was persuaded to carry on, until things became too much for him and he gave up the seals of office on 4 January 1939.[1] The fall of his Cabinet temporarily resolved the domestic imbroglio by removing both Suetsugu and Ikeda from office.

The new Cabinet was headed by Baron Hiranuma, who chose Marquis Kido as Home Minister, but retained Arita, Itagaki, and Yonai in their respective posts. The choice of Hiranuma as Konoye's successor appeared at first sight to be a victory for the pro-Axis and totalitarian party, for until 1936 Hiranuma had been the leader of the extremist society known as the Kokuhonsha. This had been dissolved after the Army mutiny of February 1936, and Hiranuma had become President of the Privy Council. As Premier, Hiranuma revealed himself as an upholder of the traditional Japanese policy. Japan, he repeatedly averred, was in neither the democratic nor the totalitarian camp, she was *sui generis*, and possessed a peculiar polity of her own, summed up in the term Kodo—the Imperial Way. Stripped of its mysticism and verbiage, this was a correct representation of Japan's form of Government. Theoretically an absolute monarchy, it was in fact an oligarchy, in which policy was formulated by discussion and compromise between the various groups within the ruling caste. It was a system which militated against swift decisions and clear-cut policies, as well as against sudden changes of front. Hence the 'dynamic diplomacy' of the Axis Powers was alien to the long deliberations in which policy was formulated in Tokyo.

Meanwhile, early in January Mussolini, who hitherto had hesitated, announced his readiness to conclude the pact, whereupon Ribbentrop produced a revised draft.[2] This draft differed from the previous one, in that the preamble laid more stress on the common interests of the three Powers in Europe and Asia, as compared with defence against the Comintern. The articles followed those of the previous draft, with an additional provision for ratification. The secret additional protocol now provided for a

    [1] According to the *Saionji–Harada Memoirs* (28 Oct. 1938), Konoye wanted to succeed Kurahei Yuasa, who was in bad health, as Lord Keeper of the Privy Seal. Saionji was opposed to this on the ground that it would increase the influence of the Army in Palace circles.
    [2] Ciano on 2 January telephoned Ribbentrop and also wrote telling him that Mussolini was now ready to sign the pact. Ribbentrop replied on 9 January to say that 'a few days ago' he had given the draft pact and an additional secret protocol to Attolico and to Oshima. He proposed that the pact should be signed in Berlin on 28 January (*D Ger.FP*, series D, iv. 545–6).

permanent committee, composed of the three Foreign Ministers or their representatives assisted by sub-committees of experts, to work out the details of assistance. There were also to be permanent committees, for information and press services, set up in Berlin, Rome, and Tokyo, and composed of the Foreign Minister and diplomatic representatives of the other two signatories.[1]

Oshima sent the text of the draft treaty by courier to Tokyo. He may presumably have telegraphed a summary of the contents.[2] The revised proposal was discussed at a conference of the Japanese Inner Cabinet which, on 19 January, decided to send to Europe a special mission with a detailed instruction on the Japanese standpoint for communication to Oshima and Shiratori.[3] The members of the mission were Nobufumi Ito, formerly Minister to Poland, Lieut.-Colonel Tatsumi, of the Army General Staff, and Rear-Admiral Abe, of the Naval General Staff.[4] The composition of this mission indicated that agreement had been reached between the Foreign Ministry and the Services, and the real motive for its dispatch was to impress Oshima and Shiratori with this and to keep a restraint on them. Oshima was informed by telegram of the dispatch of the mission which was expected to reach Berlin on 28 February.[5] The reason given for its dispatch was the need to preserve secrecy about the details of the negotiations.

Both Ribbentrop and Ciano were impatient at the delay which this procedure involved since they wanted the tripartite pact concluded before they made the fresh moves in Europe which they knew would arouse Anglo-French apprehension and hostility. Ribbentrop urged Oshima to get his Government to telegraph the details which they wanted modified, but Tokyo would not

---

[1] For text see RIIA, *Documents, 1939–46*, i. 152.

[2] Oshima and Usami make no mention of the January 1939 draft. Ribbentrop, in his telegram to Ott of 26 April, said that Oshima had participated in the framing of the new draft and had sent it by special courier to Tokyo. This also appears from a memorandum of Weizsäcker of 13 January 1939. He had urged Oshima to have everything ready for signing by 28 January. Oshima said the final version of the text was on its way to Japan by courier and would arrive there on the 20th (*D Ger.FP*, series D, iv. 697–8). Itagaki, however, said that the new proposal was received in Tokyo 'at the beginning of January' (IMTFE, *Record*, p. 30315). If so its contents must have been telegraphed.

[3] Evidence of Itagaki (IMTFE, *Record*, p. 30315); *Saionji–Harada Memoirs*, 20 Jan. 1939.

[4] Interrogation of Nobufumi Ito, 1 April 1946 (IMTFE). The 'Ito Directive' was dated 23 January (evidence of Itagaki, IMTFE, *Record*, p. 30316).

[5] 'My mission was in fact primarily that of persuasion, to tell these two Ambassadors the real situation of the country which did not permit us to go as far as these two desired' (Interrogation of Ito, IMTFE).

concur.[1] The general nature of the Japanese Government's desiderata were, however, fairly apparent to both Oshima and Shiratori, especially as Arita had, on 21 January, told the Diet that the more the Anti-Comintern Pact was expanded and strengthened the greater would be the guarantee of world peace, but that the Pact was intended for mutual defence against the destructive activities of the Comintern and that it could have no other purpose.[2]

The Ito mission came to Berlin via Rome, where Shiratori and his first and second secretaries, Sakamoto and Nagai, joined it *en route* to the German capital.[3] In Berlin Ito revealed his directive, the essence of which was that the Japanese Government wanted to accompany the treaty with a secret written mutual understanding that Japan would not have to render military aid against countries other than the Soviet Union, unless such countries went Communist, and also that if inquiries were made of her by third Powers as to the real nature of the treaty, she should be free to explain to them that it was simply an extension of the Anti-Comintern Pact.[4] This in fact meant that Japan would give no active aid to her partners, except against the Soviet Union.

Both Shiratori and Oshima declared that the directive was unacceptable and, according to Ito, Oshima would not present it officially to Ribbentrop. Hiranuma had told Ito that the decision was final, but he suspected that while he was still in Berlin information came to Oshima from Tokyo that the last word had not been spoken there. Consequently he failed to bring them to heel and he returned feeling that Hiranuma had let him down. Oshima and Shiratori had indeed urged Tokyo to reconsider.[5] According to Ribbentrop and Ciano they threatened, if this were not done,

[1] Toscano, *Patto d'acciaio*, pp. 60–61. Ribbentrop in particular wanted the Pact signed by the beginning of March at the very latest.

[2] According to Ciano (*Diary*, pp. 23–24) Shiratori told him that the Japanese counter-proposal would be of a kind which he should not accept. Shiratori at his trial denied this and said he only remarked that it might not prove to be Tokyo's last word (IMTFE, *Record*, p. 35038). Hiranuma was said to have told Arita: 'I am of the same opinion as you. I am opposed to the strengthening of the Axis Anti-Comintern Pact to the extent of waging war against England and France. Should the Army coerce us, I shall resign together with you' (*Saionji–Harada Memoirs*, 5 Jan. 1939).

[3] Statement of Nagai. He says there were no discussions in Rome (IMTFE, *Record*, pp. 34942–3). The Ito mission left Japan on 2 February and reached Berlin at the beginning of March.

[4] Evidence of Oshima (ibid. pp. 34002–3). The versions given by Usami and Ribbentrop agree, except for slight variances in phrasing, with that of Oshima.

[5] *Saionji–Harada Memoirs*, 10 March 1939.

to resign and so provoke a Cabinet crisis in Tokyo.[1] Oshima pointed out that he had already committed Japan to a pact of general validity, and in this had acted on instructions previously received. The Ito directive was accompanied by an explanatory statement which implied that Tokyo would not have accepted the treaty text committing Japan to general obligations had there not been an original misunderstanding on the extent to which Japan was ready to go. Oshima asked who was held responsible for this; to which Arita replied at the end of March that no one in particular could be blamed.[2]

Oshima and Shiratori joined in a telegram to warn Arita that Germany and Italy would not now accept Japan's proposed limitation of her obligations and to suggest that the pact should be concluded without any secret understanding, but that the extent of Japan's military obligations should be left for later discussion.[3] Shiratori also independently warned Arita that if Japan did not conclude the treaty there was a probability that Germany would seek an accord with the USSR, in order to free her hands for action against the Democracies; he was more concerned at this possibility than was Oshima who did not believe in it.[4] Nor did Arita, who thought that the Germans were simply trying to bring pressure on Japan to conclude the pact on their terms.

The issue was now plain. If Japan wanted the pact she would have to accept some military commitments against the Democracies, and not only against the USSR. On this issue the battle was joined in Tokyo, the chief antagonists being Itagaki and Yonai. During March and April 1939 the apparently triumphant progress of German and Italian aggression in Europe, as exemplified in Czechoslovakia and Albania, strengthened the hand of the advocates in Japan of meeting the wishes of the Axis Powers. So did the opening of Anglo-Soviet negotiations, because of Japanese

---

[1] Toscano, *Patto d'acciaio*, pp. 69–71, and Ribbentrop's telegram of 26 April. But both Ambassadors denied these allegations at their trials in 1946–7 (IMTFE, *Record*, pp. 34136–7).

[2] Evidence of Oshima (ibid. pp. 34000–4).

[3] Evidence of Usami (ibid. pp. 33730–44).

[4] Evidence of Shiratori (ibid. p. 35042) and of Nagai (ibid. p. 34943). The Ito mission was not empowered to negotiate with Germany; it remained a short time in Berlin and then returned to Japan. While it was in the German capital, Oshima called a conference of other Japanese diplomats in Europe. This was unauthorized and disapproved by Arita when he learned of it. Among those who came was Togo, who told Ito to return and advise against any pact. (Evidence of Ito, ibid. p. 35459.)

fears that an accord between Great Britain and the USSR might include the Far East. All this increased the pressure upon the Hiranuma Cabinet to conclude the general military alliance. The result was that on 25 March a new directive was drawn up, in which the Japanese Government somewhat receded from the position they had taken in the Ito directive. They accepted in principle the obligation of military assistance against the Democracies, but explained that for political and especially for economic reasons, Japan was as yet unable to come out openly against them. Therefore, the Tokyo Government still wished to have a secret written agreement to provide that for the time being Japanese aid against the Democracies should be limited to measures short of war and to allow Japan, if questioned, to explain that the public pact was solely directed against the Comintern. They also wanted the duration of the pact reduced from ten to five years.[1]

Oshima received these instructions at the end of March and communicated their substance to Ribbentrop at the beginning of April. Ribbentrop, after consultation with Hitler, told Oshima that Germany would agree to the pact being limited to five years' duration. (Hitler reckoned on war long before the expiration of that period.) But he said that since the Japanese Government had now accepted in principle military obligations against the Democracies, he could not consent to their desire to give a different interpretation of the pact in explanations to those Powers. He declared that Japan would not be asked to do more than it was in her power to perform, and again suggested that there was no need for any secret understanding since the details of the aid to be rendered could be settled after the signature of the treaty. Ribbentrop was evidently resolved to concede nothing to the Japanese that would weaken the effect of the pact as a deterrent to the Democracies, especially the United States. He was willing to have an oral agreement, after the public pact had been signed, which would practically absolve Japan from joining in active hostilities against any Power except the USSR. But he objected to any *written* agreement on this because if this became known to others, it would seriously weaken the value of the pact.[2]

During April a series of Inner Cabinet conferences took place

---

[1] Evidence of Oshima (ibid. pp. 34005–6), of Usami (ibid. pp. 33730–44); Ribbentrop to Ott, 26 April 1939 (ibid. p. 6101).

[2] Evidence of Oshima (ibid. pp. 34006–7) and of Usami (ibid. pp. 33730–44).

in Tokyo in which the question of the Axis alliance was further
debated, but the Navy Minister still remained inflexibly opposed
to any commitments which might involve Japan with Great
Britain and the United States.[1] On 19 April Admiral Yonai
confidentially informed the American Ambassador, Mr. Grew,
that Japanese policy had been decided, and that the element which
desired Fascism for Japan and a tripartite Pact with Germany
and Italy had been suppressed.[2] On 20 April, at a reception on the
occasion of Hitler's birthday, Ribbentrop warned Oshima and
Shiratori that, should Japan continue to delay, Germany might be
forced to seek a non-aggression pact with the USSR.[3] But this
did not produce the desired effect since both Oshima and Arita
regarded it as simply bluff, and Shiratori's warnings to the contrary were ignored.[4] On 24 April a reply was received in Berlin
in which the Japanese Government took an even stronger line
against any military commitments, except in the case of the USSR.[5]
Both Oshima and Shiratori declared that the last word had not
been spoken in Tokyo and were urged in reply to get a final
decision from their Government.[6] They were correct in thinking
that the battle was by no means over. In Tokyo Marquis Kido, the
éminence grise of Japanese politics, was afraid of a military coup
d'état and was exercising his influence to secure a compromise
between the conflicting views of the Army and the Navy, and
so avert the overthrow of the Cabinet and the assassination by
extremists of the opponents of the pact.[7]

On 4 May Baron Hiranuma, in an attempt to find a way out of
the impasse, sent a personal message to Hitler, and a similar one
to Mussolini, through the German and Italian Ambassadors in

[1] Yonai declared: 'If problems such as this bring about bad results the entire
responsibility of national defence will fall to the Navy' (*Saionji–Harada Memoirs*,
5 May 1939).
[2] J. C. Grew, *Ten Years in Japan* (London, Hammond, 1944), pp. 245–6.
Grew, on instructions from Hull, had been unofficially using his influence against
the Pact (Hull, *Memoirs*, i. 627–8).
[3] Oshima's evidence (IMTFE, *Record*, p. 6079). Ribbentrop had said that
he must have a definite answer by 28 April.
[4] ibid. pp. 16003–4.
[5] Toscano, *Patto d'acciaio*, p. 125.
[6] It was at this time that Oshima and Shiratori tried to put pressure on the
Cabinet by asking to be recalled. The evidence of Attolico on this (ibid.) is
borne out by the *Saionji–Harada Memoirs*, 5 May 1939, which note that Arita
had said that Oshima and Shiratori had requested their recall.
[7] Kido's Diary, 19 April, 2 May 1939 (IMTFE, *Record*, pp. 16235–6). He
was also worried over the Emperor's opposition to a pact of general application
(*Saionji–Harada Memoirs*, 24 April 1939).

Tokyo.[1] In his letter the Japanese Premier declared that Japan was honestly desirous of concluding the pact and sincere in her readiness to extend aid, including military assistance, to Germany and Italy, should they be assailed by third Powers, and even should the Soviet Union not be among these. But in Japan's existing situation she was not able to render effective military aid, at the moment or in the near future, although she would do so when circumstances should permit. Hiranuma therefore asked that Germany and Italy agree to the secret understanding which Japan wanted, to excuse her from the obligation of military assistance for the time being, and to allow her to give an innocuous explanation of the pact when this was published. He added that to doubt Japan's sincerity would destroy the real basis of the agreement and make its signature impossible.[2]

Ott, who on 26 April had been told by Ribbentrop to report on the situation in Tokyo, on 6 May summarized the views of Japanese General Staff officers on the Hiranuma message. The Army had proposed that Hiranuma should define the 'changed circumstances' which would make effective aid possible, and that he should exclude in any case the possibility of Japanese neutrality. They blamed Arita for the omission of these points. But they pointed out that the treaty would bind Japan to the Axis Powers, that the very elasticity of the proposed reservations might be better than a more hard and fast formula, and that Hiranuma had pledged his word of honour. He had, in face of a serious cleavage in the entire Government, secured a compromise which retained the principle of an alliance of general application. If no agreement were reached on the basis of the Hiranuma declaration, the Japanese Government might fall, with serious consequences, both at home and abroad.[3]

But Hiranuma's plea failed to convince the German and Italian Governments of his good faith. They suspected that if they agreed to a secret written understanding of the kind he wanted, the Japanese Government would use the public pact as a threat to try to blackmail the Democracies and, if this proved successful, would then reveal the secret articles to them in proof that Japan was not irrevocably committed to war against them if they took up arms

---

[1] This step had been decided on at an Inner Cabinet Conference on 24 April (*Saionji–Harada Memoirs*, 5 May 1939).
[2] IMTFE, *Record*, pp. 6103–7.   [3] ibid. pp. 6108–11.

against the Axis Powers in Europe.[1] The negotiations now became even more complicated and tortuous. In Milan on 6–7 May Ribbentrop agreed with Ciano to push on with the conclusion of a bilateral pact, without waiting for Japan, but to frame it so as to permit her to adhere to it later on, if she wished.[2] Meanwhile Oshima had instructed two of his subordinates, Usami and Takeuchi, to collaborate with Gaus in the drafting of yet another draft of a tripartite pact.[3] On 13 May, after Ribbentrop had returned from Italy, Oshima called on him and warned him of the unfavourable reactions that the conclusion of a German-Italian pact might provoke in Tokyo. Ribbentrop, while he justified the conclusion of a separate German-Italian pact, proposed that a tripartite pact might also be signed at the same time and he secured Italian consent to make considerable concessions to the Japanese point of view.[4] The upshot was that on 15 May Ribbentrop sent to Ott the drafts of the latest versions of the proposed tripartite agreement.[5]

These consisted of the public arrangement—a preamble and four articles, worded as the Japanese had wanted: i.e. the preamble stressed defence against Communism as the motive for the agreement; and the duration of the pact was limited to five years. There was to be an additional article on the relation of the tripartite to the German-Italian pact. The pact was to be accompanied by a signing protocol which stated that a threat to or attack upon Manchukuo was to be considered equivalent to such action against Japan, and also that if the situation contemplated in Articles 2 or 3 had actually come into being at the time the pact was due to expire, this should be prolonged until such a situation had ended.[6]

The secret additional protocol provided that 'the competent

---

[1] 'I believe that Germany began to get suspicious that Japan was attempting to weaken the treaty by a separate secret pact, of which she might in turn inform certain nations' (evidence of Oshima, IMTFE, *Record*, pp. 6069–70). As has been seen, Konoye and Arita *had* cherished some such design, while Hiranuma's overture to Roosevelt (see below, pp. 122–3) indicates that he was thinking along the same lines.   [2] RIIA, *Documents, 1939–46*, i. 167.

[3] Evidence of Oshima (IMTFE, *Record*, pp. 6068–9). According to the *Saionji–Harada Memoirs* for 6 May, Arita said Usami telegraphed that Gaus had submitted unofficially a new draft. This retained the German stipulations about Japanese participation in war. Arita upon inquiry found that it had been originally submitted by the Japanese Army through the Japanese military attaché. He was very angry about this. He was also upset about Oshima having told Ribbentrop that if Germany and Italy were engaged in war (under the provisions of the pact), Japan would consider herself in a state of war also.

[4] Toscano, *Patto d'acciaio*, pp. 175–6.

[5] IMTFE, *Record*, pp. 6115–19.   [6] ibid. pp. 22541–6.

authorities of the three contracting Powers' should, immediately after the pact came into force, investigate the various possibilities of conflict and the nature and extent of the assistance to be given in each case. It also precluded the making of a separate armistice or peace and gave the articles of the pact precedence over any conflicting provisions in existing treaties with third Powers. This protocol was not to be made public except by common consent of the three signatories, and was to have the same duration as the public pact.[1]

There was also the draft of a Note, which was to be presented in writing by the Japanese Ambassador before he signed the pact, and which set forth the explanations the Japanese Government could give in response to inquiries as to the purport of the public pact. They might say that it was purely defensive, intended to maintain peace, and aimed at no country in particular; that it was the consequence of the union of the three contracting parties in common defence against the Comintern and that it was from Communist efforts emanating from Soviet Russia that Japan apprehended 'the most imminent danger for the pact' (i.e. the likeliest *casus belli*). They could also say that if one of the contracting parties were the object of unprovoked aggression, the consequences for the Powers themselves were provided by the text of the pact, but that until third Powers threatened or attacked the contracting parties, the obligations to lend support and give help and assistance would not apply.[2] That meant that in conversations with the Western Democracies the Japanese Government could lay stress on the defensive aspects of the Pact and indicate that they regarded it as primarily intended against the USSR, but that they could *not* give assurances that it would operate against that Power *alone*, or that they would in no circumstances take up arms against the Democracies.

Furthermore, prior to signing the pact, Oshima was to make the following *verbal* declaration:

On instruction by my Government I ask your Excellency to take note that Japan can carry out the obligations accepted in Article 3 of the pact, to render help and assistance in a military respect, at the present and in the immediate future only to a restricted extent. The details

[1] ibid.
[2] The text of this note was not included in the records of the Tokyo Trials. The details are in a telegram of Attolico to Ciano of 13 May, quoted by Toscano, *Patto d'acciaio*, pp. 175–6.

as to the military assistance to be rendered from time to time in the future, shall be reserved to the discussions provided in the secret accessory protocol.[1]

Ribbentrop had thus made substantial concessions to the Japanese. He instructed Ott to say that the tripartite negotiations were not prejudiced by the decision of Germany and Italy to sign a bilateral pact of alliance; to urge the Japanese Government to accept the new proposals in time for both agreements to be signed simultaneously; and to point out that the consolidation of Japan's position in East Asia depended on the Axis Powers in Europe being superior to the Democracies; therefore she should not allow these to assume that they could count on her neutrality in the event of their coming into conflict with Germany or Italy.[2]

The receipt of Ribbentrop's overture of 15 May caused a fresh crisis in Tokyo. The Army wanted to accept the new draft and to get the tripartite pact signed at the same time as the German-Italian pact; but Arita and Yonai still opposed any commitment to war against the Western Powers, although Hiranuma seems to have wavered. A compromise was reached at an Inner Cabinet conference on 20 May, which, as telegraphed by Arita to Oshima, did not commit the Japanese Government to declare war in the event of a conflict between the Axis Powers and the Democracies.[3] According to Ribbentrop, Oshima refused to communicate this officially to the German Government and protested against it, while he told Ribbentrop about it confidentially.[4]

In Tokyo it was officially announced on 21 May that the Government had decided upon the policy to be adopted in respect of the European situation, but the precise decision was not revealed and Hiranuma issued a statement which indicated that while Japan sympathized with Germany and Italy in desiring changes in the territorial *status quo* she was maintaining her freedom of action.[5] On 22 May the Italo-German 'Pact of Steel' was formally signed,[6]

[1] IMTFE, *Record*, pp. 6118–19.
[2] ibid. p. 6119.
[3] ibid. pp. 30503–6; telegram Ott to Ribbentrop, 27 May (ibid. pp. 37408–10); *Saionji–Harada Memoirs*, 23 May 1939.
[4] Ribbentrop to Ott, 28 May (IMTFE, *Record*, pp. 15990–2). Oshima, however, denied having refused to communicate officially any proposals of his Government. (Evidence of Oshima, ibid. p. 34010). But an entry in the *Saionji–Harada Memoirs* for 23 May says that Oshima and Shiratori had rejected the draft.
[5] *The Times*, 22 May 1939.
[6] RIIA, *Documents, 1939–46*, i. 168–70.

and on 28 May Ribbentrop complained to Ott 'we can no longer understand here what can be going on in Tokyo.'[1]

But the controversy in Tokyo had not been ended, nor had all possibility departed that Japan would line up with the Axis. The Japanese Government were alarmed about a possible Anglo-Soviet accord in Europe, which they feared would be a preliminary to a similar understanding in the Far East. On 17 May Mr. Dooman, the American chargé d'affaires in Tokyo, had reported a conversation with Arita, in which the Japanese Foreign Minister declared that although the British Ambassador had given him definite assurances that any Anglo-Russian agreement would not apply to the Far East, this was not sufficient to allay Japanese alarm. Arita declared that any agreement between Great Britain, France, and the USSR for close collaboration in Europe was bound eventually to bring about a similar collaboration in the Far East. Consequently a decision over Japanese policy with regard to Europe would have to be withheld until the results of the Anglo-Soviet negotiations became known.[2]

At about the same time Itagaki told Kawabe, who had succeeded Oshima as military attaché in Berlin, and who was urging the need for a quick decision, that 'the matter of the Treaty is now under earnest discussion within the Cabinet and, as the atmosphere is turning favourable to its decision we had better remain silent for the time being. I have no thought whatever of overthrowing the Cabinet.'[3] From this it may be deduced that the 'decision' of 20 May was far from being final. Hiranuma and Arita had gained time to see what would result from the overture which, as will be seen, they were making to the United States. The Army leaders were hoping that events would force the Cabinet to accept the German proposals. The Inner Cabinet on 5 June decided to instruct Oshima to inform Ribbentrop that Japan would not, for the time being, enter into war against the Democracies and that she insisted on a written understanding to this effect.[4] Ribbentrop in reply stood firm in refusing to accept anything more than an oral declaration to this effect by the Japanese signatory. On this

---

[1] Ribbentrop to Ott, 28 May.
[2] US, Congress, Joint Committee on the Investigation of the Pearl Harbor Attack, *Hearings* (Washington, USGPO, 1946), pt. 20, Exhibit 177, pp. 4147–50 (subsequently referred to as *Pearl Harbor Attack*).
[3] Evidence of Kawabe (IMTFE, *Record*, pp. 33769–70).
[4] Evidence of Oshima (ibid. pp. 34011–12).

point the negotiations remained deadlocked, and the Ribbentrop–Oshima discussions came to an end in mid-June.[1]

But the pro-Axis party in Tokyo were very far from defeated and evidently still reckoned on gaining their objective, especially should an Anglo-Soviet agreement be concluded and be followed by general war in Europe. In that event could Japan afford to stand aloof? Ribbentrop's argument was always that she could not, that her fate was inseparably linked with that of Germany. If Great Britain, France, and the USSR, who were all opposed to Japanese policy in China, lined up against Germany and Italy in Europe and defeated them, the three Powers would then be free to turn against Japan, who would be isolated. Therefore Japan could not afford to see the defeat of the Axis Powers in Europe and should join them without any more delay. The United States would be hostile to such a move, but she was opposed to Japan in the Far East anyway and must be reckoned as a potential enemy. Furthermore, public opinion in the United States was as yet too divided to permit the Washington administration to join with the European Democracies, much less with the Soviet Union. If, while America was undecided, the three dissatisfied Powers struck their blow and won the victory over their European enemies, what then could the United States do against them in either Europe or Asia?

Hiranuma opposed these views because he doubted if Germany and Italy could win the war in Europe and because he thought that American intervention might have to be faced. So it would appear that the policy he preferred was to avoid a final and irretrievable commitment to the Axis, but to use the threat of it to secure a further measure of appeasement on the part of the Democracies. He had taken note of the message of President Roosevelt to Hitler and Mussolini on 14 April.[2] To him the American démarche was an indication that, in the event of war, the United States might join in against the Axis Powers; at the

---

[1] ibid. On 21 June Weizsäcker telegraphed Ott to continue talks with the Japanese but not to press for an agreement by any particular date (ibid. p. 24719). By this time Hitler and Ribbentrop were becoming increasingly interested in the possibility of an understanding with the USSR. The Soviet Ambassador had hinted at this in an interview with Weizsäcker on 17 April and this was followed a month later by verbal overtures from the Soviet chargé, Astakhov, and by Molotov, who became Minister of Foreign Affairs on 3 May, to the German Ambassador in Moscow (*Nazi-Soviet Relations*, pp. 1–17).

[2] RIIA, *Documents, 1939–46*, i. 204–7. Roosevelt proposed that they give a pledge of non-aggression. This would be followed by discussions on disarmament and on international economic problems.

same time it suggested a means by which the impending conflict might be averted and the ground cut from beneath the feet of the pro-Axis group in Japan.

Therefore, on 18 May, when Grew was about to go to Washington on leave, Arita gave him a letter from Hiranuma to deliver to the Secretary of State and to bring to the notice of the President. Hiranuma referred to the menace of war in Europe and the dangers to civilization which this would involve. It was, he averred, the duty of the United States and Japan, as the two non-European Great Powers, to do all they could to prevent such a catastrophe. Germany and Italy might be advised to be more patient in their demands, but Great Britain and France ought also to reconsider their attitude of preserving the *status quo*. It was the ardent wish of the Japanese Government that all nations should have their proper place in the world and thus true world peace could be established. There was here a possibility of much closer co-operation between Japan and America, which might lay the foundations of a deeper understanding between them.[1]

Hiranuma on 23 May followed up this overture by inviting Dooman secretly to dinner at his private house in the suburbs of Tokyo. He told Dooman that, in his view, Japan could not tie herself to any foreign Government whose stability depended on the continued existence of one individual. Both in Germany and in Italy there were political currents beneath the surface which gravely affected confidence in any alliance with these two Powers. In time of war, Hiranuma declared, these dissident elements would make themselves felt and would be a menace to the success of German and Italian arms. Hiranuma went on to suggest that an international conference should be called to discuss all the problems, political and economic, which were threatening to cause a world war. If the President would sound Great Britain and France on their willingness to come to such a conference, Hiranuma would do the same with Germany and Italy. Should the four Powers agree to attend, then Hiranuma would be pleased to see President Roosevelt issue a formal invitation to them under such conditions as might be agreed upon through the normal diplomatic channels.[2]

Dooman warned the Japanese Premier that the United States Government would not be disposed to collaborate in this manner

---

[1] *Pearl Harbor Attack*, pt. 20, pp. 4135–8.   [2] ibid. pp. 4160–1.

with the Japanese Government so long as the latter were pursuing a policy in China which appeared to the United States to be similar to that followed by the aggressor States in Europe. 'The adjustment of the conflict in China on terms satisfactory to all concerned would have to be a condition precedent to the degree of collaboration between the United States and Japan which could reasonably be expected to bring about the desired results in Europe.'[1]

Hiranuma replied that if the American Government took the view that the settlement of the China conflict must be a condition precedent to any joint American-Japanese efforts to avert war in Europe, then any hope of these would have to be abandoned. He declared that the objectives of Japan in China were essential to her in a world of sanctions, embargoes, the closure of markets and the lack of free access to raw materials. So long as such conditions existed, any modification of Japanese peace terms to China could not be considered. But Japan would be willing to have the Far Eastern situation included in the agenda of the proposed conference, and Hiranuma said that if conditions were established which assured to all nations adequate markets and supplies of raw materials, the importance to Japan of securing such facilities in China would greatly diminish.[2]

Grew delivered the Japanese Premier's message to the State Department on 12 June. Hull regarded it with suspicion and disfavour.[3] The American reply to Hiranuma's letter was dispatched on 8 July and was in effect a refusal. As both Grew and Dooman had warned would be the case, Japan was told, in polite phraseology, that the best contribution she could make to world peace would be to terminate her aggression upon China. The reply referred to the steps already taken by the United States Government to preserve peace in Europe and said that the Government did not perceive what additional measures they could usefully take, although they would be glad to have any amplification of Hiranuma's proposals.[4]

This last was simply politeness. Hull told Dooman, in answer to his query, that the reply was intended to answer both the message which the American Ambassador had brought and the proposals

---

[1] ibid. p. 4153.   [2] ibid. pp. 4158-9.
[3] 'I was more than skeptical of Hiranuma's approach. Japan was benefiting so hugely from the impending chaos in Europe that we wondered what ulterior motive lay in the Premier's mind' (*Memoirs*, i. 631).
[4] *Pearl Harbor Attack*, pt. 20, pp. 4173-4.

communicated at the Japanese Premier's private interview with the American chargé.[1]

Dooman delivered the reply on 8 August and intimated to Hiranuma through a confidential intermediary that it was also an answer to his private overture of 23 May.[2]

While Hiranuma was awaiting a reply to his overture to the United States, he was facing a renewed onslaught by the advocates of an alliance with the totalitarian aggressors in Europe. The general course of world events, which included the development of the Anglo-Japanese crisis over Tientsin, the Soviet-Japanese hostilities at Nomonhan, the denunciation by the United States of the Treaty of Commerce of 1911 with Japan, the German-Polish crisis and the growing certainty of war in Europe, all furnished an excellent opportunity for the renewal of pressure on the Japanese Government to adhere to the Italo-German military Pact concluded in May.

Consequently at the beginning of August the crisis boiled up again. On 4 August Kido recorded in his Diary that whereas the people generally wanted to see an end of the China conflict and a successful issue to the Anglo-Japanese conference about Tientsin, Itagaki had told him that the Army was resolved on the conclusion of the Axis Pact. If Itagaki could not get the Cabinet's consent he would have to resign, and so precipitate the fall of the Cabinet. Kido urged him to avoid any such action in view of the disorder which it would provoke, but to continue to seek a compromise with the Navy.[3]

This Itagaki endeavoured to do. In view of the open hostility of the Navy, the veiled hostility of the Court circles for whom Kido spoke, and the disinclination of the general public for fresh military adventures, a coup d'état by the Army might have turned out badly for its authors. Therefore, Itagaki did not wish to bring down the Cabinet so long as there was a chance of securing the pact by other means. At a conference of the Inner Cabinet on 8 August he urged a modification of the stand taken on 5 June, but was opposed by all

---

[1] ibid. p. 4194.

[2] ibid. p. 4209. On 10 July Hull had told the Japanese Ambassador that 'nations cannot but take notice that Japan herself is engaged in military operations for purposes of conquest. This situation well calls for an ending if Japan is to exercise her fullest influence, along with the United States and other countries, to compose threatened military conquest in other parts of the world' (*Memoirs*, i. 633).

[3] IMTFE, *Record*, pp. 16237–9.

his colleagues.[1] Then he, on 11 August, sent General Machijiri to see Ott and Auriti (the Italian Ambassador), with a compromise proposal on behalf of the Army. This was apparently that Berlin and Rome should agree to the Japanese stipulations of 5 June, while Itagaki would get the Japanese Cabinet to include in the secret accessory protocol a guarantee that Japanese obligations under the treaty really would be carried out when Japan felt able to do so.[2]

But while Hiranuma had been sounding the Washington Government and the Japanese service chiefs had continued their quarrel, Hitler had made up his mind to accept the Soviet overtures for political accord. He wanted to attack Poland at the end of August and, to do this, he needed to come to terms with Stalin.[3] An agreement with the USSR was of far more value to Hitler than any pact with Japan. For a German-Soviet accord might deter Great Britain and France from coming to the aid of Poland and, even if it did not, it would free Germany from the menace of the two-front war, since Hitler counted on crushing Poland quickly. The hesitations and divisions of opinion in Japan strengthened Hitler's determination to throw her over, and made him the readier to bury the hatchet with the USSR. He told Mussolini that

Japan would probably agree to an alliance against Russia, which would have only a *secondary* interest, under the prevailing circumstances, for Germany, and in my opinion, for Italy also. She would not, however, undertake such definite obligations against England, and this, from the standpoint not only of Germany, but also of Italy, was of decisive importance.[4]

The news that Germany was about to conclude a non-aggression pact with the Soviet Union came as a stunning shock to Oshima.[5]

---

[1] ibid. pp. 30106, 30317; *Saionji–Harada Memoirs*, 14 Aug.
[2] Ott to Ribbentrop, 11 August 1939 (ibid. pp. 34141–3). Itagaki's overture was made without the knowledge of the Foreign Office. He asked for a reply by 15 August, but evidently did not get one, for Ott on 18 August reported that the political crisis in Japan continued undiminished (ibid. pp. 34143–5). Harada on 23 August noted that the situation remained unchanged. Prince Chichibu had, according to Harada, suggested that Hiranuma pay a personal visit to Hitler, but Kido opposed this as undignified.
[3] Hitler told Ciano of his intention to attack Poland at their meeting on 13 August 1939 (International Military Tribunal, *Nazi Conspiracy and Aggression* (Washington, USGPO, 1946), viii. 526–9). For his decision not to do this unless he was sure of Stalin, see Weizsäcker, *Memoirs*, pp. 199–200.
[4] Letter from Hitler to Mussolini, 25 August 1939 (*Nazi-Soviet Relations*, pp. 80–81).
[5] On 21 August Ribbentrop broke the news to Oshima in a telephone message (ibid. p. 70). Oshima protested that it would be an act of bad faith and a contravention of the Anti-Comintern Pact (evidence of Oshima, IMTFE, *Record*,

Despite the hints Ribbentrop had given and Shiratori's warnings, Oshima had refused to believe that Germany would really take such a step. It came as an equal surprise to Tokyo, where Arita had heeded neither Shiratori nor British and Polish advices that a German-Soviet political accord was impending.[1] His incredulity was not without reason since towards the end of July the German Foreign Ministry had denied any such intention.[2]

The German-Soviet Pact destroyed the whole basis of Japanese policy towards Europe and there was little concealment of the dismay and bitterness in Tokyo. The Pact came at a time when a full-scale battle was raging between Japanese and Soviet forces at Nomonhan and at first it appeared to have set the USSR free to throw her full strength against Japan. The manner in which Germany had acted in negotiating the Pact with the USSR was especially humiliating. The Japanese public did not know that Germany had violated a definite treaty commitment—Article 2 of the secret protocol to the Anti-Comintern Pact—but it was clear enough that Germany had thrown Japan over, had rendered the pact worthless, and had made Japan look ridiculous in the eyes of the world. She had also sealed the doom of the Hiranuma Cabinet whose 'foreign policy had been betrayed', as Hiranuma declared, and who were in the unhappy position of having wrongly advised the Emperor to 'strengthen' the Anti-Comintern Pact.[3] One of the last acts of the tottering Hiranuma Government was to instruct Oshima to make a formal protest to the German Government on the ground that their Pact with the USSR constituted 'a serious violation of the secret agreement attached to the Anti-Comintern Pact'. He was also to inform the German Government that Japan

p. 34014). Weizsäcker says that when Oshima came to his house on 22 August at midnight, 'the news that Ribbentrop was flying to Moscow to conclude the Pact took him completely by surprise. . . . His face became rigid and grey' (*Memoirs*, p. 201).

[1] Craigie says that 'some months before the event' he warned Arita that there was reason to believe that such a step was seriously contemplated by Germany, that he heard that Arita had inquired of the Japanese Ambassadors in Berlin and Rome and that Oshima had dismissed the warning as simply British propaganda (*Behind the Japanese Mask*, p. 71). On 7 June the Polish Ambassador had told Arita that the Polish Government had indisputable evidence from both German and Soviet sources that a German-Soviet rapprochement was being actively canvassed (*Pearl Harbor Attack*, pt. 20, p. 4157).

[2] Usami on 20 July questioned the German Under-Secretary of State, Woermann, on newspaper reports of negotiations for a German-Soviet non-aggression pact. Woermann said all such news was 'nothing but a swindle' (memo. by Woermann, 20 July 1939, IMTFE, *Record*, pp. 24180–4).

[3] *Saionji–Harada Memoirs*, 23 Aug. 1939.

regarded the conclusion of the Non-Aggression Pact as finally terminating the negotiations between Japan and Germany for a tripartite pact with Italy.[1] Arita informed Ott of this on 25 August. The latter, in accordance with instructions, declared that Germany had been left with no alternative owing to the critical European situation. He also urged that the German-Soviet Pact would be of benefit to Japan since it would enable Germany to use her influence at Moscow for the improvement of Soviet-Japanese relations. Arita replied that Japan was compelled to make the protest but was willing to continue friendly relations with Germany.[2]

Arita reserved his opinion on the suggestion of German-Soviet-Japanese collaboration.[3] Oshima, however, seems to have quickly swung round to this idea, which had been urged on him by Weizsäcker on 22 August.[4] When he took his note of protest to Weizsäcker the latter persuaded him to postpone it, on the ground that it would be a serious embarrassment to Germany at a time of critical negotiations over the Polish question. Oshima obligingly agreed, while he informed Tokyo that he *had* obeyed its instructions.[5] Ribbentrop, on 9 September, told Ott that in a recent conversation with Oshima he had urged German mediation to effect a Soviet-Japanese accord, which would free Japan's hands and enable her to extend her power in East Asia and to advance towards the south. Ribbentrop declared that Oshima had agreed.[6] Ott was told to propagate the same idea among the Japanese General Staff. He was also instructed to try to persuade the Japanese Government to retain Oshima in Berlin.[7]

Meanwhile, after some days of political manœuvring, a new Cabinet had been formed in Tokyo. When Hiranuma had announced that he would resign, Hirota was at first suggested as his successor. Konoye, Kido, and Yuasa all favoured this, but the Army opposed it, and on 26 August Hirota had to decline. Konoye

---

[1] Ott to GFM, 25 Aug. 1939 (IMTFE, *Record*, p. 6123).
[2] ibid.   [3] ibid.
[4] Memo. by Weizsäcker, 22 Aug. (*Nazi-Soviet Relations*, pp. 70–71).
[5] Memo. by Weizsäcker, 18 Sept. 1939 (IMTFE, *Record*, pp. 6124–6); also evidence of Oshima (ibid. p. 34015).
[6] Ribbentrop to Ott, 9 Sept. 1939 (ibid. pp. 6127–30).
[7] ibid. Ott did so (ibid. p. 6130), but unsuccessfully, as Oshima resigned and was replaced by Kurusu. When Oshima on 18 September once more apologetically proferred the Japanese Note of protest of 26 August, Weizsäcker refused to receive it officially. Oshima himself suggested that it should be accepted, but no reply was made and the matter let lapse, which was apparently what happened (Weizsäcker's memo. of 18 Sept. 1939).

himself was sounded but was disinclined to come forward at this time. No other prominent figure was generally acceptable, so military and political circles eventually compromised on General Nobuyuki Abe.[1] He was a retired general who had seen little active service and who had even less experience in the political field. He also took the portfolio of Foreign Affairs for the time being, with General Hata as War Minister and Admiral Yoshida as Minister of the Navy.[2] His administration was aptly described by the correspondent of *The Times* as 'a Cabinet of Caretakers'.[3]

On 31 August General Abe issued a broadcast statement in which he said that his Cabinet would take all necessary measures for the execution of Japan's 'immutable policy' in China. The Government would pursue an independent course in their dealings with foreign Powers, Japan would co-operate with those who were willing to co-operate with her and would 'inflexibly oppose those who obstructed her mission.'[4] Then came the outbreak of war in Europe. On 4 September, after a Cabinet meeting, General Abe issued the following statement: 'Faced by the European War which has just broken out Japan intends not to be involved in it. She will concentrate her efforts on a settlement of the China Affair.'[5]

For the time being Japan intended to wait and see. Although there were elements who would have had her follow the German example, make a pact with the USSR and turn upon Great Britain and France, these were held in check.[6] Ribbentrop was still urging such a course. General Terauchi had gone on a visit to Germany, which included a tour of the Polish battlefields.[7] On 20 September he was received by Hitler and Ribbentrop at Zoppot.[8] Both set forth the necessity of Japan and Germany joining hands, as two dissatisfied nations. Ribbentrop asserted that he had long believed in the necessity of a Soviet-Japanese agreement, that he would

---

[1] *Saionji–Harada Memoirs*, 1 Sept. 1939. The Emperor insisted upon having either Hata or Umezu as War Minister; the Army agreed on Hata (ibid.).
[2] ibid.   [3] 30 Aug. 1939.
[4] *Saionji–Harada Memoirs*, 31 Aug. 1939.   [5] ibid. 5 Sept. 1939.
[6] Saionji declared that Oshima had agreed to Ribbentrop's suggestion that Japan conclude a non-aggression pact with the USSR—'an attitude disloyal to his own Emperor' (*Saionji–Harada Memoirs*, 10 Sept. 1939). On 3 September Arita told Harada that 'the group which had changed from the left wing to the right wing were the prime power behind the movement to have Japan join the German-Soviet non-aggression pact and strike at England with an alliance of Germany, Russia and Japan' (ibid. 11 Sept. 1939).
[7] He was said to have the backing of a 'young officer' group (ibid. 2 Oct. 1939).
[8] GFM memo. on visit of Terauchi to Zoppot (IMTFE, *Record*, p. 6134).

have striven for it even had a German-Japanese-Italian pact been concluded, and that he had told Oshima so, over a year previously. He regretted that the efforts of Oshima and himself to bring about the tripartite pact had failed. Germany had been compelled to seek an accord with the Soviet Union alone, but he had talked to Stalin about the question of a Soviet-Japanese agreement, and according to Ribbentrop, Stalin had declared 'if the Japanese desire war, they can have war, if they desire an understanding they can have that too.'[1]

Oshima declared that he had already proposed to Tokyo a Japanese southward advance and an attack on Hong Kong. He suggested, 'as his personal opinion', that the Netherlands should be detached from Great Britain by the offer of a non-aggression pact; this could be followed by an agreement between the Netherlands and Japan which would allow her to exploit the raw materials of the Dutch East Indies.[2] Terauchi said little and did not commit himself.[3] At a later meeting, on 23 September, with Knoll and with General Brockdorff, Terauchi was said to have agreed with his host's suggestion that Japan would do well to end the China war by a reasonable settlement, and then turn south.[4]

But as yet no such policy was possible for Japan. The humiliation inflicted by Germany had resulted in a severe setback for the political power of the Army in Japan, and for pro-Axis elements in general. Furthermore, whatever the machinations of ex-Communists now professing rightist opinions, they could not overcome the general dislike and fear of the Soviet Union, which was little diminished by the peaceful conclusion of the Nomonhan affair. Until the summer of 1940 the prevalent opinion in Tokyo remained in favour of the policy of non-involvement, while utilizing the possibility of another course as a means of putting pressure on Great Britain and France to acquiesce in the Japanese domination of China.

[1] ibid. pp. 6135–6.
[2] ibid. p. 6137.
[3] ibid.
[4] ibid. pp. 6138–9.

CHAPTER V

The Western Democracies and the Sino–Japanese Conflict, 1937 to July 1940

THE continuation of the Sino-Japanese conflict resulted in a mounting threat to the treaty rights and interests in China of Great Britain, the United States, and France. The armed operations, which extended over an ever-widening sphere, took an increasing toll in death and injury to the nationals of these Powers, and caused widespread destruction and damage to their business and educational properties. For some of this the Chinese were responsible, especially in the opening months of the war, but by far the major responsibility lay with the Japanese; in particular with their air arm. While the hazards of war and the inaccuracy of aerial bombardment might reasonably be taken to account for a good deal of this havoc, the element of design was not entirely wanting. Protests and claims for reparation became too numerous to recount.[1] The climax to a long series of such incidents came on 12 December 1937, when American and British warships and merchant vessels on the Yangtze were attacked by Japanese shore batteries and aircraft, as a result of which the American gunboat *Panay* was sunk, with considerable casualties, and the British gunboat *Ladybird* was damaged.[2] The moving spirit in this was the local Japanese military commander, Colonel Kingoro Hashimoto, and despite his denials at his trial after the Pacific War, there can be no reasonable doubt that the attacks were deliberate. Apparently Hashimoto hoped to provoke war between Japan and the Western Powers as a means of facilitating the 'Showa Restoration' i.e. a military dictatorship in Japan.[3]

The Japanese Foreign Ministry was prompt in expressing apologies and promises of indemnity, especially to the United States. The Tokyo Government were genuinely shocked and alarmed, as well they might be, for the reaction in America might

[1] By 1939 the British and US Governments had each lodged several hundred claims for reparation with the Japanese Government (Craigie, *Behind the Japanese Mask*, p. 52; Grew, *Ten Years in Japan*, p. 267).
[2] RIIA, *Survey, 1937*, i. 309–10, 312–13.
[3] Craigie, *Behind the Japanese Mask*, pp. 52–53.

well have been a demand for war, such as had resulted from the destruction of the *Maine* at Havana in 1898.[1] In fact, however, the affair served to demonstrate the predominantly isolationist mood of the American people. The advocates of strong action against Japan were more than offset by those who, *per contra*, urged the withdrawal of American vessels and nationals from the areas of combat in China, while the majority of the people waited for a lead from Washington.[2]

On 13 December Hull expressed to the Japanese Ambassador, the President's 'shock and concern' at the affair and, at Roosevelt's order, requested that the Emperor be directly informed of this.[3] A formal Note to Tokyo, followed on the same day, in which the Japanese Government were required to express regret, to make complete indemnity, and to give an assurance that they were taking definite measures to prevent any future assaults by the Japanese armed forces upon American nationals or properties in China.[4] The following day the British Ambassador expressed to Hull the disappointment of the British Government that Washington had not waited to concert joint action with Great Britain in the matter. The British Foreign Secretary considered that a show of force on a large scale was needed to restrain the arrogance and recklessness of the Japanese military.[5] Hull, however, was opposed to any such step, which might have provoked war, in view of the exalted mood of the Japanese military, flushed with their victories in Shanghai and Nanking. The considerations that weighed with him were that America was not prepared for war, that the vast majority of her people were opposed to it, and that, if it came, the United States, in his view, would have had to shoulder the main burden.[6] So, despite increasing evidence of the premeditated character of the attack, he accepted the Japanese reply of 23 December, which gave assurances that the required steps would be taken, but maintained that the affair had been accidental.[7] The Japanese Government made a similar response to British protests and demands for indemnification, and with this the British Government had perforce to profess satisfaction.[8] Hashimoto was indeed recalled to Japan, where he continued to agitate for a totalitarian policy at home and abroad.[9] While nothing comparable to this

[1] Grew, *Ten Years in Japan*, pp. 204–6.
[2] Hull, *Memoirs*, i. 563.   [3] ibid. p. 560.   [4] ibid. p. 561.
[5] ibid.   [6] ibid. pp. 562, 570–1.   [7] ibid. p. 562.
[8] RIIA, *Survey, 1937*, i. 310–12.   [9] IMTFE, *Judgment*, pp. 384–6.

happened again prior to Pearl Harbour, Japanese air bombings of Chinese cities became more unrestrained and foreign protests went virtually unheeded.[1] The affair, indeed, served to throw into sharp relief the unreadiness of the United States to take any effective action to check the Japanese in China and the inability of Great Britain, in view of the deepening crisis in Europe, to move without her.

The breakdown of the German-sponsored peace overtures, followed in January 1938 by the decision of the Japanese Government to support the creation of a new régime in China, constituted a fresh and ominous development. It soon became apparent that the Japanese military authorities in China, with the tacit support of the Tokyo Government, were using the plea of 'military necessity' to hamper foreign business and commercial activities in China, while facilitating those of their own people. There was, furthermore, an increasing disposition on the part of Tokyo to utilize this situation as a bargaining point to induce the Western Powers to abandon diplomatic recognition of the legitimate Chinese Government. The great port and distributing centre of Shanghai remained largely severed from its hinterland in the Yangtze valley area through the continued closure of that great riverine artery to all but Japanese vessels. As the Japanese were quick to point out, the Chinese had originally closed the river by establishing a defensive boom at Kiangyin. But, after the Japanese had demolished this obstacle and had advanced upstream to Nanking and beyond it, they still refused to permit third Powers to exercise their treaty right of navigation on the river, alleging military necessity and the existence of mines and other perils. Meanwhile evidence accumulated that Japanese vessels were carrying commercial cargoes as well as military supplies.[2] The establishment of the North and the Central China Development Companies and of other monopolistic concerns, the introduction of a Japanese-sponsored currency in North China, the interference with foreign

---

[1] Chungking and other Chinese cities were subjected to mass air raids. Japan had signed, but had not ratified, the rules on air war formulated at The Hague in 1922. At the Tokyo Tribunal Japanese defence witnesses claimed that instructions were issued to their airmen to bomb only military objectives and to avoid third nations' property as far as possible (IMTFE, *Record*, pp. 21374-6, 21507-12). But the recommendations of the Chief of Staff of the Japanese Central China Army in July 1939 included the bombing of strategic points in the interior of China to create terror and excite anti-war sentiments (ibid. p. 3666).

[2] 25 May 1938, H C Deb., vol. 336, col. 1282; Craigie, *Behind the Japanese Mask*, pp. 84-85; Grew, *Ten Years in Japan*, p. 229.

shipping and wharf facilities all served to indicate that, as had already occurred in Manchukuo, foreign business concerns in China were going to be squeezed out, and foreign import and export trade channelled through Japanese monopolies. At the same time increasing Japanese pressure was exerted upon the foreign-administered Concessions and Settlements in China, in particular upon the International Settlement in Shanghai, of which the principal industrial and docking sections remained in Japanese military occupation and interdicted from control by the Municipal Council of the Settlement.[1]

Great Britain and the United States were on somewhat delicate ground in combating these practices. Since neither Japan nor China had declared formal war, the legal rights of the Japanese troops in China were open to question, but this was a matter which neither London nor Washington wished to raise. For if Japan *did* declare war she could establish a full blockade of the Chinese ports and she might also occupy the foreign-administered areas on the ground that, since they were still under Chinese sovereignty, they were not neutral territory. For the American Government, too, there was the further consideration that a formal state of war between Japan and China would compel the application of the American Neutrality Act of 1937, under which belligerent Powers were required to pay cash for their purchases of raw materials and to transport them in their own ships. This would have told heavily in favour of Japan, who, in contrast to China, possessed both the cash and the ships.[2]

The imposition of economic sanctions upon Japan, or the rendering of assistance to China by financial credits or other means, might also have precipitated Japanese measures of blockade and seizure of the Concessions and Settlements, and so created a state of affairs in which the Western Powers would be faced with the choice of humiliation or of war. Therefore both London and Washington proceeded cautiously and for the time being contented themselves with repeated representations and protests. This practice avoided letting their case go by default, while it did not outwardly reject the Japanese Government's professions of respect for the 'Open Door' and pleas of 'military necessity' as excuse for infringements of that doctrine.

There was also the possibility that Japan, who had become

---

[1] Jones, *Shanghai and Tientsin*, pp. 63–66.   [2] Hull, *Memoirs*, i. 557–8.

engaged upon hostilities of a scale far greater than she had envisaged in 1937, might be brought to offer peace terms of an acceptable character to China. This appeared the more likely when the Chinese rallied after the fall of Nanking and the Japanese were lured on ever deeper into the interior. It was believed that the Japanese economy could not long stand the strain, an idea sedulously propagated by the Chinese, who were ever fearful that other Powers might follow Germany's example in siding with Japan. The known divisions of opinion in Japan and the uncertain temper of the Soviet Union were other factors which might lead to a Sino-Japanese accommodation.

At the same time the anti-foreign attitude of the Japanese military in China, which was exacerbated by their belief that Western support constituted the main prop of continued Chinese resistance, made it advisable, especially for Great Britain, to seek some *modus vivendi* with them. British investments in China, outside of Manchuria, were the largest of any foreign holdings; they had already suffered considerably and would be altogether imperilled by any action which should provoke a fresh outbreak of extremism of the Hashimoto brand.

British policy, therefore, was devoted to gaining time in the Far East and meanwhile to avoidance of a frontal clash with Japan. The Premier, Neville Chamberlain, was working for an accord with Italy and still hoped to reach one with Germany; at the same time British rearmament was progressing, although a vast amount of leeway had to be made up. Had 'appeasement' produced any enduring betterment in relations with the European Axis Powers, Great Britain would have been in an improved position to adopt a sterner policy towards Japan; unless and until that happened it was wiser, if inglorious, to 'bear with patience and good humour actions which we should like to treat in very different fashion', as Chamberlain remarked.[1]

American policy was not fundamentally dissimilar, but the American Government, relatively less preoccupied with European considerations and with a much smaller financial and industrial stake in China than had Great Britain, could afford to take a theoretically stronger line and to deprecate compromises on immediate issues. Thus, on 3 May 1938, after several months of

[1] In a letter to an American friend on 16 January 1938 (Feiling, *Chamberlain*, p. 324).

negotiation, an Anglo-Japanese Agreement was reached upon the Chinese Maritime Customs funds accruing in ports in Japanese occupation. The Japanese Government agreed to make available from these revenues quotas sufficient to continue the full servicing of the foreign loans and indemnities which were secured upon the Customs revenue. But the custodian of the funds collected in Japanese-occupied areas was to be the Yokohama Specie Bank instead of the British Hong Kong and Shanghai Banking Corporation, and the Japanese Government also stipulated that they should be paid the arrears and future instalments of their loans and share of the Boxer Indemnity.[1] On 6 May the Chinese Government refused their assent to these arrangements, which consequently never came into full effect.[2]

The appointment of General Ugaki as Japanese Foreign Minister seemed to presage the abandonment of the policy of January 1938, and the renewal of direct negotiations for peace with the Chinese National Government. This the British Government both publicly and privately endeavoured to further.[3] At the same time unofficial conversations took place during the summer and early autumn of 1938 between Craigie and Ugaki. These covered virtually the whole field of British rights in China, in particular freedom of riverine navigation.[4] But, conceding Ugaki's personal sincerity in wishing to remedy some of the outstanding foreign grievances, he was under powerful pressure to do no such thing unless Great Britain openly abandoned the Chinese cause and espoused that of Japan. Reports of concessions on his part leaked out and resulted in attacks upon him, while the prospect of war in Europe over the Czech question played into the hands of his opponents.[5] So did the

---

[1] H C Deb., vol. 335, coll. 845–50.
[2] ibid. vol. 336, coll. 7–8. Only one payment was made, in June 1938. On 14 January 1939 the Japanese Embassy spokesman at Shanghai announced Japan's refusal to carry out the agreement until the Chinese paid the arrears of the Japanese loan. On 15 January 1939 the Chinese Government announced that they could no longer service foreign loans. They had kept up the full service until then.
[3] On 21 and 27 June the Under-Secretary of State for Foreign Affairs told the Commons that the British Government was ready to do all in their power to further a termination of hostilities (ibid. vol. 337, coll. 905–6, 1500). The Prime Minister, on 26 July, said much the same (ibid. vol. 338, coll. 2961–2). According to the *Saionji–Harada Memoirs*, 27 July 1938, the British Ambassador in China forwarded an offer from Chiang of terms that would have been very advantageous to Japan, but Konoye preferred to wait— presumably for the fall of Hankow.   [4] Craigie, *Behind the Japanese Mask*, p. 61.
[5] He was said to have assured Craigie that Canton and Hainan island would not be attacked (*Saionji–Harada Memoirs*, 13 July 1938).

peaceful settlement of the Changkufeng affray, which relieved the Japanese of fear of war with the USSR and cleared the way for the operation against Canton, which was already being planned.[1] The fall of Ugaki at the end of September destroyed whatever chance there had been of a *modus vivendi* on British interests in China or of British mediation in the Sino-Japanese conflict. Ugaki's resignation was quickly followed by a further Japanese defiance of the League of Nations. On 19 September the League Council, in response to a formal request of the Chinese Government, had invited the Japanese to send representatives to Geneva under the provisions of Article 17 of the League Covenant.[2] The Japanese Government refused, thereby rendering themselves technically liable to the penalties embodied in the preceding Article 16. The League Council on 30 September resolved that the members of the League were entitled to adopt individually the measures prescribed in Article 16. There was, as indeed the resolution intimated, small likelihood of this occurring.[3] On 3 October the Japanese Foreign Ministry spokesman declared that by invoking Article 17 the League had recognized the existence of a state of war between Japan and China 'which is inconsistent with the attitude of its Member States, which with regard to the question of respect for their interests in China, profess that no state of war exists between the two countries.'[4] He declared that counter-measures would be taken in the event of any member of the League applying sanctions against Japan. He furthermore indicated that Japan would now withdraw from all co-operation with the social and technical organs of the League.[5] Her formal withdrawal from these bodies was announced on 2 November.[6]

In view of Japan's hardening attitude the Department of State, on 1 October, sent Grew a long Note, which reviewed the whole field of Japanese violations of the Open Door, and injuries to American rights and interests. Owing to an error in decoding Grew thought that the message came direct from Roosevelt. He lost no time in seeing Konoye, who was Acting-Foreign Minister, and orally communicating to him the substance of the Note.[7] The Note itself was formally presented on 6 October. It was couched

[1] According to the *Saionji–Harada Memoirs*, after preliminary discussions between the Army and Navy Staffs the attack on Canton was sanctioned on 7 September 1938   [2] RIIA, *Documents, 1938*, i. 376.
[3] ibid. pp. 376–7.   [4] ibid. p. 378.   [5] ibid.
[6] ibid.; IMTFE, *Exhibit 271*.   [7] Grew, *Ten Years in Japan*, pp. 231–2.

in sharp language and contained a hint that continuation of the practices complained of might affect the Treaty of Commerce of 1911 between Japan and the United States.[1]

Konoye had told Grew that there would be no change in China policy and that the principle of equality of commercial opportunity would be respected.[2] The hollowness of these promises was soon revealed. The fall of Canton and of Hankow and the intrigues of Wang Ching-wei in Chungking appeared to Tokyo to foreshadow the collapse of Chinese resistance. So, on 3 November, Konoye proclaimed the establishment of the New Order in East Asia and intimated that third Powers would have to adjust themselves to it. The new Foreign Minister, Arita, made it clear that Japan intended to monopolize such Chinese products and industries as she considered essential for her own economy; outside of that there would still be a field for foreign enterprise.[3] On 7 November the Governments of Great Britain, France, and the United States addressed parallel Notes to Tokyo in protest against the closing of the Yangtze, but were met with a virtual refusal to open that river.[4] All this constituted a virtual reply to the American Note of 6 October, although the formal answer to this was delayed until 18 November, and was unsatisfactory and defiant in tone.[5]

It was clear that harsh words alone would not move Japan from the course upon which she was set. During the Anglo-French conversations in Paris on 24 November, the French Foreign Minister, Bonnet, remarked that he had tried to obtain American support for common action over the Yangtze question and the Konoye statement, but that nothing urgent had transpired.[6] Chamberlain replied that the American Government had asked if Great Britain had any views about retaliation should a negative reply be received to the demand for the reopening of the Yangtze. But Washington had submitted no ideas of its own, and probably

[1] RIIA, *Documents, 1938*, i. 354–8.
[2] Grew, *Ten Years in Japan*, p. 232.
[3] He told correspondents 'it is imperative that the economic activities of other Powers should be subject to certain restrictions dictated by the requirements of the national defence and economic security of the countries grouped under the new order. . . . But, even if these restrictions are put in force, there will remain vast fields of commercial and economic activity open to the people of other Powers' (RIIA, *Documents, 1938*, i. 352).
[4] Grew, *Ten Years in Japan*, p. 229.
[5] RIIA, *Documents, 1938*, i. 358–61.
[6] E. L. Woodward and R. Butler, ed., *Documents on British Foreign Policy, 1919–39*, 3rd series, iii. 308–9 (hereafter referred to as *D Brit. FP*).

had none to put forward. The Chinese Government had approached London for help in maintaining the stability of the Chinese currency; this matter was under consideration and if the decisions were favourable, the United States would be asked to take similar action. The British Government had no other measures in contemplation.[1]

Here was the old trouble. Hull was suspicious of Great Britain and France and would not take the initiative; at this time, too, he agreed with Grew in opposing any sanctions against Japan. Chamberlain said that the British Government would have done more had Washington been ready for joint action. But he was probably not ill pleased at having the excuse of American unwillingness to move. He mentioned to Bonnet the Chinese belief that if they could hold out long enough Japan would eventually become exhausted.[2] He had told Parliament at the beginning of November not to take too gloomy a view of British trade; at the close of the Sino-Japanese conflict large quantities of capital would be required for the reconstruction of China, and in this British participation would be essential.[3]

The attitude of the Western Powers now began to stiffen. On 31 December an American Note to Japan, in answer to the Japanese Note of 18 November, denied that country's right to establish a New Order by its own fiat, or unilaterally to abrogate treaties. It expressed, however, readiness to discuss, in collaboration with other Treaty Powers and with China, any reasonable proposals which Japan might submit.[4] The British Government, on 14 January 1939, addressed a communication to Tokyo which dealt more especially with the Konoye statements of 3 November and 22 December 1938, and declared that the British Government were 'at a loss to understand' how Konoye's assurances of respect for Chinese territorial integrity and sovereignty could be 'reconciled' with the declared intention of the Japanese Government to compel the Chinese people by force of arms to accept conditions involving the surrender of their political, economic, and cultural life to

---

[1] ibid. p. 309.
[2] ibid.
[3] 'When the right hon. Gentleman [Mr. Attlee] appears to contemplate a future in which Japan will have the monopoly of Chinese trade and we shall be excluded from it altogether, I say that is flying in the face of the facts. It is quite certain that when the war is over and the reconstruction of China begins, she cannot possibly be reconstructed without some help from this country' (H C Deb., vol. 340, col. 82).   [4] RIIA, *Documents, 1938*, i. 362–6.

Japanese control.[1] The British Government meant to uphold the Nine-Power Treaty, under the provisions of which the Chinese had been developing an effective and stable Government, to the advantage of all Powers, including Japan. Great Britain would, however, be ready to consider any constructive Japanese suggestions for the modification of any of the multilateral agreements relating to China. She was also prepared to renew the negotiations for the abrogation of British extraterritorial rights 'with a fully independent Chinese Government when peace has been restored.'[2] On 17 January the French Government also announced their intention of upholding the Nine-Power Treaty, though they, too, promised consideration of any future Japanese proposals for its modification.[3]

The three Powers had thus proclaimed their opposition to the Japanese New Order. Their stand was reinforced by measures of financial and commercial assistance to the Chinese National Government. These were ostensibly taken for the furtherance of their own trade, but their significance was plain enough. The Chinese, in anticipation of the loss of the trade route via Hong Kong and Canton, had been constructing the famous 'Burma Road' from Kunming to Lashio. In December 1938 the American Government, through their financial organ, the Export-Import Bank, advanced China a credit of $25 million, much of which was used for the purchase of lorries and petrol for use on the new road. Great Britain promptly followed suit by ear-marking funds for Chinese purchases under the Export Guarantees Bill. The initial export credit, of £450,000, was small, but it served as a precedent for future action and showed that Great Britain, like the United States, was now prepared to move, albeit cautiously, to encourage continued Chinese resistance. In this they were successful; despite the defection of Wang Ching-wei, Chiang Kai-shek and the great majority of the military and political leaders of the Kuomintang stood firm in refusal to consider the Konoye terms.

The Japanese Army leaders were now in a quandary. For reasons which have already been seen, they were averse to a further full-scale campaign to expel the Chinese National Government from Chungking. They hoped eventually to wear down Chinese resistance as well as to secure a measure of control of the occupied

[1] ibid. pp. 366–8.
[2] ibid. p. 368.　　　　　　　　　　　[3] ibid. pp. 368–9.

territories sufficient to allow of their effective economic exploitation. But this wearing-down process would be a lengthy one, involving a continued strain upon the Japanese economy and increasing hardships for the Japanese people. It would be a tedious and burdensome war of attrition, and, were it to be unduly prolonged, it might well arouse such popular ill-will in Japan as to jeopardize the prestige and political power which the Army had secured since 1931.

Consequently the Army needed a scapegoat, and it found one by denouncing the attitude and policy of the Western Powers—apart from Germany and Italy—as primarily responsible for encouraging the Chinese to continue the struggle and so far robbing Japan of the fruits of her victories. Great Britain, France, the United States, and the Soviet Union were all attacked on this score. But, since the USSR was regarded as a political and ideological enemy anyway, and because France was felt to be following the example of Great Britain and the United States, these last two Powers were chiefly singled out for opprobrium. In 1938–9 Great Britain was the main target because the Japanese thought her more susceptible to pressure, and, if she could be compelled to abandon the Chinese National cause, France and the United States might well follow suit.

In this pillorying of the Western Powers, the Japanese Army Chiefs were not simply adopting a pose. They saw that the aid China was receiving from abroad, although it was limited in scope, was a factor of importance in enabling her to continue the struggle and one that would assume additional weight the more that struggle came to be waged by economic and financial, as distinct from military, weapons. The Chinese Government, while naturally pleading for more assistance, as well as for direct measures to hamper Japan's war effort, were fully cognisant of the value of the aid which they were already receiving. Furthermore, the knowledge that they had the support of the majority of the Powers, and the belief that all-out help would one day be forthcoming, were moral factors of incalculable importance to the Chinese. The Japanese were equally clear that if these Chinese hopes could be shattered and a 'Far Eastern Munich' be brought about, Japan's task would be correspondingly lightened.

One desired method of achieving this was to conclude an alliance with the Axis Powers in Europe and to utilize this as a means of blackmailing Great Britain and France. But, as recounted above, the Army failed to bring this about in 1939.[1] The second line of policy was to deny to the nationals of these Powers the full exercise of their commercial and business rights under the Treaties and to endeavour to subject the foreign-administered Settlements and Concessions to Japanese control. The Japanese military in China regarded these enclaves of territory with rising animosity. They formed a refuge for influential Chinese financial and mercantile groups who continued to support the legitimate Chinese Government and whose hoarded wealth the Japanese longed to enlist forcibly in support of their currency schemes. They were equally angered by the existence of a free Chinese press, which, within the limits imposed by the municipal authorities, continued to keep alive Chinese national sentiment. Thus the foreign-administered areas —apart of course from Japan's own Concessions in Tientsin and Hankow—were stumbling blocks in the Japanese path. At the same time, since they were islets in the ocean of Japanese-occupied territory, they were practically hostages in Japanese hands. The Chinese National Government which benefited considerably from the existence of the foreign-administered areas, added to the difficulties of the foreign municipal authorities by permitting a campaign of terrorism and assassination against Chinese who went over to the Japanese to be waged in and from the Settlements. This was understandable, but short-sighted, since it played into Japanese hands.

The Japanese answered the Western Powers' démarche against the new order by a number of threatening moves. In February 1939 they occupied Hainan island, ostensibly in furtherance of their operations against the Chinese, but also because it was adjacent to the Singapore–Hong Kong sea route. They followed this up in March by asserting their sovereignty over the Spratley islands, to which France also laid claim. This was calculated to perturb both the French in Indo-China and the Americans in the Philippines.[2]

At the same time the Japanese renewed their attempts to gain a major share of control of the International Settlement at Shanghai. On 4 January 1938 the Japanese military and consular authorities

---

[1] See Ch. IV above.
[2] Hull, *Memoirs*, i. 618. He received Japanese explanations 'with lively skepticism'.

in Shanghai had demanded that the Municipal Council of the Settlement appoint Japanese subjects to 'controlling positions' in all branches of the municipal administration. It was also to improve the status and enlarge the numbers of the Japanese branch of the Settlement police force.[1] The Council, backed by the British and United States Governments, had on 18 March 1938 returned a polite refusal to the first demand, but proposed a scheme which went a good way to meet the second.[2] Here for the time being the matter rested. The Council furthermore issued stringent proclamations against anti-Japanese terrorism, in which it prescribed expulsion from the Settlement of persons in unlawful possession of arms, and the surrender to the Japanese of those who actually committed acts against them.[3] But these measures, against which the Chinese Government protested, did not put an end to violence, some of which, however, was fomented by the Japanese and their Chinese auxiliaries. In February 1939 more murders of officials of the Nanking régime provoked warnings and threats against the International Settlement by the Japanese Foreign Minister and the new Premier, Baron Hiranuma. The Japanese Consul-General demanded that his consular police should have the right to take independent action for the suppression of terrorists. The Council, backed by the American and British Governments, refused, and on 4 March another compromise was reached whereby, subject to the consent of the Municipal Police Commissioner, his forces would co-operate with the Japanese consular police in rounding up terrorists.[4]

In the following May the Japanese returned to the charge. The Japanese naval authorities in Shanghai on 2 May declared that the measures taken by the Municipal Council to suppress anti-Japanese elements in the Settlement were inadequate and supported demands made by Fu Siao-en, the Mayor of the Shanghai City Government which controlled the Chinese-administered parts of Shanghai. Fu demanded that his police be allowed to enter the Settlement to help in suppressing terrorists; that the Chinese national flag should not be allowed to be flown in the Settlement and that the Settlement Chinese Courts as well as title-deeds to property and other documents of the Chinese Land

---

[1] Jones, *Shanghai and Tientsin*, p. 42.
[2] ibid. pp. 43–44.
[3] ibid. p. 69.   [4] H C Deb., vol. 344, col. 887.

Office there should be turned over to his régime.[1] Then, on 3 May the Japanese Vice-Minister for Foreign Affairs communicated his Government's desires concerning the International Settlement in the form of an *aide-mémoire* to the British Ambassador. A separate but identical communication was on the same day made to the American Ambassador. The Japanese desiderata included a revision of the Land Regulations, which formed the legal basis of the Settlement administration, so as to give the Japanese a larger share in representation on the Council and in the administration of the Settlement; close co-operation between the municipal authorities and the Chinese City Government, including the surrender to it of the land records of the former Chinese municipal régime, and a stricter control of anti-Japanese activities in the Settlement.[2] Once more the Japanese press adopted a threatening tone and declared that failure to comply with these demands might result in a forcible Japanese occupation of the Settlement.

The Shanghai Municipal Council indicated its readiness to meet such of the demands as did not encroach upon its administrative independence, and it joined with the French Concession authorities in issuing a joint proclamation which prohibited all political activities of whatever kind in the two areas and proclaimed their strict neutrality in the Sino-Japanese conflict. But the Japanese demands for a revision of the Land Regulations and a reorganization of the administration of the Settlement were rejected by the American and British Governments in their replies to the Japanese Government, delivered on 17 and 19 May respectively. Both Governments held that the revision of the Land Regulations and the question of the Chinese Courts in the Settlement should await the development of more stable conditions in Shanghai. They praised the energy and efficiency of the Municipal Council in dealing with disorders in that part of the Settlement which remained under its control and expressed confidence that the municipal authorities would continue to make adjustments to meet reasonable Japanese requests.[3]

The dissatisfaction of the Japanese Government with this answer was evident in a statement made on 24 May by the director of the Intelligence Bureau of the Foreign Ministry, Mr. Kawai. He declared that the Settlements in China were not foreign territory,

---

[1] China Association (London), *Annual Report*, 1939-40, p. 53.
[2] H C Deb., vol. 347, coll. 5-6.   [3] 21 May 1939, ibid. col. 1395.

but merely areas in which foreigners exercised administrative rights. Chinese sovereignty over these areas was suspended but not extinguished. Therefore, as Japan was engaged in hostilities with China, Chinese sovereignty in the foreign-administered areas was, as in the Japanese-occupied regions, subject to Japanese control. Anti-Japanese terrorism in the Settlements was part of the Chinese resistance to Japan, and she was consequently legally justified in eliminating such resistance by force. He went on to say that it was the existing situation in the Settlements that made imperative the strengthening of Japanese administrative rights in them; the reforms proposed by Japan were a matter of necessity and she sincerely desired the co-operation of foreign Powers in securing such changes.[1]

Point was given to Kawai's remarks by events in the tiny International Settlement on the island of Kulangsu, opposite the port of Amoy, which was under Japanese occupation. Here, on 11 May Hung Li-hsun, the pro-Japanese Chairman of the Amoy Chinese Chamber of Commerce, had been fatally wounded. The following day the Japanese landed 200 marines in the Settlement and conducted a search for the assassins. They furthermore presented sweeping demands to the Kulangsu Municipal Council, which they accused of negligence in the suppression of terrorism.[2] They required that Japanese nationals should be given the posts of Chairman of the Council, Chief Secretary, and Police Commissioner, that Formosan residents should be given the franchise and representation on the Council, that three vacancies in the Council should be filled by Chinese ratepayers, and that Japanese consular police should co-operate with those of the Municipality in dealing with anti-Japanese activities on the part of terrorists in the Settlement. Acceptance of these demands would have made the Council a Japanese-controlled body, but the Council rejected all but the last of them, protested against the Japanese action in landing troops, and declared that the murder of Hung was not a political crime and that the Japanese were simply making it a pretext to invade Kulangsu.

Kulangsu itself was of minor importance.[3] It was nevertheless

[1] China Association, *Annual Report*, 1939–40, p. 54.
[2] H C Deb., vol. 347, coll. 968–9.
[3] It had a foreign population numbering some 250. The Municipal Council was composed of three Chinese members, two British, two Japanese, and one American; the Chairman was a Dutch subject.

evident that, should the Japanese attain their ends here, they would be emboldened to adopt similar measures at Shanghai. Therefore Great Britain, France, and the United States took prompt action in support of the Kulangsu municipal authorities. In addition to protests made both to the local Japanese consular authorities and in Tokyo the three Powers sent warships to Kulangsu, and on 17 May parties of American, British, and French sailors were landed there. The Japanese denounced this action as 'unfriendly' and declared that, while most of their marines had been withdrawn, some would remain until the Municipal Council agreed to at least the second of the demands made upon it.

However, the Japanese were in fact checkmated and they had also been indirectly warned of the serious consequences to Anglo-Japanese relations which would follow if they tried a similar coup in the International Settlement at Shanghai.[1] The Japanese then tried to force the Kulangsu Council to yield by cutting off supplies of food from the mainland and by maintaining a virtual state of siege. Since they did not venture to prevent supplies reaching the island by sea in foreign ships the Council managed to hold out until the Japanese dropped their major demands. An agreement was reached on 17 October, between the Kulangsu Municipal Council and the Japanese Consul-General, and was approved by the consular body. The Council agreed to appoint additional Japanese members to its police force and to co-operate with the Japanese authorities in the suppression of terrorists, but it maintained its administrative rights unimpaired. At the outbreak of the European War the British and French landing parties had been withdrawn from Kulangsu, but the American contingent, of equal strength with the Japanese force there, had remained. On the day following the signature of the agreement the American and Japanese forces were simultaneously withdrawn.[2]

The Japanese had failed to attain their major objectives at Shanghai and Kulangsu because they had encroached upon the interests of all the other major Treaty Powers and had met with collective resistance. In particular, the United States was involved in the defence of the International Settlements and the Japanese Government were wary of unduly provoking her.

Ever since the Japanese conquest of North China in the autumn of 1937 the Japanese military and political authorities there had

[1] H C Deb., vol. 347, col. 969. [2] ibid. vol. 352, col. 1904.

been at feud with those of the British and French Concessions in Tientsin. The Japanese complained that Chinese guerrillas in the surrounding countryside received supplies of arms and of money from Chinese Nationalist organizations in the Concessions and that the Concession authorities were making no real effort to suppress these activities. The Japanese demanded that any Chinese in the Concessions whom they accused of anti-Japanese activities should be surrendered to them. This the foreign municipal officials declined to do unless, as was rarely the case, the Japanese could submit evidence of guilt on the part of the persons named.[1] They themselves arrested and detained suspected Chinese terrorists, but to hand these over to the tender mercies of the Kempeitai was contrary to Western notions of justice and would have aroused the ill-will of the Chinese Nationalist Government.

Behind the constant friction over this matter lay a deeper source of trouble. In November 1935 the Chinese Government had introduced monetary reforms which had included the introduction of a managed currency and the demonetization of silver. The Japanese military from the first regarded this reform with aversion as tending to strengthen the prestige and authority of the Chinese Central Government. They had consequently exerted pressure to prevent the silver stocks of the Chinese Government Banks in Peiping and Tientsin from being sent to Shanghai. In view of the threatening attitude of the Japanese the silver bars in question were deposited for safe-keeping in the British and French Concessions in Tientsin and in the foreign Legation quarter in Peiping.[2]

After the formation of the Japanese-sponsored Provisional Government in North China, this body, on 11 February 1938, inaugurated the Federal Reserve Bank as a new organ of note issue. The Bank was in fact organized and partly financed by the Japanese in an attempt to drive out the fapi, or Chinese National currency, from North China. But this it failed to do, since its notes had not sufficient specie backing and were not freely convertible. The Western banks in North China would not accept the notes of the Federal Reserve Bank except for holding in special accounts which were not convertible into Chinese national currency, which was freely convertible.[3] Consequently the Japanese during 1938–9 found the new currency universally distrusted by the Chinese

[1] Jones, *Shanghai and Tientsin*, pp. 172–3.
[2] ibid. pp. 163–4.   [3] ibid. pp. 164–5.

populace, while their efforts to call in fapi for use in procuring foreign exchange were partially frustrated by measures taken by the Chinese National Government, with the quiet backing of Western financial organs in China.

The Japanese therefore wanted to get hold of the silver in the foreign Concessions and Legation quarter for use as specie backing for the new currency, but the authorities of those areas refused either to allow the Japanese or their minions access to it, or to compel its removal into Japanese-occupied territory. This infuriated the Japanese military authorities in North China, and, in August 1938, they ordered Japanese subjects resident in the British and French Concessions to evacuate them, so as to clear the way for action against these areas.[1] By the following December the Japanese civilians had reluctantly obeyed orders and the Japanese military then began to harass the Concessions by interfering with food supplies from the outside and by instituting examination and search of foreigners and Chinese entering or leaving the two Concessions. British and French protests resulted in some temporary relaxation of these measures, but in March 1939 they were re-enforced.[2]

So far from yielding to Japanese pressure and threats, the British Government took further steps to aid the Chinese cause. On 8 March 1939 the Chancellor of the Exchequer announced that a Chinese currency exchange-stabilization fund would be established, with a backing of £10 million, a half of which was to be provided by the British Hong Kong and Shanghai Banking Corporation and the Chartered Bank of India, Australia, and China, if Parliament would sanction a Government guarantee of this loan.[3] This Parliament did on 24 March.[4] In the following month further export credits were granted to cover Chinese purchases from British manufacturers. These steps were officially justified as stimulating British trade with China, but their effect was to strengthen China, especially in the financial and economic war now being waged with Japan. The Japanese Government affected to minimize their consequences, but the Japanese press did not conceal its ire and was prolific in threats of reprisals.

On 9 April 1939 the Chinese manager of the Federal Reserve

---

[1] RIIA, *Survey, 1938*, i. 564.
[2] ibid. pp. 564–5; Jones, *Shanghai and Tientsin*, p. 174.
[3] H C Deb., vol. 344, coll. 2147–9.   [4] ibid. vol. 355, coll. 1602–17.

Bank was assassinated in the British Concession in Tientsin. This was the first political murder to occur within its boundaries. The British municipal authorities arrested a number of suspects, among whom were four declared by the Japanese authorities to have been concerned in the murder. These men were handed over to the Japanese for questioning and two of them made confessions in which they implicated themselves. However they later retracted these when returned to the custody of the British municipal authorities.[1] As the Japanese failed to submit independent evidence to make out a case against the men, the British Concession authorities declined to hand them over to the local Chinese District Court in Japanese-occupied territory. The British Consul-General proposed that they should be held in his custody and eventually expelled from the Concession, should the Japanese produce no further evidence against them. Any future political crimes would result in the culprit being handed over to the *de facto* Chinese authorities for trial, or by expulsion from the Concession.[2] But the Japanese refused to accept this and reiterated their demand for the surrender of the four men. They declared that a strict blockade of the British Concession would be instituted if this were not done. The British Government then suggested that the case be considered by an advisory committee of three: one British, one Japanese, and one neutral member. This was refused and on 14 June the blockade of the British and French Concessions began. A live-wire barricade was erected around them and persons entering or leaving were searched and sometimes publicly stripped by Japanese guards. British subjects, both men and women, suffered these indignities. At the same time supplies of provisions and fuel were largely cut off.[3]

The Japanese objective was clearly to force Great Britain not only to submit to the demand to give up the four suspects, but to co-operate with Japan over the silver question and related issues. This placed the British Government in an extremely difficult position. Public indignation rose high, accompanied by demands for reprisals, which the Government intimated might be made. But, humiliating as the alternative was, any such steps would have been disastrous. The British Government had accurate information on the division of opinion in Japan over the tripartite pact

---

[1] H L Deb., vol. 113, coll. 549–51.   [2] ibid.
[3] ibid.; Craigie, *Behind the Japanese Mask*, pp. 72–73.

negotiations.[1] Reprisals against Japan would have played into the hands of the pro-Axis faction, while there was always the danger that the local military firebrands in North China might seize the Concession by force, with the object of provoking war with Great Britain and stampeding Tokyo into signing the pact. It was impossible for Great Britain to send her fleet to the Far East in view of the critical European situation, accentuated by Hitler's threat to Poland and the British guarantee to that country.[2] No effective help over Tientsin was forthcoming from the United States. The only favourable omens were the border hostilities between Japanese and Soviet forces at Nomonhan and Japanese nervousness lest the Anglo-Soviet negotiations result in an agreement covering the Far East as well as Europe.

Nevertheless, with an impasse between the British and the Japanese authorities in Tientsin and with the Japanese Army organizing and financing anti-British demonstrations, both in occupied China and in Japan itself, the situation was daily becoming more dangerous. The British Government had information that the Japanese General Staff had its plans worked out for war with Great Britain, and that a strong faction in the Army was pressing for war on the Tientsin issue, on which they reckoned there would be no active intervention by the United States.[3] In that calculation they were undoubtedly correct; although American opinion was hardening against Japan, there was no thought of going beyond economic measures of retaliation. It was indeed fortunate for Great Britain that division of opinion in Japan acted as a check upon the advocates of force, for otherwise the British Government would either have had to acquiesce in the forcible seizure of the British Concession, or plunge into war with Japan which, in view of the German menace, would have been suicidal. The policy

---

[1] *D Brit.FP*, 3rd series, iv. 5, 70–71, 161.

[2] Early in 1938 there had been discussions in London between the American Director of the War Plans Division, Navy Department, and his British opposite number on co-operation in the event of an Anglo-American war with Japan. At that time the Admiralty were prepared to send some ships to Singapore, but would not commit themselves on numbers (*Pearl Harbor Attack*, pt. 9, pp. 4274–5). But on 22 March 1939 Halifax told the American Ambassador that Britain had promised Australia that she would send a fleet to Singapore, but now felt unable to do so and wondered if the United States would send its fleet back to the Pacific. The French Government had said that if the British Mediterranean Fleet were to be sent to Singapore, France would not co-operate in any further opposition to Hitler in central and eastern Europe. On 15 April the United States Fleet was ordered back to the Pacific (Hull, *Memoirs*, i. 630).

[3] Craigie, *Behind the Japanese Mask*, p. 73.

London in fact adopted was, in these circumstances, the only sane one, to endeavour to transfer the negotiations to Tokyo, to be prepared to yield on some points, but to play for time and to give way as little as possible.[1]

After some preliminary discussion, it was agreed that an Anglo-Japanese conference on the Tientsin question should be held in Tokyo. But on 15 July Arita informed Craigie that, as a preliminary, the British Government must recognize that the Japanese Army was conducting large-scale operations in China and should agree not to assist the Chinese in the areas occupied by Japanese forces and not to hinder the objectives of the Japanese Army in them.[2] This Craigie objected to as too sweeping, and pointed out that the responsibility for the maintenance of peace and order in the occupied areas lay with the Japanese Army. But it was evident that some general statement would have to be issued before the Japanese military would agree to await the results of the proposed conference. On 24 July a compromise formula, reached between Craigie and Arita, was made public. This stated that the British Government recognized that large-scale hostilities were in progress in China, that the Japanese Army had to safeguard its own security, maintain order in regions under its control, and to prevent any actions which would obstruct it or benefit the enemy. British officials and subjects in China would be instructed to avoid any actions prejudicial to the measures taken by the Japanese to this end.[3]

Did the purposely vague phraseology of the Tokyo formula mean simply that Britain would not obstruct the Japanese in the suppression of terrorism in the occupied areas, or did it cover the

---

[1] Baron Hiranuma was also in favour of opening negotiations in Tokyo and made a secret overture to Craigie to secure this (F. S. G. Piggott, *Broken Thread* (Aldershot, Gay & Polden, 1950), p. 320).

[2] *Saionji–Harada Memoirs*, 15 July 1939; Craigie, *Behind the Japanese Mask*, pp. 74–75.

[3] 'His Majesty's Government in the United Kingdom fully recognize the actual situation in China where hostilities on a large scale are in progress and note that, as long as that state of affairs continues to exist, the Japanese forces in China have special requirements for the purpose of safeguarding their own security and maintaining public order in regions under their control and that they have to suppress or remove any such acts or causes as will obstruct them or benefit their enemy. His Majesty's Government have no intention of countenancing any act or measures prejudicial to the attainment of the above-mentioned objects by Japanese forces and they will take this opportunity to confirm their policy in this respect by making it plain to British authorities and British nationals in China that they should refrain from such acts and measures' (H L Deb., vol. 114, coll. 368–9; H C Deb. vol. 350, coll. 994–5).

financial and economic policy of the Japanese Army as well? The
British Government, in interpreting the formula to a puzzled and
alarmed Parliament, took the first view; the Japanese Government,
in statements for home consumption, the second.[1] Which interpretation would prevail depended upon circumstances, which at the
time did not seem to favour Great Britain. The Chinese Government were alarmed, and British business and commercial circles
in China voiced their apprehensions.

In Washington Hull also was perturbed. He recalled the
Lansing–Ishii Agreement of 1917, and the use which Tokyo had
made of the mention of Japan's 'special interests' in China.[2] So
Roosevelt and Hull agreed that the time had come to take a step
which both had been contemplating for some time—the denunciation of the Commercial Treaty of 1911 with Japan. A further
motive was the desire to forestall Congressional action in this
respect, which would have been accompanied by debates liable to
inflame tempers on both sides of the Pacific. That the administration did not want—their object was to keep Japan uncertain of
what action would follow the expiration of the Treaty, in the hope
that thereby she might be induced to modify her China policy. So,
on 26 July, Hull served formal notice of the denunciation of the
Treaty, which under its terms, became effective after six months,
i.e. on 26 January 1940.[3]

The American action disconcerted Tokyo, but it brought no
relief to Great Britain; indeed in one way it proved an embarrassment to the British Government, since it gave rise in the House of
Commons to demands that Great Britain take similar action, which
the Government were in no position to do.[4] When the conference
on the Tientsin issues opened in Tokyo on 27 July the British
negotiators were confronted with Japanese demands for the
surrender of the four Chinese suspects and for co-operation
between Japanese and municipal police in repressing anti-Japanese
activities in the Concession, this co-operation to include the right
of the Japanese police to make arrests within the Concession.[5] The
Japanese authorities produced evidence against the four Chinese,
and on 12 August the British Government announced that they

---

[1] For the British official explanations see H C Deb., vol. 350, col. 2025; for
Hiranuma's interpretation, *The Times* 24 July 1939.
[2] Hull, *Memoirs*, i. 635–6.　　　　　　　　[3] ibid. pp. 636–8.
[4] H C Deb., vol. 350, col. 2868.
[5] Craigie, *Behind the Japanese Mask*, p. 75.

would be given up.[1] The Chinese Government protested, to which the British Government replied in a Note made public on 26 August, which upheld the British decision, but denied that it constituted any recognition of the Peking régime.[2] A provisional draft agreement was also reached about the policing of the British Concession, by the terms of which Japanese police could supply information about suspects and be present when the municipal police took action against these, but could not make independent arrests.[3]

The Japanese Government had also demanded the surrender of the Chinese silver stocks in the Concession and co-operation by the British municipal authorities in enforcing the use of Federal Reserve Bank notes and the prohibition of fapi.[4] On these matters the British Government stood firm and would not go beyond an offer to keep the silver sealed in the foreign bank vaults, so that neither side could use it. This the Japanese rejected; therefore, on 18 August, Craigie declared that, since the silver and currency questions went beyond the scope of the purely local Tientsin issues, the British Government would discuss these questions with other interested Governments before proceeding further in the matter.[5] So on 20 August the Tokyo Conference adjourned *sine die* and the British Foreign Office publicized the stand which it had taken,[6] while the Gaimusho replied that if this meant third-party intervention it would not be tolerated.[7]

The British Government could afford to be stiffer on these issues, which affected all foreign trade in North China. Then came the news that the USSR was about to conclude a non-aggression pact with Germany. This was a heavy blow to British diplomacy, but a worse one to Japanese; since fighting on a considerable scale had been going on at Nomonhan, the Japanese forces had sustained a severe reverse, and a general Japanese-Soviet conflict seemed likely. In consequence the Hiranuma Government fell, the silver and currency questions for the time being lapsed, and the danger of an Anglo-Japanese war in the summer of 1939 passed away.

One crisis had thus been surmounted, but the root of the trouble

---

[1] China Association, *Annual Report*, 1939–40, p. 43.   [2] ibid.
[3] Craigie, *Behind the Japanese Mask*, pp. 75–76.   [4] ibid. p. 76.
[5] ibid.   [6] RIIA, *Documents, 1939–46*, i. 556–8.
[7] ibid. pp. 558–9; *The Times*, 21 Aug. 1939.

still remained. Japan had proclaimed her New Order in East Asia and Great Britain, France, and the United States had voiced their opposition to this, although they had left themselves a loophole by professing readiness to discuss possible modifications in the Nine-Power Treaty. With the outbreak of the European War it was clear that Japan's neutrality—or non-involvement, as she preferred to call it—would be used as a bargaining counter in her efforts to get Great Britain and France to abandon all support of the Chinese National Government, and, in effect, to acquiesce in Japanese policy. On 5 September the Japanese Government informed the European belligerents that the continued presence of their warships and troops in China 'might result in unfortunate incidents and in a condition of affairs ill adapted to Japan's "non-involvement policy".'[1] Consequently Japan gave them 'friendly advice' voluntarily to withdraw these forces and offered to undertake the protection of the lives and property of their citizens.[2]

Since Germany had no forces in China it was obvious that this was simply another move in Japan's campaign to get the foreign-administered areas at her mercy. This put the British and French Governments in a quandary. They knew that Germany was working to get Japan to settle her differences with the USSR and that Japanese military circles were responsive to this idea, which would free Japan for action against the Western Powers. To refuse the Japanese demand might precipitate this. So they turned to the United States for advice and support. Hull on 7 September had told the Japanese Ambassador that his Government were trying to force the Western Powers out of China, but that American troops would remain there. He also hinted that the Congressional advocates of economic reprisals against Japan might be given free rein.[3] But he could do no more. On 11 September he advised the British Government to make no reply to the Japanese.[4] This was Hull's favourite policy of 'keeping them guessing'. It had the effect of irritating the Japanese without materially deflecting them from their course, and it would not do for Great Britain, especially when the news came of a Soviet-Japanese armistice at Nomonhan. On 19 September the British Government intimated that they would withdraw their garrison from Tientsin unless they were assured of American support. That in fact meant a promise of

---

[1] *The Times*, 7 Sept. 1939.
[3] Hull, *Memoirs*, i. 719–20.
[2] ibid.
[4] ibid. p. 720.

definite aid in the event of a Japanese attack, and such a promise
Hull could not give. He could only inform London of the vague
threats he had made to Horinouchi, and reiterate that American
forces would not be withdrawn from China.[1]

So the British Government decided to yield. On 3 October they
announced that five of the British gunboats on the Yangtze would
be withdrawn; the official reason given was that the ships could be
more usefully employed elsewhere.[2] The British Ambassador on
20 October told Hull that the bulk of the British forces would be
withdrawn from Peking and Tientsin, though not from Shanghai.
Hull declined comment upon this decision, of which he clearly
disapproved. He urged that the British Government should continue financial and economic aid to China and should discourage
private capital from co-operating with Japanese interests. Lord
Lothian replied that the Burma Road would be kept open.[3] In
November the British and French Governments announced that,
save for token forces to preserve their rights under the Boxer
Protocol, they were evacuating their forces from North China.[4]

It was impossible for Roosevelt and Hull to give Great Britain
any definite assurance that, in the event of an Anglo-Japanese clash
over the China issue, concrete American aid would be forthcoming.
They had already, on 2 November, turned down a proposal by
Chiang Kai-shek that an international conference should be called
to discuss a settlement of the Far Eastern situation and that, if
Japan should refuse to attend, economic sanctions should be
inflicted upon her.[5] American Congressional and public opinion
was not yet ripe for any such measures, nor was the United States
militarily prepared to meet the possible consequences. Hull was
therefore right in being cautious and non-committal.

But his grasp of the broader issues appeared limited. For Great
Britain and France the first essential was to keep Japan from
joining with Germany. This, as the course of events had shown,
influential elements in Japan were averse from doing. But the
Japanese military leaders had to extricate themselves from the
China conflict on terms which would justify the blood and treasure
which they had poured out. Furthermore, as Grew realized, they
had general support in Japan in seeking to secure economic con-

[1] ibid.
[2] *The Times*, 3 Oct. 1939.   [3] Hull, *Memoirs*, i. 722.
[4] *The Times*, 13 and 14 Nov. 1939.   [5] Hull, *Memoirs*, i. 723-4.

cessions in China which would in large measure free Japan from her dependence for strategic raw materials upon the United States and Great Britain.[1] Mutterings about sanctions and the abrogation of commercial treaties tended only to confirm the Japanese in this conviction. Consequently, if Japan were to be kept permanently out of the Axis camp, there was good reason to seek a compromise settlement of the Sino-Japanese conflict, and to save what could be saved of foreign rights and interests in China. The time for this seemed opportune since the war in China had developed into a stalemate, which in itself was an inducement to Japan to moderate the more extreme of her demands. Furthermore German influence in Japan had not recovered from the setback caused by the Soviet-German Non-Aggression Pact, the German conquest of Poland had evoked mixed feelings in Japan, and the spectacle of British command of the sea had impressed Japanese naval and commercial circles.[2]

Therefore, during November and December 1939, the British and French Governments approached the Department of State with suggestions for a compromise in the Far East. The British Ambassador said that his Government favoured an accord 'on a basis which would be fair and equitable to both sides, but with the realization on the part of both China and Japan that each side would have to make concessions.'[3] The American Ambassador in Japan, Grew, appeared to be thinking along the same lines.[4] But Hull would not consider such a policy.[5] He did not believe that Japan could reach a definite accord with the USSR; on that he proved correct at the time, but the future remained uncertain and the British and French Governments, while unable to be at open cross-purposes with the United States in the Far East, were justifiably worried.

Meanwhile, on 23 September Admiral Kichisaburo Nomura had become Minister of Foreign Affairs in Japan.[6] He was no career diplomat, but had formerly been naval attaché in Washington and

[1] Grew, *Ten Years in Japan*, pp. 262–3.
[2] Craigie, *Behind the Japanese Mask*, p. 79.
[3] Feis, *Road to Pearl Harbor*, p. 43.
[4] So it would appear from his dispatch of 1 December 1939, in which he argued very strongly against sanctions, and declared that 'to await the hoped-for discrediting of the Japanese Army is to await the millennium'. He added that the United States Government should not compromise with principle, but referred to the possible modification of the Nine-Power Treaty by 'orderly processes', i.e. international agreement (*Ten Years in Japan*, pp. 260–5).
[5] Hull, *Memoirs*, i. 727.   [6] *The Times*, 23 Sept. 1939.

had been well known and popular in American naval circles. This appointment was intended as a friendly gesture towards the United States. On 2 October he repeated previous assurances that the New Order would not extinguish foreign rights and interests in China, but went farther in saying that Japan must give concrete proof of this.[1] This was followed by conversations between Nomura and Grew during November and December which resulted in the settlement of some of the outstanding American claims to reparation for injury to their citizens and damage to their property in China. But, on the wider issue of the Open Door, Nomura soon ran into difficulties. On the one hand the Japanese Army in China and the vested interests which had grown up around it were bitterly opposed to making any substantial concessions which might undermine the Japanese industrial and trading monopolies.[2] On the other, Hull refused to consider either the negotiation of a new commercial treaty or the conclusion of a temporary *modus vivendi*, 'unless Japan completely changed her attitude and practice towards our rights and interests in China.'[3] On 18 December Nomura informed Grew that the Yangtze, between Shanghai and Nanking, would be opened to general navigation in about two months' time. But he added that this would be subject to certain restrictions owing to the continuance of military operations in China. He could give no assurances about economic monopolies or Japanese-sponsored currencies in China.[4]

Grew urged the Department of State either to conclude a *modus vivendi* or to begin negotiations for a new treaty of commerce, which need not be made effective until Japan had carried out her promises.[5] He believed that some concessions to the Japanese Government would strengthen their hand against the recalcitrant Army. Hull disagreed, and Roosevelt concurred with his view. Therefore, while they decided to avoid the imposition of any discriminatory duties or tonnage dues on Japanese goods and vessels after the 1911 Treaty expired, they also refused to replace it by any new instrument. Grew was so informed on 20 December.[6] This was a bitter disappointment to Nomura, who had already been assailed for truckling to the United States and who was now more vehemently attacked since he had promised something and

---

[1] ibid. 3 Oct. 1939.   [2] *Saionji–Harada Memoirs*, 13 Dec. 1939.
[3] *Memoirs*, i. 725–6.   [4] Grew, *Ten Years in Japan*, p. 269.
[5] Hull, *Memoirs*, i. 727.   [6] ibid. pp. 726–8.

got nothing in return. Assailed on both foreign and domestic matters the Abe Cabinet resigned in mid-January 1940. It was succeeded by that of Admiral Yonai, with Hachiro Arita as Foreign Minister. Arita took a stiffer line with the United States; he did not continue the conversations with Grew, and on 17 February he told the Diet that the Yonai Cabinet was not bound by the promise of its predecessor to open the Yangtze.[1] The War Minister on 4 March declared that the Army would decide whether this should be done or not, and in fact it was not done.[2]

Hull's obduracy was thus matched by an equal stubbornness on the side of the Japanese. Grew had favoured a less rigid attitude because he was aware of the mounting public discontent in Japan at the apparently endless war in China, and of the conflict over China policy in the inner circles of the Government. Some indication of this was afforded by the preliminaries to the establishment of a Japanese-sponsored Central Government in China, headed by Wang Ching-wei.

The Abe Cabinet, on 13 September 1939, had declared their intention to render positive assistance to the formation of the new régime.[3] But progress was at first slow. One obstacle lay in the localism of the Japanese authorities in North China, who wished to keep the region under the control of the Peking Provisional Government independent of Wang. Until his death in February 1940, they were still angling for Wu Pei-fu. A more serious difficulty arose over the character of the peace terms which were to be concluded between the Japanese Government and the 'National Government' of Wang Ching-wei. A strong party in Tokyo wanted these terms to be a bait for Generalissimo Chiang Kai-shek. It was hoped that, once they were formally concluded and publicized, the Generalissimo would see his way to accepting them, or, should he remain obdurate, that enough of his followers would secede to Wang, so as to leave Chungking powerless. This was hinted at by General Yanagawa, the Director-General of the China Affairs Board, who in February 1940 told the Japanese Diet that peace with China would come when the Chungking Government either asked for peace, allowed themselves to be absorbed in the new régime, or co-operated with it.[4]

---

[1] Grew, *Ten Years in Japan*, p. 274; *NYT*, 18 Feb. 1940.
[2] *NYT*, 5 March 1940.
[3] *Tokyo Gazette*, October 1939, p. 142.   [4] *NYT*, 23 Feb. 1940.

But to achieve this aim the terms of peace needed to be moderate. General Abe, just before assuming office, had publicly contrasted the 'crafty liberality' of the Western Powers towards China with the 'illiberal and stingy way' in which Japan treated her.[1] Wang Ching-wei and his associates, Tang Leang-li and Chou Fu-hai, had been saying much the same in articles which appeared in their own organs in Shanghai and occasionally in the Japanese press and periodicals. Thus, in an editorial of 23 November 1939, in his paper *Central China Daily News*, Wang declared that Japanese leadership in East Asia depended upon her ability to co-operate with China in the spirit which marked British and French co-operation with that country. He asserted that, except for garrisons in Mongolia, all Japanese troops should be evacuated from China and that Chinese economic rights should remain intact and independent.[2] Since Wang was entirely dependent upon Japanese support, he would not have ventured to write in such a fashion without encouragement. There is some evidence that this came from the War Minister, General Hata, who had been appointed by the Emperor despite opposition from some of the Army chiefs. According to General Ryukichi Tanaka, Hata wanted to effect a material reduction in the number of Japanese troops in China, as a gesture to Chiang and as the prelude to a peace offer which should include the evacuation of Japanese troops from China, but he encountered strong opposition.[3] Undercover peace overtures were still being put out to Chiang via Hong Kong, and Abe appears to have favoured asking Great Britain to mediate.[4] This she evidently would have done if she could have secured American approval; so also would France. In view of the opposition of influential Army leaders at home, and in China, to any peace which did not give Japan far-reaching concessions in central and southern, as well as in North China, it cannot be confidently asserted that the mediation of the Western Powers would have swung the balance in favour of the moderates.

As things were, the discussions between Wang Ching-wei and representatives of the Japanese Army in China resulted in the formation of 'basic peace terms' at the end of December. These were reportedly approved by the China Affairs Board on 7 January

[1] *Daily Telegraph*, 2 Oct. 1939.
[2] *Peking and Tientsin Times*, 24 Nov. 1939.
[3] IMTFE, *Record*, pp. 29410–11.   [4] ibid. pp. 29112–13.

1940.[1] But then occurred a contretemps. On 13 January Kao Tsung-wu and Tao Hsi-sheng, who had defected to Wang, fled from Shanghai to Hong Kong, where on 21 January they published in the Hong Kong edition of the *Ta Kung Pao* the text of the agreement which they said had been concluded between Wang and Lieut.-General Kagesa on 30 December 1939.[2] Two days later a Chinese Government spokesman declared that Tao and Kao had sent photostat copies of the agreement to Chungking. They had explained that Wang had shown them his preliminary agreement with the Japanese, that when they saw it they realized how wrong they had been ever to join him, and that they had taken photostatic copies of it to send to Chungking.[3] For this patriotic action they were pardoned and restored to favour.

There may have been more to this than met the eye. Both men had been trusted supporters of Chiang; Kao, as has been seen, had twice before been employed on peace *pourparlers* with the Japanese. They may well have attached themselves to Wang for the purpose of discovering what concrete terms the Japanese were prepared to offer. Wang, too, may not have been as dismayed as he professed to be at the premature disclosure of terms which were much more severe than those which he had hoped to obtain.

The peace terms, according to Kao and Tao, were that China was to recognize Manchukuo and to join the Anti-Comintern Pact. Japan agreed to withdraw her troops from central and southern China in two years' time, provided that the new régime had secured effective control of those regions. But permanent Japanese garrisons were to be stationed in Inner Mongolia and in North China; a joint Sino-Japanese administration was to be established in the former region and the latter was to be a semi-autonomous area. Hainan island was to be permanently occupied by Japan, while throughout China the Japanese were to have special privileges in the exploitation of mineral resources, the development of industrial undertakings, and the management of communications.[4] Wang's supporters declared that these terms were only the Japanese initial demands, which Wang had got modified in the definite treaty. Kao and Tao retorted that the final agreement was the same as the one they had published except for slight changes in two articles.[5]

[1] *The Times*, 6 and 8 Jan. 1940.   [2] *NYT*, 14 and 22 Jan. 1940.
[3] ibid. 23 and 24 Jan. 1940.   [4] ibid.   [5] ibid. 24 Jan. 1940.

The terms were fiercely denounced in the press of free China and Chiang himself, in a manifesto to the Chinese Army and the people in general, stigmatized Wang as a traitor and declared that his agreement with the Japanese was 'ten times more deadly' than had been the Sino-Japanese Treaty of May 1915. This affair, together with the fall of the Abe Cabinet, resulted in the postponement of the establishment of Wang's régime. While outwardly the succeeding Yonai Cabinet reiterated the intention to set up a new Chinese Central Government, behind the scenes the conflict of policy continued, and there was talk of a new direct approach to Chiang through the medium of Akiyama, a close associate of Konoye.[1] On 2 February the Diet was enlivened by a thinly veiled attack upon the policy of the Army in China. This was delivered by Takao Saito, a leading member of the Minseito. He hinted that the Army was really trying to subjugate China and that the fine phrases of the Konoye statement were not to be taken seriously.[2] But, although his views were privately shared by certain political, industrial, and financial groups, these dared not come into the open. For his temerity Saito was compelled to resign from his party and, on 7 March, was expelled from the Diet.[3] Two days later the Lower House passed a resolution which declared that Japan's policy for the settlement of the China Affair was firmly and clearly established and which pledged the House to support of the objectives of the 'holy war'.[4] On 12 March Wang formally announced his intention to establish a new régime, and Yonai the next day pledged support for it.[5] Three days later it was announced that the ex-Premier, General Abe, would go as Ambassador and special envoy to the new régime.[6] This was inaugurated in Nanking on 30 March, when the Japanese Government issued a further statement which reaffirmed their support for Wang and for the New Order, but which denied any intention of excluding 'such peaceful economic activities of third Powers as conform with the new situation in East Asia' and suggested that these Powers should recognize the new régime.[7]

The legitimate Chinese Government replied by reiterating their

---

[1] *Saionji–Harada Memoirs*, 13 and 29 March 1940.
[2] *Trans-Pacific* (Tokyo), 8 Feb. 1940.
[3] *The Times*, 7 March 1940.   [4] *Japan Chronicle*, 10 March 1940.
[5] *The Times*, 14 March 1940.   [6] ibid. 17 March 1940.
[7] *Tokyo Gazette*, April 1940, p. 417. But the 'Basic Treaty' was for the time being shelved, and undercover peace overtures to Chungking were continued.

intention of continuing resistance until the Japanese were completely driven from Chinese territory. They furthermore served
notice that they would regard *de jure* or *de facto* recognition of the
Nanking Government as an unfriendly act and a violation of international law and treaties.[1] They were assured of American support, for Hull had already rejected Japanese suggestions that
foreign Powers might give the new régime *de facto* co-operation,
even if they avoided formal recognition.[2] On 7 March the American
Government had given Chungking a further credit, and on 30
March Hull publicly declared that the establishment of the new
régime was another stage in the Japanese programme of creating
a political and economic hegemony over China, and that the United
States would continue to recognize the National Government of
Chiang Kai-shek.[3]

Since the United States was not involved in war, Hull could
afford to continue the policy of encouraging the prolongation of
Chinese resistance in the hope that ultimately Japan would be
forced to cut her losses and abandon her design for the New Order
in East Asia. The British Government were in a more difficult
situation. They were still uneasy over the prospect of a possible
Soviet-Japanese accord which would leave Japan free for an assault
upon British possessions in the Far East to coincide with a German
onslaught in the West.[4] Also, while the immediate prospect of
war between the Western Democracies and the Soviet Union had
passed with the conclusion of a Soviet-Finnish peace on 12 March,
relations remained strained in view of the economic assistance
which the USSR was rendering Germany. For Great Britain the
primary purpose was to do nothing to drive Japan into the arms of
Germany. The Yonai Cabinet had continued the policy of its
predecessor in discouraging the advocates of such an alliance in
Japan; it had, too, shown moderation in the compromise settlement of the *Asama Maru* affair which in January 1940 had caused
a sharp crisis in Anglo-Japanese relations.[5] But the Tientsin issues

---

[1] *The Times*, 31 March 1940.
[2] Hull, *Memoirs*, i. 724–5.   [3] ibid. p. 725.
[4] Harada said that he reassured Craigie on this in a private interview at Oiso,
on 23 March 1940 (*Saionji–Harada Memoirs*, 29 March 1940).
[5] The *Asama Maru* had on board a number of German merchant seamen
who were trying to get home via Japan and the USSR. On 21 January 1940 she
was stopped by a British cruiser thirty-five miles from Japan, and twenty-one
of the Germans were removed. The Japanese press raved about the insult to
Japan 'in proximity to the Imperial Palace'. However, after some exchange of
arguments, a compromise was reached, by which Britain released nine of the

remained unsolved, the blockade of the British Concession continued, and, in face of Japanese demands for co-operation with the
Wang régime, Britain had to proceed cautiously. On 21 March the
Japanese Ambassador in London, Shigemitsu, had a conversation
on this subject with Mr. Butler, the British Under-Secretary of
State for Foreign Affairs. He told Butler that the Wang régime
would be set up on 30 March, that it would seek to include all but
Communist elements and that 'it must be a matter for congratula-
tion if some compromise could be found between the new Central
Government and the Chungking Government.' Shigemitsu
reported that Butler had replied that the British Government
could not change their policy of recognition of the Chungking
Government but 'he understood my explanation and hoped that
the new Government would be successful.'[1] Shigemitsu added
that Butler had referred to the necessity of beating the Soviet
Union by blockade or other means in the extension of the war
against Germany and had agreed on the possibility of future Anglo-
Japanese understandings.[2] On 28 March the British Ambassador
in Tokyo told the Japan–Britain Society that both Great Britain
and Japan were ultimately striving for lasting peace and that it was
surely not beyond the powers of constructive statesmanship to
bring the aims of their national policies into full harmony.[3] This
aroused unfavourable comment in the Commons and the British
press. On 3 April the British Foreign Secretary denied any
intention of withdrawing recognition from the Government of
Chiang Kai-shek, though he added that this need not prevent
Britain from cultivating good relations with Japan.

If Japan could have been induced to modify her policy in China
and to evacuate at all events the southern and central portions of
the country, which was what Hata and a section of the General
Staff appeared to be working for, the way might have been cleared
for Anglo-Japanese co-operation in the event of the USSR becoming a full partner of Germany. But the German conquest of

Germans and Japan secretly agreed to refuse passage in her ships to Germans
of military age (*Correspondence . . . regarding the removal of German Citizens
from the Japanese Ship 'Asama Maru'*, Cmd. 6166, 1940; Craigie, *Behind the
Japanese Mask*, pp. 82–84).   [1] IMTFE, *Record*, p. 9676.
   [2] ibid. pp. 9675–9. The British Government wanted Japan to co-operate in
stopping strategic imports from reaching Germany via Japan and Vladivostok
(*Saionji–Harada Memoirs*, 6 April 1939). For Anglo-Japanese conversations on
this matter, March–June 1940, see W. N. Medlicott, *The Economic Blockade*,
vol. i (London, HMSO and Longmans, Green, 1952), pp. 403–11.
   [3] *The Times*, 28 March 1940.

Norway in April, followed by their successful onslaught in the Low Countries, caused a resurgence of the pro-German elements in Japan and set in motion the train of events which led to the Tripartite Pact of September 1940.

These cataclysmic events produced a furore in Japan. The pro-Axis elements were exultant. 'The Army, the reactionaries, the southern "expansionists" raised their heads once more. Soon these factions were openly exalting in the Allied defeats as their friends the Huns swept forward in France.'[1] But to the Japanese Government the problem was not simply one of climbing on to the German band-wagon. Admiral Yonai and Japanese naval circles in general were responsive to warnings that Hitler would not easily overcome British sea power and that the end was not yet. They got such warnings from, among others, Shigemitsu in London, who also said that the British people were rallying behind the Churchill Government.[2]

Furthermore, would a complete German victory prove an unmixed blessing for Japan? The Japanese Government were uneasily conscious that neither their obstructive attitude over the proposed Tripartite Pact of 1939, nor their virtual acquiescence in Britain's exercise of belligerent rights at sea, as exemplified by the *Asama Maru* agreement, would be likely to earn them Hitler's goodwill. Would he, if victor in Europe, acquiesce in their 'New Order in East Asia', or would he, the great apostle of Aryan racialism, seek to extend German domination over the Asiatic dependencies of the vanquished European countries? It was clear to Tokyo that Japan must lose no time in staking out her claims in these regions against all comers, including if need be, Germany. Shigemitsu, with the freedom accorded to an experienced diplomat, was urging this course upon Arita.[3]

To free her hands for any contest which might arise over the 'South Seas' heritage, it was all the more advisable for Japan to terminate the China conflict. The capitulation of France and the dire peril in which Britain stood presented Japan with an unrivalled opportunity to compel those Powers to withdraw their forces from China and to close the routes under their control along which supplies could still reach Chungking. Such an abandonment

---

[1] Craigie, *Behind the Japanese Mask*, p. 87.
[2] Shigemitsu to Arita, 13 May 1940 (IMTFE, *Record*, pp. 9684-5).
[3] Shigemitsu to Arita, 13 May, 19 June 1940 (ibid. pp. 9686, 9692-3).

would, so Tokyo hoped, bring Chiang Kai-shek to terms, or else promote further defections from his side to that of Wang Ching-wei.

On 19 June the British Government announced that an agreement had been concluded in Tokyo on the issues of silver, currency, and police affecting the British municipal area in Tientsin. One-tenth of the silver was to be sold and the proceeds devoted to the relief of the distress among the Chinese population caused by the floods in the Tientsin area in 1939. The remainder was to be left in the vaults of the Chinese Bank of Communications in the British Concession under the consular seal of the parties concerned, pending a decision as to its ultimate disposal. The circulation of fapi (Chinese National notes) in the British Concession was to continue, but stringent measures were to be taken to prevent its misuse for purposes of gambling or smuggling. FRB (Japanese-sponsored) notes were to continue to circulate side by side with the fapi. The police arrangements provided for closer co-operation between the British municipal authorities and the local Japanese authorities in cases against persons in whose criminal activities the latter were interested. It was emphasized that in such cases the necessary action would always be taken by the municipal police and that the administrative integrity of the British Concession was fully preserved.[1]

The British Government said that they had consulted the Chinese Government 'at all material stages' of the negotiations over the silver question.[2] They had obtained the assent of the Chinese Government to that part of the Tientsin Agreement relating to the disposition of the silver. But the Chinese Government protested to that of Great Britain about the currency and police arrangements.[3]

In consequence of this Agreement the Japanese Army ended its long-continued blockade of the British municipal area, and the Japanese authorities in North China undertook 'to do everything in their power to suppress anti-British action or agitation in regions under their control'.[4]

Having obtained at least something of what they wanted in Tientsin, the Japanese proceeded to exert pressure to secure the removal of the European garrisons from the foreign-administered areas, including the International Settlement at Shanghai. Already on 11 June, a day after Italy entered the war in Europe, the

[1] H C Deb., vol. 362, coll. 140–1.   [2] ibid. vol. 360, col. 720.
[3] ibid. vol. 362, coll. 140, 1139.   [4] ibid. col. 141.

Japanese Government had intimated to the British, French, and Italian representatives in Tokyo their 'strong desire' that the European belligerents should avoid any action which might cause untoward events in China.[1] The meagre Italian force in Shanghai had no desire to start any trouble, and on 13 June it was announced that an agreement had been reached to prevent any hostilities in Shanghai.[2] This did not satisfy the Japanese, and the Wang Ching-wei régime continued to demand the withdrawal of belligerent forces from China and also declared that it would refuse to recognize the transfer of belligerent rights and interests to another Power.[3]

On 24 June the Japanese Government requested that the British Government take measures to stop the transit to China by way of the Burma Road of war materials and certain other classes of goods and they made a similar demand in respect of Hong Kong. They declared that the continuance of the transit of these goods would have a serious effect upon Anglo-Japanese relations.[4] To give point to this threat 5,000 Japanese troops were concentrated along the border of the Kowloon Leased Territory, and the situation became for a while so menacing that the military authorities at Hong Kong ordered the destruction of the frontier rail and road bridges over the Shumchun river.[5] The Hong Kong Government decreed the compulsory evacuation of British women and children to Manila and Australia.[6]

The British Government, engaged in a death grapple in home and Mediterranean waters and now menaced by Japan in the Far East, turned to the United States for aid. On 27 June Lord Lothian, accompanied by the Australian Minister to the United States, Mr. Casey, called upon the Secretary of State and said that the collapse of French resistance compelled the British Government to reconsider the policy which they had hitherto pursued of endeavouring to reach agreement with Japan on minor issues—such as those at Tientsin—but of standing in accord with the United States in rejecting Japanese plans for a New Order in China. Japan had now demanded that British troops be withdrawn from Shanghai and that the Burma Road and the Hong Kong border be closed.[7]

[1] *The Times*, 12 June 1940.   [2] ibid. 13 June 1940.
[3] ibid. 14 June 1940.   [4] H L Deb., vol. 116, col. 1039.
[5] *The Times*, 25 and 27 June 1940.
[6] ibid. 30 June 1940.   [7] Hull, *Memoirs*, i. 896.

The British Government, said Lothian, realized that yielding to Japan would result in her making further demands and that continual giving way to them would in the end compromise both the security of the British Commonwealth and the interests of the United States in the Far East. But the British felt that it was impossible for them to oppose aggression in both Europe and the Far East. In this situation the British Government believed that there was a choice of alternatives. The first was for the United States to increase pressure on Japan, either by imposing a full embargo on exports to Japan, or by sending American warships to Singapore—which Britain would make available to them.[1] The second course was for the United States and Britain to join in mediating a peace settlement between Japan and China. If the United States would adopt the first course (of embargo), Britain would co-operate. If not, would the United States join with Great Britain in making proposals for a Far Eastern settlement? These proposals would be on a basis of leaving China independent; securing respect for Western rights and interests in the Far East, and preserving Japanese neutrality in the European War. If Japan would concede these things, the United States and Great Britain would afford her financial and economic assistance, while the Allied Governments would ask a guarantee against re-exports to Axis countries of any materials which they might make available to Japan. The future of the foreign-administered areas in China could be settled after the restoration of peace in Europe and in Asia. Such were the proposals of the British Government as communicated by Lothian and embodied in an *aide-mémoire*.[2]

Hull replied that the American fleet could not be sent to Singapore as this would leave the Atlantic seaboard of the United States exposed to a possible attack. He went on to give Lothian and Casey a summary of the Grew–Nomura conversations and said that these had developed encouragingly until the French surrender, but that since then the military group had been moving in the direction of Hitler and Hitlerism and there was little hope of weaning them from this. The United States had nothing tangible in the Far East that she could offer to Japan and was not willing to offer her concessions at the expense of third Powers.[3]

---

[1] According to the Hopkins memoirs, Churchill had previously suggested this in a cable to Roosevelt on 15 May (R. E. Sherwood, *The White House Papers of Harry L. Hopkins* (London, Eyre & Spottiswoode, 1948), i. 143).
[2] Hull, *Memoirs*, i. 896–7.   [3] ibid. pp. 897–8.

Lothian then asked if there would be any objection to Great Britain and Australia endeavouring to bring about peace between Japan and China. Hull said that there would be no objection to Britain and Australia agreeing among themselves as to what concessions they could give Japan and then approaching Japan and China to inquire what concessions each of them was ready to make to secure peace. But he added that in any such negotiations the principles of the Japanese New Order would need to be negatived or at least seriously modified and that no properties or interests of China should be offered to Japan by Britain or the United States. He thought that the best policy would be one which neither made sweeping concessions to Japan nor, on the other hand, took any action against her which was likely to provoke her to war. He did not think that Japan was yet ready for war but that she would continue to nibble off what she could without engaging in a major conflict so long as Britain continued to resist Germany and the American fleet remained in the Pacific.[1]

This reply was in effect a rejection of both the British suggestions. Hull was inviting Great Britain to stand firm against the Japanese demands on the assumption that the Japanese were only bluffing when they threatened war. But what if the Japanese decided that they could fall upon the virtually defenceless British possessions in the Far East without incurring any serious danger of American intervention? They were not ignorant of the strength of isolationist sentiment among the American people, nor of the fact that it was Presidential election year in the United States. What the British Government had to fear was that the Axis Powers might, as in fact they did, promise acquiescence in Japanese domination in China and South East Asia in return for Japanese participation in war against Great Britain. The Yonai Government might resist such blandishments but it was already being undermined by the resurgent militarists. Hull was asking Britain to take a very grave risk at a time when he could promise her no really effective aid if she were attacked by Japan.

Nevertheless, the British Government did not at first give way to the Japanese demands. On 8 July the Japanese Foreign Ministry issued a communiqué stating that Arita had informed Craigie that a reply received from Great Britain about the Burma Road was unsatisfactory. The Japanese Foreign Minister demanded an

[1] ibid. p. 899.

immediate reconsideration of the British attitude and the Japanese press was full of war threats. Faced with this crisis the British Government gave way. On 12 July Lothian told Hull that Japan would declare war on Britain at any time unless the British Government closed the Burma Road. He said that the British Government would either close the Road for three months to any larger freight than had passed over it during the previous year, or else stop the transit of all war materials for three months and utilize this interval to make an effort to bring about a settlement of the Sino-Japanese conflict. Hull expressed his 'regret and disappointment' at any such course.[1]

On 14 July it became known that an Agreement had been reached in Tokyo, embodying the second alternative, as regards the Burma Road, mentioned by Lothian. Hull on 16 July issued a statement that the American Government 'has a legitimate interest in the keeping open of arteries of commerce in every part of the world' and 'considers that action such as this, if taken, and such as the action taken recently in relation to the Indo-China railway, would constitute unwarranted interpositions of obstacles to world trade.' This 'created a flurry in London' and Hull assured Lothian that his chief purpose had been to direct attention to the lawless conduct of Japan.[2]

Meanwhile, on 15 July the Acting Governor of the Straits Settlements was reported as saying in a broadcast that 'believing that an honourable peace is the real desire of the Chinese and Japanese peoples, His Majesty's Government will go to the greatest length to avoid seconding and prolonging the war in the East and will put forward every effort it can afford to that end.'[3] This provoked a statement by Chiang Kai-shek on 17 July in which he said

should she [Great Britain] try to link the question of the Burma Route with the question of peace between China and Japan this would practically amount to assisting Japan to bring China to submission. So long as China has not attained the object for which she has been fighting and suffering, namely, the preservation of her sovereignty and her territorial and administrative integrity, she will not lay down her arms.[4]

On 18 July the Anglo-Japanese Agreement was communicated to Parliament by the Prime Minister in the House of Commons

[1] ibid. p. 900.   [2] ibid. p. 901.
[3] China Association, *Annual Report*, 1940–1, p. 5.   [4] ibid. pp. 5–6.

and the Foreign Secretary in the House of Lords. The full text was as follows:

On 24th June the Japanese Government requested His Majesty's Government to take measures to stop the transit to China via Burma of war material and certain other goods. A similar request was made in respect of Hong Kong. The continuance of the transit of these materials was represented as having a serious effect upon Anglo-Japanese relations. An agreement has now been reached with the Japanese Government as follows:

Hong Kong.—The export of arms and ammunition from Hong Kong has been prohibited since January, 1939, and none of the war materials to which the Japanese Government attach importance are in fact being exported.

Burma.—The Government of Burma have agreed to suspend for a period of three months the transit to China of arms and ammunition as well as the following articles: petrol, lorries and railway material. The categories of goods prohibited in Burma will be prohibited in Hong Kong.

In considering the requests made by the Japanese Government and in reaching the agreement to which I have referred, His Majesty's Government were not unmindful of the various obligations accepted by this country, including their obligations to the National Government of China and to the British territories affected. His Majesty's Government were however also bound to have regard to the present world situation, nor could they ignore the dominant fact that we are ourselves engaged in a life and death struggle.

The general policy of this country towards the Far Eastern troubles has been repeatedly defined. We have persistently asserted our desire to see assured to China a free and independent future, and we have as frequently expressed our desire to improve our relations with Japan.

To achieve these objectives two things were essential—time and a relief of tension. On the one hand it was clear that the tension was rapidly growing owing to the Japanese complaints about the passage of war material by the Burma route. On the other, to agree to the permanent closure of the route would be to default from our obligations as a neutral friendly Power to China. What we have therefore made is a temporary arrangement in the hope that the time so gained may lead to a solution just and equitable to both parties to the dispute and freely accepted by them both.

We wish for no quarrel with any nation in the Far East. We desire to see China's status and integrity preserved, and as was indicated in our Note of 14th January, 1939, we are ready to negotiate with the Chinese Government, after the conclusion of peace, the abolition of extraterritorial rights, the rendition of concessions and the revision of treaties on the basis of reciprocity and equality. We wish to see Japan attain that state of prosperity which will ensure to her population the welfare and economic security which every Japanese naturally desires. Towards the attainment of the aims of both these countries we are prepared to offer our collaboration and our contribution. But it must be clear that if they are to be attained, it must be by a process of peace and conciliation and not by war or threat of war.[1]

The effect upon China was moral rather than material, as the volume of supplies passing over the Burma Road was small. Moreover the duration of the arrangement coincided with the rainy season in Burma and Yunnan, during which traffic was very materially reduced. To Great Britain the chief value of the Agreement was that it weathered another dangerous Anglo-Japanese crisis. It is true that, as has been revealed since, Japan was not yet ready for war with Great Britain and that the Navy in particular was averse to it.[2] But it does not necessarily follow from this that, had the Japanese demands been rejected, war would not have resulted, either in consequence of an extremist coup d'état in Tokyo, or through action by the Japanese Army in China.[3] Indeed, it is arguable that Japan missed her best chance of victory by *not* attacking in 1940, when she could have swept through South Eastern Asia with even greater ease than she did in 1942, and when considerable sections of American opinion had already written off Great Britain as lost. As it was Great Britain gained time—the crucial three months during which the Battle of Britain was fought and it became clear that there was to be no swift and complete victory for Hitler. Further, this precious time was bought at the

---

[1] H C Deb., vol. 363, coll. 399–400.   [2] See Ch. VII below.

[3] On 4 July a Shimpeitai plot to assassinate Yonai, Arita, and several members of the Court party was detected and most of the conspirators arrested (*Saionji–Harada Memoirs*, 10 July 1940). At the same time the Army leaders were becoming openly hostile to the Cabinet and the Kempeitai were menacing Arita (ibid.). On 17 July the Yonai Cabinet was compelled to resign. In the interval between its fall and the formation of the succeeding Cabinet fifteen British subjects in Japan were arrested for 'espionage'. This was done by the gendarmerie, supported by a pro-German clique in the War Ministry. One of those arrested was Mr. Melville Cox, Reuter's correspondent in Tokyo, who died while under examination at the gendarmerie headquarters, according to the Japanese, through jumping from a window. The whole affair appears to have been a deliberate attempt to precipitate war with England. After the formation of the Konoye Cabinet the British Ambassador took the matter up with the new Japanese Foreign Minister, Matsuoka, who co-operated in getting some of the accused released and others given 'suspended' sentences, which meant that they were able to leave Japan (Craigie, *Behind the Japanese Mask*, pp. 111–12).

price of relatively minor concessions to Japan, thanks in part to the continuance of the internal strife over domestic and foreign issues in Tokyo.[1]

[1] On 9 August it was announced that the remaining British troops were to be withdrawn from North China and from the International Settlement at Shanghai, where they had been garrisoning 'B' and 'D' Sectors. The Japanese Naval Landing Party wanted to take over both sectors, and on 15 August refused to accept a majority decision by the foreign commanders that they should receive only 'D' sector, while 'B' sector, in the heart of the Settlement, should be taken over by the American Marines. So, as a temporary arrangement, the Shanghai Volunteer Corps took over this sector. This remained the situation until the outbreak of the Pacific War.

CHAPTER VI

The USSR and the Sino-Japanese Conflict, 1937 to July 1940

THE Soviet Union, as the one Great Power which bordered on the combatant Chinese and Japanese, and which possessed strong military forces in the Far East, was unique in being able, should she choose, to exercise an immediate and decisive influence upon the course of the struggle. Upon her, therefore, the hopes and fears of the belligerents were centred to an especial degree. Despite her known weaknesses, armed intervention by the Soviet Union in support of China would have placed the Japanese armies in dire straits, particularly in 1938 when they were heavily engaged in Central China, and were suffering from ammunition shortages.[1] The possibility of this was a nightmare to the Japanese General Staff, and accounts in some degree for the piecemeal character of their operations in China, which contributed to rob them of decisive victory.[2] It was also a factor in their decision in 1939 to undertake no further general advance in China and to endeavour to achieve their ends by political and diplomatic, rather than by military, means. They wished to limit their expenditure of men and materials in the China conflict, even though they utilized this to secure from the Diet the appropriations for the expansion of armaments and war industries, under the 1936 programme.[3] This was planned to place the Japanese Army in a position of full readiness for war with the USSR by about 1940, or several years before that Power, as Tokyo calculated, would have finished *her* current programme of expansion in industry, communications, and general military and economic development in the Far East.[4]

Prior to the outbreak of the Sino-Japanese conflict the Soviet Government had been endeavouring to further improved relations with China. This was a slow process, because of Chinese sus-

---

[1] See above, pp. 73–76.   [2] See above, p. 73.   [3] See above, pp. 82–85.
[4] So General Machijiri is said to have told Kido in 1936 (*Saionji–Harada Memoirs*, 8 Jan. 1938). In March 1939 the Chief of Staff of the Kwantung Army was reported as saying that the Army was not yet ready to attack the USSR, but would like to do it before 1944 because by then the second Trans-Siberian line would be completed.

picions of the USSR and irritation over the *de facto* severance of
Outer Mongolia from China. It was of primary importance to the
Soviet Union that Chiang Kai-shek should not yield to Japanese
pressure and enter the anti-Comintern ranks and the progress of
the 'united front' policy in China after the Sian coup of December
1936 was doubtless viewed with satisfaction in Moscow. In April
1937 Bogomolov, the Soviet Ambassador to China, who had been
discussing with Sun Fo the terms of a projected Sino-Soviet
commercial treaty, returned from a visit to Moscow with suggestions that China should propose a conference of Pacific States;
and that she should conclude a non-aggression pact and a mutual
assistance pact with the USSR.[1] This appears to have been an
attempt to offset the overtures to Nanking of the Japanese Foreign
Minister, Naotake Sato. The Nanking Government, for several
reasons, thought a Pacific conference undesirable; and, for fear
of Japan, they would not look at the proposal for a Sino-Soviet
mutual assistance pact, although they were willing to open discussions for a non-aggression pact.[2] After the outbreak of hostilities
at Lukouchiao, the Chinese Government were ready to reconsider
their attitude towards the proposal for a mutual aid pact, but now
the Soviet envoy drew back, expressing some doubts on Chinese
will and capacity to resist Japan.[3] The Sino-Soviet Non-Aggression Pact was, however, concluded on 21 August 1937. This
bound the Soviet Union not to enter into any bargain with Japan
at the expense of China; on the other hand it, at any rate by implication, precluded China from lining up with the anti-Comintern
front.[4]

In addition to their diplomatic support of the Chinese cause,
especially at the Brussels Conference, the Soviet Government were
prompt in affording China material and technical assistance.
During the opening months of the Sino-Japanese struggle the
USSR sent arms and ammunition to China to the value of 100
million Chinese dollars prior to the conclusion of a definite loan
agreement.[5] In the autumn of 1937 General Yang Chieh, who
later became Chinese Ambassador to Moscow, went there to
arrange for further supplies, but was told by Voroshilov, the
Commissar for War, that a definite agreement for the repayment

---

[1] Aitchen K. Wu, *China and the Soviet Union* (London, Methuen, 1950),
p. 264.   [2] ibid.   [3] ibid.
[4] See above, p. 49.   [5] Wu, *China and the Soviet Union*, p. 268.

of the first loan was a prerequisite for the provision of any further assistance.[1] Early in 1938 Sun Fo, the head of the Russophil group within the Kuomintang, went to Moscow to urge that a second loan be granted. He had an interview with Stalin, who proposed that the value of the original loan should be fixed at US $50 million, and that a second loan of equal value should be made. Sun Fo wanted this to be larger, a suggestion which Stalin countered by promising a third loan after the second should be exhausted.[2] In May 1938 the first and second loan agreements were formally signed in Moscow.[3] By November 1938 the second Soviet loan had been almost all spent and renewed Chinese appeals for a further credit met with no immediate response. The Soviet Government were possibly waiting to see whether Chinese resistance would continue after the fall of Canton and Hankow. In April 1939 Sun Fo again visited Moscow, but was unable to see Stalin until 13 May. At this interview Stalin proved cordial and, according to General Yang Chieh's account of the conversation, said 'You may have a loan of any amount you require without putting forward any reasons.'[4] The third Sino-Soviet Agreement, for a loan of US $150 million, was concluded in June 1939. On 16 June Sun Fo and Mikoyan, the Soviet Commissar for Trade, also signed a Sino-Soviet Treaty of Commerce, which provided, *inter alia*, for most-favoured-nation treatment and for the establishment in Chungking of a Soviet trade delegation, with diplomatic privileges and immunities.[5]

Thus during the first two years of the Sino-Japanese conflict the USSR extended total credits of US $250 million to China, for the purchase of Russian arms and ammunition at prices fixed in American currency. The loan agreements provided for an interest rate of 3 per cent. and for repayment by China, over a period of years, in raw materials, chiefly brick-tea, wool, and tungsten.[6] During 1937–8 Soviet supplies came by sea from Odessa,[7] but after the fall of Canton, the land route from Alma Ata, on the

[1] ibid.   [2] ibid.   [3] ibid.   [4] ibid. p. 269.
[5] The USSR ratified the Treaty on 5 January 1940 and China followed suit on 23 January (ibid. p. 271).
[6] ibid. p. 269. The Soviet authorities agreed that the prices for their arms and ammunition supplies should be cheaper than American prices. In calculating the value of Chinese deliveries in repayment the pre-war exchange rate of the Chinese dollar was accepted as a basis.
[7] ibid. According to General Yang Chieh 60,000 tons of military supplies came via Odessa during 1937–9 (ibid.).

Turkestan-Siberian Railway, through Sinkiang (Chinese Tur-
kestan) to Lanchow, became the main artery of Sino-Soviet
traffic. During 1937–9 the Chinese authorities mobilized a great
mass of peasant labour to modernize this route sufficiently for it
to carry lorries loaded with ammunition and supplies, while camel
trains were organized to convey supplies of petrol to the various
fuelling stations along the route of over 2,000 miles.

These developments tended to consolidate Soviet influence in
the great province of Sinkiang, with its predominantly non-Chinese
population. That influence had been growing since 1933 when the
Russians had assisted Sheng Shih-tsai, the Governor of the region,
to defeat a Tungan (Chinese Moslem) rebellion, led by Ma Chung-
yin. This they had done, first, by allowing Chinese troops driven
from Manchuria by the Japanese to travel via Siberia to Sinkiang.[1]
In 1934 when, despite this reinforcement, Sheng Shih-tsai was on
the point of defeat, the Soviet Government responded to his appeal
by sending in two brigades of their own troops, with artillery,
tanks, and aircraft, to overthrow Ma Chung-yin and his allies.[2]

The Soviet Government justified these proceedings on the
ground that in aiding Sheng, whose appointment as Governor had
been endorsed by Nanking, they were upholding the authority of
the Chinese Government in Sinkiang, and helping to crush a
rebellion which the Japanese were said to have supported.[3] They
denied any intention of annexing Sinkiang, nor, indeed, was this
their policy, since it would have been an unnecessary affront to
Nanking. Until 1941 Sheng had perforce to rely upon Soviet
friendship; he appointed Soviet advisers to key positions in the
provincial administration, concluded loan agreements with the
USSR, and facilitated a virtual Soviet monopoly of the external
trade of the region.[4] Thus, with at first the active co-operation of
Sheng Shih-tsai, Communist propaganda made great headway in
the province, education on Marxist lines was extended, 'reaction-
ary' elements were eliminated, and students encouraged to go to
Alma Ata and Tashkent for further training. The Tungan–Turki
revolt of 1937–8 under General Ma Ho-san and Mahmoud She-
jang was a reaction against the spread of Communist ideas, which

---

Sir Eric Teichman, *Journey to Turkistan* (London, Hodder & Stoughton,
1937), p. 187.
[2] In April 1939 Stalin told Sun Fo that these troops had been disguised in
Chinese military uniforms (Wu, *China and the Soviet Union*, p. 258).
[3] So Stalin told Sun Fo (ibid. pp. 257–8).   [4] ibid. p. 258.

tended to undermine Islamic influence and authority. After the suppression of this revolt, at the beginning of 1938, also with Soviet armed assistance, no effective internal opposition was left.[1] Soviet garrisons were stationed at Ili and Hami, Soviet engineers were engaged in coal and oil extraction and, in September 1939, a Sino-Soviet Aviation Company was established for an air service between Hami and Alma Ata, with equal Chinese and Soviet shares of capital, and a Sino-Soviet Board of Directors. This air route linked, on the one hand, with a Chinese Government line from Chungking to Hami and, on the other, with a Soviet air line from Alma Ata to Moscow.[2]

With internal revolt crushed, 'anti-imperialist' propaganda was increasingly directed against the British Consulate-General at Kashgar and British Indian traders in southern Sinkiang. In 1939 many of these had their property confiscated and were forced to make the hazardous journey across the mountains to India.[3] Sheng Shih-tsai, himself, who was not a Communist, and who was mainly concerned in maintaining his own authority, was unable to prevent these developments, and indeed, found his own position increasingly threatened by the Soviet-trained officials in the Sinkiang administration. He had been initially willing to appoint these but now, despite his summary methods, found them a growing menace. Prior to the outbreak of the Soviet-German War, he dared not openly break with the Russians and their proteges, while the Chinese Central Government had to conceal their distaste of what was happening in Sinkiang, because of their need for continued Soviet diplomatic support and material assistance in their struggle with Japan.

Apart from Sinkiang, Soviet policy in regard to Chinese internal affairs was carefully circumspect in the first years of the Sino-Japanese conflict. Soviet supplies of arms and ammunition were delivered to the Chinese Central Government apparently without any stipulation that they should be shared with the Chinese Communist forces.[4] In the autumn of 1937 the first Soviet 'volunteer' airmen came to China to fly combat missions and to aid

---

[1] N. L. D. McLean, 'Sinkiang Today', *International Affairs*, July 1948, p. 381.
[2] Wu, *China and the Soviet Union*, pp. 260–1.
[3] McLean in *International Affairs*, July 1948, p. 381.
[4] Wu says the munitions were sent to Chungking and then distributed to the Chinese armies, including the Communist forces. The route from Hami to Chungking was under the control of the Kuomintang forces (*China and the Soviet Union*, p. 270).

in training the Chinese air force. Four fighter and two bomber squadrons were sent, the personnel being constantly rotated, so as to give actual battle experience to as many Soviet airmen as possible.[1] Soviet artillerists and other technicians were also sent to China to assist in the utilization of the equipment purchased from the USSR. But the Russians established their own hostels and kept very much to themselves.[2] They remained until the summer of 1938, when they were withdrawn in view of the menace of war in Europe.[3]

It was sound policy for the USSR to avoid any partisanship as between the Kuomintang and the Chinese Communists since this would have played right into the hands of the Japanese by further-ing disruption in China and so strengthening Wang Ching-wei and the 'peace group' within the Kuomintang. The Chinese Com-munists themselves, while quietly working to strengthen their position in the guerrilla areas, remained studiously moderate in tone, so that outward accord between the two parties was pre-served, although by 1939 it was beginning to show signs of breaking down. The Japanese put out frequent reports of Communist plans to establish a separate State in north-west China but they did not really believe this themselves, though they thought that it might be attempted in the event of a collapse of Kuomintang resistance to Japan.[4]

Soviet support of the Chinese cause, together with the measure of material aid which the USSR gave, served to offset the defection of Germany and to keep alive Chinese hopes of eventual full-scale Soviet intervention. Thus Soviet policy was an important factor in stimulating continued Chinese resistance, and resentment in Tokyo was correspondingly bitter. During 1938 Japanese protests against Soviet arms sales to China were rejected by the Soviet Government,[5] while general Japanese policy in China and the Far East was denounced in the harshest terms by Zhdanov, Molotov,

---

[1] Chennault, *Way of a Fighter*, pp. 61–62.
[2] ibid.
[3] E. F. Carlson, *The Chinese Army* (New York, IPR, 1940), p. 73.
[4] The appreciation of the situation in July 1939 by the Chief of Staff of the (Japanese) Central China Expeditionary Army said: 'the Communist Party is under the control of the National Party and has no capacity to create a new trend in the situation.' After the fall of Chiang the Communist Party 'will come under the sway of the Soviet Union and will settle in the North-West, in concert with Outer Mongolia' (IMTFE, *Record*, p. 3668).
[5] M. Beloff, *The Foreign Policy of Soviet Russia* (London, Oxford University Press for RIIA, 1948–9), ii. 184.

and Litvinov.[1] Equally bellicose statements came from the Japanese side, where no secret was made of Japanese military preparations to crush Soviet intervention if this became necessary.

Apart from the China issue, there were a number of other causes of quarrel between the USSR and Japan. Prominent among these was the perennial question of the Siberian fisheries. This dated back to the Russo-Japanese Treaty of Portsmouth of 1905, of which Article eleven provided that Japanese fishermen should have the right to pursue their calling in Russian Far Eastern waters. This broad provision was implemented by a Russo-Japanese Fishery Convention in 1907, under which the Japanese fishermen could establish canning factories at points on the Russian littoral, in return for payment of rent. After the Russian revolution the Japanese for a time enjoyed these rights without payment. In January 1925 the general Treaty which established relations between the Japanese and Soviet Governments recognized Japan's fishing rights under the Treaty of Portsmouth and agreed that a new fisheries convention should be concluded. The upshot was the Soviet-Japanese Fishery Convention of January 1928, which was to run for eight years. Under its terms fishing grounds were to be auctioned to various private companies, including Japanese. These privileges of fishing and of establishing fish-canning establishments were very valuable to the Japanese, not only because fish ranked along with rice as a staple item in the Japanese diet, but also because of the increasing Japanese exports of tinned fish.

But the Soviet Government regarded these concessions with a jaundiced eye. From the ideological standpoint they resented the exploitation of Soviet resources by foreign capitalists; from the strategic angle the concessions were an element of danger because of the opportunities they gave for espionage, and economically, the Japanese were competitors of the Soviet fishing interests, which Moscow desired to build up.[2] Consequently, while careful to avoid provoking Japan too much, the Soviet Government worked to limit as much as possible the privileges of her nationals under the 1928 convention. In 1928 the Japanese companies had leased

---

[1] ibid. pp. 189–91. Litvinov on 23 June 1938 declared that 'Japan in her programme of aggression likewise is not limiting herself by the boundaries of China and likewise [i.e. like Germany] sometimes permits herself to dream about Soviet lands' (RIIA, *Documents, 1938*, i. 319).

[2] D. J. Dallin, *The Rise of Russia in Asia* (London, World Affairs Book Club, 1950), pp. 245–6.

80 per cent. of the fishing grounds, but in subsequent years they encountered increasing rivalry from ostensibly private Russian fishing interests, with the result that by 1931 the Japanese share of the fishing grounds had fallen to 50 per cent. Japanese protests led to an agreement in 1932, the text of which was kept secret, but which appeared to have 'frozen' the existing situation by allowing Japanese fishing concerns to retain a stipulated number of fishing lots, without further auction, until the 1928 Treaty should expire.[1]

Soviet-Japanese negotiations for a new treaty at first made no headway and were suspended in June 1935. They were resumed in March 1936 and in the following May the 1928 Convention was extended until the end of the year. Prolonged negotiations led to the initialing of a new Fishery Convention in November, but upon the news of the German-Japanese Anti-Comintern Pact the Soviet Government, in retaliation, refused to sign the Convention.[2] They consented, in December 1936, to prolong the 1928 Convention for a further year, and, at the end of 1937, this process was repeated. But this left the Japanese fishing interests in a precarious condition and Moscow remained deaf to Tokyo demands that either the draft convention of 1936 should be ratified, or negotiations for a fresh one initiated.

By the Treaty of 1925 Japan had agreed to evacuate the northern half of the island of Sakhalin, which her troops had occupied; in return for this she was granted the right to exploit oil lands and coal mines in that area, subject to a yearly rental. Accordingly, in December 1925, two Japanese concerns, the North Sakhalin Petroleum Company and the North Sakhalin Mining Company, were established to develop these concessions.[3] Though not as important as the fisheries, they were valuable to Japan, especially in view of her poverty of resources in oil. The Soviet Government regarded them with equal dislike, and, as general Soviet-Japanese relations worsened in the nineteen-thirties, so the difficulties of the Japanese companies grew. They complained that the Soviet authorities would neither supply adequate Russian labour, nor

---

[1] ibid. pp. 246–7.

[2] The Fisheries Convention was to have been signed on 20 November, but news of the imminent signature of the Anti-Comintern Pact leaked out in Tokyo before that date, which laid the Japanese Government open to criticism by its political opponents (Grew, *Ten Years in Japan*, pp. 174–5). The conclusion of the Pact was criticized by some of the Privy Councillors because it had endangered Japan's valuable fishing privileges.

[3] Dallin, *Rise of Russia in Asia*, p. 248.

allow them to bring in enough Japanese workers. There was constant trouble with the Russian workers, fomented, so the Japanese alleged, by the Soviet authorities.[1]

The Soviet Government had grievances on their side, especially in connexion with the terms of the sale of the Chinese Eastern Railway to Manchukuo in 1935. The Manchukuo Government, which of course in fact meant the Japanese, suspended the promised payment of pensions to former employees of the Chinese Eastern Railway. In March 1938 Manchukuo refused to pay the final instalment of the purchase price for the line, on the ostensible ground that there were unpaid debts owing to the line from the Soviet Government. Japan held the stronger position here; Soviet protests to Tokyo were referred to Hsinking, to the irritation of the Soviet Government, which knew and declared that Manchukuo was but a puppet of Japan.[2]

All these matters were susceptible of peaceful settlement, but the mutual animosity and distrust made proposals for an accommodation abortive. The result was a general tension, and, while responsible officials on both sides desired to avoid war, there was always the danger of an armed clash being provoked through the action of less prudent elements.

In July 1938 such an armed clash occurred at Changkufeng, a hill near Lake Khassan, on the Manchukuo-Soviet border, not far from Possiet Bay. At the time of the affray the place was declared to have considerable strategic importance, but neither side had hitherto troubled about this, nor had any question of the boundary been raised.[3] The initial fighting was little more than

[1] *NYT*, 22 July 1939.
[2] The Japanese Government had guaranteed the full payment of the sale price.
[3] The Soviet General Grebennick, who in 1938 was a Colonel commanding the Soviet border guards in the Zhozernaya (Changkufeng) region, told the Tokyo Tribunal that there was no border problem and that his guards knew precisely where the boundary line was. The eastern slope of the hill was Soviet territory and the western was Manchurian (IMTFE, *Record*, pp. 38284–300). He accused the Japanese of beginning the trouble, but Japanese defence witnesses declared that Soviet patrols began it by occupying the crest of the hill, where hitherto Korean villagers had held periodic festivals without being interfered with by the Russians. Aitchen K. Wu, who was Chinese Consul-General at Vladivostok at the time, calls the affair 'a direct Soviet challenge to Japan—"Manchukuo"' (*China and the Soviet Union*, p. 273). One consequence of the affair was the removal of Marshal Blücher from his command of the Soviet forces in the Far East and his disappearance from public life. According to Ivan Krylov, Blücher 'believed that war with Japan was necessary and provoked the "two hills incident" which ultimately cost him his life'. Krylov says that Blücher was imprisoned in the Lubianka where he hanged himself (*Soviet*

patrol skirmishes, but each side brought up reinforcements, including heavy artillery and tanks, and a considerable battle ensued in which the Japanese appear to have got rather the worst of it. On 2 August the Japanese Cabinet decided to settle the matter by negotiation, if possible, and Shigemitsu, then Ambassador to Moscow, was instructed accordingly.[1] His initial claims that the disputed area belonged to Manchukuo were firmly rejected by Litvinov, who produced a map which he declared had been attached to the Russian copy of the protocol of 1886 which supplemented the Russo-Chinese Treaty of Hunchun of 1869, and which justified the Soviet claims. Shigemitsu, finding that no progress could be made along these lines, asked Tokyo for authority to conclude a temporary truce agreement pending a later definition of the boundary.[2] Tokyo agreed, and Litvinov was also agreeable, but he insisted that Soviet forces should retain the positions they held, and suggested that the Japanese forces should fall back a kilometre, so as to leave a no-man's-land in the disputed zone.[3] To this Shigemitsu, after further consultation with Tokyo, consented, and so the hostilities ended on 11 August.[4] Litvinov had proposed that the truce should be followed by the appointment of a joint boundary commission to define the frontier, but this was never done, since no agreement could be reached on the validity of the Hunchun protocol and map.[5]

Staff Officer (London, Falcon Press, 1951), p. 9). But it is doubtful how much reliance can be placed upon Krylov's reminiscences.

[1] *Saionji–Harada Memoirs*, 2 Aug. 1938.
[2] ibid. 10 Aug. 1938.
[3] IMTFE, *Record*, pp. 23905–10.
[4] ibid. also *Saionji–Harada Memoirs*, 13 Aug. 1938.
[5] The Changkufeng affair was included in the Soviet case against Japan at the International Military Tribunal hearings in Tokyo. Here the Russians produced a photostatic copy of the Russian text of Annex I of the Sino–Russian protocol of 1886, which defined the boundary in the Hunchun area (IMTFE, *Exhibit* 753). The defence applied to the Chinese Ministry of Foreign Affairs for a copy of the Chinese text of this instrument. The Chinese replied that a search had been made, but the document and maps were not available for production or copy (*Record*, pp. 34500–1). They referred to a 1936 collection of Sino-foreign treaties as containing an accepted text of the protocol and Annexes, but the prosecution objected to this as not being the original (ibid.).

The majority judgment of the IMTFE held that the Japanese had initiated the hostilities at Changkufeng, and that the attack had been planned by the Japanese General Staff and by Itagaki, then Minister of War (*Judgment*, p. 833). This decision was influenced by an entry in the *Saionji–Harada Memoirs* for 28 July 1938, according to which Matsudaira had told Harada that Prince Kanin, the Chief of Staff, and Itagaki had forced an audience with the Emperor and advocated war with the USSR, declaring that the Foreign Minister and the Navy Minister had agreed to this. This the Emperor knew to be untrue, and he severely reprimanded them. Itagaki, however, strongly denied this story in the

While a general conflict was thus averted, Soviet-Japanese relations grew worse in the ensuing months. Tojo, then Vice-Minister of War, on 28 November told a gathering of Japanese munition makers that Japan had to prepare to fight both China and the Soviet Union. When the Diet met in January 1939 some members criticized this speech. Itagaki replied that the Army had no intention of making an attack upon the Soviet Union, but 'against any unjustifiable aggression on their part, I reiterate that we are prepared to beat them back and destroy them without hesitation.' He added that the connexion between a settlement of the China Incident and military preparations against the Soviet Union was so close as to make these two policies identical.[1] As has been seen, the Army and the Cabinet were agreed that the proposed military pact with Germany and Italy should be primarily directed against the USSR, with the object of either forcing that Power to abandon support of China, or confronting her with a two-front war.[2] Moscow had some knowledge of these negotiations, and this served still farther to exacerbate Soviet relations with Japan.[3] The Japanese, for their part, were alarmed at the Anglo-Soviet negotiations in the spring and summer of 1939, which they feared might result in an Anglo-Soviet line-up against them in the Far East.[4]

During the first half of 1939 the local issues of the fisheries and the Sakhalin concessions produced fresh embitterment. In December 1938 the Soviet Government refused to prolong the life of the 1928 Fisheries Convention for a further year unless the Japanese agreed to give up some forty of the fishing grounds. Discussion on this matter between Togo and Litvinov during the first two months of 1939 were fruitless. The Soviet Government then declared their intention of holding an auction on 13 March, at Vladivostok, at which the fishing lots thrown open to bids would include those

course of his defence (IMTFE, *Record*, p. 30477), and was supported in this by General Usami, who had been chief ADC to the Emperor in 1938. But as Usami was not very sure of his dates and could not say he had been present at the actual interview, his affidavit was rejected by the Court. Other entries in the *Saionji–Harada Memoirs* themselves go to show that Itagaki, whatever his initial attitude had been, did his best to limit the conflict, in line with the decision of 2 August, in face of some recalcitrance on the part of the Kwantung Army (*Saionji–Harada Memoirs*, 5 and 10 Aug. 1938).

[1] *NYT*, 26 Feb. 1939.   [2] See above, p. 107.
[3] On 17 November 1938 Litvinov told Viscount Chilston, the British Ambassador, that he had 'sure knowledge' that the Anti-Comintern Pact was to be transformed into an alliance (*D Brit.FP*, 3rd series, iii. 280).
[4] See above, p. 120.

which the Japanese claimed should be reserved to Japanese companies. The Japanese Foreign Ministry in reply declared that Japan would not accept the results of the auction and that she might be constrained to act in self-defence should the Soviet Union resort to such unilateral action.[1] The Japanese press underlined this by threats that Japanese fishermen would continue to use the disputed fishing grounds, and would be backed by a naval escort.

Whether on account of this, or because of the renewed crisis in Europe, the Soviet Government modified their attitude. They indeed held the auction, but the Soviet State fishery organization bought only four lots. On 20 March it was announced that further auctions would be postponed until 3 April, because of the lack of buyers.[2] But at the latter date a Soviet-Japanese agreement was announced, by the terms of which thirty-seven former Japanese fishing grounds were given up, but ten new ones were conceded to Japanese companies. At the same time the 1928 convention was extended until the end of 1939.[3]

In the summer of 1939 renewed trouble over the Japanese oil concessions in Sakhalin was likewise tided over. The local Russian Workers' Union had sued the Japanese North Sakhalin Petroleum Company for non-fulfilment of its labour contract, and Soviet local courts in Sakhalin had sentenced it to pay heavy fines under pain of confiscation. The Company officials complained that Soviet obstructive tactics had reduced oil production to almost nothing. Tokyo protested to Moscow on 16 July, but the protest was rejected and mutual recriminations followed.[4] However, in early August a new agreement between the Japanese concession-naires and the Soviet oil workers, by which the latter received increased wages and other benefits, caused the trouble to subside.[5] The Japanese Government had made it clear that they would not be jockeyed out of the concessions, and Moscow could afford to wait.

More serious than these affairs was the outbreak of another conflict, this time on the border between the Mongol People's Republic and Manchukuo. This began in May 1939, in the district south-east of Buir Nor where the territory of the Mongol People's

---

[1] *NYT*, 16 March 1939.   [2] *The Times*, 20 March 1939.
[3] *NYT*, 5 April 1939. The Japanese were said to have acquired 366 fishing grounds, 264 of these on a 'permanent' basis.
[4] ibid. 16 July 1939.   [5] ibid. 12 Aug. 1939.

Republic formed a salient between the Manchukuo Province of North Hsingan and the Inner Mongolian Province of Chahar. Here the Khalka River flows north-eastward to empty into Lake Buir. On the right bank of the Khalka are some hillocks, called the Bolshegol heights, of which Nomonhan, some 150 feet high, is the largest.[1] The heights had some strategic value because of the level plain all around. The Manchukuo Government claimed that the Khalka River was the boundary between Manchukuo and Outer Mongolia, whereas the Government of the Mongol People's Republic declared that it lay some miles east of that river.[2] The fighting began in May, each side as usual accusing the other of initiating it.[3] It soon swelled to considerable proportions, with aircraft on both sides in operation. In June-July the Kwantung Army brought up a large force from their railhead at Halunarshan and drove back the Soviet and Outer Mongol forces to the Khalka.[4] But their triumph was short-lived, for the Russians dispatched strong reinforcements of first-line troops, with heavy flame-throwing tanks, which the Japanese could not match. On 20 August these attacked and inflicted a heavy defeat upon the Japanese, who were driven out of the disputed territory. The Tokyo War Ministry later admitted that the Kwantung Army had sustained 18,000 casualties while the Russians claimed that the Japanese Sixth Army had been destroyed.[5] To the bitterness of defeat was added the disquieting revelation of Japanese technical inferiority to the Russians, and this at a time when the conclusion of the German-Soviet Non-Aggression Pact appeared to have set the USSR free to turn her whole attention to the Far East.

Up to this time the struggle had been nominally one between Manchukuo and Outer Mongolia; the Japanese troops were engaged as allies of Manchukuo by virtue of the Japan–Manchukuo Treaty of Mutual Assistance of 1932, and the Soviet forces as

[1] ibid. 9 and 10 July 1939.
[2] The Soviet Major Bykov, who in 1939 commanded a battalion of Soviet troops stationed in Outer Mongolia and who fought at Nomonhan, told the Tokyo Tribunal that the frontier lay from twenty to twenty-five kilometres east of the Khalka, and was marked by boundary posts with inscriptions on them (IMTFE, *Record*, p. 38368).
[3] The Tokyo Tribunal held that hostilities were initiated by the Kwantung Army but that there was no evidence of complicity on the part of the General Staff or the Government in Tokyo (IMTFE, *Judgment*, pp. 837–9).
[4] *The Times*, 11 July 1939.
[5] ibid. 13 July 1940. Among those who participated in the battle on the Soviet side was the future Marshal Zhukov. He gave an account of it to foreign correspondents in Berlin in June 1945 (*NYT*, 11 June 1945).

allies of Outer Mongolia under the Pact of Mutual Assistance
concluded in 1936. But in early September it seemed as though
these fictions would be discarded and that the two principals
would come out into the open in direct and general conflict. The
defeated Japanese general issued a proclamation declaring that the
Army must avenge its defeat and inflict a crushing blow upon the
enemy, while General Ueda, the Japanese Commander-in-Chief,
hurried up reinforcements and enforced air-raid precautions and
other emergency measures over all Manchuria.[1]

But neither Tokyo nor Moscow wanted a general war. In
Tokyo the new Government headed by General Abe, badly shaken
by Japanese diplomatic and military reverses, opened negotiations
for a settlement with the USSR. The Soviet Government, intently
watching the swift progress of German arms in Poland, and anxious
to make sure of the promised share of the booty, were equally ready
for peace. Accordingly, Togo and Molotov reached agreement
upon an armistice, which came into effect on 16 September. It provided that the respective armies at Nomonhan should remain where
they were, which in fact left the Russians in possession of the area in
dispute, and that a Commission should be appointed, with equal
Japanese–Manchukuoan and Soviet–Outer Mongol representation,
to endeavour to settle the boundary in the theatre of hostilities.[2]

During the latter part of 1939, following the armistice at Nomonhan, there was a slight improvement in the relations between Japan
and the USSR. On 27 October 1939 the two Powers reached an
agreement for the mutual release of fishing vessels detained on
charges of poaching.[3] On 6 November the arrival of Mr. Smetanin
as Soviet Ambassador to Japan where for sixteen months the
USSR had been represented only by a chargé d'affaires, marked
a further easing of tension between the two countries. In Moscow
the discussions between Togo and Lozovsky resulted in an agreement on the formation of a mixed commission to settle the boundary

---

[1] IMTFE, *Judgment*, p. 837.
[2] *NYT*, 16 Sept. 1939. One consequence of the affair was the removal of
General Ueda. On 17 September Admiral Nomura told Harada that Abe had
offered him the portfolio of Foreign Affairs, but that he had said he could not
accept unless the Kwantung Army was restrained from waging war on the
USSR. Abe replied that the Commander-in-Chief had been changed and it was
intended also to replace the staff officers of the Kwantung Army (*Saionji–Harada
Memoirs*, 17 Sept. 1939). The probable object of the Kwantung Army was to
push back the frontier to the Khalka to give more protection for a planned rail
line from Halunarshan to Hailar. See Jones, *Manchuria Since 1931*, p. 111.
[3] *NYT*, 27 Oct. 1939.

questions between Outer Mongolia and Manchukuo and between Manchukuo and the USSR. The commission held its first meeting in Chita on 7 December, and after seven further sessions on 25 December reached an agreement as to procedure. It then removed to Harbin to get down to the real work of boundary delimitation.[1]

Togo had opened negotiations for the conclusion of a long-term fisheries agreement and for a commercial treaty, and in these spheres also some progress was made. Preliminary discussions for a commercial treaty resulted in an agreement in principle on 19 November, and this was followed by conversations in Moscow between Togo, together with Matsushima, Minister to Sweden and a former head of the Commercial Bureau of the Gaimusho, and Molotov and Mikoyan.[2] On 31 December a Soviet-Japanese *modus vivendi* provided for the extension of the existing fisheries agreement for another year, pending the conclusion of a long-term treaty, and for the payment of the last instalment of the purchase price of the Chinese Eastern Railway.[3]

These promising developments were destined to be interrupted during the spring of 1940. The Soviet-Japanese Boundary Commission, after holding eight conferences in Harbin between 5 and 30 January, came to a complete deadlock over the Nomonhan area, since neither side was willing to accept the maps put forward by the other, and on 31 January it was announced that the Commission had found agreement impossible and would disband.[4] Arita on 10 February told the Japanese Diet that negotiations with the USSR had broken down, but he added that they would be resumed. He said that while there was no room for optimism with regard to a successful readjustment of Soviet-Japanese relations, undue pessimism would also be unjustified.[5]

In mid-March the trade talks reached an impasse and a month later Matsushima returned to Sweden. At the same time the negotiations for a new fisheries treaty were reported to have reached a standstill.[6]

[1] IMTFE, *Record*, p. 23100.
[2] *NYT*, 20 and 25 Nov. 1939. The treaty of 1925, which inaugurated diplomatic relations between Japan and the USSR, had contemplated subsequent commercial negotiations, but hitherto nothing had been done. After the outbreak of the European War the severance of seaborne trade between Japan–Manchukuo and Germany accentuated the importance of transit trade via the Soviet Union. Direct Soviet–Japanese trade was of minor importance.
[3] *The Times*, 6 Jan. 1940.   [4] *NYT*, 31 Jan. 1940.
[5] ibid. 11 Feb. 1940.   [6] ibid. 8 and 15 April 1940.

In his speech on foreign affairs delivered before the Supreme Soviet on 29 March Molotov, while referring to the questions which 'not without some difficulty' had been settled at the end of 1939, declared that 'we cannot express great satisfaction in regard to our relations with Japan'.[1] He denounced suggestions in the Japanese Diet that the USSR might sell north Sakhalin and the Maritime Province to Japan and remarked that *per contra* the Japanese might think of selling the southern part of Sakhalin to the USSR.

Behind this recrudescence of trouble lay the question of the general political relations of the two countries. Ever since the conclusion of the German-Soviet Non-Aggression Pact the German Government had been urging the Japanese to follow suit. This would facilitate a Japanese southward move at the expense of Great Britain and also ease the way for the development of German-Japanese-Manchukuo trade across the Soviet Union.

Ott in Tokyo was instructed to work for a Soviet-Japanese non-aggression pact and he was reinforced by Stahmer, Ribbentrop's personal agent, in February 1940.[2] Oshima and Shiratori, after their return to Tokyo, became ardent sponsors of a Soviet-Japanese pact and gained some adherents. But resentment at the German action, fear of Communism, and suspicion of the Soviet Union were formidable obstacles to overcome.

Shigenori Togo was also an advocate of a Soviet-Japanese pact, although not on account of any love for the Axis, at least on his own showing and that of his diplomatic subordinates.[3] According to the evidence of Saburo Ota, who was at this time Third Secretary of the Japanese Embassy at Moscow, Togo 'at the end of 1939 or beginning of 1940' sent Saito, another Secretary of the Japanese Embassy, to Tokyo to urge that he be given permission to open negotiations for a Soviet-Japanese pact, and Arita gave him instructions to proceed.[4] Neither Ota nor Togo in his own evidence was precise on when the instructions were received, but Togo said that they came 'at length', and the probability is that he did not get them until the late spring or early summer of 1940.[5] Stahmer and

---

[1] ibid. 8 April 1940.   [2] IMTFE, *Record*, pp. 6127–30, 6141–2.
[3] For Togo's opposition to the proposed Tripartite Pact of 1939 see above, p. 105. He told the Tokyo Tribunal that he had advised a Soviet–Japanese pact as early as 1933 (IMTFE, *Record*, p. 35638).   [4] ibid. p. 23103.
[5] On 13 May Arita told Harada that the Cabinet was discussing the conclusion of a Soviet–Japanese Non-Aggression Pact. This was considered an essential preliminary to the conclusion of a military pact between Japan, Germany, and Italy (*Saionji–Harada Memoirs*, 22 May 1940).

Ott, in their reports to Ribbentrop during early 1940, made it clear that the weight of opinion in Japan, especially among the Court party and the Cabinet, was hostile to the USSR and this was borne out by Japanese official pronouncements.

Thus Arita, in the course of his speech to the Japanese Diet on 31 January 1940, declared that Japan would continue her policy of close relationship with all the Powers who had signed the Anti-Comintern Pact. He added that the USSR 'should cease interfering in the industrial concessions of North Sakhalin, modify her policy of supporting the anti-Japanese régime in China, and collaborate for the realization of general peace in Eastern Asia'.[1] On 22 March he again referred to the continued existence of the Anti-Comintern Pact.[2] Soviet assistance to Chungking and the hostile attitude of the Soviet press towards Japanese policy in China were major stumbling blocks in the way of a rapprochement between the two Powers, especially since the involvement of Great Britain and France in the European War made Soviet aid to China of more importance than before.

The Soviet-Finnish War and the possibility, which in early March, almost became an actuality, of Anglo-French intervention on behalf of Finland, opened up a new prospect to the Japanese Government. If the Western Allies had become involved in war with the USSR, they might have been prepared to come to terms with Japan about China, in return for her assistance. The hardening of the Japanese attitude towards the USSR, and the drawing up by the Japanese General Staff of a new plan of campaign against the USSR, which was approved by the Emperor in March,[3] were very probably connected with such anticipations.[4]

But the Soviet-Finnish peace and the German offensive in Western Europe changed the situation. The Soviet Union was freed from the Finnish entanglement and from danger of war with the Allies; to that degree its position *vis-à-vis* Japan was strengthened. On the other hand the collapse of France and the prospect of a complete German victory could hardly be regarded without misgivings in Moscow, which would be the less inclined to risk

[1] *The Times*, 1 Feb. 1940.   [2] ibid. 23 March 1940.
[3] IMTFE, *Record*, pp. 7526–8.
[4] The Japanese paper *Chugai Shogyo* on 17 December 1939 had declared that the Allies would sooner or later be involved in war with the USSR, and that as the USSR was so situated geographically that no foreign Power, except Japan, could effectively check her, Japan might have an important role to play. See also above, p. 162.

embroilment in the Far East. Japan, however, was still bogged down in China, and her Army, after Nomonhan, had less zest for engaging the USSR in addition. Moreover, Japan wanted a Soviet assurance that she would not be attacked by the USSR should she embark upon some southward adventure. On the whole, therefore, she was in the weaker diplomatic position, and so had to give way on the Nomonhan question.

Consequently, in March 1940 Togo resumed negotiations upon the disputed Manchukuo–Outer Mongolia border and, after protracted discussions, an Agreement was reached on 9 June between Togo and Molotov, which defined the boundary in the Nomonhan area according to the Soviet claims.[1] On 18 July a joint Border Commission was agreed upon.[2]

According to Yoshio Noguchi, who acted as interpreter between Togo and Molotov, it was in early July that Togo made proposals for a political agreement. These were that the two Powers should confirm that the basic treaty (of 1925) should continue to govern their relationships; that if either of them were to be attacked by a third Power or Powers, the other should remain neutral throughout the conflict, and that the pact should last for five years. Molotov 'some days later' agreed in principle and in mid-August declared that the USSR was prepared to accept the proposed pact on condition that the Japanese gave up their coal and oil concessions in north Sakhalin. Togo recommended to Tokyo that this stipulation should be accepted, and the pact concluded.[3] But by this time the Yonai Cabinet had fallen and had been replaced by one with Konoye at the head and Yosuke Matsuoka as Foreign Minister. At this time, as will be seen, Matsuoka, so far from agreeing to surrender the Sakhalin concessions, was hoping to purchase the Soviet half of that island. He expected to accomplish this, as well as the larger aim of inducing Moscow to abandon support of Chungking, through the conclusion of a treaty between Japan and the Axis Powers in Europe. This he reckoned would bring the Soviet Union into line with Japanese policy, an idea which Ribbentrop and Stahmer sedulously fostered. So, on 29 August, Togo

---

[1] 'The frontier line between the Mongol People's Republic and Manchukuo in the above-mentioned area runs as it is shown on the map published by the Red Army General Staff in 1935, Scale: $1 = 200,000$, which is attached to the present agreement' (IMTFE, *Record*, p. 7851).

[2] ibid. pp. 23101–2.

[3] ibid. pp. 35380–2.

was recalled and was ordered to suspend the negotiations for a Soviet-Japanese pact, pending the arrival of his successor.[1]

[1] ibid.; also evidence of Togo (ibid. p. 35619). According to the *Saionji–Harada Memoirs*, an Inner Cabinet Conference was held on 19 August, at which it was decided to conclude an alliance with Germany and Italy, and also a non-aggression pact with the Soviet Union. The latter was to have a duration of five or ten years, during which time Japan could build up her military forces and war potential *vis-à-vis* the USSR, while she took advantage of the immediate situation to establish the Greater East Asia Co-Prosperity Sphere at the expense of the British, Dutch, and French.

CHAPTER VII

Japan, Germany, and the USSR

1940–1

THE German victories in Europe sealed the fate of the Yonai Cabinet. They had failed to reach any agreement with Great Britain and the United States which would have facilitated the longed-for disposal of the China Incident and they were now accused of having 'backed the wrong horse'. Japan desired to reach an understanding with Germany upon the division of the spoils once Great Britain was overthrown, which seemed to be but a matter of time. But the German Government received Japanese overtures with some coolness and made it apparent that they were not prepared to work with a Government which hitherto had kept aloof from them.[1] This policy had the intended effect; the Japanese military leaders resolved to get rid of the Yonai Cabinet and to replace it by one which could achieve the desired co-operation with the Axis in foreign affairs, and fashion a totalitarian structure at home.

Marquis Kido, who had become Lord Keeper of the Privy Seal on 31 May 1940, had, as his own diary reveals, been working for some time to secure the appointment of Konoye as successor to Yonai.[2] He wanted to placate the Army for fear of another coup d'état,[3] and both he and the military leaders knew that Konoye, however reluctantly, would swim with the tide. So both the Kido group at Court and the Army were agreed upon Konoye as leader of the 'new political structure' which was being formed to replace the parliamentary parties, and as the next Premier.[4]

It remained to get rid of the Yonai Cabinet, and, as Yonai

---

[1] Ott, on 19 June 1940, reported to Berlin that he had been sounded out by the Japanese on the possibility of Germany giving Japan a free hand in Indo-China. He suggested that Berlin avoid any commitment so as to promote the fall of the Yonai Cabinet and its replacement by 'one which would be close to us' (IMTFE, *Record*, pp. 6164–5). See also below, pp. 221–2.

[2] ibid. pp. 6242–3.

[3] On 4 July the police arrested a group of the Shimpeitai, and seized a cache of arms. The plotters planned to kill Yonai, Harada, and Matsudaira, among others (*Saionji–Harada Memoirs*, 10 July 1940).

[4] Konoye resigned on 24 June as President of the Privy Council to free himself for these new tasks (ibid. 28 June 1940).

refused to be accommodating, the Army had recourse to its favourite device. On 16 July it brought about the resignation of the War Minister, General Hata, and refused to recommend a successor, which compelled the resignation of the Yonai Cabinet.[1] The Emperor did not want to see the Cabinet overthrown and showed some resentment, but he dared not make any open stand against the Army. Meanwhile, Kido had already formulated a plan for the choice of a new Cabinet. The aged Genro, Prince Saionji, was to be consulted as a matter of form, but the real decision was to be taken at a meeting of Kido and Hara, the new President of the Privy Council, with the six ex-Premiers. Here Kido proposed to be responsible for securing unanimity of opinion.[2] This plan was duly carried into effect and the choice, as expected, fell upon Konoye.[3] Saionji, who was nearing his end, appears to have washed his hands of the whole affair, so that Kido could tell the Emperor that the Genro did not disapprove and Konoye received the imperial command to form a Cabinet.[4]

In choosing the members of his Cabinet Konoye, even had he desired, could not have avoided the selection of General Hideki Tojo as War Minister, for this decision rested with the Army Chiefs.[5] But, if Kido may be believed, the Army left the choice of

---

[1] The prime movers in this were Anami, the Vice-Minister of War; Muto, the head of the Military Affairs section of the War Ministry; and Prince Kanin, the Chief of the Army General Staff. Hata was almost certainly an unwilling participant in the affair. General Shigeru Sawada, who at this time was Vice-Chief of the General Staff, testified before the Tokyo Tribunal that when Kanin heard that the Cabinet, in contrast to the Army, was against an Axis Pact, he ordered Sawada to consult with Anami on how to get over this. Anami said that in his view, though it was not shared by Hata, the Cabinet must go. Sawada then, on Kanin's order, wrote a letter, which Kanin signed, for delivery to Hata. Sawada declared that the letter said that there must be a new and stronger Cabinet to secure German help in ending the China Incident and in effect told Hata to resign which, after receipt of it, he did (IMTFE, *Exhibit* 3205). The letter itself could not be found for production in Court (*Record*, pp. 29010–16). Yonai told the Court that 'when I received General Hata's resignation I believed that he was forced to resign, not of his own will, but through outside forces. I am today still convinced that this was so' (ibid. p. 28918). There is, however, an entry in the *Saionji–Harada Memoirs*, 12 July 1940, which says that Hata told Yonai that Anami and Muto were expressing their personal views, but that he (Hata) thought it best the Cabinet should resign. This may have been because he realized what the Army would do if it did not.

[2] *Saionji–Harada Memoirs*, 20 July 1940. The ex-Premiers were Wakatsuki, Okada, Hirota, Hayashi, Hiranuma, and Konoye himself.   [3] ibid.

[4] Saionji said: 'Only when it suits them do they make me responsible. Leave it to Kido' (ibid.).

[5] General Noda, at this time Chief of the Personnel Bureau of the War Ministry, testified that 'it was the feeling in Army circles that no one except Lt.-General Tojo would do' (IMTFE, *Record*, pp. 29395–6).

a Foreign Minister to Konoye, and the Emperor advised him to exercise prudence in the matter.[1] His powers of selection were in fact somewhat restricted for he needed someone who could get along with the Army and who would be well-regarded in Germany, with whom Japan wished to strike a bargain. That, for the one reason or the other, ruled out Arita, Shigemitsu, Togo, and Hirota. Shiratori, who was angling for the post of Vice-Foreign Minister, was hardly of sufficient seniority for the higher position, and was probably regarded by the cautious Court party as too pro-Axis. So Konoye decided upon Yosuke Matsuoka, probably because he felt that Matsuoka would not be too subservient to either Army or Axis. But as things turned out he could not have made a worse choice, for Matsuoka, apart from not being a professional diplomat, was completely lacking in stability. He was, indeed, very much the Japanese counterpart of Ribbentrop.

The new Foreign Minister was naturally self-assertive, conceited, and garrulous. To these innate qualities his education in the United States had added a blunt and direct manner which was not typical of his countrymen, who are normally outwardly polite, reticent, and unobtrusive. After his graduation at Oregon Law College, Matsuoka had spent some years in the Japanese Foreign Service, where he was very much a fish out of water. His colleagues mostly detested him, a sentiment which he heartily reciprocated, declaring more than once that he hated diplomacy and diplomats.[2] In 1921 he found more congenial employment with the South Manchuria Railway Company, of which he became Vice-President in 1927, and President from 1935-9. In the meanwhile he had been chief Japanese Delegate to the League of Nations Assembly during the Manchurian crisis and had brusquely announced Japan's departure from the League after her actions in Manchuria had been condemned. Since 1930 he had been active in politics, and had been prominent in demanding an end of the old parties and the establishment of a totalitarian structure. He was also a fervent believer in the establishment of Great East Asia, with Japan as the paramount Power.[3]

[1] ibid. pp. 6243, 6255. According to the *Saionji–Harada Memoirs*, Konoye in mid-June had asked Harada how Matsuoka would do as Foreign Minister.

[2] One of his first actions as Foreign Minister was to 'purge' the diplomatic and consular services; the dismissals and enforced resignations were ostensibly for political reasons to get rid of those unsympathetic to a pro-Axis alignment—but no doubt Matsuoka took the opportunity to pay off old scores.

[3] He had written several pamphlets on these subjects during 1933-40, and

Matsuoka appears to have been confident that he could make use of the Axis Powers, while not committing himself too fully to their side.[1] He told Shigemitsu that Italy would be subordinated to Germany in the future, but that Japan, because of her geographical situation, could preserve her independence. She should pursue what he termed 'an independent parallel policy, similar to that of the Soviet Union'. Japan should take advantage of the German victories in Europe to descend upon the territories of France, Holland, and Portugal in the Far East, and thus secure the maximum of benefit with the minimum risk of involvement in war.[2] But he also believed that Great Britain would be crushed by Hitler, that Japan could then seize upon her Far Eastern possessions, and that the United States could be prevented from aiding Great Britain by the threat of Japan's active intervention on the other side. These misconceptions led him to pursue a course which gave Japan the worst of both worlds. The Axis Powers mistrusted her, not without reason, and never gave her their full confidence, while the Democracies regarded her as an enemy who was simply awaiting her opportunity. Thus Matsuoka's fatal year of office saw Japan get into a situation from which she could extricate herself only by accepting humiliation or by risking her all in war.

The four chief Ministers in the new Cabinet—Konoye, Tojo, Matsuoka, and Yoshida (the Navy Minister)—agreed upon the principle of an Axis pact at the same time as they accepted office. Muto and Oka—the head of the Naval Affairs Bureau of the Navy Ministry—were ordered to prepare a draft agreement.[3] Then on 1 August Matsuoka in Tokyo and Kurusu in Berlin renewed the Japanese soundings of Germany with respect to her attitude to the Greater East Asia Sphere.[4] Matsuoka's overtures received a more favourable response from Hitler and Ribbentrop than that accorded to those of his predecessor, Arita. This, it may be inferred, was owing not only to the fact that the new Japanese Cabinet was regarded by Berlin as more trustworthy than that of Yonai, but also

in May 1941 published a book entitled *The Great Task of Reconstructing Asia*, in which he urged 'Nipponism' at home and expansion abroad.
    [1] Konoye had wanted Shiratori to be Vice-Minister of Foreign Affairs, but Matsuoka preferred Chuichi Ohashi, a fellow 'Manchurian'. Shiratori was made adviser to the Foreign Ministry but said that he had no influence and was not consulted (IMTFE, *Record*, p. 35049).
    [2] Matsuoka to Shigemitsu, 5 Aug. 1940 (ibid. pp. 9712–13).
    [3] Preliminary interrogation of Matsuoka at Sugamo, 15 March 1946.
    [4] IMTFE, *Record*, pp. 6280–5, 6331–5.

because German hopes of a quick end to the European conflict were fading after the failure of Hitler's peace feeler to Great Britain in his speech of 19 July. A long and hard struggle lay ahead and one in which the possibility of American participation could not be entirely ruled out. Furthermore, the first signs of rift in the German-Soviet partnership were appearing, and Hitler was meditating an attack upon the USSR. It was therefore deemed necessary to secure Japan's adhesion to the Axis and to pay her price for this.

Accordingly, towards the end of August, Ribbentrop again sent Heinrich Stahmer to Tokyo with instructions to find out what the real intentions of the Japanese Government were, as there had been some variance between Ott's reports and the information given by Kurusu. If the Japanese proved ready to conclude a pact, Stahmer was, in conjunction with Ott, to open negotiations for this, but was to report all details to Berlin for approval as he went along.[1] Stahmer left Berlin on 23 August and arrived in Tokyo on 7 September.[2]

Meanwhile on 4 September the Japanese Inner Cabinet had decided on the bases of the negotiation. These were: political and economic co-operation between the Axis Powers to establish the New Order in Europe and Africa on the one hand, and in Greater East Asia on the other. For the purpose of the negotiations the latter sphere was to include 'the region from Burma eastwards and New Caledonia northwards'.[3] Ultimately it was to extend to India, Australia, and New Zealand, but if need be India could be recognized as coming within the Soviet sphere, should this be necessary to induce the USSR to fall into line with the policy of the three partners.[4] Japan was to take all measures short of war to aid the Axis Powers to overthrow Britain and to prevent American 'interference'. If, however, the China Incident looked like coming to an end, or if the international situation took a turn which permitted of no further delay, war could be entered upon, either with Great Britain alone, or with the United States as well.[5]

---

[1] Evidence of H. Stahmer (ibid. pp. 24404–6). Also Ribbentrop distrusted Ott, as the latter knew (Interrogation of Ott, 20 Feb. 1946).
[2] Evidence of Stahmer.   [3] IMTFE, *Record*, p. 6314.
[4] ibid. The Japanese were still uncertain as to German intentions, and the decisions of the Cabinet Conference included agreement upon an understanding with Germany and Italy on action in the contingency of war with the USSR, if Japan's prospective allies should ask for this to be included in the pact.
[5] ibid. pp. 6318–19.

On 9 September Stahmer met Matsuoka at his private residence and gave him an exposition of Ribbentrop's views on the situation. Germany did not want the European War to develop into a world war, but desired to end it as soon as possible; in particular, she wished to prevent American participation, which was indeed unlikely, but not impossible. At the moment it seemed more probable that the United States would move against Japan, and therefore Germany considered that an agreement between herself and Japan would be mutually advantageous in deterring the United States from intervention in either the European or the Far Eastern conflicts. Germany did not at this juncture seek Japanese military aid in the war against Great Britain, but desired her only to help in restraining the United States. Germany was ready to acknowledge Japanese leadership in Greater East Asia and asked merely for economic privileges and assistance in securing strategic raw materials. She would furthermore be willing to act as an 'honest broker' in bringing about a rapprochement between Japan and the USSR, but she thought it best to reach agreement with Japan first, before approaching the Soviet Union, with whom she had not yet conferred on the subject.[1]

This explanation cleared the way for negotiations for a Pact of Alliance. The actual discussions were between Matsuoka and Stahmer; in the preparation of the drafts Matsuoka was assisted by his 'advisers', Toshio Shiratori and Yoshio Saito, and by Shunichi Matsumoto, head of the Treaty Section of the Tokyo Foreign Ministry. Matsumoto gave the Tokyo Tribunal a detailed account of the negotiations.[2] The chief difference arose over the wording of what became Article 3, in which the three contracting parties defined their obligations in the event of outside attack. The original Japanese draft of this was vaguely worded and Stahmer submitted a more precise counter-draft which provided that if a party to the pact were attacked by a Power not involved in the European War or the Sino-Japanese conflict, the other members would assist it with all political, economic, and military means.[3] This was tentatively agreed upon on 11 September and then reported to Ribbentrop.[4] His revisions were communicated to Matsuoka on 14 September. He wished the military obligations

---

[1] ibid. pp. 6323–7.
[2] IMTFE, *Exhibit* 3145; also *Record*, pp. 27983–28007.
[3] *Record*, pp. 27985–6.   [4] ibid. p. 27986.

of Article 3 to operate 'when one of the three Powers concerned shall *either openly or in concealed form* be attacked by a Power not at present involved in the European War or the Japanese-Chinese conflict.'[1]

It is obvious that what Ribbentrop had in mind were measures of American assistance to Great Britain, short of formal belligerency. Matsuoka evidently saw this as well; he objected to this addition and was successful in getting it deleted. Agreement was also reached on what became Article 5 of the pact, in which its members affirmed that it did not 'in any way affect the political status which exists at present' between them and the USSR.[2]

But all was not yet over. The draft Pact was considered at a special Cabinet session in Tokyo on 16 September and by a Liaison Conference three days later, with explanations by Matsuoka.[3] Ribbentrop went to Rome on 19 September and conferred with Mussolini and Ciano on the impending Treaty.[4] On 21 September Stahmer presented the Japanese with a further revision of Article 3, which was now to provide that if a Power not involved in the existing conflicts in Europe and the Far East 'commits an act of aggression against one of the contracting parties, Japan, Germany, and Italy undertake to declare war on such Power and to assist one another with all political, economic and military means.'[5]

The Germans urged that 'America would certainly hesitate ten times before entering the war if the Pact stated in clear and impressive terms that America would then automatically be at war with three great Powers.'[6] But the definite obligation to declare war was strongly opposed by the Japanese Navy, and in further discussions between Matsuoka and Stahmer and Matsumoto and Ott, the Germans gave way on the matter.[7]

Meanwhile on 19 September Saito had presented Stahmer with a draft secret protocol to the Pact.[8] This provided for the establishment of joint military, naval, and economic commissions, and stipulated that the respective Governments were to determine

---

[1] ibid. p. 27987. Matsuoka told the Liaison Conference of 19 September that in answer to his query about this phraseology, Stahmer had said that it would cover such cases as the British allowing the United States to occupy a base in the Mediterranean, or a secret Anglo-American Treaty for the use of Singapore by the United States fleet. But Matsuoka still objected and Stahmer agreed to drop the phrase, subject to Ribbentrop's concurrence, which was secured (ibid. pp. 6336–7).

[2] ibid. p. 27987.

[3] ibid. p. 27987.

[4] Ciano, *Diary*, p. 291.

[5] IMTFE, *Record*, pp. 27987–8.

[6] ibid. pp. 28000–1.

[7] ibid. pp. 28006–7.

[8] ibid. p. 27987.

whether or not an open or secret attack had been made on one of the contracting parties. If the decision were in the affirmative, the commissions, subject to the approval of their Governments, would determine the measures to be taken. Germany and Italy were to agree that they would do all they could to tie up the forces of a hostile Power in the Atlantic; they were also, in the event of an attack upon Japan, to come to her assistance in the Pacific Ocean with all possible strength.[1] Germany and Italy were to use their good offices to improve Soviet-Japanese relations, while all three partners were to 'make the utmost efforts to induce the USSR to act in accord with the main purposes of the present Pact.' The protocol further provided that the three Powers should furnish each other with all new inventions and weapons of war, with industrial equipment, technical assistance, and raw materials for war purposes.[2]

The Germans, as well they might, considered these proposals as altogether too one-sided and in Japan's favour. They would not accept them, even when somewhat modified, in the form of a protocol, which would have had the same binding force as the Treaty.[3] Ultimately a letter was drafted by Ott for formal presentation at the time the Pact was signed. This missive contained a much watered-down version of the original Japanese desiderata.[4]

On 23 September general agreement was reached, but now the Japanese received another shock when Stahmer informed them that Ribbentrop wanted the Pact signed in Berlin.[5] Matsuoka was chagrined; he said that so far all the participants had been negotiating on the assumption that the Pact would be signed in Tokyo. He asked if Ribbentrop insisted on the signature taking place in Berlin. He also wanted to know if the English text, on which they had been working, could be taken as the official one, because otherwise, if the Pact were in three languages, the three versions would all have to go to the Privy Council for comparison, which would delay ratification.[6] He also inquired whether the exchange of letters which were to accompany the Pact could take place in Tokyo, between Ott and himself. Ribbentrop insisted upon the Pact itself being signed in Berlin, but he conceded the other points.[7] The pact received final approval at a conference of

[1] ibid. p. 28001.   [2] ibid. p. 28002.
[3] ibid. p. 27989.   [4] ibid. pp. 28013–14.
[5] ibid. p. 27989.   [6] ibid. pp. 28015–16.
[7] ibid. On 25 September a reply came from Ribbentrop to say that the agreed

the Japanese Cabinet with the Investigation Committee of the
Privy Council on 26 September. Despite the reassurances given
by Matsuoka, Tojo, and Konoye, considerable misgivings were
expressed during the course of the conference, especially with
regard to the effect of the Pact upon Japanese-American relations;
the amount of help to be expected from Germany should Japan
become involved in war under Article 3, and the prospects of a
Japanese-Soviet rapprochement.[1] The formal signature of the
Pact took place in Berlin on 27 September and was publicly proclaimed two days later; the Japanese Government, evidently
unsure of the public reaction, took the unusual step of having the
pact announced by an Imperial rescript.[2]

The Tripartite Pact was accompanied by an exchange of secret
understandings between Ott and Matsuoka in Tokyo on 27
September. By the first of these Germany agreed that whether or

draft of the pact, in the English language, would be signed in Berlin, as a temporary measure; later on texts in Japanese, German, and Italian were to be
secretly substituted. The letters from Matsuoka to Ott were to be in Japanese,
with an English translation; those from Ott to Matsuoka were to be in German,
with an English translation. These letters were to be kept secret from the
Italians (ibid. p. 27992).

[1] ibid. pp. 6352–78. It is clear from the tone of some of the interpellations
that the distrust of Germany in consequence of the German-Soviet Pact was
still very much alive, and also that there was a considerable pro-Anglo-American
group among the Privy Councillors. These appealed to the Government not to
make the promulgation of the pact an occasion for stirring up popular feeling
against Great Britain and the United States, and Konoye agreed with this view.
With this understanding the Committee approved of the Pact. The full Privy
Council met on the evening of the same day; its approval was a foregone conclusion after the Committee proceedings. Grew says that he heard indirectly
from a member of the Imperial family that both the Emperor and Konoye were
against the Pact, but that the Emperor was warned that he might not survive a
refusal (*Ten Years in Japan*, p. 300). Kido, the Lord Privy Seal, declared that
he told the Emperor on 16 September that if the Pact were concluded, it would
divide the world into two parts, despite the opinions of Konoye and Matsuoka to
the contrary. The Emperor also thought that the Pact would lead to war, but
custom dictated his approval once the Cabinet had agreed upon it (IMTFE,
Record, pp. 30909–10). According to the *Saionji–Harada Memoirs*, 20 September, the Emperor asked Konoye what the Navy would do in the event of
a Japanese-American War. He had heard that in the Naval Staff College exercises Japan always came out the loser in such a war. What would happen to
Japan if she were vanquished? Another strong opponent of the Pact was
Admiral Isoroku Yamamoto, Commander-in-Chief of the Combined Fleet. On
14 October he told Harada that he considered the policy outrageous. 'Even if a
non-aggression pact is concluded with Russia, she cannot be relied upon entirely.
While we are fighting with the United States who can guarantee she will observe
the Pact and not attack us from the rear?' He added that in the event of war he
himself would probably die fighting, that Tokyo would probably be burned to
the ground, and that Konoye and the Cabinet might get torn limb from limb by
the people (*Saionji–Harada Memoirs*, 15 Oct. 1940).

[2] For text see Appendix 1.

not one of the Parties had been attacked within the meaning of Article 3 should be decided by consultation between the three Powers.[1] In the event of such an attack upon Japan, Germany promised full economic and military assistance, and in the meantime would render Japan all possible technical and material aid in preparing for such an emergency. She furthermore promised to do all in her power to promote a friendly understanding between Japan and the USSR.[2] The second exchange of Notes embodied an understanding that, in the event of war between Japan and Great Britain, Germany would afford all possible assistance to Japan.[3] The third understanding concerned the former German colonies in the Pacific. It was agreed that the Japanese mandated islands, which had formerly belonged to Germany, should remain in Japanese possession, in return for some compensation for their final relinquishment by Germany. The remaining ex-German possessions were to be restored to Germany upon the conclusion of the European War, but Germany would then open negotiations for their sale to Japan.[4]

Such was the Tripartite Pact and its accompanying understandings. Why did Matsuoka, despite his parade of Japanese independence as compared with the subservient position of Italy, prove so ready to compromise that independence? First, because he was convinced that Germany would defeat Great Britain and emerge victorious from the European War, and he feared that, without an understanding to the contrary, she would then seek to establish herself in the Far East and Pacific.[5] Secondly, he saw clearly enough that no improvement in Japanese-American relations could be expected while Japan continued her efforts to dominate China. He said that the United States believed that Japanese strength was being weakened by the continuance of the China

---

[1] IMTFE, *Record*, p. 6398. Matsuoka had told the Privy Councillors that in the event of the United States entering the European War, there would first be a consultation between the military and naval authorities; then a decision by the Cabinet on the basis of the agreement reached by the armed Services, and then a consultation with Germany and Italy. Thus Japan would be free to choose her own time for entering the war (ibid. pp. 6346–9).

[2] ibid.   [3] ibid. pp. 6400–1.

[4] ibid. p. 6402. The Japanese had been nervous lest Germany, if she won the European War, should demand back the Pacific colonies she had held prior to the First World War. Matsuoka told the Privy Council that the compensation to Germany for Japanese retention (in the form of annexation) of the mandated islands would be 'very little, almost nominal' (ibid. p. 6359).

[5] He expressed this fear in the Privy Council discussions of 26 September (ibid. p. 6362).

conflict; if Japan remained isolated, American pressure upon her might increase; consequently Japan's best policy was to join hands with the Axis Powers.[1] He agreed with Ribbentrop that the Pact would deter the United States from intervening in either Europe or Asia, and thus would leave Japan free to fall upon the colonial possessions of France, Holland, and Great Britain in the Far East. Finally, he was persuaded that the Tripartite Alliance would induce the Soviet Union to conclude a pact with Japan, which would involve Russian abandonment of the Chinese cause.[2] It does not appear that Matsuoka ever thought of the loopholes in Article 3 of the Pact as constituting a bargaining counter with the United States, although it is possible that Konoye did. Matsuoka claimed in his memoirs that he intended the Pact as an instrument of peace, but the peace he envisaged was one of conquest, and he seems to have looked forward, as the architect of that conquest, to becoming a national dictator in Japan.[3] Such were the motives of the man who set Japan upon the slippery slope that led to war.

Konoye supported the Pact because he hoped that it would result in a Soviet-Japanese non-aggression pact, concluded with Germany's assistance. Through this, and, in addition, with German good offices, a compromise peace might be arranged with Chiang Kai-shek.[4] More peace feelers were being made at this time between Tokyo and Chungking. According to the *Saionji–Harada Memoirs* (1 September 1940) Konoye declared that an overture had been received from Chiang to suggest that if the Japanese Government rescinded their declaration of 16 January 1938—that they would have no further dealings with the Chinese National Government—peace negotiations could be opened. Konoye was not prepared to go so far and was suspicious of the genuineness of the offer, but he replied in a personal letter to Chiang, which was sent to Itagaki, in the hope that a meeting between him and Chiang could be brought about in Changsha. But nothing came of this, and Konoye declared that he had been

---

[1] ibid. p. 6343.

[2] He told the Privy Council that he did not believe Stahmer's statement that no negotiations had yet taken place between Germany and the Soviet Union on the question of the latter aligning herself with the three proposed Axis partners (ibid. p. 6357).

[3] Grew noted in his Diary for 2 August 1941: 'It is generally believed that his [Matsuoka's] ambition is to become Prime Minister (God help Japan if he does)' (*Ten Years in Japan*, p. 333).

[4] *Saionji–Harada Memoirs*, 16 Sept. 1940.

hoaxed.[1] If both German and Soviet pressure could be brought to bear upon Chungking to make peace, better results could be expected. Both Konoye and the General Staff were more than ever anxious to end the wearisome China conflict which was 'the chain on her feet' for Japan.

Furthermore, it was of prime importance for Konoye and Matsuoka to secure a pact with the USSR for, as things stood, there was nothing to prevent her from attacking Japan, and should she do so, Article 5 of the Tripartite Pact could be invoked to exempt Germany from coming to Japan's assistance. This had already aroused criticism of the Tripartite Pact. But, although a pact with the USSR was eventually secured, it was made under very different circumstances than those which Konoye and Matsuoka envisaged in September 1940.

On instructions from Ribbentrop the German chargé d'affaires in Moscow on the evening of 26 September informed Molotov of the impending conclusion of the Tripartite Pact and of its general purport.[2] The Soviet Foreign Minister in reply said that he had received reports from the Soviet Embassy in Tokyo that such an agreement was being made and he asserted that the Soviet Government, by virtue of Articles 3 and 4 of the Soviet-German Non-Aggression Pact, had a right to see in advance the text of the Tripartite Pact, including any secret protocols, and to express their views upon it.[3]

The German reply, which was not delivered until 4 October, after the conclusion and publication of the Pact, was that the question of prior consultation did not arise since the Pact expressly provided that the relationship of the signatories to the Soviet Union remained unaltered. Ribbentrop also declared (falsely) that 'there were no secret protocols nor any other secret agreements.'[4] Molotov was clearly not satisfied, but, in view of his impending visit to Berlin, did not go farther into the matter at this time.[5]

The Soviet Government feared that, despite the professions of its signatories to the contrary, the Tripartite Pact might be a revival, in a more dangerous form, of the three-Power anti-Comintern bloc.[6] It was ominous since it came close after the Vienna Award and the Italo-German guarantee to Rumania,

---

[1] ibid.   [2] *Nazi–Soviet Relations*, pp. 145–6, 197–9.
[3] ibid. p. 198.   [4] ibid. pp. 202–3.   [5] ibid. p. 204.
[6] G. Gafencu, *Prelude to the Russian Campaign* (London, Muller, 1945), p. 87.

events which were disturbing Soviet relations with the Axis Powers. Again, despite the soothing assurances of Togo that the Pact was in no way directed against the USSR, with whom the Japanese Government desired to maintain the closest relations, the Soviet Government were nervous about Japanese intentions.[1] The negotiations for a Soviet-Japanese neutrality pact had come to a standstill; Togo was under recall, and his designated successor was a military man, General Yoshitsugu Tatekawa, who had been aide-de-camp to General Nogi, the conqueror of Port Arthur in the Russo-Japanese War. Soviet apprehensions were not lessened when the new envoy declared in Hsinking, while en route to Moscow, that Soviet-Japanese relations 'should be restored to a clean slate'.[2] However, when Tatekawa arrived in Moscow at the end of October he proposed the conclusion of a non-aggression pact, which should be similar in character to the German-Soviet Pact and should include an agreement on spheres of interest in Asia. The Soviet Government in reply 'put a number of questions' to Tatekawa, and one of these was evidently the renunciation of the Japanese concessions in north Sakhalin.[3]

On 12–13 November Molotov was in Berlin where Hitler and Ribbentrop sought to allure him with the prospect of a division of the Old World into spheres of influence—that of the USSR to include Iran and India. With regard to Japan, Ribbentrop said he knew that she was anxious to conclude a non-aggression pact with the USSR, and while Germany had not been asked by Japan to mediate in this matter, she would be glad to do so if desired. Ribbentrop intimated that the Japanese Government wanted the pact concluded first, and that then they would be willing to 'settle all other issues in a generous manner', including the recognition of Outer Mongolia and Sinkiang as within the Soviet sphere.

The Japanese Government was disposed to meet the Soviet wishes half-

[1] ibid. p. 86.

[2] Evidence of Yoshio Noguchi, secretary interpreter of the Japanese Embassy in Moscow, October 1939 to November 1940. He said that Molotov told Togo that the sudden change of Ambassador in the midst of an important negotiation was incomprehensible and that he repeatedly asked what the intentions of the Japanese Government were. Togo gave such reassurance as he could (IMTFE, *Record*, pp. 35382–3).

[3] This would appear from the Ribbentrop–Molotov conversations in Berlin. See below p. 204. Gafencu (*Prelude to the Russian Campaign*) says that the Russians wanted Japan to retrocede Southern Sakhalin, but this was not mentioned in the Berlin conversations nor included in the Soviet proposals of 26 November.

way in regard to the oil and coal concessions on Sakhalin Island, but it would first have to overcome resistance at home. This would be easier for the Japanese Government if a non-aggression pact were first concluded with the Soviet Union.[1]

Molotov in reply said that negotiations for a pact could not be entered upon until the Japanese Government had replied to the questions asked them and that even then the negotiations 'could not be separated from the remaining complex of questions'.[2] In other words Japan would not get the pact unless she paid the price.

Other Far Eastern matters discussed in Berlin included the precise limits of the Greater East Asia Sphere. Molotov showed himself very suspicious of this and he repeatedly pressed for greater information about it. Ribbentrop professed not to be well versed in the matter although he repeated the assurance that nothing in the Tripartite Pact was intended to injure Soviet interests.[3] The possibility of peace between Japan and China was also canvassed; on this Molotov said that 'it was certainly the task of Russia and Germany' to attend to the settlement of Sino-Japanese relations, but that 'an honorable solution would have to be assured for China', especially as Japan now stood a chance of getting Indonesia.[4]

In his final conversation with Molotov Ribbentrop presented verbally a proposed pact of three articles by which the USSR should declare its concurrence with the aims of the Tripartite Pact and its readiness to co-operate politically with the signatories of that instrument, while all four Powers should respect each other's spheres of influence, and none should join any combination of Powers hostile to any one of them. This was to be a public agreement, but was to be accompanied by a secret protocol in which 'the focal points in the territorial aspirations' of the four Powers could be defined.[5]

Ribbentrop remarked that the aspirations of Japan remained to be clarified through diplomatic channels, but possibly a line could be fixed 'which would run south of the Japanese home islands and Manchukuo.'[6]

[1] *Nazi-Soviet Relations*, p. 251.
[2] ibid. pp. 251–2.   [3] ibid. pp. 224–5.
[4] ibid. pp. 224 and 247.   [5] ibid. pp. 248–50.
[6] ibid. p. 249. An undated written version of the Pact appears on pp. 255–8, from the secret files of the German Embassy in Moscow. It contained an extra clause to Article 2; this provided for recognition and respect for 'the present extent' of the possessions of the Soviet Union. There were also two secret

Molotov returned to Moscow on 15 November, and delivered the Soviet reply on 26 November. This was that the Soviet Government were prepared to accept the draft of the four-Power pact outlined by Ribbentrop on 13 November, subject to a number of conditions which were to be embodied in five secret protocols.[1] One condition was that Japan should renounce her concessions for coal and oil in northern Sakhalin.[2] The others were mainly concerned with Finland, Bulgaria, and Turkey. It was on account of the Soviet demands in these regions that Hitler decided on war with the USSR which he had been meditating since June. On 18 December he issued his Directive No. 21 for 'Operation Barbarossa'.[3] No reply was vouchsafed to Molotov's communication; on 17 January 1941 he expressed surprise at this and asked for an early reply. The German Ambassador said that the questions raised must first be discussed with Italy and Japan and an answer would be given when these discussions were ended.[4] Ribbentrop on 21 January instructed Weizsäcker to make a similar reply to Dekanosov, the Soviet Ambassador in Berlin, and to say that the German Government hoped to be able to resume the political discussions with the Soviet Government in the near future. Similar instructions were sent to the German Ambassador in Moscow.[5] But in fact the German Government had abandoned hopes of bringing the Soviet Union into line with the Tripartite Pact and were already preparing another *volte-face* in policy.

Meanwhile direct Soviet-Japanese negotiations were not making much headway. Moscow had returned to the project of a neutrality pact, but still wanted Japan to relinquish her concessions in northern Sakhalin. When Tatekawa hinted at Japanese readiness to purchase the Soviet half of that island, Molotov asked whether 'that was meant for a joke'.[6] On 15 November 1940 Tass denied a foreign press report that the Soviet Union and Japan had reached agreement on their spheres of influence in Asia, and that the Soviet Union had undertaken to give no further help to China.[7]

In respect of China Matsuoka suffered another disappointment.

protocols, by the first of which Japanese territorial aspirations were to centre 'in the area of Eastern Asia to the south of the Island Empire of Japan' and those of the USSR 'south of the national territory of the Soviet Union in the direction of the Indian Ocean'.

[1] ibid. pp. 258–9.
[2] ibid. p. 259.
[3] ibid. pp. 260–4.
[4] ibid. p. 270.
[5] ibid. p. 272.
[6] ibid. pp. 308–9.
[7] Beloff, *Foreign Policy of Soviet Russia*, ii. 370.

Despite the establishment of the Wang Ching-wei régime on 30 March, the Japanese Government still cherished hopes of coming to an agreement with Chungking, and had deferred the formal promulgation of the peace treaty with Wang.[1] After he took office Matsuoka made a renewed attempt to bring about peace by direct negotiations with Chungking. He sent Counsellor Tajiri and Mr. Matsumoto to Hong Kong to contact Chungking and at first the negotiations seemed promising, but in the event came to nothing.[2] In Berlin Kurusu had been sounding out Chungking through the German Foreign Ministry and the Chinese Ambassador there.[3] But once again no concrete result was achieved.

Meanwhile negotiations had been going on between Abe and Wang Ching-wei in Nanking, as the result of which a draft Treaty was initialed on 10 October. In early November a Manchukuo representative arrived in Nanking and a draft Japan–Manchukuo–China Declaration was agreed upon on the eighth of that month. On 13 November the China Treaty and accompanying protocols were formally sanctioned at an Imperial Conference in Tokyo. They received final approval by the Privy Council on 27 November. Three days later the treaty and accompanying documents were formally signed in Nanking, and the public parts of them were promulgated.[4]

The public 'Treaty concerning Basic Relations between China and Japan' consisted of nine articles. The two first provided for mutual respect for sovereignty, and for co-operation in the political, economic, and cultural spheres. By Article 13 the two countries were to undertake joint defence against Communism, for which purpose Japan was to maintain forces in Inner Mongolia and North China. Detailed provision for this was to be made the subject of a separate agreement. So were arrangements for the evacuation of

[1] See above, p. 160.

[2] Evidence of Kido (IMTFE, *Record*, p. 30913). Kagesa also spoke of Matsuoka's overture to Chungking (ibid. p. 24002).

[3] Ribbentrop told Molotov in Berlin that he had heard of efforts at compromise between Japan and China, and that he had told the Chinese Ambassador that Germany would be glad to see such a compromise. He denied that Japan had suggested this action, or that he had offered to mediate (*Nazi-Soviet Relations*, p. 224). But on 29 November Weizsäcker had a conversation with Kurusu, in which 'the Japanese Ambassador repeated what he had said in his last visit to the Reich Foreign Minister, that on account of the peace feelers between Japan and China, it was necessary to wait to see what instructions the Chinese Ambassador will now receive from Chiang Kai-shek' (IMTFE, *Record*, p. 6428).

[4] IMTFE, *Exhibit* 464.

Japanese forces in general after peace was restored (Article 4); and provision for the stationing of Japanese warships in Chinese waters (Article 5). Article 6 laid down that there was to be 'close economic co-operation between the two countries in conformance with the spirit of complementing each other and ministering to each other's needs.'[1] Special reference was made to the mineral resources of Inner Mongolia and North China in this respect, as well as to 'specific resources in other areas which are needed for national defence'. 'Specially close co-operation' was to be the rule in reference to trade and commerce on the lower Yangtze and in Japanese commerce with North China and Inner Mongolia. The Japanese Government were to lend assistance in the rehabilitation and development of industries, finance, transport, and communications in China.[2] Under Article 7 Japan promised to abandon her extraterritorial rights and concessions in China in return for freedom of trade and residence for Japanese subjects throughout that country. Article 8 provided that separate agreements should be made to cover specific matters; the last article brought the Treaty into force immediately upon its signature.[3]

Under a protocol to the Treaty the Nanking régime accepted all Japanese measures taken in pursuance of the existing military conflict, while Japan promised to complete the evacuation of her forces—except from the special anti-Communist areas—within two years of the cessation of hostilities. In additional 'Terms of Understanding' Japan promised to turn over to Nanking fiscal agencies and industrial establishments which were under the control of the Japanese forces in China.[4]

These publicized instruments were accompanied by two secret annexes, an exchange of Notes and a letter from Wang to Abe. By the terms of the first secret annex, it was agreed that 'in order to promote the common interests of both countries and to secure peace in East Asia, diplomacy based upon mutual concert shall be effectuated and that no measures which are contrary to this principle shall be taken in relation with other third countries.'[5] Wang promised to accept all the requirements of the Japanese forces which were to be stationed in the 'anti-Communist areas', with respect to communications, waterways, harbours, and other facilities.

[1] ibid.   [2] ibid.   [3] ibid.   [4] ibid.
[5] *Exhibit* 465.

By the second secret annex Japanese warships were to enjoy navigational and harbour facilities along the Yangtze and the south China coast. Furthermore 'to maintain and safeguard the security of traffic lines in the China Sea' there was to be 'close military co-operation' between Japan and China 'in specified islands along the south China coasts and connecting spots thereof '. There was further to be 'intimate co-operation' in the development of 'resources necessary for national defence' in Amoy, on Hainan island, and in adjoining islands.[1]

The secret Notes committed Wang to recognize the Mengchiang (Inner Mongolian) régime as an autonomous area, to concede wide powers, especially in relations with Japan, to the North China Political Committee—the new name for the former 'Provisional Government of North China'—and also to the local pro-Japanese administration in Shanghai and its environs, which was to be another region of 'specially close co-operation'.[2]

Finally, in his letter to Abe, Wang agreed that 'during the period in which Japan continues in the territories of the Republic of China the warlike operations she is now carrying on the Government of the Republic of China [i.e. Wang's régime] will positively co-operate towards the full attainment of the purpose of the said warlike operations of Japan'.[3]

While these latter provisions were to remain for the time being secret, the public agreements alone clearly amounted to Japanese political and economic hegemony over China. On 1 December the legitimate Chinese Government in Chungking issued a counter-blast, in which they denounced Wang as an arch-traitor, condemned the treaty he had made as null and void, and reiterated their resolve to fight on.[4] But behind this bold front there was distress and anxiety in Chungking, where economic hardships were increasing and spirits were flagging. The German Government were urging Chiang Kai-shek to come to terms with Japan, or he would find himself completely abandoned.[5] The incessant propaganda of Wang and his henchmen that the longer the war dragged on the more likely it was that China would fall prey to Communism was having its effect, especially with the deterioration of the relations between the Kuomintang and the Chinese Communist Party. So

[1] ibid.   [2] ibid.   [3] ibid.
[4] China, Ministry of Information, *China Handbook, 1937–43* (New York, Macmillan, 1943), p. 138.
[5] See above, p. 206; also Feis, *Road to Pearl Harbor*, pp. 134–5.

Chiang once again appealed to the United States for aid and was supported in this by the American Ambassador in Chungking, who gave warning of a possibility of the collapse of Chinese resistance.[1] The American Government responded by extending a further credit of $100 million to Chungking, by promising supplies of fighter aircraft, and by facilitating Chinese recruitment of American volunteers as airmen or air instructors. A proposal to supply China with a bomber force to attack Japan was dropped as impracticable, since there were no such aircraft to spare.[2]

In his efforts to hold out against Japan, Chiang was further cheered by continued support from the USSR. On 5 December Tass reported that the Japanese Government had assured the Soviet Government that the anti-Communist clauses in the Treaty with Nanking were not aimed at the USSR, and that the Treaty was no barrier to better Soviet-Japanese relations. The reply, delivered through the Soviet Ambassador in Tokyo, was that 'the policy of the USSR had not changed in the least in regard to its relations with China.'[3] Here was another rebuff for Matsuoka, and it was given point by the conclusion of new Sino-Soviet trade agreements in December 1940 and January 1941, and by the completion of a motor road from Ulan Ude on the Trans-Siberian Railway, to Ulan Bator, in Outer Mongolia, whence goods could be transported by camel to Free China.[4] Thus Soviet aid to China was continued, and German and Japanese prophecies to the contrary were proved false.

All this was highly disquieting to Matsuoka because it meant that his domestic opponents, open and secret, were accumulating a formidable case against him. The Tripartite Pact was not producing the major results which he had predicted—the USSR had not come into line; China was still resisting, and the United States, so far from being frightened, was becoming more hostile to Japan. All he could set against these unfavourable developments was German goodwill and diplomatic assistance in the penetration of Indo-China.[5] But Japan dared not venture farther south until she was sure that her formidable northern neighbour would remain quiet, and unless Matsuoka could somehow ensure this his tenure of the Foreign Ministry was likely to be a 'tiger's head,

[1] ibid. p. 135.   [2] ibid. p. 140.
[3] Beloff, *Foreign Policy of Soviet Russia*, ii. 370.
[4] Dallin, *Soviet Russia's Foreign Policy, 1939–42* (Newhaven, Yale University Press, 1942), p. 341.   [5] See Ch. VIII below.

snake's tail' affair.[1] He therefore decided to pay a visit to Europe, to find out what was happening to German-Soviet relations and to see what he might accomplish in person in Moscow.

On 19 December 1940 Ott reported that Matsuoka was considering Ribbentrop's invitation to come to Berlin, and was also thinking of visiting Rome and Moscow.[2] Matsuoka had emphasized to Ott the need to overcome the deadlock in the negotiations with the USSR and China and 'to make a strong gesture' in favour of the Tripartite Pact.[3] Matsuoka received a welcoming reply on 24 December and said he would secure permission from the Cabinet and the Army for his visit, which, however, he would delay until Oshima, who had been reappointed to the Berlin Embassy to replace Kurusu, should have arrived and presented his credentials.[4] Matsuoka secured the needed permission in early February, but delayed his departure until he had concluded his 'mediation' between Thailand and France over Indo-China.[5]

Matsuoka went via the Trans-Siberian Railway and stopped in Moscow where on 24 March he had a conversation with Stalin and Molotov. He treated the Soviet leaders to a lecture on Japanese 'moral Communism' as opposed to the 'individualism' and 'egoism' of the Anglo-Saxons who were the common enemies of Germany, Japan, and the USSR.[6] But he also broached the question of 'the fundamental problems' in Soviet-Japanese relations, although he deferred consideration of them until his return from Berlin.[7]

Matsuoka reached Berlin on 26 March and during the next three days had long conversations with Ribbentrop and Hitler. He then paid a brief visit to Rome and on his return to Berlin had further conversations with the Führer and the Reich Foreign Minister on 4 and 5 April. He was told by Ribbentrop that there

---

[1] A Japanese way of describing a pretentious start and feeble ending.

[2] Matsuoka told the British Ambassador that Ribbentrop had made such an invitation at the time of the signature of the Tripartite Pact (Craigie, *Behind the Japanese Mask*, p. 115).

[3] IMTFE, *Record*, pp. 6449–50.   [4] ibid. pp. 6451–2.

[5] Ott to Ribbentrop, 10 February 1941 (ibid. p. 6453). Matsuoka expected the Thailand–Indo-China negotiations to be settled by the end of February; in fact they were not concluded till 11 March.

[6] So he told Hitler on 27 March (*Nazi-Soviet Relations*, p. 297), and apparently also the United States Ambassador in Moscow, Steinhardt. (See Grew, *Ten Years in Japan*, pp. 327 and 330–1).

[7] Schulenburg to GFM, 24 March 1941, reporting what Matsuoka told him. He thought Matsuoka had said more to the Russians than he admitted (*Nazi-Soviet Relations*, p. 280).

never had been any question of inviting the USSR to become a full partner in the Tripartite Pact,[1] and that the negotiations for a separate pact of association were now in abeyance, because the Soviet conditions, of which he was given details, were unacceptable to Germany.[2] Ribbentrop said that relations with the USSR were now correct, but not friendly, and there was no certainty how they would develop. If the USSR made any hostile move in Europe Germany would strike her down and had a great army concentrated and ready for such an emergency. Similarly, if the USSR attacked Japan, Germany would immediately attack the USSR.[3] Hitler, in the interview on 27 March, declared that the United States and Great Britain were hoping to bring in the USSR against Germany in 1941 or 1942. If Germany saw any danger of this happening she would strike at once against the USSR, though Hitler said that he did not believe that the danger would arise.[4] He added that, with 150 German divisions concentrated on her western frontier, the Soviet Union would not dare to intervene against Japan if the latter made a move against Great Britain.[5]

The German object in all this was to persuade Japan to strike at once against Singapore, without waiting for any pact with the USSR.[6] They had been urging this for some time and had manifested impatience with the Japanese preoccupation with Chinese and Russian questions.[7] But Matsuoka was evidently not convinced by these assurances. He told Ribbentrop in the course of their second conversation on 28 March that 'Japan was prepared to permit Russia an ice-free outlet to the sea by way of India or Iran, but would not tolerate the Russians on the Chinese coast'.[8] He asked whether, upon his return journey, 'he should remain in Moscow for a somewhat longer period in order to negotiate with the Russians on the Non-Aggression Pact or the Treaty of Neutrality. He emphasized in this connection that direct acceptance of Russia into the Tripartite Pact would not be countenanced by the Japanese people'.[9]

---

[1] ibid. p. 304.   [2] ibid. pp. 284–5, 304–5.
[3] ibid. pp. 299–303.   [4] ibid. p. 291.   [5] ibid. p. 292.
[6] For the conversations on Singapore, see Ch. VIII below.
[7] 'I expressed doubts to Oshima whether the order of problems which he had mentioned (settlement with the USSR, peace with China, attack on Singapore), fits the demand of the historic hour which would probably never return' (memo. of conversation between Weizsäcker and Oshima, 22 February 1941; IMTFE, *Record*, p. 6438).
[8] *Nazi-Soviet Relations*, p. 301.   [9] ibid. p. 302.

Ribbentrop said that such direct Soviet adherence was out of the question and recommended Matsuoka, if possible, not to raise in Moscow the matter he had mentioned 'since this probably would not altogether fit into the framework of the present situation'.[1] There was, however, no objection to the conclusion of Soviet-Japanese fishery and commercial agreements. Ribbentrop returned to the matter in the conversation of 29 March and told Matsuoka that a conflict between Germany and the USSR was 'always within the realm of possibility'. If it happened 'the Soviet Union would be finished with in a few months'.[2]

Matsuoka replied that as he had made the original non-aggression pact proposal, he would be forced to discuss the matter in Moscow. Moreover, he hoped to buy northern Sakhalin, with its valuable oil deposits, which he thought might produce an annual 2 million tons of oil under full exploitation. He was not sanguine about this, however, and mentioned Molotov's sour rejoinder to Tatekawa, as described on a previous page.[3] Ribbentrop opined that 'only a purely formal, superficial handling of these points was advisable' and that the Sakhalin question could also be settled later. He gave Matsuoka another broad hint in saying that

if the Russians should pursue a foolish policy and force Germany to strike, he would—knowing the sentiments of the Japanese Army in China—consider it proper if that army were prevented from attacking Russia. Japan could best help the common cause if she did not allow herself to be diverted by anything from the attack on Singapore. With a common victory, the fulfillment of the wishes named above would, so to speak, fall into Japan's lap like ripe fruit.[4]

Here then was Ribbentrop saying as plainly as he could that

---

[1] ibid.   [2] ibid. p. 303.
[3] ibid. pp. 308-9. According to the record of conversation Matsuoka then said 'At any rate Japan was ready in return to replace the treaties of Portsmouth and Peking by other agreements and also give up her fishing rights'. It is likely that, in addition to the surrender of the concessions, the Soviet Government wanted Japan to retrocede southern Sakhalin and to give up her fishing rights and that these things were their price for a non-aggression pact. But it is clear that Matsuoka had *not* hitherto been willing to pay such a price—hence the failure of the Molotov–Tatekawa conversations. Nor was Matsuoka more yielding on his return to Moscow; as will be seen, he preferred to drop the idea of a non-aggression pact altogether. So it seems likely that there is a mistake here in the record of the conversations and that what Matsuoka really said was that Japan might abandon her attempt to purchase northern Sakhalin, but would *not* agree to giving up southern Sakhalin, and the fisheries. In view of the strategic and commercial disadvantages of such a surrender and the indignation it would arouse in naval, military and business circles, it is incredible that any Japanese Government would have contemplated it at that time.   [4] ibid.

there *was* going to be a German-Soviet war, and that Japan need not make any concessions to the USSR since she could pick up what she wanted after the Russian defeat. But one all-important matter Hitler and Ribbentrop did *not* tell Matsuoka—they did not reveal the existence of the Barbarossa plan. Hitler on 5 March had issued a directive on collaboration with Japan to the German High Command in which he had forbidden any reference to 'Barbarossa'.[1] Admiral Raeder on 18 March advised Hitler to tell Matsuoka about it so as to spur him on to attack Singapore immediately.[2] Weizsäcker on 24 March also raised the point with Ribbentrop.[3] But Hitler evidently did not trust Matsuoka to keep the secret. When he saw Matsuoka on 4 April, after the latter's return from Rome, he told him that the USSR would not be attacked if she remained friendly and continued to observe her pact with Germany. Further, he acquiesced in a Soviet-Japanese pact.[4]

Matsuoka returned to Moscow on 7 April and reopened negotiations with Molotov for the conclusion of a non-aggression pact and the purchase of northern Sakhalin. In his conversations with Schulenburg, the German Ambassador, Matsuoka avoided giving him any details of the first talks with Molotov.[5] On 14 April, however, the German chargé in Tokyo, Boltze, reported a conversation with the Japanese Vice-Minister, Ohashi, in which the latter said (presumably from information sent by Matsuoka) that Molotov had at first demanded 'certain concessions in the sense of a revision of the Treaty of Portsmouth', but that Matsuoka had replied that he was neither ready nor empowered to make such concessions.[6]

Matsuoka then, on 10 April, dropped his non-aggression pact proposals and took up instead the project of a simple Pact of Neutrality. But the Soviet Government demanded that Japan should agree, in an annex to the Pact, to surrender her concessions in north Sakhalin. Matsuoka would not consent to this and the negotiations seemed on the point of failure.[7] However, on 12 April, in a conversation between Matsuoka and Stalin, a compromise

---

[1] *NCA*, i. 847–9.   [2] ibid. vi. 966–7.

[3] 'A clear statement which course our relations to Russia may take is unavoidable in order to protect him (Matsuoka) from surprises' (Weizsäcker to Ribbentrop, 24 March 1941, IMTFE, *Record*, p. 6477).

[4] A. Martienssen, *Hitler and his Admirals* (London, Secker & Warburg, 1948), pp. 102–3. Weizsäcker (*Memoirs*, pp. 249–50) says he tried independently to warn Matsuoka and Oshima of a coming rift in German-Soviet relations.

[5] Schulenburg to GFM, 9 April 1941 (*Nazi-Soviet Relations*, p. 321).

[6] Boltze to GFM, 14 April 1941 (IMFTE, *Record*, pp. 6555–6).

[7] Schulenburg to GFM, 10 April 1941 (*Nazi-Soviet Relations*, pp. 321–2).

was reached. Stalin dropped his demand for the immediate surrender of the concessions, while Matsuoka agreed to do his best to persuade the Japanese Government to surrender them within a few months.[1] On this understanding the Soviet-Japanese Pact of Neutrality was signed on 13 April.

The Pact of Neutrality provided for the maintenance of peaceful and friendly relations between Japan and the USSR and for mutual respect for territorial integrity. Each Power pledged neutrality for the duration of the conflict should the other 'become the object of hostilities on the part of one or several third Powers'. The Pact was to endure for five years from the date of signature. It was accompanied by a Frontier Declaration, by which the USSR pledged herself to respect the territorial integrity and inviolability of Manchukuo, and Japan gave a similar undertaking in respect of the Mongolian People's Republic.[2]

The Pact was in reality a triumph for Soviet diplomacy and a defeat for that of Matsuoka. He had, as has been seen, recalled Shigenori Togo for urging agreement to the very terms which now he had himself, with but slight modification, accepted.[3] In view of the impending German-Soviet war, he could have let the matter of a Pact drop altogether and then, when Hitler struck, have been free either to join in against the USSR or to demand the cession of north Sakhalin as the price of Japanese neutrality.

The Soviet prosecutor at the Tokyo Trials declared that Matsuoka tried to deceive the USSR, that he concluded the Pact in the hope that, on the strength of it, the Soviet troops would be withdrawn from the Far East to Europe to meet the German invasion, and that then Japan would seize upon the defenceless Soviet Far Eastern regions. In fact, however, the Soviet Government were not caught napping and did not denude their Far Eastern zone of its garrison.[4]

Now while, as will be seen, Matsuoka, after the outbreak of the German-Soviet War, *did* urge a Japanese attack on the USSR despite the Neutrality Pact, his motives at the time he concluded the Pact were in all probability not so Machiavellian as the Russians

---

[1] Schulenburg to GFM, 13 April 1941 (ibid. pp. 322–3). Matsuoka gave a written pledge to Molotov to bring about the rendition of the concessions (Schulenburg's No. 884 of 13 April, ibid. pp. 323–4). On 31 May Tatekawa informed the Soviet Government that the concessions would be given up within six months, but this pledge was not carried out. The Russians published the fact of these pledges on 1 April 1944, at the time when Japan *was* constrained to fulfil the promise.   [2] *The Times*, 14 April 1941.
[3] See Ch. VI above.   [4] IMTFE, *Record*, p. 7269.

later supposed. The likeliest explanation of his conduct is that, while he believed in an *ultimate* German-Soviet conflict, after the anticipated defeat of England, he did not expect an *immediate* clash. He believed what Hitler had told him—that there would be no attack upon the USSR unless she herself provoked it by showing signs of joining Great Britain and, despite the bad feeling over the Balkans, he did not think that Stalin would make any such move. He had found Stalin hostile to the 'Anglo-Saxon Powers' and anxious to avoid giving offence to Hitler.[1] Therefore, while he was not ready to make sweeping concessions to the USSR to secure a non-aggression pact, he *was* ready to pay a more limited price for the Neutrality Pact, partly because he did not want to return to Tokyo empty-handed, and partly because Japanese suspicions would not be allayed by mere verbal promises on Hitler's part to strike at the USSR should she attack Japan. The Pact was a fairly solid guarantee that when Japan moved southwards she would have nothing to fear from the USSR. Stalin, for his part, was quite happy to encourage Japan in any move that would embroil her with Great Britain and the United States and leave the Soviet Union unscathed.

During his second sojourn in Moscow, Matsuoka again talked with Steinhardt, the American Ambassador, and told him, *inter alia*, that 'unless the Soviet Union substantially reduced its delivery of supplies to Germany, the Germans would not invade Russia, although they were fully prepared to do so. He thought it was for the purpose of frightening the Soviets into continuing supplies that the Germans had given out rumours of a possible attack.'[1] The diary of Marquis Kido goes to show that this was an honest expression of opinion. On 6 June 1941 Kido noted that Konoye had telephoned to say that Oshima had seen Hitler at Berchtesgaden and that Germany had decided to attack the USSR. Konoye on receipt of this news had called a liaison conference at which Matsuoka declared that, in spite of Oshima's report, the chances were 60 per cent. in favour of agreement between Germany and the USSR and only 40 per cent. for war between them.[3] He appears to have persisted in this view right down to the actual outbreak of the war.[4]

[1] So he told Ott on 6 May 1941 (IMTFE, *Record*, pp. 9883–4).
[2] Grew, *Ten Years in Japan*, p. 331.
[3] IMTFE, *Record*, pp. 9980–1.   [4] ibid. p. 10000.

The enthusiasm which Matsuoka endeavoured to arouse in Japan for the Pact soon waned. His colleagues in the Cabinet were annoyed with him for having given the pledge to give back the Sakhalin concessions, which he had not been authorized to do.[1] The Japanese press and public had been led to expect a radical change in the Soviet attitude to China as a result of the Pact. The Chinese Government were at first alarmed and also irritated at the implied Soviet recognition of Manchukuo, but it soon became apparent that, as the Chinese Communists from the first declared, there was to be no change in Soviet policy to China.[2]

On 11 June a five-year Soviet-Japanese trade agreement was reached, and also an agreement on Japanese-German trade via the Trans-Siberian Railway.[3] In May and June representatives of Manchukuo and Outer Mongolia met at Chita to resume the interrupted negotiations for a border demarcation in the disputed Nomonhan area. They reached agreement on 14 June and began the actual work of boundary surveying on the spot on 27 June. The work was finished on 17 August and the Commissioners drew up a protocol embodying the results of the survey. This was signed in Harbin on 15 October, but was not finally ratified till 15 May 1942.[4] These ameliorations in Soviet-Japanese relations, while welcome in themselves, were small compared with what Matsuoka had led the Japanese to anticipate from the Pact and his stock, which had soared immediately after his return from Europe, fell heavily in the ensuing months.[5]

Oshima on 22 June telegraphed the news of the outbreak of war between Germany and the Soviet Union. This precipitated a crisis in the Japanese Government. Konoye, Hiranuma, and Kido had previously agreed on the policy to be followed in that event— i.e. neutrality in the war and a further move southwards—and Kido had informed the Emperor accordingly.[6] But Matsuoka was

---

[1] Grew, *Ten Years in Japan*, p. 333. Grew did not know what the undertaking was and thought it had to do with the number of troops on the Siberian border.
[2] Molotov gave an assurance to this effect to the Chinese Ambassador on 16 April (Beloff, *Foreign Policy of Soviet Russia*, ii. 376).
[3] Dallin, *Soviet Russia's Foreign Policy*, p. 349.
[4] Evidence of Ota (IMTFE, *Record*, pp. 23103–4).
[5] Matsuoka had told Schulenburg that the Pact 'would make a powerful impression on Chiang Kai-shek and would appreciably ease Japanese negotiations with him' (*Nazi-Soviet Relations*, p. 323). Stalin had also hinted to Matsuoka that the USSR might later on fall into line with the Tripartite Pact (IMTFE, *Record*, p. 9888). When neither of these things occurred the Japanese press and people were correspondingly disappointed.
[6] IMTFE, *Record*, pp. 10021–2.

of a different opinion. On 6 May he had told Ott that 'no Japanese Premier or Foreign Minister could keep Japan neutral in the event of a German-Soviet conflict. Japan would be driven by force of necessity to attack the Soviet Union at Germany's side and no Neutrality Pact could change this'.[1] He now went over Konoye's head to the Emperor and urged that Japan should join in the attack on the Soviet Union as well as making ready for a southward move. Kido, who again saw the Emperor after Matsuoka's audience, found him in a state of agitation. He told Kido what Matsuoka had said and remarked that such a policy would overtax Japan's resources and would not command the support of either Cabinet or Army. Kido at once warned Konoye and Hiranuma of Matsuoka's action and the Premier demanded an explanation from his Foreign Minister. Matsuoka said he had not advocated immediate action, but this naturally did not appease Konoye and relations between the two became very strained.[2]

Matsuoka continued his intrigues for Japanese intervention against the Soviet Union. He again, on 22 June, told Ott that Japan would not remain neutral,[3] and on 24 June, in answer to an inquiry by the Soviet Ambassador, Smetanin, he said that Japan's policy had not yet been formulated, and would be largely influenced by a determination as to where the responsibility for the outbreak of war lay. He added that the Tripartite Pact remained the basis of Japanese foreign policy, and that if the Neutrality Pact proved to be at variance with that then the Pact would not remain in force.[4]

The German Government were also urging Tokyo to intervene against the USSR. On 28 June Ribbentrop told Ott that Oshima had agreed to influence his Government in that direction, and he instructed Ott to do the same. Ott was to say that, as Japan did not appear to be ready to attack Singapore, she should now join with Germany to eliminate the Soviet Union and so make herself quite free to make a southward drive later.[5]

---

[1] Ott to Ribbentrop, 6 May 1941 (ibid. p. 9888).
[2] ibid. pp. 10022-3. See also Konoye Memoirs, in *Pearl Harbor Attack*, pt. 20, p. 3993. From this it appears that Matsuoka wanted an immediate attack on the USSR and war with the United States as well if she entered the war against Germany. 'Ultimately Japan would be fighting the Soviet, America and England simultaneously.'
[3] IMTFE, *Record*, p. 7955.   [4] ibid. pp. 7956-7.
[5] ibid. pp. 6562-5. Ott had asked whether his previous instructions to work for a Japanese advance southwards still held good. The change in German policy may have been owing to their suspicion of Japanese good faith in the projected attack on Singapore. See Ch. VIII below.

But powerful forces were working the other way in Tokyo. Hiranuma was strongly opposed and bitterly hostile to Matsuoka.[1] So, according to his own account, was Kido, who says that on 23 June he told Konoye that as Germany had reversed the policy of promoting good relations with the Soviet Union—which had been an important factor in securing Japanese adhesion to the Tripartite Pact—Konoye ought to consider the abandonment of the Tripartite Pact.[2] This does not appear to have been seriously considered, but in the five Liaison Conferences which were held between 25 June and 1 July, it became apparent that the weight of opinion was against Matsuoka. Tojo on 28 June told Kido that the Army considered that 'a calm and prudent' attitude should be taken towards the German-Soviet War.[3] Ott, reporting to Ribbentrop on the same day, said that Konoye and a majority of the Cabinet were against intervention as likely to injure Japan's military position in China.[4]

On 2 July an Imperial Conference was held and this decided to prosecute the plan of an advance in Indo-China and Siam even at the risk of war with Great Britain and the United States. With regard to the German-Soviet War, the Russians were to be officially informed that Japan would continue to observe the Neutrality Pact. Should the war go in Germany's favour then Japan would intervene finally 'to secure stability in the northern regions'.[5] On the same day Smetanin was orally informed by Matsuoka that Japan would respect the Neutrality Pact.[6] Matsuoka on the following day told Ott that this statement was meant to deceive the Russians while Japan completed her military preparations against them.[7] This did not satisfy Ribbentrop, who on 5 July told Ott to remind Matsuoka of his statement on 6 May that Japan would intervene on Germany's side.[8]

But Matsuoka could do no more. His own position was precarious and there was a feeling that, since he had tied Japan's hands by concluding the Neutrality Pact, he ought now to resign.[9]

[1] Hiranuma was almost certainly 'the former Prime Minister' whom Grew describes as planning to impeach Matsuoka with having failed all along the line in his foreign policy (*Ten Years in Japan*, p. 342).
[2] IMTFE, *Record*, p. 30931.   [3] ibid. p. 10036.
[4] ibid. pp. 10034-5.   [5] ibid. pp. 6567-9, 7961.
[6] ibid.; Grew, *Ten Years in Japan*, p. 346.
[7] IMTFE, *Record*, p. 7962.   [8] ibid. p. 7955.
[9] So the Japanese Ambassador in Rome told Mackensen, the German Ambassador there (ibid. pp. 7962-3).

There was resentment against Germany for having once again made Japan look ridiculous in the eyes of the world, and there was also a belief, based on the Japanese Army's unhappy experience at Nomonhan, that Hitler would not find the Russians such easy victims as he supposed. Tatekawa was among those who held this view. Consequently the general disposition in Tokyo was to wait and see.

The American Government now took a hand in the game. On 6 July (United States time) President Roosevelt sent a personal message to Konoye to express the hope that there was no truth in the reports that Japan intended to attack the Soviet Union and to ask for an assurance to that effect.[1] Konoye replied on 8 July (through Matsuoka) that the Japanese Government had not so far considered the possibility of war with the Soviet Union and gave the American Ambassador a copy of the statement made to Smetanin on 2 July. Matsuoka added that future developments would largely determine Japan's policy. When asked what he had in mind he instanced the possibility of an alliance between Great Britain and the USSR and any attempt by the United States to send military supplies to the USSR via Vladivostok.[2]

Indeed, the American démarche appears to have aroused considerable nervousness in Tokyo about possible Soviet-American collaboration. Matsuoka asked whether the United States really intended to intervene in the European War, to which the Secretary of State replied, on 16 July, that American policy in the face of Germany's plans for world conquest was solely one of self-defence, but that the United States could not be expected to permit Germany to secure strategic advantages that would directly threaten American security.[3] Matsuoka replied, through Ohashi, on 17 July; he contested the American indictment of Germany and declared that no Government could invoke without limit the so-called right of self-defence.[4] This was Matsuoka's swan song, for on 16 July the Konoye Cabinet had resigned for the express purpose of getting rid of him, and then reconstituted itself on 18 July with a new Foreign Minister, Admiral Teijiro Toyoda. But the Japanese Government continued to be alarmed about Soviet-American relations. On 15 August Oshima was informed by Toyoda that Smetanin had again asked about Japanese intentions. He had been

---

[1] Hull, *Memoirs*, ii. 1012.   [2] Grew, *Ten Years in Japan*, p. 344.
[3] Hull, *Memoirs*, ii. 1012.   [4] Grew, *Ten Years in Japan*, p. 344.

told that Japan intended to abide by the Neutrality Pact, but had been warned that if the Soviet Union ceded or leased any of its territory in East Asia to a third Power, or offered it facilities for military bases, or concluded any alliance with a third Power against Japan, the latter would not overlook such a threat. Smetanin in reply denied that his Government had any such intentions and said that they would rigidly observe the terms of the Neutrality Pact.[1]

The reply appears to have calmed Japanese fears and to have made the Japanese Government less disposed than before to heed German suggestions of intervention. Ott on 4 September reported that the Japanese General Staff, which still remembered Nomonhan, was averse to any attack on the USSR while the Soviet Far Eastern Army remained in being.[2]

So Hitler must have had reason to repent of the boastful language which he and Ribbentrop had used to Matsuoka. They had declared that, in the event of war, the Soviet régime would be eliminated in a few months and that Japan need not aid in this. Now the Japanese were taking them at their word and were in effect refusing to intervene. Thus the summer of 1941 saw a marked divergence between the policies of Germany and Japan, and this was to have momentous consequences for the future course of the world struggle.

[1] IMTFE, *Record*, pp. 7987–9. [2] ibid. pp. 7971–2.

CHAPTER VIII

Japan Advances Southwards

EVER since their capture of Canton had brought into prominence the supply route to Free China by way of Haiphong, the Tongking railways, and the French-owned Yunnan railway to Kunming, the Japanese had been bringing pressure upon France to interdict the transport of military supplies over this route. Prior to June 1940 they had got little satisfaction, while the French had made counter-protests against Japanese bombing of the Yunnan railway. The collapse of France and her surrender to Germany profoundly altered the situation and the Japanese were quick to seize their advantage. On 19 June the Japanese Government demanded that the frontier between Indo-China and China should for the time being be closed to traffic and that the French authorities should agree to the dispatch of Japanese inspectors to ensure the permanent prohibition of any transit traffic which would aid Chungking's war effort.[1] The French Government replied on 20 June that they had already, on 17 June, closed the frontier to supplies of gasoline and trucks; that they would extend the prohibition to cover a wide range of other materials, and that they had no objection to the dispatch of a Japanese inspectorate.[2] On 29 June a Japanese mission under General Nishihara arrived in Hanoi and proceeded to establish control stations in Haiphong, Hagiang, Laokay, Caobang, Langson, and Fort Bayard.[3]

But the Japanese wished to go farther than this. Ott on 19 June reported a conversation with the head of the European Department of the Gaimusho, who said that the Japanese Ambassador in Berlin had been instructed to point out Japan's special interest in the future of French Indo-China. This, it was explained to Ott, meant that Japan wanted Germany to give her a free hand in Indo-China[4] and presumably to put pressure on the Vichy Government to that end. In Berlin on 19 June Kurusu, the Japanese Ambassador,

[1] IMTFE, *Record*, p. 6713.
[2] *The Times*, 20 June 1940. The Chinese Government protested unavailingly against the French acquiescence in Japan's demands.
[3] IMTFE, *Record*, p. 6713. Fort Bayard is in the (then) French leased zone of Kwangchouwan, which was administratively attached to the Indo-Chinese Union. [4] ibid. p. 6164.

had referred to a coming visit by Naotake Sato, a former Foreign Minister, and had talked in large terms about post-war economic co-operation between the New Order in Europe and that in Asia.[1] On 24 June Ott reported that General Muto had told the German military attaché that the Japanese Army would welcome German mediation to conclude the China War, and that Japan was also much interested in Indo-China for this reason. Ott himself had been sounded on the Indo-China question by General Koiso, Minister of Overseas Affairs.[2] Muto and Koiso also canvassed the possibility of a Soviet-Japanese non-aggression pact. The idea was apparently that, if the Japanese came to terms with the USSR, and also occupied Indo-China, then Chiang Kai-shek, finding himself isolated, might agree to a peace of the sort Japan wanted, especially if he were offered a piece of Indo-China as a bribe.[3]

The Germans received these various Japanese overtures with coolness. Ott, in his telegram of 19 June, expressed mistrust of Yonai and Arita, who wished to compromise with Great Britain and the United States. He hinted that, if Germany evaded any declaration that Indo-China was to be left to Japan, the fall of the Yonai Cabinet might be brought about and its replacement by one 'which would be close to us'.[4] He told Koiso (24 June) that Germany would probably not object to Japan taking action in Indo-China provided Japan committed herself to tie down America in the Pacific, perhaps by a promise to attack the Philippines and Hawaii in the event of America intervening in the European War.[5]

In Berlin Wiehl, the head of the Economic Division of the German Foreign Ministry, in a memorandum of 19 June, complained bitterly of the way in which Japan had acquiesced in the Anglo-French blockade of Germany. Only in recent months had she allowed a few shipments of raw materials such as tin and wolfram, to go through Japan to Germany. In January 1940 Japan had concluded a monopoly agreement with Manchukuo for soya beans without informing Germany and, despite German remonstrances, had to date released only 70,000 tons of beans for shipment to Germany. Japan had, he considered, repaid with ingratitude

[1] ibid. p. 6170.   [2] ibid. pp. 6175–7.
[3] As a preliminary, Indo-China, or part of it, would have been given to the Wang Ching-wei régime (*NYT*, 20 June 1940).
[4] IMFTE. *Record*, pp. 6164–5.   [5] ibid. p. 6177.

Germany's action in stopping war supplies to China and hence forfeiting valuable Chinese raw materials.[1] Knoll, in a memorandum of 20 June, said Sato had better be told that Germany expected a more obliging attitude from her with respect to the supply of raw materials from East Asia.[2]

Sato had his interview with Ribbentrop on 8 July; Kurusu and Stahmer were also present. Sato talked about Japan having made Germany's task easier by her activities in the Far East, which had diverted the attention of the British, French, and American Governments. Japan was trying to establish a New Order in Asia, as was Germany in Europe, and there should in future be close co-operation between the two, especially in respect of any intervention by the United States in European or Far Eastern matters. Japan was trying to end the China War in order to gain a free hand for this purpose. Sato then referred to Japanese nervousness about the future of French Indo-China and the Netherlands Indies.[3]

Ribbentrop was non-committal in his reply. He referred to the failure of the negotiations for a tripartite pact in 1939; these had failed because, 'as appeared again from the latest speeches of Japanese statesmen,' Japan was not interested in European affairs. So now it was not at all clear what she meant by strengthening German-Japanese collaboration.[4]

Arita anxiously inquired of Sato whether Germany had any ambitions in respect of the French and Dutch colonies in the Far East, or whether she was using these as a bait to secure Japan's participation in the war. Sato replied that he did not gather that either of these was in Germany's mind; she seemed not to attach much importance to Japanese participation at the moment.[5] Ribbentrop, however, told Kurusu there was no truth in reports that Germany was cool towards Japan and he responded favourably to a suggestion of a more definite exchange of views on the mode of German-Japanese collaboration.[6]

Sato's failure to get any pledges from Germany in respect of Indo-China and the Netherlands East Indies, and Ribbentrop's hint that a more concrete approach was expected of Japan resulted

---

[1] ibid. pp. 6166–8.   [2] ibid. pp. 6972–3.   [3] ibid. pp. 6174–81.
[4] ibid. pp. 6181–2. Ribbentrop apparently referred to Arita's broadcast of 22 June, in which he had again mentioned Japan's policy of non-involvement in the European War.
[5] ibid. pp. 6187–40.   [6] ibid. p. 9705.

in the Foreign Ministry drafting the outlines of a German-Japanese agreement, and, on 12 and 16 July, discussing it with representatives of the Army and the Navy.[1] The draft proposals were that Germany should recognize that the South Seas region, including French Indo-China and the Dutch East Indies, were part of Japan's sphere of influence and should support Japanese ambitions there. She should furthermore assist Japan in disposing of the China Incident, and should accord Japan a favoured position in trade with the Euro-African bloc. Japan in return should recognize German leadership in Europe and Africa, should assist Germany, though by measures short of war, to bring about the surrender of Great Britain, and should accord Germany a favoured position in trade with Greater East Asia. The two Powers should co-operate in maintaining peace with the USSR, but if either were threatened by that Power both should confer on the measures to be taken; and if either were at war with the USSR, the other should give no aid to the Soviet Union. Germany and Japan should also co-operate to prevent American interference with their respective plans in Europe and Asia.[2] A generally similar pact was to be negotiated with Italy.[3] The reluctance of Yonai and Arita to fall in with these proposals coupled with the obvious German dislike and distrust of the Yonai Cabinet, impelled the Army to get rid of it in the manner which has been already told.

The new Government in Tokyo were eager to incorporate Indo-China in the Greater East Asia Sphere, both economically and strategically. Japan needed and coveted its resources in rice, rubber, coal, and tin, while, if she could install her armed forces there, she could not only materially further her operations against China, but would be poised for a swoop farther southwards should Great Britain suffer the fate of Holland and France.

General Catroux, Governor-General of the Indo-Chinese Union, had appealed to the Governments of Great Britain and the United States for aid in resisting the Japanese demands in June, but in

---

[1] The members were Ando and Ishizawa, Section chiefs of the Foreign Ministry; Lt.-Colonel Takayama, of the War Ministry; Major Tanemura, of the Army General Staff; Commander Shiba, of the Naval Ministry, and Captain Ono, of the Naval General Staff.
[2] ibid. pp. 6203–6. The first draft was dated 12 July 1940. There were some subsequent modifications as the result of the conference discussions. The negotiations with Germany were to be preferably at Berlin; those with Italy at Rome; these were thus to be parallel with, but separate from, those with Germany.
[3] ibid. pp. 6206–7.

vain.[1] He had dispatched a mission, headed by Colonel Jacomy, to the United States, in an effort to purchase aircraft and other weapons, but this also proved unsuccessful, while the Japanese applied pressure upon the Vichy Government to stop such 'anti-Japanese' measures.[2] In this situation Catroux, although personally in favour of the de Gaullist movement, judged it best to discourage any anti-Vichy activities in Indo-China, lest these precipitate a Japanese invasion.[3] When in mid-July General Nishihara raised the question of air bases and transit rights in Indo-China, General Catroux professed willingness to co-operate with Japan in preventing the entry of Chinese troops, and to make commercial concessions; but he declared that any Japanese military occupation must be a matter for negotiation between the Governments of France and Japan.[4] On 20 July Catroux turned over his office to the Vichy appointee, Vice-Admiral Decoux.[5] As will be seen, Decoux also followed his predecessor in yielding where he must, resisting where he could, and procrastinating as much as possible. All things considered, he put up a very creditable performance in a position of extreme difficulty.

The second Konoye Cabinet resolved to conduct negotiations on political and military matters with the Vichy Government, through the medium of their Ambassador in Tokyo, Arsène Henry, but to leave economic affairs to discussions between the Japanese Consul-General in Hanoi, Suzuki, and the French Indo-China authorities.[6] General Nishihara was summoned to Tokyo for consultations with the Government, and left Hanoi on 28 July; Colonel Kenryo Sato, who represented the Japanese South China Army, was made acting head of the Japanese military mission in Indo-China.[7]

[1] W. L. Langer, *Our Vichy Gamble* (New York, Knopf, 1947), p. 78 n.

[2] For the State Department's unwillingness to sell arms to French Indo-China, see Hull, *Memoirs*, i. 907. Japanese reactions to the attempt are recounted in the Report of the South Seas Bureau of the Gaimusho for 1940 (IMTFE, *Record*, p. 6868). Catroux was blamed by Vichy for acceding to the Japanese demands in June, and on 25 June was recalled. (J. Decoux, *À la Barre de l'Indochine* (Paris, Plon, 1949), p. 66.)

[3] So Catroux declared after his arrival in London to join de Gaulle (*Manchester Guardian*, 19 September 1940).   [4] IMTFE, *Record*, p. 6877.

[5] Decoux had received his official appointment as Governor-General on 30 June (*L'Indochine*, p. 58).

[6] IMTFE, *Record*, p. 6878. Vichy agreed to this on 27 July (Decoux, *L'Indochine*, p. 93).

[7] *The Times*, 30 July 1940. Nishihara returned on 10 August. Sato meanwhile had presented Decoux with a virtual ultimatum, but Tokyo disavowed him (Decoux, *L'Indochine*, p. 94).

The initial conversation between Matsuoka and Henry took place on 1 August. The Japanese Foreign Minister demanded that France provide bases and transit facilities in Indo-China for Japanese troops. Henry objected that this was tantamount to asking France to go to war with China. He also said that if it were accepted there was no saying what Japan would demand next. Matsuoka in his usual blustering style threatened force if France did not yield.[1] On 9 August Ohashi gave Henry a draft of the proposed Franco-Japanese exchange of Notes on political and military affairs in Indo-China. The French Ambassador at once declared that the requests as drafted were couched in too vague a form and might imply the use of airfields and the stationing of Japanese troops anywhere in Indo-China. Despite Ohashi's assurance that the privileges demanded were intended only as an aid to Japan in the China conflict, Henry stood firm and said that his Government would not accept the proposals as they stood.[2] His firmness was rewarded the next day when Ohashi gave him a revised draft which specified the Province of Tongking as the area in which the Japanese required these military concessions to be made. Henry still objected and asked that the particular points needed for airfields should be specified. This Ohashi refused, pleading the need for military secrecy as his excuse. Henry then, under protest, accepted the demands in principle.[3]

But Vichy still refused to sign any kind of a blank cheque and demanded a guarantee of the territorial integrity of French Indo-China and some advance definition of what the precise demands would be with regard to air bases and the transit of troops.[4] On the night of 21 August the Japanese Foreign Ministry, after consultation with the Army, informed Henry that 'for the time being' only three air bases would be asked for, at Hanoi, Phulan Thuang, and Phutho, and that the Japanese military personnel at these should not exceed 5,000–6,000 men. The routes of passage for the Japanese Army should be via the Haiphong–Hanoi–Laokay and the Hanoi–Langson railway lines; but it was impossible to state how many troops would be sent along these routes.[5] Despite renewed threats of force by Matsuoka the French still held out and submitted another counter draft on 25 August, which, while evidently

[1] IMTFE, *Record*, pp. 6887–8.
[2] ibid. pp. 6888–90.   [3] ibid. pp. 6892–3.
[4] ibid. pp. 6912–13.   [5] ibid. p. 6921.

going a long way towards acceptance of the Japanese demands, was not entirely satisfactory to Tokyo.[1]

Meanwhile Matsuoka had been endeavouring to bring German pressure to bear on Vichy. On 2 August he told Ott of the Japanese demands, and asked Germany not to object to them, but to influence the French Government to agree. Again on 15 August Ott reported that the Japanese Foreign Ministry had told him that the French were making difficulties, and had repeated its requests for German support. Ott was told that Berlin would accord this but that 'our influence on French policy was limited'.[2] Thus the German Government at this time appear to have given at the most, but lukewarm support to Japan. Ribbentrop had apparently accepted Ott's hint in June that the Indo-China situation might be used as a bargaining counter to tie Japan to the Axis.[3]

The Vichy Government did not want to give way to Japan. Baudouin on 17 August informed the Chinese, in general terms, of the negotiations. The Chinese Government on 26 August threatened to send in *their* troops if the Japanese were allowed into Tongking. Baudouin said that the French would not resist the Chinese, if they came in answer to a Japanese invasion. This would have turned the province into a Sino-Japanese battlefield.[4]

The distraught Vichy régime could see no prospects of effective support against Japan from any quarter. The American Government had, on 7 August, made inquiries in Tokyo about the rumoured Japanese demands, and, on 26 August, had pressed Vichy not to accept them.[5] But Vichy had to fear that, if it procrastinated too long, the Japanese Army in south China would invade Tongking, with or without the sanction of the Government in Tokyo. If that happened, there would be an end of French sovereignty over and administration in Indo-China; and this was what Baudouin, the Vichy Foreign Minister, was anxious to prevent.[6] So, on 30 August, agreement was reached in the form of

---

[1] ibid. p. 6922. [2] ibid. pp. 6295–6.
[3] See p. 222 above.
[4] Decoux, *L'Indochine*, pp. 247–8.
[5] Hull, *Memoirs*, i. 903. The Japanese answered the 7 August representations a week later with a reply 'written in pencil' which in effect told the United States Government not to meddle with what did not concern them (ibid. pp. 906–7).
[6] Baudouin had once been head of the Banque de l'Indochine. The French had one card to play, i.e. that if the Japanese wrecked the French administration and turned Indo-China into a battlefield, they would largely ruin their own hopes of economic and military gain. Decoux says that he sent three telegrams

an exchange of Notes in Tokyo between Henry and Matsuoka. France recognized the economic and political predominance of Japan in the Far East and agreed to concede to her economic privileges in Indo-China superior to those accorded to third Powers. On the understanding that the military privileges required were intended only to facilitate the ending of the Japanese conflict with China, and that they would therefore be limited and temporary in character, the French Government were prepared to order the General Officer Commanding their forces in Indo-China to settle the details with the Japanese general in command at Hanoi. France was not to be involved in any expenditure and was to receive compensation should the Sino-Japanese conflict spread to Indo-China as a consequence of the facilities granted to the Japanese forces. In return for these concessions to Japan, France asked for a guarantee that Japan would respect French rights and interests in the Far East, and in particular French sovereignty over Indo-China and the territorial integrity of the region. The Japanese reply gave the required guarantee, accepted the French propositions concerning the grant of facilities in Indo-China, and asked that the French Government should speedily issue instructions to the French authorities in Indo-China.[1]

Despite the Henry–Matsuoka Agreement, both Vichy and Hanoi still tried to procrastinate, perhaps in the hope of last-minute assistance.[2] When Nishihara on 30 August called on Decoux, he found that the Governor-General had received no instructions to open negotiations.[3] Renewed pressure by Tokyo on Vichy, through Sawada, the Japanese Ambassador there, resulted in Decoux getting instructions on 2 September.[4] But Decoux,

urging Vichy not to give way and saying that Indo-China could be defended. He admits that the Japanese forces in South China were underestimated by General Martin, Commandant of the Indo-China forces (*L'Indochine*, pp. 101–2).

[1] IMTFE, *Record*, pp. 6936–9.

[2] The Vichy Government asked the United States to secure assurances from Japan similar to those given to France. Hull declined this and lectured Vichy severely for having agreed to Japanese hegemony in the Far East in the agreement of 30 August. But, while he renewed his protests to Tokyo against the Japanese demands, he was unwilling to go farther and join with the British Government in rendering military assistance to Indo-China, which Lothian proposed on 16 September. Hull would not go beyond protests and economic reprisals, and he warned Lothian that if the United States were involved in a Pacific war, it would mean a serious curtailment of American supplies to Britain (*Memoirs*, i. 904–7).

[3] Nishihara presented Decoux with a military convention which he said must be accepted by 2 September (Decoux, *L'Indochine*, p. 102).

[4] IMTFE, *Record*, p. 6928.

backed by the Indo-China Conseil du Gouvernement, rejected the Japanese ultimatum.[1] Nishihara then threatened that the Japanese Army would advance into Indo-China on 5 September and warned Suzuki to prepare to evacuate Japanese nationals on the previous day.[2] The Japanese Government in Tokyo brought renewed pressure to bear on Vichy and, as a result of all this, a Military Agreement was signed between General Nishihara and General Martin, commander of the French Indo-China forces, on the morning of 4 September.

This Agreement provided that the number of Japanese personnel, including non-combatants, at the bases to be granted them, should never exceed two-thirds of the 25,000 troops for which they were demanding passage through Tongking. Until a final agreement on details should be reached no Japanese troops were to enter. Should they do so, it would constitute a breach of the agreement and would entitle the French to regain freedom of action.[3] Nishihara expected the agreement on details to be concluded on 6 September, but on that day a Japanese battalion crossed the border near Langson.[4] Despite Nishihara's explanation that this action was unauthorized, Decoux declared it to be a breach of the agreement of 4 September and broke off the negotiations.[5] They remained at a standstill until 13 September when Decoux declared that he had received instructions to resume them.[6]

On 11 September Henry raised in Tokyo the question of Siamese border aggressions and asked Japan to have them stopped.[7] Despite a rejoinder from Ohashi on the following day that Japan had no concern with this matter, the French Ambassador on 16 September asserted that Japan was backing Siam and that therefore the delay in concluding the Indo-China negotiations was Japan's own fault.[8] Ohashi in reply threatened that the Japanese Army might advance at any time.[9] On 17 September the French Indo-China authorities signified their general assent to the

[1] Decoux, *L'Indochine*, p. 104.
[2] IMTFE, *Record*, pp. 6928–9.
[3] ibid. pp. 6930, 6940–8.
[4] ibid. p. 6930.   [5] ibid.
[6] ibid. p. 6931. Decoux was taking a stiff attitude because he and Martin believed the Japanese forces in Yunnan were in poor condition and might be successfully resisted. His instructions from Vichy were to resist the Japanese if they came in without an agreement, but to let them in should the Chinese invade Indo-China in answer to the Matsuoka–Henry accord (*L'Indochine*, pp. 104–6).
[7] IMTFE, *Record*, p. 6931.
[8] ibid. pp. 6931–2.   [9] ibid.

Japanese demands.[1] But two days later Nishihara presented fresh demands to Decoux, including the permanent stationing of 32,000 troops in Indo-China,[2] while Ohashi told Henry that 'after zero hour on 23 September the Japanese Army would enter Tongking whether the agreement on details had been concluded or not'.[3] This was followed by the evacuation of Japanese nationals from Hanoi and Saigon and by Japanese naval demonstrations in the Gulf of Tongking. The Japanese South China Army, under General Saburo Ando, concentrated for an attack on Dong Dang and Langson.[4]

Despairing of effective help from abroad, the French on 22 September came to an Agreement with Japan. This was signed by Nishihara and a representative of the French Indo-China Army on board the Japanese warship *Kawachi*.[5] The Agreement provided for the establishment of three Japanese airfields in Tongking, with a garrison of not more than 6,000 troops, and for the possible transfer of a maximum of 25,000 men through Tongking against Yunnan. The Japanese division massed on the border near Langson might be evacuated through Indo-China, but this was to be the subject of a separate agreement.[6] But the Japanese South China Army, apparently irritated because permission had not been accorded it to come in via Langson, attacked nevertheless and on 25 September inflicted a heavy defeat on the ill-prepared and demoralized French forces at Langson.[7] Decoux appealed to

----

[1] ibid. Decoux (*L'Indochine*, p. 108) says that the Japanese modified their original demand for unlimited troop entry.

[2] So the French delegation to the Franco-German Armistice Commission told General von Stuelpnagel, head of the German delegation (IMTFE, *Record*, p. 6790). Decoux says Nishihara demanded that the Japanese Army come in via Langson and that it should set up a Headquarters in Hanoi (*L'Indochine*, pp. 110–11).

[3] IMTFE, *Record*, p. 6932.

[4] *NYT*, 20 and 21 Sept. 1940.

[5] Baudouin on 23 September said that the agreement had been reached after long negotiations; and that France had accepted 'as the only means of saving what could be saved for France in Indo-China'. He alleged that the American Government on 31 August had declared that they could not help to defend Indo-China and that they understood the necessity of the French making concessions to Japan. He denied any German pressure on France to conclude the agreement (ibid. 24 Sept. 1940). Hull on 23 September denied ever having approved the French concessions to Japan (ibid. also Hull, *Memoirs*, i. 907).

[6] Decoux, *L'Indochine*, p. 112.

[7] The Annamite contingents were disaffected to the French and so was the considerable number of Germans in the Foreign Legion (A. T. Steele in *Chicago Daily News*, 7 Oct. 1940). Steele in subsequent dispatches from Hanoi described the arrogance of the Japanese, their encouragement of Annamite disaffection, and the spirit of defeatism among French officials who complained of lack of

Tokyo through Henry and the Emperor issued a personal order to the troops to stay their advance, which they did. On 2 October Nishihara was replaced by General Sumita. The Japanese apologized for the affray, released their prisoners, and returned Langson to the French forces. The belligerent Japanese division was evacuated via Haiphong.[1]

While overborne by the Japanese in front, the French administration in Indo-China was also menaced by a flank attack from Siam. The hopeful experiment in constitutional monarchy which had been inaugurated in that country in 1932 had subsequently degenerated into a military oligarchy, especially after 1938 when Marshal Luang Pibul Songgram became Premier and virtual dictator.[2] In domestic policy he aped the methods of European dictators, while in foreign affairs he encouraged chauvinism and irredentism. Thus he fostered the development of a pan-Thai movement which preached the inclusion in the Siamese kingdom of all peoples of Thai extraction, especially those in the Shan States of Burma and western China and in the Indo-China Protectorates of Laos and Cambodia. One aspect of this was a decree of Luang Pibul that Siam should henceforth be officially styled 'Thailand' and its people 'Thai'. The names were not new, but the intent was significant.[3] More extreme nationalist claims envisaged the incorporation into Siam of all territories over which her kings had ever exercised suzerainty, whether inhabited by people of Thai extraction or not; these claims included all of Cambodia and part of Lower Burma. They also encompassed the four Malay States of Kedah, Perlis, Kelantan, and Trengganu, suzerainty over which had been abandoned by Siam in favour of Great Britain by the Anglo-Siamese Treaty of 1909.[4] These more extreme aims, however, remained partially concealed until December 1941.

help, especially from the United States, in explaining the surrender to Japan (ibid. 3, 4, 5, and 7 Dec. 1940).

[1] Decoux, *L'Indochine*, pp. 117–21. Tojo, in his defence statement to the Tokyo Tribunal, said that he removed the general in command and his staff, and court-martialled the subordinate officers (IMTFE, *Record*, pp. 36203–4).

[2] Sir J. Crosby, *Siam; the Crossroads* (London, Hollis & Carter, 1945), pp. 82–91.   [3] ibid. pp. 111–12.

[4] ibid. pp. 112–13. In 1904 Siam had ceded to France that part of Luang Prabang which was situated on the west bank of the Mekong, and by a further Treaty in 1903 she had similarly ceded the Cambodian provinces of Battambong and Siemrap. There was latent resentment in Siam at these enforced cessions, at least among the nationalist intelligentsia. In the mid-nineteenth century Siam had got the upper hand of Annam in the long conflict between them for control over the Lao regions and the weak kingdom of Cambodia. The coming of the

The Japanese, whose influence in Siam had grown *pari passu* with the rise of the military party there, did their utmost to encourage these aspirations, as a means of undermining British and French influence in Siam and of inducing her to look to Japan as the 'big brother' who would one day help her to pay off old scores. They also endeavoured to exploit for their own ends the Siamese fear of and hostility to China. Formerly the numerous Chinese immigrants into Siam had usually intermarried with the Siamese and become largely assimilated. After the rise of the Kuomintang, the Chinese in Siam, even if born there, were claimed as citizens of the Chinese Republic and encouraged to preserve their separate identity especially through the establishment of their own schools. This alarmed the Siamese and added political estrangement to the resentment already felt at the economic stranglehold which the Chinese had secured upon Siam. After 1932 the Siamese Government retaliated by imposing limits, through the medium of an admission tax, on immigration; by the assertion of the Siamese nationality of all children born in Siam; and by insisting on the use of the Siamese language as the chief medium of instruction in all schools. They further endeavoured, through the organization of semi-official concerns, to break the virtual foreign (including Chinese) monopoly of commerce and industry. This policy called forth loud protests from the Chinese communities in Siam. These were supported by the Chinese Nationalist Government, which demanded the conclusion of a treaty to enable China to establish diplomatic and consular representatives in Siam. The Siamese were unwilling to agree to this unless the Chinese Government would first renounce their claim that all persons of Chinese blood born in Siam were Chinese citizens and entitled to the protection of the Chinese State.[1] To the Siamese therefore, China, rather than Japan, was a potential danger, and the Japanese attack upon China was in the nature of a relief to them. But should China happen to emerge from the struggle stronger, more united, and even more shrilly nationalist, Siam would be in no comfortable position. So, while they had no particular liking for the Japanese, it was not unnatural that the Siamese leaders should feel that, to some degree, the fortunes of Japan and of Siam were linked.

French altered matters to Siam's disadvantage. But the primitive Thai people of Laos had no desire to be ruled by Bangkok, while the Cambodians to some degree regarded the French as their protectors.

[1] Crosby, *Siam*, pp. 70–76.

Nevertheless, the traditional policy of Siam had been one of preserving peaceful relations with the powerful states in her vicinity; it was in fact due to the shrewdness of her monarchs in pursuing this policy that she, alone out of the countries of South East Asia, had succeeded in preserving her political independence. It was in line with this policy that, on 12 June 1940, the Siamese Government signed at Bangkok Treaties of Non-Aggression with Great Britain and with France. The idea of such a pact had originated with the French; the Siamese Government had at first welcomed it and extended it to include Britain and also Japan. The British and French Governments had been in consultation and had agreed on the terms of the proposed treaties. In both cases these provided for respect of the territorial integrity of the contracting parties and bound each of them to accord no assistance to any third Power with which the other should be at war.[1]

Japan preferred an independent procedure. On the same day as the Anglo-Siamese and Franco-Siamese Treaties were signed, the Japanese Government signed in Tokyo a Treaty with Siam, which, in addition to provisions of a similar character to those of the British and French Agreements, stipulated that the two countries should exchange information and should consult upon matters of mutual interest.[2]

The ratifications of the Anglo-Siamese Treaty were exchanged on 31 August 1940.[3] But the Franco-Siamese Treaty was never ratified. The Siamese Government had for some time been asking Paris to agree to a modification of the Mekong river frontier to make the thalweg, or deep-water channel, the actual boundary, so as to give the islands on the Siamese side to Siam, instead of all the islands being French, as was the case under the existing treaties. This was a minor claim and a reasonable one, but the French Government had stood on their legal rights and refused to heed the advice of their Minister in Bangkok to concede the point. After the fall of France the Vichy Government did agree, and proposed the appointment of a Franco-Siamese Commission to redefine the boundary.[4]

But the defeat of France in Europe and the Japanese demands

[1] ibid. p. 56. Decoux criticizes M. Lepissier, then French Minister at Bangkok, for urging Paris to conclude this treaty, which he says was done without any official consultation with the Governor-General of Indo-China (*L'Indochine*, pp. 128–31).   [2] Crosby, *Siam*, pp. 56–57.
[3] ibid. p. 56.   [4] ibid. pp. 117–18.

in Indo-China fanned the flames of Siamese irredentism. On 13 September the Siamese Government made a formal demand on Vichy for the retrocession of territories on the west bank of the Mekong River as far as the frontier of Cambodia and of the Cambodian provinces of Battembong, Siemrap, and Sisophon.[1] The French Government on 19 September rejected any territorial cessions.[2] Luang Pibul refused to ratify the non-aggression treaty with France unless his claims were conceded. He renewed them on 28 September, with the additional demand that if and when the French Government renounced sovereignty over Indo-China they should cede all of Laos and Cambodia to Siam.[3] The French again refused and sporadic land, air, and naval hostilities broke out between Siam and Indo-China.

It appears that when the Siamese Government made their demands they were confidently expecting the collapse of the French administration in Indo-China in face of the Japanese attack. When this did not occur and the French came to terms with Japan, the Siamese were in somewhat of a quandary, as they had not the strength to force submission to their demands.[4] This situation provided an excellent opportunity for Japan to intervene; she was in the position of the fisherman in the Chinese fable, who came upon a kingfisher which had pecked at an oyster and got caught by the beak and who promptly bagged both of them.

From the account of the negotiations found in the archives of the Japanese Foreign Ministry it appears that the Japanese had not instigated the Siamese demands on Indo-China. These were, indeed, something of an embarrassment to Tokyo, which was endeavouring to get the French to yield to Japanese requirements without fighting.[5] The Japanese had, indeed, a plan for the partition of Indo-China in certain eventualities. They were ready to give Tongking to China if by this means Chiang Kai-shek could be bribed to conclude peace with Japan. If necessary they also envisaged the cession of Cambodia to Siam and the setting up of the rest of Indo-China as an Annamese State professedly independent but really in Japanese political and economic leading-strings.[6] In the meantime, they preferred to keep Indo-China as a going

---

[1] IMTFE, *Record*, p. 6869. [2] ibid. [3] ibid. p. 6870.
[4] ibid. pp. 6870–1. [5] ibid. p. 6871.
[6] This scheme is to be found in an unsigned memorandum dated 28 September 1940, from the archives of the JFM and reproduced in IMTFE, *Record*, pp. 6977–8.

concern, and to let the French administration continue to function, since this made it easier for them to exploit the country.

On the other hand Matsuoka wanted to bring Siam into the Greater East Asia sphere, both for economic and for strategic reasons. He desired to secure Siamese rice and raw materials; while he also wanted to get control of the country as a stepping-stone for the attack on Malaya and Singapore which he planned to launch when the time should be propitious.[1] So he was willing to help Siam if she were ready to pay the price.

On 20 September a Siamese 'goodwill mission', with the Vice-Minister of War at its head, arrived in Tokyo.[2] In response to its overtures the Japanese Government at first professed neutrality in the Siamese quarrel with Indo-China and during the following month watched the Siamese get more deeply involved in trouble. In early October the American Government signified their disapproval of Luang Pibul's proceedings by stopping exports of American aircraft to Siam and by warnings against any disturbance of the *status quo* in Indo-China.[3] The Vichy Government on 15 October announced their rejection of Siamese territorial demands in Laos and Cambodia.[4] Pibul responded with threats of war, but despite his bluster, he evidently did not feel confident of the result.[5]

This provided the Japanese Government with the opportunity to intervene. At a meeting of the Inner Cabinet on 5 November it was decided to offer assistance to Siam in the fulfilment of her territorial aspirations in return for her agreement to cooperate both politically and economically in the establishment of Greater East Asia. A second Inner Cabinet meeting on 21 November agreed to back up Siam if she limited her demands to the territory on the west bank of the Mekong and the Pakse region.[6] Pibul, caught in a net of his own making, had to accept the Japanese terms.[7] On 28

---

[1] IMTFE, *Record*, p. 6872.

[2] This mission, led by Luang Prom Yodi, went by way of Indo-China. Its chief suggested to Decoux an Indo-Chinese accord with Siam against Japanese expansion. The price for this was to be the cession to Siam of the territory on the right bank of the Mekong. Decoux rejected the proposal out of hand (*L'Indochine*, p. 132).

[3] *NYT*, 11 and 15 Oct. 1940. Hull on 13 January 1941 warned the Siamese Minister in Washington against Japan's designs and urged that Siam compose her differences with Indo-China. But he told the British Government that he did not think much could be done as Japan was 'probably directing and controlling the cause and attitude of Thailand' (*Memoirs*, ii. 985).

[4] *NYT*, 16 Oct. 1940. [5] ibid. 21 Oct. 1940.
[6] IMTFE, *Record*, p. 6873. [7] ibid.

November Matsuoka proposed to the Vichy Government a 'peaceful arbitration' of the Siam–Indo-China disputes, to which they replied on the following day that while they appreciated Japan's good intentions they were not prepared to cede any territory. Matsuoka advised 'reconsideration' of this attitude, 'which would not be to the French advantage'.[1]

Meanwhile Decoux had appealed to Vichy for reinforcements. Vichy responded by ordering four battalions of Senegalese troops to sail from Djibouti, but their ship was ordered back by British cruisers, and, despite appeals to London through Washington, the British Government would not let the troops proceed.[2] Decoux considers that the British envoy in Bangkok was working to placate the Siamese at the expense of Indo-China; he also accuses the French representative at Bangkok of inclining to the same course, until his recall in November 1940.[3] In mid-January a French offensive designed to secure better covering positions in Cambodia met with defeat, but this was offset by the French naval victory of Koh-chang on 17 January, when the Siamese Navy lost its best ships.[4] Decoux had also sent an emissary to Singapore, in the hope of enlisting the diplomatic support of the British authorities there. The Japanese got to know of this and protested to Vichy. Matsuoka told Henry that the British Minister at Bangkok had offered British mediation in the Siam–Indo-China quarrel.[5] Garreau, the new French Minister in Bangkok, said he believed that Crosby's attitude was that 'it was better to have the Siamese on the Annamite chain, than the Japanese in Thailand'.[6] Certainly a settlement sponsored by Great Britain, which included some sops to the Siamese expansionists, would have strengthened British influence in Siam and lessened that of Japan. This Tokyo was resolved to prevent.

So on 21 January the Japanese Government again offered mediation and two days later the Vichy Government, under heavy pressure, were constrained to accept, and to agree to a cessation of hostilities effective from 28 January.[7] The next day armistice negotiations opened on board the Japanese cruiser *Natori* in Saigon harbour, and agreement was reached on 30 January. By the terms of this both sides were to withdraw to positions ten

[1] ibid. p. 6874.   [2] Decoux, *L'Indochine*, p. 136.
[3] ibid.   [4] ibid. pp. 140–1.   [5] ibid. pp. 142–3.
[6] ibid. p. 145.   [7] *NYT*, 29 Jan., 3 Feb. 1941.

kilometres from those they were holding when the fighting stopped. To make sure that her 'mediation' would be successful Japan poured fresh troops into Haiphong and Hanoi and made little secret of her intention to use force against Indo-China unless her 'solution' were accepted.[1]

The Franco-Siamese negotiations began in Tokyo on 7 February 1941. The French delegation was headed by the French Ambassador to Japan, Arsène Henry, and the Siamese by Prince Varnvaidya. They completely failed to agree and Henry told Matsuoka on 17 February that further discussion was useless. The armistice was due to expire on 25 February and the French were ready to fight Siam rather than yield. But Matsuoka insisted on an extension of the armistice till 7 March and then produced his compromise plan. To this the Siamese had perforce to agree and the French were threatened with dire consequences unless they, too, accepted the proposals.[2] Very unwillingly and protesting that they 'yielded to Japan, not to Thailand', the Vichy Government submitted. On 6 March a joint communiqué from the Japanese, Siamese, and French negotiators announced that agreement had been reached on the principal points. On 11 March the agreement was initialed and its terms revealed.[3] Japan's price took the form of an exchange of letters between her Government and those of her two victims in which she guaranteed the 'final and inviolable' character of the settlement, while they each agreed to conclude no arrangements with third Powers which might involve them in any political, economic, or military collaboration, direct or indirect, against Japan.[4] The German Government had also, at Japan's request, put pressure on Vichy to yield. Ohashi on 21 November 1940 had told Ott of Japan's intention to mediate to prevent Siam

[1] IMTFE, *Record*, pp. 6718–19.   [2] ibid. pp. 6719–20.
[3] By the agreement France ceded to Siam the part of Laos situated on the west bank of the Mekong, and an area of Cambodia bounded by the Mekong River to Stung Treng, thence by a line running to the Tonle Sap (Great Lake) and from there south-west to the Gulf of Siam. The ceded area was to be demilitarized and equality of treatment was to be accorded to Siamese and Indo-Chinese in matters of entry, residence, and occupations. The Siamese Government were to respect the mausoleum and royal palace of the King of Luang Prabang. The Mekong River frontier was to follow the main channel of the river, but the islands of Khong and Khone were to be under joint Franco-Siamese administration. The award meant that Siam got about one-third of Cambodia, in addition to the districts formerly a part of the Laos Protectorate.
[4] The formal treaties were concluded in Tokyo on 9 May 1941 (IMTFE, *Record*, p. 6721). The text of the letters exchanged between Matsuoka and Arsène Henry are in ibid. pp. 6994–7.

from being won over to the Anglo-Saxon camp. On 6 February 1941 Berlin was informed of Japan's intention to bind both Indo-China and Siam by a secret protocol. On 17 February Tokyo told Berlin of difficulties in the negotiations owing to the excessive demands of Siam. The German Government were shown the Japanese compromise proposals and asked to influence Vichy to accept. This they evidently did, for, on 12 March, Ohashi asked Boltze to convey to Ribbentrop 'the sincere gratitude of the Japanese Government for his extraordinarily valuable and effective support of Japanese mediation in the dispute between Thailand and French Indo-China.'[1]

While Japan thus succeeded in bringing French Indo-China into the Greater East Asia Sphere and had taken a long step towards imposing the same fate upon Siam, she met with failure in her efforts to incorporate the Netherlands East Indies into her New Order. They were a much tougher nut to crack, not only because of the proverbial stubbornness of the Dutch character, which was frequently exemplified in the course of the negotiations, but also because Japan was not nearly so well placed to use force in the East Indies as she was in Indo-China and Siam. Although the Netherlands had been overrun by Hitler's armies their Government had not surrendered; they were still carrying on the struggle as allies of Great Britain and a direct attack upon their Far Eastern empire might well involve Japan in hostilities with Great Britain. Furthermore, the United States had large economic interests in the Netherlands East Indies and had reacted promptly to Japanese pronouncements about the *status quo* there in April and May 1940.[2] Therefore the Japanese Government had to reckon that they could not seize the Netherlands East Indies without almost certain war with Great Britain and possible war with the United States. Again, the Dutch disposed of considerable forces in the East Indies which could fight a delaying action for long enough to allow of the destruction of oil stocks and of the equip-

---

[1] ibid. pp. 6444–7.
[2] The Department of State was kept informed of the Japanese-Netherlands conversations and encouraged the Netherlands to make no concessions that would impair the political or economic independence of the East Indies. On 11 July 1940 Grew pointed out to Arita that in 1937 15·8 per cent. of the total foreign trade of the Netherlands East Indies had been with the United States, as compared with 11·6 per cent. with Japan, and emphasized the interest of the United States in the continuance of the 'open door' in that area (Hull, *Memoirs*, i. 895–6).

ment of oil wells; this the Japanese Navy in particular was anxious to avoid. Therefore direct action against the Netherlands East Indies was to be deferred until after Great Britain had been invaded or forced to surrender to Germany, when Japan intended to seize upon Malaya and Singapore. Then would come the turn of the East Indies, which would be forced to declare independence of the Netherlands and afterwards made into a Japanese protectorate.[1]

In the meantime Japan proposed to pave the way for this by endeavouring, through mingled cajolery and threats, to draw the Netherlands East Indies into her political and economic orbit.

The process had begun as early as 2 February 1940, when the Japanese Government, through their Minister at The Hague, presented a Note to the Netherlands Government. This asked for the repeal or modification of restrictions on Japanese import and export trade with the Netherlands East Indies, and for greater facilities for Japanese enterprises there, both extant and contemplated.[2] The Netherlands Government were still considering their reply when the German invasion took place.[3]

Meanwhile in anticipation of this event the Japanese Government had made a public démarche. On 15 April 1940 the Japanese Foreign Minister told the Japanese press that Japan had intimate economic relationships with the South Seas region, especially the Netherlands East Indies. These economic ties would be adversely affected, should war in Europe involve the Netherlands and their East Indies. Consequently Japan would be deeply concerned over any development that might affect the *status quo* of the Netherlands East Indies.[4] The *Asahi* of the same date said that, if the Netherlands became involved in war, either Great Britain might seek to

---

[1] The Dutch produced as part of their case against Japan a Japanese Foreign Ministry document entitled 'Tentative Plan for Policy towards the Southern Regions', dated 4 October 1940. This referred to the desirability of avoiding the destruction of the natural resources of the Netherlands East Indies through a Dutch 'scorched earth' policy. Japan should first secure Singapore, after which the Netherlands East Indies should be coerced into declaring their independence, and a governing council should be established, composed of Dutch, natives, Chinese, and Japanese, but with the Dutch in a minority. The next step would be to weed out the Dutch, and to secure a treaty of alliance between the 'independent State' and Japan, which should provide for the appointment of Japanese 'advisers' to influential positions, and for the lease of military and naval bases to Japan (ibid. pp. 11724–7). The Kobayashi and Yoshizawa missions were evidently intended as a preliminary 'softening up' process.

[2] H. J. van Mook, *The Netherlands Indies and Japan*, (London, Allen & Unwin, 1944), pp. 24–26.

[3] ibid. p. 26.

[4] IMTFE, *Record*, p. 11637.

control the East Indies or else the Netherlands Government might take refuge there and appeal for the protection of the United States. The Japanese press in general talked in a bellicose way of what Japan would do should anything of the sort occur. On 16 April the Japanese Minister at The Hague raised the matter with the Netherlands Foreign Minister, who replied that his Government had not sought nor would seek any country's protection of the East Indies and would refuse any offers of protection or intervention of any kind. A similar assurance was given on 18 April by the Netherlands Minister at Tokyo to the Japanese Foreign Minister.

These Japanese moves caused speculation abroad upon Japan's own possible design to seize upon the East Indies. On 16 April the American Ambassador in Paris reported to Washington a suggestion of the French Foreign Ministry that Britain, France, and the United States should make a joint démarche in Tokyo by reminding the Japanese that, at the time of the Four-Power Treaty of 1921, its signatories had promised to respect Dutch rights in the Pacific.[1] Hull, however, preferred to take separate action, which took the form of a statement to the American press on 17 April. In this Hull challenged the Japanese claim to any special interest in the fate of the Netherlands Indies and declared that any alteration of the *status quo* by other than peaceful processes would be prejudicial to peace and security in the entire Pacific.[2] In a conversation with the Japanese Ambassador on 20 April[3] Hull had some acid comments to make upon Japanese press claims of a Japanese 'Monroe Doctrine' for East Asia and the South Seas.

There things rested until 10 May, when the Germans invaded the Netherlands. Hull on that day suggested to the British Ambassador that Great Britain should pledge herself not to interfere with the East Indies. He feared that, should any Allied troops be sent there, Japan would seize the excuse to move.[4] The next day Arita handed copies of his statement of 15 April to the British, French, and German Ambassadors and said that events in Europe had accentuated the deep concern of the Japanese Govern-

---

[1] Hull, *Memoirs*, i. 888–9. After the signature of the Four-Power Treaty of 13 December 1921, the signatory Powers had individually, on 4 February 1922, notified the Governments of Holland and of Portugal that they would respect the insular possession of those countries in the Pacific.

[2] ibid. p. 889.   [3] ibid. p. 890.

[4] The Australian Minister was also told that the United States Government desired to see no Allied landings in the Netherlands East Indies, unless at the request of the Dutch Government and under Dutch command (ibid. p. 891).

ment over the status of the Indies. He also expressed to the Netherlands Minister the hope that the Dutch Government would maintain their attitude of preserving the existing *status quo*. Hull, fearing that this might presage some Japanese military move, issued a further press statement on 11 May, which referred to previous commitments to respect the *status quo* in the East Indies and added that these could not be too often reiterated. Roosevelt and Hull urged the British Government to give Tokyo a similar assurance, which they did on 13 May.[1] The French three days later informed the Japanese Government that they also had no intention of intervening in the Netherlands East Indies. Craigie further told Arita that there would be no interference with exports to Japan of raw materials from the East Indies.

Meanwhile Britain and France had sent troops to Curacao and Aruba, in the Dutch West Indies, a step which aroused fresh nervousness and suspicion in Japan, despite a statement by the Netherlands Minister in Tokyo on 15 May that Great Britain, France, and the United States had no intention of intervening in the East Indies, where, in contrast to the situation in the West Indies, the Dutch had ample forces. On 16 May Hull had a long and acrimonious conversation with Horinouchi, the Japanese Ambassador, who had questioned him at length about the Dutch West Indies.[2] Hull was convinced that the Japanese Government were trying to find a pretext for intervention in the East Indies and asserts that

if we had not adopted a firm attitude from the very outset, and if we had not brought immediate pressure on Britain and France to explain their actions in the Dutch West Indies and deny any intention to move into the Dutch East Indies, Japan might well have made a decisive move toward the East Indies in the summer of 1940.[3]

In fact, however, Hull exaggerated Japan's immediately aggressive intentions. Japan certainly coveted the Indies and hoped at some future time to secure them, but she was not yet ready for such an adventure, which would almost certainly involve war with Britain. On 10 August 1940 Kido recorded in his Diary that Prince Fushimi, chief of the Naval General Staff, had said that the Navy

---

[1] Feis, *Road to Pearl Harbor*, pp. 56–57.
[2] Hull, *Memoirs*, i. 893. On 10 May Hull had sharply criticized the British action and Roosevelt had followed this up by urging a public pledge to withdraw from the Dutch West Indies as soon as possible. This also was done (ibid. pp. 815–16).
[3] ibid. p. 893.

wished at present to avoid the use of force against the Netherlands East Indies and Singapore and that since at least eight months would be required to prepare for such an attack after a decision to make it was taken, the later war came the better.[1] It also appears that, while the Army disliked the efforts of the Yonai Cabinet to reach a settlement with Great Britain and the United States and was plotting the overthrow of the Cabinet, it did not wish Japan to be involved in war until the China Affair was settled and until Soviet intentions were more certainly known. The Japanese are apt to be most truculent when they are at heart afraid and they were worried in the spring of 1940 about their supplies of overseas raw materials, especially of oil, rubber, and tin. The wartime needs of Great Britain and of France had caused those Powers to put restrictions upon the export of raw materials from their colonies; while economic relations with the United States remained in a state of uncertainty, with the possibility of an American embargo on oil and other exports to Japan always present. If the Netherlands Indies came under British or American control supplies from that quarter might also be restricted. What Japan wanted was to keep everybody else out of the East Indies until she was ready to move in; hence, on the one hand, her insistence on the maintenance of the *status quo* there, and, on the other, her dislike of the American proposal that Japan and the United States should exchange Notes guaranteeing the *status quo* of the Pacific territories of the European belligerents.[2]

The German invasion of the Netherlands was followed by fresh Japanese demands upon the East Indies. On 20 May Arita presented a Note to the Netherlands Minister in Tokyo, General J. C. Pabst, in which he demanded that the Netherlands East Indies supply Japan annually with a specified tonnage of certain raw materials, including a million tons of mineral oil.[3] On 28 May he required an immediate answer, and made a veiled threat of force.[4]

The policy of the Netherlands Government was, as of necessity it had to be, to avoid a too direct rebuff to Japan, while yielding as

---

[1] IMTFE, *Record*, p. 11718.

[2] Hull told Grew to propose this on 22 June and Grew did so two days later. Arita told Kido that it was inadvisable at this time to have Japan's activities, including those in the Netherlands East Indies, restricted. He was willing to consider only a guarantee of Japanese and American insular possessions in the Pacific (Hull, *Memoirs*, i. 895; IMTFE, *Record*, p. 11709).

[3] van Mook, *Netherlands Indies and Japan*, pp. 27–28.

[4] ibid. p. 28.

little as possible and playing for time. Accordingly, they returned on 6 June a dignified but cautious answer, which laid stress on their general policy of nondiscrimination with regard to foreign nationals, enterprises, and commerce in the East Indies, rejected Japanese proposals for a preferred position, accepted the more reasonable Japanese requests with regard to exports of raw materials, and suggested that negotiations on details should take place in Batavia between the Japanese Consul-General there and the local Netherlands authorities.[1]

The Japanese Government continued to ask for more comprehensive negotiations at Batavia. They had avoided sending their envoy in Holland to London, and it became clear that they wanted to enter into political as well as economic talks in Batavia as a means of detaching the colony from the Netherlands Government in London.[2] The Netherlands Government combated these moves; they insisted that any discussions should be confined to economic affairs, and they also objected to General Koiso, who was at first proposed by the Konoye Cabinet as head of the Japanese delegation.[3] Finally, on 27 August the Japanese Government announced that Ichiro Kobayashi, Minister of Commerce and Industry in the Cabinet, had been appointed as special envoy to the Netherlands East Indies.[4] The Netherlands Government appointed Dr. H. J. van Mook, Director of Economic Affairs, as their chief delegate.[5] To this the Japanese Government strongly objected. They wanted the Netherlands Government to confer special powers upon the Governor-General of the Netherlands East Indies for the discussions with Kobayashi. It was clear that what they were aiming at was to detach the Government of the Netherlands East Indies as much as possible from the Netherlands Government in London and that the primary purpose of the Kobayashi mission was not economic, but political.[6] But they found themselves frustrated; in reply to their remonstrances

---

[1] ibid. pp. 29–36.   [2] ibid. pp. 38–39.

[3] Koiso had told Japanese press reporters on 3 August that the Netherlands Indies Government had always oppressed the natives there. So the Netherlands Government refused to accept him unless he retracted this statement (ibid. p. 39).

[4] ibid. Kobayashi was a successful business man, but no diplomatist. His chief advisers were T. Ota, chief of Section in the Tokyo Foreign Ministry and O. Saito, Consul-General in Batavia, who was overbearing and aggressive in character (ibid. pp. 38–39).

[5] ibid. p. 40. He was assisted by Dr. Enthoven, Director of Justice, and Dr. van Hoogstraten, Chief of the Bureau of Commerce (ibid.).

[6] ibid. pp. 39–40.

the Netherlands Government raised van Mook to the rank of Minister-Plenipotentiary, and agreed to a few general conversations between Kobayashi and the Governor-General, but would go no further.[1]

Kobayashi, accompanied by a numerous suite, which included military and naval officers, arrived in the East Indies on 12 September 1940. He was received with all due ceremony, but his overtures for general 'co-operation' with Japan were politely but firmly declined, and it was made clear to him, especially after the Tripartite Pact of 27 September, that the Netherlands would continue the negotiations only on the understanding that Japan had no hostile intentions towards the East Indies and did not claim any hegemony over them.[2] To this Kobayashi had reluctantly to concur, in a joint statement of 16 October.[3] He thus attained none of his political objectives. In economic matters the Japanese were themselves vague as to what they wanted; they produced some fantastic demands for annual oil supplies, to be guaranteed by the Netherlands East Indies Government, but their demands were scaled down in the course of the negotiations and the request for a guarantee was dropped.[4] On 22 October Kobayashi left for Japan, ostensibly because he was needed in his Ministry, in reality because he had failed in his errand of bringing the Netherlands East Indies into the Co-Prosperity Sphere.[5] He left the negotiations to his subordinates, but in fact they were at a standstill, while the numerous Japanese 'experts' attached to the mission were ferreting out all the information they could secure in preparation for the contemplated future invasion.[6] In view of this the Netherlands Government on 15 November informed the Japanese Govern-

---

[1] ibid. p. 40.   [2] ibid. pp. 42–45.
[3] ibid. pp. 44–45. Kobayashi reported to Matsuoka on 13 September that the Governor-General refused to discuss political problems and that it was useless to continue negotiations with him (IMTFE, *Record*, pp. 11813–14).
[4] They asked for 3,150,000 tons annually, over and above the 600,000 tons they were buying already. Eventually contracts were agreed on for an annual total of about 1·8 million tons (van Mook, *Netherlands Indies and Japan*, pp. 45–60). But the Japanese were not mainly interested in oil purchases; what they were after was leases of land for oil prospecting and getting control of the oil companies. This is revealed by a telegram of 3 September 1940 from Matsuoka to Saito, and another from Kobayashi to Matsuoka of 18 September, which show clearly that what Japan wanted was to enlarge her foothold in the country (IMTFE, *Record*, pp. 11813–14, 11828).
[5] van Mook, *Netherlands Indies and Japan*, pp. 60–61. The oil contracts signed with the oil companies on 18 October resulted in the actual delivery to Japan of about 900,000 tons of oil up to the 'freezing' of Japanese assets in July 1941 (ibid. pp. 54–55).   [6] ibid. pp. 64–65.

ment that the negotiations had come to an end for lack of subject-matter, and suggested that they be formally discontinued.[1] The Japanese Government replied on 20 November that a new special envoy would be appointed; he proved to be K. Yoshizawa, a member of the Japanese House of Peers and a former Foreign Minister. He arrived on 28 December.[2]

Yoshizawa, unlike his predecessor, was an urbane and skilled diplomatist, but his objective was the same, to bring the Netherlands East Indies into the economic and political orbit of Greater East Asia. Moreover, whatever effect his suavity of approach might have had was nullified by the threats and bluster indulged in by Matsuoka and by the Japanese press.[3] On 16 January 1941 Yoshizawa presented a memorandum which asserted the economic interdependence of Japan and the South Sea area and which embodied a number of sweeping demands for enlarged Japanese participation in the industrial and commercial life of the East Indies.[4] These, if accepted, would have gone far to give the Japanese an economic stranglehold on the country. The Netherlands authorities had no intention of conceding these demands; indeed they wished to reduce drastically exports to Japan of vital raw materials, both because of the uncertainty of her intentions, and because of the danger that these commodities would find their way into German hands.[5] But on balance it seemed desirable to

---

[1] ibid. p. 64.   [2] ibid.

[3] Matsuoka on 21 January 1941 told the Japanese Diet that the Netherlands East Indies were already involved in the Greater East Asia Sphere (ibid. p. 71). On 28 January he telegraphed Yoshizawa, telling him to refrain from any expressions that might deny Japanese hegemony within the Greater East Asia Co-Prosperity Sphere (IMTFE, *Record*, p. 11743). This was very embarrassing for Yoshizawa, who was trying to allay Dutch suspicions. The Netherlands Minister in Tokyo on 31 January 1941 informed the Japanese Foreign Ministry that they repudiated any idea of the Netherlands East Indies being incorporated in a 'New Order in Asia'. A Japanese Government spokesman suggested to the foreign press that the Netherlands Government in London was without legal status and only a puppet of the British Government. This caused a suspension of the negotiations until the end of February, when some sort of retractation was obtained from the Japanese (van Mook, *Netherlands Indies and Japan*, pp. 71–75).   [4] ibid. pp. 67–71.

[5] ibid. pp. 76–78. Japan offered to guarantee that any rubber and tin secured from the Netherlands East Indies would be used only in Japan itself. The Dutch regarded such a guarantee as valueless (ibid. p. 80). In this they may have over-rated Japan's solicitude for her quasi-ally. A telegram from Ott to the GFM dated 9 February 1941, shows that Japan was facilitating deliveries of rubber from Indo-China to Germany via Dairen and the Manchuria-Siberian route, but was making difficulties about rubber from Malaya and the Netherlands Indies and saying that she could not get enough from these sources to meet her own needs (IMTFE, *Record*, pp. 6985–90).

spin out the negotiations as long as possible and to avoid giving open offence to Japan, despite the disadvantages of having a virtual espionage ring in the East Indies and of the general public uneasiness created by the 'war of nerves' which the Japanese were waging.[1]

Therefore the conversations were continued. The Japanese delegation, because their Government also were disposed to await events and were not yet prepared to force the issue, proved ready to reduce their demands. But even their revised proposals, which were submitted in the form of a second memorandum on 14 May, still embodied the concept of a preferred economic position for Japanese in the Netherlands Indies.[2] This was firmly controverted in the final Netherlands answer, delivered on 6 June, which, while it offered minor concessions, amounted to a refusal of all the major Japanese demands.[3] On 17 June Yoshizawa had an audience with the Governor-General and said that, as the Netherlands reply was entirely unsatisfactory, he was instructed to ask for its reconsideration, failing which the Japanese Government had decided to discontinue the negotiations. The Governor-General regretted that such reconsideration was not possible. Yoshizawa replied that, despite the disagreement, his Government wanted to see general trade and economic relations continued as before.[4] A joint communiqué was agreed on which embodied this view.[5] Thus the negotiations ended in an atmosphere of outward cordiality. But this was manifestly hollow; the Dutch had no illusions about what Japan would do if and when the time seemed ripe. They had, however, prevented her from getting control of the Netherlands Indies by piecemeal infiltration which was the purpose behind the Kobayashi and Yoshizawa missions. The technique which had been so successful in Indo-China did not work in the East Indies. That meant that, while the fate of the Netherlands East Indies was only postponed and not averted, Japan was at least prevented from getting their resources intact into her hands.[6]

[1] van Mook, *Netherlands Indies and Japan*, pp. 75–78.
[2] ibid. pp. 81–87. The tables giving Japan's detailed requirements in goods were not presented till 22 March.
[3] ibid. pp. 88–96.   [4] ibid. pp. 97–98.
[5] 'Both the Netherlands and the Japanese Delegations greatly regret that the economic negotiation, which has been conducted between them, has unfortunately come to no satisfactory result. It is needless, however, to add that the discontinuation of the present negotiation will lead to no change in the normal relations between the Netherlands Indies and Japan' (ibid. p. 99).
[6] Matsuoka when in Berlin told Ribbentrop that 'if it could somehow be

Japan's military penetration of French Indo-China, immediately followed by her adherence to the Tripartite Pact of 27 September 1940, seemed to the British Government to be the prelude to an attack upon the British possessions in the Far East and Pacific. To Great Britain, fighting for her life against her German and Italian enemies and with no forces to spare to stem the onslaught of a fresh foe, this was a deadly menace. If the Japanese overran Malaya and seized Singapore, they would deprive Great Britain of the vital tin and rubber supplies from this region. Their powerful Navy would dominate the Indian Ocean and cut off the supplies of food, raw materials, and troop reinforcements sent from India and Australasia to Suez or to Great Britain via the Cape. Such a stroke might well prove decisive.[1] Even Cordell Hull agreed that 'this would be more damaging to British defense in Europe perhaps than any other step short of a German crossing of the Channel.'[2]

The Tripartite Pact was signed at a time when unofficial and exploratory Anglo-American Staff talks were going on in London. They were preliminary and tentative in character and, with an election in sight and isolationist feeling running high, Roosevelt turned a deaf ear at the time to suggestions that they be made more concrete.[3] Nor could he respond to British suggestions that the American Pacific fleet be sent to Singapore as a deterrent to further Japanese aggression, both because American isolationist opinion would have denounced such a move as a defence of 'British imperialism' and because the American Chiefs of Staff considered it to be unsound strategy.[4]

avoided he would not touch the Dutch East Indies, as he feared that in case of a Japanese attack on those regions the oil fields would be set on fire. Then they could not be brought into production again for one or two years' (*Nazi-Soviet Relations*, p. 310).

[1] Early in February 1941 Hopkins cabled to Roosevelt: 'I want to emphasize to you the British belief that Japan, under the influence of Germany, is considering making a positive move against British territory in the near future. Eden fears that Japan would be able at least for the time being to cut off the transport route around the Cape from their Thailand bases. From the same bases they could also cut off the route from the Eastern Mediterranean to Australia and New Zealand. Eden believes that a recent temporary blocking of the Suez Canal was a German move to impress the Japanese with their ability to close the Canal' (Sherwood, *White House Papers*, i. 259).

[2] Hull, *Memoirs*, ii. 1017.   [3] Sherwood, *White House Papers*, i. 271.

[4] For British suggestions that Singapore be used by the United States Navy see Hull, *Memoirs*, i. 897, 914; ii. 986–7. The preliminary Anglo-American staff talks in 1940 led to more concrete ones in Washington, during January to March 1941. They resulted in an agreement known as the ABC I Staff Agreement. This laid it down that if Great Britain and the United States became involved in war with both Germany and Japan, the concentration of force should be

In early 1941 some sharp exchanges took place between the British and Japanese Governments. On 7 February Eden had a stormy interview with Shigemitsu. Eden said that Japanese professions that the Tripartite Pact was meant to preserve peace were hard to credit in view of belligerent speeches by Matsuoka and the enlargement of Japan's claims to a sphere of influence in East Asia. The British Government could not accept Japan's claim to a right of mediation in Far Eastern conflicts and considered that her mediation was but a pretext to secure military and political concessions from Siam and French Indo-China. Now a report had been received from Craigie that a crisis was likely in the Far East within two or three weeks. Was Great Britain to assume from this that her territories in the Far East were in danger of a Japanese attack? Eden gave warning that they would be defended to the limit and said he hoped that Japan would remember that she had been best off when she was on friendly terms with Great Britain and the United States.[1] Shigemitsu retorted that it was only natural that Japan should hold the leading position in Eastern Asia. He furthermore complained of British assistance to Chiang Kai-shek.[2]

Matsuoka on 13 and 14 February told Shigemitsu that there was no intention to make trouble with Britain and that Craigie's report was a 'ridiculous fantasy'.[3] He dispatched a memorandum to Eden in which he disclaimed any aggressive intentions against Great Britain, and again declared that the purpose of the Tripartite Pact was to prevent the war in Europe from spreading.[4] He denied

against Germany, until she was beaten; a containing war of attrition was to be waged against Japan (Sherwood, *White House Papers*, i. 273). 'If Japan does enter the war, the military strategy in the Far East will be defensive. The United States does not intend to add to its present military strength in the Far East, but will employ the United States Pacific Fleet offensively in the manner best calculated to weaken Japanese economic power and to support the defense of the Malay Barrier by diverting Japanese strength away from Malaysia' (*Pearl Harbor Attack*, Pt. 15, pp. 1491–2). This decision was followed by a conference of American, British and Dutch military representatives at Singapore, 21–27 April 1941 (ibid. pp. 1551–84). Here disagreement arose over Singapore, to which the Americans considered that the British attached exaggerated importance. The defence plan ultimately produced was rejected by Admiral Stark and General Marshall on 3 July 1941 'mainly because the whole thing pivoted on Singapore' (S. E. Morrison, *History of US Naval Operations in World War II* (London, Oxford University Press, 1948), iii. 55).

[1] IMTFE, *Record*, pp. 9782–7; Sherwood, *White House Papers*, i. 258.

[2] IMTFE, *Record*, pp. 9789–91.

[3] ibid. pp. 9794–9802. But compare this with Matsuoka's statement to Ott on 10 February, p. 250 below.

[4] This memorandum appears in IMTFE, *Record*, p. 10046, under date 17 February. But Matsuoka referred to it in a conversation with Craigie on 15 February.

the charges made in connexion with Japan's mediation between Siam and Indo-China and ended up with what was perhaps only one of his rhetorical flourishes: 'Japan, deeply impressed as she is with an early restoration of peace, is fully prepared to act as a mediator, not only in Greater East Asia, but anywhere the world over, or to take whatever action is calculated to recover normal conditions.'[1]

The British Government took this as an offer to mediate between Great Britain and Germany, prompted by the latter Power. The matter became public through an indiscretion—apparently calculated—of Ishii, deputy spokesman of the Information Bureau, who gave parts of the memorandum to the press.[2] This brought down a storm on Matsuoka's head; the German Government were angry at the suggestion that they needed peace and indignant at any such move being made without their prior knowledge.[3] So were the pro-German elements in Japan, and Matsuoka had hurriedly to deny that Germany and Italy had ever suggested mediation. He explained that, as an old acquaintance of Eden's, he had merely been expressing to him his personal sentiments.[4] The affair resulted in an interchange between Churchill and Matsuoka, in which the Prime Minister repudiated any idea of a negotiated peace and expressed his confidence in final victory. At the same time, while he deplored the strained relations between Great Britain and Japan and denied any desire on the part of Great Britain to become embroiled with her, he declared if this did happen, it would not affect the eventual outcome of the war.[5] Matsuoka in reply affected an equal desire to avoid a clash with Great Britain, again denied

[1] ibid. p. 10046.

[2] Craigie, *Behind the Japanese Mask*, p. 114; Grew, *Ten Years in Japan*, p. 322. Grew describes Matsuoka's anger at British suggestions that this showed that Germany was in a bad way and needed peace, 'which was the last thing he had intended to convey'.

[3] Oshima on 25 February reported an interview with Ribbentrop who had been inclined to regard it as a betrayal of the Tripartite Pact. Oshima had reassured him in this point. Ribbentrop appeared mollified but said he hoped that there would be no misunderstanding in Japan of Germany's real intentions (IMTFE, *Record*, pp. 9826–7).

[4] So he informed Shigemitsu that he had told Craigie on 15 February. Craigie seemed relieved (ibid. p. 9813).

[5] 'It would be a matter of profoundest regret to H.M. Government if by any circumstance Japan and this country were to become embroiled, and this not only because of their recollection of the years during which the two countries were happily united in alliance, but also because such a melancholy event would both spread and prolong the war without however in the opinion of H.M. Government altering its conclusion' (Foreign Office memo. 24 Feb. 1941, enclosed in Shigemitsu to Matsuoka, 24 Feb. 1941, ibid. pp. 9818–23).

that he had any intention to propose formal mediation, but at the same time, while he reaffirmed the peaceful intent of the Tripartite Pact, he asserted that Japan would unhesitatingly carry out her obligations under it.[1]

While Matsuoka was giving these assurances to the British Government, the projected attack on Singapore was being discussed in Japanese military and naval circles and was being vigorously urged upon Japan by the Germans. Ott on 31 January reported that 'activist circles' in Japan were urging a surprise attack on Singapore so as to exclude any possibility of its use by American forces.[2] Ott said that he had discussed with the German military and naval attachés the advantages and disadvantages to Germany of such a Japanese move. On the one hand it would mean a heavy blow to Great Britain, on the other it would almost certainly bring the United States into the war, and create a new theatre of war in the Pacific far removed from German influence. Furthermore, while Japan would secure rich territories in Malaya and the East Indies, she would need their resources for her own war effort and would no longer be able to supply Germany. So Ott asked for instructions as to the attitude he should take towards the projected attack.[3] On 10 February he reported a conversation with Matsuoka, in connexion with the latter's impending visit to Germany. Matsuoka declared that he had told Nomura (the new Ambassador to the United States) to emphasize Japan's loyalty to the Tripartite Pact and to urge upon Roosevelt that the entry of the United States into the war would be senseless, since it could not prevent the defeat of Great Britain. However, should such American action appear imminent Japan would consider an attack on Singapore as a means of preventing America from waging war in the Western Pacific. Matsuoka added that Japan would take such a decision only in complete agreement with Germany. Meanwhile the Japanese armed forces were making preparations for such an eventuality.[4]

Hitler and Ribbentrop had none of Ott's doubts. They wanted Japan to attack Singapore at once as a means of bringing Great

---

[1] ibid. pp. 9835–6. The reply was dated 27 February.
[2] He mentioned Suetsugu and Shiratori, as among them. It should be recalled that Ott admitted to the Military Tribunal in Tokyo that he had in his reports to Ribbentrop habitually exaggerated the influence of these and other 'extremists' so as to please the Nazis and avoid trouble for himself.
[3] IMTFE, *Record*, pp. 6430–4.   [4] ibid. p. 6455.

Britain to her knees and forcing her to sue for peace. Ribbentrop on 23 February told Oshima that the occupation of Singapore 'must take place with lightning speed and, if at all possible, without a declaration of war and in the midst of peace.' This would cripple England and deter the United States from coming into the war.[1]

Oshima replied that preparations for the occupation of Singapore were going on and would be completed by the end of May. But it was felt in Japan that for safety's sake these preparations must envisage war with the United States as well as with Great Britain. The attack on Singapore must come from the land as it was judged too difficult to attempt it by sea alone. The plan of operations provided for the occupation of Hong Kong and also the Philippines in case of need, and it would be carried out in co-ordination with the development of the war in Europe.[2]

This was not at all what Ribbentrop wanted and he again urged his idea of an immediate surprise attack upon Singapore alone. Oshima possibly out of politeness, expressed agreement and said that Konoye and Matsuoka were also in favour of an early attack on Singapore. Ribbentrop replied that he hoped Matsuoka would bring with him the final decision to attack Singapore soon, as the details could be worked out in Berlin. He urged the closest co-operation between Japan and Germany, especially with regard to publicity, in which connexion he referred to Matsuoka's mediation gaff, evidently still a sore point with Berlin.[3]

On 27 February Ribbentrop instructed Ott to 'work with all the means at your command to the end that Japan takes possession of Singapore as soon as possible by surprise.'[4] On 3 March Hitler issued a directive to the Wehrmacht on collaboration with Japan, in which he declared that the object was to bring Japan to active operations in the East so as to tie down British forces there and to divert American attention to the Pacific.[5]

But the Japanese had no intention of fighting Germany's battles for her. Raeder on 18 March told Hitler that, while Japan ought to attack Singapore immediately, Japanese officers had indicated that she would do this only if and when German forces landed in Great Britain.[6] Weizsäcker, in a memorandum to Ribbentrop of 24 March, said much the same thing. He declared that, while

---

[1] Ribbentrop to Ott, 27 Feb. 1941, reporting conversation with Oshima at Fuschl on 23 Feb. (ibid. pp. 6461–3).   [2] ibid. pp. 6463–4.
[3] ibid. pp. 6464–6.   [4] ibid. p. 6468.
[5] ibid. pp. 6470–2.   [6] ibid. p. 6475; also IMT, Nuremberg, iii. 378.

Germany could offer certain inducements to Japan, such as re-nunciation of all claims to the Netherlands East Indies, and to former German possessions in the Pacific, as well as mediation in the China conflict or the recognition of the Wang Ching-wei régime, he did not think these offers would have much effect. He considered that Japan's entry into war with Great Britain depended on further German victories.[1] Ott, who had been recalled to Berlin to take part in the conversations with Matsuoka, reported that the Chiefs of the Army and of the Navy General Staffs in Japan had both said that they were preparing for the attack on Singapore. But the Navy Chiefs were worried about American submarine and air warfare against Japan's lines of communication, should the Philippines be left unsubdued. They were also nervous about a possible transfer of British naval forces from the Mediterranean to the Pacific. The Army leaders, for their part, wanted to be quite sure that the USSR would make no hostile move, and were not prepared to get involved with Great Britain without such an assurance.[2]

Such was the background to the Hitler–Matsuoka conversations. In them both Hitler and Ribbentrop strove to convince Matsuoka that the war against Great Britain was as good as won. Their assurances with respect to the USSR have already been described.[3] With regard to Great Britain, Hitler declared that she was tied down in Europe and the objective was now the destruction of the British World Empire. The United States was not yet ready to intervene, and now was the most favourable moment for Japan to strike and to help in the destruction of British power. He added that if this favourable moment were let slip and the European conflict ended in some sort of compromise, France and England would, after a few years, recover and would be joined by America as a third enemy of Japan. Germany and Italy, on the other hand, had no interest in East Asia and no objection to Japan realizing her ambitions there. Therefore, Japan should join with Germany and Italy in securing the complete overthrow of Great Britain.[4]

---

[1] IMTFE, *Record*, pp. 6476–7. 'Matsuoka's companion, Sakamoto, revealed more clearly than did Matsuoka himself that his Government intended to inter-vene in South East Asia, that they would do so when the British Empire was obviously becoming shaky, and that they would most certainly do so if we landed in Britain' (Weizsäcker, *Memoirs*, p. 249).

[2] Note on the situation of Japan (undated, possibly also of 24 March, ibid. pp. 6478–9).   [3] See Ch. VII above.

[4] Interview between the Führer and Matsuoka, 27 March 1941 (*Nazi-Soviet Relations*, pp. 289–93).

Ribbentrop, echoing his Führer's ideas, in particular pressed for a speedy Japanese attack on Singapore.[1]

Matsuoka's reply is illustrative of his bombastic character. According to the German records of the conversation he declared that he had been in favour of the alliance with the Axis long before the outbreak of the European War. When that conflict occurred he had urged an immediate Japanese attack on Singapore 'since he did not favor the idea that Japan should join the alliance without having made some contribution toward bringing about the collapse of England.' But he had been overruled. He agreed that Japan should seize Singapore as soon as possible. But, he said, 'there were in Japan, as in other countries, certain intellectual circles which only a powerful individual could hold firmly under control.' He meant by intellectual circles the sort of persons 'who would like to capture the tiger cub', but who were not 'prepared to go into the den and take it away from its mother.'[2] Some of these people were in influential positions and he had to bring them round to his point of view. In this he was certain of ultimate success. 'But at the present moment he could under these circumstances make no pledge on behalf of the Japanese Empire that it would take action. . . . He could make no definite commitment, but he would promise that he personally would do his utmost for the ends that had been mentioned.'[3]

This was not very pleasant hearing for the leaders of the Reich and, in a later conversation, Ribbentrop again dwelt upon the impending collapse of Britain and the great opportunities which lay before Japan if only she would take the plunge. He also endeavoured to assure Matsuoka that there was little danger of American intervention.[4] Matsuoka professed agreement and said that 'his tactics were based on the safe assumption that the whole Japanese Nation could be united at one stroke by the sudden attack on Singapore.'[5] He declared that

he was doing everything to soothe the British with regard to Singapore. He was acting as if Japan had no designs whatsoever on this key point of England in the East. It might therefore be that in his words and acts he would assume a friendly manner toward the English. But Germany should not be misled by that. He was assuming that manner not only in

[1] ibid. p. 287.   [2] ibid. p. 294.   [3] ibid. p. 295.
[4] Ribbentrop–Matsuoka conversation, 28 March 1941 (ibid. pp. 298–300).
[5] ibid. p. 307.

order to soothe the British, but to mislead the pro-British and pro-American elements in Japan, until he should one day suddenly attack Singapore.[1]

He requested German assistance in the attack, to which Ribbentrop replied that he had already asked Oshima to supply maps of Singapore 'so that the Führer, who certainly must be considered the greatest expert of modern times on military matters, could advise Japan as to the best method for the attack on Singapore.'[2] Matsuoka said that 'some junior naval officers who were experts on such matters and who were good friends of his were of the opinion that it would take three months to capture Singapore', though 'as a cautious Minister of Foreign Affairs, he had doubled that time.'[3]

In his final interview with Hitler Matsuoka again pressed for 'German help in the way of furnishing the latest operational experience and the newest technical improvements and discoveries.'[4] Hitler agreed and with reference to possible American intervention, said that, while Germany wished to avoid war with the United States, she had made all preparations for it.

If Japan got into a conflict with the United States, Germany on her part would take the necessary steps at once. It made no difference with whom the United States first came into conflict, whether it was with Germany or with Japan. They would always be intent upon disposing of one country first, not with the idea of then coming to an agreement with the other country, but with the idea of disposing of it next. Therefore Germany would . . . promptly take part in case of a conflict between Japan and America, for the strength of the allies in the Three Power Pact lay in their acting in common. Their weakness would be in allowing themselves to be defeated separately.[5]

Matsuoka replied that he had always declared that if Japan continued along her present course she would some day have to fight the United States and that this conflict might better occur sooner than later. But many people refused to follow this line of thought and considered him 'a dangerous man with dangerous ideas.'[6] Therefore he must inform Hitler

of the regrettable circumstances that he (Matsuoka) as Japanese Foreign

---

[1] ibid. p. 306.   [2] ibid. p. 309.   [3] ibid. p. 310.
[4] Hitler–Matsuoka interview, 4 April 1941 (ibid. p. 313).
[5] ibid. p. 314.
[6] ibid. He had said something of this sort at the first meeting of the Konoye (Inner) Cabinet but drew in his horns when this was received with dismay by his colleagues (*Saionji–Harada Memoirs*, 24 July 1940).

Minister, in Japan itself did not dare to say a word about the plans which he had set forth to the Führer and the Reich Foreign Minister. In political and financial circles it would do him much harm. . . . Also . . . he could not state how soon he would be able to hold a conference with the Japanese Prime Minister or with the Emperor about the questions which had been discussed. He would first have to go into developments in Japan closely and carefully, in order to determine a favorable occasion on which to give Prince Konoye and the Emperor the true picture about his real plans.[1]

In the meantime he would say, if asked, that the question of Singapore had been discussed only hypothetically and asked that, to preserve secrecy, nothing about it should be mentioned in telegrams. He had confidence in German discretion, but could not, unfortunately, say the same thing for Japanese.[2]

Had Matsuoka lived to stand his trial for conspiracy and aggression, he would almost certainly have said that in these conversations he was simply fooling the Germans, that he professed readiness to attack Singapore in order to extract valuable technical information on military and naval matters, that he had carefully avoided committing his Government to action, and that he had provided himself with an avenue of escape in the stress he had laid on the strength of the anti-war elements in Japan.[3] Such an exculpation would probably have had this much of truth in it, that Matsuoka, for all his bold talk, was not going to run any more risks than he could help, that he too was not going to steal any tiger cubs until he was sure that the tiger was dead or mortally wounded. But he undoubtedly hoped and believed that the Tripartite Pact would deter the United States from entering war against Germany, that the latter power would succeed in dealing Great Britain a fatal blow, and that then Singapore and all that went with it could be safely seized.

Matsuoka had a good conceit of himself, but it is unlikely that he deceived Hitler, always a shrewd judge of persons. It is significant, as already observed, that the Führer told his guest nothing of the 'Barbarossa' plan, and it is likely that doubt as to Japanese

---

[1] *Nazi–Soviet Relations*, pp. 315–16.
[2] ibid.
[3] In his own notes on the visit Matsuoka asserted that he refused to discuss Singapore with Hitler and said Japan would decide for herself if and when she would attack it. But these notes were apparently written much later and little reliance can be placed on them (IMTFE, *Analysis of Documentary Evidence*, vol. i, Document no. 492).

intentions was a factor in his decision to put that plan into execution.[1]

Nor did Matsuoka's professions of peaceful intent succeed in deceiving the British Government; indeed, they exaggerated his immediately belligerent intentions. On 12 April 1941 Churchill sent him a memorandum, through the medium of the British Embassy in Moscow. This was described as 'a friendly message of sincerity and goodwill' to suggest 'a few questions which deserve the attention of the Imperial Japanese Government and people.' The questions were framed in such a way as to supply their answers—as the British Prime Minister saw them. They amounted to a declaration that if Japan entered the war on the side of the Axis Powers she would be defeated along with them, and that she had better wait and reflect.[2] Matsuoka replied on 22 April in lofty but evasive language.[3]

When Matsuoka returned he found that American-Japanese conversations had been initiated in Washington, of a tenor which, if successful, looked like making Japan's adhesion to the Tripartite Pact largely nominal. Matsuoka did his best to obstruct the negotiations and also revealed them to Germany and Italy, who were duly indignant and dismayed. But he could not prevent their continuance, and in these circumstances the projected attack on Singapore, while not lost sight of, was hushed up. With the outbreak of the German-Soviet War the German Government turned to urging Japan to join in against the USSR since from their standpoint the Singapore operation had lost its immediacy. So did Matsuoka, but he was again overborne and the southward advance was resumed.

[1] On 22 May Raeder asked Hitler for his opinion on Japan's attitude. Hitler replied that he had no clear picture of the situation, but that obviously there were internal political difficulties in Japan (A. Martienssen, *Hitler and his Admirals* (London, Secker & Warburg, 1948), p. 107). 'The elimination of Russia means, at the same time, a tremendous relief for Japan in East Asia, and thereby the possibility of a much stronger threat to American activities through Japanese intervention' (Hitler's letter to Mussolini, 21 June 1941, *Nazi-Soviet Relations*, p. 351).
[2] Thus, question no. 4 was: 'If the United States entered the war at the side of Great Britain and Japan ranged herself with the Axis Powers, would not the naval supremacy of the two English-speaking nations enable them to deal with Japan while disposing of the Axis Powers in Europe?' (IMTFE, *Record*, pp. 9869–71; W. S. Churchill, *The Second World War*, iii. 167–8).
[3] After affirming that Japanese policy, based on the principles of Hakko Ichiu, was determined upon after a very careful weighing of all the circumstances, Matsuoka concluded, somewhat amusingly, that it 'will be carried out with resolution, but with the utmost circumspection, taking in every detail of changing circumstances' (IMTFE, *Record*, p. 9872).

In September 1940 the professed object of the Japanese Government in exacting air bases and military facilities in Tongking had been to further their war against China. Nor was this mere camouflage; there was a strong body of opinion in Japan which held that the China conflict must be brought to an end, by arms or diplomacy, before Japan ventured upon any openly hostile move against Malaya and the East Indies. So the Japanese Army seems for a while to have contemplated an offensive against Kunming from Indo-China, while Japanese aircraft, operating from the Tongking bases, bombed the Burma Road. At the same time secret peace overtures continued to be made to Chiang Kai-shek, despite the formal signature of the 'peace treaty' between Japan and the Nanking régime of Wang Ching-wei.[1]

Although from September 1940 to June 1941 the Japanese proceeded to tighten their military grip on Tongking and to attempt to get an economic stranglehold on Indo-Chinese resources, especially of rice and rubber, they did not as yet go further. They used Siamese aggression for their own ends, but did not at that time exact the concession of bases in southern Indo-China and Siam. Matsuoka when in Berlin told Ribbentrop that the Japanese Army had wanted to do this, but that he had rejected the scheme because it would arouse British suspicion of an attack on Singapore.[2] The truth was that Japan was not then ready for such an open avowal of her designs.[3]

Moreover, the military situation in Europe during the early months of 1941 was such as to make Japan pause. The Germans had so far failed to invade and conquer England, while their Italian allies were staggering under the defeats in Africa, Greece, and at sea. This seemed to belie the boasts of Hitler and Ribbentrop, while the sturdy confidence of Churchill was probably not without its effect on Matsuoka.

By the summer of 1941 the situation had changed to Britain's disadvantage. She had been driven from Greece and Crete,

[1] On 10 February 1941 Matsuoka told Ott that he had continued highly confidential soundings of Chiang Kai-shek, who was showing signs of a greater readiness for an understanding with Japan in order to avoid the increasing danger from the Chinese Communists (IMTFE, *Record*, p. 6435).

[2] *Nazi-Soviet Relations*, p. 310.

[3] On 30 July 1941 Mr. Eden told the House of Commons that, on instructions from London, Sir Robert Craigie had repeatedly warned Matsuoka of the serious effect which would be produced on Anglo-Japanese relations by any attempt on the part of Japan to secure bases in southern Indo-China and Siam (H C Deb., vol. 373, coll. 1414–16).

defeated in Africa, and her Navy had been badly mauled by the Luftwaffe in the Mediterranean. If the Germans followed up their victories it seemed that nothing could stop them from overrunning all the Middle East. The enemies of Britain were exultant and her friends despondent. So the time seemed favourable for a further Japanese advance.

The immediate motive for this was the Japanese Navy's concern about oil supplies. Matsuoka had said in Berlin that if, in the event of war with the United States, the latter were to send her battle fleet into the western Pacific, the Japanese Navy were confident of defeating it and rather hoped for such a move. But the Naval Staff did not think it likely; they expected that the main American fleet would be held back, and that the United States would endeavour to wear down Japanese resources by years of air and submarine attack.[1] This was a prospect which worried the Japanese Naval Staff in view of the limited nature of Japanese resources, especially in oil.

Meanwhile, since July 1940, the American Government had been exerting a steadily widening economic pressure upon Japan. On 26 July exports of high-grade aviation fuel, lubricants, and certain types of scrap iron and steel were made subject to official licence.[2] This was not a serious hardship, since Japan could and did, purchase other grades of American oil and convert it into aviation spirit.[3] In the following September the extension of what was in fact an embargo on all iron and scrap exports to Japan did constitute a heavy blow, though not a fatal one, to the Japanese steel industry.[4] After the Presidential election of November 1940, the ban on exports to Japan was further widened to include iron ore, pig iron, steel, and a variety of steel products.[5] In January 1941 copper, brass, and zinc were added to the controlled list, and shortly afterwards American supplies to Japan of oil-drilling equipment and oil storage tanks were stopped.[6] In May 1941 these controls were extended to the Philippines.

[1] This was a pretty good estimate of American intentions, as formulated in the Anglo-American Staffs conversations of March 1941. Fear of American carrier-borne air raids on Japanese cities and the public repercussions which would follow in Japan decided Admiral Yamamoto in favour of an initial offensive against the American fleet, instead of a defensive policy (*Saionji–Harada Memoirs*, 5 Nov. 1940).
[2] Feis, *Road to Pearl Harbor*, pp. 88–93. He shows how Morgenthau very nearly put across an embargo on *all* oil and scrap exports at this time.
[3] ibid. p. 99 n.   [4] ibid. p. 106.   [5] ibid. p. 142.
[6] ibid. p. 157. Morgenthau, on 28 December 1940, proposed that all foreign

The official reason for these measures, and the ground on which Japanese protests were rejected, was that these various materials were needed for America's own defence, but this of course did not deceive the Japanese, nor was it expected to do so. At the same time American aid to Great Britain was increasing, while the information the Japanese got through their agents about Anglo-American discussions on military and naval measures in the Pacific and Far East may have led them to exaggerate the immediately hostile intent, especially of the United States, just as the information which the British Government occasionally received from sources apart from the Tokyo Embassy tended to exaggerate that of Japan.

In addition, several members of Roosevelt's Cabinet, especially the Secretary of the Treasury, Morgenthau, had long been pressing for a complete embargo on oil exports to Japan. So, latterly, had the British Government.[1] Congressional opinion in favour of such a step was growing. Only Hull's caution and the warnings of the Chiefs of Staff that America was not yet ready for war had hitherto prevented it. It is impossible to suppose that the Japanese were entirely ignorant of what was going on in Washington. To them it appeared as an attempted encirclement of Japan, which, if not countered, would eventually render her helpless by cutting off all her supplies of vital materials and then compel her either to accept a humiliating abandonment of the Greater East Asia policy, or to fight in hopeless circumstances. Therefore, even before the outbreak of the German-Soviet War, the Japanese Government resolved to take counter-measures.[2]

funds in the United States should be put under American Government control, i.e. 'frozen'. Hull managed to stave it off for the time being (ibid. pp. 143–4).

[1] ibid. pp. 158–9.

[2] Tojo told the Tokyo Tribunal that the decision to send troops to southern Indo-China was taken ten days before the outbreak of the German-Soviet War and was definitely not caused by that war (IMTFE, *Record*, p. 36237). He declared that the Japanese had intelligence that the British authorities in Singapore were working on influential elements in Siam and Indo-China to cut down supplies of rice and rubber to Japan (ibid. pp. 36249–50). The United States was bidding for Indo-Chinese rubber and tin and Great Britain for its rice (Feis, *Road to Pearl Harbor*, p. 234 n.). But on 6 May 1941, after long negotiations in Tokyo, an economic accord had been concluded whereby an exchange of commodities between Japan and French Indo-China was to be effected, the amounts to be fixed annually; Decoux says he did all he could to keep these to the minimum and to protect the Indo-Chinese economy. The amount of rice exported to Japan for 1941 was fixed at 700,000 tons but actually Japan got less (Decoux, *L'Indochine*, pp. 427–30). But this was not the primary cause of the move into southern Indo-China, which was to secure a jumping off place for the seizure of the Netherlands East Indies. Tojo himself said that news of the failure

As has been seen, the Japanese Government had hoped, through a mixture of cajolery and threat, to draw the Netherlands East Indies into their economic orbit, without having to resort to force. In this they had failed, and therefore, in order to ensure adequate supplies of oil, they considered it necessary to seize upon the East Indies. But, as a preliminary to this operation, bases must be secured at Camranh Bay and other points in southern Indo-China. Matsuoka on 21 June avowed this to Ott. He said that there would be no renewal of negotiations with the Netherlands East Indies, that the existing tension was unbearable, and that for proceedings against the East Indies bases in southern Indo-China were needed. Therefore he had instructed Oshima to ask the German Government to secure Vichy's consent to this.[1]

As has been related, when the German-Soviet War broke out, Matsuoka wanted to postpone the southern move for a while and to turn on the USSR, but he was overruled.[2] The Imperial Conference of 2 July 1941 decided to wait and see what happened to the USSR, but to expedite the southward move and to carry it out even at the risk of war with the United States and Great Britain.[3] Matsuoka on 3 July told Ott of the decision to occupy *points d'appui* in French Indo-China and the next day Ott reported that Saigon would be occupied 'in the not too distant future'.[4] On 10 July he said that the move was imminent, but that the Japanese Government were again asking German aid in getting Vichy to consent, as Oshima had been told that German mediation between Tokyo and Vichy on Indo-Chinese matters was not advisable. The Japanese Government intended to propose to Vichy military

of the negotiations in Batavia was received on 10 June, and that a Liaison Conference on 13 June, decided to expedite the southern policy (IMTFE, *Record*, p. 36327).

[1] IMTFE, *Record*, p. 7009. On 4 July the German Minister to Bangkok reported a conversation between the German military attaché there and the Secretary of the Japanese Embassy. The latter had said that the failure of Japan's negotiations with the Netherlands East Indies obliged her to take over the oil resources there by force, since otherwise her fleet would be incapable of action. Prior to this there was to be a Japanese military occupation of jumping-off points in Indo-China. The occupation of Thailand was not envisaged. The preparations and execution of the operations were to be made by the staff of the South China Army at Canton under General Ushiroku (ibid. pp. 7032–3).

[2] See Ch. VII above.   [3] IMTFE, *Record*, p. 6568.

[4] ibid. p. 7030. Sumita 'early in July' told the French Indo-China authorities that Japan would shortly demand bases in southern Indo-China. Decoux warned Vichy of this and also informed Henry, the French Ambassador in Tokyo. Decoux declared that he was not prepared to agree to anything beyond the existing agreements. But the Japanese went over his head to Vichy (Decoux, *L'Indochine*, p. 151).

co-operation for joint defence of Indo-China. They were hoping to keep this secret and had denied any such intention in conversations with the American and British Ambassadors. They wanted to present the United States and Great Britain with a *fait accompli*, though they were prepared to fight these Powers should they interfere. They did not expect any serious resistance from the French.[1]

On 12 July Kato, the Japanese Minister to Vichy, was told of the impending move and instructed to open negotiations with the Vichy Government. The French Ambassador in Tokyo was suspected by the Japanese Government (although quite wrongly) to be a Gaullist and was believed to have revealed the course of the previous negotiations over Indo-China to the American and British Ambassadors. So this time the negotiations were to take place in Vichy. Kato was instructed to deal directly with Pétain, or at any rate with Darlan, and to warn them to keep the negotiations secret. He was to tell the French Government that if they agreed to the Japanese demands the guarantee of the independence and territorial integrity of French Indo-China would be renewed, but, if they refused 'a grave change might occur in the situation of Indo-China.' Furthermore the military occupation was scheduled to start on 20 July, so if the French wanted the occupation to be peaceful, they should agree by that date.[2]

The Japanese demanded French consent to the dispatch of 'the necessary number' of troops, fleet units, and air units to southern Indo-China; the establishment of air bases at eight places in Cambodia and Cochin-China, and of naval bases at Camranh Bay and Saigon.[3] The Japanese troops were to have full freedom of movement and the limitations on this in the Nishihara–Martin Agreement were to be removed.[4] The Note which embodied the demands was accompanied by a personal message from Konoye to

[1] IMTFE, *Record*, pp. 7035–6. German coolness towards the Japanese project reflected Berlin's irritation at Japan's failure to join in the war against the USSR, and also the suspicion that if she could get a settlement with the United States she would not hesitate to throw over the Tripartite Pact.
[2] ibid. pp. 7037–40.
[3] ibid. pp. 7047–8.
[4] On 10 May the Chief of Staff of the Japanese Army in Indo-China had complained to the Vice-Minister of War in Tokyo that French permission had to be sought for Japanese manœuvres and for travel; that the French provided Annamese primary schools as billets for the Japanese troops, so as to cause ill-feeling between Japanese and Annamese and that they charged high rents for the airfields. All this should be changed (ibid. pp. 7001–6).

Pétain, urging their acceptance and promising Japanese respect for French sovereignty and for the territorial integrity of the colony.[1] Kato presented the demands on 14 July. The ostensible reason for them was joint defence of Indo-China against the Gaullist activities supposedly backed by Great Britain. This had some appeal to Darlan, at that time the real head of the Vichy Government. He hated the Gaullists and the British, whom he believed and hoped would be beaten. But on the other hand he knew what faith to put in Japanese promises and he did not want to see Indo-China involved in war against Great Britain and the United States, lest France lose it whichever side won. So he replied that the acceptance of the Japanese demands must not be interpreted as a hostile action by France against Great Britain and the United States, and that the French Government could not decide without previous consultation with the German Government.[2] He may have hoped that the fall of Matsuoka might result in an abatement of Japanese pressure. If so, he was soon undeceived. Admiral Toyoda, the new Foreign Minister, told Ott on 20 July that the change made no difference to Japanese policy in Indo-China, while Ohashi said that Japan was pressing Vichy for a reply and if it was not satisfactory force would be used.[3] Darlan was served with an ultimatum which said that an answer was expected in Tokyo at 6 p.m. on 22 July, and that on the expiration of this time the Japanese troops would move in anyway.[4] So Darlan decided to capitulate, and on 21 July signified assent to the Japanese demands.[5] On 24 July a Vichy spokesman revealed that Japan had asked for bases in southern Indo-China 'as a temporary military measure to defend Indo-China against the de Gaullists, Chinese and British,' and intimated that consent would be given. He declared that events in Syria had obliged the French Government to come to this decision.[6] On 24 July 40,000 Japanese troops were poured into southern Indo-China. The Franco-Japanese protocol was signed at Vichy on 29 July. It was accompanied by an exchange of letters between Kato and Darlan, in which the specific Japanese demands

---

[1] ibid. pp. 7055–6; also *Exhibit* 651.
[2] So he told the German occupation authorities in Paris on 21 July (ibid. pp. 7056–7).
[3] ibid. p. 7052.   [4] ibid. p. 7057.
[5] ibid. Ott reported from Tokyo on 22 July that Kato had telegraphed to say he was expecting unconditional acceptance 'early tomorrow'. Ohashi said 40,000 troops would begin landings on 24 July (ibid. p. 7068).
[6] *The Times*, 25 July 1941.

were agreed to in return for an undertaking that French political and territorial rights would be respected.[1]

Meanwhile, despite Japanese efforts at secrecy, their intentions had become known. Messages reporting the Imperial Conference decision of 2 July had been intercepted and decoded.[2] On 14 July an intercepted message from Japanese Army headquarters in Canton to Tokyo revealed the military details of the intended occupation and also its ultimate purpose of providing concentration points for an attack on the Netherlands Indies and Singapore. Early in July the British Ambassador had asked if it were true that Japan intended to occupy southern Indo-China and had said that Great Britain would take a serious view of such a step. Ohashi had denied it at that time.[3] On 16 July Admiral Leahy, the American representative at Vichy, had an interview with Darlan who said that Japan would 'in the immediate future occupy bases in Indo-China with the purpose of projecting military operations to the southward.'[4]

Thus the Japanese action did not come as any surprise to the American and British Governments, nor were they deceived as to its purport. Consequently they received with scorn Japanese explanations that the occupation was entirely defensive in character, and that it was not a prelude to yet a further advance. On 23 July the British Foreign Secretary told the House of Commons that there was absolutely no truth in Japanese reports of aggressive British designs on either Indo-China or Siam.[5] On 25 July he denounced the Japanese action in Indo-China as a plain threat to British territory and indicated that defensive measures were being

[1] IMTFE, *Record*, pp. 7104–5.

[2] ibid. pp. 7043–4. The American Naval Intelligence had broken the Japanese diplomatic and military codes. Since January 1941 they had passed on information thus received to the British Admiralty. The Foreign Minister's summary of the Imperial Conference decisions, sent out to Japanese envoys abroad, was thus made known to high officials in Washington on 8 July. This summary, however, did *not* include the decision to prepare for war with the United States if the diplomatic negotiations broke down (*Pearl Harbor Attack: Report of Joint Committee*, Appendix D, pp. 295–6).

[3] So Ohashi told Ott on 22 July. He said that the British inquiry had been made fourteen days previously. An entry in Kido's diary for 5 July recounts Matsuoka as saying that 'something seemed to have leaked out' about Japan's intentions in Indo-China and that Craigie had delivered a protest to Ohashi (IMTFE, *Record*, p. 10156). Eden's statement to the House of Commons on 30 July said that Ohashi on 5 July had categorically denied any intention of occupying southern Indo-China. Craigie had repeated his warnings to both Toyoda and Ohashi (H C Deb., vol. 373, coll. 1414–16).

[4] Langer, *Our Vichy Gamble*, p. 177.

[5] *The Times*, 24 July 1941.

taken in Malaya and that the British Government were in consultation with the Dominion Governments and the Government of the
United States about methods of retaliation.[1]

These consultations had in fact been going on for some time.
On 10 July the Acting Secretary of State, Sumner Welles, told the
British Ambassador that

if Japan now took any overt step through force or through the exercise
of pressure to conquer or to acquire alien territories in the Far East, the
Government of the United States would immediately impose various
embargoes, both economic and financial, which measures had been
under consideration for some time past and which had been held in
abeyance for reasons which were well known to the Ambassador.[2]

This was followed by discussions between American and British
officials on the means to be employed and also between the State
and Treasury Departments in Washington.[3] By 15 July the
American Government were apprised (through 'Magic') of the
content of the Japanese demands, and a few days later it became
clear that the fall of Matsuoka meant no change in Japanese policy.
So, on 21 July, agreement was reached on the freezing of Japanese
funds, although at that time it was contemplated that a strictly
limited export of oil might be licensed.[4]

But Admiral Turner, head of the War Plans Division of the
Navy Department, who had been told by Nomura of the impending
Japanese action in French Indo-China, had on 19 July submitted
a memorandum to Admiral Stark, Chief of the Naval Staff, in
which he advised against any immediate embargo upon Japan,
which he thought might precipitate war, and be prejudicial to
naval operations in support of Great Britain in the Atlantic. Stark
in general concurred and passed on the memorandum to the
President.[5] So Tokyo was warned, through its representatives in
Washington, of the serious consequences which would follow any
occupation of Indo-China. But Toyoda replied that this could not
now be prevented.[6] On 24 July, Roosevelt decided upon the
freezing of Japanese assets, and the news was made public on the

---

[1] ibid. 26 July.　　　　　　　　　[2] Feis, *Road to Pearl Harbor*, p. 227.
[3] ibid. p. 228.　　　　　　　　　　[4] ibid. pp. 229–30.
[5] *Pearl Harbor Attack*, pt. 5, pp. 2382–4. Admiral Turner thought that Japan
had decided against an early attack on the British and Dutch, but meant to
strengthen her position in Indo-China and to attack the Russians in Siberia.
He therefore wanted to postpone any embargo until Japan *was* involved against
the Soviet Union.　　　　　　　　　　[6] See Ch. IX below.

evening of the next day.[1] The British Government, which had been concerting action with the Dominions, had announced to Washington on 23 July their readiness for this.[2] So, on 26 July, orders were issued in the United States, Great Britain, and the British dominions for the freezing of Japanese funds in these countries. Great Britain in addition denounced the Anglo-Japanese Treaty of Commerce and Navigation of 1911, the Commercial Agreement of 1934 in respect of India, and that of 1937 on Japanese trade with Burma. On 28 July the Netherlands Indies authorities made all Japanese trade and financial transactions subject to official permits.[3]

At first it was not clear whether no licences would be issued and so a complete embargo on Japanese trade be effected, but in fact this became the case.[4] So those who had long advocated such a policy got their way. Japan had now to choose between submission and war.

---

[1] Feis, *Road to Pearl Harbor*, p. 237. This was prior to his proposals to Nomura that Indo-China be neutralized.   [2] ibid. p. 235.
[3] The Dutch hesitated because they were not sure of American support if Japan attacked them, nor did they know whether the freezing measure meant a complete embargo on Japanese trade or not. They got no clear guidance on either point (ibid. pp. 245–6).   [4] ibid. pp. 247–8.

CHAPTER IX

Japan Confronts the United States

DURING the summer and autumn of 1940 the relations between the United States and Japan had gone from bad to worse. The formation of the second Konoye Cabinet and, in particular, the appointment of Matsuoka as Foreign Minister, were taken in Washington as clear evidence that Japan's expansionist policies would henceforth be pursued with greater determination than before, and that Japan meant to cast in her lot with the Axis Powers.[1] Grew, who had hitherto advised against coercive measures against Japan, on 12 September dispatched his 'green light' telegram, in which he said that the time had come for a policy of firmness as the only means of restraining Japan in the Pacific until such time as Germany should have been defeated, after which the whole problem of the Pacific could be readjusted 'to the permanent benefit both of the United States and of Japan—on a just basis.'[2]

This was a contingency of which the Japanese Government were themselves aware. They had not fully established the 'New Order in East Asia'—that euphemism for Japanese political and economic hegemony there—and they did not need the frequent admonitions of Hitler and Ribbentrop to perceive that, once the United States and Great Britain had their hands free in the Pacific, Japan would have to abandon all hopes of its establishment. She would have to beat a retreat, get out of China—with little or nothing to show for the blood and treasure she had spent since 1937—give up her dreams of *Lebensraum* and resign herself to a large measure of economic dependence on the United States and the British Commonwealth.

But should Germany defeat Great Britain, then not only would the latter Power be eliminated, but also the United States, in face of a German-dominated Europe, would have to devote her whole attention to this menace. That, so the pro-Axis elements argued, would leave Japan free to achieve her ambitions. Without Ameri-

---

[1] 'I had long considered him (Matsuoka) to be as crooked as a basket of fish-hooks' (Hull, *Memoirs*, i. 902).
[2] Grew, *Ten Years in Japan*, pp. 289–98.

can aid, Great Britain appeared doomed to defeat; hence the Tripartite Pact, which Matsuoka fondly hoped would cow the United States into withholding that aid.

To Cordell Hull the Pact was simply a formal ratification of a state of affairs which had long existed. As he makes plain in his *Memoirs*, he did not believe that there was any real difference between the ruling groups within the Japanese oligarchy, and he considered that the professed opposition between soldiers and civilians was largely a sham. He was right to this extent—that they both believed in the divine right of Japan to dominate the Orient. But they were divided as to the means. Tojo and those who thought like him declared that now was 'the chance of a thousand years' for Japan to achieve her ambitions, and they were ready to fight the United States and Great Britain rather than give way. Konoye and Kido were not; they thought the risk too great, and they would in the last resort have preferred a policy of *reculer pour mieux sauter*.[1] But, because their opposition was based on expediency and not morality and because they feared a coup d'état, they were at a fatal disadvantage. The egregious Matsuoka stood somewhere between the two; he did not really want to fight, but he thought that a parade of belligerency would make the American Government quail and leave both Japan and Germany free to achieve their ends.

The Tokyo Government, however, at the time of the making of the Pact with the Axis, did not believe that the United States really meant to fight either Japan or Germany.[2] In view of the apparently hopeless situation of Great Britain and also of the divided state of American opinion, this view was not unreasonable. If, therefore, Washington could be convinced that the Tripartite Pact meant no more than it said, and that neither Japan nor Germany would attack the United States provided she did not intervene against them, it seemed to the Japanese Government that she could be deterred from such intervention and perhaps persuaded to sponsor a compromise peace in both Europe and Asia.

---

[1] That is, to avoid a breach with the United States and Great Britain, to keep out of the European War, and to await its outcome, when Japan, if she preserved her strength intact, might eventually succeed in her aims without fighting. The Emperor, some of the Court party, and the older business groups, who feared domination by the Army, at heart would have preferred economic and not territorial expansion.

[2] On this point see Frederick Moore, *With Japan's Leaders* (New York, Scribners, 1942), pp. 161–3.

One of the victims of Matsuoka's 'purge' of Japanese diplomatic representatives abroad was Horinouchi, the Ambassador in Washington, though he did not leave until some three months after his recall. To replace him the Government turned to Admiral Kichisaburo Nomura, who had been living in retirement since his short-lived tenure of the Foreign Ministry in the Abe Cabinet. Nomura did not want to go, and twice declined, but the assurances he received that he would be supported in a policy of rapprochement with the United States combined with his sense of duty to overcome his doubts.[1] His appointment was approved on 8 November.

Nomura's hesitations were well founded. He was known as an advocate of peace and friendship between Japan and the United States and he was liked and respected in American naval circles. But this was an insufficient qualification for the ambassadorial post; indeed, in one way it was a drawback because it gave rise to the suspicion that the appointment of such a man was an attempt to deceive the American Government about Japan's real intentions.[2] Further, Nomura was not a career diplomat, as his predecessors had been, and his lack of professional skill soon became painfully evident, both in Washington and in Tokyo.[3] Although it is highly improbable that any Japanese envoy could have averted the ultimate catastrophe, yet the Japanese might better have retained Horinouchi, or replaced him by a professional diplomat of experience.

Nomura arrived at his post in early February 1941. Meanwhile the Japanese Government had put out an unofficial 'feeler' to Washington through the medium of two Catholic dignitaries, Bishop Walsh and Father Drought, respectively Superior-General and administrative secretary of the Catholic Foreign Mission Society of America at Maryknoll, New York.[4] Upon their return

---

[1] Grew, *Ten Years in Japan*, 304; *Saionji–Harada Memoirs*, 29 Sept., 5 Oct., 5 Nov. 1940. On 6 November he agreed, though still doubtful (ibid. 11 Nov.).

[2] Moore, who knew him well, asked him about Washington suspicions that he was a false front. He replied 'That may be. I do not know. But I don't think so.' He told Moore he had received assurances from high Army and Navy officers that he would be supported in readjusting relations with America (Moore, *With Japan's Leaders*, pp. 173–4).

[3] On this point see Grew, *Ten Years in Japan*, pp. 317–18; Hull, *Memoirs*, ii. 1030–1; Konoye Memoirs, p. 3997. Nomura's recall was considered in September, but decided against (ibid. p. 4006).

[4] This was in November–December 1940. They talked with Konoye, Matsuoka, and Muto, among others. They got the impression, though not from Matsuoka, who was indefinite about the terms of an agreement, that the Japanese

from Japan in January 1941 they secured, through the good offices of the Postmaster-General, Frank C. Walker, an interview with the President and the Secretary of State.[1] At the same time, another unofficial emissary from the Japanese Government arrived in Washington. This was Tetsuma Hashimoto, who had previously been in touch with Grew and Dooman, who was strongly critical of the alliance with the Axis, and who now came with the backing of Konoye, Hiranuma, Kido, Oikawa, and Tojo, but not of Matsuoka.[2]

Roosevelt and Hull had little faith in those overtures but they agreed that, in view of the necessity of avoiding war in the Pacific while the situation in Europe was so threatening, it would be inexpedient to turn them down. Consequently it was decided that Walker and the two Catholic priests should continue their talks with Colonel Iwakuro and Tadeo Wikawa, who had been sent over as 'advisers' to Nomura.[3]

Nomura himself, when he arrived, had no specific proposals to make.[4] But he took part in the talks with Walker, Walsh, and Drought, who on their side kept in touch with the Department of State. On 9 April Walker submitted to Hull the draft of a proposed arrangement, on which all the participants in the informal talks had agreed. By this Japan would declare that she was bound to go to war only if one of her partners in the Tripartite Pact was 'aggressively attacked'. The United States was to agree to avoid aggressive alliances, and both sides were to guarantee Philippine independence. The President of the United States was to request Chiang Kai-shek to conclude peace with Japan on a basis of recognition of Manchukuo; no territorial annexations or indemnities; no

Government were ready in fact, though not formally, to nullify the Tripartite Pact, and to restore the *status quo ante* in China. (Affidavit of Walsh, IMTFE, *Exhibit* 3441.)
    [1] Walker was 'one of the most prominent Catholics in the administration' (Hull, *Memoirs*, ii. 984).
    [2] Tetsuma Hashimoto, *Untold Story of Japanese-American Negotiations* (Tokyo, Shiunso Press, 1946), pp. 45–72.
    [3] ibid. pp. 984–6; Konoye Memoirs, p. 3997. Iwakuro was attached to the Military Affairs Bureau of the War Office. Wikawa was President of the Co-operative Bank. They had been in contact with Walsh and Drought in Japan. Iwakuro said Konoye initiated the overture and that Muto was also in favour of it. He said that Muto after Dunkirk told him England would hold out, with United States aid, and that the war would be protracted (evidence of Iwakuro, IMTFE, *Exhibit* 3442). Muto himself told the Tokyo Tribunal that his advocacy of concessions to America got him into trouble with the General Staff and that his life was menaced by some of the extremists (*Exhibit* 3454).
    [4] Hull, *Memoirs*, ii. 989.

large-scale Japanese immigration into China; the coalition of the Chungking and Nanking régimes; the withdrawal of Japanese troops in accordance with a subsequent Sino-Japanese agreement; and recognition of the Open Door principle—the detailed application of this to be the subject of a future American-Japanese agreement. The peace terms would also include arrangements based on the three Konoye principles. Should Chiang refuse, the United States was to cease all aid to him. The plan provided for the resumption of normal trade relations between the United States and Japan, for an American gold loan to Japan, and for American 'co-operation' with her in securing vital raw materials. It also suggested a conference at Honolulu between Roosevelt and Konoye.[1]

Hull was keenly disappointed with these propositions, which would have left Japan free to put her own interpretation upon Article 3 of the Tripartite Pact, and to establish the preferential political and economic position in China for which she had been fighting. But although he had no belief that an understanding could be reached, it was inexpedient to exclude all possibility of this at the start.[2] So on 14 and 16 April he held conversations with Nomura and on the latter date gave him a statement of the four principles upon which, in Hull's view, any agreement must rest. These were: respect for the territorial integrity and the sovereignty of each and all nations; support of the principle of non-interference in the internal affairs of other countries; support of the principle of equality, including equality of commercial opportunity; non-disturbance of the *status quo* in the Pacific unless the *status quo* may be altered by peaceful means. If the Japanese Government accepted these principles, the informal proposals of 9 April could serve as a basis for discussions between the two Governments.[3]

Nomura sent the proposals to Tokyo where they were received on the night of 17 April and transmitted to Konoye the next day.[4] He at once summoned a Liaison Conference of the Inner Cabinet and the Supreme Command. This decided to accept the proposals as a basis of negotiation, but with revisions which should lay stress upon Japanese fidelity to the Tripartite Pact and upon the New

---

[1] US, Dept. of State, *Foreign Relations of the United States: Japan, 1931–41*, ii. 398–402; Hull, *Memoirs*, ii. 991–2.
[2] Hull, *Memoirs*, ii. 991–4.
[3] ibid. pp. 994–5; Konoye Memoirs.   [4] Konoye Memoirs.

Order in East Asia. Terasaki, then Chief of the American Bureau of the Foreign Ministry, wanted to inform Nomura that Japan accepted the proposals in principle, but Ohashi insisted that no answer be given until after Matsuoka returned from his European tour.[1]

Matsuoka reached Dairen on 20 April and Konoye informed him by telephone of the proposal. Matsuoka at first thought that it had resulted from his conversations with Steinhardt in Moscow. When he reached Tokyo two days later and found that this was not the case, he gave a display of ill temper at a second Liaison Conference, and manifested opposition to the proposed negotiations.[2] He then retired to his home on a plea of illness. However, when he had calmed down, he devoted himself to a study of the original proposals and of the revised draft prepared by representatives of the Army, Navy, and Foreign Ministries on 21 April. This latter he subjected to further revision. A third Liaison Conference was held on 3 May at which Matsuoka's revisions were approved. But he insisted that before the revised draft was submitted to the United States, she should first be offered a neutrality pact as a test of 'sincerity'. He furthermore demanded that the vexed question of whether or not to inform Germany of the proposed conversations should be left to his discretion. On both points he got his way.[3]

He then sent two instructions to Nomura; one was to propose a non-aggression pact; and the other was an oral statement from Matsuoka to the effect that the German and Italian leaders were confident of victory, that American participation in the war would serve only to prolong it and cause the downfall of civilization, and that Japan could not act in any way injuriously to her Axis allies.[4] When Nomura saw Hull on 7 May the Secretary of State promptly turned down the non-aggression pact proposal.[5] Nomura then brought out the oral statement, in which, he said, there were many

[1] ibid. pp. 3986–7.
[2] He had told Steinhardt in Moscow that if the United States intervened against Germany, Japan would certainly come in against the United States (Matsuoka's diary, IMTFE, *Analysis of Documentary Evidence*, vol. i, Document no. 491). In instructions of 22 January and 7 February 1941 he had warned Nomura to make this clear to the United States Government. In his dispatch of 7 February he had prophesied that a Japanese-American war would result in the USSR sweeping all over China and bolshevizing the greater part of Asia. He had also said that 'even if America could make Japan surrender and enforce a cruel treaty upon the Japanese people . . . Japan could break such fetters or bonds within thirty years' (IMTFE, *Record*, pp. 9643–55).
[3] ibid. pp. 3987–8. [4] ibid. p. 3988.
[5] ibid.; Hull, *Memoirs*, ii. 997.

things that were 'wrong'. Hull glanced at it and advised Nomura
to retain it since it would only be a bar to further conversations if it
were presented officially. So Nomura kept it back.[1] Hull warned
Nomura against further delay in the conversations and indicated
that the United States intended to prevent German domination of
the seas.[2]

Nomura urged Tokyo to lose no further time and declared that
any demands by Japan at this juncture for mediation in the European War or for recognition of the New Order would do more
harm than good.[3] The Japanese military and naval attachés in
Washington also signified their opposition to Matsuoka's 'gesture
diplomacy'.[4] But on 4 May Matsuoka had informed Germany and
Italy of the proposed Japanese-American conversations and of his
oral statement and neutrality pact proposal.[5] He did not want to
send the revised draft of 3 May until he had heard from the Axis
Powers. On 8 May he obtained an audience with the Emperor to
whom he declared that if the United States entered the war against
Germany, Japan must join with Germany, and threatened resignation if there were any weakening of such a stand.[6] Konoye, who
saw the Emperor two days later, indicated that Matsuoka's
opinions were not those of all the Cabinet, and that despite division
of opinion, he meant to do his best to reach a settlement with the
United States.[7] On 12 May Matsuoka was constrained to send
the Japanese revised proposals to Nomura, without waiting any
longer for the views of the Axis Powers.[8]

[1] Hull already knew its contents through 'Magic', i.e. the deciphering of
Japanese Government messages by United States code experts.
[2] Hull, *Memoirs*, ii. 998.
[3] Konoye Memoirs, p. 3989.   [4] ibid.
[5] ibid. On 6 May he asked for Ribbentrop's views on the matter. He told Ott
that the American proposals originated from Steinhardt's report to Washington
in consequence of Matsuoka's conversation with him. He said 'he would try to
keep the United States from entering the war although he had little hope of this
and he was considering a warning to the United States that her patrolling activities in the Atlantic might result in war' (IMTFE, *Record*, pp. 9884–7). He told
Grew on 14 May that in his view, if war with Germany resulted through American convoying of ships to Great Britain, Japan would regard the United States
as an aggressor in the sense of Article 3 of the Tripartite Pact (Grew, *Ten Years
in Japan*, p. 336).   [6] Konoye Memoirs, p. 3989.
[7] ibid. pp. 3980–90. Kido told Konoye that Matsuoka's reasoning had become
so flighty after his visit to Europe that the Emperor was considering getting
rid of him.
[8] ibid. p. 3990. Roosevelt was due to speak on 14 May, Pan-American Day,
and the Japanese wanted to reply before this. As it happened the speech was
postponed till 27 May, ostensibly on the grounds of Roosevelt's ill-health, in
reality because of the divided state of American opinion (Sherwood, *White House
Papers*, i. 293).

Nomura on 12 May presented the revised draft to Hull. There were significant points of difference between it and the proposals of 9 April. Section 2 dealt with the attitude of the two countries to the European War. The Japanese Government declared that the Tripartite Pact was intended to prevent nations not directly affected by the European war from entering it, and stated their intention to give armed aid to their allies should the situation envisaged in Article 3 of the Pact arise. The American Government were to disclaim any present or future intention of taking sides in the European conflict. Both Powers were to co-operate 'speedily to restore peace in Europe'.[1] Thus, despite Nomura's warnings, Matsuoka had persisted in his idea that the United States could be threatened into abandoning Great Britain and in sponsoring a 'mediation' which would leave Germany predominant in Europe.

Section 3, which dealt with China, provided that the President should urge Chiang Kai-shek to make peace with Japan on the basis of the Konoye principles, the Japan–Nanking Treaty of Peace of 30 November 1940, and the Japan–Manchukuo–China Joint Declaration, of the same date, which professedly embodied those principles.[2] In an explanatory Note which accompanied the revised draft, Japan asked for a secret understanding that the United States would stop aid to Chiang should he refuse the peace overtures.[3]

Another point of difference was the deletion by the Japanese Government of the suggestion of a meeting between the President and the Japanese Premier. At this stage of the talks it was the Japanese Government which preferred an agreement first, with the conference possibly to come later.[4]

As it stood the Japanese draft afforded but faint possibilities of agreement, but Hull and Roosevelt hoped to get the Japanese to modify their stand. A series of conversations therefore followed during the rest of May between Hull, Nomura, and their respective aides. Meanwhile the German Government had replied to Matsuoka. They said that Japan should make it clear to the United States that the patrolling and convoying activities which her vessels were carrying on in the Atlantic were deliberately provocative of war; that in the event of war resulting from them Japan

---

[1] Hull, *Memoirs*, ii. 1000.   [2] ibid.; Konoye Memoirs, pp. 4017–18.
[3] Hull, *Memoirs*, ii. 1000.   [4] ibid. p. 1001.

would come into it; and that Japan's readiness to enter upon negotiations for a settlement with the United States was contingent upon the latter terminating such activities. Berlin, evidently suspicious, asked to be consulted before Japan sent a reply to the American overture. The Italian Government signified their concurrence with these views.[1]

When Ribbentrop learned that Japan had replied to the United States without awaiting his views, he was furious. Ott was instructed to express Germany's 'immense regret' at this and to demand that she be immediately informed of the American reply and admitted to full participation in any future Japanese-American negotiations.[2] Matsuoka in reply protested his loyalty to the Tripartite Pact. He declared that he had no belief in the success of the negotiations and that he believed that the United States would enter the war. He was only trying to postpone this and so to delay increased American aid to Britain. But he would not agree to the German desire for complete participation in the conversations, though he promised to keep Berlin informed of them. Ott told Ribbentrop that evidently Matsuoka had been compelled to yield to influences hostile to the Tripartite Pact.[3]

Bitter protests also came from Oshima. He was justly incensed, because he had first heard of the Japanese-American conversations from Ribbentrop, who had told him of them on 3 May, remarking that apparently his own Government had meant to keep them secret from him. On 9 May Ribbentrop had shown him Ott's report and a summary of Matsuoka's interim overture. Ribbentrop declared that when Matsuoka was in Berlin he had said that Japan would attack Singapore; now it seemed that he had changed his mind. If Japan concluded an agreement with the United States this would in reality render the Tripartite Pact meaningless, no matter what phraseology might be used in an attempt at reconciliation. Ribbentrop therefore wanted Japan to make no such agreement. Oshima suggested that she might make one with a stipulation that the United States should maintain a strictly neutral attitude towards the European war. Ribbentrop was dubious and said he would need to consult Hitler. On 10 May Oshima went to Rome to find out what the Italian attitude was. The German Ambassador there, Bismarck, on 12 May showed him the instructions sent to

---

[1] Konoye Memoirs, p. 3990.
[2] Ott to Ribbentrop, 18 May 1941. This quotes Ribbentrop's instruction of 15 May. (IMTFE, *Record*, p. 9910.)   [3] ibid. p. 9911.

Ott in reply to Matsuoka, and said that the Italian Government concurred. From their tenor Oshima gathered that Hitler had differed from Ribbentrop and was ready to see the Japanese conversations with the United States continue provided they served to deter her from helping Great Britain.[1]

Then on 13 May Ribbentrop flew to Rome, where he saw Mussolini and Ciano that day. Oshima met Ribbentrop the next day, who told him that the Japanese Government had replied to Washington without waiting for the views of their allies, and expressed deep resentment. Ciano, obviously primed by Ribbentrop, said the same.

On 17 May Oshima returned to Berlin where he saw Weizsäcker who showed him a summary of the Japanese reply to the United States, telegraphed to Berlin by Ott on 14 May. Weizsäcker said that the German Government attached great importance to Matsuoka's statement that Japan would attack the USSR if the latter were involved in war with Germany. He asked if Matsuoka, when in Berlin, had understood the true state of affairs between Germany and the USSR (i.e. that Germany meant to attack the USSR) and Oshima replied that he was sure that Matsuoka *did* understand.[2]

From this it may be deduced that Hitler had decided that he could not count on the Japanese, either to attack Singapore, or to honour their obligations under the Tripartite Pact. But as they had always been more anti-Soviet than anything else, he thought that it would be easier to ensure their co-operation in the war that he planned to loose against the Russians. Also, with the USSR knocked out, Japan might be emboldened to take up arms against Great Britain and, if need be, against the United States.

Oshima himself strongly remonstrated with Matsuoka. He said that Japan's 'two-faced diplomacy' would earn her the contempt and hatred of both sides in the European struggle and she would find herself isolated. If she made an agreement with the United States which allowed the latter to extend her aid to Great Britain, although not nominally entering the war, then this might affect the outcome of the struggle. But if it did, the United States would

---

[1] Oshima to Matsuoka, 20 May 1941 (ibid. pp. 9920–4).
[2] ibid. pp. 9925–8. But, as has been seen, Matsuoka had not understood that Hitler meant an immediate assault on the USSR. He told the Emperor that since America's participation in the European war would result in its prolongation, there might be the danger of a German-Soviet collision, in which case Japan would have to abrogate the neutrality treaty and advance at least as far as Irkutsk (Konoye Memoirs, p. 3989).

turn on Japan afterwards and Japan 'might suffer from some unexpected calamity'. Therefore Japan should demand that the United States cease her assistance to Great Britain and preserve neutrality.[1] Oshima gave copies of his telegrams of 20 May to the Japanese military and naval attachés in Berlin for transmission to the military and naval chiefs in Tokyo.[2]

So far as Matsuoka was concerned, Oshima was preaching to the converted. But the remonstrances from Berlin and Rome strengthened him in his opposition to the conversations with the United States. He inveighed against Nomura, whom he accused of having initiated them.[3] In the joint conferences, in conversations with Grew and in public, he insisted upon fidelity to the Tripartite Pact, and declared that if American patrolling and convoying activities in the Atlantic led to a clash with Germany Article 3 of the Pact would become operative.[4]

Matsuoka's bellicosity reacted unfavourably upon the conversations in Washington. Hull asked Nomura whether Japan genuinely desired peace, or whether she was seeking to extricate herself from the China conflict in order to be free to strike elsewhere. Nomura endeavoured to reassure him, but Hull remained unconvinced.[5] On 31 May he submitted a redraft of the proposals. In this a sentence was inserted that 'obviously, the provisions of the [Tripartite] Pact do not apply to involvement through acts of self-defense'.[6] He had previously made it clear to Nomura that the United States regarded the measures she was taking to assist Britain as defensive, in view of the menace to her which an Axis victory would entail.[7] But on 15 June the Japanese submitted a counter-draft which omitted this safeguarding clause.[8] There was thus a deadlock over the critical question of the interpretation of Article 3 of the Tripartite Pact.

The two sides had also been drifting farther apart on the China question. It became clear that the Japanese Government wanted

---

[1] Oshima's no. 569 to Matsuoka, 20 May 1941 (IMTFE, *Record*, pp. 9930–2), 'I feared very much that if the Japanese-American negotiations should fail, Japan would fall into a worse state of diplomatic isolation than ever, as the United States would look down upon Japan, and Germany and Italy would not trust her any more' (Oshima's evidence, ibid. p. 34029).
[2] ibid. pp. 9933–4.   [3] Konoye Memoirs, p. 3992.
[4] ibid. p. 3991; Grew, *Ten Years in Japan*, p. 336. Grew thought that Matsuoka dared not admit that he had been mistaken in believing that the Tripartite Pact would frighten America into complete isolationism (ibid. p. 339).
[5] *Memoirs*, ii. 1006–7.   [6] ibid. p. 1007.
[7] ibid. p. 1001.   [8] ibid. p. 1010.

the United States to suggest peace to China, but desired the terms to be settled direct between Tokyo and Chungking. These terms would include the permanent stationing of Japanese troops in Inner Mongolia and part of North China in furtherance of Sino-Japanese 'co-operative defence against Communistic activities'. Iwakuro in particular was firm in saying that this would be an absolute condition of any settlement with China.[1] Japanese troops elsewhere in China would be removed over a period of two to three years. Hull urged that lasting peace between Japan and China would depend on total evacuation of Japanese forces. Nomura professed personal agreement, but indicated that Tokyo would not concur.[2] The American redraft of 31 May provided for the withdrawal of Japanese military and naval forces from China as promptly as possible in accordance with an agreement to be concluded between Japan and China. Co-operative Sino-Japanese defence against Communism was to be made subject to further discussions.[3]

Nomura on 2 June said that he and his associates were in agreement with the American draft of 31 May, 'with the exception of some of the phraseology'.[4] But Hull felt that the changes of wording which the Japanese subsequently put forward were intended to enable Japan to put her own interpretation on the provisions of the agreement and that she was steadily narrowing down the concessions which she had originally made. He complained of this in an oral statement of 6 June.[5] On 21 June Hull gave Nomura a fresh redraft. This omitted any suggestion of joint efforts for peace in Europe and again sought to make the Tripartite Pact inapplicable to American involvement in the war through acts of self-defence. It also left Sino-Japanese co-operation against Communism to a later agreement, but included general terms of peace between Japan and China.[6] This redraft was accompanied by an oral statement in which Hull said that while he did not doubt that many Japanese leaders shared the desire of Nomura and his associates to bring about a better understanding between Japan and the United States and to establish peace in the Pacific, there was accumulating evidence

that some Japanese leaders in influential official positions are definitely

[1] ibid. pp. 1004-5.   [2] ibid. p. 1005.
[3] ibid. p. 1007.   [4] ibid.   [5] ibid. pp. 1008-9.
[6] *Japan, 1931-41*, ii. 486-92; Hull, *Memoirs*, ii. 1010.

committed to a course which calls for support of Nazi Germany and its policies of conquest, and that the only kind of understanding with the United States which they would endorse is one that would envisage Japan's fighting on the side of Hitler should the United States become involved in the European hostilities through carrying out its present policy of self-defense.[1]

Hull intimated that if this attitude continued there could be no hope of a successful outcome to the conversations. This, as Hull made clear to Nomura, was aimed at Matsuoka.[2] On 22 June Hull hinted to Nomura that the German attack on the USSR gave Japan a chance of freeing herself from the Tripartite Pact, but Nomura said that Tokyo would not do this.[3] Intercepted Japanese messages on 2 July indicated that Japan intended to use the new situation to her advantage, and in particular to make a further move southwards.[4]

The American draft of 21 June was debated at Liaison Conferences in Tokyo on 10 and 12 July. Matsuoka, furious at the oral statement, which he interpreted as a demand for his removal, wanted the statement rejected and the conversations broken off. But he was overborne and a compromise worked out which, in regard to the Tripartite Pact, said that in the event of the European War spreading, the Japanese Government would determine their attitude solely according to the national welfare and safety.[5] Matsuoka still remained obdurate; he revealed the new proposal to the Germans, and in defiance of Konoye, on 14 July sent instructions to Washington which termed the oral statement an 'incomplete and improper document' and said that unless it were withdrawn Japan could not continue with the conversations.[6] This was the last straw and on 16 July the Konoye Cabinet

---

[1] Hull, *Memoirs*, ii. 1010.

[2] ibid. pp. 1010–11. Roosevelt had made his postponed speech on 27 May. He had not mentioned Japan, but he intimated that more help was to be given to Britain and her allies against Germany. 'It was official policy then to avoid provoking Japan, so as to keep her out of the war' (Sherwood, *White House Papers*, i. 297). But on 29 May the President was said, in an American press report, to have told Congressional leaders that financial interests in Japan would bring about the virtual nullification of the Tripartite Pact. Konoye wanted to ban this story in Tokyo, but Matsuoka insisted that it be published and made a statement of refutation, insisting on Japan's loyalty to the Pact (Konoye Memoirs, p. 3992).   [3] Hull, *Memoirs*, ii. 1011.

[4] ibid. pp. 1012–13.   [5] Konoye Memoirs, p. 3995.

[6] ibid. pp. 3995–6. Matsuoka had also on 10 July accused Nomura of exceeding his instructions and used words, said Nomura, 'such as one would not dare to use in talking to a common soldier.' So Nomura wanted to resign, but was urged to remain by the Navy Minister (Nomura's diary, 10–11 July 1941. IMTFE).

resigned; it was reconstructed two days later, with Admiral Toyoda as Foreign Minister.[1]

So ended Matsuoka's ill-opened tenure of the Foreign Ministry, but his fall could not change the drift to disaster which he had set in motion. For the third Konoye Cabinet remained bound by the decisions of the Imperial Conference of 2 July and whatever good effect the removal of Matsuoka might have had was nullified by the Japanese occupation of southern Indo-China.[2] Nomura on 23 July, prior to his interview with Welles, warned Toyoda of the growing opinion in Washington that the Japanese Government were not sincere in their peaceful professions, but were merely trying to deceive the United States while all the while preparing to attack Singapore and the Netherlands Indies. He asked for information as to the new Cabinet's policy.[3] Then came the American decision to suspend the conversations. On 24 July Nomura saw Roosevelt who proposed that Japanese troops should evacuate Indo-China, in return for which he would endeavour to secure guarantees of its neutralization from all interested Powers.[4] On 31 July Welles repeated the neutralization proposal and extended it to include Siam.[5]

The rupture of the conversations and the imposition of economic sanctions came as a staggering blow to Tokyo. Konoye blames Nomura for this unexpectedly strong reaction. One of the last acts of the second Konoye Cabinet had been to send Nomura the Japanese reply to the American proposals of 21 June, but the Admiral had not delivered this to the Department of State, partly because of the political change in Tokyo, partly because he did not think that the reply would be acceptable. Moreover Konoye says that Tojo got Imperial Headquarters established in the Imperial

[1] Konoye Memoirs, pp. 3996–7. The Army had broken with Matsuoka, Tojo declaring that it was no longer possible to co-operate with him (ibid. p. 3996). His opposition to the occupation of southern Indo-China and demand for an attack on the USSR was a factor in this (Craigie, *Behind the Japanese Mask*, p. 118). But to dismiss him alone would have left him free to declare that the Government had bowed to an American demand for his removal. Hence the decision to resign *en bloc*, taken in Matsuoka's absence. He was at home ill and was greatly annoyed when the Chief Secretary of the Cabinet arrived to present him with the *fait accompli* and demand his seal of office. Konoye proposed Hiranuma as the new Premier, but the council of ex-Premiers summoned by Kido preferred Konoye to continue (Konoye Memoirs, p. 3995; Kido's diary, 15–17 July 1941, IMTFE, *Record*, pp. 10162–8).
[2] Konoye says that he advised the abandonment of the invasion, but, if so, he was unable to prevent it (Konoye Memoirs, p. 3994).
[3] IMTFE, *Record*, pp. 10177–8.
[4] Hull, *Memoirs*, ii. 1014.   [5] ibid.

Palace and also obtained permission for Liaison Conferences to be held there, the idea being to give their decisions greater authority and to silence malcontents. But, according to Konoye, Nomura did not grasp the significance of this and failed to explain it to the Americans.[1]

It is most unlikely that, even if he had, it would have affected the American attitude. The root trouble was that the decisions of the Liaison Conferences themselves were compromises between conflicting opinions, and of a kind which gave Japan the worst of both worlds. For she could neither stand in firm alignment with her Axis partners, a policy which would at least have had the merits of consistency, nor bring herself to abandon them and to meet the American viewpoint. No political reshufflings or institutional changes could affect this fundamental incoherence of policy, which, as Oshima had warned, caused Japan to be distrusted and condemned everywhere.[2]

The economic sanctions imposed on Japan in consequence of the 'freezing' measures of 26 July effected one radical change in the situation to her detriment. Before their imposition it had been the American Government which had manifested some impatience at the lack of progress in the conversations and the uncertainty as to Japanese intentions. After 26 July the time factor was against Japan. Her imports of raw materials from the Co-prosperity Sphere were far from sufficient to offset the crippling effects of the embargo on those from the United States, the British Empire, and the Netherlands East Indies. She must consequently live on her stockpiles, which would slowly dwindle. If that process were protracted the time would eventually come when she would be in no shape to fight a major war at all, and when her bargaining power would be gone. Therefore after 26 July it was Tokyo which pressed for a settlement, while Washington held off.

The conflict of opinion in Tokyo continued; after four Liaison Conferences another compromise proposal emerged on

[1] Konoye Memoirs, pp. 3997–8.
[2] Toyoda on 20 July told Ott that Japan's policy would remain based on the Tripartite Pact and that her attitude to Germany and Italy would undergo no change (IMTFE, *Record*, 10171). He said much the same to Grew on 25 July (Grew, *Ten Years in Japan*, p. 351). While he complained to Oshima that Germany had started the Russian war at a time most inconvenient to Japan, he implied to Ott that Japan would attack the USSR later on (*Pearl Harbor Attack*, pt. 12, pp. 8–10, 15–16). These messages relayed to Nomura were picked up by American Naval Intelligence and increased Hull's distrust of Japan.

4 August.[1] This evaded a direct reply to Roosevelt's neutralization proposal and was intended as a means of reopening the general conversations.[2] Japan was to agree not to advance beyond Indo-China, to withdraw her troops from that region after the settlement of the China Incident, and to guarantee the neutrality of the Philippines. The United States in return was to discontinue military preparations in the south-west Pacific, lift her economic restrictions against Japan, mediate peace between Japan and China, and recognize Japan's special position in Indo-China.[3] Nomura submitted these proposals to Hull on 6 August, but the Secretary of State indicated that they were unacceptable and on 8 August replied formally that they were 'lacking in responsiveness to the suggestion made by the President.'[4] Meanwhile on 4 August Konoye had proposed to the War and Navy Ministries that he should meet Roosevelt in personal conference. His arguments for this course, as given in his memoirs, show pretty clearly that what he had in mind was a deal, by which Japan should in reality scrap the Tripartite Pact, in return for American concessions to Japan in the Far East.[5] The Navy

---

[1] Konoye says that he consulted Mitsuru Toyama, among others, in the hope of getting the support, even of extremist opinion (Konoye Memoirs, p. 3999).
[2] ibid. [3] Hull, *Memoirs*, ii. 1016–17. [4] ibid.
[5] 'The Prime Minister should meet personally with the President and express straightforwardly and boldly the true intentions of the Empire. If the President still does not understand, I shall, of course, be fully prepared to break off the talks and return home. It is therefore an undertaking which must be carried out while being fully prepared for war against America. . . . If, after a direct meeting with the President, an understanding cannot be obtained, the people will know that a Japanese-American war could not be avoided. This would aid in consolidating their determination. . . . It is not necessary to assume from the start that the conversations will fail. Japan will insist, of course, on the firm establishment of the Greater East Asia Co-Prosperity Sphere. American claims will be based on the provisions of the Nine-Power Pact. The contents of these are at odds with each other. However, America has stated that "it is ready at any time to discuss making revisions to the Nine-Power Pact through legal means." Japan's ideal, of course, is to bring about the firm establishment of the Greater East Asia Co-Prosperity Sphere. In view of the national potential it is too much to expect this ideal to be fulfilled at once. Therefore, I do not believe that Japanese-American talks are an impossibility if they are carried out with broad-mindedness. This conference must be held soon. The outlook of the German-Soviet war indicates that the peak will become apparent in about September. If . . . a stalemate is brought about, Germany's future cannot be viewed with optimism. If that does happen, the American attitude will stiffen and she will no longer entertain the thought of talking with Japan. On the other hand, even if the German-Soviet war develops favorably for Germany this conference would not necessarily bring about unfavorable results for Japan. Even if Germany's attitude towards Japan becomes cool, since there is no chance of a German conquest of the world or of a complete victory over Britain and America, there are many ways in which Japanese-German relations can be altered. Therefore, we need not feel much anxiety because of favorable developments for Germany in the German-Soviet war. On the contrary, in consideration of possibly

Minister expressed agreement with Konoye's suggestion, but Tojo was unenthusiastic. His reply was that the Army did not think the meeting would be successful, but was prepared to agree to it on the definite understanding that there should be war if it failed, and that Konoye should assume leadership in that war.[1] Konoye's plan was sanctioned at a Liaison Conference on 6 August and by the Emperor. Instructions were sent to Nomura the next day. Nomura conveyed the proposal to Hull on 8 August but found him unresponsive, while other members of the American Cabinet were equally pessimistic, and said that the proposed meeting was inadvisable since it had no chance of success.[2]

Meanwhile Roosevelt and Churchill were meeting at Argentia. The British Prime Minister urged that parallel warnings against further aggression, couched in the strongest terms, should be delivered to Japan by the American, British, and Netherlands Governments. He now believed that Japan would not dare to move if she were sure that the result would be war.[3] He therefore submitted a draft of the proposed warning. Roosevelt wished to continue negotiations with the Japanese, so as to gain time, even if only a month. He agreed, however, to include in his reply to the Japanese proposals of 6 August the warning drafted by Churchill.[4]

unfavorable developments for Germany, it is of the utmost urgency that we reach an accord with America without a day's delay' (Konoye Memoirs, pp. 3999–4000). This passage deserves quotation in full, because it shows that Konoye was prepared to make some concessions in the Far East and was ready to drop the alliance with Germany.

[1] 'If . . . it is the Prime Minister's intention to attend such a meeting with determination to firmly support the basic principles embodied in the Empire's Revised Plan . . . and to carry out a war against America if the President of the United States still fails to comprehend the true intentions of the Empire even after this final effort is made, the army is not necessarily in disagreement' (ibid. p. 4000).

[2] ibid. pp. 4000–1; also *Pearl Harbor Attack*, pt. 12, pp. 17–18. According to Kido, Admiral Nagano, Chief of the Naval Staff, was opposed to war with the United States, which he did not believe Japan could win, owing to the oil supply problem. He also thought that the negotiations could not succeed while the Tripartite Pact remained. Kido says he was opposed to Japan's repudiating the Pact, which would bring her into contempt with America, but he thought that Japan should back down in Asia, as she had done in 1895, and wait until her economy had become stronger (Kido's diary, 31 July, 2 and 7 August 1941, IMTFE, *Record*, pp. 10184–6, 10196–7, 10199–201).

[3] 'The State Department . . . believed, as I did, that Japan would probably recoil before the ultimately overwhelming might of the United States' (Churchill, *Second World War*, iii. 522).

[4] 'Any further encroachment by Japan in the South-West Pacific would produce a situation in which the United States Government would be compelled to take counter-measures even though these might lead to war between the United States and Japan' (ibid. p. 390). The Hopkins papers contain a further sentence from the British draft. The drafts are also in *Pearl Harbor Attack*,

When Hull on 15 August saw the draft he thought it too provocative and liable to precipitate a conflict for which the United States was not yet prepared. So he not only toned down the wording, but also proposed that, on the one hand, the warning should be delivered, but on the other, that at the same time an offer should be made to resume the interrupted conversations. He saw Nomura on 16 August and, while he rebutted the Ambassador's plea that Japan had gone into Indo-China for economic rather than military reasons, he proved more responsive to the proposed Roosevelt–Konoye meeting.[1]

Roosevelt himself, on his return, approved Hull's changes in the draft of the warning statement and also of the offer of renewed conversations. He and Hull met Nomura on 17 August. The President read the two prepared statements, the latter of which ended with a request that the Japanese Government submit a clearer statement of their attitude and intentions than they had yet

pt. 14, pp. 1270–1. 'If any third Power becomes the object of aggression by Japan in consequence of such counter-measures or of their support of them, the President would have the intention to seek authority from Congress to give aid to such Power. (His Majesty's Government would give all possible aid to such Power).' Roosevelt feared that so 'tough' a line would drive the Japanese to war. He also wanted to extend the scope of any warning to include an attack on the USSR (Sherwood, *White House Papers*, i. 354–7).

[1] Hull, *Memoirs*, ii. 1018–19. Sumner Welles, the Under-Secretary of State, brought from Argentia what Hull describes as a draft which had been agreed upon between Roosevelt and Churchill. The concluding paragraph read: 'The Government of the United States, therefore, finds it necessary to state to the Government of Japan that if the Japanese Government undertakes any further steps in pursuance of the policy of military domination through force or conquest in the Pacific region upon which it has apparently embarked, the United States Government will be forced to take immediately any and all steps of whatsoever character it deems necessary in its own security, notwithstanding the possibility that such further steps on its part may result in conflict between the two countries.' Hull toned this down to read: 'Such being the case this Government now finds it necessary to say to the Government of Japan that if the Japanese Government takes any further steps in pursuance of a policy or program of military domination by force or threat of force of neighboring countries, the Government of the United States will be compelled to take immediately any and all steps which it may deem necessary toward safeguarding the legitimate rights and interests of the United States and American nationals, and toward insuring the safety and security of the United States' (ibid. p. 1018). This was the warning given to Nomura on 17 August. Churchill was disappointed that it was not stronger and the proposed parallel warnings by the British Dominions and Netherlands Governments were never made (Sherwood, *White House Papers*, ii. 358). Churchill told Attlee on 12 August: 'We have laid special stress on the warning to Japan which constitutes the teeth of the President's communication. One would always fear State Department trying to tone it down; but President has promised definitely to use the hard language.' He told Menzies, the Australian Premier, that he hoped to see the United States, the British Commonwealth, the Netherlands, and perhaps the USSR line up in a warning to Japan that war would follow any fresh aggression (*Second World War*, iii. 397–9).

given. Subject to this, he agreed in principle to the meeting with Konoye and suggested that it might be held in Juneau, Alaska, around 15 October.[1]

On 28 August Roosevelt received a personal message from Konoye, in which the Japanese Premier urged that the meeting be held as quickly as possible, since 'the present situation was developing swiftly and might produce unforeseen contingencies.' At the same time a second communication from the Japanese Government said that they would withdraw their troops from Indo-China as soon as the China incident was settled or a just peace established in East Asia, and that they would take no military action against the Soviet Union so long as she observed the neutrality pact and did not menace Japan or Manchukuo, nor would they 'without provocation' use force against any neighbouring country.[2]

Roosevelt was at first enthusiastic over the prospects of the meeting, but Hull was very much the reverse. He scented the possibility of a 'Far Eastern Munich' if Roosevelt and Konoye got together and he was resolved to prevent it. Therefore he insisted that an agreement on details should precede the meeting, and the kind of agreement he had in mind was one in which Japan should give way both on the Tripartite Pact and on the Chinese question. Nomura suggested that, in view of the wide differences with regard to China, this matter might be dropped from the agenda of the meeting, but Hull replied that this was 'one of the pivotal' matters which could not remain unsettled.[3]

On 3 September Roosevelt gave Nomura his reply to Konoye's message. The tone of this made it clear that Hull had won the day and that there would be no meeting prior to a detailed settlement of outstanding questions.[4] In an accompanying note Japan was asked to 'clarify her attitude' upon the outstanding points of difference.[5] Hull on 4 September saw the Chinese Ambassador and told him that exploratory conversations with Japan were going on, but that no common basis for negotiations had been reached. He repeated his pledge to discuss matters with China and other

---

[1] Hull, *Memoirs*, ii. 1019–20.

[2] ibid. p. 1021; *Japan, 1931–41*, ii. 573–5. The statement accompanying Konoye's letter also said that (Hull's) principles were 'the prime requisites of a true peace and should be applied not only in the Pacific area, but throughout the entire world' (ibid. p. 575).   [3] Hull, *Memoirs*, ii. 1021–7.

[4] ibid. p. 1026; Konoye Memoirs, p. 4002.

[5] Hull, *Memoirs*, ii. 1026.

interested Powers before beginning definite negotiations with Japan. Hu Shih 'seemed to feel that Japan was weakening and that within a reasonable time she would be obliged to abandon any aggressive military activities and seek peace.'[1] Hull mentioned four possible developments—a Japanese collapse; a reversal of policy in line with American requirements; an attempt at a 'facing-both-ways' agreement; and refusal of 'the governments opposed to Japan' to make any agreement 'at the present time'.[2] It is significant that he did not mention another possibility, i.e. a Japanese decision for war. Hull also informed the Chinese Government that no consideration had been or would be given to any arrangement permitting the continuance of aggression in China, that there would be no sacrifice of principles, and that the United States would continue to assist nations resisting aggression.[3]

In Tokyo on 3 September another Liaison Conference had drawn up a fresh set of proposals.[4] These were communicated to Grew on 4 September and by Nomura to Hull on 6 September.[5] By these Japan promised not to send troops from French Indo-China against any adjoining area, or to move against any region in south Asia without justifiable reason. She would make an independent decision on the interpretation and execution of the Tripartite Pact. She would endeavour to restore normal relations with China and would subsequently withdraw her troops as soon as possible in accordance with agreements between herself and China. She would not restrict American economic activities in China 'so long as pursued on an equitable basis.'[6] On 6 September Grew had a confidential interview with Konoye, in which he quoted the Japanese Premier as saying that his Government 'conclusively and wholeheartedly' agreed with the four basic principles enunciated by Hull.[7] Konoye said that he was aware that there were doubts in Washington of his ability to put through a peaceful settlement in

---

[1] ibid. pp. 1026–7. [2] ibid. p. 1027.
[3] ibid. This was done through Gauss, the American Ambassador in Chungking. [4] Konoye Memoirs, p. 4003.
[5] ibid.; Hull, *Memoirs* ii. 1027. Nomura had never submitted the Japanese counter-proposals of 15 July. On 4 September he gave Hull some proposals of his own, without authority from Tokyo. This resulted in a muddle, which took some time to clear up (ibid. p. 1030; Grew, *Ten Years in Japan*, pp. 370–1).
[6] Hull, *Memoirs*, ii. 1028–9.
[7] Grew, *Ten Years in Japan*, p. 368. But Konoye himself says he remarked that 'they were splendid as principles but when it came down to actual application a variety of problems arose. It was in order to solve these very problems that I deemed it necessary to hold the meeting with the President' (Konoye Memoirs, p. 4005).

the face of extremist opposition. He declared that he had the full support of the responsible chiefs of the Army and the Navy and that he would be accompanied by a full general and a full admiral, as well as by the Vice-Chiefs of Staff of both services. Their participation would enable him to control opposition from the pro-Axis elements in the armed forces. He again urged that the meeting should be arranged without delay.[1]

Konoye was anxious because he knew that the sands were running out. Owing to an indiscretion it had become public property that he had sent a message to Roosevelt.[2] Although the Japanese Government did their best to keep the contents secret, it was practically impossible to do so, since too many people were in a position to know what was in train. Matsuoka had kept the Axis envoys informed of the details of the conversations and they were doing their utmost to rally sentiment against their continuation.[3] Agitation against any yielding to the United States was rising, while in military and naval circles there was a growing demand that the conversations be broken off and hostilities begun on the ground that the American Government were only playing for time to complete their own preparations and to let the economic embargo weaken Japan.[4] Konoye was increasingly pressed to reach a quick decision one way or the other. As a result of numerous discussions an 'Outline for the Execution of the National Policy of the Imperial Government' was drawn up and submitted to a full-dress Imperial Conference on 6 September. This confirmed the decisions of the Imperial Conference of 2 July and laid it down that preparations for war with the United States, Great Britain, and the Netherlands should be completed by the end of October. The diplomatic negotiations should meanwhile be continued, but 'if

---

[1] Grew, *Ten Years in Japan*, pp. 367–70.
[2] According to Hull, Nomura on 28 August told American reporters that he had given Roosevelt a message from Konoye (*Memoirs*, ii. 1030). *Pearl Harbor Attack: Report of Joint Committee* (p. 308), however, says that it is not clear whether the American press got the information from Nomura or from Hull. The Japanese Government appealed to Washington for secrecy about the proposed meeting. They on 29 August issued a statement that Nomura had delivered a message from Konoye to Roosevelt (ibid.).
[3] Konoye Memoirs, pp. 4003–4.
[4] ibid. p. 4004. On 14 August Baron Hiranuma was wounded by a band of fanatics. Konoye's own life was not safe. Toyoda told Nomura on 3 September that 'since the existence of the Premier's message was inadvertently made known to the public, that gang, that has been suspecting that unofficial talks were taking place, has really begun to yell and wave the Tripartite Pact banner' (*Pearl Harbor Attack*, pt. 12, p. 25).

by the early part of October there is no reasonable hope of having our demands agreed to . . . we will immediately make up our minds to get ready for war against America (and England and Holland).'[1] A list of Japan's minimum demands and her maximum concessions were annexed to the 'Outline of National Policy'. These, while generally similar to previous Japanese proposals, were stiffer in tone and showed signs of a hardening in Japanese policy, with regard to China and South East Asia.[2]

Hull had reacted unfavourably to the Japanese proposals, received on 6 September. He felt that Japan was narrowing down the concessions she had originally been prepared to make. In particular he was averse to any permanent stationing of Japanese troops in China.[3] Nomura on 11 September cabled Toyoda that the American Government, both on account of American public opinion and of the reactions to be expected in China, would be unable to sponsor a Sino-Japanese peace which included the provisions for the stationing of Japanese forces in parts of China, embodied in the Japan–Nanking Treaty. Nomura said that the American attitude on this point had become harder, as a result, so he believed, of conversations with the Chinese. Hull had suggested that Japan agree to the complete withdrawal of her troops within two years after the conclusion of peace. He thought that the two sides were in sight of agreement on other matters, and he urged Tokyo to agree to the American proposal for troop withdrawal, as otherwise there was no hope of agreement.[4]

The point at issue was this. Japan wanted to include in the

---

[1] Konoye Memoirs, p. 4022. The Emperor, taking a stronger stand than usual with him, had rebuked General Sugiyama for saying that, in the event of war, operations in the Southern Pacific could be completed in three months. Sugiyama, Chief of Staff, had been War Minister at the time of the outbreak of the 'China Incident' and had then prophesied that it would be over in a month. When Sugiyama excused his mistake on the ground of the vast Chinese hinterland, the Emperor replied that the Pacific Ocean was much larger (ibid. pp. 4004–5). Tojo told the Tokyo Tribunal that the Japanese High Command held that November was the best month for landing operations in Malaya, &c., December was possible, but difficult, January quite impossible. They wanted a month to complete their preparations after the final decision for war, hence the decision to make early October the deadline in the Japanese-American negotiations (IMTFE, *Record*, pp. 36281–2).

[2] Konoye Memoirs, pp. 4022–3.

[3] Hull, *Memoirs*, ii. 1028. The American attitude was stiffening because of a belief that the Philippines could be held and could serve as an air base to strike at any Japanese expeditionary forces moving through the South China Sea. The Army thought this could be done by December 1941, the Navy by January or February 1942 (Feis, *Road to Pearl Harbor*, p. 263).

[4] IMTFE, *Record*, pp. 10224–5.

peace treaty with China an article which would give her the right to retain her troops in Inner Mongolia and part of North China, for the professed purpose of co-operation with China against Communism. The United States wanted no mention of this in the peace treaty, but an agreement by Japan to withdraw all her troops within a stated time. After that, so Konoye and Toyoda said, an agreement *might* be reached between Japan and China for joint co-operation against Communism, including the temporary stationing of Japanese troops in designated areas of China. Nomura and Konoye said that this was merely a matter of procedure; the United States would avoid the odium of sponsoring a peace treaty giving Japan the right to keep her troops on Chinese territory, but Japan would still get that right. But once Japan committed herself to total withdrawal of her troops, it was scarcely likely that the Chinese Government would be willing to see them brought back anywhere in China. It was also unlikely that, once a settlement of the wearisome Chinese conflict had been reached, Japanese public opinion would tolerate a renewal of the struggle because of a quarrel over this point. Thus the Japanese Army would be out-manœuvred, which was doubtless what Konoye had in mind.

But the Army Chiefs could see the danger and were consequently stubborn in their insistence that there should be no withdrawal of troops from the designated areas. In this they were supported by a section of the Cabinet, as Konoye indicates.[1] In consequence of conversations in Tokyo between Dooman and Ushiba, Konoye's private secretary, another Liaison Conference was held on 20 September at which a further general draft agreement, including detailed Sino-Japanese peace terms, was drawn up.[2] The peace terms were transmitted to Washington on 23 September, and the whole proposal on 27 September.[3] But the

---

[1] 'Lastly, in respect to the stationing of troops, there were times when the Army seemed to hold the moderate view that pretext and form were of no importance, but at the very next moment one would come up against a firm resolution not to give in on any account. Even within Japanese Government circles there was a strong tendency to feel that this constituted a real problem' (Konoye Memoirs, p. 4006). Tojo's opinion, as he told the Tokyo Tribunal, was: 'If we withdrew the troops not only would Japan bring to nought those sacrifices . . . in the course of the China Incident of more than four years' standing, but also the Chinese contempt for Japan would ever expand, if we retire from China unconditionally because of U.S. duress . . . fresh Chinese incidents would result and the repercussions of our loss of prestige would be keenly felt in Manchuria and Korea' (IMTFE, *Record*, pp. 36300–1).

[2] Grew, *Ten Years in Japan*, pp. 370–3; Konoye Memoirs, p. 4006.

[3] Konoye Memoirs, p. 4007.

proposal in general followed the pattern laid down at the Imperial Conference of 6 September. The Sino-Japanese peace terms included 'the stationing of Japanese troops and Japanese warships for a limited time in stated areas [of China] in harmony with past agreements and precedents.'[1] At the same time Toyoda again urged that the meeting between Konoye and Roosevelt should soon take place, preferably around 10 –15 October, and indicated that unless this happened the Konoye Cabinet would fall and with it all possibility of an agreement between Japan and the United States.[2] Similar warnings came from Grew to Roosevelt and Hull.[3] On 29 September Grew sent a long cable to the Department of State. In this he said that the Japanese Government dared not make specific commitments in advance, especially on the matter of the Tripartite Pact, for fear of their betrayal to Germany and to the pro-German elements in Japan. He thought that Konoye would be able to give Roosevelt guarantees that would in reality make the Tripartite Pact a dead letter, and that it was the Prince's sincere intention to bring Japan's general policy into line with that of the United States, by gradually implementing the four basic principles which he had accepted. He intimated his disagreement with the view that Japan would not dare in any event to risk war with the United States and he gave warning that if the Konoye Cabinet fell it would be succeeded by a military dictatorship which would 'lack either the disposition or the temperament to avoid colliding head-on with the United States'. He therefore urged that it was

[1] ibid. p. 4025. The version in Grew (*Ten Years in Japan*, pp. 375–6) reads 'existing agreements and usages'. Grew gathered that the Japanese were thinking of the Boxer Protocol.
[2] Toyoda's statement to Grew, 27 September (*Pearl Harbor Attack*, pt. 12, pp. 33–36).
[3] Grew wrote to Roosevelt on 22 September. In this letter he declared: 'I am convinced that he [Konoye] now means business and will go as far as is possible, without incurring open rebellion in Japan, to reach a reasonable understanding with us. . . . It seems to me highly unlikely that this chance will come again, or that any Japanese statesman other than Prince Konoye could succeed in controlling the military extremists in carrying through a policy which they, in their ignorance of international affairs and economic laws, resent and oppose. The alternative to reaching a settlement now would be the greatly increased probability of war—and while we would undoubtedly win in the end I question whether it is in our own interest to see an impoverished Japan reduced to the position of a third-rate Power. I therefore most earnestly hope that we can come to terms even if we must take on trust, at least to some degree, the continued good faith and ability of the present Government fully to implement these terms' (ibid. pt. 20, p. 4214). At the same time Nomura was warning Tokyo that there was much talk in the United States of 'inevitable' war with Japan and a belief that the United States Navy would soon be victorious (ibid. pt. 12, p. 29).

worth while holding the Roosevelt–Konoye meeting, even if it failed to produce an entirely satisfactory agreement.[1]

Hull took the opposite view, for he did not trust Konoye or any Japanese. He thought that what they wanted was an agreement on generalities which they would then interpret in their own way. He told the President that since the acceptance in principle of the proposed meeting, the Japanese had receded from the relatively liberal assurances given by Konoye on 28 August. Roosevelt on 28 September agreed with Hull's proposal to point this out to the Japanese Government, ask them to go back to their original attitude, and begin discussions again on an agreement in principle, while re-emphasizing the President's hope for a meeting.[2]

Hull told Hu Shih on 1 October 'that the chances of reaching a stage of formal negotiations with Japan had at all times been one out of twenty-five or fifty or even a hundred.'[3] Should that stage ever be reached, all pertinent questions would be discussed fully with China. On 2 October the Japanese Government were informed that their proposals of 6 September were 'a source of disappointment' to Washington. The Note indicated that there could be no qualifications or exception to the application of the four principles.[4]

The American Note of 2 October really ended all hope of a meeting or of an agreement and sealed the fate of the Konoye Cabinet. The High Command had already demanded that the decision taken on 6 September be implemented and war be decided on if no agreement had been reached by 15 October.[5] The Navy was divided in sentiment. Evidently, Oikawa wanted to back out of the decision for war, but since he had acquiesced in it at the Imperial Conference he dared not say so openly, and threw the

---

[1] *Japan, 1931–41*, ii. 645–50.

[2] Text of Hull's pencilled note to Roosevelt (undated) in *Pearl Harbor Attack*, pt. 20, pp. 4425–7, and Roosevelt's reply, ibid. p. 4423.

[3] Hull, *Memoirs*, ii. 1033.

[4] ibid. 'It seemed that because of this memorandum pessimistic arguments about the future of Japanese-American negotiations took on a darker color all at once' (Konoye Memoirs, p. 4007). Toyoda on 7 October saw Grew and insisted that Konoye on 6 September had agreed only 'in principle' to the 'four general principles laid down by Hull and that the Japanese record of the meeting showed this. He also complained that Konoye's confidential remarks, intended only for the President, had been incorporated in the American Note of 2 October and had thus obtained an embarrassing degree of circulation among Japanese Government officials (*Pearl Harbor Attack*, pt. 12, pp. 55–56; Grew, *Ten Years in Japan*, pp. 389–90).

[5] According to Tojo this demand was made at a Liaison Conference on 25 September (IMTFE, *Record*, p. 36295).

responsibility for a final decision on Konoye.[1] Konoye wanted to give way, since he felt that Japan's chances of success in war with the United States were problematical. He thought that she would do better to yield to the American demands, especially on troop withdrawal from China, avoid war, keep her Navy intact, and see what the situation was at the end of the European struggle.[2] But Tojo adamantly refused to concede that Japanese troops should be evacuated from all China.[3] He declared that, in view of Japan's sacrifices in the China conflict, she was entitled to annex Chinese territory, but since this would be a violation of the Konoye principles, it would not be done. So at the least, Japan must secure the right to retain forces in parts of the country. Furthermore, in Tojo's view, the United States herself wanted domination in the Far East, and the more Japan gave way to her demands the more overbearing she would become. Japan should fight if she had to and Tojo thought that Konoye was much too pessimistic about her chance of success.[4]

There was thus a deadlock. Tojo was able to prevent a decision to yield, but, especially in view of the lukewarm attitude of the Navy, he could not get a clear-cut decision for war. So on 14 October he proposed that the whole Cabinet should resign and that a new one should be formed under Prince Higashikuni which would not be bound by the decision of 6 September and could make a new decision.[5] Konoye on 15 October conferred with Kido and then with the Emperor himself. The Emperor said that he was in favour of peace, and that if an imperial prince did take the Premiership it would be to follow a peaceful policy. But in that

---

[1] On 12 October, just prior to another Inner Cabinet conference, the Chief of the Military Affairs Bureau of the Navy told the Chief Secretary of the Cabinet: 'The Navy does not desire a rupture in the negotiations. Thus it wishes as much as possible to avoid war. But as far as the Navy is concerned it cannot of itself bring this openly to the surface and say so. At today's conference the Navy Minister is expected to say that the decision for peace or war is entirely up to the Premier, so I beg you to keep this matter in your mind' (Konoye Memoirs, p. 4009). 'It was my opinion that if the Navy made a public announcement that it lacked confidence in fighting the United States, it would create the disruption of national opinions, cause the pitting of the Army against the Navy and consequently develop into a grave internal problem' (evidence of Oikawa, IMTFE, *Record*, p. 33341).

[2] Konoye Memoirs, p. 4028.

[3] 'The problem of the stationing of troops in itself means the life of the Army, and we shall not be able to make any concessions at all' (ibid.).

[4] IMTFE, *Record*, pp. 10252–64.

[5] Konoye Memoirs, p. 4010. Tojo agreed that he did make this proposal (IMTFE, *Record*, p. 36306).

case would the Army accept the decision?[1] Tojo, questioned on the point, made an equivocal reply—he could not guarantee submission, but certainly no one but a member of the Imperial House could obtain it.[2] This looked ominous, and Kido and the Court party therefore decided against Higashikuni becoming Premier.[3] According to Konoye, Kido wanted to have Oikawa appointed, but Konoye expressed fears of an Army revolt if this were done. Let Tojo be appointed, that would put the responsibility squarely upon the Army.[4] Furthermore, if Tojo decided to continue the conversations with the United States it might improve the prospects of success, because it would remove the former objection that it was useless to obtain assurances from a civilian Premier, since the Army would prevent him from honouring them.[5] Kido agreed, and so on 16 October the Konoye Cabinet resigned and the next day General Tojo became Premier.[6]

[1] IMTFE, *Record*, p. 10267.   [2] ibid. p. 10268.
[3] Konoye Memoirs, p. 4011. According to Kido, some of the Prince's entourage belonged to the war party. The Prince himself had no political experience and might be a figurehead, with the War Minister in actual command. 'Then if war came, the direct responsibility would rest upon the Imperial Family who, in the event of defeat, might become the target of hatred by the people' (IMTFE, *Record*, pp. 30973–4).
[4] Konoye Memoirs, p. 4011.   [5] IMTFE, *Record*, p. 10270.
[6] Konoye Memoirs, p. 4011. Konoye sent a letter to the Emperor, in which he said that Tojo regarded further negotiations as hopeless and wanted a decision for war. 'To plunge into a great war, the issue of which is most uncertain, would be something which I [Konoye] could not possibly agree to'. Tojo declared at his interrogation by the International Military Tribunal: 'My opinion was as follows. Japan was making concession after concession in order to effect a diplomatic break (? in the deadlock) before the middle ten days of October; but on the other hand America refused to budge from her position and made no concessions. . . . As War Minister my opinion was that there remained practically no hope of a diplomatic break and I suggested that the time had come when we had better make up our minds for war. The longer we delayed in making this decision, the more disadvantageous the situation would be for Japan if war were declared later' (IMTFE, *Record*, pp. 10273–4). Konoye says that there was some disagreement in the conference of Jushin (ex-Premiers) on 17 October, about recommending Tojo, but eventually they came round to Kido's views (IMTFE, *Record*, pp. 31018–28).

CHAPTER X

Tojo Decides for War

WHEN he became Prime Minister, Tojo continued to hold his former position as Minister of War and, in addition, took over the Home Ministry.[1] This concentration of power in the hands of a man who was also a full general on the active list of the Japanese Army was intended as a demonstration to the country and to the outside world that, whatever doubts might have been entertained about Konoye, the new Premier would wield sufficient authority to carry through any policy which should be decided upon, whether for peace or for war. The choice of Shigenori Togo, as Foreign Minister, was also significant. He had always worked for improved Russo-Japanese relations, he was *persona grata* in Moscow, and his appointment was evidently intended as a gesture of appeasement to the USSR, and as a proof that Japan was not intending to join Germany against the Soviet Union, a possibility that had aroused concern in Washington. The Vice-Minister of Foreign Affairs, Haruhiko Nishi, was another expert in Russo-Japanese affairs; he was a friend and former colleague of Togo in Moscow.[2]

At the time of his appointment Tojo received through Kido a message from the Emperor which set him free from the decisions of the Imperial Conference of 6 September and enabled him to continue the conversations with the United States.[3] The Foreign Minister, Togo, was therefore able to tell Nomura, who had twice asked to be recalled, that 'the new Cabinet differs in no way from the former one in its sincere desire to adjust Japanese-United States relations on a fair basis.'[4] But he sounded an ominous note: 'Our country has said all she can say in the way of expressing of

[1] Tojo said he feared 'internal confusion' if peace was decided upon instead of war. 'To meet such a state of affairs I felt I should make myself answerable as Home Minister as well as War Minister' (IMTFE, *Record*, p. 36311).

[2] Grew, *Ten Years in Japan*, p. 398.

[3] IMTFE, *Record*, p. 10292. Togo declared that he only accepted the Foreign Ministry on Tojo's assurance that the whole position would be re-examined, including the question of stationing Japanese troops in China (ibid. p. 35671).

[4] Nomura cabled on 18 and again on 20 October asking to be allowed to resign. In his second cable he complained that the Navy had not supported his efforts and he also declared that there was no hope of a modification of the American attitude (*Pearl Harbor Attack*, pt. 12, pp. 79–80).

opinions and setting forth our stands [*sic*]. We feel that we have now reached a point where no further positive action can be taken by us except to urge the United States to reconsider her views.'[1]

Nomura had no hope of any such reconsideration and on 22 October made a further pathetic appeal to be relieved, saying that while the American Government knew of his sincerity, they also knew how little influence he had in Japan. He added bitterly, 'I don't want to continue this hypocritical existence, deceiving other people.'[2] But Togo replied urging him to remain at his post.[3]

Nomura was right in thinking that he could do little to reconcile the basic Japanese-United States differences. On 24 October Wakasugi, the Japanese Minister in Washington, had an interview with Sumner Welles, who told him 'that the United States position was fully set forth in its draft proposals of June 21 and the statement delivered to Ambassador Nomura on October 2, and that for this reason he did not think any counterproposals by the United States were called for.'[4] Nomura and Wakasugi reported to Tokyo that there was little immediate hope of any change in the American attitude.[5] Wakasugi suggested that Japan should wait on events, saying that by 'good-naturedly continuing the talks there would be opened up ways of breaking down differences if we make the best use of world developments.'[6]

In Tokyo, however, the Supreme Command was insisting that a decision should be reached soon. Although the resolutions of the Imperial Conference of 6 September were supposed to have been expunged, the General Staffs were still making war preparations on the basis of that Conference. The Vice-Chief of the Army General Staff was especially vehement in declaring that there was no hope of a successful issue to the talks, so they should be ended, 'and action taken in self-defence.'[7] The Navy, too, was now veering round to this point of view. Togo said that only after a hard

[1] ibid. p. 81. Togo told the Tokyo Tribunal: 'With all public opinion which manifested itself approving of and supporting Japan's course during and since the Manchurian Incident, it was unthinkable for any Cabinet even to consider ignoring all of the changed conditions which had resulted from those years of warfare, as the United States was demanding of us—in fact no Japanese, even those of us who had most strongly opposed aggressive courses, felt that we should do so' (IMTFE, *Record*, p. 35680).
[2] *Pearl Harbor Attack*, pt. 12, p. 81. He meant deceiving the Japanese people into thinking an accord was possible.
[3] ibid. p. 82.
[4] *Pearl Harbor Attack: Report of Joint Committee*, Appendix D, p. 332.
[5] ibid.   [6] ibid.
[7] IMTFE, *Record*, p. 35683.

struggle, and a threat to resign, did he get agreement on the sub-mission of fresh propositions to Washington.[1]

In a long Liaison Conference of the Supreme Command and the Cabinet on the night of 1–2 November the choices before Japan were exhaustively discussed. Togo, backed by Kaya, the Finance Minister, urged that even if the conversations with America failed, Japan should not go to war, but should wait and see how the inter-national situation developed.[2] But the representatives of the Supreme Command were adamant against this. They declared that, if the military and naval operations which they were preparing were not undertaken by the end of the year, unfavourable weather conditions would compel their postponement for almost another year.[3] This would give America and Britain time to increase their forces in South East Asia to a dangerous degree, especially since Japan had to keep the bulk of her forces in Manchukuo—in case the USSR made any agreement with America—and in China.[4]

Furthermore Japan's stockpiles of raw materials would steadily decrease, and, if she did nothing to offset the economic blockade to which she was being subjected, she would eventually find herself in a position in which she would be unable to fight with any hope of success and so would have to submit to any terms the United States chose to offer her. The crucial question was that of oil. Japan's stocks were already dwindling, despite the fact that civilian consumption had been cut to the minimum and that no very large-scale military operations were going on in China.[5] In August 1941 General Suzuki, President of the Cabinet Planning Board, had been asked by Konoye to investigate the oil problem and to report on the possibility of Japan's obtaining self-sufficiency by the development of synthetic oil supplies.[6] Suzuki at *that* time said that this might be achieved after some years, provided that the necessary capital and materials were devoted to it.[7] Apparently on

[1] ibid. p. 35688.   [2] Evidence of Togo (IMTFE, *Record*, p. 35690).
[3] Evidence of Tojo (ibid. p. 36321).
[4] ibid. p. 36332. Sugiyama said that Japan could not afford to employ more than 11 divisions in South East Asia and the Pacific.
[5] She had a reserve of 51 million barrels in 1939; this had fallen to 43 million barrels in December 1941. The Navy at that date had 21·7 million barrels of fuel oil (Jerome B. Cohen, *Japan's Economy in War and Reconstruction*, Minne-apolis, University of Minnesota Press for IPR, 1949, pp. 134–5).
[6] Evidence of Suzuki (IMTFE, *Record*, pp. 35200–1).
[7] ibid. According to Konoye, Suzuki said that with the expenditure of 2,000 million yen on the expansion of the synthetic oil industry, Japan could secure by this means an annual production of half a million tons of oil by the end of 1943 and of 4 million tons by the end of 1944 (Konoye Memoirs, p. 4012).

the basis of this the Konoye Cabinet approved a plan for the expansion of the synthetic oil industry with the object of securing an eventual annual production of 4 million tons.[1]

At the end of October, after the fall of the Konoye Ministry, Kaya, the Finance Minister, asked Tojo about this scheme. Tojo in turn questioned Suzuki and also Kikusaburo Okada, Chief of the Preparation Section of the Mobilization Plans Bureau of the War Ministry.[2] Suzuki at this time said that the prospects were not bright.[3] Okada replied that the plan was impossible of fulfilment. Japan lacked the necessary technique, she was very short of cobalt, and the amount of coal and iron that would be needed for any such scheme could be supplied, if at all, only by cutting into other essential naval and military requirements.[4]

What if Japan went to war? The Supreme Command reckoned that their existing oil stocks would last for two years, by which time the Netherlands East Indies would be in Japanese hands, any destruction of oil-well equipment made good, and the oil problem solved. Then they would be ready to face any counter-attack. The Army chiefs, Tojo and Sugiyama, were confident of final victory; the Navy ones, Shimada and Nagano, were not so certain about this, they thought that much would depend on the international situation. But they held that Japan could establish an impregnable position in South East Asia and could defeat the American Navy if it ventured to attack it.[5]

So the decision was taken to make a last attempt at diplomatic negotiation, and, if it failed, to fight.[6] Tojo on 2 November reported this to the Emperor.[7] It was further submitted to the Supreme

[1] Evidence of Kikusaburo Okada (IMTFE, *Record*, p. 24860).
[2] ibid. p. 24861.   [3] Evidence of Suzuki (ibid. p. 35216).
[4] Evidence of Okada (ibid. pp. 24855–61). His view confirmed opinions which Tojo had previously expressed, and Konoye thought the Army had a political motive in its pessimism; they *per contra* rather suspected Suzuki of having been deliberately optimistic. But all Japan's experience with the synthetic oil industry shows that Tojo and Okada were right. The Synthetic Oil Industry Law of 1937 had inaugurated a seven-year plan of expansion, under which Japan was to produce 7·8 million barrels in 1941. The actual production in that year was 1·2 million. In 1943 it was just over 1 million barrels, as against a planned production of 14 million (Cohen, *Japan's Economy*, p. 137). For examples of Japanese technical inferiority in this matter, see ibid. pp. 138–9.
[5] Evidence of Togo (IMTFE, *Record*, pp. 35692–4).
[6] Togo and Kaya left the Conference without having agreed, and Togo said he consulted Hirota on whether he should resign, but Hirota said 'No, stay in office and do all you can to maintain peace'. So Togo concurred in the majority decision, as Kaya had already done (ibid. pp. 35695–7).
[7] Evidence of Tojo (ibid. p. 36327). According to him the Emperor said: 'If the state of affairs is just as you have stated now there will be no alternative

War Councillors on 4 November, and, after their approval, ratified at a formal Imperial Conference on the next day.[1]

On 2 November Togo informed Nomura that Liaison Conferences to discuss Japanese-American relations had been held for several days and that a final decision would be taken at an Imperial Conference to be held on 5 November. 'This will be our Government's last effort to improve diplomatic relations. When we resume negotiations every aspect of the situation makes it urgent that we reach a decision at once.'[2] Two days later Togo sent another cable to Nomura to say that the Japanese Government had decided to make a last counter-proposal and that if it were rejected the conversations would be broken off. 'Then, indeed, will relations between our two countries be on the brink of chaos. I mean that the success or failure of the pending discussions will have an immense effect on the destiny of the Empire of Japan.'[3] Togo went on to assert that Japan, for the sake of peace, had already yielded too much to the United States. Now this was her 'last possible bargain', beyond which she would not go. 'Nay, when it comes to a question of our existence and our honour, when the time comes we will defend them without recking the cost.'[4] Nomura was urged to continue to do his utmost, to follow Togo's instructions to the letter and, as soon as he received word of the result of the Imperial Conference, to impress on Roosevelt and Hull Japan's determination to secure a final decision, one way or the other. Two further cables were sent to Nomura at the same time; one gave him the terms of the counter-proposal, and the other informed him that Saburo Kurusu was being sent to assist him.[5]

The Imperial Conference of 5 November formally decided that if the conversations had not produced a successful result by 25 November Japan would make war on the United States and Great Britain. In that case she would inform Germany and Italy of her decision to open hostilities, and ask them to join with her against the United States and to agree with her to make no separate

but to proceed with the preparations, but I still hope that you will further adopt every possible means to tide over the difficulties in the American-Japanese negotiations' (ibid.).   [1] ibid. pp. 36328–38.
   [2] *Pearl Harbor Attack*, pt. 12, p. 90.   [3] ibid. pp. 92–93.
   [4] ibid. p. 93. Grew, who had received warnings from 'a reliable Japanese informant', on 3 November cabled the State Department that Tokyo was not just sabre rattling and that 'Japan's resort to measures which might (make) war with the United States inevitable may come *with dramatic and dangerous suddenness*' (*Pearl Harbor Attack: Report of Joint Committee*, pp. 335–6).
   [5] *Pearl Harbor Attack*, pt. 12, pp. 94 and 97.

peace. Should Germany demand that Japan go to war with the USSR, Japan was to reply that this was impossible for the present, and was to maintain this stand, even if it meant postponement of German participation in war against the United States. It was, indeed, laid down at the Conference that, in the event of a Japanese-United States war, Japan should try to mediate for peace between Germany and the USSR so as to restore the communications between Japan and Germany.[1]

Other resolutions of the Conference, to be effective in the event of war, provided for an agreement with Siam to permit the passage of Japanese troops through her territory, in return for a guarantee of her independence and a promise that she should receive territorial acquisitions in Burma and Malaya. No war was to be declared against Chungking, but foreign Settlements and Concessions in China were to be seized and another peace approach was to be made to Chiang Kai-shek, with the foreign-administered areas as a bait.[2]

The final proposal for a definitive peace settlement, called by Togo Proposal A, authorized Nomura to pledge the Japanese Government to carry out the principle of non-discrimination in trade in the whole Pacific area, including China, provided that the principle was applied to the entire world. With regard to the Tripartite Pact, he was to make it clear to the American Government that Japan would not enlarge upon her interpretation of the right of self-defence and to repeat that she desired to prevent the European War from spreading into the Pacific. Upon the conclusion of a Sino-Japanese peace, some of the Japanese troops already in China would remain stationed for 'a suitable interval' in North China, Inner Mongolia, and on Hainan island. If questioned about the 'suitable interval', Nomura was to answer 'vaguely' that it meant around twenty-five years.[3] The Japanese troops in other parts of China would be removed within two years from the conclusion of peace. Nomura was instructed to say that the Japanese Government respected the territorial integrity of French Indo-China and would remove their troops from there

[1] IMTFE, *Record*, pp. 10333–8. It is significant that the Japanese Government were not sure of German participation at this date and were deciding to fight the United States alone, if necessary.

[2] ibid.

[3] Togo told the Tokyo Tribunal that after a hard fight with the Army chiefs he got them to accept the idea of a time-limit, and he also got them to exclude Shanghai and Amoy from the 'prescribed areas' (IMTFE, *Record*, pp. 35686–7).

when Sino-Japanese peace was established, or the China Incident successfully concluded. He was, however, told that the Japanese Government, as a matter of principle, were anxious to avoid having this pledge written into any formal agreement with the United States.[1]

In his explanatory comment on these proposed terms Togo intimated that while the question of non-discrimination in trade was put on a world-wide basis, the Japanese Government really wanted a regional agreement, and he supposed that understanding could easily be reached on this. He believed, too, from what Nomura had reported, that there would soon be agreement about the interpretation of the Tripartite Pact. He felt that Proposal A completely accepted the American demands on two out of the three major points at issue. But he made it clear that the third, complete evacuation of Japanese troops from China, was unacceptable and that Japan was now offering her last possible concession on this matter.[2]

In the event of no immediate agreement being possible on Proposal A, Togo included a second set of terms, called Proposal B, as a stop-gap 'to prevent something happening'. By these terms the two Governments were to agree that neither would invade any area in South East Asia or the South Seas, except French Indo-China; they were to co-operate with one another in securing the raw materials they needed from the Netherlands East Indies and were to return to the situation prior to their respective 'freezing' measures. The United States was to agree to furnish Japan with the petroleum which she needed, and was to engage in no activity which would hamper Japan in her efforts to secure peace with China. If necessary, Proposal B could include the first two points of A and a general promise by Japan to evacuate her troops from China after peace was made.[3]

On 5 November Togo gave Nomura the word to submit Proposal A to the American Government. He was not to bring up Proposal B without prior consultations with Tokyo. Nomura was again warned that time was exceedingly short and that the situation

---

[1] *Pearl Harbor Attack*, pt. 12, pp. 94–95.

[2] 'How hard, indeed, have we fought in China for four years! What tremendous sacrifices have we made! They must know this, so their demands in this connection must have been only "wishful thinking". In any case, our internal situation also makes it impossible for us to make any further compromise in this connection' (ibid. p. 96). [3] ibid. pp. 96–97.

was very critical, though he was instructed not to give the impression that Japan was presenting an ultimatum.[1] A separate instruction advised him to avoid having the agreement drawn up in the form of a treaty, which would require ratification by the American Senate. Togo believed that the American Government also desired to avoid this and would prefer an Executive Agreement.[2] In yet another cable the Foreign Minister told Nomura that 'because of various circumstances, it is absolutely necessary that all arrangements for the signing of this agreement be completed by the 25th of this month.'[3]

These instructions were all picked up and decoded by the cryptographic experts of the American Navy and, in view of the tenor of the last one, Hull at the Cabinet meeting of 7 November gave warning that a military attack by Japan might come 'anywhere at any time'.[4] On the same evening Nomura, accompanied by Wakasugi, called on Hull and gave him the terms of the Japanese Proposal A, asked for a speedy reply, and also solicited an interview with the President.[5] This took place three days later, when Nomura read an explanation of the Japanese proposals and again pressed for a quick decision.[6] Roosevelt replied in terms which deprecated any undue haste, and gave no definite answer.[7] Togo on 11 November complained that apparently the American Government were still not fully aware of the critical stage which had been reached; he again warned Nomura that 25 November

[1] ibid. p. 99.   [2] ibid. p. 98.
[3] ibid. p. 100. Nomura was told that this would save Japanese-American relations from falling into a chaotic condition. He was *not* told then or later precisely what would happen if there were no agreement. According to F. Moore, Nomura used to say 'the crime (war) will be committed! But it will not be. There are still men of reason in Tokyo' (*With Japan's Leaders*, p. 212).
[4] Hull, *Memoirs*, ii. 1057–8. On 6 November Roosevelt broached to Stimson, the Secretary of State for War, the idea of a six months' truce in the Pacific, with no movement of troops or armaments, 'and then if the Japanese and Chinese had not settled their arrangement in that meanwhile, we could go on on the same basis.' But Stimson objected that it was vitally important to go on reinforcing the Philippines, and that the Chinese would feel deserted (*Pearl Harbor Attack: Report of Joint Committee*, p. 346).
[5] *Pearl Harbor Attack*, pt. 12, 104–5; Hull, *Memoirs*, ii. 1058–9. During the conversation, Hull asked what the Japanese response would be if the Chinese said they desired real friendship with Japan and would work with her along peaceful ways. Hull said that this was just his own idea. The Japanese Government took it as meaning he would bring the two parties, Japan and China, together and then leave the discussion of peace terms to them. This was just what Tokyo wanted, but not what Hull meant at all, so that the only result was to confuse the issue (*Pearl Harbor Attack*, pt. 12, pp. 106–8; Hull, *Memoirs*, ii. 1058–9).   [6] *Pearl Harbor Attack*, pt. 12, pp. 113–16.
[7] Hull, *Memoirs*, ii. 1059.

was the deadline and urged him to make renewed efforts to secure an immediate answer.[1] Togo had also, on 10 November, informed Grew of the new proposals which Nomura had been given. He warned the American Ambassador that Japanese national sentiment 'would not tolerate further protracted delay in arriving at some conclusion.'[2] Moreover, Togo declared that the American Government should 'realize the possibility that the Japanese people, if exposed to the continued economic pressure, might eventually feel obliged resolutely to resort to measures of self-defence.'[3]

Togo also told Grew that the Japanese Government desired that the British Government should conclude an agreement simultaneously with the United States.[4] Before the fall of the Konoye Cabinet, Toyoda had approached Craigie to urge that the British Government should play a more active part in the negotiations. Shigemitsu, who had returned from London on leave of absence, was the intermediary in this and discussions took place at the Tokyo Foreign Office between him, Toyoda, and Craigie, in which the British Ambassador was asked to do all he could to avert a breakdown in the conversations.[5] But Craigie was 'precluded by my instructions from taking an official part in discussing the matters under negotiation in Washington.'[6] Now, on 11 November, Togo warned Craigie that, so far from being merely preliminaries, the negotiations were in their final stage, and he sharply criticized Churchill for threatening war without knowing what was happening in the negotiations.[7]

The Japanese Government hoped that London would prove more accommodating than Washington, since in the past the British Government had shown readiness to compromise with Tokyo.[8] But British policy was now dominated by Churchill, and

[1] *Pearl Harbor Attack*, pt. 12, pp. 116–17.
[2] *Pearl Harbor Attack: Report of Joint Committee*, p. 347.
[3] ibid. p. 348.   [4] ibid. p. 347.
[5] Affidavit of Sir R. Craigie (IMTFE, *Record*, pp. 34546–7).
[6] ibid. p. 34547. According to Toshikazu Kase (*Eclipse of the Rising Sun*, pp. 58–59), he also sought to get the British Government to intervene. 'Sir Robert Craigie readily concurred in my view and we tried to awaken the British Government to the situation. However, his plea that his Government take an active part in the negotiations unexpectedly met a sharp rebuff. Sir Robert was rather bluntly told to keep silence, since the negotiations were in the best hands, those of the United States, which knew what was best to do.'
[7] *Pearl Harbor Attack*, pt. 12, pp. 117–19.
[8] 'While Washington was often obdurate, London was usually more elastic and capable of wider accommodation' (Kase, *Eclipse of the Rising Sun*, p. 58).

he, as has been seen, believed that Japan would climb down before a firm front. He was disappointed that the draft warning to Japan, agreed upon between Roosevelt and himself at Argentia, had been turned down, and he had shortly after stated publicly that, in the event of a Japanese-American war, Britain would range herself unhesitatingly at the side of the United States. British naval reinforcements were moving to the Far East, including the ill-fated *Prince of Wales* and *Repulse*.[1] At the beginning of November Chiang Kai-shek, alarmed at the dispatch of Japanese military and air reinforcements to Tongking, a move which he thought presaged a Japanese attack through Indo-China upon Kunming, to cut the Burma Road, appealed for aid to Churchill and Roosevelt.[2] He wanted British air units sent to help him repel such an attack, and also asked for American co-operation in this. Churchill on 5 November told Roosevelt that he was prepared to 'send pilots and even some planes if they could be spared in time'.[3] He also urged that Washington and London issue parallel warnings to Japan not to attack Yunnan.[4] Roosevelt referred the matter to the Joint Chiefs of Staff and they advised very strongly against any action which would lead to war with Japan, although they favoured all aid to China short of war.[5] So, on 7 November, Roosevelt replied to Churchill that he doubted if the Japanese intended to attack Yunnan in the immediate future, and that he thought that the proposed warning would have no good effect.[6] On 10 November, however, Churchill, in the course of his Guildhall speech, once more gave warning that if there were war between Japan and the United States, 'the British declaration will follow within the hour'.[7] It was to this that Togo referred in his talk with Craigie on 11 November.

---

[1] R. Grenfell, *Main Fleet to Singapore* (London, Faber, 1951), pp. 92–95.
[2] Churchill, *Second World War*, ii. 526–8.
[3] *Pearl Harbor Attack: Report of Joint Committee*, p. 340.   [4] ibid.
[5] Their specific recommendations were 'That the dispatch of United States armed forces for intervention against Japan in China be disapproved. That material aid to China be accelerated consonant with the needs of Russia, Great Britain, and our own forces. That aid to the American Volunteer Group be continued and accelerated to the maximum practicable extent. *That no ultimatum be delivered to Japan.*' They also said that 'military action against Japan should be undertaken only in one or more of the following contingencies: (1) A direct act of war by Japanese armed forces against the territory or mandated territory of the United States, the British Commonwealth, or the Netherlands East Indies. (2) The movement of Japanese forces into Thailand to the west of 100° East or south of 10° North; or into Portuguese Timor, New Caledonia, or the Loyalty Islands' (ibid. pp. 341–2).
[6] ibid. p. 342.   [7] *Second World War*, iii. 528.

Subsequent conversations in Washington between 12 and 15 November served only to emphasize the fact that the American and Japanese Governments were as far apart as ever, and that Togo had been mistaken in thinking otherwise. Hull considered that the proposals submitted to him on 7 November were no real advance on previous Japanese terms for a settlement. He reiterated that the Tojo Government should give a definite pledge of their peaceful intentions, should subscribe definitely to the principle of equal commercial opportunity, and should make the Tripartite Pact a dead letter.[1] He further insisted that the talks were only preliminary conversations, whereas to the Japanese they were the last stages of a protracted negotiation.[2]

Nomura on 14 November told Togo that 'I believe I will win out in the long run in these negotiations', but at the same time warned him that the United States would meet with force any further Japanese move, in whatever direction. He declared that while there were divergent opinions in the United States about war with Germany, there was 'not the slightest opposition to war in the Pacific'. Contrary to what he had at first expected, there was no inclination to compromise with Japan. He intimated that Japan might find herself at war with the United States, Great Britain, and the USSR, and that victory would be to the side which could hold out longest. He urged the Japanese Government to be 'patient for a while in order to get a clear view of the world situation'. This was a plain intimation that the Japanese Government must not expect a settlement on the basis of Proposal A but that nevertheless they would be wise to avoid precipitate action and to wait and see how the European War went.

In a reply dated 16 November Togo referred to his no. 725 of 4 November. He also said that Nomura's proposal to wait was out of the question and that there would be no change in the date set for the conclusion of the negotiations. He urged Nomura to press for a solution and not to 'allow the United States to sidetrack us and delay the negotiations any further'.[3] Togo was now ready to

---

[1] Hull, *Memoirs*, ii. 1060-1.

[2] ibid. p. 1061. Hull on 15 November gave Nomura the draft of a joint American-Japanese declaration on economic policy. This would have bound Japan to restore complete economic, financial and monetary control to China and to pledge herself to respect the 'Open Door' there (ibid. pp. 1061-3). It was quite unacceptable to Tokyo and Togo rejected it in a dispatch to Nomura of 17 November (*Pearl Harbor Attack*, pt. 12, pp. 145-6).

[3] ibid. pp. 137-8.

present Proposal B, but in deference to Kurusu's wish delayed
instructions to do this until Kurusu should have had a chance to
try *his* powers of persuasion.[1]

Kurusu, however, had no better fortune than Nomura. Hull
disliked and distrusted him and felt that he had nothing new to
offer.[2] Moreover, his arrival coincided with a bellicose speech by
Tojo to the Japanese Diet in which he announced Japan's intention
to reinforce her troops in Indo-China, which appeared to belie the
peaceful professions of the Japanese envoys in Washington.
Kurusu on 17 November saw Roosevelt, to whom he declared
that Japan could not openly abandon the Tripartite Pact, but that
she had no intention of becoming a tool of Germany nor did she
mean to wait until the United States became deeply involved in
the battle of the Atlantic and then stab her in the back. Should
Japan and the United States reach an understanding about the
Pacific this would 'far outshine' the Tripartite Pact.[3]

Further than this he could not go and he told Hull in another
conversation on 18 November that it was impossible for Japan to
abrogate the Pact or to make it ineffective at this time.[4] Hull
intimated in reply that American public opinion would not tolerate
any agreement with Japan while she remained in association with
Hitler.[5] Thus matters again reached an impasse.

[1] ibid. pp. 130–1.
[2] 'Neither his appearance nor his attitude commanded confidence or respect.
I felt from the start that he was deceitful. . . . His only recommendation in my
eyes was that he spoke excellent English, having married his American secretary'
(Hull, *Memoirs*, ii. 1062–3). Kurusu had formerly occupied consular posts in the
United States, had risen to be head of the economic section of the Japanese
Foreign Ministry. He had been appointed Ambassador to Berlin by Nomura,
when the latter was Foreign Minister. Hull was prejudiced against Kurusu
because he had been the Japanese signatory of the Tripartite Pact. But this
was on orders from his Government; the Pact itself had been made by Matsuoka
and Stahmer in Tokyo. Moore says that Nomura never believed that Kurusu
had approved of the Pact, and some months previously, when Kurusu, after
his relief by Oshima, was in Washington en route to Japan, Nomura had asked
him to come and help in the conversations. Moore, who had formerly been
acquainted with Kurusu, says he found him a changed man, who showed some
tendency to strut (*With Japan's Leaders*, pp. 259–60, 267–8). But from the record
it would appear that Kurusu did what he could to save peace, though he evidently
had no real hope. He told Moore that 'Hull, with his sentiments and theories
was undoubtedly a fine old gentleman, but visionary and impractical in a hard
and difficult world' (ibid. p. 281). Craigie says that he heard that the Japanese
Foreign Ministry wanted to send Shigemitsu, who had returned from the London
Embassy in August, to Washington, but the Army vetoed this (*Behind the
Japanese Mask*, pp. 129–30). But, even if Shigemitsu had gone instead of
Kurusu, the result would almost certainly have been the same.
[3] *Pearl Harbor Attack*, pt. 12, pp. 142–3.
[4] ibid. p. 148.   [5] Hull, *Memoirs*, pp. 1063–5.

Kurusu expressed to Togo his belief that the President was sincere in desiring an understanding with Japan and said that he considered it most essential that Japan should do all she could to meet America's wishes about the Pact and let her become more involved in the Atlantic. This, he thought, would put Japan in a better position to settle the China Incident and also benefit her in respect of the international situation after the European War. He had expressed to Roosevelt Japanese fears of an Anglo-American combination against them when the European War ended and Roosevelt had replied that the agreement under consideration would cover all such points.[1]

The conversation on 18 November made it clear that there was no possibility of an immediate agreement. Kurusu and Nomura therefore sounded Hull on the possibility of a temporary *modus vivendi* to tide over the critical state of affairs. In return for this they suggested that Japan might withdraw her troops from southern Indo-China.[2] Hull intimated that he would not be willing simply to revert to the situation prior to the imposition of the 'freezing' orders, because Japan might use the troops she withdrew from Indo-China for some 'equally objectionable movement elsewhere'.[3] Although he agreed to sound the British and Dutch Governments on the question of a *modus vivendi*, he considered that the Japanese Government should give some concrete evidence of their alleged peaceful intentions.[4]

Both Nomura and Kurusu advised Tokyo against presenting Proposal B in its entirety and suggested instead concentration upon securing the removal of the 'freezing' orders.[5] Nomura reported that they had been told by an (unnamed) member of the American Cabinet that all but two members of the Cabinet approved in

---

[1] *Pearl Harbor Attack*, pt. 12, pp. 150–1. Kurusu warned Tokyo that the United States, while desirous of a settlement with Japan, so as to be free to concentrate upon the European problem, was nevertheless ready for war with Japan if necessary. According to Masuo Kato, Tojo had told Kurusu, just before the latter left for Washington, that the United States would not dare to fight Japan, and that therefore Kurusu should take a strong line in the negotiations, which Tojo thought would make the United States back down over China (*The Lost War* (New York, Knopf, 1946), pp. 54–55). Kurusu was now warning him that he was wrong.

[2] This was in the course of the conversation of 18 November. Nomura suggested that Japan should evacuate southern Indo-China and in return the United States should rescind the 'freezing' order (*Pearl Harbor Attack*, pt. 12, p. 149). [3] Hull, *Memoirs*, ii. 1067.

[4] ibid.; also *Pearl Harbor Attack*, pt. 12, p. 149.

[5] *Pearl Harbor Attack*, pt. 12, p. 152.

principle of an understanding, and that if Japan would do something substantial, such as evacuating her troops from Indo-China, it would open the way for a resumption of normal trading relations.[1]

Togo replied on 19 November to reprove Nomura for having made the suggestion of a *modus vivendi* without first consulting Tokyo.[2] He said that the internal situation in Japan did not permit the Government to agree to withdraw from southern Indo-China merely in return for the abandonment of the 'freezing' orders. Such withdrawal could only be made if Proposal B were accepted by the American Government and Togo now instructed Nomura to present that proposal. Should it be rejected the Japanese Foreign Minister declared that the negotiations would be broken off.[3] In another dispatch of the same date Togo told the envoys to make it clear that, in the event of the United States entering the European War, Japan would make an independent decision upon whether this constituted an attack in relation to Article 3 of the Tripartite Pact. They could further declare that there were no secret articles. But they were not to make these explanations unless they saw prospects of agreement on Proposal B.[4] In another dispatch of the same date Tokyo warned its envoys to listen to the Japanese daily short-wave news broadcast for a code warning of an emergency which would be the signal for them to destroy all ciphers and confidential documents in the Embassy.[5]

These instructions crossed another cable from Nomura which urged that Japan should not embark upon a fresh war after four years of the China Incident, and again suggested a temporary truce 'in the spirit of give and take'. He asked that these views

---

[1] ibid. p. 154. The conversation took place on the evening of 17 November, the American official referred to appears to have been the Postmaster General, Walker (*Pearl Harbor Attack: Report of Joint Committee*, pp. 355–6).

[2] Togo thought Hull's statement about definite evidences of a peaceful policy by Japan referred to the question of the Tripartite Pact. Thus it was evident that the United States did not want simply to revert to the situation before the 'freezing' orders; on the other hand, neither did Japan. So, said Togo, Nomura's suggestion, made without consultation with his Government, could result only in delay and failure in the negotiations (ibid. p. 155). [3] ibid.

[4] ibid. p. 157. In yet another instruction of 19 November they were told not to include any reference to non-discrimination in trade or to the Tripartite Pact in the actual Proposal B. These were the two points of A which Togo on 4 November had said might be tacked on to B. But they were to include a pledge by the Japanese Government to withdraw their troops from southern to northern Indo-China, 'upon the conclusion of the present agreement' (ibid. pp. 157–8).

[5] This was the 'winds' code: East wind rain = Japan–U.S. relations in danger: North wind cloudy = Japan–USSR relations in danger: West wind clear = Japan–British relations in danger (ibid. p. 154).

should be conveyed to Tojo.[1] But he received a reply which rejected his proposal, confirmed the instructions given him to present Proposal B, and said that Tojo was absolutely in accord with them.[2] So on 20 November—Thanksgiving Day in the United States—Nomura and Kurusu presented Hull with Proposal B.[3] Nomura reported Hull as being 'terribly aroused' by the fifth point—the discontinuance of aid to China.[4] Hull declared that the purpose of American aid to China was the same as that underlying aid to Britain, and intimated that the assistance to China would continue so long as Japan remained allied with Hitler and insisted upon her New Order in East Asia.[5] Togo replied on 22 November to say that if the United States would accept the Japanese Proposal B, Tokyo would have no objection to Roosevelt exercising his good offices to bring Japan and China to peace negotiations. Once a Sino-Japanese armistice were established there would be no need for continued American aid to Chungking.[6] In an earlier dispatch of the same date Togo extended the deadline, hitherto maintained as 25 November, to 29 November, provided that agreement could be secured by that date with the United States, Great Britain, and the Netherlands. 'After that [i.e. if there was no agreement] things are automatically going to happen.'[7]

Hull regarded the Japanese terms of 20 November as 'of so preposterous a character that no responsible American official could ever have dreamed of accepting them.'[8] But he felt that an

---

[1] ibid. p. 158. [2] ibid. p. 160.
[3] The five points of Proposal B as finally presented were:
   (1) Japan and the United States to make no [new] armed advance into any region in South-East Asia and the South-West Pacific area.
   (2) Japan to withdraw her troops from Indo-China when peace was restored between Japan and China or an equitable peace was established in the Pacific area. Meanwhile Japan to withdraw her troops from southern to northern Indo-China upon conclusion of the present agreement, which would later be embodied in the final agreement.
   (3) Japan and the United States to co-operate toward acquiring goods and commodities that the two countries needed in the Netherlands East Indies.
   (4) Japan and the United States to restore their commercial relations to those prevailing prior to the freezing of assets, and the United States to supply Japan with a required quantity of oil.
   (5) The United States to refrain from such measures and actions as would prejudice endeavours for the restoration of peace between Japan and China.
   (Hull, *Memoirs*, ii. 1069; *Japan, 1931–41*, ii. 755–6.)
[4] *Pearl Harbor Attack*, pt. 12, p. 161.
[5] ibid.; Hull, *Memoirs*, ii. 1071.
[6] *Pearl Harbor Attack*, pt. 12, p. 166.
[7] ibid. p. 165.
[8] Hull, *Memoirs*, ii. 1070. The State Department generally concurred in this view. So did Roosevelt (Feis, *Road to Pearl Harbor*, p. 310).

abrupt rejection of them would precipitate the conflict and throw on the United States the onus of a rupture of the conversations. Moreover, the Chiefs of Staff of War and of the Navy were pleading with him to gain more time for them to complete their preparations to meet a Japanese attack.

The State Department had since early November been working upon a draft *modus vivendi*, as a stop-gap arrangement.[1] On 18 November Hull told the British Minister, Sir Ronald Campbell, of the Japanese Ambassador's suggestion of a temporary agreement. The next day he gave similar information to the Ministers of Australia and the Netherlands.[2] Hull on 22 November discussed with the diplomatic representatives of Australia, Britain, China, and the Netherlands the Japanese proposals of 20 November and the draft reply. They all, except the Chinese Ambassador, expressed approval of the American draft.[3] Later the same day Hull saw the Japanese Ambassadors and told them that he had discussed the Japanese proposals with the envoys of the four interested countries. These would need to consult their respective Governments and Hull could therefore give no definite reply until 24 November.[4] But, when on that date Hull again met the four envoys he found that only the Netherlands Minister had received instructions. These were that his Government would support the American draft *modus vivendi*. Hull expressed his disappointment 'at the lack of interest and lack of a disposition to cooperate'.[5] Later on the same day Roosevelt, at Hull's suggestion, cabled Churchill giving him a summary of the proposed *modus vivendi*.[6]

On 25 November Hull showed the final revised draft to the Secretaries of War and of the Navy.[7] Stimson noted that there was no chance of the Japanese accepting it, and Hull was evidently of the same mind, for at noon on the same day he told the 'War Council' 'that there was practically no possibility of an agreement being achieved with Japan', and gave warning of a possible surprise attack.[8]

Under the proposed *modus vivendi*, which would have lasted for

[1] *Pearl Harbor Attack: Report of Joint Committee*, p. 366.
[2] ibid. pp. 363–4.   [3] Hull, *Memoirs*, ii. 1073.
[4] ibid. pp. 1074–6.   [5] ibid. pp. 1076–7.
[6] Roosevelt added to the message: 'This seems to me a fair proposition for the Japanese, but its acceptance or rejection is really a matter of internal Japanese politics. I am not very hopeful, and we must all be prepared for real trouble, possibly soon' (*Pearl Harbor Attack: Report of Joint Committee*, p. 373).
[7] ibid.   [8] ibid. pp. 373–4.

an initial period of three months, Japan was to agree to make no further advance either southwards or northwards; she was at once to withdraw her forces from southern Indo-China, and to reduce her total troops there to the number as of 26 July 1941 (or approximately 25,000). In return for this the United States would modify her freezing and export restrictions so as to permit imports from Japan to enter freely, and to allow a limited export to Japan, including raw cotton of a monthly value of $600,000, and petroleum 'within the categories permitted general export, upon a monthly basis for civilian needs.'[1]

On 25 November Hull received the British and the Chinese reactions to these proposals. The British Foreign Secretary, in contrast to the British Ambassador in Tokyo, evidently thought that the Japanese would not really fight.[2] He suggested that the proposal should stipulate for total withdrawal of all Japanese troops and air forces from Indo-China and for the suspension of further military advances in China as well as elsewhere. He further objected to the resumption of any oil supplies to Japan, for 'we know the Japanese have no shortage except for military purposes.'[3] While saying that the British Government had complete confidence in Hull's handling of the negotiations and that he was the best judge of what it was best to do, Eden evidently would have preferred that the Japanese proposal should be rejected, with a hint that Tokyo should think again and produce a better offer.[4]

Churchill's reply to Roosevelt was received either late on the same day or early the next morning.[5] In it the Prime Minister declared:

Of course it is for you to handle this business and we certainly do not want an additional war. There is only one point that disquiets us. What about Chiang Kai-shek? Is he not having a very thin diet? Our anxiety is about China. If they collapse our joint dangers would enormously increase. We are sure that the regard of the United States for the Chinese cause will govern your action. We feel that the Japanese are most unsure of themselves.[6]

[1] *Pearl Harbor Attack*, pt. 14, pp. 1150–4.
[2] 'We feel sure that . . . the Japanese will try to force a hurried decision by magnifying the dangers of delay' (ibid. p. 1164). 'It had always been my view that a breakdown of the Washington negotiations would, in the light of all the other portents, be the signal for war and I had of course reported this opinion to my Government' (Craigie, *Behind the Japanese Mask*, p. 133).
[3] Hull, *Memoirs*, ii. 1165.   [4] ibid. p. 1164.
[5] Feis (*Road to Pearl Harbor*, pp. 317–18) thinks that its substance was known on the night of 25 November.   [6] *Pearl Harbor Attack*, pt. 14, p. 1300.

At the time they made these replies neither Churchill nor Eden knew that Hull had from the first intended to present to the Japanese, along with the draft *modus vivendi*, proposals for a comprehensive settlement, which included the recognition by Japan of the Chungking régime and the withdrawal of all Japanese troops from China.[1] Churchill has since indicated that, had they known, their reaction would have been different.[2] Presumably the same applies to Chiang Kai-shek, whose attitude was one of violent opposition and of accusations of American intended appeasement of Japan at the expense of China. These views were expressed not only in a Note from the Chinese Foreign Ministry, but also in direct cables from Chiang to Churchill and to T. V. Soong, who was then in Washington.[3] Soong was instructed to show Chiang's message to Stimson and Knox, which he did.[4] Chiang declared that if the embargo on Japan were at all relaxed, the effect upon Chinese morale would be such that a collapse of Chinese resistance would follow. He urged that there should be no relaxation of the freezing regulations until the Japanese had agreed to withdraw their armies from China.[5]

The hysterical opposition of the Chinese, which was expressed both privately and publicly, together with the doubtful attitude of the other Governments concerned, made Hull decide to drop the projected *modus vivendi*.[6] In a memorandum to the President which he presented on the morning of 26 November, Hull said that he wanted to give the Japanese the comprehensive peace proposal, but to withhold the *modus vivendi*.[7] 'The President promptly agreed.'[8]

[1] In his reply Eden had said: 'We feel that to prevent misrepresentation by Japan it will have to be made public that any interim agreement is purely provisional and is only concluded to facilitate negotiation of an ultimate agreement on more fundamental issues satisfactory to all parties concerned (*Pearl Harbor Attack*, pt. 14, p. 1165).   [2] *Second World War*, iii. 530–1.

[3] Hull, *Memoirs*, ii. 1077–8; *Pearl Harbor Attack*, pt. 14, p. 1161.

[4] Hull, *Memoirs*, ii. 1077–8, also *Pearl Harbor Attack: Report of Joint Committee*, pp. 376–7.   [5] ibid.

[6] Welles says that T. V. Soong, through 'a former official who had recently taken up the practice of law in Washington', stirred up accusations of American appeasement of Japan in the press and among Congressmen and Senators. 'Chinese opposition was successful. The project was shelved' (*Seven Decisions*, p. 88).

[7] Hull told the Pearl Harbor Committee that: 'It was manifest that there would be widespread opposition from American opinion to the *modus vivendi* aspect of the proposal especially to the supplying to Japan of even limited quantities of oil. The Chinese Government violently opposed the idea. The
[*Note continued on next page.*]

[8] Hull, *Memoirs*, ii. 1082.

The history of this 'comprehensive proposal', which was embodied in the fateful American Note of 26 November, is of interest. The basis of it was a draft prepared by Morgenthau, the Secretary of the Treasury, and sent to the State Department on 18 November.[1] This was revised by the Far Eastern Division of the State Department and then submitted to the Chiefs of Staff. They submitted proposed amendments and deletions on 21 November, at a meeting with Hull.[2]

Morgenthau's draft contained, *inter alia*, a proposal that the American Government should use their influence to cause the British Government to sell Hong Kong to China, the purchase price to be loaned China by the United States.[3] This, however, was deleted at the instance of Admiral Stark. It would be pleasant to record that this was because he realized what a gross and unmerited affront to Britain this suggestion constituted, but unhappily this was not the case; the Admiral thought that the British should surrender the Colony freely.[4]

Morgenthau's draft also included the stipulation that Japan should evacuate all her forces from China, exclusive of Manchuria. She was to withdraw the bulk of her troops from Manchuria, except for security forces, provided the USSR did the same in the Far Eastern region.[5] This provision was objected to by both Stark

other interested governments were sympathetic to the Chinese view and fundamentally were unfavourable or lukewarm. Their co-operation was a part of the plan. It developed that the conclusion with Japan of such an arrangement would have been a major blow to Chinese morale. In view of these considerations it became clear that the slight prospects of Japan's agreeing to the *modus vivendi* did not warrant assuming the risks involved in proceeding with it, especially the serious risk of collapse of Chinese morale and resistance and even of disintegration of China. It therefore became perfectly evident that the *modus vivendi* aspect would not be feasible' (*Pearl Harbor Attack: Report of Joint Committee*, p. 381).

[1] Text in *Pearl Harbor Attack*, pt. 14, pp. 1098–102. Hull says: 'Although this was a further example of what seemed to me to be the Secretary of the Treasury's persistent inclination to try to function as a second Secretary of State, some of its points were good and were incorporated in our final draft' (Hull, *Memoirs*, ii. 1073). This does rather less than justice to Morgenthau's contribution.

[2] *Pearl Harbor Attack: Report of Joint Committee*, pp. 366–7. General Gerow deputized for General Marshall.

[3] Text of Morgenthau's draft in *Pearl Harbor Attack*, pt. 14, p. 1099.

[4] 'As I mentioned this morning I just don't like the idea of our buying Hongkong from the British and giving it to China. If this is to be done I think the British at least might make this contribution to a cause more important for the British Commonwealth than for the United States. Portugal should likewise give up Macao' (memo. by Admiral Stark, 21 Nov. 1941, ibid. p. 1105).

[5] ibid. p. 1101.

and Gerow, on the grounds that it would probably be unacceptable to the Russians, and would not be in the interests of the United States.[1] It is, however, of interest as indicating that it was not intended to demand that Japan abandon Manchuria and restore it to China. But because in the final version as presented to Japan there was no mention of Manchuria, the Japanese appear to have thought that this was the intention, since the American Government had never recognized Manchukuo.[2]

Hull was almost certainly right in his belief that the *modus vivendi* would have been rejected by the Japanese Government.[3] Togo on 24 November had reiterated that Japan required the acceptance of all points of Proposal B and that she would make no further concessions.[4] Nevertheless it may be wondered why Hull did not stand firm and insist upon the presentation of the *modus vivendi*. The British Government were not unalterably opposed to the idea of a *modus vivendi* and were ready to leave the terms to Hull's decision. The Chinese were simply trying out a form of blackmail. They had obvious reasons for wanting the United States to get involved in war with Japan and their attitude could have been anticipated and largely discounted.

The answer would appear to be found in the state of American Congressional and general opinion. As Nomura had told Tokyo, this might be divided on the question of participation against Germany, but it was solidly anti-Japanese. Hull could not risk giving any colour to accusations, skilfully fomented by the Chinese, that he was ready to sell out China to Japan in order to be free to concentrate against Germany. This would only have given too good

---

[1] ibid. pp. 1105–6.
[2] Tojo said he took it that Manchuria was included (IMTFE, *Record*, p. 36355). Togo told the Tribunal that he had also thought so (ibid. p. 36127).
[3] 'I knew there was but a very slight chance of Japan's accepting it, but I was nevertheless very much in favour of presenting it because it would contribute to keeping the record clear. It would help emphasize for all time to come that we were doing everything we could to avoid war'...(Hull, *Memoirs*, ii. 1080).
[4] *Pearl Harbor Attack*, pt. 12, p. 176. In another cable of the same date he told the Ambassadors that the time-limit set in his dispatch of 22 November was in Tokyo time, i.e. 29 November in Tokyo, 28 November in Washington. In a dispatch of 26 November Togo instructed Nomura to tell the American Government, if an agreement was being reached on Proposal B, that Japan wanted to import 4 million tons of petroleum per annum from the United States and an additional million tons of petroleum per annum from the Netherlands East Indies. He said that these figures roughly corresponded to the amount of Japan's oil imports from those sources prior to the embargo. He would, however, have been prepared to accept somewhat less (ibid. p. 177). But this was vastly different from the limited export which Hull had in mind.

a case to the numerous enemies of the Roosevelt administration. Hence his promptness in dropping the proposed *modus vivendi* and Roosevelt's ready acquiescence in this.

On the afternoon of 26 November Nomura and Kurusu went to their fateful conference with Hull. They had already abandoned hope of a settlement on the lines desired by Tokyo and had made a last appeal to Togo on that morning. They suggested an exchange of messages to express the desire of both sides for peace, and that the Japanese Government should propose the neutralization of Indo-China, Thailand, and the Netherlands East Indies. They asked that their message should be shown to the Minister of the Navy, evidently in the hope of getting the support of that Service for this last-minute effort to preserve peace.[1]

The Japanese Ambassadors came to the Department of State in the anticipation that Hull would reject Proposal B, but also that he would present them with a counter draft for a *modus vivendi*. They were given instead the proposal for a comprehensive settlement and they were both aghast at its contents.[2]

Japan was asked to join in a proposed multilateral non-aggression pact among the principal Powers interested in the Pacific, and in a pledge to respect the territorial integrity of French Indo-China and the principle of equality of commercial opportunity therein. She was to withdraw all her armed forces from China and from Indo-China, to promise to support no régime in China except the National Government then in Chungking, and agree to surrender her extraterritorial rights to China.[3] She was further to pledge herself not to interpret the Tripartite Pact in such a way as to conflict with the purpose of the proposed accord—the establishment and preservation of peace in the Pacific area. In return she was offered a new commercial treaty with the United States, on liberal terms, the removal of the 'freezing' restrictions, and the

[1] ibid. pp. 180–1.
[2] Text of the American Note of 26 November in *Japan, 1931–41*, ii. 768–70. Hull intimated that the Japanese proposal B was rejected and that the American Government had dropped the idea of a *modus vivendi*. When they had glanced over the American Note the envoys said they did not even know whether they should report it to Tokyo. Kurusu said that if they did the Japanese Government would be likely 'to throw up its hands' (*Pearl Harbor Attack*, pt. 12, pp. 183–5; Hull, *Memoirs*, ii. 1084–5).
[3] In his conversation with the Japanese Ambassadors Hull said that the United States was not necessarily asking that the evacuation of China be effected immediately. It would be carried out by negotiations. The same consideration applied to the Open Door principle (*Pearl Harbor Attack*, pt. 12, pp. 183–5).

stabilization of the dollar–yen rate by means of a fund, half of which would be supplied by the United States.

It is true, as Hull points out, that the American Note only made explicit what had been implicit in the American attitude from the beginning of the negotiations.[1] It is also true that the Note was not an ultimatum in the sense that the United States intended to make an armed attack upon Japan if she rejected these terms.[2] But Hull made it clear that there would be no *modus vivendi* and that the terms would not be modified. That meant that, unless and until Japan accepted them, the economic pressure upon her would continue. She was faced with the alternatives of making a public surrender of all that she had for years been fighting for in the Far East, or of undergoing slow economic strangulation. She had herself to blame for being in this situation, as Hull had repeatedly intimated. But moral lectures are not conducive to peace, especially when the moral standards of the lecturer's country have not always been quite as high as those he advocates.[3] Furthermore the very economic sanctions which were intended to teach Japan to mend her ways were an object-lesson to the Japanese on the need to build up an economically self-sufficient empire if they could.

Neither Roosevelt nor Hull believed that Japan would accept the terms embodied in the American Note. Why, then, did they proffer it? It has been charged that they meant to provoke Japan to attack the United States so that the latter might get into war with Germany 'by the back door'. But, apart from other objections to this theory, the American Government at this time could not be sure that Hitler would support Japan in arms if she attacked the United States. He was not bound to do so under the letter of the Tripartite Pact. An attack by Japan upon the United States, even a 'provoked' attack, was not the same thing as an attack by the United States upon Japan unless Hitler chose to interpret it so.

[1] 'The document . . . was essentially a restatement of principles that had long been basic in United States foreign policy (Hull, *Memoirs*, ii. 1084).

[2] ibid.

[3] Kurusu once burst out to Moore: 'I know what governments say and I know what they do. I was for a long time, as you know, in charge of commercial relations in the Foreign Office and I know from that experience how reluctant other countries were to deal fairly with us.' Moore said he supposed the United States had been the worst. 'No', said Kurusu, 'I cannot say that. The British were the worst' (Moore, *With Japan's Leaders*, pp. 278–9). Nomura too had once told Hull, 'You Americans are in an advantageous position relative to the various nations when it comes to commercial negotiations. We do not have the advantageous bargaining position that you have' (*Pearl Harbor Attack*, pt. 12, p. 150).

Japanese behaviour towards Germany after the fall of Matsuoka would have warranted his refusing such an interpretation and paying the Japanese back in their own coin.[1] Had he taken this course there would have been formal war between the United States and Japan, but not between the United States and Germany. In that case American opinion would have compelled their Government to concentrate upon the Pacific theatre of war, which was exactly what Roosevelt and Churchill wished to avoid. It was not until 1 December that an intercepted message from Oshima to Tokyo made it appear that Hitler was not going to take this course, but meant to declare war, if Japan did.[2]

The real reason for the preparation and delivery of so uncompromising a Note appears to have been to refute the charges of appeasement of Japan and of preparing a 'Far Eastern Munich', which were being bandied about in Washington, thanks to the outcry the Chinese were making. Hull's openly expressed anger at this reveals the extent of his anxiety about it.[3] The rumours

[1] Toyoda on 16 October had told Nomura that he had refused to give confidential information about the Washington conversations to the German and Italian Ambassadors. He further said that the German Government had repeatedly demanded that Japan tell the United States Government that their policy (of assistance in the Atlantic to Britain) would bring them into war with Germany and Italy and that this would bring Article 3 of the Tripartite Pact into operation. But Japan had delayed doing anything as long as she could. Now a warning message was sent, for Nomura to deliver. This expressed the 'deep concern' of Japan, as a signatory of the Pact, over the danger of war between Germany and the United States and her 'sincere desire' that there should be an easing of the existing tension in German-American relations (ibid. p. 72). But it was careful to omit all mention of what Japan *would* do if war did occur. Hull realized that it was a very watered-down version of what Germany wanted (*Memoirs*, ii. 1034). Togo on 11 November told Nomura that the Germans had made two further representations. Apparently they wanted another Japanese démarche in Washington, but Togo on 6 November gave an answer which was really a polite refusal (*Pearl Harbor Attack*, pt. 12, p. 117). These messages were intercepted, so that Roosevelt and Hull knew that the Japanese were playing fast and loose with their Axis partners.

[2] Oshima reported on 29 November a long conversation with Ribbentrop in the course of which the latter said that, if Japan engaged in war with the United States, Germany would join in immediately and that Hitler was determined on this. The message was decoded on 1 December (ibid. pp. 201–2).

[3] When Halifax came on 29 November to ask what had happened about the *modus vivendi* Hull complained that Chiang Kai-shek, without a complete understanding of the facts, had sent numerous hysterical cables to different Cabinet members outside the State Department. 'When Churchill received Chiang's loud protest about our *modus vivendi*, it would have been better if he had sent Chiang a strong cable to brace up and fight with the same zeal as the Japanese and Germans were displaying. Instead, he passed on the protest to us without objection on his part, thereby virtually killing what we know were the individual views of the British Government toward these negotiations' (*Memoirs*, ii. 1089).

made it impossible to keep the conversations secret any longer, and on 27 November Hull gave an outline of the situation to the press.[1]

Hull declares that the proposals—which would in any case have been delivered—with or without the *modus vivendi*—were drawn up with a view to keeping the conversations going, thus gaining time and also, if accepted, to forming the basis of a comprehensive settlement.[2] From this it appears that he thought it just possible, despite the contrary evidence of the intercepted messages, that Japan would still go on talking, and that when it came to the pinch, she would not dare to fight. Churchill admits that this was his view and Roosevelt at heart seems to have believed the same.[3]

It is certain that there were many in, or close to, American and British governmental circles who held that view. It was not an unreasonable one, in view of the fact that the Japanese had initiated the conversations, had gone on talking for the best part of a year, and despite their constant threats, had hitherto taken no irrecoverable step. They had, indeed, shown a considerable anxiety to avoid war with the United States, and had made, or offered, striking concessions. If the United States stood firm, might not Japan climb down still more? In this connexion the peace party in Japan probably did a disservice to their cause by representing the power of the military in Japan as more impaired than in fact was the case, and by exaggerating the war-weariness and economic strain caused by the China War. Chinese propaganda worked to the same end, and, because of her failure to force China to accept peace, Japan was dangerously underrated as a military Power.[4]

---

[1] ibid. pp. 1086–7.　　　　　　　　　　[2] ibid. p. 1073.

[3] Harry Hopkins quotes Churchill as saying, at an Anglo-American conference in London in mid-July, that 'he was convinced that the Japanese would not enter the war until they were certain that the British Empire was beaten. He was convinced that the Japanese did not want to fight the United States and the British Empire together. (This conviction shared by Roosevelt was of enormous importance in the formulation of policy prior to Pearl Harbor)' (Sherwood, *White House Papers*, i. 316). Churchill writes: 'It had seemed impossible that Japan would court destruction in war with Britain and the United States, and probably Russia in the end. A declaration of war by Japan could not be reconciled with reason.' He adds that Roosevelt, Hull, Stimson, Knox, Marshall, and Stark all thought it 'an act of suicide' for Japan to attack the United States (*Second World War*, iii. 585–6).

[4] The Joint Intelligence Sub-Committee of the British War Cabinet thought that Japan's first move would be to occupy Siam 'which Japan might think would involve the least risk of a major conflict' (Sherwood, *White House Papers*, ii. 425). This appreciation was passed on to Washington on 21 November. Intercepted Japanese reports from Bangkok showed that the Japanese were intriguing with members of the Siamese Government to get Siam to allow Japanese forces in and to ally herself with Japan, but that the Siamese

On 27 November a Liaison Conference was held in Tokyo. All were agreed that the American Note was unacceptable, and that Japan must now fight.[1] But it was decided that the matter should be first laid before the Jushin (ex-Premiers), prior to a formal Imperial Conference on 1 December.[2] The next day Togo had conversations with Tojo, Shimada, and Kido, who all agreed that the last-minute suggestion of Nomura and Kurusu was impracticable. Kido remarked that acceptance of the American Note might lead to civil war in Japan.[3] So, on 28 November, Togo informed Nomura and Kurusu that the American terms could not be accepted and that 'with a report of the views of the Imperial Government which I will send you in two or three days, the negotiations will be *de facto* ruptured.'[4] In the meantime they were to avoid giving the impression that this was to happen. He further told them that the Navy Minister had turned down their suggestion for a last-minute breaking of the deadlock as entirely unsuitable.[5] But the peace party still made a last effort to avoid war. At the conference of the Jushin on 29 November Konoye and Yonai urged that, even though negotiations with the United States had

---

were trying to avoid committing themselves (*Pearl Harbor Attack*, pt. 12, pp. 175–6, 202–4). Nomura and Kurusu thought that their Government intended the occupation of Siam and warned Tokyo that in response to this British and American forces might occupy the Netherlands East Indies and *then* Japan would attack them (ibid. pp. 181, 197). Marshall and Stark, in an appreciation of the situation on 28 November, evidently thought that Siam was the likeliest Japanese objective (*Pearl Harbor Attack: Report of Joint Committee*, pp. 390–1). The weight of political and service opinion in both Great Britain and the United States was that Japan would avoid a direct clash with these Powers, at any rate while the German-Soviet war was undecided. A point in connexion with this was that although the Japanese Government had protested against American tankers carrying oil to Vladivostok and the Japanese press had threatened naval action to stop this, the tankers sailed and nothing happened. Moore says that this 'tended to give American officials the impression that Japan would not accept war with the United States' (*With Japan's Leaders*, pp. 243–4).

[1] 'The reaction of all of us to it was, I think, the same. Ignoring all past progress and areas of agreement in the negotiations, the United States had served upon us what we viewed as an ultimatum containing demands far in excess of the strongest positions theretofore taken. We felt that clearly the United States had no hope or intention of reaching an agreement for a peaceful settlement, for it was plain to us, and must have been plain to the Americans, that this document demanded as the price of peace total surrender by Japan to the American position. Japan was now asked not only to abandon all the gains of her years of sacrifice but to surrender her international position as a Power in the Far East. That surrender, as we saw it, would have amounted to national suicide. The only other way to face this challenge and defend ourselves was war' (evidence of Togo, IMTFE, *Record*, p. 35706).

[2] Evidence of Tojo (ibid. p. 36357).

[3] Evidence of Togo (ibid. pp. 35707–8).

[4] *Pearl Harbor Attack*, pt. 12, p. 195.   [5] ibid.

failed, peace should be maintained, in the hope that international developments might tell in Japan's favour. Konoye once more referred to the possibility that Japan might be able to carry on economically, despite the embargo.[1] But, as before, Tojo maintained that this was impossible especially in the matter of oil.[2] Wakatsuki said that if it was a matter of the national existence Japan should fight rather than surrender, but she should not risk war for the maintenance of the Greater East Asia Co-Prosperity Sphere.[3] Tojo, however, insisted that war was the only course and he held the advantage, not only because he was clearly the dominating character, but because the Jushin had to rely upon the information he gave them concerning the economic and military situation, and accept his assurance that victory could be won.[4] So they concurred, although sadly and doubtfully.

Tojo, however, got a shock on the next day when the Emperor summoned him and said that Prince Takamatsu had told him that the Navy desired to avoid war.[5] But he was equal to the occasion. He replied roundly that the decision of the Liaison Conference could not be revised and that the High Command were convinced of victory. If the Emperor had any doubts he had better consult with the Navy Minister and the Chief of the Naval Staff.[6] Tojo knew that he had won over Shimada and Nagano. On that evening Kido telephoned Tojo to say that the Emperor agreed to the holding of the Imperial Conference on 1 December.[7] That meant that the peace party had capitulated.

Thus the Imperial Conference of 1 December, which ratified the decision for war, was largely a formality. The Emperor, as usual, said nothing.[8] Hara, the President of the Privy Council, said that a prolonged war should be avoided as there was danger of a national collapse. Tojo replied that there would still be no war if the United States made concessions at the last moment, and that all care would be taken to preserve the morale of the home front.[9] So the fateful decision for war was finally taken. In his

[1] Konoye Memoirs, p. 4012; evidence of Kido, IMTFE, *Record*, p. 31035.
[2] Evidence of Tojo, ibid. p. 36367.
[3] Evidence of Kido, ibid. p. 31035.
[4] Tojo told them that the High Command was confident of success in occupying strategic points, and areas which contained vital raw materials. Then Japan could propose peace terms, especially to China and Britain, perhaps through the good offices of the USSR or the Vatican (evidence of Tojo, ibid. p. 36370).
[5] ibid. [6] ibid. pp. 36370-1. [7] ibid. p. 36371.
[8] Evidence of Tojo (ibid. p. 36378). [9] ibid. pp. 36376-7.

evidence before the Tokyo Tribunal Tojo absolved the Emperor from all responsibility for this. The Emperor, he said, did nothing without advice and it was unheard of for him to go against the recommendations of the Cabinet and the Supreme Command. He did not even offer suggestions except on the advice of the Lord Keeper of the Privy Seal.[1] This was certainly normal constitutional procedure, but the times were abnormal and the Emperor, *de jure* absolute, might have broken through the constitutional trammels and declared for peace. Kido, indeed, declared that a plan to have him do this was on foot, but that the American Note of 26 November caused it to be abandoned.[2] He thought that the result of such an attempt would have been internal upheaval, and he was very probably right in this.

Meanwhile Togo on 29 November had told Nomura and Kurusu to make a last effort to get the American Government to reconsider their attitude. But even without the knowledge of Japanese naval and military movements in the direction of Siam and Malaya gained through the intercepted telegrams, a bellicose public speech by Tojo to mark the anniversary of the Anti-Comintern Pact would have frustrated Togo's purpose.[3] The Ambassadors themselves remonstrated about this in a trans-Pacific telephone conversation with Kumaichi Yamamoto, head of the American Division of the Japanese Foreign Ministry.[4] The effect of Tojo's speech was to cause Roosevelt to cut short a brief vacation at Warm Springs. Nomura, on instructions from Tokyo, did his best to minimize the significance of the speech and of other belligerent public statements in Japan, and to explain away the Japanese military movements in Indo-China.[5]

Nomura and Kurusu continued to urge moderation upon Tokyo

---

[1] ibid. pp. 36380–1. [2] Evidence of Kido (ibid. p. 31035).
[3] He was reported as saying that Chiang's continued resistance was 'only due to the desire of Britain and the United States to fish in the troubled waters of East Asia by pitting the East Asiatic peoples against each other and to grasp the hegemony of East Asia. . . . For the honour and pride of mankind we must purge this sort of practice from East Asia with a vengeance.' His speech was made at a Convention of the Imperial Rule Assistance Association, and several other Japanese officials rivalled him in belligerency (*Pearl Harbor Attack: Report of Joint Committee*, p. 401). Associated Press reports of his speech came in to Washington on 29 November.
[4] *Pearl Harbor Attack*, pt. 12, pp. 206–7, 212–13. Tokyo said that Tojo had been mistranslated by Domei and that his speech was not so threatening as the American press had reported (ibid. p. 225).
[5] Tokyo told them to say that this was to counter Chinese military activity on the border (ibid. p. 224), which they did on 5 December. Hull was openly contemptuous of this excuse (*Memoirs*, ii. 1093).

and suggested on 1 December that perhaps a meeting might still be arranged between Konoye and Wallace, the Vice-President, or with Harry Hopkins, Roosevelt's friend and confidant.[1] In an interview with Welles on 2 December they reported him as saying that 'the American proposals of the 26th were brought about by the necessity to clarify the position of the United States because of the internal situation here.' They took this as a hint that, if the conversations continued, there might still be some modification in the American stand.[2]

But Tokyo's course was set. On 6 December Togo cabled the long and bitter Japanese reply to the American Note of 26 November.[3] The Japanese memorandum denounced the whole attitude of the United States throughout the negotiations, accused her of conspiring with Great Britain and other Powers to encircle Japan and exert inhuman economic pressure upon her, as well as to prolong the war between her and China. It rejected the American proposals covering China and the Tripartite Pact, accused the United States of pursuing a policy of imperialistic exploitation in the Far East, and ended with the statement that 'the earnest hope of the Japanese Government to . . . preserve and promote the peace of the Pacific through cooperation with the American Government has finally been lost.' Therefore it was impossible to reach an agreement through further negotiations.[4] On 7 December (Tokyo date) Nomura was instructed to deliver the memorandum at 1 p.m. on 7 December, United States time.[5] This was in order to time the delivery twenty minutes before the scheduled hour of the attack on Pearl Harbour (7.50 a.m. on 7 December Honolulu time) in an effort to clear Japan of the charge of an attack without warning.[6]

---

[1] *Pearl Harbor Attack*, pt. 12, pp. 213–14. Togo replied on 3 December rejecting this proposal (ibid. p. 224).

[2] ibid. pp. 222–3.

[3] Togo told Nomura to keep it secret for the time being until he got another instruction on the time of presentation. He was meanwhile 'to put it in nicely drafted form' (ibid. pp. 238–9).

[4] *Pearl Harbor Attack: Report of Joint Committee*, pp. 461–5. Togo regarded this phraseology as tantamount to a declaration of war (IMTFE, *Record*, p. 35719).   [5] *Pearl Harbor Attack*, pt. 12, p. 248.

[6] The Japanese Striking Force, under Admiral Nagumo, had concentrated in Tankan Bay, Etorofu Island, in the Kuriles on 22 November. It sailed for Hawaii on 26 November. On 2 December it got the code wireless signal from Admiral Yamamoto to attack (Climb Mount Niitaka) on 8 December (Japanese time). (Morison, *US Naval Operations in World War*, iii. 88–93.) Togo told the Tokyo Tribunal that Nagano and Ito (Vice-Chief of the Naval Staff) at first wanted no reply at all to the United States Note, so as to make the surprise complete. But he talked them out of this. Then they said the Japanese reply

Meanwhile the American Government, knowing that a Japanese blow was impending, but not knowing just where it would fall, were considering their course of action. The idea of a personal message from Roosevelt to the Japanese Emperor had been under consideration for some time.[1] On 6 December it was sent, to ask the Emperor for the sake of humanity to withdraw his forces from southern Indo-China.[2] There was no hope of a favourable response —the message was really 'for the record'. The known Japanese military and naval movements now indicated an imminent invasion of Siam and a probable attack on the British and Dutch possessions in the Far East. The Siamese Government had been terrified at the Japanese military occupation of southern Indo-China in July, and had made repeated appeals to Washington and to London for arms and ammunition, including artillery and aircraft.[3] But they had got very little, because there was little to spare. On 25 November the British Ambassador in Washington passed on a report from Sir Josiah Crosby that unless some practical aid was given them the Siamese Government would again come under Japanese influence.[4] This was reinforced by warnings from the Siamese Minister in Washington that a Japanese attack upon Siam was imminent. He again appealed for arms supplies.[5] On 30 November Churchill once more suggested to Roosevelt the issuance of a joint

should be delivered at 12.30 p.m. on 7 December, Washington time. But on 5 December the Vice-Chiefs of Staff, Tanabe and Ito, said they wanted the time changed to 1 p.m. They would not tell him when the attacks were to be made, but assured him that there would be time for prior delivery of the Japanese Note, so Togo agreed. Later (after Pearl Harbor) Ito said 'I am very sorry for you, we cut it too fine' (IMTFE, *Record*, pp. 35712–24).

[1] The message had been under consideration since October. Hull was not in favour of sending it, except as a last resort, because he considered the Emperor a mere figurehead and that addressing him directly would only annoy Tojo and make him think the United States was weakening. On 6 December a Japanese combined expedition was reported en route from Indo-China to the Kra peninsula (Hull, *Memoirs*, ii. 1093).

[2] The President's message was received at the Japanese telegraph office at noon on December 7 (Japanese time) but was not delivered to the American Embassy until 10.30 p.m. Grew gave a copy to Togo on 12.15 a.m., 8 December. This was but half an hour before the Pearl Harbour attack. Grew asked for an audience with the Emperor which Togo said he would convey to him. Togo the next morning said he had seen the Emperor, apparently at 3.0 a.m., but that the Japanese memorandum (the one sent to Nomura on 6 December) was the answer (Grew, *Ten Years in Japan*, pp. 420–4). There was not much the Emperor could have done, if he had got the message before Pearl Harbour, but the military took no chances. They had apparently heard that such a message might come and they ordered the censorship on 7 December to hold up all telegrams for ten hours.

[3] *Pearl Harbor Attack: Report of Joint Committee*, pp. 405–6.
[4] ibid. pp. 407–8.   [5] ibid. p. 408.

declaration or a parallel warning to Japan against any further forward move.[1] On the same day the British Government informed Washington that there were indications that Japan was about to attack Siam and intended to seize the Kra isthmus. Great Britain had plans to occupy the region first, so as to secure a good defensive line covering Malaya. She wanted to know what the American Government's reactions would be.[2] Hull said that he would lay these matters before the President upon his return from Warm Springs.[3]

The Japanese Government had, on 23 November, decided, in the event of war, to ask Bangkok for permission to send their troops through Siam. But they evidently hoped that the British would make the first move, so that they could come in as defenders of Siam against British aggression.[4] The pro-Japanese faction in Siam was working with the Japanese to this end; an intercepted message of 29 November from the Japanese Ambassador in Siam to Tokyo, said that, in order to accomplish it 'Japan should carefully avoid Thai territory, and instead land troops in the neighbourhood of Kotaparu in British territory, which would almost certainly force Britain to invade Thailand from Patanbessa.'[5]

So Roosevelt deferred replying to the British inquiries, while the British Government deferred their proposed move into Siam, pending a clear indication of the American attitude.[6] Meanwhile they drew up a draft warning to Japan, which was intended to be subscribed to by all the Commonwealth nations, that she would invade Siam at her peril. This was communicated to Roosevelt for his comments on 7 December.[7]

Roosevelt was in a difficult position. He wanted to give full support to Great Britain and the Netherlands in the event of a Japanese attack upon their Far Eastern territories or a Japanese invasion of Siam which would be the prelude to it. But he could not be sure of Congressional support if he got into the position of 'firing the first shot' against Japan in defence of European colonial possessions. He was considering whether or not to send a parallel warning to the one proposed by the British Government, when the

---

[1] ibid. p. 403.
[2] ibid. pp. 403–4; Churchill, *Second World War*, iii. 534.
[3] *Pearl Harbor Attack: Report of Joint Committee*, p. 404.
[4] Evidence of Tojo (IMTFE, *Record*, p. 36401).
[5] *Pearl Harbor Attack: Report of Joint Committee*, p. 405.
[6] Churchill, *Second World War*, iii. 534. Also Crosby was urging London not to send armed forces into Siam (*Pearl Harbor Attack: Report of Joint Committee*, p. 439).
[7] ibid. pp. 429–30.

whole problem was solved for him by the Japanese attack on Pearl Harbour.[1]

Owing to the slowness of his staff in deciphering and translating the Japanese Note of 6 December Nomura was not ready to deliver it at the scheduled time and he and Kurusu did not see Hull until 2.30 p.m. on 7 December, by which time the attack on Pearl Harbour had been delivered and Hull had received a copy of Admiral Kimmel's first dramatic message, 'Air Attack on Pearl Harbor. This is not a drill.'[2] He describes the Ambassadors as 'cowering' when he told them that in fifty years of public service he had 'never seen a document that was more crowded with infamous falsehoods and distortions.'[3]

In Tokyo Togo summoned Grew to the Foreign Ministry at 7.30 a.m. on 8 December and gave him a copy of the Japanese Note which Nomura had delivered to Hull.[4] Craigie, who was asked to come at 8.0 a.m., received another copy.[5] This was some hours after the attack on Pearl Harbour and the opening of hostilities in Malaya. Formal notifications of a state of war were handed to the American and British Ambassadors around 11 a.m. the same morning, at about the time the Imperial Rescript declaring war was issued.[6] The next day, following a presidential message, Congress responded with a declaration of war upon Japan.[7]

As has been seen, after the fall of Matsuoka, the Japanese Foreign Ministry had consistently refused to keep the Germans informed about the content and progress of the conversations in Washington.[8] Tokyo was also careful to leave Oshima in ignorance. The German Government, however, learned something of the conversations through secret channels.[9] Despite official reassurances from Tokyo that Japan would stand firm in upholding the Tripartite Pact, Berlin was deeply suspicious of her, for which,

---

[1] Sherwood, *White House Papers*, i. 433.
[2] Hull, *Memoirs*, ii. 1095–6. He blames Nomura for not coming at 1 p.m. to deliver what had been translated by that time.
[3] ibid. p. 1096.   [4] Grew, *Ten Years in Japan*, p. 484.
[5] Craigie, *Behind the Japanese Mask*, pp. 134–5.
[6] Grew, *Ten Years in Japan*, p. 425; Craigie, *Behind the Japanese Mask*, p. 136.
[7] Hull, *Memoirs*, ii. 1100. The British Government had already issued their declaration on 8 December.   [8] See above, p. 315.
[9] Weizsäcker, in a memorandum of 12 July 1941, said that Oshima was very poorly informed; he was not told of the date of the Japanese descent on southern Indo-China or of the progress of the Washington negotiations. 'I do not believe that Oshima is aware that an answer from Washington is in Tokyo, a fact which came to our knowledge first from a certain source through the Italian Ambassador in Tokyo' (IMTFE, *Record*, pp. 37919–21).

indeed, there was good reason.[1] But Hitler never objected to the
Japanese-American conversations as such; he apparently considered that they might be beneficial, if only Japan would make it
clear to Washington that she would not remain neutral should the
United States enter the war against Germany.[2] At this juncture
he did not want war with the United States and he reacted to
American patrolling and convoying activities in the Atlantic with
unaccustomed forbearance. Although he was finding the task
harder than he had expected, he still counted upon decisively
defeating the Russians, after which he could turn with full force
upon Great Britain, who would then find American help 'short of
war' to be insufficient to save her. Meanwhile he continued to urge
Japan to join in against the USSR, but Tokyo evaded any commitment to do so.[3] The Japanese Government in fact were resolved
to avoid war with the USSR, even if they thereby forfeited German
aid against the United States. By mid-October, however, Hitler
had convinced himself that the Russians were beaten and that their
collapse was only a matter of time. So, for the moment, he changed
his mind about Japanese intervention.[4]

In late November, Japan began to sound Germany as to her attitude in the event of a Japanese-American war, and on 21 November Ribbentrop gave an assurance that Germany would come in.[5]

[1] Oshima, on 1 October 1941, told Toyoda 'that the Foreign Office staff from
Weizsäcker downwards and also everyone in general were thoroughly disgusted
with Japan.' He gave warning that 'if Japan goes ahead with her negotiations
without consulting Germany, there is no telling what steps Germany may take
without consulting Japan' (ibid. pp. 24733–4).

[2] 'As far as I know Germany also did not wish for a collision between Japan
and the United States and expressed her approval to the Japanese-American
negotiations in so far as they would induce the United States to observe
neutrality' (evidence of Oshima, IMTFE, *Record*, pp. 34029–30).

[3] When in the summer and autumn of 1941 Germany approached Japan,
asking her to intervene in the German-Russian war, there never was a clear-cut
Japanese reply of 'yes' or 'no' (evidence of Kretschmer, German military attaché,
Tokyo, ibid. pp. 24618–19).

[4] Weizsäcker (*Memoirs*, p. 262) says that on 21 October he heard that Hitler
did not expect much from the new Tojo Cabinet, and he was even somewhat
alarmed at the possibility that Tojo might declare war on Russia. 'For', he said,
'if Russia now collapses and England wants to make peace with us, Japan would
only be in our way.'

[5] On 20 November Kretschmer was asked by Major-General Okamoto if
Germany would declare war on the United States should there be a Japanese-
American conflict. Okamoto was evasive on how the war might arise, or whether
Japan intended to attack United States territory. Okamoto referred him to
Ott, who questioned Ribbentrop. On 23 November Tojo, as Minister of War,
expressed his deepest gratitude for the favourable reply made by Ribbentrop
(evidence of Kretschmer, IMTFE, *Record*, pp. 24643–4; also *Exhibits* 601,
603 A).

He repeated this pledge in an interview with Oshima on 28 November, in which he told the Ambassador that he had received word that there was practically no hope of a successful issue to the Japanese-American negotiations, and added that 'if Japan determined on war against Britain and America, not only would this be to the common advantage of Japan and Germany, but he believed that it would also be to Japan's advantage.'[1] Oshima on the next day duly reported this to his Government, remarking that the attitude of Germany towards the United States had considerably stiffened and that she would not refuse to fight her if necessary.[2] On 30 November (Japan time) Togo instructed Oshima to tell Hitler and Ribbentrop that the Japanese-American conversations were ruptured, that England and America were taking a provocative attitude, and were making troop movements in the Far East, which Japan would have to counter. The instruction continued: 'Say very secretly to them that there is extreme danger that war may suddenly break out between the Anglo-Saxon nations and Japan through some clash of arms and add that the time of the breaking out of this war may come quicker than anyone dreams.'[3]

If asked about Japanese policy in respect of the USSR Oshima was to reply that, unless that Power joined with Great Britain and

[1] *Pearl Harbor Attack*, pt. 35, p. 676.
[2] ibid. Ribbentrop had just been in conference with Hitler, Goering, and other leading civil and military personages. He told Oshima, in answer to the latter's queries, that the most important military operations in Russia had been concluded and that a large part of the army would be withdrawn to Germany; the rest would in the following spring drive Stalin into Siberia (ibid.). Germany had no intention of making peace with Britain and meant to expel her from the Mediterranean and the Near East (ibid.). It would thus appear that Hitler had modified his optimism of the previous October to the extent of expecting that the USSR and Great Britain would remain in the field over 1942. Consequently, Japan was needed as a counter-weight to American Lend-Lease assistance to these Powers. If she attacked British possessions in the Far East she could inflict serious, and possibly crippling damage upon the British war effort. Should, in consequence, America become involved in war with Japan, Hitler hoped that American naval forces would be withdrawn from the crucial battle of the Atlantic, and American supplies to Great Britain and to the USSR be limited. Mussolini seems to have been of like mind. Neither suspected Japan's intention of striking immediately at the United States, nor, as Ribbentrop testified, did they want her to do that. 'Japan did neither the one thing we wanted (attack Singapore) nor the other (attack the USSR); rather she did a third thing. She attacked the United States at Pearl Harbor' (evidence of Ribbentrop at Nuremberg, 30 March 1946, IMTFE, *Exhibit* 2692). If Hitler had suspected that Japan had made up her mind to fight the United States anyway, he might have avoided a pledge to join her. But he, like Roosevelt and Churchill, underrated her immediately belligerent purposes. She had threatened, but done little, so often before. So he gave the pledge to join her in the hope that it would screw up her courage to attack Britain.
[3] *Pearl Harbor Attack*, pt. 12, pp. 204–5.

the United States, Japan preferred, for the time being, not to
attack her.[1] In a separate dispatch which contained a resumé of
the conversations in Washington, Togo was careful to lay stress
upon the quarrel over the Tripartite Pact as the main cause of the
rupture, and to allege that the crisis had come because the United
States had insisted that Japan should abandon her Axis partners.[2]

In an interview with Ott on 30 November Togo took the same
line; he declared that Japan had insisted upon maintaining her
treaty obligations and that her faithfulness to the Pact had been
the main obstacle to the success of the negotiations in Washington.
Ott repeated the assurance that Germany would stand side by side
with Japan should the latter be involved in war with the United
States.[3] Oshima, who had not dreamed of the imminence of war,
had gone to Vienna to attend the Mozart festival.[4] He was called
back to Berlin by the Counsellor of Embassy and returned on
2 December to find Togo's instructions to him to initiate negotiations for a No-Separate-Peace agreement.[5] He interviewed
Ribbentrop the same day, who said that he could not alone decide
the grave question of whether Germany should immediately intervene in the event of a Japanese-American conflict. Hitler must be
consulted.[6] The Führer was at the Russian front, endeavouring
to cope with the critical situation caused by the onset of winter and
Russian counter-attacks. On 3 December Oshima again saw
Ribbentrop, who said that he did not want to use the telephone and
that aircraft could not be dispatched because of weather conditions.
Therefore, Ribbentrop himself would go to Hitler's headquarters

[1] ibid. p. 204.
[2] 'The Imperial Government adamantly stuck to the Tripartite Alliance as the
cornerstone of its national policy regardless of the vicissitudes of the international
situation', and Japan had based her hopes for a solution in the adjustment of
diplomatic relations between Japan and the United States 'definitely within the
scope of that alliance' (ibid. p. 205).
[3] Ott to Ribbentrop, 30 Nov. 1941 (*NCA*, v. 566).
[4] Evidence of Oshima (IMTFE, *Record*, p. 34031). He had received a telegram from Togo, dated 28 November, which said that the American counter-
proposal of 27 November (Japan time) could not be considered for a moment
and that there would probably be a rupture (*Pearl Harbor Attack*, pt. 35, p.
683; also evidence of Oshima).
[5] ibid. p. 34033. This was almost certainly included in Togo's dispatch of
30 November, one part of which was not intercepted and deciphered in
Washington. Oshima was not the brightest of Ambassadors, but even he would
scarcely have gone off to a music festival after receiving an instruction of that
kind. Togo told the Tokyo Tribunal that it was on 30 November that he
instructed the Japanese Ambassadors in Berlin and Rome to begin negotiations
for a No-Separate-Peace agreement (ibid. p. 35736).
[6] Evidence of Oshima (ibid. p. 34033).

(in East Prussia) and await the Führer's return, which would be on either 4 or 5 December. Ribbentrop added that he personally approved of the No-Separate-Peace proposal, and believed that Hitler would consent, but no official reply could be given until Hitler *had* been reached.[1]

On balance it does not appear that this was a subterfuge for delay as Ciano apparently supposed.[2] Hitler *was* at the front; he had gone to the Rostov area, where General von Kleist had just sustained a sharp repulse. Oshima told Tokyo that he was fairly confident that the Germans would agree to come in.[3] Furthermore, being completely ignorant that 7 December (European time) had been fixed by the Supreme Command as the date of the opening of hostilities, he had still not grasped the urgency of the matter. On his own showing, he had on 2 December told Ribbentrop that it was not clear whether war would come.[4]

On 3 December Mussolini had told the Japanese Ambassador in Rome that, if Japan declared war on the United States, Italy would immediately follow suit. He made no conditions and did not raise the question of Japanese participation against the USSR.[5] His willingness to intervene is curious if he had any reason to suppose that Hitler was not prepared to do so.[6]

At 3 a.m. on 5 December Ribbentrop sent for Oshima and gave him a formal acceptance of the Japanese requests. He also submitted a draft of an agreement.[7] Evidently, Hitler had been reached and had concurred. The draft treaty was in conditional form; it provided that if a state of war arose between Japan and the United States, Germany and Italy would also go to war and conduct it with all the armed forces at their disposal. Japan was to assume similar obligations in the event of war between the two Axis Powers and the United States. Under Article 2 the three Powers bound themselves not to conclude any armistice or peace with the United States, save by full mutual agreement among themselves. The same stipulation applied to Great Britain, in the event of an Anglo-

---

[1] Oshima to Togo, 3 Dec. 1941 (*Pearl Harbor Attack*, pt. 9, p. 4200).
[2] Ciano, *Diary*, pp. 405–6.
[3] Oshima to Togo, 3 Dec. 1941 (*Pearl Harbor Attack*, pt. 9, p. 4200).
[4] IMTFE, *Record*, p. 34033.
[5] *Pearl Harbor Attack*, pt. 12, pp. 228–9. 'The Duce was pleased by the communication and said, "Thus we arrive at war between continents, which I have foreseen since 1939"' (Ciano *Diary*, p. 405).
[6] He did reserve the right to consult with Berlin (ibid.).
[7] Oshima to Togo, 5 Dec. 1941 (*Pearl Harbor Attack*, pt. 35, p. 684).

Japanese war. The treaty was for the time being to be secret and was to have the same duration as the Tripartite Pact of 1940.[1]

The whole tenor of this shows that the Germans were quite unaware of the imminence of war between Japan and the United States. They appear to have suggested that, in this eventuality, Japan might stop the transport of supplies from America to Vladivostok in Soviet ships. This Togo refused to accept, even if it affected the German decision to come in against America.[2] On 7 December he told Oshima that while Japan agreed to the German treaty proposals, war might come before the formal conclusion of the agreement, which would render the first article obsolete. So he asked Oshima to tell Ribbentrop that Japan expected the immediate participation of the Axis Powers even if war with the United States came before the signature of the treaty. He further instructed him to negotiate only for a No-Separate-Peace agreement.[3]

On the evening of 7 December Oshima was told of the first broadcast reports from London of the attack on Pearl Harbour.[4] He could not confirm them when questioned by Ribbentrop, who had been himself, at first, incredulous, but told Oshima that it might be true, that, if so, immediate participation in the war by Germany and Italy was a matter of course, and that the draft treaty was obsolete.[5] The next day Oshima got official confirmation from Tokyo. When he called on Ribbentrop to request that Germany fulfil her promise to intervene he was told that Hitler had already issued orders to the German Navy to attack American ships wherever they found them and was at the moment conferring with General Headquarters on how a formal declaration of war could be made in a way to make a good impression upon the German people.[6]

Ribbentrop and Oshima, together with Gaus, Kase, and Uchida, then drafted a revised tripartite agreement. This provided (1) for the prosecution of the war until victory was secured; (2) for no separate armistice or peace; and (3) for co-operation after the war

[1] Text in ibid. p. 685.
[2] This appears from a telegram of 6 December from Togo to Oshima (*Pearl Harbor Attack*, pt. 12, pp. 245–6).   [3] ibid. pt. 35, p. 686.
[4] IMTFE, *Record*, p. 34035. See also Ribbentrop's statement at Nuremberg, 30 March 1946, that the attack came as a complete surprise both to him and to Oshima (IMTFE, *Exhibit* 2692; also IMT, Nuremberg, x. 346–97).
[5] Oshima to Togo, no. 1432, 8 Dec. 1941 (*Pearl Harbor Attack*, pt. 35, p. 687).
[6] ibid. pt. 12, p. 253.

in the establishment of an equitable New Order.[1] This last appears
to have been Ribbentrop's idea and Togo did not like it. He suggested to Ott that it might be deleted, or else, if the German
Government insisted upon its retention, that a reference to the
Tripartite Pact of 1940 should be added.[2] This would limit its
duration to that of the Tripartite Pact. The Germans agreed to
this latter suggestion and on 10 December the text was agreed
upon and ratified by the Privy Council in Tokyo.[3] Oshima arranged
for its formal conclusion on the following day, the eleventh. That
day, 11 December, Germany and Italy declared war upon the
United States, who at once responded in kind. So the grim circle
of world conflict was completed.

[1] Oshima to Togo, 8 Dec. 1941 (ibid. pt. 35, pp. 687–8).
[2] Togo to Oshima, 9 Dec. 1941 (ibid. p. 691).
[3] ibid. pp. 690–1. The final text (ibid. pp. 691–2) was as follows: 'In the
inflexible resolve not to lay down their arms till the joint war against the United
States and England has been successfully concluded, the Japanese, German
and Italian Governments have jointly agreed as follows:
Article 1. Japan, Germany and Italy will fight together with all the resources
at their command until victory is achieved over the United States and
England.
Article 2. Japan, Germany and Italy undertake not to make a separate armistice or a separate peace with the United States or England without full
mutual understanding.
Article 3. Japan, Germany and Italy will after the victorious conclusion of
the war collaborate closely in establishing an equitable New Order in the
spirit of the Three-Power Treaty signed on 27 September 1940.
Article 4. This Pact shall come into force at the date of signature.'

CHAPTER XI

Greater East Asia

I. THE 'ALLIED NATIONS'

DURING the first six months of the Pacific War the Japanese advanced from victory to victory. Their initial crippling of the American fleet at Pearl Harbour left them for a considerable time free from any interference from that quarter. They were thus able to develop their offensive movements in South Eastern Asia with the advantage of complete naval and air superiority. This, together with the skill and daring of their operations, enabled them to gain control of a vast land and sea area in a shorter time and with smaller losses than they had themselves anticipated. Hong Kong fell into their hands on 25 December 1941; on 15 February 1942 the conquest of Malaya was completed with the surrender of the British forces at Singapore, the greatest disaster to British arms that history records, as Churchill himself described it. A bare three weeks later Java had capitulated and the Japanese were bringing under their control the rich and varied resources of the Netherlands East Indies, including the vital oil supplies. On 6 May, with the surrender of the defenders of Corregidor, the Philippine Islands likewise came under Japanese sway. At the same time the shattered remnants of the British and Chinese forces in Burma were struggling over the mountain trails into Assam, and yet another great and rich region had fallen to the Japanese conqueror.

The Japanese were exultant, as well they might be. From Pearl Harbour to Colombo the Japanese Navy had swept the seas. In April 1942 the carrier and battleship force under Admiral Nagumo, which had dealt the blow on Pearl Harbour, was sent into the Bay of Bengal, where it wrought grievous loss upon British merchant shipping, sank several naval units, and compelled a British battleship squadron to retreat into African waters.[1] India itself appeared to be in danger until it became apparent that the Japanese had secured their immediate strategic objectives and were not planning to advance farther westwards.

[1] Churchill, *Second World War*, iv. Ch. 10.

Japan had now brought under her control a congeries of races and peoples in different stages of political and economic development. Already, on 20 November 1941, a Liaison Conference in Tokyo had laid down the broad principles of policy for the regions which Japan expected to dominate. This Conference decided upon an initial period of military administration for them, pending a later decision as to their final form of government. The military authorities were to respect local customs and were to make as much use as possible of the existing administrative organs. But the needs of the native inhabitants were to be subordinated to those of the military who were to utilize local supplies of food and raw materials so far as was possible. The acquisition by Japan herself of the 'resources vital for national defence' was, as might be expected, given priority. With this end in view, the military authorities were to exercise strict control over communications, industry, trade, and finance. Enemy—i.e. American, British, and Dutch—nationals were to be made to co-operate with the military administration; for recalcitrant elements deportation 'or other appropriate measures' were to be employed. The existing rights and interests of nationals of the Axis Powers were to be respected, 'but any future extension of them will be restricted as far as possible.'[1] The Japanese remained as adverse to letting the Germans secure any preferred position in the East Indies as they had already shown themselves to be in the case of occupied China.

The important Chinese communities in South East Asia were to be compelled to renounce all allegiance to Chungking, to support the Wang Ching-wei régime, and to co-operate with the Japanese administration. Japanese subjects who wanted to emigrate to the newly acquired territories were to be carefully examined to decide upon their fitness to do so. Japanese who had been resident in Malaya, in the Netherlands East Indies, and in other regions of South East Asia, but who had gone home in view of the imminence of war, were to be given preferential facilities for returning.[2]

Any modifications or changes in overall colonial policy—as it may be termed—were to be decided at subsequent Liaison Conferences. The Conference of 20 November evidently envisaged the gradual termination of military administration and the creation of local organs of self-government, though it went on record as

[1] IMTFE, *Exhibit* 877.   [2] ibid.

opposed to the encouragement of 'premature independence movements'.[1]

The Imperial Rescript which proclaimed a state of war with the United States and Great Britain declared that the objectives of the struggle were to ensure the peace and stability of East Asia and to protect that region against Anglo-American exploitation. This became the main theme of Japanese propaganda to the peoples in the occupied regions and to the world in general, as well as to the populace in Japan proper. The war was termed *Dai Toa Senso* (the Greater East Asia War), and its purpose was the establishment of *Dai Toa Kyoeiken* (the Greater East Asia Co-Prosperity Sphere), in which the participants would all co-operate to fashion a self-sufficient economic zone.

Tojo on 22 January 1942 told the Diet that Japan intended to establish permanent peace in Greater East Asia. To ensure this, he went on, 'we have a mind to bring under our power those areas which are absolutely indispensable for the defence of Greater East Asia and to deal with the others in accordance with traditions and the culture of every race.' He referred in particular to Hong Kong and Malaya as strategically vital for the defence of the Greater East Asiatic Sphere.[2] At the same time he promised independence to the Philippines and Burma, provided their peoples 'understood our true intentions', and were prepared to co-operate in the building of Greater East Asia. The peoples of the Netherlands East Indies were given a vaguer pledge of support for their development and welfare, provided they also gave willing assistance to Japan.[3]

After the Japanese surrender, some evidence of the Government's concrete plans for the ultimate disposal of the conquered territories was discovered in the form of a draft scheme, drawn up in the Foreign Ministry, under the date of 14 December 1941.[4] Togo, however, when questioned about this, declared that he had never seen or heard of it and that it must have been drafted by some subordinate official.[5] However this may have been, something akin to the plan would have been put into effect had Japan been able to retain her conquests. In some matters, indeed, it foreshadowed steps which Japan did take during the war.

[1] ibid.　　　　　　　　　　　　　　　[2] IMTFE, *Exhibit* 1338 B.
[3] ibid. A similar promise was given to Australia which Tojo apparently hoped might be induced to make a separate peace.
[4] *Exhibit* 1333 A.　　　　　　　　　　[5] *Record*, p. 35754.

According to the draft scheme, Singapore island, the Straits Settlements, British North Borneo, and Sarawak were to be made Japanese territory and to be ruled by a Japanese Governor-General resident at Singapore. The rest of Malaya, with the exception of the four northern Malay States, was to constitute a Japanese protectorate, under the suzerainty of the Governor-General at Singapore, who was to have a similar authority in respect of Brunei. The northern Malay States were to be given separate consideration, which meant that they might be restored to Thailand, as indeed was later done.[1]

The Netherlands East Indies were to be grouped in an Indonesian federation, but the outer regions—Dutch New Guinea, Dutch Borneo, and the Dutch part of Timor—were to remain under Japanese control, although termed 'dominions of the federation'. The Philippines were to be made independent, but subject to Japanese special privileges in military and economic affairs. Hong Kong was also to be Japanese territory, although its retrocession to China might be considered after the restoration of peace.[2]

The general Japanese concept of Greater East Asia was one in which Japan herself stood forth as the leader in all walks of life— military, political, economic, and cultural. Around her were to be grouped the satellite States, varying in the degree of political subordination to Tokyo, but all in common looking to Japan as the superior country, whose ways they should endeavour to imitate and with whom they should all faithfully co-operate. For the Japanese the successful establishment of Greater East Asia meant not only the attainment of the long-desired goal of economic self-sufficiency, but also of something else which would satisfy a psychological craving—the recognition of Japan's ethical and cultural superiority, the acceptance of Japan at her own valuation as the 'light of Asia'. Indeed, whether consciously or not, the Japanese aspired to play the part which the Chinese had once played in the great days of the Celestial Empire, when the Son of Heaven in Peking 'swayed the wide world', and when China was regarded by her neighbours as the exemplar and fountain-head of civilized life. It is not without significance that, in the regions of South East Asia which the Japanese armies overran, they were apt to treat the Chinese communities with especial

[1] IMTFE, *Exhibit* 1333 A.   [2] ibid.

suspicion and severity, particularly in the initial stages of the occupation.[1]

To emphasize the special relationship which was to be created between Japan and the occupied regions, Tojo early resolved upon the creation of a special organ to supervise and correlate policy towards them. The first step towards this was taken in March 1942, by the establishment of the Greater East Asia Deliberative Council, as an advisory body to the Prime Minister.[2] This was the prelude to the Greater East Asia Ministry. The organizational plan for this was drafted by the Cabinet Planning Board in the summer of 1942.[3] Togo, who appears first to have heard of it through the Home Minister, Michio Yuzawa, was bitterly opposed to the scheme.[4] The jurisdiction of the Foreign Ministry had been progressively reduced by the creation of the Manchurian Affairs Board in 1935 and the China Affairs Board three years later. Now, in matters affecting the countries of South East Asia, the Foreign Ministry was to be restricted to 'pure diplomacy' which, according to what Naoki Hoshino, President of the Planning Board, told Togo, meant ceremonial—the official reception of envoys and the formal signature of treaties.[5] Togo resolved to fight this plan and he at first hoped that by refusing his assent to it and also refusing to relinquish his post he would compel the resignation of the whole Tojo Cabinet, with whose general conduct of affairs he was increasingly dissatisfied.[6] But he found that Tojo was too firmly entrenched. The Army and the Navy, as their emissaries warned Togo, were favourable to the creation of the new Ministry, and, while evidently Yuzawa and other civilian members of Tojo's Cabinet were doubtful, they were not prepared to stand with Togo in any attempt to bring about the downfall of the Cabinet.[7]

The matter was thrashed out at a stormy Cabinet meeting on 1 September 1942. Tojo presented the draft plan and insisted upon its adoption. He declared that the other countries of Greater East Asia stood in a special relation of kinship to Japan and hence this new Ministry was needed for dealings with them.[8] Togo rejoined that they were more likely to resent the creation of the Ministry as

---

[1] *Shonan Times*, 23 Feb. 1942; R. Hastain, *White Coolie* (London, Hodder & Stoughton, 1947), p. 72.
[2] IMTFE, *Exhibit* 3673.   [3] Evidence of Togo (*Record*, p. 35756).
[4] Evidence of Yuzawa (ibid. p. 35575).
[5] Evidence of Togo (ibid. p. 35757).   [6] ibid. p. 35760.
[7] ibid.; also evidence of Yuzawa (ibid. p. 35575).
[8] ibid.; also evidence of Tojo (ibid. pp. 36444–5).

an outward indication that they were to be subordinated to Japan; that if the new organ was to be anything like the China Affairs Board, which, he declared, had done nothing but arouse Chinese antagonism, this would certainly be so.[1] He furthermore argued that to create two separate diplomatic organs would make for confusion and division in Japanese foreign policy. Togo also pointed out that Japan had by no means won the war and that the Cabinet would do better to concentrate upon that and to leave any considerations of the permanent relationship of Japan to the occupied regions until later.[2] But Tojo was obdurate and the Foreign Minister, finding that his hopes of bringing down the Cabinet were illusory, and unable to persuade Tojo to accept any compromise, was finally compelled to resign.[3] For the time being Tojo himself took over the Foreign Ministry, in addition to his other posts.[4]

With Togo gone, Tojo was able to secure Cabinet acceptance of the plan for the Greater East Asia Ministry. But when it was submitted to the Investigation Committee of the Privy Council, it encountered sharp criticism from several members of that body.[5] They echoed Togo's arguments about the confusion it would cause to have two separate bodies handling diplomatic affairs, and about the adverse effect it might well have upon opinion in the countries to which it was to apply. Tojo's claim that the new Ministry was essential to unify policy towards Greater East Asia was considerably weakened by his admission that its authority would be excluded from regions under military administration.[6] He declared, however, that military would give place to civil rule as soon as possible, and that the Army itself desired this. In answer to one Councillor, who pertinently remarked that even in Formosa the administrative personnel was almost wholly Japanese, and asked where the staff was to be found for all the newly occupied regions, Tojo declared that the inhabitants of such regions would be allowed to participate in their government through a series of gradual reforms. The Committee was not wholly satisfied with the explanations given by Tojo and by his new and more subservient Foreign Minister, Masayuki Tani. They wanted to amend the original

[1] Evidence of Togo (ibid. p. 35758). General Suzuki said that the Koain had not been a failure but Togo replied that everybody knew that it was!

[2] ibid.

[3] ibid. Nishi, the Vice-Minister of Foreign Affairs, also resigned.

[4] ibid. On 17 September Masayuki Tani was appointed Foreign Minister.

[5] The Investigation Committee held eight meetings during the period 8–21 October 1942 (IMTFE, *Exhibit* 687). [6] ibid.

scheme, but Tojo refused to accept this proposal and, in the end, his will prevailed.[1]

The Greater East Asia Ministry was formally established by Imperial Ordinance on 1 November 1942. It was divided into the four Bureaux of General Affairs, Manchurian Affairs, China Affairs, and Southern Region Affairs. Consequently the Manchurian Affairs Board, the Kwantung Bureau, the China Affairs Board, the East Asia and the South Seas Bureaux of the Foreign Ministry, as well as the Northern and Southern Development Bureaux of the Overseas Ministry, were to be absorbed into it. It was, however, excluded from any jurisdiction over Korea, Formosa, or Japanese Sakhalin.[2]

The functions of the new Ministry included the control of all former subordinate officials of the Japanese Foreign Service in the Greater East Asia sphere, except in the restricted field of 'pure diplomacy'. It supervised the activities of all other Japanese nationals throughout the area; selected and trained Japanese administrative personnel who were to be sent there, and was charged with the direction of the activities of Japanese development companies in these regions. It was furthermore entrusted with the promotion and supervision of cultural links between Japan and the associate countries within the sphere.[3]

The new Ministry was staffed, in part by the existing personnel of the Manchurian and China Affairs Boards, in part by officials transferred from the now defunct East Asia, South Seas, and American Bureaux of the Foreign Ministry, and in part also by Army and Navy officers. Kazuo Aoki, a former Minister of Finance and Supreme Economic Adviser to the Wang Ching-wei régime, was appointed Minister of Greater East Asia Affairs, with Kumaichi Yamamoto, formerly Director of the American Bureau of the Foreign Office, and for a short time in 1942 Vice-Minister of Foreign Affairs, as Vice-Minister.[4]

In point of fact the main reasons for the creation of the Greater East Asia Ministry would seem to have been, first, the desire of the armed services to relegate the Foreign Ministry to obscurity, and, secondly, to promote the Nipponization of the occupied regions. Its share in major decisions on policy towards the con-

---

[1] ibid.   [2] IMTFE, *Exhibit* 90.   [3] ibid.
[4] Evidence of Kumaichi Yamamoto (IMTFE, *Record*, pp. 17912–13; 17982–3).

quered areas was, at most, an advisory one; questions of what measure of local self-government should be permitted in any of them were a matter for the Cabinet and the Supreme Command to thrash out between themselves. According to the testimony of Yamamoto, it had no authority in countries like the East Indies which were under direct military rule, although his evidence was regarded with suspicion, since he was obviously anxious not to be implicated in the harsher features of Japanese rule.[1]

The main activities of the Greater East Asia Ministry were in the field of cultural propaganda. It sponsored the dispatch of instructors in the Japanese language all over the occupied areas, in an attempt to replace English or Dutch by Japanese as the second tongue of all the peoples who had been brought within Japan's orbit. It arranged for 'goodwill missions' to Japan from the regions of Greater East Asia, and supervised the activities of the carefully selected groups of students who were chosen to spend a period of study in Japanese universities. It organized periodic Greater East Asia literary and scientific conferences, and promoted various cultural associations throughout the area. Its mission, indeed, was to rally the peoples of East Asia behind Japan in the war for their liberation from Western exploitation, as the Japanese depicted the conflict, and to convince them that Japan was superior to the West in ethics, philosophy, and culture, as well as its equal in scientific attainments. Japan, not the Occident, was henceforth to be the guide and teacher of the Asiatic peoples.

The heyday of the Greater East Asia Ministry came in the autumn of 1943 when it organized the Greater East Asia Conference in Tokyo, which was attended by representatives of the allegedly independent allies of Japan—Manchukuo, China, Thailand, Burma, and the Philippines. The situation—theoretical and actual—in each of these countries may be briefly surveyed.

Manchukuo is of interest as the prototype of the new-style Japanese political architecture. It was professedly an independent State in alliance with Japan under the terms of the Protocol of 15 September 1932, by which Japan and Manchukuo agreed to co-operate for the preservation of the national security of each, to which end Japanese forces were to be stationed in Manchukuo. A secret military arrangement concluded at the same time placed all Manchurian forces under Japanese command in the event of

[1] ibid.

invasion or internal upheaval.[1] In fact the Manchukuo administration, from the Emperor Kang Teh (Pu Yi) downwards, was firmly under Japanese control; policy was shaped by the Japanese Director-General of the General Affairs Board and executed largely by the Japanese Vice-Ministers in the various departments. Japanese ex-officials in the Manchukuo administration who gave evidence for the defence at the Tokyo Trials claimed that the Chinese members of the Government had some measure of independence in the discussion and passage of legislation. They also said that this tended to increase as time went on and a better class of Chinese official was secured as a result of training in Japanese-sponsored academies.[2] Something of this may have happened, but Japanese control of the political and economic life of the country remained unimpaired down to the Soviet invasion and final collapse of Manchukuo in 1945. Pu Yi, the ex-Emperor, who was temporarily released by the Russians for the purpose, gave evidence in 1946 of the complete control exercised by the Japanese over himself and the country generally. Although there is little doubt that he was, at any rate initially, a more willing tool of the Japanese than he professed to be, and while much of his evidence was so highly-coloured as to be practically worthless, it remains true that the independence of Manchuria was a fiction. It suited the Japanese to maintain it because thereby they could repudiate charges of territorial expansion by declaring that they had not in fact annexed any territory, and they could deny responsibility for measures taken in Manchukuo which were adverse to third-Power commercial and industrial interests there.

At the opening of the Pacific War Japan had been in control of Manchuria for a decade, resistance to her rule had practically everywhere been driven underground, and the political and economic methods and instruments of domination had been created and applied. The war years therefore witnessed an intensification of Japanese economic exploitation of Manchuria, but little that was new in the political sphere. It was otherwise in the case of Japanese-occupied China, nominally under the control of the so-called

---

[1] Evidence of Tadashi Katakawa (IMTFE, *Record*, pp. 37108–11). He had been on the staff of the Kwantung Army and said that he helped to draft the secret military agreement.

[2] See e.g. evidence of Tamotsu Matsuki, who was, *inter alia*, Deputy Chief of the General Affairs Board (ibid. pp. 20153–74) and of Tomio Muto, Councillor of the Legislative Bureau of the Board (ibid. pp. 20386 ff.).

Central Government at Nanking under Wang Ching-wei. That régime had made 'peace' with Japan by virtue of the Treaty of 30 November 1940, but the harsh terms of that instrument, combined with the obvious actuality of Japanese domination, in themselves gave the lie to Japanese propaganda claims to be fighting for the liberation of China in common with the rest of East Asia.[1] The legitimate National Government in Chungking had been prompt to declare formal war upon Japan after the outbreak of the Pacific War and to stimulate overt and covert resistance to her in the occupied areas by holding out the hope of liberation when she should have been defeated by the coalition of her enemies. The initial Japanese victories which left free China more isolated than ever, and deprived her of all but the thinnest trickle of material aid, were a heavy blow to morale in free China. The Japanese in 1942 appear to have considered mounting an offensive against Chungking, but abandoned this plan when the tide of battle began to turn against them at Guadalcanal.[2] Until 1944 they continued to avoid major military operations in China and confined themselves to endeavouring to consolidate their hold in the regions which they had already penetrated. They hoped that the mounting financial and economic difficulties of free China, combined with warweariness and resentment at long-deferred aid, might yet bring about its collapse. The increasing rift between the Kuomintang and the Chinese Communists, together with resentment in Chungking at American unsought-for advice in this matter, further encouraged Japanese hopes of a Chinese secession from the Allied camp.

To promote such a development and to lend strength to the peace movement of Wang Ching-wei and his associates, it was necessary for the Japanese to give that régime the outward status of an ally and an equal. Tojo, who was not without imagination in these matters, appears to have grasped this. His perception was no doubt sharpened by the increasingly unfavourable aspect of military developments, both in the Pacific and in Europe. The influence of Mamoru Shigemitsu, first as emissary to Nanking and, in April 1943, as the successor of Tani in the Japanese Foreign Ministry, was also important. He appears to have seen in the 'new

[1] See Ch. VIII above.
[2] According to the evidence of Lieut.-General Shinichi Tanaka, Chief of Operations Division, General Staff, October 1940 to December 1942 (IMTFE, *Record*, pp. 23341–3).

China policy' a means of securing peace with Chungking, as a prelude to a possible accommodation with the Western Powers.[1] For Tojo the policy was probably more a device for rallying Chinese sentiment to Japan, but whatever his motives, he accorded it his active support and collaboration.

In December 1942 Wang Ching-wei came to Tokyo and held discussions with the Japanese Cabinet.[2] This was followed, on 9 January 1943, by a formal declaration of war by the Nanking Government upon Great Britain and the United States.[3] At the time Tojo, in a speech expressing appreciation of this step, declared that it was 'only natural and proper that Nippon should at this juncture resolutely re-establish her relations with China upon new foundations. . . .'[4] He declared that the Japanese Government had decided to surrender their extraterritorial rights and their Concessions in China, to turn over to her the International Settlement in Shanghai and that at Kulangsu, as well as enemy properties in China which had been seized by the Japanese forces.[5]

This announcement was no doubt intended to counter the effect of the impending relinquishment by Great Britain and the United States of their extraterritorial rights in China. They had announced their intention of entering into negotiations with China for this purpose on 10 October 1942, and the treaties were on the point of signature, a fact of which the Japanese, who knew most of what went on in Chungking, were probably aware. The formal signature of the Sino-American and Sino-British treaties took place on 11 January 1943, and was made an occasion for special celebration in Chungking as marking the end of the era of the 'unequal treaties'.[6]

The Japanese stigmatized the provision in the British treaty for the rendition of the British Municipal Area at Tientsin and of the British Concession at Shameen as a mere empty gesture, since these were in Japanese possession.[7] They took a similar view of the surrender of American and British administrative rights in the International Settlement at Shanghai, from which, as their propaganda organs gleefully pointed out, the *taipans* had been expelled

---

[1] Kase, *Eclipse of the Rising Sun*, p. 69.
[2] *Syonan Sinbun*, 23 Dec. 1942.   [3] ibid. 9 Jan. 1943.
[4] ibid. 11 Jan. 1943.   [5] ibid.
[6] Hull, *Memoirs*, ii. 1257–8; *China Newsweek*, 10 Oct. 1942; 23 Jan. 1943.
[7] They had been formally handed over to the 'National Government of China' in March 1942, but the Japanese military remained in *de facto* control (*Shonan Times*, 26, 29, 30 March 1942).

and where the Municipal Council was now made up only of Japanese and Chinese members.[1] But the complete surrender of American and British special rights, especially at Shanghai, left the Japanese no option but to follow suit and to implement the promise they had made in November 1940.

Accordingly, on 9 February 1943 it was announced that a Sino-Japanese Commission had been established to work out the details of the rendition of Japanese Concessions.[2] On 14 March an agreement was reported whereby the Japanese Concessions at Hankow, Tientsin, Shasi, Soochow, Hangchow, and Amoy were to be rendered, without compensation, to the Chinese Government (i.e. the Wang Ching-wei régime). The Chinese were to enjoy full administrative rights in these areas, although the agreement safeguarded the property holdings of Japanese residents in them.[3] This step apparently caused misgivings among the Japanese in China, for the announcement of the agreement, effective on 30 March, was shortly followed by a visit of Tojo himself to Shanghai and Nanking, during which he took the opportunity of declaring that, while the Japanese Government were deeply concerned with the position and interests of their residents in China, they were resolved to adhere to the policy of considering Chinese interests first and foremost, and he asked for co-operation in this policy from the Japanese in China.[4] At the end of the month, after his return to Japan, he told a conference of Japanese economic officials and industrialists that Japanese business men in China should cease to entrench themselves behind the bulwark of special rights and interests and should work with the Chinese on a basis of equality.[5]

Further steps in the new policy included the handing over to the Wang Ching-wei régime of the small International Settlement area at Kulangsu on 27 March.[6] On 30 June an agreement was reached in Nanking for Chinese administrative control over the International Settlement at Shanghai. By the terms of this the Nanking Government were to take over the assets and liabilities of the Municipal Council, the positions and emoluments of the existing administrative staff were to be maintained, as also were the property rights of Japanese nationals in the Settlement.[7]

[1] *Syonan Sinbun,* 1 Jan. 1943.   [2] ibid. 12 Feb. 1943.
[3] ibid. 15 March 1943.   [4] ibid. 16 March 1943.
[5] ibid. 30 March 1943.   [6] ibid. 29 March 1943.
[7] ibid. 1 July 1943.

Meanwhile, on 18 May, the French (Vichy) representative in Nanking had concluded a general agreement for the rendition of French Concessions in China.[1] On 22 July a special agreement covering the rendition of the French Concession in Shanghai was likewise concluded in Nanking.[2] These agreements on the International Settlement and the French Concession came into force on 1 August. At this time a further Sino-Japanese agreement was announced by virtue of which Japanese civilians in China were made liable to Chinese taxation, subject to certain safeguards.[3]

On 15 June Tojo told the Diet that the Government intended to effect a fundamental revision in the Basic Treaty of 30 November, 1940.[4] Masayuki Tani, who had replaced Shigemitsu as Ambassador to Nanking, entered into negotiations for this end. In early September Aoki, the Greater East Asia Minister, paid a visit to Nanking and returned with reassurances for those who were evidently dubious about the 'new China policy'.[5] On 30 October a Pact of Alliance was signed in Nanking by Tani and Wang Ching-wei.[6]

The preamble to this Treaty said that the two Governments were resolved to co-operate as equals in the establishment of a Greater East Asia, and to eradicate all sources of difficulty, and had therefore agreed upon the new Pact.[7] This comprised six articles: the first provided for permanent relations of amity and friendship, with mutual respect for sovereignty and territorial integrity; the second for co-operation and assistance in the establishment of Greater East Asia; the third for close economic co-operation on the basis of reciprocity; while the fourth made provision for future discussions on details. By Article 5 the Treaty of 30 November 1940, 'together with all the instruments annexed thereto', were to be null and void from the date of the coming into force of the new Treaty, which by the sixth article was the date of its signature.[8]

In a protocol to the Treaty of Alliance Japan undertook to with-

[1] ibid. 19 May 1943.   [2] ibid. 23 July 1943.
[3] ibid. 1 and 2 Aug. 1943. Italy on 22 July had agreed to relinquish her treaty rights in the International Settlement at Shanghai (ibid. 23 July 1943). When Italy surrendered to the Allies the Japanese disarmed her forces and seized her properties in the Far East (ibid. 15 September 1943). On 14 July 1944 an agreement was signed between the Nanking Foreign Minister and the Italian chargé d'affaires for the rendition of the Italian Concession in Tientsin (ibid. 15 July 1944).   [4] ibid. 19 June.
[5] ibid. 8 Sept. 1943.   [6] ibid. 1 Nov. 1943.
[7] IMTFE, *Exhibit* 466; *Record*, pp. 5333–4.   [8] ibid.

draw her troops from China when general peace between the two countries was restored and the state of war had ceased to exist. She furthermore renounced the right which she possessed to station troops in China under the Peking (Boxer) Protocol and supplementary agreements.[1]

A statement by the Japanese Government Board of Information declared that, since the outbreak of the Greater East Asia War, a radical change had occurred in the situation in China. It referred to the declaration of war by Nanking upon Great Britain and the United States 'whose influence had thus been expelled from China', and said that Japan and China were adjusting their treaty relations so that untrammelled by all past circumstances, they could revert to their normal and proper status as good neighbours.[2]

All this 'new policy' could be, as it indeed was, denounced as a sham and a façade, since the Nanking régime remained dependent upon Japanese support and could not have existed without it. But this is to miss the significance of the Treaty. What Japan gave to Nanking she was really proffering to Chungking. She had now gone on public record as abandoning her former demands to station troops over a long period in parts of China, or to secure neutralized zones, as ready to give up her pre-war rights under the Boxer Protocol which had served to bring about the Lukuochiao affair, and to surrender her Concessions and her extraterritorial privileges. In return she still asked for general political and economic collaboration. She was in fact saying to Chiang Kai-shek that if he abandoned the West and joined her, he would be treated as an equal and an ally. Japanese propaganda to Chungking now took the line that the original Sino-Japanese hostilities had been caused by misunderstanding fomented by Anglo-American intrigue, and that since Japan had now clearly conceded Chinese sovereignty and integrity there was nothing left to fight about.[3] Chiang was warned that, if he continued to struggle he would only serve the interests of the Western Powers, and the Japanese took advantage of his controversy with General Stilwell in 1944 to point out that after all, the Americans might abandon him in favour of the Chinese Communists.[4]

Chiang remained deaf to these blandishments because he

[1] ibid. [2] *Record*, p. 5335.
[3] Aoki's statement to the Diet, 25 Jan. 1944 (*Syonan Sinbun*, 27 Jan. 1944).
[4] ibid. 28 April 1944.

expected that Japan would be completely defeated and that as a result of this China would emerge as the Great Power of the Far East, and would regain all that she had ever lost to Japan, including Manchuria and Formosa.[1] While he was angered at American interference in Chinese domestic affairs, he had his own ways of circumventing this and he evidently did not believe that the United States ever would or could stand by and see China fall a prey to Communism—the one fatal miscalculation he made. Nevertheless his situation during much of 1944 was very precarious, with war-weariness and apathy rife throughout free China. Had not things gone so disastrously for Japan on other fronts, as well as for Germany in Europe, there might have been a collapse of Chinese resistance to Japan. As it was, the death of Wang Ching-wei in Japan on 10 November 1944 removed the one influential collaborator with Japan.[2] Chen Kiung-po, who became 'Acting President' of the Nanking régime, had none of the standing and prestige that Wang had once enjoyed in the Kuomintang. The 'new policy' in China thus failed of its immediate objectives and the Nanking régime, which had pledged itself 'to die or live with Nippon', perished with her fall. But, while the anti-Western propaganda which it had for years poured out did not in the long run benefit Japan, this was not without some consequence in preparing the ground for the very similar propaganda of the Chinese Communists and so may be said to have contributed to their success in mobilizing Chinese opinion against the West. Moreover, the necessity to outbid Japan in China was one factor in concessions to China by the Western Powers, which made it certain that while Japan's New Order was overthrown, the old order could never be restored.

Of all the 'allied' nations in the Greater East Asia Sphere Thailand stood in a specially favoured position. The growth of Japanese influence in Thai political circles has already been described, although Western, especially British, influence had previously formed a strong counter to this, aided by the financial and economic ties which bound Thailand to Great Britain.[3] Of her own choice Thailand would have preferred to remain neutral, and even Luang Pibul might have elected to resist the passage of

---

[1] As had been promised him at the Cairo Conference. See Ch. XIII below.
[2] *Syonan Sinbun*, 13 Nov. 1944. He had come to Japan in the spring of 1944 to undergo an operation.   [3] See Ch. VIII above.

Japanese troops through his country had he been assured of greater initial assistance.[1]

The Japanese had hoped that Great Britain would become the initial violator of Thai neutrality, in order to secure a shorter defence line in the Malay Peninsula.[2] On 1 December 1941 the Japanese Ambassador in Bangkok, Teiji Tsubokami, was instructed to be prepared to open negotiations with the Thai Government for either a full-fledged alliance, or, at any rate, the peaceful passage of Japanese troops through Thailand.[3] But he was not to broach the subject until he received a further instruction. This came to him from General Terauchi, Commander-in-Chief of the Southern Area, who told him to see the Thai Foreign Minister at 10 p.m. on 7 December.[4] Luang Pibul, whether by accident or design, was away from the capital, and the other Thai Ministers would not agree to Tsubokami's demands, even though he warned them that the Japanese troops would in any case enter the country the next morning.[5] This the Japanese forces began to do early on 8 December and were at first resisted. But Pibul hurried back to Bangkok and ordered the cessation of resistance.[6] At 9 a.m. on 8 December he and Tsubokami reached agreement for the peaceful transit of the Japanese forces.[7]

On 10 December alliance negotiations began between Tsubokami and Pibul and were quickly completed.[8] The Japan–Thailand Alliance was formally signed on 21 December. It provided for mutual respect for sovereignty and independence, for full political, military, and economic assistance in the event of conflict with a third Power, and forbade any separate armistice or peace. It was accompanied by a secret protocol by the terms of which Japan undertook to assist Thailand to regain her lost territories, and Thailand undertook to give Japan all the assistance specified in Article 2 of the Treaty, in the existing war with Great Britain and the United States. This Treaty and accompanying protocol superseded the agreement of 8 December, thus ensuring a much wider

---

[1] See Ch. X above.

[2] The Japanese began landing at Singora and Patani, in southern Siam, during the night of 7–8 December. The British forces did not cross the Siamese frontier until 11 a.m. on 8 December and were opposed by the Siamese troops (Grenfell, *Main Fleet to Singapore*, p. 110).

[3] Interrogation of Teiji Tsubokami at his home in Tokyo, 18 April 1946 (IMTFE).

[4] ibid.   [5] ibid.

[6] Evidence of Tojo (IMTFE, *Record*, pp. 36401–2).

[7] Interrogation of Tsubokami.   [8] ibid.

scope of action to the Japanese forces in Thailand.[1] On 25 January 1942 Thailand declared war upon Great Britain and the United States.

The Japanese stationed a large garrison force in Thailand and took over airfields, railways, and harbour facilities. A Liaison Bureau was established to ensure military co-operation between the Japanese and the Siamese armies. The latter were mostly retained in Thailand to preserve internal order, although some of them participated in the invasion of the Shan States.[2] As will be seen, two of these States, Kengtang and Mongpan, were transferred to Thailand in the autumn of 1943. These were then garrisoned by Siamese forces, who had occasional skirmishes with the Chinese.

Since Thailand had a Government and an army of its own, and trouble there would have been awkward for their troops in Burma and Malaya, the Japanese had to be circumspect in their treatment of the country. The Siamese authorities retained control over their own nationals although the Japanese military police 'co-operated' with them in cases involving aliens—Japanese civilians, Chinese, and Indians. The Chinese and Indians were organized, through the usual mixture of propaganda and pressure, into pro-Japanese associations. Bangkok, indeed, for a while became the headquarters of the Japanese-sponsored Azad Hind, or Free India, movement.

The Japanese established numerous prisoner-of-war camps in Thailand, chiefly for captive British, Australian, and Dutch soldiers. These, together with great numbers of conscript Tamil, Javanese, Annamese, Malayan, and Chinese labourers, were employed in the construction of the Thailand–Burma railway.[3] This project, intended to give the Japanese Army through rail communication to Moulmein, was authorized by Japanese Imperial Headquarters in June 1942. Work upon it began the following November and it was originally scheduled for completion by the end of 1943.[4] But in February 1943 the Japanese High Command, worried by increasing losses of shipping on the Singapore–Rangoon route, ordered the completion of the line by the end of August 1943.[5] This was an impossibility. The route traversed some of the most difficult mountain and jungle country in the world. There were no excavating machines or engineering equipment; the work was

---

[1] ibid.   [2] *Syonan Times*, 29 May 1942.   [3] Hastain, *White Coolie*, p. 146.
[4] IMTFE, *Record*, pp. 5524–5.   [5] ibid.

carried on almost entirely by manual labour. Food was inadequate and medical supplies were scanty. The wretched prisoners of war and the coolie labourers were driven on mercilessly throughout the monsoon season and died like flies of disease and starvation.[1] The railway of 415 kilometres in length, was completed on 17 October 1943.[2] The Japanese themselves estimated that it had cost the lives of 10,000 of their own troops, 10,000 prisoners of war, and 30,000 coolie labourers, and this was an underestimate as regards the two latter categories.[3] When it was completed the Japanese held a religious ceremony in honour of all who had died that the line might be built.[4] In their own way they were no doubt sincere about this, horrible and incomprehensible as it appeared to their victims and to Western opinion in general.

The Siamese people as a whole had no love for the Japanese and often showed, as far as they could, friendship and sympathy towards the unhappy prisoners of war.[5] Popular ill will towards the Japanese grew as the economic consequences of Thailand's adhesion to the Japanese made themselves increasingly apparent. In April 1942 a Thai economic mission, headed by Nai Vanich Panananda, went to Tokyo to arrange for imports of consumer and capital goods from Japan, in lieu of such supplies from Great Britain and the United States, and to secure the best terms they could for Siamese exports of rice, rubber, and tin to Japan. On 22 April it was announced in Tokyo that an agreement had been reached for yen-baht parity. Thai exports to Japan were to be increased while Japan promised to supply goods to Thailand without raising their prices.[6] These arrangements told against Thailand. The currency agreement represented a considerable devaluation of the baht, which, especially as the war went on, commanded a much higher rate of exchange on the black market. In the case of Thailand, as with other countries included in the yen-bloc area,

[1] Hastain, *White Coolie*, pp. 134–58, 179.
[2] IMTFE, *Record*, p. 5550.
[3] ibid. p. 5568. Hastain (*White Coolie*, p. 179) says that some 63,000 died, of whom approximately 16,000 were British and Australian prisoners of war.
[4] ibid. p. 158. A Japanese defence witness, Tadakazu Wakamatsu, who in 1943 was head of the Transport and Communications Section of the General Staff, said that he inspected the railway work in the summer of 1943 and reported the unsatisfactory conditions to Tokyo, which resulted in their extending the time-limit until October. He blamed the incessant rains, epidemics of disease, and the difficulty of keeping up food supplies owing to floods, for most of the deaths (IMTFE, *Record*, pp. 14633–5).
[5] Hastain, *White Coolie*, pp. 114–15, 119, 125.
[6] *Syonan Times*, 23 April 1942.

the Japanese were quite unable to provide adequate supplies of manufactured goods. The conversion of Japanese industry to war production meant that Japan had very little to export in the way of textiles and other consumer goods, nor had she any surplus capital equipment. Hence exports from Japan were few and far between and prices were high, whereas Japan drew heavily upon Thailand, especially for supplies of rice. But a favourable balance of trade with Japan brought no benefit to Thailand, since the credits which piled up to her account in Japanese banks remained 'frozen' for the duration of the war.

These grievances were increased by the behaviour of the Japanese Army in Thailand, which often paid for its needs by printing and issuing Thai currency, thus damaging credit and promoting inflation.[1] The Chinese, who had so much of the internal trade of the country in their hands, responded by speculation and hoarding, so that food shortages began to appear in what was normally a land of plenty, with resultant distress in Bangkok and other towns.[2] Japan's increasing economic grip upon the country, furthered by some complaisant officials, took the form of Japanese 'partnership' in a good many industrial and commercial State enterprises, and added to the growing apprehension and dislike.

Outwardly Japanese-Thai relations continued to be cordial during 1942–4. In April 1942 a Thai special mission, headed by General Phya Bahol, who as a colonel had taken a prominent part in the military coup d'état of 1932, went to Tokyo, professedly to affirm Thailand's adhesion to the ideals of Greater East Asia.[3] The Japanese responded by sending a 'Grand Mission of Goodwill' to Bangkok, with Koki Hirota at its head. This arrived in mid-July, and was the occasion of more official expressions of amity and co-operation between Japan and Thailand.[4] Luang Pibul gave Hirota a personal letter to Tojo, in which he expressed the hope that the Japanese Premier himself would be able to visit Thailand.[5] Other signs of outward cordiality were the appointment of a Thai Minister to Manchukuo, on 29 June,[6] the recognition by Thailand of the Wang Ching-wei régime on 7 July,[7] and the conclusion on

[1] USOSS, *Japanese Domination of Thailand* (Washington, 1944), p. 31; Hastain, *White Coolie*, p. 132.
[2] *Japanese Domination of Thailand*, p. 178.
[3] *Syonan Times*, 28 April 1942.
[4] ibid. 23 June, 15 and 24 July 1942.   [5] ibid. 30 July 1942.
[6] ibid. 1 July 1942.   [7] ibid. 10 July 1942.

11 July in Saigon of the Siamese-Indo-China boundary demarcation agreement, after the boundary had been surveyed and marked by a tripartite commission, of Japanese, Siamese, and French delegates.[1]

Thailand was thus assured, as far as it lay in Japan's power to do so, of sovereignty over the regions which she had been awarded by the enforced Japanese mediation of the previous year.[2] But, despite the secret protocol to the Treaty of 21 December 1942, the Japanese were in no hurry to make further concessions to her. By the spring of the following year, however, signs of Thai discontent were seemingly making themselves apparent. In April 1943 Aoki, the Greater East Asia Minister, visited Bangkok, in the course of a tour of South East Asia, and had discussions with Luang Pibul and Nai Vichitr, the Thai Foreign Minister. The official communiqué on 25 April of course revealed nothing and simply declared that complete accord had been reached on measures for the prosecution of the war.[3] But shortly after Aoki's return to Tokyo the question of handing over to Thailand the four Malay States—Perlis, Kedah, Kelantan, and Trengganu—which Great Britain had secured from Thailand in 1909—as well as the two Shan States, Kengtung and Mongpan, was raised by Tojo. He told the Tokyo Tribunal that at the time he encountered opposition from the Japanese Army in Bangkok, but that he overcame this.[4] The decision to turn over the territories to Thailand was formally made at an Imperial Conference of 31 May 1943.[5]

On 15 June Tojo told the Diet that Thailand was 'marching valiantly and vigorously forward, surmounting numerous difficulties. . . .' He declared that Japan was sympathetic to Thailand's aspirations and was prepared to afford her further co-operation in securing these.[6] On 3 July Tojo and Pibul met in Bangkok, and two days later it was publicly announced that the four Malay and the two Shan States were to be transferred to Thailand.[7] On 20 August a formal treaty providing for the transfer was concluded at Bangkok. By its terms the territories to be incorporated with Thailand were to retain their existing boundaries and all Japanese administration was to cease within sixty days from the signature of the treaty.[8]

When the treaty came before the Investigation Committee of

[1] ibid. 14 July 1942.
[2] See Ch. VIII above.
[3] *Syonan Sinbun*, 26 April 1943.
[4] IMTFE, *Record*, pp. 36458–9.
[5] ibid.
[6] *Syonan Sinbun*, 19 June 1943.
[7] ibid. 7 July 1943.
[8] ibid.

the Japanese Privy Council it encountered considerable criticism. It was pointed out with some force that since Japan had no legal right to the territories she equally had no right to cede them to Thailand, and that her action in so doing would create an unfavourable impression abroad, as an indication that she considered herself to be in permanent possession of the regions she had occupied.[1] This was contrary to official denials that Japan intended to annex these areas. But Tojo, as usual, got his way. In January 1944 Tojo told the Diet that he was fully aware that the cession of territory to Thailand was not in conformity with Japanese economic interests, but that the action was in accord with the principles which governed the relationship of the nations of Greater East Asia.[2]

The Japanese action may have served for a while to strengthen the position of the Siamese dictator, Luang Pibul, who was effusive in his thanks. But it could not for long offset the mounting discontent in Thailand at the financial and economic hardships which accompanied the Japanese occupation. Furthermore, as the tide of battle continued to turn against Japan, it became apparent that Thailand's territorial gains were illusory, since the victorious Allies were not likely to allow her to keep them. Further association with Japan, indeed, might jeopardize the independence of Thailand itself after the war. Consequently the pro-Western party, some of whom had maintained secret contacts with the Allies, gained in strength.[3] The fall of Tojo, on 21 July 1944, sealed the fate of his Siamese associate. On 24 July, the Thai Assembly, by rejecting some domestic changes proposed by Pibul, brought about his resignation.[4] His Cabinet was replaced by one headed by Major Kuang Aphaiwongse, while Luang Pradit re-emerged as sole regent for the absent monarch. This really meant the formation of an anti-Japanese and pro-Allied Government in Thailand. The new régime, however, could not openly break with Japan and outwardly professed co-operation with her; on the other hand the Japanese, although not deceived, wished to avoid a coup d'état and direct military rule in Thailand since this would have too obviously negated their claim to be fighting for the independence of East Asiatic nations. Thus, during the last months of the

[1] IMTFE, *Record*, pp. 36460–1; also *Exhibit* 1275.
[2] *Syonan Sinbun*, 26 Jan. 1944.
[3] Their chief leader was Luang Pradit, who had resigned rather than be associated with the war policy.   [4] *Syonan Sinbun*, 31 July 1944.

Pacific War a curious situation obtained in Siam; with the active connivance of the Siamese Government British and American intelligence agents were able to establish themselves in Bangkok and send out wireless reports of Japanese military activities. At the same time the Siamese Government, with Allied assistance, were preparing for uprisings to coincide with an anticipated Allied invasion which, however, was forestalled by the Japanese surrender. They were also intimating their readiness to restore the territories they had been given by the Treaty of August 1943 and to submit to the United Nations the question of those secured in 1941 from Indo-China. In this they were encouraged by the American Government, although Great Britain and France were, understandably, less disposed to be lenient towards them, as Siamese policy ever since 1940 had been clearly opportunist.[1]

Japanese interests in Burma had been relatively small prior to 1941, but contacts had been established with Burmese politicians who were dissatisfied with the country's progress towards full self-government, rapid though this had been since its administrative separation from India. Among these were the Thakin Party, who had in the early nineteen-thirties been theoretical Communists, but who were later inclined to Fascist totalitarian ideas.[2] A group of thirty of these, headed by Aung San, left for Japan shortly after the outbreak of the European War and received military training by a Colonel Minami. Other Burmese politicians who had previously shown pro-Japanese proclivities included U Saw, who was Prime Minister during 1940–1. He visited London in November 1941, in the hope of securing the concession of full

---

[1] The United States had never declared war on Siam and did not regard itself as at war with her (Hull, *Memoirs*, ii. 1587–8). The American Government also supported the 'Free Thai' movement, organized by the Siamese Minister in Washington. The British Government *did* regard themselves as at war with Siam, and they were not prepared to recognize the 'Free Thai' movement. According to Hull (ibid. p. 1588), the British Government in 1944 were inclined to demand of Siam strategic guarantees in respect of the Kra isthmus. But contrary to rumours at the time, no such demands were made, either in the Military Agreement of September 1945, or in the Anglo-Siamese Peace Treaty of January 1946. By the latter Siam was required to restore the British territories she had acquired in 1943, to compensate British subjects for property losses, and to deliver a maximum of $1\frac{1}{2}$ million tons of surplus rice. But this could not be collected until Great Britain, in the following May, agreed to purchase it (A. Peterson, 'Britain and Siam: the Latest Phase', *Pacific Affairs*, December 1946, pp. 364–72).

[2] Thakin = master, or lord, was a courtesy title given to Europeans. The Party took the name to assert equality with the British (U Tun Pe, *Sun Over Burma* (Rangoon, Rasika Ranjani Press, 1949), pp. 32–37).

dominion status for Burma, in which he was disappointed. On his way home he was arrested and kept out of Burma by the British authorities, on a charge of having been in contact with the Japanese since the outbreak of the Pacific War. Failing him the Japanese turned to Ba Maw, who had a fairly considerable political following, especially in Upper Burma. He had been Prime Minister during 1937-9, but had fallen from power partly because his social reform policies proved too expensive, partly because he was suspected of dictatorial ambitions. In the summer of 1940 he was arrested for seditious activities and sentenced to imprisonment.

Hence at the time of the Japanese invasion Ba Maw was in Mogok prison, from which, however, he escaped in the confusion attendant upon the Allied retreat. For a time he seems to have been in contact with the Chinese, but did not respond to the suggestion of one of their generals that he should go to Chungking.[1] He was then, according to his own account, found by the Japanese military police, who took him to Maymyo, where he was interviewed by Colonel Nasu, Deputy Chief of Staff to General Iida, the Japanese conqueror of Burma. Nasu told him that the Japanese had been looking for him, as they wanted him to head the Civil Administrative Committee, which they were in process of forming.[2] This was because the Thakins were proving unsatisfactory, their armed forces—the so-called Burma Independence Army—were paying off old scores against their political opponents and in particular attacking the Karens of Upper Burma. This threatened to cause widespread disturbances behind the Japanese lines, until the Japanese stopped it by disbanding the original Burma Independence Army, and putting Ba Maw at the head of a coalition administration, in which the Thakins were represented, but were not predominant. Ba Maw was at first made Chairman of the Preparatory Executive Committee and proved useful to the Japanese in getting most of the Burmese civil service officials to remain at, or to return to, their posts.[3] On 1 August 1942 a Burmese Executive Administration was set up in Rangoon with Ba Maw as its head.[4]

Ba Maw and his fellow collaborators appear to have been naïve enough to suppose that the Japanese would concede them real

[1] ibid. p. 51.
[2] Interrogation of Ba Maw, in Sugamo, 22 May 1946 (IMTFE).
[3] *Syonan Times*, 23 June, 24 July, 4 and 5 Aug. 1942.
[4] ibid. 5 Aug.

independence. They were soon undeceived; in all important matters, central and local, they had to follow the dictates of Japanese military advisers, while any recalcitrance was dealt with by the Kempei, whose addiction to pulling out the finger nails of their victims gave rise to the grim jest 'do your nails need a manicure?'[1] One disillusioned member of the Thakin Party remarked: 'We often told you the British were sucking the blood out of you. Well, the Japanese are here to suck the marrow out of your bones.'[2]

Ba Maw himself declared that he found General Iida sympathetic to Burmese nationalist aspirations, but that his staff officers were not, and declared that any talk of independence was premature. Ba Maw thought that they were considering the establishment of a grandson of the last king of Burma, Thibaw, as a puppet ruler, but, if so, they did not persevere with this idea.[3]

Outwardly, the Japanese praised the Burmese as providing the most thorough co-operation in the establishment of Greater East Asia and held them up to the Filipinos as an example in this respect. Ba Maw responded with speeches and articles in which he attacked British rule in Burma, praised the Japanese as liberators, and professed full acceptance of the concept of the Greater East Asia Co-Prosperity Sphere.[4] General Iida, on 1 August 1942, declared that the Japanese Army would afford the utmost assistance towards the creation of a Burma for the Burmese provided that the Burmese continued to co-operate with Japan as they had been doing.[5] In late August he went on a tour of Burma and upon his return to Rangoon declared that the conduct of the Japanese in Burma must be 'careful and discreet', since owing to the proximity of Burma to India, what happened in Burma would have an effect upon opinion in India.[6]

In his speech to the Diet of 22 January 1942, Tojo had declared that Japan's aim was to make Burma independent.[7] On 28 January 1943 he promised that this should be done within the year.[8] In the following March Ba Maw went to Tokyo to thank Tojo for this promise.[9] He declared that he was ordered to do this by Colonel

---

[1] Khin Kyo Chit, *Three Years Under the Japanese* (Rangoon, 1945), p. 41.
[2] U Tun Pe, *Sun Over Burma*, p. 40.
[3] Interrogation of Ba Maw, 22 May 1946 (IMTFE).
[4] *Syonan Times*, 9 and 16 June, 23 July, 5 Aug. 1942.
[5] *Syonan Sinbun*, 5 Aug. 1942.   [6] ibid. 4 Sept. 1942.
[7] IMTFE, *Record*, p. 36450.   [8] ibid.
[9] *Syonan Sinbun*, 20 March 1943.

Ishamira, who had succeeded Colonel Nasu as Deputy Chief of Staff, and that his interview with Tojo was limited to the expression of formal thanks. At a later meeting Tojo told him that it was Burma's duty to join in the war against Great Britain and the United States.[1] In May an Independence Preparatory Commission was established, with Ba Maw as Chairman. But, according to his own story, the local Japanese military, who grudged even token independence to Burma, did the real work of Constitution-making. In July, when he returned from his conference with Tojo at Singapore, he found that Colonel Ishamira had presented a draft of the Burmese Declaration of Independence, and of the accompanying Basic Treaty, together with a secret military agreement whereby the Japanese Commander-in-Chief could take any measures he deemed necessary for the furtherance of Japanese military operations, could command the co-operation of the Burmese Government in these, and could nullify any of its actions of which he disapproved.[2]

On 1 August 1943 the Burmese Declaration of Independence was issued and a new administration formed with Ba Maw as Nainggandaw Adipadi, or Head of the State. At the same time Burma declared war upon Great Britain and the United States and a Treaty of Alliance was signed with Japan, the signatories being Renzo Sawada, who had been designated as Japanese Ambassador to Burma, and Ba Maw. This provided for full military, political, and economic co-operation between the two countries in the prosecution of the Greater East Asia War, as well as for future co-operation in the construction of the Co-Prosperity Sphere.[3] General Kawabe, who had succeeded Iida as Commander-in-Chief in Burma, gave formal notification of the abolition of the Japanese Military Administration.[4]

Ba Maw was installed as Adipadi with almost royal honours, and, within the limits allowed him by the Japanese, exercised dictatorial powers, to the increasing disgust of his colleagues.[5] He had, however, a rival in Aung San, who was made a Major-General by the Japanese, was head of the Burma Defence Army—later called the Burmese National Army—and also Minister of Defence. But the Japanese Army remained in fact supreme. Ba Maw said that when

---

[1] Interrogation of Ba Maw.   [2] ibid.
[3] *Syonan Sinbun*, 2 and 4 Aug. 1943.   [4] ibid. 2 Aug. 1943.
[5] U Tun Pe, *Sun Over Burma*, pp. 97–98.

he saw Tojo in Singapore he complained to him of the arbitrary
and brutal practices of the Kempei and of the overbearing attitude
of the Japanese military advisers. Tojo promised that these matters
should be redressed and said that the military advisers should be
replaced by civilian ones drawn from the Greater East Asia Ministry.
He kept his word in this, but the civilian Japanese were too much
under the thumb of the General Staff of the Japanese Army in
Burma to effect any real amelioration, and the same was true of
Sawada.[1]

Ba Maw's régime in any case faced formidable financial and
economic difficulties. In the initial fighting great havoc had been
wrought in the towns and in parts of the countryside. Rail and
river transport was dislocated and, when got into some sort of
working order again, was largely monopolized by the Japanese
Army. The Army requisitioned large supplies of rice, and also
slaughtered bullocks for food, which hampered agricultural recovery and led to local food shortages and distress.[2] The Japanese
military paid for their requirements in paper money, including
forged Indian rupee notes, with the usual inflationary consequences.
As was the case with other countries of the Co-Prosperity Sphere,
the Japanese were quite unable to supply imports of manufactured
goods to replace those from Western countries; on the other hand,
so long as they had the shipping, they took what they could get of
Burmese raw materials—minerals, cotton, and timber. Thus
economic conditions deteriorated, while lawlessness and banditry
increased. Such efforts as Ba Maw and his colleagues made to
cope with these problems were of little avail.[3]

The Japanese also drew heavily upon Burmese labour, by both
voluntary recruitment and conscription. The more fortunate were
those recruited for the Heiho, or Auxiliary Service Branch, of the
Japanese Army. They were mostly used in transport work; they
accompanied the Army and received reasonably good pay and
rations. Those who were enrolled in the general Labour Service
Battalions were much worse off; they were employed in the repair
of roads and railways and in the construction of airfields.[4] Many
thousands were utilized in the construction of the Burma–Siam

[1] Interrogation of Ba Maw.
[2] USOSS, *Japanese Administration of Burma* (Washington, 1944), pp. 9–20.
[3] ibid.; also Interrogation of Ba Maw.
[4] Khin Kyo Chit, *Three Years Under the Japanese*, p. 19; USOSS, *Japanese Administration of Burma*, pp. 32–35.

railway and the mortality among these was very heavy. Ba Maw declared that he twice asked the Japanese for permission to inspect the working conditions of Burmese employed in building the line, but was refused, although he did eventually get the right to send inspectors who tried to do something to improve the appalling conditions in which the men worked. He estimated that 30,000 Burmese died in the construction of the line.[1] This may have been an exaggeration, although the Japanese themselves declared in March 1944 that Burma had contributed a greater amount of labour service than had any other of the southern regions.[2]

On 25 September 1943 a Treaty was concluded in Rangoon whereby the Japanese agreed to the incorporation with Burma of the Shan States, except the two given to Thailand, of the Karenyi States and of the Wa region.[3] This was a bribe intended to offset the territorial concessions made to Siam, the ancient rival of Burma, but it had little effect in checking the growing animosity against the Japanese; still less did the peoples of the regions affected relish being placed, even theoretically, under the direct rule of Rangoon. Ba Maw said that the first resistance movements against the Japanese began to develop in June 1944. They were savagely repressed by the Kempei and Ba Maw himself was threatened by Kawabe when he protested against the ruthless methods of the Japanese. Under General Kimura, who succeeded Kawabe in August 1944, the Japanese were somewhat more conciliatory.[4]

In November 1944, Ba Maw paid another visit to Tokyo. He declared after the war that he had done so in the hope of arranging for a Japanese evacuation of Burma which would prevent further fighting and destruction. He had an interview with General Koiso, the new Japanese Premier, who referred him to the Chief of Staff, General Sugiyama. But he got little comfort, for Sugiyama pointed to the havoc that was occurring in the Philippines, and said that this was because the Filipinos had not co-operated as they should with Japan. If the Burmese co-operated whole-heartedly with Japan, they would be spared this fate.[5] Ba Maw got more sympathy from Shigemitsu, who expressed some indignation at the recital of Burmese sufferings at the hands of the Japanese Army, but it was the attitude of the latter which counted. They

[1] Interrogation of Ba Maw.
[2] *Japanese Administration of Burma*, p. 35.
[3] *Syonan Sinbun*, 26 Sept. 1943.
[4] Interrogation of Ba Maw.   [5] ibid.

evidently did not trust the Burmese and were prepared to deal harshly with any backsliding. Thus upon his return Ba Maw found it politic to express his faith in Japan's ability to defend Burma against invasion and to win the final victory.[1] So, for the time being, did Aung San.[2] In the spring of 1945 when the defeat and dissolution of the Japanese Army in Burma was all but completed, he went over to the victors, and placed his forces, now renamed the Anti-Fascist People's Freedom League, at the disposal of the British Commander, General Slim. He was able to do this under the pretext of proceeding to the front to join in a last ditch stand against the Allied forces. Ba Maw was in no such position, with the fall of Rangoon and the collapse of his administration in May 1945, he went with the retreating Japanese to Moulmein and thence to Japan.

In their occupation of the Philippines the Japanese were faced with a different and more intractable problem than that which confronted them elsewhere. Three centuries of Spanish rule had resulted in a considerable admixture of European blood among the upper-class Filipinos. It had also witnessed the conversion to Roman Catholicism of the bulk of the population, excepting only the Moros of Mindanao and the Sulu archipelago, and some of the primitive Negrito tribes of the mountain districts. Thus by 1900, when Spanish rule ended, the Philippines were already more akin to a Latin American country than to the neighbouring States of Asia. The subsequent forty years of American rule had furthered the process of Westernization, especially in the development of a widespread educational system and also of representative political institutions. Economically, too, the Philippines were dependent upon the United States, because of the growth of sugar, hemp, and other products for sale in the American market.

At the outbreak of the Pacific War, the Government of the Philippines, as organized in 1935 under the terms of the Tydings–McDuffie Act of the previous year, consisted of a President and Congress, who functioned in accordance with a Constitution, which was largely patterned on that of United States Federal institutions. This, however, was subject to the surveillance of the United States High Commissioner and to the control of foreign affairs by Washington. Under the Tydings–McDuffie Act the

---

[1] U Tun Pe, *Sun Over Burma*, pp. 106–7.
[2] *Syonan Sinbun*, 6 Jan. 1945.

Philippines were scheduled to receive full independence in 1946. Thus the slogan of 'Asia for the Asiatics and the overthrow of white imperialism' had little meaning for the educated Filipino, whose heritage was more European and American than Asiatic and who saw his political ambitions on the way to realization.

There were, however, certain factors of which the Japanese might take advantage. Political power was in the hands of the Nationalist Party, headed by the President, Manuel Quezon. There were personal rivalries among his followers: apart from this, since they were representative of the wealthier landowning class, some of them were nervous about the possible growth of radicalism among the peasantry. Coupled with this went apprehension about the economic and political future of the Islands. What would happen to the staple exports of the Philippines, especially sugar, when they were put outside the American tariff barrier? Could the Islands hope to stand alone in a world of rival ambitions and warring States? These fears produced some tendency to revision-ism or postponement of independence. This, however, was scarcely practicable, not only because of nationalist sentiment in the Philippines, but also because of the sugar and other interests in the United States which favoured the grant of independence as a means of ridding themselves of competition from Philippine products, and who could do some effective lobbying in Washington.

In this situation some Filipino politicians looked to Europe, to Spain and Italy, with their authoritarian and Catholic traditions, which were, after all, more deep-rooted in the Philippines than were American democratic ideas. But Europe was remote and could do little to solve the economic problem. Japan, on the other hand, was nearby; she could supply manufactured goods, and, while she did not want Philippine sugar which would compete with the Formosan product, she was interested in promoting the export of raw cotton and of iron ore from the Islands. Japanese commercial and economic interests in the Philippines, though small compared with American, had been growing. There was also a considerable Japanese colony in and around Davao, in southern Mindanao, and some of the Filipino politicians who later served in the pro-Japanese régime had, as lawyers, aided the Japan-ese to get round the limitations placed on Japanese land holding.[1]

[1] USOSS, *The Government of the 'New Philippines'* (Washington, 1944), pp. 15, 31–39.

Thus the average Filipino politician was torn two ways; on the one hand he had no sympathy with the Greater East Asia concept and certainly did not want to exchange American rule for Japanese; on the other hand, could the Philippines, once the tie with the United States was severed, avoid drifting into the economic orbit of Japan? There was also a definitely pro-Japanese minority. The leading figures in this were Benigno Ramos, who had organized the totalitarian Sakdalista Party and had fled to Japan to avoid arrest; Arturo Ricarte; Pio Duran; and the aged General Emilio Aguinaldo, who had fought against the Americans in 1900 when their intention to make the Philippines a dependency had become plain.

The Japanese conquest of the Philippines struck a heavy blow at American prestige. The American authorities had grossly underestimated Japanese striking power and had led the Filipinos to believe that any Japanese invasion would be defeated.[1] When it came the Filipino forces, ill-trained and ill-equipped, fought gallantly along with the Americans as part of the United States Armed Forces in the Far East, but were overwhelmed at Bataan and Corregidor.[2] Before the final débâcle, General MacArthur, Commander of the USAFFE, had, in obedience to instructions, left for Australia. Shortly afterwards President Quezon and his chief lieutenant, Sergio Osmena, also left, and eventually reached Washington. Some other prominent members of the Nationalist Party fled from Manila and became leaders of the resistance movement; several paid with their lives for this. But most remained to await the coming of the invader and to take office under his aegis.

After the end of the war some of them claimed in exculpation of their conduct that they had acted in accordance with an intimation from Quezon to 'go ahead and do the best you can. Make

[1] 'When some Filipino military officials testified before the National Assembly, behind closed doors during its last sessions of July-August 1941, they gave a wrong impression of the striking power of Japan. One of them told the Appropriations Committee that Japan, to his best knowledge, did not have any long-range bombers that could bomb Manila from their existing bases. Thus when hostilities broke out, the possibility of a successful invasion was still far from the minds of most Filipinos' (Maximo M. Kalaw, 'Filipino Opposition to the Japanese', *Pacific Affairs*, December 1945, p. 341).

[2] General MacArthur, when military adviser to the Commonwealth, had said that, until 1946, the United States was responsible for Philippine defence and that there was no need to buy military equipment which would be obsolete by that time (ibid. p. 340).

what bargains you have to with these people. Try to keep the Philippines together in one piece.'[1] Jorge Vargas, who had been Cabinet Secretary, and who became the leading collaborationist in 1942, declared when in Tokyo that Quezon himself would have stayed if he could.[2] They furthermore claimed that by taking office under the Japanese they prevented the real pro-Japanese group, headed by Ramos, from coming into power. Because these were too obviously instruments of Japan, the Japanese themselves preferred to keep them in the background as long as possible.[3] In further extenuation it was said that the collaborationists did something to screen the people from the full rigours of direct Japanese military rule, that they did what they could to thwart the Japanese and gave secret aid to the active resistance movements, and that the Japanese themselves declared that the Filipinos were 95 per cent. pro-American and 5 per cent. liars.[4]

No doubt few of them were at all sincere supporters of the Japanese, especially as time went on and the prospect of Japan's defeat became clearer. On the other hand they did enable Japan to establish her so-called Philippine Republic and they did pour out pro-Japanese and anti-American propaganda. Perhaps the best clue to their attitude is to be found in a remark attributed to Laurel: 'I believe the war will last at least six years and we cannot tell who will win. What are we going to do in the meantime? It is our duty to do what we can to mitigate the sufferings of our people and to ensure the survival of the Filipino race.'[5] Certainly after the war a lenient view was taken of their activities and the most of them, including Laurel, who had been President of the 'New Philippines' during 1943–5, returned to political life.[6]

Immediately after their occupation of Manila, which had been left an open city, the Japanese Army, on 2 January 1942, issued a draconian proclamation in which they threatened to reduce the country to ashes should the population offer resistance, and pro-

---

[1] C. M. Recto, *Three Years of Enemy Occupation* (Manila, People's Publishers, 1946), p. 9.

[2] Vargas's address to the Federation of South Seas Associations, Tokyo, 17 March 1944 (Philippine Islands, Ministry of Foreign Affairs, *Bulletin*, April 1944, p. 119).

[3] Recto, *Three Years of Enemy Occupation*, p. 13.   [4] ibid. pp. 18–19, 89.

[5] F. S. Bustos, *And Now Comes Roxas* (Manila, Bustos, 1945), p. 193. He also says that Quezon did not want to leave (ibid. pp. 47–48).

[6] Manuel Roxas, whose activities during the Japanese occupation were regarded by many as at any rate equivocal, became President of the Philippines in 1946, with the support of MacArthur, and remained so until his death in 1948.

claimed the death penalty for a wide variety of offences.[1] Having thus first brandished the mailed fist they held out an olive branch in a further proclamation in which they said that they had come to emancipate the Filipinos 'from the oppressive domination' of the United States and to enable them to establish the 'Philippines for the Filipinos' as a member of the Co-Prosperity Sphere in East Asia.[2]

Tojo, in his speech to the Diet on 21 January, declared that 'as regards the Philippines, if the peoples of those islands will hereafter understand the real intention of Nippon and offer to co-operate with us as one of the partners for the establishment of the Greater East Asia Co-Prosperity Sphere, Nippon will gladly enable them to enjoy the honor of independence.'[3] This set the tone of Japanese propaganda, issued both by the Army organs, and, at their behest, by the Philippine Executive Commission, established by the Japanese Military Administration on 23 January 1942.[4] This was made up of a Chairman (Vargas) and six departments, each headed by a Commissioner.[5] Each department had its Japanese adviser and assistant advisers, while the acts of the Commission were subject to the approval of the Director-General of the Japanese Military Administration.

In December 1942 the Japanese authorized the organization of the Kalibapi, or Association for Service to the New Philippines.[6] Vargas was made its *ex officio* Chairman, but chief influence in it was wielded by Aquino, as Director-General; Pio Duran; Martinez; and Ramos.[7] Like the Imperial Rule Assistance Association in Japan, the Concordia Society in Manchukuo, or the Hsin Min Hui in North China, the Kalibapi was intended to replace the old political parties by an all-embracing association devoted to propaganda for the cause of Japan and the Co-Prosperity Sphere, pacification work in guerrilla areas, and economic reconstruction on the lines desired by the Japanese. An associated Women's Corps and a Youth Corps were also subsequently organized.

---

[1] *Official Journal of the Japanese Military Administration* (Manila, Nichi-Nichi Shimbun Sha), vol. 1, pp. 1–2. [2] ibid.
[3] ibid. vol. 5, p. vii. [4] ibid. vol. 1, pp. 7–8.
[5] These were Agriculture and Commerce (Alunan); Finance (Las Alas); Interior (Aquino); Justice (Laurel); Education, Health, and Public Welfare (Recto); Public Works (Paredes). All were prominent members of the Nationalist Party.
[6] The full title was *Kapisanan sa Paglilingkod sa Bangong Pilipinas*.
[7] *Official Journal of the Japanese Military Administration*, vol. 8, pp. 9–26.

The Japanese further encouraged the formation of neighbour-hood associations, similar to the *tonarigumi* of Japan, or the *pao chia* in China. Their functions included the preservation of order through the prompt denunciation of any disaffected members, or suspicious strangers, with harsh penalties for the whole group in the event of any remissness.[1]

As in the other occupied regions the Japanese began by tem-porarily closing all the schools, later permitting them to reopen, after a hasty revision of the textbooks to eliminate pro-American sentiments, pending the issue of new ones designed to promote the ideals of Greater East Asia.[2] They proclaimed that in future Japanese and Tagalog were to be the official languages, although the use of English was to be permitted for the time being. But they strove by all means in their power to spread the knowledge of Nippongo—the Japanese language—which it was their ambition to make the common second tongue of Greater East Asia.[3]

Japanese propaganda to the Filipinos took the line that because of their resistance they might have been treated as a conquered people and put indefinitely under direct Japanese rule, but that of her generosity Japan did not wish to do this. Her ambition was that the Philippines should achieve political independence as one of the associated group of Greater East Asiatic nations. To obtain this they must co-operate wholeheartedly and sincerely, not merely in words, with Japan—a point on which Japanese officials and publicists grew more shrilly insistent as it became more apparent that the great mass of the people were not prepared to do anything of the sort. Great stress was laid upon the necessity for the Fili-pinos to throw off their cultural bondage to Europe and America and remember their Asiatic origins. Thus the Japanese Com-mander-in-Chief, in an address to the Philippine people on 31 July 1942, denounced American influences as materialist, hedonistic, and disruptive. He was especially severe upon 'the corruptive custom of showing excessive esteem toward the weaker sex, which led to the breakdown of the time-honoured principle of the East —to respect the head of the family.' The Filipinos, he declared,

---

[1] ibid. vol. 6, p. 98.   [2] ibid. vol. 1, pp. 16–17.
[3] 'When it is realized that the Japanese language is destined to become the common tongue within the vast limits of the Greater East Asia Co-Prosperity Sphere and that there will be no other medium than Japanese for the introduction of Oriental culture and new knowledge, the importance of acquiring the language will require no further emphasis' (ibid. vol. 6, p. xxx).

must throw off the degenerate influence of American culture and become once more a genuine Oriental people. He added, not very happily: 'As a leopard cannot change its spots you cannot alter the fact that you are Orientals.'[1]

In economic matters the Japanese denounced what they termed 'the crafty policy' of the United States in allowing the expansion of sugar production and export. They announced that the cultivation and refining of sugar would be continued to an extent sufficient to meet the local demand and to produce liquid fuel and alcohol for Japanese military purposes. The rest of the sugar plantations were to be progressively turned over to the cultivation of cotton, in accordance with a five-year plan for the expansion of cotton production and export. Philippine cotton would find markets in Japan and other countries of the Co-Prosperity Sphere, and the Philippines would 'hold one of the key positions as a member of the Sphere.' Eight Japanese firms were each allotted portions of the area to be converted and a Philippine Cotton Growers' Association was organized under the supervision of the Army.[2] But the lukewarm attitude of the Filipinos, together with guerrilla control of some interior districts, prevented much progress from being made before the reconquest of the Islands by the American forces. The encouragement of food production was another major point in Japanese agrarian policy, but here also the results were relatively meagre. General trade and industry were placed under Japanese military control, and made subject to a permit system and to the operations of special associations licensed by the Army.[3] These were, for the most part, Japanese firms who took over former American properties and secured a dominating position in finance, overseas trade, mining, and factory industry.[4]

Despite Japanese blandishments, threats, and reprisals, local resistance movements continued and spread. Some of these originated with detachments of the USAFFE scattered through the Islands who refused to participate in General Wainwright's surrender, others were local peasant uprisings.[5] There was at first little co-ordination between the various groups and rivalry between

---

[1] ibid. vol. 8, p. xx.
[2] ibid. vol. 6, pp. 29–33.   [3] ibid. p. 14.
[4] Recto, *Three Years of Enemy Occupation*, pp. 10–11.
[5] These included the Hukbalahaps or People's Anti-Japanese Army, which soon became Communist-controlled. There was also a great deal of outright banditry and killings for private vengeance.

some of the Filipino leaders, but from the spring of 1943 onwards contact was established by radio and submarine with General MacArthur's forces in Australia. This was followed by the dispatch of agents and supplies, to foster resistance, and to organize it in preparation for the day when it could play an effective part in hamstringing Japanese communications, in conjunction with the liberation forces.

The Japanese could hardly have been wholly unaware of this state of affairs or of the passive hostility to them of the majority of the people; indeed their constant exhortations for 'sincere and active' co-operation and their ruthless reprisals revealed their dissatisfaction. But outwardly they professed to believe that disturbances were confined to a few bandit elements who would eventually be pacified or destroyed. At the end of January 1943 Tojo told the Diet that he sincerely hoped 'that the Filipinos will further strengthen their cooperation with our country and thus consummate at the earliest possible moment the independence of their land.' The Director-General of the Japanese Military Administration preached a sermon on this text in which he said that if the Filipinos wanted their independence soon it was up to them to show by tangible evidence a greater degree of co-operation than they had hitherto done, and that it was a matter of regret to the Japanese Army that Burma would get its independence first.[1]

Despite similar exhortations by Vargas and other members of the Executive Commission, there was no perceptible response. Nevertheless, Tojo himself paid a flying visit to Manila and, in the course of a public speech on 6 May, expressed great satisfaction at the progress made and declared that he was more than ever convinced of the propriety of early independence.[2] On 18 June the Military Administration gave instructions to the Kalibapi to organize a Preparatory Commission for Philippine Independence.[3] This was promptly followed by a special national convention of the Kalibapi which selected the members of the Commission.[4] The twenty members included most of the outstanding figures whom the Japanese had secured as collaborators. They produced a draft Constitution, which they signed on 4 September and which was

[1] *Official Journal of the Japanese Military Administration*, vol. 8, pp. xxiv–v.
[2] ibid. vol. 11, p. xv.　　　　　　[3] ibid. vol. 13, p. x.
[4] ibid. pp. xxxii–xxxiii.

ratified by another convention of the Kalibapi three days later. On 20 September the Kalibapi also elected a National Assembly which met five days later and elected José Laurel as President. He, together with Vargas and Aquino, was then summoned to Tokyo to discuss the Pact of Alliance with Japan. They returned on 6 October, and on 14 October the Pact was signed. The same day the independence of the Philippines was proclaimed and the Military Administration formally ended.[1]

The terms of the Pact were similar to those Japan had already concluded with Thailand and Burma. But Laurel managed to secure one important concession from the Japanese; he, for the time being, avoided any declaration of war upon the Western Powers. He was thus able to declare that the Philippines were not at war with anybody, and that there would be no conscription and no obligation to perform any military service outside of the Islands.[2] Shozo Murata, who had been chief Japanese adviser to the Philippine Executive Commission, was appointed Ambassador to the new Republic, while Vargas, perhaps because the Japanese were doubtful of him, was picked as Philippine Ambassador to Tokyo, although he did not present his credentials until the end of February 1944.

Recto who, together with Murata, signed the Pact of Alliance, and who became Foreign Minister in the Laurel administration, declared that there was bad faith on both sides. The Japanese never intended that the Philippines should be truly independent and the Filipino officials meant to nullify the Pact in every way they could. 'All these things were no secret, either to the Japanese, the Filipinos, or to the Americans themselves.'[3] This, allowing for his natural desire to exculpate himself and his colleagues, was no doubt largely true, especially as by the time the Pact was concluded, the war was going against Japan and the promise of MacArthur to return was likely to be implemented. While the Japanese Army remained in control, it had to show some outward respect to the supposedly independent Government and to work through them. This enabled them to do a certain amount of successful obstruction

---

[1] Recto, *Three Years of Enemy Occupation*, p. 33.
[2] ibid. Laurel in 1923 had been Secretary of the Interior, but had later resigned over a dispute with General Wood, then the American Governor. In 1936 he had become Assistant Justice of the Philippine Supreme Court. He had acted as attorney for Japanese firms, and had sent his sons to be educated in Japan (USOSS, *The Government of the 'New Philippines'*, pp. 16–17).
[3] Recto, *Three Years of Enemy Occupation*, p. 40.

and also to give secret information and assistance to the guerrillas.[1] Among other things Laurel is said to have encouraged the Philippine Constabulary Force, trained under Japanese auspices for anti-guerrilla operations, to desert to the resistance movement, which most of them succeeded in doing.[2]

In April 1944 a Philippine 'Gratitude Mission', headed by Aquino, visited Tokyo; in the course of their sojourn there fulsome speeches were made by Aquino and responded to by Tojo and Shigemitsu.[3]

But with the loss of Saipan, the fall of the Tojo Ministry and the approach of the American forces, the pretence began to be abandoned. Recto himself, on 20 June 1944, addressed a letter to the Japanese Ambassador, Shozo Murata, and to the Chief of Staff of the Japanese Army, General Wati. This communication was in fact one long condemnation of Japanese military practices and an indirect assertion that independence was a sham. It intimated that the common people were filled with resentment through face-slappings, beatings, the torture of suspects, communal punishments for the acts of individuals, and confiscation of property without any adequate compensation, while the educated classes could 'distinguish between truth and propaganda, sincerity and pretence'.[4] The Filipino leaders were trying to persuade the people that Japan was sincere in her professions, but the harsh Japanese treatment of the Filipino peasantry had nullified the effect of these professions.[5] As Recto's stated purpose was to explain why it was that the Japanese-sponsored régime could not obtain the co-operation which they were outwardly urging, the Japanese recipients of this communication could not very well punish him for this outspoken reproof.

The Japanese military authorities were increasingly irritated at the unresponsiveness of Laurel and his associates to suggestions that they should declare war upon the United States and Great Britain. If Laurel had opposed this in 1943, he was even less inclined to it in the following year when Japan's cause was visibly failing. His attitude was that the Philippines were anxious only to

[1] ibid. pp. 40–41, 56.
[2] Roxas also is declared by his biographer, Bustos, to have been active in secret assistance on the resistance movement (Bustos, *And Now Comes Roxas*, pp. 209–23).
[3] Philippine Ministry of Foreign Affairs, *Bulletin*, April 1944.
[4] Recto, *Three Years of Enemy Occupation*, pp. 117–18.
[5] ibid. pp. 118–19.

preserve their independence and would not fight unless attacked. But when, in August and September 1944, American carrier-borne aircraft began to make raids upon the Islands, the Japanese insisted that he treat this as a *casus belli*. On 23 September he proclaimed a state of war, giving the air attacks as his reason. He is said to have told Roxas that the Japanese had threatened him with death if he did not do so, and Roxas to have counselled submission but the avoidance of any conscription law, thus making the declaration a mere paper one.[1] Japanese distrust of the Laurel régime resulted in their promotion of a new organization, the Makapili, or League of Patriotic Filipinos, headed by Ramos and pledged to full co-operation with the Japanese Army. But this came late in the day and the forces raised by Ramos themselves either deserted or were killed by the resistance elements.[2] General Tomoyuki Yamashita, the conqueror of Singapore, was sent to the Philippines to organize the defence against the imminent American invasion. But the American landing on Leyte cut off his forces in Luzon from those in Mindanao, and, after the crushing defeat of the Japanese Navy in the Battle of Leyte Gulf, 25–26 October 1944, he was in a hopeless position. Faced by American naval and air supremacy and hampered by guerrilla attack upon his communications, he could not concentrate his forces to meet the successive American landings. His troops were in consequence defeated piecemeal, but they fought desperately and also savagely retaliated upon the Filipinos, especially in Manila, which was largely destroyed.[3] In December 1944, when the Americans were nearing Manila, Laurel and his Cabinet were sent by the Japanese to

[1] Bustos, *And Now Comes Roxas*, p. 299. Bustos says further that by the Constitution of 1943 a three-fourths majority of the Assembly was needed for a declaration of war, but that the Japanese could get only 23 out of 140 together, the rest having on Roxas's advice absented themselves (ibid. pp. 299–300).

[2] Recto, *Three Years of Enemy Occupation*, p. 57; Bustos, *And Now Comes Roxas*, p. 224.

[3] Office of Resident Commissioner to the Philippines, *Report on the Destruction of Manila and Japanese Atrocities* (Washington, 1945). Laurel on 1 December tried to get Manila declared an open city and Yamashita was inclined to agree. He went to Tokyo on 10 December, but upon his return ten days later he removed the Philippine Government to Baguio. The Japanese then began preparations to defend the city. Yamashita was not in Manila in February 1945, when the fighting and massacre took place. After his surrender he was arrested and tried in the Philippines by an American tribunal as a war criminal. He was convicted, and an appeal to the United States Supreme Court having failed, he was hanged in February 1946. But it is a moot point how far he was personally responsible. See A. F. Reel, *The Case of General Yamashita* (University of Chicago Press, 1949).

Baguio, where they remained as virtual prisoners, until in the following March some of them were taken to Japan.[1]

It may be wondered why the Tojo Government went to all the trouble of Constitution-making, declarations of independence, and treaties of alliance, when the reality was so very different from the appearance. One obvious answer is that it was simply intended as a propaganda weapon against the Allies, as shown by the timing of the treaties with the Philippines and China. These took place in October 1943, when the Japanese were anticipating an Allied Conference and a declaration on policy in the Far East.[2] On 5 November an Assembly of Greater East Asiatic Nations convened in Tokyo. This was attended by Chang Ching-hui (Manchukuo); Wang Ching-wei (China); Prince Wan Wai Thayakon (Thailand);[3] Ba Maw (Burma), and Laurel (Philippines). On 6 November the Assembly adopted a Joint Declaration. This condemned the 'aggression and exploitation' of the United States and Great Britain in the Far East and enunciated the principles of mutual respect for sovereignty and independence, and of political, economic, and cultural co-operation among the nations of Greater East Asia.[4]

However great was the contrast between the high-flown language of this Declaration and the reality of affairs in the Japanese-occupied regions, it did constitute a policy and was a challenge to the Allies to say what were *their* war aims in the Far East. It was no doubt to a considerable degree aimed at Indian opinion. The Japanese original overall strategic plan did not contemplate any full-scale invasion of India, despite propagandist talk of this. What they did hope to effect was a revolt against British rule. Tojo in numerous speeches urged the Indian people to refuse to have anything to do with the British war effort—in this appealing to the neutralist sentiments of Gandhi and of a large part of Congress—and disclaiming any Japanese designs upon India.[5] In June 1942 the Japanese organized an 'Indian Independence League' conference at Bangkok which voted for severance from Britain.[6] By a mixture of cajolery and threat the Japanese whipped up support for this among the Indian communities in Siam, Malaya, Burma,

[1] Roxas escaped and joined the resistance forces (Bustos, *And Now Comes Roxas*, pp. 242–3).   [2] Kase, *Eclipse of the Rising Sun*, p. 72.
[3] Luang Pibul excused himself from coming on the plea of ill health.
[4] For the text of the Joint Declaration see Appendix, p. 2.
[5] *Syonan Times*, 12 March, 7 April 1942.
[6] *Syonan Sinbun*, 17 and 23 June 1942.

and elsewhere in countries under their control. Similarly they promoted the formation of an Indian National Army, recruited from Indian prisoners of war. Their chief Indian collaborator was at first Rash Behari Bose, who had for long been working with them. But in 1943 his much more influential namesake, Subhas Chandra Bose, came from Berlin to Tokyo and became the head of the pro-Japanese organization. In October 1943 the Provisional Government of Free India was set up, with Bose at its head.[1] He attended the Assembly of Greater East Asiatic Nations as an 'observer'. In January 1944 the 'Provisional Government of Free India' was transferred to Burma and the Indian National Army took part in the Japanese offensive against Assam.[2] But the eventual defeat of that attack, followed by the expulsion of the Japanese from Burma, ended all hopes of stimulating a general uprising in India.[3]

The Japanese may also have hoped to drive a wedge between Great Britain and the United States by playing upon American 'anti-colonial' sentiments. They had their sources of information in Chungking and they may have known something of the pressure that was being put upon the British Government by Roosevelt and Chiang Kai-shek to establish some kind of national government in India during the war.[4]

Apart from these calculations of immediate advantage, Japanese policy was not without its long-term objectives. By promoting the cause of Asian independence and whipping up sentiment against the white peoples, they were doing what they could to ensure that, whatever the outcome of the existing war, the *ante bellum* state of affairs could never be restored. In this respect, their talk of 'a hundred years' war' was not all hyperbole—viewed in this light the Second World War was simply the first round in a protracted struggle in which Japan might hope to emerge victorious in the end even though initially she suffered defeat. If she could seriously weaken Western domination in the Far East, she might still hope at some future date to achieve her own ambitions. This, at least, is a reasonable explanation of her actions in Indo-China and the East Indies, taken at a time when her defeat was in fact accomplished.

[1] ibid. 22 Oct. 1943.   [2] ibid. 10 Jan. 1944.
[3] Subhas Chandra Bose left Burma in May 1945. On 18 August 1945, while en route from Singapore to Japan, he received mortal injuries in an air crash at Taihoku, Formosa (ibid. 24 May 1945).
[4] For this see Churchill, *Second World War*, iv. 181–97, and Hull, *Memoirs*, ii. 1483–96.

CHAPTER XII

Greater East Asia

II. THE EAST INDIES, MALAYA, AND INDO-CHINA

THE Japanese conquest of Malaya and the Netherlands East Indies constituted the achievement of a long-cherished ambition. With these rich prizes in her hands Japan, as Tojo exultantly declared, was no longer a 'have-not' nation.[1] The tin, the rubber, and, above all, the oil resources which she had coveted were now in her possession. It is therefore understandable that she should have regarded these territories as the very heart of the Co-Prosperity Sphere. They were the ones over which she was the most anxious to preserve firm control, and to retain, if she could, at the compromise peace settlement which she hoped to secure. Furthermore, Japan hoped that the racial, linguistic, and religious differences of the peoples who inhabit these regions would serve to make her task easier. She was not here confronted by any firmly rooted and largely Occidentalized nationalist movement as in the Philippines, by the tradition of a relatively recent independent kingdom as in Burma, or, except among the Chinese minorities, by an old-established, cohesive, and tenacious society of a character similar to her own. By overthrowing the British administration in Malaya and that of the Dutch in the East Indies Japan severed the ties which bound the respective peoples of those areas in such unity as existed; she expected then to create new ones of her own devising, which would, however, leave her in supreme control. What the Japanese actually accomplished, at first despite themselves and later by design, was something very different.

Immediately upon the conquest of the Dutch East Indies, the Japanese established a Military Administration for Java with headquarters at Batavia, which they renamed Djakarta.[2] Sumatra, however, was for a while placed under the Military Administration of Malaya.[3] The Japanese made much of the racial affinity of the

---

[1] On 2 February 1943 Tojo told the Diet that Japan had become a 'have' country, far richer than Great Britain or the United States (*Syonan Sinbun*, 3 Feb. 1943).
[2] ibid. 10 Dec. 1942.　　　　　　　　　　[3] ibid. 24 Oct. 1942.

Malays of Sumatra and those of Malaya—apparently as part of
a policy of bolstering the Malay population against the Indian
and Chinese inhabitants of Malaya, who, taken together, were
numerically superior.[1] Also, the administrative detachment of
Sumatra seemed to discourage ideas of an 'Indonesian' State
inclusive of the whole East Indian archipelago, a concept which
the Japanese initially frowned upon. Later, however, Sumatra
was detached from Malaya and placed under a separate military
régime. Dutch Borneo, the Celebes, and the Lesser Sunda islands
were under Japanese naval administration, with its headquarters
at Macassar.[2] As will be seen, the Japanese Navy, at least until the
latter part of the war, was even less inclined than was the Army to
concede any voice in the administration to the inhabitants.

Despite this division of the conquered territories between the
two armed services, their administrative organization and procedure were in general devised on similar lines throughout the
islands. Thus in Java, the most important and by far the greatest
centre of population, the Dutch administrative system was destroyed and replaced, under ordinance of 7 March 1942, by a central
Military Administration headed by a Gunseikan, or Chief Military
Administrator, and organized into the nine departments of General
Affairs, Internal Affairs, Finance, Justice, Police, Public Works,
Economic Affairs, Audition, and Propaganda.[3] A second administrative ordinance, of 5 August 1942, divided Java into two provinces, seventeen Residencies (*Syun*), and a special municipality
(Batavia).[4] There were also two bureaux for the supervision of the
four Sultanates of Central Java. The *Syun* were subdivided into
smaller units. Thus the Japanese created a rigidly centralized and
bureaucratic system, approximating to that of their homeland.

A Japanese military court was established to deal with violations

[1] ibid. 4 March 1943.
[2] Statement of Klaas A. de Weerd (IMTFE, *Exhibit* 1351). He was a former
official of the Department of Justice of the Netherlands East Indies Government,
who was called up and became a major in the Artillery. As a prisoner of war of
the Japanese he acted as camp translator of the newspapers in Malay, which the
Japanese, until 1944, permitted to circulate. He kept records and thus accumulated much material on the Japanese administration. After the Japanese surrender
Major de Weerd was put in charge of an Intelligence group charged with the
task of collecting information in the East Indies and in Tokyo about Japanese
rule in the East Indies.   [3] ibid.
[4] *Shonan Sinbun*, 7 Aug. 1942; Statement of de Weerd. The former provinces of West, Central, and East Java were eliminated (ibid.). According to the
Shonan Sinbun, Java and Madura were divided into the two provinces of Djok-
jakarta and Surakarta.

of Army ordinances, while, in September 1942, the existing judicial system was reorganized on the Japanese pattern, and in 1944 a new and severe penal code was promulgated.[1] The Police Department was similarly reorganized, and an auxiliary police force, or Keibutan, was set up in the towns and villages. As happened in all Japanese-occupied territories the chief power in police and judicial affairs was wielded by the Kempei and exercised with their usual ruthlessness. To facilitate their operations they trained and organized a Javanese branch, which became an object of especial hatred and fear on the part of the populace in general.[2]

The social consequences of the Japanese conquest were profound. All Dutch officials were removed and interned, together with the Dutch civilian population in general, totalling over 60,000. The Dutch officials were replaced by Japanese, who came mainly from Japan itself, Korea, and Formosa.[3] In 1945 over 23,000 Japanese were in the employment of the Japanese Military Administration.[4] Javanese and other indigenous inhabitants were mainly confined to subordinate positions in the Administration; the few who were admitted to higher office had Japanese 'advisers' at their elbow.[5] The hand of the Japanese descended heavily upon the considerable Eurasian population of Java, whom they suspected and disliked as a source of continued Western influence. Many were imprisoned or interned and the remainder closely watched and restricted, although later on there was some relaxation in their treatment, since the Japanese found that they could not altogether be dispensed with.[6] The large Chinese community also suffered severely. Those suspected of pro-Chungking proclivities were dealt with by the Kempei, while the Chinese in general were dragooned into associations professing support for Japan and for the Wang Ching-wei régime in China.[7]

Japanese educational policy followed familiar lines. As happened in other occupied areas, all schools were initially closed and then reopened with their textbooks and curricula reshaped to inculcate anti-Western, pro-Japanese, and pan-Asiatic doctrines. The use of the Dutch language was forbidden; Japanese and Indonesian—a variant of Malay—were made the official languages. A censorship of books was established, while the press and radio were brought under Japanese control and operation. The death penalty was

[1] Statement of de Weerd.   [2] ibid.   [3] ibid.
[4] ibid.   [5] ibid.   [6] ibid.   [7] ibid.

imposed and inflicted for listening to Allied broadcasts and spreading any news gleaned therefrom.[1]

Thus the native peoples of the East Indies saw the old social order overturned. Although they were themselves oppressed and ruthlessly dealt with if suspected of any activity inimical to Japanese rule, they saw the Europeans, Eurasians, and Chinese even worse treated and they were encouraged to regard them as foreigners and inferiors. In the linguistic sphere the Japanese were largely successful in eliminating the use of Dutch, since this had not become the lingua franca of the islands. But, as elsewhere in South East Asia, Japanese attempts to spread the knowledge of their own complex and difficult language met with very limited success, although had they been given the time, this situation might have altered. On the other hand, Indonesian, as a standard form of Malay, had been making rapid progress before the occupation, stimulated as it was by the rise of nationalist movements.[2] The Japanese were therefore compelled to utilize it as the only immediately practicable medium of communication. In consequence of this its use spread rapidly, assisted by its absorption of words and phrases from the various regional dialects and its acquisition to some degree of a modern terminology drawn from foreign languages.[3] This had important effects in stimulating a consciousness of unity among the indigenous peoples of the East Indian archipelago, and in making the term 'Indonesian' something more than a mere appellation of convenience.

Other features of Japanese rule combined to produce the same effect. The centralized uniformity of the Military Administration tended to diminish local particularism. At the same time the host of officials brought in by the Japanese was to a large degree composed of men, who, however trained as administrators, had no previous experience or knowledge of the East Indies. Many of them proved ignorant, incompetent, and venal, to the surprise of the Indonesians who had expected the Japanese to prove more efficient than the Dutch. The consequence of this was that the Indonesian subordinates of the Japanese, thanks to their knowledge of the country, the language, and the people, in fact came to exercise a good deal of actual power, which gave them self-

[1] ibid.
[2] Takdir Alisjahbana, 'The Indonesian Language: By-Product of Nationalism', *Pacific Affairs*, December 1949, pp. 388-9.
[3] ibid. pp. 389-90.

confidence and some training for the anticipated time when they would be in full control.[1] While Japanese propaganda against the Dutch and other Western peoples, aided by the spectacle of Japan's victory over them, met with a ready reception, Japanese efforts to portray their own country as the protector of Asia, the leader of Asia, and the light of Asia were largely frustrated by the ever-recurrent examples of brutality, venality, and incompetence set by the police, soldiery, and officials of Nippon.

Similar consequences attended the financial and economic hardships which soon followed in the wake of Japanese rule. The issue of paper money by the Japanese produced the usual inflationary effects, until by the time of the Japanese surrender this currency was worth only a fortieth of its face value.[2] The Japanese seized the property of the Dutch and other Allied nationals, and, apart from factories, mines, and plantations operated by the Military Administration or turned over to Japanese companies, a good deal of money, valuables, and other property was sequestered by the Enemy Property Administration Bureau and turned over to Japanese or to their collaborators.[3] This largely weakened the economic basis of Western control. At the same time the disruption of the overseas trade of the East Indies caused a severe shortage of consumer goods, and, especially in densely populated Java, of food supplies. The Japanese were unable to remedy these deficiencies, or, as their shipping losses mounted, to absorb the staple products of the islands.[4] They strove to replace plantation economy by subsistence agriculture, their goal being to make each of the islands virtually self-sufficient in food production, in view of the difficulties of marine transport, which their encouragement of wooden shipbuilding did little to ameliorate.[5] They did have some success in expanding food production, but this was offset by the needs of their own armies of occupation and of their camp followers. By the end of the war, even these were ragged and under-nourished, while the populace in general were even more so. These developments produced, as elsewhere, no enthusiasm for the ideals of the Co-Prosperity Sphere. Neither did the Japanese organization of the Romusha, or Labour Service Corps, into which a host of Javanese labourers were conscripted. According to

[1] *History of Indonesia's National Movement* (New York, Republic of Indonesia Office, 1949). [2] Statement of de Weerd.
[3] ibid. [4] ibid. [5] ibid.

Japanese figures 270,000 of these were sent overseas, of whom only a fraction survived.[1]

For two decades prior to the Japanese occupation of the Indies, the Dutch had been faced with a rising nationalist movement which, in contrast to previous activities of this kind, eschewed a primarily Moslem basis and sought to unite the Moslem, Hindu, and Christian native communities in a common programme of political independence from Holland. The Netherlands East Indies Government during 1932–4 had retaliated by arresting the chief leaders, Soekarno, Mohammed Hatta, and Soetan Sjahrir and exiling them to New Guinea. In 1937 a recrudescence of the movement, led by Amir Sjarifoeddin, offered co-operation against Japan, in the event of war, in return for the organization of an Indonesian army and the promise of independence, but the Dutch again refused to listen to such demands. There was also an Indonesian Communist movement which had been organized by Tan Malakka and Semaoen. These leaders had been exiled and the Communist Party proscribed, but in 1941 it was still active beneath the surface.[2]

When the Japanese conquered the East Indies they released the imprisoned nationalist leaders and brought them back to Java.[3] Soekarno and Hatta were among those who were willing to collaborate with the Japanese and to pay at any rate lip service to the concepts of Greater East Asia.[4] Sjahrir and Amir Sjarifoeddin were unwilling to do so, and with their following went underground.[5] The Communist elements also continued in resistance. Soekarno and Hatta appear to have initially believed that, in return for nationalist collaboration, the Japanese would be willing to concede a real measure of independence. They were soon undeceived. The Japanese military authorities, while ready to utilize them in stirring up popular feeling against the West, sharply reacted against any idea of uniting the islands in an Indonesian State, and forbade any flying of the Indonesian flag or singing of the Indonesian national anthem. Those who disobeyed fell into the clutches of the Kempei.[6] Japanese policy, indeed, during 1942–3 was largely

[1] ibid.
[2] J. A. Verdoorn, 'Indonesia at the Crossroads', *Pacific Affairs*, December 1946, pp. 341–6.   [3] Statement of de Weerd.
[4] *Shonan Sinbun*, 15 July 1942. It quoted Soekarno as saying that Indonesians now had a golden opportunity to realize their dream of independence.
[5] Verdoorn, loc. cit. p. 346.   [6] Statement of de Weerd.

one of *divide et impera*. They encouraged Indonesian nationalism as against the non-Indonesian minorities, but at the same time tried to be all things to all men by favouring a pan-Islamic movement which would have cut across the national ideal and by paying court to the Hindu and Christian communities.[1] While they made the usual promises of political concessions in return for genuine co-operation, they were studiously vague on the extent of any Indonesian State which might be set up under their auspices.

This question was discussed in Tokyo in the spring of 1943. Tojo and Shigemitsu would apparently have favoured a commitment to accord eventual independence, but the Supreme Command were altogether against it.[2] So, at that time, were the local military and naval authorities in the East Indies. Apart from opposition on the ground that Japanese strategic and economic interests might be endangered it was also declared that, if Japan went on record as promising independence to the East Indies, she would be thereby committed and would be in a difficult position in any peace negotiations.[3] The idea was that if Japan, as was anticipated, held out long enough against enemy counter-attacks to bring her opponents to consider a compromise peace, she needed something to bargain with.

These views prevailed and the decision was reached, and ratified at an Imperial Conference of 31 May 1943, to treat the East Indies as Japanese territory, but to permit their inhabitants, according to their abilities, to have some voice in the administration.[4] Accordingly Tojo, in his speech to the Japanese Diet of 15 June 1943, declared, apropos of the East Indies, that, in view of their praiseworthy co-operation, the Japanese Government intended to take measures, step by step, to allow the people of the islands to participate in their Government to the extent commensurate with their abilities, and he indicated that this would occur most quickly in Java.[5] This was shortly followed by a visit by Tojo to Batavia early in July.[6]

[1] ibid. They wanted to get the Moslem leaders to proclaim a holy war against the Allies, but the Moslems were not unreasonably suspicious of people who were quietly introducing Shinto rites and compelling people to bow towards the Imperial Palace in Tokyo, not towards Mecca.
[2] Evidence of Tojo (IMTFE, *Record*, pp. 36466–7); also *Exhibit* 1344: 'Course of Events Leading up to Decisions on Political Control and Reversion of the East Indies in the Second World War', JFM, Records Section, 1946.
[3] IMTFE, *Exhibit* 1344.
[4] ibid.; also evidence of Tojo (*Record*, pp. 36466–7) and of Kumaichi Yamamoto (ibid. pp. 17992–3).
[5] IMTFE, *Exhibit* 1324.   [6] *Syonan Sinbun*, 14 July 1943.

The Japanese had initially swept away the partly nominated, partly elected Volksraad, which had been established by a Netherlands Government law in 1916 and enlarged in membership and functions in 1925, as well as all local councils. On 1 August 1943 the Japanese Commander-in-Chief in Java, Lieut.-General Kumakichi Harada, announced that regional councils and also a central advisory council would be established in Java, that Indonesians would be given more posts in the administration, and that, if the co-operation of the populace merited it, further concessions of this nature would be made to them.[1] In pursuance of this decree local committees, partly elective, were established in the residencies and in Djakarta. These sent eighteen members to the Central Council, which contained in addition twenty-three nominees of the Military Administration and twelve of the Sultanates. The functions of both local and central councils were limited to giving advice on such matters as the authorities laid before them. The Japanese further appointed an Indonesian as head of the Department of Religious Affairs, and two others as chiefs of Residencies; they also brought in Indonesians as advisers in several of the departments of the Military Administration.[2] The first session of the Central Advisory Council for Java was convened in mid-October, Tojo and Marshal Terauchi, the Japanese Supreme Commander in the Nampo (South Seas Area) sending their congratulations upon this event.[3] Provincial Councils were likewise established in Sumatra, while the naval authorities followed suit by setting up local councils in the areas under their jurisdiction, but no central council.[4]

In March 1942 the Japanese military authorities in Java had sponsored the organization of the Poetera, an Indonesian organization, similar to the Kalibapi in the Philippines, devoted to the elimination of Occidental influences, the fostering of co-operation with Japan, the promulgation of the concepts of Greater East Asia, and collaboration to assist in the economic objectives of the occupation.[5] Membership in the Poetera, of which Soekarno became the Director, was not open to Chinese, Eurasians, or other minority groups; hence it could be utilized to foster Indonesian nationalism. The Japanese Navy, significantly, did not allow any

[1] ibid. 3 Aug. 1943.   [2] Statement of de Weerd.
[3] *Syonan Sinbun*, 18 Oct. 1943.
[4] ibid. 11 and 26 Nov. 1943; Statement of de Weerd.
[5] Statement of de Weerd.

similar movement to take shape in the regions over which it ruled.[1]
An Indonesian Youth Movement was also organized in Java.[2] In
August 1943 the Japanese Commander in Java had hinted pretty
clearly that he expected further co-operation from the inhabitants
in the form of a volunteer corps—or home guard—to assist in
suppressing resistance movements and in the defence of the island
in the event of an Allied invasion. Petitions to form a Volunteer
Corps were duly forthcoming from members of the Poetera, and
in October 1943 General Harada was pleased to give his assent to
these.[3] Volunteer Defence Battalions were gradually established,
though the Japanese were at first very careful about arming these,
and issued weapons only at drill times. This defence organization
was distinct from the Heiho, or auxiliaries of the Japanese armed
forces, into which Indonesians were also recruited.[4]

In mid-November 1943 Soekarno went to Tokyo, ostensibly to
thank the Japanese Government for the concessions which they
had made. In reality his object was to appeal to Tojo for a grant of
independence similar to that accorded to Burma and the Philippines, but he got no satisfaction and came away deeply disappointed.[5] Indeed, during the first half of 1944 the Japanese
somewhat modified their previous policy of favouring the Indonesians. The Chinese and Eurasians received some amelioration of their former harsh treatment and in March 1944 the
Poetera was dissolved as being too nationalistic and as having
failed to influence the ordinary village people to a sufficient degree
of co-operation. The Poetera was replaced by a new organization
—the Corporation for Communal Services in Java; this included
all associations, even that of the Japanese residents themselves.
It had a central directorate which was exclusively Japanese, and its
ramifications extended down to the neighbourhood associations
which the Japanese promoted in the East Indies, as elsewhere.[6]
Its object was to promote the 'total mobilization' of the populace
in achieving the objects of the Greater East Asia War and of the
Co-Prosperity Sphere.[7]

The Allied advance in New Guinea, the fall of Saipan, and the
resignation of the Tojo Cabinet resulted in a further change in
Japanese policy. The Japanese Military Administration in Java

[1] ibid.   [2] ibid.   [3] ibid.   [4] ibid.
[5] IMTFE, *Exhibit* 1344.   [6] Statement of de Weerd.
[7] *Syonan Sinbun*, 13 March 1944.

was now ready to make further concessions to the Indonesian nationalists in the hope of thereby rallying the populace to its side against an Allied invasion. The matter came up for discussion at the first meeting of the Supreme Council for the Direction of the War, established by the Koiso Cabinet. The Army chiefs were now ready to agree that the Government should promise independence to the East Indies, but the naval authorities were strongly opposed to any such declaration.[1] The upshot was the usual compromise, formulated on 2 September 1944.[2] It was agreed that General Koiso should inform the Diet that the people of the East Indies should be accorded their independence in the future— the date being left unspecified. What precise form independence should take and what the future relationship of the East Indies to Japan should be were left over for later consideration, so was the exact area to be included in the proposed declaration. It was agreed that certain immediate concessions should be made in Java, with corresponding measures in other territories 'as far as consistent with actual conditions.'[3]

Koiso on 7 September duly gave the public promise of eventual independence for the East Indies.[4] In line with the decisions of 2 September the people of Java were permitted, on stated occasions, to fly the Indonesian flag and sing the Indonesian anthem. More Indonesians were appointed as local governors and as advisers in the Bureaux of the Military Administration. Special sessions of the Central Advisory Council were held in September and November 1944, to deliberate on measures of co-operation with the Japanese in the defence of the East Indies.[5] A statement by the Commander of the Japanese forces in Sumatra indicated that the local administration there would keep in step with that of Java.[6] In January 1945 it was announced that a Central Advisory Council, similar to that in Java, would be established in Sumatra.[7]

The territories under Naval Administration remained unaffected by these changes. But after the battle of Leyte Gulf the Navy could no longer keep open communications with the East Indies and had no further reason to oppose the policy of political concessions.[8] In February 1945 the Naval Administration established

[1] IMTFE, *Exhibit* 1344.
[2] 'Policy in Regard to the Independence of the East Indies', 2 Sept. 1944, *Exhibit* 1348.   [3] ibid.   [4] ibid.
[5] Statement of de Weerd.   [6] *Syonan Sinbun*, 8 Sept. 1944.
[7] ibid. 6 Jan. 1945.   [8] *Exhibit* 1344.

an advisory council of thirty members for South Borneo, the Celebes, and the Lesser Sunda Islands.[1] It also proceeded to appoint more Indonesians to administrative posts.[2]

During April and May 1945 discussions took place at Singapore, under the auspices of General Itagaki, the Commander-in-Chief there, on the question of East Indian independence. Itagaki at first appears not to have been in favour of this; he told Marshal Terauchi that the time was not yet ripe, although the Japanese Headquarters in Java thought that it might take place in about a year's time.[3] In Java a preliminary Committee with Japanese, Chinese, and Eurasian, as well as Indonesian, members, was organized in May and held two meetings, in May and July. It drew up a draft Constitution, but it had no power to do more and was excluded from consideration of anything but Java.[4]

But the progress of the Allied offensive rendered these proceedings obsolete. By July 1945 Australian and Dutch forces had made successful landings in Borneo, Japanese resistance had all but ended in the Philippines, and Okinawa had fallen after a desperate resistance. It may be wondered why, at this juncture, the Japanese troubled further about political schemes for the Indies, which they could not now expect for long to hold. The Army, however, hoped by a last-ditch resistance to avoid unconditional surrender. Furthermore, Tokyo was still pinning its faith on Soviet mediation, and, especially in the junior echelons of the Army, there was a hope that a breach between the Western Powers and the Soviet Union might induce the latter to aid Japan. Admiral Maeda, who was Naval Liaison Officer at Batavia, appears to have regarded the Javanese Communists with at any rate a tolerant eye.

On 17 July 1945 the Supreme Council for the Direction of the War decided that the independence of the East Indies was to be recognized as soon as possible. An Independence Preparatory Committee was to be organized and the whole territory was to be included in the proclamation of independence.[5] At the beginning of August Terauchi was instructed to hasten preparations for this, so that the independence of Indonesia could be proclaimed in September 1945, instead of early in 1946 as he had apparently at first contemplated. He accordingly sent for Soekarno and other leading nationalists and, on 11 August, informed them of the

---

[1] *Syonan Sinbun*, 22 Feb. 1945. [2] ibid. 30 May 1945.
[3] Statement of de Weerd. [4] ibid. [5] IMTFE, *Exhibit* 1350.

Imperial Decree. This was to the effect that the entire territory of the Netherlands East Indies would be included in the proposed new State; that the date of its proclamation remained at the discretion of the Japanese Government, and that an independent régime would be first installed in Java.[1] Soekarno returned on 14 August and an Independence Preparatory Committee was organized, under his chairmanship, with thirteen members from Java, three from Sumatra, and five from the Outer Islands. These were picked by the local Japanese commanders.[2]

The first meeting of the Committee had been fixed for 19 August, but on 15 August its members were secretly informed of Japan's capitulation to the Allies. No public announcement of this was permitted until 21 August, when the Japanese Emperor's broadcast of 15 August, announcing the decision to surrender, was published. Word of it, however, had got around, and Soekarno and Hatta were urged by the Indonesian Youth Corps, which was in touch with underground elements, to proceed with the declaration of independence. They on 16 August consulted with Admiral Maeda, who agreed to present their case to the military authorities. The latter were at first reluctant, pointing out that they had received no instructions from Tokyo. But their opposition was overcome, at least to the point of taking no active measures against Soekarno's proceedings. He and his colleagues made hasty alterations to the draft Constitution which they had drawn up in May, and, on 17 August, the independence of Indonesia was proclaimed from Soekarno's house.[3] On this score it is claimed that the Indonesian Republic was not created by Japan, since the matter was taken out of Japanese hands. But the Japanese forces could easily have maintained control if they had desired; they had Soekarno and his associates under their hand in Batavia, and needed only to seize upon them to deprive the movement of leadership. Under the surrender terms they should have done this and retained control until the arrival of Allied forces, as they did do in Malaya. Instead they permitted the newly proclaimed Republic to assume administrative functions, and supplied it with arms. The Dutch military and civilian internees remained under duress, with Indonesian guards replacing their former Japanese jailers. All this ensured

[1] Statement of de Weerd.
[2] ibid.; *Syonan Sinbun*, 17 Aug. 1945.
[3] Statement of de Weerd.

that the authority of the Netherlands could never be peacefully restored.

In Malaya the Japanese established the usual centralized Military Administration headed by a President, or Gunseikan who from April 1942 until July 1943 was a civilian, Wateru Watanabe.[1] He was responsible to the Commander-in-Chief of the Seventh Area Army, with headquarters in Singapore. The first Commander-in-Chief was General Tomoyuki Yamashita, the conqueror of Malaya. Singapore itself, which the Japanese renamed Shonan, or Light of the South, was made a special municipality, with a civilian Mayor, Shigeo Odate, who had formerly been an official in the Manchukuo régime; he held office until July 1943, when he was succeeded by another Japanese official, Kanichi Naito.[2]

The rest of Malaya was divided into eight provinces, each headed by a Japanese administrator.[3] The former distinction between the Straits Settlements, the Federated and the Unfederated Malay States was swept away. The Japanese gave themselves credit for having removed what they asserted was a British device to keep the people disunited.[4] The Sultans of the Malay States, having duly offered submission, were retained in their positions and were made heads of the Bureaux of Religious Affairs, established in each province, as part of the Japanese policy of conciliating the Moslems. But the Sultans were left with little authority, they were rebuked for the contributions they had made to the British war effort, and their stipends were reduced.[5]

---

[1] *Shonan Times*, 29 April 1942. When the Japanese conquered Singapore they seized the offices and equipment of the old-established English-language paper the *Straits Times*. This appeared as the *Shonan Times* for a while, then, after a squabble between the adherents of the Hepburn system of romanization and those of a later 'nationalist' system of phonetics, it became the *Syonan Times* and, finally, in December 1942, the *Syonan Sinbun*—an English-language edition of a Japanese newspaper. It continued until the British reoccupation in September 1945.   [2] *Syonan Sinbun*, 20 July 1943.
[3] *Shonan Times*, 12 March 1942.   [4] ibid. 25 April 1942.
[5] ibid. 13 April 1942. The *Shonan Times* of 18 April said that the Sultans had come to Singapore, paid their respects to the Japanese military authorities, and were all looking forward to peace and prosperity but had no idea how this was to be secured. 'Nor did they suggest, considering the heavy contributions that they have all made to British war funds, to what extent they contemplated subscribing to Nippon war funds.' The Sultans 'with their vast wealth and influence' should become leaders in the great task of reconstruction. On 21 January 1943 the Sultans again assembled in Singapore and were harangued by the Chief of the Military Affairs Department, who said: 'In consideration of the financial stringency brought about by the reduction in taxes, coupled with the fact that the people are still suffering from the horrors of war, and as a fine gesture on your part to share joys and sorrows with Nippon, your remuneration will be on a lesser scale than before.' As the Sultans had been confirmed in the property

The whole area was renamed Malai and the Japanese made it clear that it was to become an integral part of the Japanese Empire. Thus on 23 March 1942 the Japanese Consulate-General in Singapore was officially closed, the Second Secretary of the Japanese Embassy in Thailand performing this ceremony, because 'the Malay Peninsula is now Nippon territory.'[1] On 7 April a Japanese Military Court was established in the former premises of the Singapore Supreme Court to deal with any peace breakers 'in the Nippon territory of Malaya and Sumatra Island.'[2] On 29 April 1942, the birthday of the Japanese Emperor, a public holiday was decreed and a one-minute silence imposed during which all the inhabitants of Shonan were to stand facing north-east towards the Imperial Palace.[3] On this occasion General Yamashita, in a public message, spoke of 'the newly joined Nippon subjects of Malaya and Sumatra' as celebrating the imperial birthday.[4] Watanabe, the President of the Military Administration, spoke in the same vein of 'you, the newly absorbed subjects of Tenno Heika—citizens of Dai Nippon.'[5] On 7 May 1942 Yamashita laid the foundation-stone of the pagoda and shrine at Bukit Timah in memory of those killed in the battle for Malaya and Sumatra.[6]

At the same time the *Shonan Times* spoke of 'our great general' (Yamashita) and 'our great admiral' (Yamamoto). A frequent contributor of articles to this paper was one who signed himself Charles Nell. He repeatedly averred that Malaya was now Nippon territory and, among other things, wrote an article on Japanese achievements in Korea, which was 'an integral part of the Nippon Empire, which, if I may venture to make a guess, will be the status of Malaya'.[7]

Tojo, who paid a visit to Singapore in July 1943, called it 'the erstwhile citadel of Britain . . . which has now been converted into a key point for the construction of Dai Toa.'[8] That he considered Malaya as Japanese territory is shown by his action, described above, in forcing through the cession to Thailand of the four northern Malay States.[9] This step was not well regarded by the local Japanese administration in Malaya, because it meant

they already possessed, he hoped they would not mind this (*Syonan Sinbun*, 22 Jan. 1943).   [1] *Shonan Times*, 24 March 1942.
[2] ibid. 7 April 1942.   [3] ibid. 20 April 1942.
[4] ibid. 29 April 1942.   [5] ibid.   [6] ibid. 8 May 1942.
[7] ibid. 14 April 1942. 'Today by right of conquest every bit of Malaya is Nippon territory' (ibid. 25 April 1942).
[8] *Syonan Sinbun*, 6 July 1943.   [9] See Ch. XI above.

placing Malayan Moslems under the rule of the Siamese and ran counter to the policy of favouring the Malay people and of avoiding any offence to their religious susceptibilities. The Siamese appointed Army officers as administrators and also proceeded to discriminate against the Moslems by such devices as banning polygamous marriages and imposing extra taxes upon those who could not read and write Siamese.[1]

As elsewhere in the regions they occupied, the Japanese made special efforts to promote the study and use of the Japanese language. The schools were reopened, with revised curricula, including courses in Japanese; special schools were established for its teaching; newspapers and periodicals carried a series of lessons in Japanese. The use of English, although it had to be permitted, was frowned upon and discouraged as much as possible.[2] On 14 January 1943 it was announced that, as from the following July, all private correspondence would have to be in the Japanese, Malay, Chinese, Indian, or Thai languages; the use of English would be prohibited. This, however, did not extend to official documents or to periodicals.[3] In fact, despite the pressure they brought to bear, the Japanese had the same difficulties in popularizing their language in Malaya as they experienced elsewhere.

From the autumn of 1943 onwards there were signs of a change in Japanese policy, despite the absence of any concrete statement to that effect. But Sumatra was detached from the Malayan administration and henceforth developments there followed the course of those in Java. References to Malaya as Japanese territory ceased and were replaced by talk of co-operation in building a 'New Malai'. In October 1943 Consultative Councils were established in Singapore and in the provinces. These did not amount to much; in Singapore the Mayor was *ex-officio* Chairman; in the provinces the Japanese administrator presided, with the Sultan of the State as Vice-Chairman. The Councillors were carefully hand-picked and were summoned only when the Mayor or Governor thought fit. Nevertheless this was a move, albeit a very cautious one, in the direction of some measure of autonomy. So was the contemporary increase in the number of Malayan officials in the

[1] *Syonan Sinbun*, 17 Sept. 1943; USOSS, *Japanese Administration in Malaya*, p. 5.
[2] 'We regret that we are forced to use the language of the enemy. . . . It is a disgrace to use the language of people who exploited and suppressed us' (*Syonan Times*, 15 Sept. 1942).   [3] *Syonan Sinbun*, 14 Jan. 1943.

Japanese administration.[1] At the celebration of Kigensetsu—the anniversary of the founding of the Japanese Empire by Jimmu, the first emperor—on 11 February 1944, the *Syonan Sinbun* suggested that the future status of Malaya would be that of a 'self-contained, self-respecting member of the Toa family of nations.'[2] The Japanese, however, to the last evaded any definite promise of independence. On the third anniversary of the fall of Singapore the Gunseikan declared that Malaya had completed three years as a member of the Co-Prosperity Sphere. The Chinese had been given their freedom; the Indonesians had been promised it, everyone must have confidence that Nippon would do her best for the New Malai.[3] When on 8 August 1945 the news that Indonesia was to be given independence was published, the *Syonan Sinbun* editorial on this said that the future of Malaya would be closely linked with that of Indonesia.[4] The same paper quoted a Malay member of the Shonan Advisory Council as saying that Malaya would be included with Indonesia in receiving independence.[5] But on 12 August General Itagaki, the Commander-in-Chief in Malaya, made a public statement in which he said that the Malays must have been deeply stirred to learn that their kindred race in the East Indies were shortly to attain complete independence. They should themselves now redouble their efforts in co-operating with the Nippon Army and so working for the realization of a glorious Malai.[6] That was as far as he went, and, as will be seen, the course of events in Malaya between the Japanese decision to surrender and the British reoccupation was completely different from what happened in Java.

In Malaya, as throughout the Far East, the Japanese lost no opportunity of humiliating their white captives, whether military or civilian, and of holding them up to the hatred and derision of Asiatic peoples.

Today in Syonan and wherever the victorious Nippon armies have brought the New Order, Europeans may be seen, nude to the waist, doing jobs that Asians only were made to do before. Many of them cut ludicrous figures slouching their way through work which even Asian women are able to tackle with greater ability.[7]

British rule in Malaya was depicted as one of unbridled exploita-

[1] ibid. 3 and 5 Oct. 1943.   [2] ibid. 11 Feb. 1944.
[3] ibid. 15 Feb. 1945.   [4] ibid. 8 Aug. 1945.
[5] ibid. 10 Aug. 1945.   [6] ibid. 14 Aug. 1945.
[7] *Syonan Times*, 25 Feb. 1942.

tion, with no care for the welfare of subject races: this was contrasted with Nipponese frugality and unselfishness in being ready to make sacrifices for the establishment of the New Order.[1] Curiously enough, amid the chorus of denunciation of Great Britain, there was an occasional nostalgic reference to the bygone days of the Anglo-Japanese Alliance. Thus the *Shonan Times* of 26 February 1942 referred to the suppression by Japanese troops of an Indian forces mutiny in 1915 and said that 'Nippon helping the British at that time was really God's act'. The Japanese diplomat who came from Bangkok to close the Japanese Consulate-General at Singapore remarked that before the Washington Conference Singapore had been a base of the Nippon-British Alliance to guard the peace of Asia; after that Conference it became a British base directed against Nippon.[2] But the general line of propaganda was that the British had become luxurious, decadent, and spiritless, unable to bear hardships or to fight as the Japanese could.[3]

The Eurasians also came in for Japanese condemnation as being too Westernized and as yearning after the fleshpots of British rule. They were initially compelled to assemble and to be registered; on this occasion they were given a homily by a Japanese officer who said that unless they altered their ways 'we must think of heavy punishments for you'.[4] They were enjoined to regard themselves as Asiatics, to adapt themselves to the new order, which meant 'the end of the previous system of preferential treatment as a buffer between white and coloured races.' They should cease to hanker after clerical posts and be prepared to take up farming or shopkeeping.[5]

The Eurasian community, while thus periodically hectored and admonished, did not constitute any serious problem for the Japanese. It was otherwise with the Chinese, who form the great majority of the population of Singapore itself, and a substantial proportion of that of the rest of the country. They had, in general, been content enough under British rule, which left them free to pursue their avocations in peace. There were rival Nationalist, Communist, and Wang Ching-wei influences at work among them, but few, especially among those who had direct connexions with China itself, had any illusions on what Japanese rule would mean. The Japanese occupation of Singapore was initially marked by an

[1] ibid. 23 Feb. 1942.
[2] ibid. 24 March 1942.
[3] ibid. 23 and 25 Feb. 1942.
[4] ibid. 6 March 1942.
[5] ibid. 24 March 1942.

outburst of slaughter and rapine, and, while this was soon checked, arrests by the Kempei of what the Japanese termed 'hostile and rebellious Chinese with pro-Chungking sympathies' continued, although protection was promised to those who would co-operate.[1] The Chinese were told that all of them who had in any way opposed or resisted the Japanese were deserving of death or slavery; only through Japanese clemency and devotion to the high ideals of the Greater East Asia Co-Prosperity Sphere were they spared this fate.[2]

As a mark of appreciation and a sign of readiness to co-operate the Chinese community was required to make a 'free gift' to Japanese Army coffers. A representative body was organized from the various Chinese associations and this assessed the amount each Chinese was required to pay.[3] When all the contributions had not been forthcoming by the original date set, the laggards were given a severe scolding and threatened with a double assessment.[4] Finally, on 25 June 1942, the sum of 50 million Straits dollars was handed over to General Yamashita.[5] The *Syonan Times* made this the occasion for another scolding; it declared that the sum was a mere bagatelle compared with what the Chinese had raised for the (Chungking) China Relief Fund prior to the Japanese conquest. It also upbraided the Chinese for not co-operating to suppress 'Communist slum rats', and for indulging in racketeering and black-market practices.[6] These were complaints which were to be frequently reiterated during the occupation period.

In general, allowing for a pro-Wang Ching-wei minority and the usual element of sycophants and time-servers, the attitude of the Chinese community was one of passive resistance and obstruction, especially of Japanese financial and economic controls.[7] In the interior guerrilla bands kept up resistance; these were mainly, though not entirely, members of the Communist Anti-Japanese Malayan People's Party. The Japanese responded with merciless reprisals against Chinese villagers suspected of harbouring guerrillas or failing to report their whereabouts; the guerrillas were equally merciless upon those who did inform.[8]

---

[1] ibid. 23 Feb. 1942.
[2] ibid. 28 Feb. 1942.
[3] ibid. 9 April 1942.
[4] ibid. 19 June 1942.
[5] ibid. 26 June 1942.
[6] ibid. 27 June, 1 July 1942.
[7] Hastain, *White Coolie*, pp. 192–3.
[8] F. Spencer Chapman, *The Jungle is Neutral* (London, Chatto & Windus, 1949), pp. 152 ff., 210–11, 307.

In their initial conquest of Malaya the Japanese received guidance and aid from a section of the Malay population and, in general, the Malays, bewildered at the rapid sequence of events and the swift collapse of British power, were prepared to co-operate with the victorious Japanese, although from the first there were exceptions to this rule.[1] Fear and dislike of the Chinese, which the Japanese were quick to make the most of, also played its part in the originally receptive attitude of the Malay populace to the Japanese. But the harsh methods of the invader, coupled with the growing economic hardships, were not long in promoting sullenness and hostility.

Much the same considerations apply to the Indian community in Malaya. The Japanese recruited the Sikh and Pathan police force into their own police and auxiliary police organizations, and utilized them in anti-guerrilla operations.[2]

The unwarlike Tamils were conscribed into labour battalions and a considerable proportion of them went from Malaya to labour on the Burma–Siam railway. A local Indian Independence League was organized and affiliated to the general Japanese-sponsored movement headed by Subhas Chandra Bose.[3] But, however gratified some of the Indian population may initially have been to see the downfall and captivity of the British, they soon, in common with the Chinese and Malays, discovered that in the Japanese they had far harder taskmasters.[4] The New Order, they were periodically informed, meant sacrifices; these the Japanese had a right to demand because they themselves were pouring out their blood and treasure to establish Greater East Asia.[5]

Mounting economic hardships made the people as a whole less appreciative of this point of view. The effect of the Japanese conquest was to disrupt the economy of Malaya, which depended upon exports of rubber and tin and upon imports of rice and consumer goods. Even had the Japanese been able to maintain normal shipping services, which was not the case, they could not have absorbed all the Malayan export products. Nor could they provide adequate supplies of food and consumer goods. As elsewhere in South East Asia they took what they could of the export

[1] ibid. pp. 25, 137–8, 307, 428–9. [2] ibid. pp. 230, 290.
[3] *Syonan Times*, 22 July; 2 and 13 Aug. 1942; *Syonan Sinbun*, 21 May, 19 June, 9 July, 22 and 26 Oct. 1943.
[4] Hastain, *White Coolie*, pp. 114, 192–3.
[5] *Syonan Times*, 8 Oct. 1942; *Syonan Sinbun*, 1 Jan. 1943, 25 May 1944.

staples, sent an occasional trickle of textiles and other consumer goods, and, for the rest, preached the virtues of self-sufficiency.[1] They encouraged increased production of rice and vegetables and promoted agricultural colonies, especially at 'New Syonan' near Endau in Johore, and at Bahau in Negri Sembilan.[2] But these settlements, although made much of by Japanese propagandist organs, were on a comparatively small scale, and could do little to alleviate the problem of food supplies. This was especially severe in Singapore, where the official rice ration was progressively reduced, and where Japanese attempts to stabilize prices and prevent inflation proved ineffectual.[3] By 1945 the economy of Malaya was in a thoroughly run-down condition. Thus the capitulation of Japan came as a welcome relief to all sections of the population, more especially as they were spared the destruction and suffering which would have attended the last-ditch struggle which the Japanese were preparing, and in connexion with which they had drafted many of the able-bodied Malayans into the Giyu-gun or auxiliary defence force.[4]

At the same time, fortunate as it was in these respects, the peaceful British reoccupation of Singapore could not entirely offset the catastrophe of 1942. Then, too, the Japanese Army Headquarters in Singapore made the most they could of the circumstances of Japan's decision to capitulate. As happened in Java, they endeavoured to keep it secret until a week after it had happened and meantime denounced unofficial reports of it as idle rumours. When, on 20 August, they allowed the text of the Imperial Rescript of 15 August to appear, they accompanied it by a proclamation of their own. In this they declared that the Japanese Army in Malaya had lost none of its honour and dignity since it had been fully ready to fight a decisive battle.[5] The same was true of other Japanese armies in Indonesia, China, and in Japan itself. But the Americans, disregarding all principles of humanity, had made use of the deadly and inhuman atom bomb, against innocent

---

[1] The first shipment of Japanese consumer goods arrived in Singapore in July 1943 (ibid. 16 July 1943).

[2] ibid. 5 and 18 Jan., 21 and 25 March 1944, 15 June 1945.

[3] ibid. 2 Feb. 1943. On 27 June 1943 the paper declared that food prices had risen by nearly 300 per cent. since December 1941; that the controlled prices were ignored; and that even imported Japanese goods had found their way into the black market.

[4] *Syonan Sinbun*, 13 Jan., 23 May 1944, 9 and 22 Jan., 30 June 1945. Malayans also supplied their quota to the Heiho, or transport units, of the Japanese Army.

[5] ibid. 20 Aug. 1945.

civilians. This meant that had the war continued the whole
population of East Asia would have been exposed to destruction.
Therefore, out of his regard not only for the people of Nippon, but
also for those of East Asia as a whole, the Emperor had commanded
his troops to lay down their arms, and this command they must
obey.[1]

Glosses on this text were provided at press conferences and in
newspaper comment. The Allies, it was asserted, must have possessed the atom bomb for some time, yet they had not used it
in the war in Europe, but only against Asiatics.[2] The doubts
expressed in some American newspapers about the use of the
bomb were eagerly seized upon—'What they use against others
will be used against them tomorrow'.[3] In a final press conference,
on 21 August, the Japanese military spokesman declared that

by imperial command the Dai Toa Senso is coming to an end, but our
ideas for the existence of Nippon and the stabilization of Greater East
Asia will never die. To strive to realize these ideals in the face of in-
describable difficulties and hardships to come is the only way for the
Nippon nation to live.[4]

This piece of face-saving probably had little effect upon the
populace in general, who were glad enough to see the backs of the
Japanese 'liberators'. But, although the Japanese occupation of
Malaya was not attended by the political and social upheaval
which occurred in Indonesia, the injury to white prestige and the
stirring up of racial hatreds between East and West produced
effects, which cannot be certainly evaluated, but which it would be
dangerous to underrate. Common fear and dislike of the Japanese
did something to overcome the divisions between Malay, Chinese,
and Indian, and probably had more effect in producing some consciousness of Malayan unity than all the Japanese propaganda
about it. Furthermore, in the three weeks which elapsed between
the Japanese surrender and the re-entry of British forces, a state
of near-anarchy prevailed in Malaya.[5] Much of the interior fell
into the hands of guerrilla forces, who busied themselves in paying
off old scores. The Japanese withdrew into the towns where they
tried to maintain some semblance of order and issued proclamations

---

[1] ibid.   [2] ibid. 15 Aug. 1945.
[3] ibid. 17 Aug. 1945.   [4] ibid. 21 Aug. 1945.
[5] O. W. Gilmour, *With Freedom to Singapore* (London, Benn, 1950),
pp. 84–86.

against looting, which, however, in the circumstances were largely ignored.[1] For all these reasons a general spirit of unrest had been engendered, and a new degree of political consciousness had taken hold of the peoples of the Malay Peninsula.[2]

Until the Japanese coup of 9 March 1945, Indo-China remained in a strangely anomalous position. Despite her professed objectives in the Greater East Asia War—to sweep away Western rule and to further the independence of the peoples of the Far East—Japan continued to acknowledge French sovereignty over Indo-China. The French administration continued to function, and French troops remained responsible for the maintenance of internal peace and order which entailed the repression of any uprisings against French rule. Japanese troops were stationed in Indo-China under the agreements of September 1940 and July 1941.[3] These arrangements were supplemented by a further agreement of 9 December 1941, which was concluded between Admiral Decoux and General Tyo, the new head of the Japanese military mission. Decoux claims that this agreement in fact represented a modification of the original demands of the Japanese, that he successfully refused any collaboration in Japanese military operations outside of Indo-China, that he avoided any direct control by the Japanese of the local French military forces, and that Japanese civilians in Indo-China remained subject to French law and jurisdiction.[4]

The agreement reiterated the principle of Franco-Japanese 'common defence' of Indo-China, which had been enunciated in the previous July. Thus, at least in theory, the Japanese champions of Asiatic independence were pledged to help defend a French Asiatic colony. It was a highly artificial situation, which the Japanese maintained because it suited them (as long as they got the most of what they wanted in the political, military, and economic spheres) not to destroy the French administration. They had not the administrative personnel to ensure continued peace and order should they overthrow the existing régime, and they could not afford the chance of disorder in a country of such strategic and economic importance to them. They knew that, so long as Allied forces remained far distant from Indo-China, Decoux

---

[1] ibid.; *Syonan Sinbun*, 25 August, 1945.
[2] Gilmour, *With Freedom to Singapore*, p. 87. It was also psychologically unfortunate, though perhaps unavoidable, that the first reoccupying troops consisted of an Indian division (ibid. p. 94).
[3] See Ch. VIII above.　　　　[4] Decoux, *L'Indochine*, pp. 157–8, 230.

could not oppose them in anything of vital importance; consequently they could afford, for the time being, to leave him in power.

Decoux understood this and perceived that, precarious as was his position, he had a chance of preserving it if he could avoid anything happening which would provoke the Japanese to carry out a coup d'état and set up puppet Annamese and Cambodian administrations. He wanted to preserve French rule until such time as the Japanese were defeated in the general war, when he hoped to negotiate a peaceful evacuation, so that the colony might return to France intact.[1] In this he failed, which is not surprising; in view of the manifold difficulties and perils with which he had to contend, the wonder is, indeed, that he was able to hold on for as long as he did. He had to contend not only with the Japanese, but also with Annamese unrest, with Chinese intrigues, with the Gaullists, within and without Indo-China, and with the Allies, particularly with the Americans.

While the Japanese Government, for reasons of expediency, were not willing to sweep away French rule in Indo-China, they could not avoid its being discredited in the eyes of the inhabitants by the fact of its enforced subservience to Japan. Nor were they averse to this, for they trusted Decoux as little as he trusted them, and they wanted to be ready with an alternative to him if necessary. They therefore encouraged, up to a point, Annamese nationalist aspirations; in particular they lent support to the Cao Daist movement, with which they had previous connexions, and of which the leader, Cuong De, was in exile in Japan.[2]

Apart from deliberate policy Tokyo was unable to restrain the actions of the Japanese military in Indo-China, among whom there was the usual 'younger officer' group who were straining at the leash and who took every opportunity to humiliate and discredit the French. In July 1943 General Iwane Matsui paid a visit to Saigon, ostensibly as a private individual on a mission of information, and took the opportunity to attack French rule and to give vent to his pan-Asiatic sentiments.[3] Decoux's protests drew a

---

[1] General Sabattier suggests that Decoux thought that when Germany fell Japan might try to secure peace through the Indo-China authorities (G. Sabattier, *Le Destin de l'Indochine* (Paris, Plon, 1952), p. 53).

[2] Decoux, *L'Indochine*, pp. 234–5. Cao Daism is a curious mixture of Oriental and Occidental philosophies and religions, with an organization largely borrowed from the Roman Catholic Church. While developing nationalist tendencies, it was otherwise essentially conservative.　　　　[3] ibid. pp. 236–7.

disclaimer from Tokyo of any complicity in Matsui's activities, but they could, if they had chosen, have prevented his visit, and such incidents showed clearly how brittle the situation was. It remained unbroken during 1943-4 because Marshal Terauchi, the Japanese Supreme Commander in the Southern Regions, did not want trouble in Indo-China any more than in Siam, and perhaps also because of the influence of the Japanese envoy, Yoshizawa, whom Decoux judged to be at heart moderate and averse to the Japanese military.[1]

China represented another ever-present menace. In December 1941, coincident with their declaration of war upon Japan, the Chinese Government warned Vichy that they would expect the same facilities that the Japanese enjoyed in Indo-China and that their troops would enter the country if necessary. Decoux warned Vichy that any Chinese move against Indo-China might well result in the Japanese seizing full control there, which would be dis-advantageous both to China and to the United States. These considerations were raised by the French Ambassador in Washington, Henry Haye, in conversations with T. V. Soong and with the Department of State. In the event no overt Chinese movement occurred.[2] But the Chinese gave sanctuary to leaders of various Annamese resistance groups and sponsored their organization into a coalition group, under the leadership of Ho Chi Minh, erstwhile head of the Indo-Chinese Communist Party. The new coalition, organized at a meeting in Liuchow in 1942, took the name of League for the Independence of Annam, or briefly, Viet Minh, endeavoured to secure support from the Allies and proceeded to encourage revolts in Indo-China. They stood for opposition to the Japanese, and also for independence from France. Communism was for the time being soft-pedalled, although the Communists were the best-organized group among them.

Decoux was anxious to prevent internal trouble which would provide the Japanese with an excellent excuse for action against the French administration. In December 1941 he had persuaded the Japanese to leave the garrisoning of the Tongking–China border to French forces. By this means he hoped to preserve a buffer between the Chinese and the Japanese armies and also to have an

---

[1] ibid. p. 313. Decoux says that Yoshizawa, when on the point of leaving in November 1944, gave him a hint that Japanese policy in Indo-China would shortly change.   [2] ibid. pp. 250-1.

avenue of escape into China should the ever-present menace of a Japanese coup d'état materialize. Consequently, while doing all he could to prevent any overt Chinese action, he was anxious to keep on as good terms with Chungking as possible. In this matter he came into conflict with the French Ambassador to China, Cosme, who in 1942 wanted Vichy to recognize the Nanking régime as a means of placating Japan. Decoux did not consider this either necessary or desirable and his view prevailed with Vichy. In October 1943 the Chinese National Government broke off relations with Vichy and soon after General Pechkov arrived in Chungking, first as representative of the Committee of Liberation at Algiers and, at the end of 1944, as Ambassador. Decoux got into secret touch with Pechkov and urged that there should be no Chinese or Allied invasion of Indo-China.[1]

Decoux, as his memoirs make clear, had no liking for de Gaulle or his movement. Thus personal inclinations combined with political expediency to induce him to repress Gaullist activities in the Indo-China administration. But this was an impossible task, especially after the Allied invasion of North Africa, the German occupation of southern France, and the fall of Vichy. In February 1943, in response to Decoux's suggestion, Vichy had conferred full powers of action upon him in the event of his being entirely divorced from communication with France. In August 1944 he assumed these powers and followed this up by sending a secret message to the Provisional Government of France urging them to refrain from any disturbance of the *status quo* in Indo-China for fear of provoking a Japanese counter-stroke.[2] He received no reply to this but in October 1944 General Aymé, Commandant of the military forces in Indo-China, informed Decoux that he and General Mordant had for some time been in secret liaison with de Gaulle and that they had been nominated chiefs of the resistance movement which would come into action in the event of a Japanese coup d'état against Decoux. The latter inquired of de Gaulle whether he should resign, but in November 1944 received the answer that he was to continue as Governor-General until further orders—which he would receive through Mordant.[3]

This created an impossible situation about which Decoux writes with understandable bitterness. Mordant was getting secret

[1] ibid. pp. 252–6.
[2] ibid. pp. 300–3.   [3] ibid. pp. 306–9.

instructions from Paris and took no notice of Decoux when the latter warned him and his associates not to organize resistance movements against the Japanese. Appeals to de Gaulle on this score also met with no response. Decoux therefore considered that the indiscipline and recklessness of Mordant and Aymé, abetted by Paris, did much to precipitate the Japanese coup which he had striven so long to avert.[1]

There is, however, another side to this. The capitulation of Indo-China to Japanese demands in 1940 and 1941 had aroused disfavour in Washington. Roosevelt, who took a most one-sided view of French achievements in Indo-China, had a pet project of detaching it from France after the war and putting it under an international trusteeship.[2] For this scheme, he declared, he had the backing of Chiang Kai-shek and also of Stalin,[3] which may well be believed. Roosevelt made no secret of his aims, which the British Government regarded with concern and of which de Gaulle cannot but have been apprised. *His* reaction may well be imagined, ardent nationalist that he was, and always resolved to avoid the slightest reproach of having been subservient to the Allies, or of losing any French territory. To counter American designs, the French Committee of National Liberation in December 1943 had promised that, after the war, Indo-China should have a new political status within the French community. But they evidently also felt that to ensure the return of Indo-China to France it would be advisable for her to take an active part in its liberation from the Japanese. The British Government were in favour of this, but Roosevelt strongly disapproved, and no agreement about it could be reached at the Quebec Conference of September 1944.[4] An 'unofficial' French military mission nevertheless went to Kandy to confer with the South East Asia Command on matters affecting Indo-China. To this Roosevelt, in November 1944, again signified his disapprobation.[5]

---

[1] ibid. pp. 315–20. Decoux was very much the Admiral in command and relied too much on naval officers for the liking of the Army. Relations between Mordant and Decoux were of the worst (Sabattier, *Destin de l'Indochine*, pp. 36–39; 146–150).

[2] On 14 January 1944 Roosevelt, in a memorandum to Hull, declared: 'I saw Halifax last week and told him quite frankly that it was perfectly true that I had, for over a year, expressed the opinion that Indo-China should not go back to France but that it should be administered by an international trusteeship. France has had the country—thirty million inhabitants—for nearly one hundred years, and the people are worse off than they were at the beginning' (Hull, *Memoirs*, ii. 1597).   [3] ibid.   [4] ibid. pp. 1597–8.

[5] ibid. p. 1598. Hull did not share Roosevelt's enthusiasm for international

In the early months of 1945 the American reconquest of the Philippines brought matters to a head in Indo-China. The country had for some time been subjected to American air raids, which, according to Decoux, did little damage to the Japanese, although they caused havoc in some cities and many civilian casualties. He also declares that damage to the railway connecting Cochin-China with Tongking and the sinking of ships en route from Saigon to Haiphong hampered the transport of food supplies and contributed to the loss of a million lives in the famine which occurred in Tongking in 1944-5.[1]

The Japanese evidently expected that, after their reoccupation of the Philippines, the Americans would attempt a landing in Indo-China. Decoux says that, in anticipation of this, he had sent secret instructions to the French local authorities to assist any such invading force, but that at the beginning of February 1945 he was ordered by de Gaulle to proclaim the neutrality of Indo-China in the case of any American landing.[2]

Late in February Decoux left Hanoi on a journey to Cochin-China to endeavour to quiet the resistance elements there and early in March he arrived in Saigon. Here, on 9 March, he met the new Japanese envoy, Shunichi Matsumoto, who declared that an American invasion of Indo-China was likely and who demanded that the French military and police forces should henceforth be fully controlled by the Japanese military authorities and that the French administration in general should accept their orders.[3] Decoux refused these terms, but endeavoured to temporize and suggested that they might be accepted in the actual event of an American invasion. But the Japanese this time refused all compromise, their troops stormed the Governor-General's residence and took Decoux prisoner.[4] All over Indo-China the Japanese sought to disarm French forces and round up French civilians. In Langson, Hagiang, and several other places, the French troops were swiftly overwhelmed and many were massacred after sur-

trusteeships; he thought that Indo-China should be returned to France, provided she pledged herself to accord it eventual independence (ibid. pp. 1598-9).
    [1] *L'Indochine*, pp. 266-7.
    [2] ibid. p. 323. Mordant on 25 January 1945 was told by Paris to proclaim the neutrality of the French forces in the event of an American landing. Only should the Japanese refuse to accept this was he to fight them (Sabattier, *Destin de l'Indochine*, pp. 102-3).
    [3] Matsumoto warned Decoux that any refusal would be met by force (Decoux, *L'Indochine*, pp. 329-30).   [4] ibid. pp. 330-4.

render, as were French civilian officials.[1] Some of the French forces in Tongking, under General Sabattier, managed to make a fighting retreat across the border into China.[2]

In his speech to the Diet on 10 March General Koiso, the Japanese Premier, accused the French administration of 'acts of treachery' which had necessitated the Japanese action.

It has been Governor Decoux's policy to perform to a minimum the obligations under the pact of joint defence, doing enough only to give Nippon no good excuse for independent action, and on the other hand tolerating indiscriminate bombing by United States forces, without making serious protest.[3]

He had 'kept down to a minimum' the Indo-China share of contribution to military expenditure and funds for economic development, as well as the commodities and the labour required by Japan. He had refused to extend recognition to the National Government of China (the Nanking régime), and had been in secret communication with Chungking.[4] He had furthermore refused to hand over to the Japanese American airmen who had been brought down over Indo-China.[5] All these charges were true enough and the recital of them shows that the Japanese were under no illusions as to Decoux's real attitude towards them.

Following their coup the Japanese, on 11 March 1945, got the Annamese Emperor, Bao Dai, to issue a proclamation, in which he abrogated the Franco-Annamese Treaty of 1884, which had provided for a French protectorate over Annam, declared its independence, and pledged co-operation with Japan in the Greater East Asia War.[6] On 13 March a similar proclamation was issued by King Norodom of Cambodia.[7] In Cochin-China the former Japanese Consul-General became for the time being civilian governor. Other Japanese were initially appointed to replace the former French Residents-Superior in Tongking and Laos.

[1] IMTFE, *Record*, pp. 15292–6.

[2] Sabattier, *Destin de l'Indochine*, pp. 131–204. General Chennault says that he wanted to send help by air to these forces but that orders came from the US War Department that under no circumstances were arms and ammunition to be given to French troops in Indo-China (*Way of a Fighter*, p. 342).

[3] *Syonan Sinbun*, 13 March 1945.

[4] ibid. Decoux declares that up to 9 March 1945 he had prevented the Japanese from pillaging the economy of Indo-China (*L'Indochine*, pp. 449–50).

[5] *Syonan Sinbun*, 13 March 1945. Decoux says that he sheltered American airmen and had frequent passages of arms with the Japanese in consequence (*L'Indochine*, pp. 267–8).

[6] *Syonan Sinbun*, 13 March 1945.   [7] ibid.

Japanese 'advisers' were stationed at the Courts of Annam and Cambodia, while Shunichi Matsumoto remained as general adviser to the Japanese Commander-in-Chief.[1]

The Japanese-sponsored administration under Bao Dai consisted of a group of Annamese nationalists, with Tran Trong Kim as Premier. They stood for independence, but in other matters they were conservative, and the bulk of the Viet Minh adherents refused to join them. The Viet Minh continued resistance to Japan, and were not attracted by concessions to nationalism in the form of the reconstitution of the old Empire of Annam, including Annam, Tongking, and Cochin-China, and the proclamation of the independence of Laos in April 1945.

Then came the Japanese capitulation, which, as elsewhere, was followed by some weeks of interregnum. Decoux, who was in captivity at Loc Ninh, heard of the Japanese surrender on 17 August, and urged the local Japanese commander, General Tsuchihashi, to release him and his compatriots.[2] Decoux hoped to regain control of the administration and with the aid of the (imprisoned) French forces to prevent the triumph of the Viet Minh. But the Japanese general replied that he could not act without orders from the Allied South East Asia Command, so that Decoux and his compatriots remained in captivity.[3] The Japanese made no effort to prevent the spread of the Vietnamese movement and even turned over arms to its members. On 22 August Bao Dai abdicated and his régime collapsed. It was succeeded by a Provisional Government under Ho Chi Minh which, on 2 September, issued a declaration of independence at Hanoi, repudiated all further connexion with France and claimed to have liberated the country.[4]

The French were powerless to prevent these developments because they had no troops in the Far East, for which de Gaulle blamed Allied slowness in providing the necessary shipping.[5] In default of these it was agreed that British troops should temporarily occupy the southern half of Indo-China, and Chinese troops the northern half, the sixteenth parallel being the line of

---

[1] ibid. 15 March 1945.　　　　　　　[2] *L'Indochine*, pp. 335–41.
[3] Decoux remained in captivity until 1 October (ibid. p. 348).
[4] *Vietnam's Fight against Fascism, 1940–45*, Vietnam Delegation in France Information Service, 1948.
[5] *NYT* 15 March 1945. But Sabattier blames De Gaulle for not securing the release of the French forces in Indo-China and not trying to employ those who had reached Yunnan. Gaullist hatred for the adherents of Vichy was the cause of this (Sabattier, *Destin de l'Indochine*, pp. 327–31).

division.[1] The first British troops, under General Gracey, arrived in September 1945. They had instructions to disarm the Japanese, to free the French and co-operate in the restoration of French authority. This was violently opposed by the Vietnamese, with the result that fighting broke out in which the British forces became involved.

The Chinese occupation of the northern half of the country was marked by disorder and looting on the part of the undisciplined Chinese forces and by virtual Chinese support of the Annamese nationalists, despite Chinese official disavowals of any designs on Indo-Chinese territory and professions of neutrality as between the French and the Annamese. In January 1946 French troops arrived to take over from the British, who were glad enough to be free of the imbroglio. In February 1946 the French, in return for substantial concessions to China, secured a promise of Chinese evacuation of northern Indo-China by the end of the following March. This undertaking was, however, only belatedly fulfilled. Thus the stage was set for the long and bitter struggle which marked the post-war years in Indo-China.

In general throughout South East Asia it may be said that the Japanese, while they failed to establish their own New Order, ensured that the old order of Western political domination could never return. But they did more than this. They attacked not only Western rule in Asia, but the whole Occidental way of life. They denounced democratic ideas as productive of individualism, materialism, and class strife. This, coupled with their initial victories over the West, was not without effect upon the peoples whom they conquered. On the other hand, they had nothing positive to offer in the way of political, social, or cultural concepts, because their own ideas on these subjects were an ill-digested assortment of traditional Japanese lore and of totalitarian ideology. They thus, unconsciously and unintentionally, paved the way for the spread of Communism. The economic and social consequences of their rule tended in the same direction. The traditional authority of the upper classes in indigenous society in the colonies was weakened, either because of collaboration with the Japanese, or through the persecutions and confiscations with which the Japanese repaid any recalcitrance or hesitations. The pre-existing

[1] Decoux says that de Gaulle preferred a Chinese, rather than an American occupation, because of his suspicion of American motives (*L'Indochine*, p. 343).

Communist groups were quick to seize their opportunity of stimulating and, as far as possible, dominating active resistance movements. Thus Japanese aggression, combined with Communist
calculation and also American anti-colonialism, created at any
rate the possibility of another 'new order' for East Asia—that of
Communism.

CHAPTER XIII

The Fall of the Japanese Empire

On 18 January 1942 Germany, Italy, and Japan concluded a military agreement in Berlin which defined their respective spheres of operation.[1] That of Japan was to be 'the waters eastward from about 70° E. longitude to the west coast of the American continent, as well as the continent and islands—Australia, the Netherlands East Indies, and New Zealand—which are situated in these waters', and also the Asiatic continent east of about 70° E. longitude. It was, however, provided that, subject to future agreement upon the matter, operations in the Indian Ocean might be carried out beyond the zone limits. The agreement furthermore stipulated that, if the American and British Navies were to devote their main efforts to the Atlantic theatre of war, Japan should send a portion of her Navy there to co-operate directly with the German and Italian fleets, while these would send similar assistance to Japan should the enemy naval concentration be primarily in the Pacific. Provision was also made for the maintenance of contact in important operational plans, for collaboration in economic war, for the exchange of military information, and for co-operation in the establishment of air and sea communications between the Axis Powers and Japan.[2]

In fact this agreement remained largely inoperative. Both German and Japanese witnesses testified after the war to the very meagre collaboration which had been effected between Germany and Italy, on the one hand, and Japan, on the other. One obvious reason for this was the difficulty of communication between the Axis in Europe and its Asiatic partner. At sea this was limited to submarines, plus an occasional armed surface raider or blockade-runner, on land to telegraphic messages, which had their drawbacks in the possibilities of interception and decoding by the enemy. But this is by no means the whole story, for the difficulties of intercourse could have been overcome had the will to do so existed.

[1] This was a purely military agreement, signed by General Keitel, General Marras, the Italian representative on the Tripartite military commission, Admiral Naokuni Nomura and General Banzai, the Japanese representatives (IMTFE, *Exhibit* 49). Togo testified that the Japanese Foreign Ministry knew nothing of it (IMTFE, *Record*, p. 35664).　　[2] IMTFE, *Exhibit* 49.

As it was, both Germany and Japan fought separate wars and were largely content to do so, a state of affairs which Italy, the junior partner, could do nothing to remedy. This failure to co-operate is one of the most striking and surprising features of the war; it stands out in sharp contrast to the intimate relationship established between Great Britain and the United States and even to the limited degree of understanding which was reached between them and the Soviet Union. It is one of the most important causes of the ultimate total defeat both of the Axis Powers and of Japan.

The causes of this lack of co-ordination were threefold. In the first place the Japanese strategists appear not to have seen the war as a whole. Their basic plan of operations, formulated in November 1941, was to occupy South East Asia and the East Indies. That accomplished, they proposed to stand on the defensive. They believed that the immense difficulties of logistics which confronted Great Britain and the United States would prevent these Powers from mounting a counter-offensive strong enough to do more than reconquer a few outer bastions of the Greater East Asia defences. Then, so Tokyo hoped, a compromise peace could be arranged. But this plan underestimated the forces which the Americans could bring to bear once their immense productive capacity was fully geared to the war effort. It also made no allowance for the inventive genius of the Americans in grappling with the problem of communications and supply.

Moreover wars are rarely won by standing on the defensive—even though it be a strategic rather than a tactical defence. In the summer of 1942 a great opportunity lay before the Japanese. Apart from climatic and geographical obstacles they had not sufficient forces to overrun India, but they could have taken Ceylon and, with that as a base, cut off Allied sea communications with the Indian subcontinent. They might also have forestalled the British in the occupation of Madagascar, and, by so doing, placed themselves across the supply routes to Egypt and to the Soviet Union via Persia. Such a move would have coincided with Rommel's initially victorious advance in Tripoli, with the German drive into southern Russia and the Caucasus, and with the slaughter of Allied merchant shipping which the German submarines were effecting in the Atlantic. The collapse of the Middle East, the defeat of the Soviet Union, the strangulation of Allied sea communications—all these grave possibilities might have become actualities had the Japanese moved westwards and striven to effect a junction with their Axis partners at a time when America had not yet recovered from Pearl Harbour and when the British fleet was partially crippled through its losses in the Mediterranean and in the Far East. The Allies feared and the Germans anticipated such a Japanese stroke. Ceylon lay within the stipulated Japanese zone of operations and the Germans would readily have agreed to a Japanese occupation of Madagascar.[1]

But the Japanese made no such move. Admiral Nagumo's squadron returned to Japan and no major Japanese naval force again appeared in the Indian Ocean. The Japanese may have feared the dangers of over-extension, yet they did yield to the temptation to go beyond the bounds which they had originally set themselves, a course which was open to the same objection. When they did this they moved deeper into the Pacific, away from their allies, and the upshot was their reverse in the Coral Sea and their disastrous defeat at Midway, which materially reduced Japanese offensive power at sea. The fact that the Japanese suffered these defeats does not of itself prove that they were altogether wrong in undertaking the operations; there was something to be said for them, looking at the war as a purely Japanese-American affair.[2] But they go to show that the Japanese did very largely look at it in this way.

Behind this localism lay the second cause of the lack of collaboration—the veiled suspicion and distrust with which Germany and Japan regarded each other. There was, after all, a fundamental incongruity in the alliance between Nazi Germany, with its theories of Nordic racial superiority, and Japan, the professed champion of Asia against Western domination. In 1940 the

---

[1] On 15 April 1942 Churchill warned Roosevelt that Japanese naval command of the western Indian Ocean 'would result in the collapse of our whole position in the Middle East, not only because of the interruption to our convoys to the Middle East and India, but also because of the interruptions to the oil supplies from Abadan, without which we cannot maintain our position either at sea or on land in the Indian Ocean area' (*Second World War*, iv. 161–2). Ribbentrop, in a telegram to Ott of 26 March 1942, said he had told Oshima on 23 March that Japan should occupy Ceylon and secure bases in Madagascar (IMTFE, *Record*, pp. 37943–4).

[2] The Coral Sea action resulted from a Japanese attempt to cut the communications between Australia and the United States. After the effervescence in Tokyo caused by the Doolittle air raid, Admiral Yamamoto planned to bring on a fleet action with the object of destroying the American navy before it again became sufficiently powerful to move against Japan. But, partly through 'Magic', things went wrong for the Japanese.

Japanese had reacted to the apparent German victory in Europe with mixed feelings. The German reaction to the Japanese victories in the opening months of 1942 was very similar. Several entries in the *Goebbels Diaries* reveal Hitler as torn between pleasure at the blows inflicted upon the Americans and British, and grief at the blow to white prestige in Asia.[1] Japanese propagandists for their part occasionally referred to the difference between their ideals for Greater East Asia and the concept of German racial superiority in Europe.[2] At heart it is probable that neither side desired the complete victory of the other. The Germans did not relish the prospect of trading with East Asia on Japanese terms and through Japanese commercial organs; the Japanese feared the possible mercantile and colonial ambitions of a Germany dominant in Europe. Early in 1943 agreements were concluded in Tokyo between Germany and Japan and Italy and Japan, which provided for economic and financial co-operation between their respective spheres during the period of the Tripartite Pact. These were signed in anticipation of a victory which never came and hence remained a dead letter.[3]

In addition to the absence of overall strategic co-ordination, there was very little German-Japanese technical military collaboration. Kretschmer, who was the German military attaché in Tokyo during 1940–5, told the Tokyo Tribunal: 'All my urgings for a closer co-operation between the German and Japanese High

---

[1] Thus, on 27 January 1942, Goebbels noted: 'The United States is trying desperately to drag us into a discussion of racial questions, especially with regard to Japan. . . . I have forbidden the German news services even to mention these somewhat ticklish and delicate problems. . . . As a matter of fact our position with Japan and the problems of eastern Asia is rather precarious, since we are uncompromising in our racial view' (*Goebbels Diaries*, p. 17). On 30 January 1942 he remarked: 'The Fuehrer profoundly regrets the heavy losses sustained by the white race in East Asia, but that isn't our fault' (ibid. p. 26). Goebbels had to take 'energetic measures' to stop discussion of the 'Yellow Peril', which 'cannot be discussed at all today, either positively or negatively' (ibid. p. 79). According to an entry in the *Von Hassell Diaries* (London, Hamilton, 1948) for 22 March 1942, Hitler was supposed to have declared that he would gladly send the English twenty divisions to help throw back the yellow men (p. 221).

[2] Thus S. Yamamoto, publisher of the *Kaizo* magazine, visited Singapore in March 1942, and declared that there was a fundamental contrast between German racial policy in Europe and Japan's desire for co-operation between all the races of Asia (*Syonan Times*, 9 March 1942).

[3] There was a general agreement on principles of post-war economic collaboration, negotiated on the Japanese side by Matsushima, the Japanese economic specialist on the Tripartite Commission, but formally signed by Oshima, in January 1943. There was also a secret protocol which provided that each party would give preferential treatment to the other over third parties in the economic blocs which they hoped to establish. More detailed trade agreements were shortly afterwards concluded in Tokyo (IMTFE, *Exhibits* 50 and 3520; evidence of Oshima, *Record*, p. 34044).

Commands were in vain. Both Supreme Headquarters seemed to be intent on waging their own wars.'[1]

The military commissions provided for under the Tripartite Pact rarely met and when they did the proceedings were confined to a propagandist review of the war situation by the Germans in the case of the Berlin commission, or the Japanese in the case of the Tokyo one.[2] Evidently neither side trusted the other sufficiently to give it a true appreciation of the state of affairs. Kretschmer declared that his appeals for a franker exposition fell on deaf ears in both Berlin and Tokyo.[3]

In the summer of 1942 the Germans sent an ordnance expert, Colonel Niemoller, to Japan. He got there by blockade-runner and then was unable to return, so he was instructed to organize German engineers similarly stranded in Japan in a group to assist the Japanese in armament production.[4] The Germans gave some help in radar and in the organization of anti-aircraft batteries, though in these matters the Japanese lagged far behind the Allies.

Japanese submarines made an occasional appearance in the Atlantic, and the German Navy wanted the Japanese to use their submarine arm primarily to attack merchant shipping. This, however, was a task for which Japanese submarines had not been designed, nor their crews trained. In the spring of 1943 Hitler presented the Japanese Navy with a couple of U-boats, which were apparently intended to serve as models for the new submarine construction which he hoped the Japanese would undertake.[5] But the Japanese accomplished relatively little in the war on merchant shipping; *per contra* it was *their* mercantile marine which was decimated by American submarine attacks, while Japanese underwater craft were increasingly employed to carry supplies to their isolated and by-passed garrisons in the Pacific islands. In this case the Japanese appear to have been willing to collaborate, but were hampered by technical difficulties.

---

[1] IMTFE, *Record*, p. 24616.
[2] Kretschmer said that the Tokyo Commission met twice, once in 1943 before Mussolini's fall, and once in 1944. 'Both meetings were only propagandist performances' (ibid.). General Komatsu, who was Japanese assistant military attaché in Berlin, 1941–3, and then succeeded General Banzai as military attaché, said that the Berlin Commission met 'two or three times' between December 1941 and the beginning of 1943 but not afterwards, and that all that happened were propagandist reports from the Germans (ibid. p. 33961). Oshima said much the same (ibid. p. 34043).   [3] ibid. p. 24619.   [4] ibid. p. 24625.
[5] Evidence of Oshima (ibid. pp. 34045–7, 34261–5), and of Admiral Yokoi, Japanese naval attaché, Berlin, 1940–October 1943 (ibid. pp. 33968–70).

But the third and probably the most important reason for the lack of German-Japanese collaboration was the fact that the German and the Japanese Governments remained at complete cross-purposes with regard to the Soviet Union. The Germans wanted the Japanese to come into the war against the Soviet Union and to strike at her in the Far East; the Japanese wanted the Germans to make a compromise peace with the USSR. As has been seen the Japanese, in July 1941, had in effect decided not to attack the Soviet Union unless that Power were to be decisively defeated by Germany, or allowed the Americans to establish air bases on her Far Eastern territory.[1] The Russians knew of this decision through accurate information supplied to Red Army intelligence by Richard Sorge, who for some years had operated a very efficient spy ring in Tokyo.[2] After the autumn of 1941, when Sorge and his associates were at last detected and rounded up, the Soviet Union could no longer be so sure of Japanese intentions. These in fact

[1] See Ch. VIII above. The Russians, through Sorge's information, almost certainly knew of the intended Japanese reaction to any Soviet-American air collaboration in Siberia and the Maritime Province. So, although Stalin professed to agree to the establishment of American bomber bases, his subordinates successfully obstructed all American efforts to implement this during 1943–5. See J. R. Deane, *The Strange Alliance* (London, Murray, 1947), pp. 223–39, 255–66.

[2] Richard Sorge was born in Baku of a German father and a Russian mother. His paternal grandfather had once been secretary to Karl Marx. Sorge himself had in fact been a Communist since 1919 and a member of the Comintern from 1924–9, when he transferred to Red Army Intelligence. He was sent to China in 1930 where he organized an espionage group, with headquarters in Shanghai. In 1933 he secured membership in the Nazi Party, which apparently failed to check on his antecedents, and came to Japan as correspondent of the *Frankfürter Zeitung*. He secured the confidence of Dirksen and of Ott, who in 1939 made him press attaché to the German Embassy. As the confidant of Ott and even of the Gestapo chief in Tokyo, Colonel Meissinger, Sorge was well informed on German-Japanese relations. His chief Japanese collaborator, Ozaki, was unofficial adviser to the Konoye Cabinet, 1938–9, and served the South Manchuria Railway in the same capacity. As a friend of Konoye and of Konoye's private secretaries, Ushiba and Kishi, Ozaki knew all about the decisions of Japanese Cabinet and Liaison Conferences. Thus, especially from 1938 to October 1941, Moscow was fully and accurately informed about Japanese political decisions and intentions; it also received a wealth of military and economic data. The spy ring was detected and rounded up by the Japanese police in October 1941. After a long investigation and trial, and the rejection of their appeal to the Japanese Supreme Court, Sorge and Ozaki were hanged in November 1944. The lesser members of the group were sentenced to varying terms of imprisonment, but the survivors (some had died) were released after the surrender and occupation of Japan. See C. A. Willoughby, *Sorge: Soviet Master Spy* (London, Kimber, 1952). There is also an account of Sorge and the Sorge case in Erich Kordt, *Nicht aus den Akten* (Stuttgart, Union Deutsche Verlagsgessellschaft, 1950), pp. 425–33. From this it appears that Sorge, although he had secured Nazi Party membership, was openly critical of the Nazi régime. This endeared him to Ott, himself no admirer of the Nazis. But nobody suspected that Sorge was a Communist.

remained much the same. Although up to 1944 the Kwantung Army was maintained at strength and its operational plans in the event of war were offensive in character, the Japanese Government were resolved to avoid war with the USSR, so far as it lay with them to do so.[1]

During the spring and summer of 1942 Ribbentrop repeatedly pressed Oshima to urge upon Tokyo the desirability of a Japanese attack upon Vladivostok and the Soviet Far East in conjunction with the forthcoming German drive. The German Foreign Minister pointed out that Japan could hold what she had gained only through a decisive victory of the Tripartite Powers. A joint German-Japanese attack would ensure the downfall of the Soviet Union. This would be followed by the elimination of British power in the Middle East and a successful junction of the Axis and the Japanese forces. With the Tripartite Powers triumphant in Asia, Africa, and Europe, the United States would be unable to effect anything decisive against them.[2]

But Ribbentrop spread his wares in vain; Tokyo refused to be tempted. On 30 July 1942 Oshima communicated to him the Japanese reply, which the Japanese Ambassador had received three days before. In this the Japanese Government declared that their operations to date had already made a substantial contribution to the general war. But Japan still had to cope with America and would also need to bring about the elimination of Chungking. Consequently any Japanese attack upon the Soviet Union would involve too great a dispersal of Japan's armed strength and might present opportunities for an Anglo-American counter-attack. Therefore Japan desired to maintain the *status quo* in the north, and to concentrate her efforts in the Pacific and Indian Ocean theatres of warfare.[3]

[1] The 'Otsu' operational plan of 1942 provided for an initial Japanese offensive against the Maritime Province, with a holding operation in Western Manchuria. There would also have been expeditions from Japan against North Sakhalin and Petropavlovsk, in Kamschatka. This was a General Staff plan, transmitted to the Kwantung Army (evidence of Lieut.-Col. Ryuzo Sejima, IMTFE, *Record*, pp. 8095–8121; of General Seiichi Kita, ibid. pp. 8126–32; and of General Tomokatsu Matsumura, ibid. pp. 8138–42). Kita commanded the Sixth Army in Manchukuo, 1941–4; Sejima was in the Operations Section of the General Staff, 1940–4, and Matsumura was on the Kwantung Army Staff, 1943–5.

[2] Ribbentrop to Ott, 26 March 1942, reporting conversations with Oshima on 23 March (IMTFE, *Record*, pp. 37943–6); memo. by Weizsäcker, 21 April 1942 (ibid. p. 37949); Ribbentrop–Oshima conversation, 9 July 1942 (ibid. p. 37925); also *NCA*, i. 856–7, v. 580.

[3] Conference between Ribbentrop and Oshima, 30 July 1942 (IMTFE, *Record*, pp. 37960–2).

According to the German record of the conversation, Oshima intimated that this was not necessarily a final refusal and that Japan might yet take action against the USSR in the autumn of 1942 or spring of 1943.[1] There is some, though by no means conclusive, evidence, that Tojo toyed with this idea.[2] But Japanese reverses in the summer and autumn of 1942, followed by the German catastrophe at Stalingrad, ended all thought of this and reinforced the contrasting policy of bringing about a Japanese-sponsored Soviet-German peace. Kretschmer declared that the Japanese General Staff, which up to that time had evaded any clear response, in the autumn of 1942 gave him plainly to understand that Japanese participation in the war against the USSR was out of the question.[3]

Ribbentrop evidently continued to importune Tokyo on the matter, but in the spring of 1943 received a definite refusal. On 6 March 1943 Oshima, on instructions from Tokyo, informed Ribbentrop that a Liaison Conference had been held there, which had decided that it was impossible for Japan to enter into war with the USSR. They intended, however, to take the offensive again elsewhere.[4] This did not satisfy Ribbentrop, who complained to Oshima that Germany was bearing the main burden of the war, that she was in danger of becoming overstrained and that Japan had a relatively small proportion of her army engaged in hostilities.[5] He refused to take no for an answer and continued to urge upon Oshima the need for a Japanese attack upon the USSR, and to assert that conditions would never be more favourable for this.[6]

But Tokyo remained obdurate. The Foreign Ministry and the

---

[1] ibid. pp. 37962–3. Oshima denied (though he was not very convincing) that he did any more than transmit Ribbentrop's appeals and the replies from Tokyo (evidence of Oshima, ibid. pp. 34026–7).

[2] F. von Petersdorf, who had been assistant military attaché in the German Embassy in Tokyo, said that in June or July 1942 Tojo had told Ott and Kretschmer that Japan intended to make a surprise attack on Vladivostok. He stuck to this story in cross-examination (ibid. pp. 38420–3, 38427, 38480). Tojo denied any intention to attack the USSR (ibid. p. 36483) and there is no corroboration of Petersdorf's story.

[3] Evidence of Kretschmer (ibid. pp. 24617–18).

[4] 'The Japanese Government absolutely recognizes the danger which threatens from Russia, and completely understands the desire of its German ally that Japan on her part will also enter the war against Russia. However, it is not possible for the Japanese Government, considering the present war situation, to enter into the war. It is rather of the conviction that it would be in the common interest not to start the war against Russia now' . . . (*NCA*, i. 857–8, ii. 658).

[5] ibid. i. 857–8.　　　　　　　　　　　　　[6] ibid. i. 858, v. 603.

Army were in unwonted harmony on the desirability of preserving neutrality in the Soviet-German struggle, although for very different reasons. After the German disaster at Stalingrad, the prevalent opinion in the Foreign Ministry was that Germany was doomed to defeat and that Japan had better reorient her policy before the German collapse came. The Japanese military leaders, on the other hand, believed that the struggle in Russia would develop into a stalemate, that the war in Europe would thereby be prolonged, and that Japan would consequently have plenty of time in which to consolidate her hold upon the regions she had conquered.[1] Ribbentrop evidently had some intimation that the Japanese Army held such views, but neither he nor Hitler could alter them.[2]

The irritation felt by Hitler and Ribbentrop at the Japanese refusal to join them against the USSR was accentuated by the favourable reports which Tatekawa, after his return to Tokyo, gave of the state of affairs in the Soviet Union and of its ability to hold out.[3] They were still more annoyed, during 1942, by Japanese efforts to bring about a compromise peace between Germany and the USSR. Shigenori Togo, who was a consistent advocate of peaceful relations between Japan and the USSR, had, just before Pearl Harbour, secured from Moscow a reassurance that the Soviet Government would continue to observe the neutrality pact of April 1941.[4] He had already intimated to Smetanin Japanese readiness to afford good offices in the restoration of peace between Germany and the USSR. In January 1942, when the Soviet Ambassador was going home on leave, Togo gave him a message to Molotov which reaffirmed Japan's willingness to act as go-between should the USSR desire to approach Germany on the subject of peace.[5] In July 1942 Togo instructed Naotake Sato,

[1] Kase, *Eclipse of the Rising Sun*, pp. 67–68.

[2] 'He (Ribbentrop) has worried silently, that certain forces work in Tokyo, who are of the opinion and who propagate it, that Germany would come through the fight victoriously and that therefore Japan should consolidate itself further at first, before it makes further and utmost efforts' (Minutes of Ribbentrop–Oshima discussion, 6 March 1943, *NCA*, i. 857–8).

[3] 'Tatekawa spoke too loudly about conditions in the Soviet Union. Our Ambassador, Ott, objected, and as a result, the Japanese Foreign Office has censured him and called him to order' (*Goebbels Diaries*, 15 April 1942, p. 121). On 25 April Goebbels noted that Tatekawa was taking a different tone (ibid. p. 134).

[4] Evidence of Norita, JFM official 1941–5 (IMTFE, *Record*, pp. 35937–8).

[5] Evidence of Y. Noguchi, member Euro-Asiatic Bureau, JFM, 1940–3 (ibid. pp. 35378–84).

who in February had replaced Tatekawa as Ambassador to the
USSR, and who was then in Kuibyshev, to lose no opportunity of
visiting Moscow and endeavouring to promote a Soviet-German
peace. Sato replied that he saw no possibility of this at the time.[1]
He got another instruction from Togo in mid-August; in this he
was given the draft of a new fisheries convention which would
provide him with an excuse for visiting Moscow and a chance
to bring up the subject of peace. But before Sato could obey
Togo had resigned, and this appears to have temporarily interrupted the peace efforts of the Japanese Foreign Ministry.[2]

Togo himself testified that his object was to bring about a peace
between Germany and the USSR, as a prelude to the restoration
of general peace at the earliest possible moment. He said that the
Emperor had expressed a desire for this to Tojo as early as
February 1942, but that he himself was left in ignorance of the
imperial wishes until July, when he reported to the Emperor upon
the refusal of the German request that Japan should attack the
USSR.[3]

It appears that, while Togo was trying to interest Moscow in
the possibility of a compromise peace with Germany, Konoye was
sounding the Italians about it. Indelli, the Italian Ambassador in
Tokyo, on 28 December 1941 reported to Ciano a conversation
with Konoye, in which the Prince had referred to the possibility
of a Soviet-German peace.[4] Mussolini was interested; he wanted
to see the end of the German-Soviet war, so as to free Germany
to concentrate against Great Britain and the United States. He
seems to have been afraid that Great Britain, in view of her defeats
in the Far East, would seek peace with Germany. This would
mean the end of Italian ambitions in the Mediterranean and Africa.
But the Duce did not think that the time was yet opportune to
approach Hitler on the subject of peace with Stalin.[5] In this he
was right, for Hitler was resolved to deal the USSR what he hoped
would be the finishing blow and he would listen to no other
counsels.

In March 1942 the General Staff of the Japanese Navy sent an
emissary to the German naval attaché in Tokyo, to propose
Japanese mediation in the German-Soviet War. The Japanese

---

[1] Evidence of Naotake Sato (ibid. pp. 35553–4).
[2] ibid.   [3] Evidence of Togo (ibid. pp. 35739–40).
[4] M. Mourin, *Les Tentatives de Paix dans la seconde guerre mondiale, 1939–45*
(Paris, Payot, 1949), p. 120.   [5] ibid. pp. 120–1.

Naval Staff believed that only through peace with the USSR could Germany be saved from bleeding to death. They had not been asked by Moscow to mediate, but, in view of Soviet congratulations to their representatives in Moscow on the Japanese victories in Malaya and the Philippines, they believed that the Soviet Government would not reject an offer of Japanese mediation.[1] The German naval attaché welcomed the Japanese overture and lost no time in reporting it to Admiral Raeder, whom he believed would recommend it to Hitler. But he got soundly rapped over the knuckles for his pains. He was told that Hitler wanted no such uncalled-for proposals from Japan and that the Führer suspected him of uttering defeatist sentiments which had prompted the 'absurd' Japanese proposal.[2]

That seems to have quieted the Japanese Navy but, at the end of June 1942, the Army General Staff took a hand in the game. They commissioned a staff officer, Lieut.-Colonel Tsuji, to contact the German Embassy through a German intermediary and propose that a special Japanese delegation, to be headed by a general and a member (unnamed) of the Japanese Cabinet should go by air to Germany in order to endeavour to effect a Soviet-German peace.[3] The Embassy was receptive, but warned Tsuji that the real object of the proposed mission had best not be revealed until it got to Berlin.[4] So Ribbentrop was told that the mission wanted to discuss co-operation in the prosecution of the war. He seems to have welcomed the idea at first, but he evidently soon got wind of the real object of the Japanese General Staff.[5] He revealed the scheme to Oshima, from whom Tsuji had wanted to keep it secret, and apparently said that the Japanese generals were lacking in courage.[6] Oshima and Banzai accepted Ribbentrop's assurances that Germany would inflict a decisive defeat upon the USSR, and reported in this strain to the Japanese General Staff.[7] So, apparently at the beginning of October, Tsuji expressed to the German Embassy the chagrin of the Japanese military leaders at this rebuff and

---

[1] Kordt, *Nicht aus den Akten*, p. 418.　　[2] ibid. p. 149.
[3] ibid.　　[4] ibid. p. 420.
[5] ibid. pp. 420–1. Kordt is not very precise on dates. If, as appears from his account, Ribbentrop was told of the proposed mission early in July, he may have thought that, after all, the Japanese were thinking of coming into the war against the Soviet Union. But, as has been seen, on 30 July Oshima informed him of their unwillingness to do so. This would arouse his suspicions about the mission which the Japanese Army was so anxious to dispatch, especially in view of the previous overture from the Navy.
[6] ibid. pp. 421–2.　　[7] ibid.

declared that they would make no further efforts at mediation unless Germany invited them to do so.[1]

However, there is some evidence that the Japanese General Staff *did* make another approach to Germany. General Halder is reported as saying that they sent a Colonel Uchigawa to Berlin at the end of December 1942, to suggest a Japanese-sponsored peace on the basis of German evacuation of Soviet territory, including the Baltic States, eastern Poland, Bessarabia, and the Bukovina; the division of the Balkans into German and Soviet spheres of influence; and German support for a Soviet-Turkish agreement on the Straits.[2] By this time Ribbentrop, alarmed at the Allied landings in North Africa and at the critical situation of the Wermacht at Stalingrad, had changed front and had come to favour an approach to Stalin for peace.[3] But Hitler would not hear of it.[4]

The objectives of the Japanese High Command in thus pressing Germany to come to terms with the USSR are clear enough. They wanted Germany to be in a position to concentrate her forces against the Americans and British, whereby the position of Japan would be greatly eased. They also desired to reopen communications between Japan and Germany across the Soviet Union, so that Japan might benefit from German technical aid in the military and industrial spheres. But they had no hope of success in 1942, for even had Hitler been less fanatically determined to destroy the

[1] ibid. Kordt says that an instruction came from Ribbentrop at the end of September saying that he had told Oshima that the Japanese General Staff should not propose mediation in the German-Soviet war, and that a few days later he received (through an intermediary) Tsuji's statement. The affair added to Ribbentrop's suspicion of Ott. This came to a head when, in October 1942, Ott demurred to an instruction from Ribbentrop which required him to ask the Japanese Government to place their British prisoners of war in fetters, as part of Hitler's reprisal policy against instructions to British commandos to fetter German prisoners. At the end of November Ott was told that he would be recalled on the ground that, after the Sorge case, the Japanese no longer had confidence in him. His successor was Stahmer (ibid. pp. 422–5). According to I. Krylov (*Soviet Staff Officer*, London, Falcon Press, 1951, pp. 200–2) the Japanese Army in September 1942 sounded Voroshilov on the possibility of Japanese mediation between Germany and the USSR, on the basis of a restoration of the territorial *status quo ante*. Voroshilov is said to have suggested, in addition, the payment of reparations by Germany, the recognition of Roumania and Bulgaria as in the Soviet zone of influence, and German acquiescence in Soviet negotiations with Turkey about the Straits. But the Politburo rebuked him for this and rejected the Japanese overture.
[2] Mourin, *Tentatives de paix*, p. 141. It is a little hard to believe that the Japanese General Staff, so soon after the rebuff they had received, would court another by suggesting such terms. Kordt, who was still in Tokyo at the end of 1942, makes no mention of any further Japanese overture to Germany.
[3] *NCA*, suppl. B, pp. 1203–6.   [4] ibid.

Soviet régime than in fact he was, Stalin, for his part, could have accepted no peace on German terms.

The situation in the spring of 1943 was somewhat different. The Germans had sustained a great disaster at Stalingrad, but they managed to avert a complete débâcle on the eastern front and eventually to halt the Russian counter-offensive. They could no longer hope to mount another attack on the scale of those of 1941 and 1942. On the other hand the USSR had suffered grave human and material loss and was greatly strained. Furthermore, although Stalin himself probably understood the reasons for it better than he was prepared to admit, the absence of any Anglo-American invasion of France had aroused deep suspicion and bitterness in Soviet political and military circles.[1] Added to this was American opposition to guaranteeing the return to the USSR of the territories which she had acquired during 1939–40.[2] These territories and much more besides still remained in German hands, but, with another great Axis defeat on the point of being consummated in Tunisia, Moscow may have thought that Hitler would be willing to surrender some of them in return for peace. In the spring of 1943 the Russians are said to have sounded the Germans, through the medium of the Japanese naval attaché in Stockholm, on the possibility of the restoration of peace on the basis of the frontiers of June 1941. The Germans are reported to have rejected these proposals, although they left the way open for future conversations.[3] Hitler at the time was planning a fresh offensive against the Russians which he hoped would bring about their collapse through exhaustion.[4] He refused to heed the appeals of Mussolini

[1] Churchill describes how, during his visit to Moscow in August 1942, when Stalin was bitter on hearing that there would be no invasion of France in that year, Molotov, in a separate interview remarked 'Stalin is a very wise man. You may be sure that, however he argues, he understands all' (*Second World War*, iv. 437).

[2] The Soviet Government had raised this question in December 1941, and continued to press it. Roosevelt and Hull were strongly opposed, and Churchill at first agreed with them. But in March 1942 Churchill wrote to Roosevelt asking 'for a free hand to sign the treaty which Stalin desires as soon as possible.' But Roosevelt would not agree. Consequently, when Molotov came to London in May 1942 he was unable to get the British Government to agree to a treaty guaranteeing the USSR her pre-war frontiers and in the end only a general Treaty of Alliance was signed (ibid. pp. 292–300; Hull, *Memoirs*, ii. 1165–74).

[3] Donald B. Sanders (pseud.), 'Stalin Plotted a Separate Peace', *American Mercury*, November 1947, p. 522. This article is said to be based in part on unpublished documentary material in the hands of the United States Government.

[4] On 20 March 1943, after an interview with Hitler in Berlin, Goebbels noted: 'The Fuehrer, of course, doesn't know exactly how long the Soviet Union can still hold out, but he believes that, once this colossus begins to totter, it will

who urged him either to make peace with the USSR, or at least to stand on the defensive in Russia.[1] But the German summer offensive around Kursk was heavily defeated and the Russians resumed their advance towards the Dnieper. These events coincided with the overthrow of Mussolini, the Allied conquest of Sicily, and the capitulation by Badoglio.

In this situation Shigemitsu who, in April 1943, had replaced Tani as Foreign Minister in Japan, resolved to make another attempt at mediation between Germany and the USSR. He believed that the surrender of Italy, whose Mediterranean and Balkan ambitions need no longer be taken into account, left Germany free to deal with the USSR over this region.[2] But his offer of mediation was declined by Berlin.[3] Hitler, while no longer outwardly so hostile to the idea, did not consider the time opportune to approach Stalin.[4] His immediate followers were divided in sentiment; Ribbentrop favoured an approach to Stalin, whereas Himmler thought it might be possible to reach an accord with the Western Powers, despite their unconditional surrender proclamation at Casablanca.[5]

Shigemitsu then turned to Moscow. On 10 September Sato asked Molotov for permission to send a special Japanese envoy to Moscow. It was intended that this personage should first exchange views with the Soviet Government and then proceed to Germany, Western Europe, and Turkey, returning to Moscow for further discussions with the Soviet Government. Sato answered in the affirmative to Molotov's inquiry whether the envoy's mission included any matters apart from the furtherance of Soviet-Japanese relations.[6] Three days later Molotov sent for Sato and said that the proposed Japanese mission was doubtless concerned with the

suffer a historic collapse. The Fuehrer thinks this will begin, not with a lack of supplies, but of manpower. The Soviets have sustained such bloody losses during the past winter that they simply cannot stand them much longer, though of course no one can say for how long. We must continue to fight stubbornly and tenaciously until the enemy is knocked out' (*Goebbels Diaries*, p. 242).

[1] Mourin, *Tentatives de paix*, pp. 149–50.
[2] Kase, *Eclipse of the Rising Sun*, p. 162.
[3] ibid.
[4] Goebbels saw Hitler on 23 September and noted: 'The Fuehrer does not believe that anything can be achieved at present by negotiations. . . . At present Stalin has the advantage' (*Goebbels Diaries*, p. 377). Ribbentrop at this time wrote a memorandum urging Hitler to make peace with Stalin. Ribbentrop declared that Hitler apparently agreed, but that he never gave him any authorization to attempt negotiations (IMT, Nuremberg, x. 298–9).
[5] Mourin, *Tentatives de paix*, pp. 178–9.
[6] Kase, *Eclipse of the Rising Sun*, p. 162.

attempts at mediation between the Soviet Union and Germany: 'Since the Soviet Government did not see any possibility of a truce or peace with Germany it therefore could not accept the proposal of the Japanese government although it appreciated the spirit in which it was made.' On this occasion Molotov read aloud a courteous note which included a statement that under different circumstances the Soviet Government would have considered it its duty to accept the Japanese offer of mediation.'[1]

On 16 September the Soviet chargé d'affaires in Washington, Gromyko, informed Cordell Hull of the Japanese overture and of the Soviet reply. 'The Soviet Government considered that any armistice or peace with Hitlerite Germany and her European satellites was absolutely out of the question, and therefore declined the Japanese proposal.'[2] Hull thanked Gromyko profusely for this communication, which he considered 'a decisively adverse reaction to Japan's approach.'[3]

Kase complains that the Japanese proposal came too late, at a time when Soviet relations with the United States and Great Britain were improving.[4] But, had it come earlier, the result would probably have been the same. Apart from Hitler's attitude, the preservation of the coalition against Germany afforded Stalin the chance of a greater gain than any compromise peace with Hitler could give him. The military situation was now such that the complete defeat of Germany was assured so long as her enemies remained united against her—and that defeat would leave the USSR the predominant Power in Europe. It would also enable the USSR to join in against Japan in the Far East—with the same consequences in that region. This was undoubtedly what Stalin really wanted, but, especially in view of the continued delay over the invasion of France, there was no harm in dropping a hint that the USSR had a possible second string to its bow. On the other hand, unless and until the time became ripe to strike at them, it was advisable not altogether to dash Japanese hopes of mediation, or Japan might even yet join Germany against the USSR.

It was at the Conference of Foreign Ministers in Moscow in October 1943 that Stalin and Molotov realized, probably to their own secret amazement, that the British and United States Governments were agreed upon the complete demilitarization, and ready

---

[1] ibid.
[2] Hull, *Memoirs*, ii. 1263–4.
[3] ibid.
[4] Kase, *Eclipse of the Rising Sun*, p. 163.

to consider the possible partition, of Germany after the war, together with a period of joint occupation, the trial of war criminals, the payment of reparations by Germany, and freedom of elections and political activities, except, of course, for the Nazis.[1] Hull describes with guileless satisfaction the enthusiasm with which Molotov and Stalin greeted these suggestions and declared that they exactly expressed Russia's thoughts about Germany.[2] Well they might, for nothing would more promote Soviet hegemony over eastern and central Europe or make easier the spread of Communism throughout Germany. They were careful to add, however, that these proposals should be considered as the minimum desiderata.[3]

Molotov was not at all enthusiastic about Hull's desire to include China as one of the 'Big Four' sponsors of the proposed post-war international organization, though he eventually agreed upon it.[4] The idea of China as a Great Power in the immediate future no doubt appeared to him as much an illusion as it did to Churchill. But there was no sense in alienating Roosevelt and Hull by opposing this pet project of theirs. Also, if they really supposed that China could act as a stabilizing force in the Far East, then they might be as ready to see the complete destruction of Japanese power as they apparently were of German. It may have been this which prompted Stalin, in the course of a farewell banquet in the Kremlin on 30 October, to tell Hull that after Germany had been defeated, the Soviet Union would join in against Japan.[5] Hull, who had been urging this course upon Litvinov in Washington, was naturally gratified, especially as Stalin made no conditions or demands for territory at that time.[6]

But all of Hull's pleadings and overtures of friendship could not persuade Stalin to come any farther than Teheran for the personal meeting with Roosevelt which the latter so much craved. So Teheran it eventually was.[7] In the meantime a separate conference had been held at Cairo between Chiang Kai-shek, Churchill, and

---

[1] These were contained in a document which Hull gave to Molotov. It was not an official proposal, but it embodied ideas which had been for some months discussed in Washington and between Washington and London. It envisaged political decentralization in Germany, but did not contain any specific proposals for partition, to which Hull was personally opposed. Eden said that the British Government favoured partition of Germany, but was divided on the question of compelling it (Hull, *Memoirs*, ii. 1284–8).

[2] ibid. p. 1285.   [3] ibid. p. 1287.
[4] ibid. pp. 1281–2, 1299.   [5] ibid. p. 1309.
[6] ibid. p. 1310.   [7] ibid. pp. 1308–9.

Roosevelt at which it was agreed that Japan was to be deprived not only of her conquests since 1931 but also of Formosa, the Pescadores, Korea, and the ex-German islands in the Pacific. She was thus to be expelled from the continent of Asia and in effect confined to her own islands.[1] At Teheran, on 28 November, Stalin assured Churchill and Roosevelt that when Germany was beaten and the necessary Russian reinforcements had been dispatched to the Far East 'we shall be able by our common front to beat Japan'.[2] He asked for nothing in return, indeed, at Teheran he would not say what territorial desires he had. Roosevelt on his own initiative suggested that the USSR might have access to Dairen, which would be a free port under international supervision, and that the Chinese 'would not—as Stalin suggested—object to this.'[3]

Roosevelt left Teheran believing that he had won the confidence and friendship of Stalin.[4] What Stalin really felt can only be conjectured and conjecture is dangerous. But from what immediately followed it is permissible to suggest that the Soviet leader went home in a puzzled and suspicious mood. Roosevelt had been affable and profuse in his expressions of desire for post-war cooperation; he had seemed to want to establish a special relationship between himself and Stalin, from which Churchill was somewhat excluded. But the President's talk about international trusteeships, the long-term future of China, the question of India and South East Asia and so forth must have seemed to the Soviet leader rather irrelevant to the existing situation. The German Army was still deep in Russia and Stalin's armies, as he had explained, were up against formidable difficulties in endeavouring to expel them. The all-important question for Stalin was the establishment of the second front—the invasion of northern France. In this Roosevelt had indeed supported him in his insistence that 'Overlord'—the code name for the projected invasion—should be carried out in

---

[1] The formal announcement of this did not appear until 1 December, but Sherwood (*White House Papers*, ii. 772) says that at their initial meeting on 28 November, Roosevelt told Stalin of the conversations with Chiang at Cairo.

[2] ibid. p. 774.

[3] ibid. p. 786. In September 1943, Roosevelt had told Sumner Welles that Dairen should be made a free port and that the Russians should get back the Kurile Islands and southern Sakhalin (Welles, *Seven Decisions*, p. 153).

[4] 'Roosevelt now felt sure that, to use his own term, Stalin was "getatable" . . . and that when Russia could be convinced that her legitimate claims and requirements . . . were to be given full recognition, she would prove tractable and co-operative in maintaining the peace of the postwar world' (Sherwood, *White House Papers*, ii. 790).

May 1944 and in discountenancing Churchill's proposals for operations in the Eastern Mediterranean in conjunction with the entry of
Turkey into the war, which Churchill was eager to bring about.[1]
Stalin, in addition to the execution of 'Overlord', wanted an invasion of southern France, possibly to precede 'Overlord'. But
when Stalin had asked Roosevelt who was to command 'Overlord',
the President had replied that this was not yet decided, whereupon
Stalin had said in so many words that he did not believe that
Roosevelt and Churchill seriously intended to execute the plan.[2]
In fact Roosevelt had wanted to nominate General Marshall, but
was faced with opposition in American military and naval circles
and was hesitating.[3] He could not tell Stalin this, and he would
not have removed the latter's suspicions if he had done so. Sherwood says that someone in the President's entourage told Stalin
unofficially that Marshall would be appointed and Stalin expressed
gratification and reassurance at this.[4] If this was so, the effect was
probably the worse when, shortly after Teheran, Roosevelt picked
Eisenhower instead.[5] Marshall was Chief of Staff and the senior
man; he had been at Teheran and 'both Stalin and Voroshilov
obviously recognized [him] as the supreme advocate of Overlord
and therefore their friend.'[6] The selection of Eisenhower, who
had been hitherto associated with the operations in North Africa
and the Mediterranean, may well have re-aroused Stalin's suspicions. Was Roosevelt really as guileless as he had appeared?
Was he at heart acquiescent in the enormous political and military
advantages which would accrue to the Soviet Union through the
collapse of German and of Japanese power, unless the Soviet
Union were itself also fatally weakened? Or was all his friendly
talk a blind to keep Stalin fighting Hitler until both were bled
white, to the ultimate profit of the Americans and the British?
What occurred immediately after Teheran suggests that Stalin,
for a while, inclined to this latter view.[7]

---

[1] ibid. pp. 774–6, 782–3. Churchill emphatically denies that he wanted an
invasion of the Balkans or a large-scale campaign in the Eastern Mediterranean
which would prevent the execution of 'Overlord' (*Second World War*, v. 303–4).
[2] Sherwood, *White House Papers*, ii. 782.   [3] ibid. pp. 755–8.
[4] ibid. p. 785. Churchill in good faith told Stalin that he was 'almost certain'
it would be Marshall (*Second World War*, v. 340).
[5] Sherwood, *White House Papers*, ii. 793.
[6] ibid. p. 778.
[7] Stalin told Churchill that 'if there was no big change in the European War
in 1944 it would be very difficult for the Russians to carry on' (Churchill,
Second World War, v. 335). The promise to execute 'Overlord' was conditional,

On 17 January 1944 *Pravda* published a report which, it said, came from its correspondent at Cairo, that negotiations for a separate peace were going on, probably at Lisbon, between Ribbentrop and representatives of the British Government.[1] When that was exposed as a fabrication, the Soviet press continued to give publicity to rumours of separate peace talks between Germany and the Western Democracies.[2] At the same time there is some evidence that the Germans had been sounding Moscow, through the good offices of the Japanese Legation in Stockholm, on the possibility of a German-Soviet accord, that the Russians had shown interest, but had been unwilling to accept German proposals for an autonomous State in the Ukraine and for Soviet economic assistance to Germany in her struggle against the Americans and the British.[3]

On 24 January 1944 Shigemitsu made another attempt to persuade Germany to come to terms with the USSR. He told the German Ambassador that Germany should approach Moscow for peace and be ready to give up the Ukraine in order to free herself to meet the Allied menace in Western Europe and the Mediterranean. He also suggested that Germany should emulate Japan by proclaiming the national independence of all countries under German occupation. But Hitler remained unconvinced.[4]

In April 1944 Shigemitsu again tried his luck with Moscow. On 8 April Sato recalled to Molotov the Japanese proposal of the previous September. Molotov asked whether Japan had been asked by Germany to mediate, since Tokyo now renewed its proposal for a special mission. Sato had to reply in the negative, whereupon Molotov on 12 April replied that, as there had been no alteration in the situation, there could be none in the Soviet attitude to the proposed special mission.[5]

In their reply to his suggestion of 24 January, the Germans had

not absolute. It depended on the strength of the German front line and reserve forces in France and the Low Countries (ibid. p. 327).

[1] Mourin, *Tentatives de paix*, p. 188. There was no accredited correspondent of *Pravda* at Cairo and the Egyptian authorities said that no such report had been sent from there (ibid.).   [2] ibid. pp. 188-9.

[3] Sanders in *American Mercury*, November 1947, pp. 525-6. The peace *pourparlers* are said to have occurred in December 1943 and January 1944.

[4] Telegram Ribbentrop to Tokyo, 13 Feb. 1944 (IMTFE, *Prosecution reject*). Shigemitsu's reference to the Ukraine suggests that he knew it to be a stumbling block to any possible German-Soviet accord.

[5] Kase, *Eclipse of the Rising Sun*, p. 164. On 13 April Gromyko informed Hull of this Japanese overture and of its rejection (Hull, *Memoirs*, ii. 1462).

intimated to Shigemitsu that they wanted to wait until they had repulsed the coming Anglo-American invasion of France before they approached the USSR. Shigemitsu had opined that it might then be too late.[1] His fears were justified by the event. The invasion came and so far from repelling it the German armies met with defeat, while in the east the Russians continued to roll relentlessly on. Surely now even Hitler would listen to reason. So in late August 1944 Shigemitsu raised the matter with Stahmer in Tokyo, while Oshima was instructed to do the same in Berlin.[2] But about the middle of September Stahmer received Hitler's answer and delivered it to Shigemitsu.[3] Hitler declared that there was no indication that Stalin was ready for any accommodation with Germany, nor was he likely to be until he was convinced that he could not successfully continue the war. If and when that happened 'a new political situation would be created'.[4] In view of these considerations Hitler asked the Japanese not to approach him again on the subject. He added that 'Stalin did not capitulate when we stood at the Don, the same now holds true for Germany.'[5]

Hitler, while still deluding himself that the Russian advance could be stopped and the Soviet Union brought to exhaustion, was right about Stalin's immediate attitude. On 16 September Sato once more asked Molotov for permission to send a special envoy to Moscow, ostensibly to help Sato. But Molotov divined that this was another attempt at mediation, as in part it would have been, and declined the proposal.[6] Once again, too, the Soviet Government told Washington what had occurred.[7]

By this time Japan's own situation was becoming so desperate that she would in fact have been ready to leave her obdurate ally to his fate, if only she could have secured a compromise peace. Ever since the battles of the Coral Sea and Midway the peace party in Japan had been raising its head again.[8] But at first there was little it could do. During 1942–3 Tojo appeared supreme. Under him the Imperial Rule Assistance Association, originally

---

[1] Ribbentrop to Tokyo, 13 Feb. 1944 (IMTFE, *Prosecution reject*).
[2] Evidence of Stahmer (IMTFE, *Record*, pp. 24483–4) and of Oshima (ibid. p. 34284).
[3] Evidence of Stahmer.
[4] IMTFE, *Exhibit* 3861; Ribbentrop to Tokyo, 6 Sept. 1944, *Exhibit* 2745, and evidence of Stahmer.
[5] ibid.   [6] Kase, *Eclipse of the Rising Sun*, p. 164.
[7] On 23 September 1944 (Hull, *Memoirs*, ii. 1462).
[8] Evidence of Kido (IMTFE, *Record*, p. 31065).

organized by Konoye in the hope that thereby he might checkmate the Army's plans for a totalitarian political structure, became an instrument of the military. In April 1942 Tojo and General Muto secured the election of a new Diet mainly packed with 'recommended' candidates of the Army. This was followed by the organization of the Imperial Rule Assistance Political Association, which was an attempt to create a single political party on Fascist lines. In this way Tojo endeavoured to bring the political parties to heel, while through the appointment of trusted subordinates to key positions in the Kempeitai he sought to utilize that formidable and feared organization to crush any domestic opposition to his policies. One example of this was the fate of Seigo Nakano and his Tohokai Party, which, although Fascist in sympathy, was opposed to Tojo. It was crushed by the Kempeitai in August 1943, and Nakano himself committed suicide in the following October.[1] After the resignation of Togo over the Greater East Asia Ministry question, Tojo for the time being had a subservient Cabinet at his command.

Yet Tojo was never a dictator in the sense that Hitler was. His power rested on insecure foundations. Lumping together the old political parties into one organization did not end the rivalries between them or result in a real equivalent to the Nazi Party in Germany. Nor, despite his readiness to dismiss or to exile to distant commands such generals as he distrusted and disliked, was his control over the Army complete or the factions within that body eliminated. He was, too, unable to prevent increasing strife and bitterness between the Army and the Navy, especially over the allocation of supplies and equipment. This hampered his somewhat belated efforts to organize and increase war production, which were further baulked by a good deal of quiet obstruction and sabotage on the part of the industrialists and by increasing apathy among the underfed and ill-clad populace in general.[2] Nor could Tojo get rid of the dichotomy between the General Staff and the Cabinet, even when in February, 1944, he himself assumed the additional post of Chief of the Army General Staff and made his

---

[1] Kato, *Lost War*, pp. 101–5.

[2] This popular apathy and undercover opposition was apparent even to British prisoners of war in Japan. (See Hastain, *White Coolie*, pp. 230–7; M. Weedon, *Guest of an Emperor* (London, Barker, 1948), pp. 36, 40, 65, 66, 81, 101, &c. For a survey of economic conditions in Japan during the war years, see Cohen, *Japan's Economy*, especially Ch. 2).

henchman, Admiral Shimada, Chief of the Naval General Staff as well as Minister of the Navy.[1]

Inter-service and interdepartmental rivalries were of course not peculiar to Japan, or, indeed, to the Tripartite Powers in general, though in some respects they do appear to have gone farther in Japan than elsewhere. Victory would have assuaged them, defeat exacerbated them. Tojo in some way compares favourably with the opportunists and waverers who first yielded to him and then turned against him when things went wrong. He was, according to his lights, a patriot, who believed that the rightful destiny of his country was to be the leader of East Asia and who set himself to secure that end. When all was lost and he himself was brought to trial as the first on the Allied list of Japanese war criminals, he did not deny that he had advocated what he still claimed to be a defensive war, and he accepted full responsibility for Japan's defeat.[2] But although he was the strongest personality whom Japan produced during this unhappy period, he was in no sense of the term a great man. He had none of the genius, albeit the erratic or even insane genius, of Hitler. He lacked the grasp of global strategy which Churchill and Roosevelt possessed. He was essentially a mediocrity who surrounded himself with sycophants. The result was that he himself was often ill informed on the true state of affairs in Japan itself and on the battle fronts. It may have been in part because of this that he committed the fatal error of promulgating false accounts of victories and of concealing defeats, a course which produced general disillusionment and scepticism when the true state of affairs could no longer be hidden.

From February 1943 onwards something like a conspiracy began to develop among the Jushin (ex-Premiers) against Tojo. The initiative appears to have come from Konoye, who foresaw defeat and feared a possible Communist uprising, a danger which always weighed upon him. He got into touch with Marquis Matsudaira and with Kido and told them of his concern. Kido, on 30 March 1943, saw the Emperor, who was equally concerned and agreed that

---

[1] 'It was rather too late then, I regret, to accomplish very much, but by this means even, I could not put a finger in matters affecting the Naval High Command' (evidence of Tojo, IMTFE, *Record*, p. 36480).

[2] 'I believe firmly and will contend to the last that it was a war of self-defence and in no manner a violation of presently acknowledged international law. As to the other question, the responsibility for defeat, I feel that it devolves upon myself as Premier. The responsibility in that sense I am not only willing but sincerely desire to accept fully' (ibid. pp. 36487–8).

the war should be ended as quickly as possible.[1] The peace group, which also included Wakatsuki, Hiranuma, and Okada, met secretly from time to time to discuss ways of overthrowing Tojo and of bringing the war to an end.[2] They had contacts inside the Government, including Hisatsune Sakomizu, a member of the Cabinet Planning Board, who was Okada's son-in-law, and who kept them supplied with confidential information.[3] In April 1943 they scored their first success when Shigemitsu replaced Tani as Foreign Minister. Shigemitsu was agreed on the necessity of bringing the war to a speedy end. In the following month Prince Takamatsu, the younger brother of the Emperor, was approached and sounded on his willingness to head a 'peace Cabinet', in the hope that a prince of the blood would command sufficient prestige to secure the acquiescence of the Army in a peace which would involve the relinquishment of Japanese ambitions to dominate East Asia.[4]

What, at any rate to begin with, the peace group appear to have hoped for was a compromise settlement. It was to this end that Shigemitsu bent his efforts to secure, as a beginning, a compromise between Germany and the USSR, but without avail. The Anglo-American demand, formulated at Casablanca in January 1943, for the unconditional surrender of Germany, Italy, and Japan does not at first appear to have been taken very seriously in Tokyo. The harsh terms announced at the Cairo Conference were regarded, by most members of the Japanese Government, as simply a device to bolster Chinese morale.[5] If Japan emerged from the conflict with her pre-war territories intact and those she had occupied recognized by both sides as independent, she would still be substantially the gainer.

Tojo was in one way more realist than were his adversaries. He held that a peace which would leave Japan in control of what she had gained could be obtained only when the Allied attack upon Greater East Asia had been decisively repelled. Hitler held similar views as to Europe, but, like Hitler, Tojo was unable to achieve such a victory. The American landing on Saipan in June 1944 and the defeat of the Japanese Navy in the battle of the Philippine

[1] Evidence of Kido (IMTFE, *Record*, pp. 31065–70).
[2] Evidence of Okada (ibid. p. 29263).
[3] USSBS, *Japan's Struggle to End the War* (Washington, July 1946), p. 3.
[4] Evidence of Kido (IMTFE, *Record*, pp. 31070–1).
[5] Kase, *Eclipse of the Rising Sun*, pp. 90–91.

Sea were the crucial events. Japan's inner defence line had been breached and the enemy brought within striking distance of her homeland. Tojo's failure to prevent this, which he could not conceal, was evidence of the bankruptcy of his policy, and of Japan's critical situation.[1]

For some time his power had been crumbling. The Diet was turning against him and opposition was developing even in the armed services.[2] Tojo in vain tried to save himself by endeavouring to associate the Jushin with his policy. He invited Yonai, Hirota, and Abe to join his Cabinet, but met with a sympathetic response only from Abe. The others refused and Abe then too held off.[3] On 17 July 1944 the Jushin met at Hiranuma's residence, and all, except Abe, agreed that Tojo must go.[4] Kido duly reported this decision to the Emperor.[5]

Tojo fought back. He had already thrown Shimada to the wolves and replaced him by Admiral Naokuni Nomura, who had returned from Berlin and who injudiciously accepted the post. On 18 July Tojo resigned as Chief of the Army General Staff in favour of General Yoshijiru Umezu, the Commander-in-Chief of the Kwantung Army. But all was in vain, two of Tojo's own Cabinet Ministers deserted him and declared in favour of a new administration. So, on 18 July, he reluctantly gave way and resigned.[6]

The Jushin had thus scored a great success, but they were divided among themselves as to the choice of a successor to Tojo. It was agreed that the time was not yet ripe for a royal prince to come forward.[7] His colleagues wanted Admiral Yonai to become Premier, but he refused to do so, in which he was no doubt wise.[8] So it was agreed that an Army man should be chosen. Marshal Terauchi, the Supreme Commander in the southern theatre of war, was at first suggested, but was opposed by Tojo who was his personal enemy.[9] So in the end the choice fell on General Kuniaki Koiso, who was then Governor-General of Korea. But

---

[1] Kase says that a friend of his, Captain Watanabe, a member of the Council of Military Affairs, on 21 June told him the truth about the Japanese defeat. Kase told Marquis Matsudaira, Kido's private secretary. Thus the news reached Kido and he told the Emperor (ibid. pp. 73–75).   [2] ibid. pp. 76–77.
[3] ibid. pp. 79–80.   [4] ibid. p. 80.
[5] Evidence of Kido (IMTFE, *Record*, pp. 31077–9) and of Okada (ibid. pp. 29263–4).   [6] Kase, *Eclipse of the Rising Sun*, p. 81.
[7] Evidence of Kido (IMTFE, *Record*, p. 31080).
[8] Evidence of Kido (ibid.).
[9] ibid., also Kido's Diary for 18 July 1944 (*Exhibit* 1278) and evidence of Okada (*Record*, pp. 29264–6).

Konoye distrusted Koiso and it was he who successfully urged that the imperial mandate should be given to both Koiso and Yonai, the latter thus being in effect Vice-Premier as well as Minister of the Navy.[1] Another struggle occurred over the War Ministry. Tojo wanted to retain it; in this he failed, but he was able to block Koiso from being restored to the active list of the Army, which would have enabled the new Premier to be Minister of War as well. As a compromise General Sugiyama obtained the post.[2] Shigemitsu continued as Foreign Minister and was also concurrently head of the Greater East Asia Ministry.

The Koiso Cabinet was really a makeshift affair, for which no one had any enthusiasm. A large part of the Army was sullen over the fall of Tojo and opposed to Koiso. Yonai, who had not wanted to be Premier at a time when, as he doubtless foresaw, fresh defeats were impending, did not assert his authority as Vice-Premier.[3] Kido and the Jushin, who had picked Koiso because an Army appointee was necessary to placate that service, appear by now to have been pretty well ready to consider the war irretrievably lost and to accept the Allied terms, at least so far as the loss of Japan's empire was concerned.[4] But they knew that the Army was not and they dared not yet openly oppose it on this issue. A too precipitate move might provoke a revolt among the 'young officer' group, and the establishment of some sort of 'national Communist' movement, which Konoye in particular greatly feared. Moreover there was the great stumbling-block of the Allied demand for unconditional surrender. The armed services were ready to fight to the death rather than accept this and the Court party feared that the Allies might be intending to overthrow the Japanese monarchy itself. Unless they could be assured that this was not the case, they could not advise the Emperor to command his forces to lay down their arms.[5]

So the business of the Koiso Cabinet was to carry on the war as best it might, while losing no opportunity to secure a compromise peace. Koiso, like his predecessor, was faced with the problem of ensuring harmony and effective co-operation between

[1] When Yonai refused, Konoye had suggested Admiral Kantaro Suzuki, but was overruled.
[2] Kase, *Eclipse of the Rising Sun*, p. 84.   [3] ibid. pp. 85–87.
[4] On 29 June 1944 Prince Takamatsu told Shigemitsu that he personally considered the war should be ended without delay, provided that the Imperial House was left intact (ibid. p. 77).
[5] USSBS, *Japan's Struggle to End the War*, pp. 5–6.

the Cabinet and the Supreme Command. With this object in view he established, in August 1944, the 'Supreme Council for the Direction of the War'. This met in the Imperial Palace and held discussions in the Emperor's presence. It normally consisted of six members: the Prime Minister, the Ministers of War, of the Navy and of Foreign Affairs, and the Chiefs of the General Staff. Other Ministers and the Vice-Chiefs of Staff could attend when necessary. This differed from the former Liaison Conference in one important respect—the Emperor being present at the discussion of policy (as distinct from the ratification of decisions already made) *could* intervene to speak the final word in the event of a deadlock. But, as with the Liaison Conference, there was a secretariat which included the director of the Military Affairs Bureau of the Army and his opposite number in the Navy. That meant that no policy could be formulated which would not at once become known to the services in general, including the 'younger officers'. Thus, under Koiso, the new body differed little from its predecessor.[1]

In the summer of 1944 the one bright spot in Japan's situation appeared to be in her relations with the USSR. The Japanese had carefully observed the Neutrality Pact of 1941, there had been no further serious boundary conflicts since 1939, and at sea the Japanese Navy had been very circumspect in its treatment of Soviet vessels. Japan had refused German requests to stop the movement of supplies across the Pacific to Vladivostok. The Japanese Navy, after the outbreak of the Pacific War, had established sea lanes for Soviet vessels to pass, and, while bringing some in for examination, had let them go, even when it was obvious that they were American ships very lately transferred to the Soviet flag.[2] In March 1944 the Japanese Government had belatedly kept the promise, made by Matsuoka at the time of the Neutrality Pact, to relinquish their coal and oil concessions in northern Sakhalin.[3]

Therefore the Japanese thought that they could look to the USSR as a mediator between them and their enemies. They had

---

[1] Kase, *Eclipse of the Rising Sun*, pp. 87–89.
[2] Evidence of Masamichi Fujita, member of Naval Affairs Bureau of Navy Ministry, 1942–5 (IMTFE, *Record*, pp. 23505–12).
[3] Kase, *Eclipse of the Rising Sun*, p. 163. In return the Russians had agreed to extend the Fisheries Convention for five years (evidence of Sato, *Record*, p. 23583).

observed that Stalin had kept clear of the Cairo Conference and the Chinese, and they were, of course, ignorant of the promises which he had made to Hull and to Roosevelt at Moscow and Teheran. Some high Japanese Army officers even thought that, after the defeat of Germany, Stalin would fall out with Great Britain and the United States, and that he might then be ready to assist Japan with supplies of raw materials, as he had done Germany during 1939–41.[1] The Japanese Government in general did not hold this view, but they thought that Soviet mediation might be purchased— and they were ready to pay a high price for it.

On 12 September 1944, at a time when the collapse of Germany seemed imminent, the Japanese Cabinet discussed a draft, placed before them by Shigemitsu, of policy towards the Soviet Union. He defined the objectives, in ascending order, as the maintenance of peace (the Neutrality Pact) between Japan and the USSR, the realization, if possible, of a Soviet-German peace, and the improvement of Japan's position, through the assistance of the Soviet Union, in the event of a German collapse.[2] Shigemitsu proposed that a special envoy should be sent to Moscow to see what could be obtained. If the Russians were prepared to agree only to the preservation of the Neutrality Pact, Japan might in turn agree to a new demarcation of the Manchukuo–Outer Mongolian border and possibly the establishment of demilitarized zones, or a mutual reduction of forces in those regions.[3] In the event of the USSR agreeing to a Japanese-sponsored peace with Germany, Japan should, if necessary, return to the USSR the north Manchurian railway and agree to a Soviet sphere of interest in north Manchuria and Inner Mongolia, surrender her fishing rights in Soviet waters and abrogate the Tripartite Pact and the Anti-Comintern Pact. If the Soviet Union sponsored a general peace, Japan should be ready in return to concede all the above things and also cede southern Sakhalin and the Kuriles. Except for the Kuriles, she should be prepared to pay the same price for a Soviet-sponsored peace with Chiang Kai-shek.[4] The Cabinet agreed upon the dispatch of a special envoy to Moscow and the opening of negotiations.[5] But, as has been seen, the Soviet Government refused their assent to the proposed special mission.

[1] Kase, *Eclipse of the Rising Sun*, p. 153.
[2] IMTFE, *Exhibit* 3557.   [3] ibid.   [4] ibid.
[5] ibid. It was intended to send Koki Hirota (Kase, *Eclipse of the Rising Sun*, p. 165).

On 15 October 1944, at the time of the Moscow Conference between Stalin, Churchill, Eden, the American Ambassador Averell Harriman, and Major-General Deane, head of the American military mission to the USSR, the Soviet leader declared that the USSR would take the offensive against Japan three months after the defeat of Germany, provided that the United States would assist in building up the necessary supplies for the sixty divisions which the Red Army needed for the operation and also that the political aspects of Soviet participation had been clarified—a hint that he wanted something in return.[1] At the third meeting on 17 October Stalin reiterated this promise and also revealed the plan for the Soviet offensive, which was to be a holding operation in north and east Manchuria and a main thrust through Inner Mongolia aimed at Kalgan, Peking, and Tientsin.[2]

On 7 November, in the course of his speech on the anniversary of the Bolshevik revolution, Stalin publicly characterized Japan as an aggressor State. This came as a great shock to Tokyo and Sato was instructed to find out what it portended. Molotov assured him that Stalin was referring only to Japan's conduct in the past and meant no criticism of her existing policy. With these smooth words the Japanese had perforce to be content.[3] For the time being, however, this episode ended any further approaches to the Soviet Union.

In mid-September 1944 the Swedish Minister in Tokyo, Mr. Widor Baggë, was approached by Bunshiro Suzuki, a director of the *Asahi* and a man with many influential political connexions. Suzuki put forward a peace proposal, which he said came from Konoye and his associates. This intimated that Japan was prepared to surrender all her wartime conquests, and possibly Manchukuo as well. Baggë was requested to forward this to Stockholm with the idea that London should be sounded upon it, the idea being that the British Government might be more receptive to it than would the American.[4] Baggë reported this to Stockholm. It would appear that the Japanese got some word in return that they would have to accept unconditional surrender, for Baggë spoke of subsequent

---

[1] Deane, *Strange Alliance*, pp. 146–7.
[2] ibid. pp. 148–9. The Russians demanded two months' supplies of food, fuel, transport equipment, etc., for a force of 1½ million men, by 30 June 1945. The Americans delivered 80 per cent. of these supplies by that date (ibid.).
[3] Kase, *Eclipse of the Rising Sun*, pp. 96–97.
[4] Affidavit of Baggë (IMTFE, *Record*, pp. 34559–60).

conversations with Suzuki in which the latter said that unconditional surrender was one of the great obstacles to peace for everyone would prefer to continue the war to the bitter end rather than see the Emperor subjected to insult.[1] In December 1944 the King of Sweden remarked to the Japanese military attaché that he felt a lively concern for the preservation of the monachy in Japan. The Swedish Prime Minister said that King Gustav's remark could be taken as a veiled invitation to ask for Swedish mediation. But the military attaché, a former supporter of the Tripartite Pact, never reported this conversation and Tokyo remained unaware of it until after the war.[2]

Suzuki's overtures had been unofficial, but in the spring of 1945, just before Baggë was due to return home, Shigemitsu had a conversation with him.[3] Shigemitsu told him that the military clique were responsible for the war and that it was now for Japanese diplomats to extricate their country from it. He asked Baggë to co-operate with Suemasa Okamoto, Japanese Minister to Sweden, in ascertaining the possibility of a negotiated peace.[4] But when Baggë got back to Sweden and called on Okamoto, he found the latter had received no instructions.[5] The fall of the Koiso Cabinet had occurred in the meantime, and Togo, the new Foreign Minister, preferred to try his hand with the Soviet Union.[6]

Undercover peace feelers from Tokyo through Shanghai or Hong Kong had been an almost constant feature of the Sino-Japanese conflict. In 1944 the Japanese peace group associated with Konoye made yet another effort. In October Konoye's younger brother, Baron Tadamaro Miyagawa, came to Shanghai and got into touch with former Chinese acquaintances of Konoye, who were, or had become, Chinese secret agents. These had been for some time in correspondence with Miyagawa and had sent him what were, or purported to be, Chinese terms for a settlement. These included the cessation of all Japanese military operations, to be followed by negotiations on the basis of the Cairo Declaration. Miyagawa came to say that in general the proposals were

---

[1] ibid. p. 34561.

[2] Kase, *Eclipse of the Rising Sun*, p. 221.

[3] Kase says that he persuaded Shigemitsu to do this (ibid. p. 220).

[4] Evidence of Baggë (IMTFE, *Record*, pp. 34561–2).

[5] ibid. pp. 34562–3. Okamoto questioned Togo, who replied that as this had been a matter handled by the previous Cabinet it would need investigation.

[6] ibid. p. 35464. Togo referred to the overture to Baggë in his evidence, but said that nothing came of it (ibid. p. 35780).

acceptable to the peace group, and to ask for some official move by the Chinese Government. But nothing came of this and it seems likely that the Chinese response to these Japanese overtures was simply intended to find out what was going on in Japan.[1] Kase remarks that the attempts at peace with China were 'mostly handled by so-called experts on China who, in spite of their professed honesty, often made a thriving business of it.'[2] In March 1945 Koiso appears to have been hoaxed by a Chinese called Miao Ping, who professed to be a confidential emissary from Chiang Kai-shek. He came to Tokyo from Shanghai on Koiso's invitation and apparently proposed that in return for Japanese withdrawal from China and abandonment of the Nanking régime, Chiang would oppose any American landing in China and was prepared to co-operate with Japan against the Communist danger. But the Supreme War Council opposed Koiso's efforts at diplomacy and suspected that the supposed Chinese agent was a fake. This affair contributed to the overthrow of Koiso.[3]

On 4 April Koiso informed Kido of his intention to resign. He had again been rebuffed by the Army when he desired to be restored to the active service list, in order to assume, concurrently with the Premiership, the post of War Minister. He was, moreover, discredited by the series of crushing defeats which Japan had sustained during his period of office. He now suggested that an 'Imperial Headquarters Cabinet' should be formed, i.e. one in which the Premier was invested with the powers of the Chiefs of Staff. But Kido ascertained that no one else was in favour of such a step.[4]

On 4 April Koiso submitted the resignation of his Cabinet and that evening Kido met the Jushin to decide on a successor. Yonai, as Navy Minister in the outgoing Cabinet, was, according to etiquette, not present. Tojo, as an ex-Premier, was; so also was Admiral Baron Suzuki, as President of the Privy Council.[5] However, Kido had previously consulted Yonai and had discovered that he wanted Admiral Suzuki as Premier. So did most of the other Jushin, including Okada, who was a relative of Suzuki.[6] But not

[1] W. R. Fishel, 'A Japanese Peace Manœuvre in 1944', *FEQ*, August 1949, pp. 387–97.   [2] Kase, *Eclipse of the Rising Sun*, p. 184.
[3] ibid. p. 108; also evidence of Kido (IMTFE, *Record*, pp. 31115–16).
[4] ibid. p. 31119.   [5] Kase, *Eclipse of the Rising Sun*, p. 111.
[6] As Kido had known. That astute individual always tried to get things cut and dried in advance.

Tojo. He brought up the real issue at stake by declaring that the choice of a new Premier should depend on the policy which was to be followed—either to fight to a finish or to make peace, even if it meant unconditional surrender. He stood for the first course and he demanded that General Hata should be selected, to head an administration which would have to cope with an invasion of Japan itself. When he met with unanimous opposition to another Army Cabinet, Tojo threatened that the Army would not co-operate with any other kind and would bring it down. But Kido countered by warning Tojo that the people, tired of the war and increasingly hostile to the Army, might turn against it. So Tojo had to give way and Suzuki was selected.[1]

Admiral Baron Kantaro Suzuki was at this time nearly eighty. He had a distinguished naval record and, after his retirement from the Navy, had become Grand Chamberlain to the Palace. In the Army mutiny of February 1936 he was badly wounded and saved from death only by the courage of his wife. He belonged to the older generation which remembered the days when Japan was an ally of Great Britain and a friend of the United States, and he had no hand in the events which led up to the Pacific War. His appointment was mainly for this very reason—it was intended as a gesture of appeasement to Japan's foes.[2]

On the other hand Suzuki *was* an admiral, and one of those who had played a part in the making of Japan as a Great Power. He no more than the others could stomach the idea of unconditional surrender, occupation, and disarmament. Shigenori Togo, whom Suzuki says he personally selected as Foreign Minister, found the aged admiral talking in terms of two or three years' more war and was consequently at first inclined to refuse the post.[3]

But Suzuki's initial attitude was in part owing to his ignorance of the true state of affairs and of the desperate plight to which Japan had been already reduced. On this matter the peace group lost no time in enlightening him, and they were close about him. Sakomizu became chief secretary to the Cabinet and Colonel Matsutani, an early adherent of the peace movement, became

[1] IMTFE, *Exhibit* 1282 (Kido's Diary); Kase, *Eclipse of the Rising Sun*, pp. 111–15.

[2] Konoye had been especially insistent that the new Premier should be a man unconnected with the politics of the past decade (ibid. p. 113).

[3] Evidence of Admiral Suzuki (IMTFE, *Record*, p. 35590) and of Togo (ibid. pp. 35578–9).

Suzuki's private secretary.[1] Moreover the advocates of peace knew that Suzuki was thoroughly loyal to the Emperor and they also knew that the Emperor was ready to come out in favour of peace so soon as this could be done without precipitating an Army revolt. Of the other leading members of the Cabinet, Yonai, who continued as Navy Minister, was one of the mainstays of the peace group and they could also count on Togo. The new War Minister, General Korechiko Anami, to the end remained opposed to unconditional surrender. So were the Chiefs of Staff, Umezu and Toyoda. Yet these three men, although counted as belonging to the war party, were not fanatics. It is significant that they did not betray the discussions of the Supreme Council for the Direction of the War, nor attempt to stir up revolt when the final decision to surrender was taken.

Soon after the inauguration of the Suzuki Cabinet it was agreed that future meetings of the Supreme Council should consist of the six regular members, exclusive of the directors of the Military and the Naval Affairs Bureaux. In this way the 'young officer' group could be kept from knowing what went on at the Council meetings. It also meant that, once Suzuki could be won over completely, the Council would be evenly balanced. Then, if a deadlock occurred, the decision could be left to the Emperor, as was to happen. Furthermore a new secretarial staff was organized. This consisted of Colonel Matsutani, as representative of the Premier and the War Minister; Admiral Takagi, representative of the Navy Minister; Toshikazu Kase, representing Togo; and Marquis Matsudaira, Kido's private secretary, as representative of the Lord Privy Seal.[2] All four were advocates of peace, including, if necessary, unconditional surrender. That Anami and the Chiefs of Staff were ready to accept such arrangements shows that they were not really diehards. They knew that the war was lost but they still hoped that

[1] Kase, *Eclipse of the Rising Sun*, p. 144. Colonel Matsutani, as a section chief of the General Staff, had in early 1944 organized group meetings of Army and Navy junior staff officers, with a view to getting them to see the realities of the military situation. He had also passed on information to Kase. In early July he was exiled to the China front by Tojo, to whom he had broached the subject of peace. After the fall of Tojo, Shigemitsu effected Matsutani's recall and appointment as ADC to the War Minister (ibid. pp. 75–76, 144).

[2] ibid. pp. 145–6. Rear-Admiral Soichi Takagi, a member of the Naval General Staff, had in March 1944 presented the results of his investigations of the war situation to Yonai. Takagi held that Japan should seek peace, even at the price of relinquishing Korea and Formosa (USSBS, *Japan's Struggle to End the War*, p. 3).

Japan might obtain some kind of terms which would avoid the disgrace of surrender and occupation. They also had to consider the prevailing attitude in the armed forces. This view, stimulated by the desperate Japanese resistance on Okinawa and the heavy losses inflicted upon the Americans, was that Japan could repel an invasion of her main islands and then could get honourable terms of peace. The peace group did not believe this. They saw that Japan's economy was fast running down, her stocks of food and raw materials were being rapidly depleted, and her cities devastated by air attack. They foresaw that, if the war was prolonged much more, complete collapse and ruin, involving the fall of the monarchy, would in all probability occur. To avoid this they were ready to surrender if they must, thereby hoping to save the dynasty, which they succeeded in doing.[1]

Meanwhile both sides were agreed that no chance should be lost of securing a negotiated peace. It was here that the choice of Togo as Foreign Minister was significant. He had always been an advocate of friendly relations with the Soviet Union and his appointment was an indirect appeal to that Power.[2] The Japanese did not know that, at the Yalta Conference in February 1945, Stalin had agreed to fall upon them in August, in return for a secret guarantee that he should receive south Sakhalin and the Kuriles, as well as railway and harbour concessions in Manchuria. On 22 February Molotov, in response to an inquiry from Sato, had assured the Japanese Ambassador that Far Eastern questions had been entirely excluded from the discussions at Yalta. He had added that Soviet-Japanese relations were conducted on a basis of neutrality and so were a matter for these two Powers alone, just as Japanese relations with Great Britain and the United States, with whom Japan was at war, concerned those three Powers alone.[3]

Then, on 5 April, Molotov called in Sato and informed him that the USSR did not intend to continue the Neutrality Pact of 1941 after its expiry in April 1946. In answer to Sato's inquiry Molotov

---

[1] 'The Army said: "Give us a last opportunity to prove our worth and vindicate our honor." We replied; "The issue of the last battle is so easy to predict that it will be far wiser to cease hostilities while the mainland still remains intact and before we have lost the power of resistance completely"' (Kase, *Eclipse of the Rising Sun*, p. 150).

[2] Marquis Matsudaira and Sakomizu both testified that they urged Togo to accept the post (IMTFE, *Record*, pp. 35394–606). Hirota, Okada, and Kido also gave him the same advice.

[3] Evidence of Sato (ibid. p. 23579).

said that the Soviet Government recognized that the Pact continued in force for another year and that their attitude to Japan
would be determined by this fact. Only after the expiration of the
full term of five years would Soviet-Japanese relations revert to
the *status quo ante*.[1]

In view of these positive assurances from Molotov and of the
increasing indications of difference between the USSR and the
Western Democracies, it was not unnatural for the Japanese
Government to suppose that their powerful and enigmatic neighbour might be induced to keep the peace with them and perhaps
even to mediate on their behalf. If the Soviet Union were going
to fall out with the United States, Moscow might have reason to
save Japan from complete defeat and occupation by American
forces.

The way for a renewed Japanese approach to Moscow was cleared
by the surrender of Germany. On 6 May Togo issued a statement
in which, after referring to the efforts of Himmler and Doenitz to
capitulate to Great Britain and the United States but to continue
the war against the Soviet Union, he declared that this was not in
accordance with the provisions of the Tripartite Pact and that
therefore Japan retained freedom of action in respect of that instrument and of her other political agreements with Germany.[2] That
meant their nullification, and, after the definite surrender of Germany, Togo on 15 May secured the denunciation of the Anti-
Comintern Pact.[3]

Thus, so far as they could, the Japanese Government had tried
to wipe out the past and to meet Stalin's reproach of 7 November
1944, as it had been interpreted to them. On 14 May the Supreme
War Council decided to approach the Soviet Union, in the first
instance for a renewal of the Neutrality Pact. Should the Soviet
response be at all encouraging a definite treaty of non-aggression

[1] ibid. pp. 23579–80.
[2] Kase, *Eclipse of the Rising Sun*, p. 127.
[3] Evidence of Togo (IMTFE, *Record*, p. 35662). On 15 May 1945 the Japanese
Foreign Ministry issued the following statement: 'Owing to the unconditional
surrender of Germany and other recent developments in Europe, the Tripartite
accord between Nippon, Germany, and Italy concluded on 11 December 1941,
the Tripartite Pact between Nippon, Germany, and Italy concluded on 26
September 1940, and various other relevant agreements providing for special
collaboration as between Nippon and Germany and other European Powers are
deemed to have ceased to be effective' (*Syonan Sinbun*, 16 May 1945). On 16
May the Nanking Government followed suit in a statement which, in abrogating
the Anti-Comintern Pact, referred to the surrender of Germany and Italy and
to the Soviet dissolution of the Comintern (ibid. 18 May 1945).

was to be proposed. Hirota, the ex-Premier and former Ambassador to Moscow, was commissioned to sound Malik, the Soviet Ambassador in Tokyo.[1]

At their first conversations, held on 3 and 4 June, Malik's reaction to Hirota's overtures seemed not entirely unfavourable. But when, a fortnight later, Hirota sought to follow up the initial talks, Malik pleaded indisposition and would not receive him.[2] However, two further interviews took place, on 24 and 29 June. At the fourth and last meeting, Hirota definitely proposed 'a non-aggression pact pledging mutual support in order to establish an enduring cordial friendship between Japan and the Soviet Union, thereby contributing toward the preservation of a permanent peace in East Asia.' In return for this he offered that Japan, at the end of the Pacific War, would withdraw her forces from Manchukuo, which might be neutralized by Soviet-Japanese agreement. Japan was also ready to relinquish her fishery rights in Soviet waters, if she could be assured of Soviet oil supplies. Hirota also hinted that Japan would be amenable to any other conditions which the Soviet Government might raise. But Malik showed indifference and promised only to transmit the offer to Moscow by the regular courier—a slow process.[3] Sato, who had been informed of the Hirota–Malik conversations and who had raised the subject with Molotov, found him indifferent.[4]

Meanwhile Japan's position was becoming daily more critical. When Germany surrendered the Japanese Government had announced their decision to continue the war.[5] At the instance of the Army a full-dress meeting of the Supreme War Council was held on 6 June, which adopted the military policy of a struggle to the end.[6] This decision was on 8 June ratified at a formal Imperial Conference.[7] These events constituted a set-back for the peace group, but its members did not lose hope. They were gaining in strength and they knew that the outwardly sacrosanct decisions of Imperial Conferences had been set aside in the past. A report on 'The Present State of Material Power', submitted at this time to the Supreme War Council, showed that, under existing conditions,

[1] Evidence of Togo (IMTFE, *Record*, p. 35782; Kase, *Eclipse of the Rising Sun*, p. 170).
[2] Kase, *Eclipse of the Rising Sun*, pp. 170–1.
[3] ibid. pp. 187–8.   [4] ibid. p. 188 n.
[5] ibid. p. 129.   [6] ibid. pp. 171–2.
[7] ibid. p. 173; evidence of Kido (IMTFE, *Record*, pp. 31146–7).

Japan could not carry on beyond the autumn.[1] Although the Army sought to rectify this by fresh drastic measures of mobilization and control of men and materials, such steps could not offset the grim fact that Japan, an island Power which had lost her fleet, was being steadily throttled.[2] By mid-June the end was at hand in Okinawa.[3] On 18 June the six members of the Supreme War Council met secretly and agreed to seek peace through the medium of the Soviet Union and to obtain terms which would at least ensure the preservation of the monarchy.[4] The peace party urged Kido to advise the Emperor to cancel the Imperial Conference decision of 8 June.[5] This the Lord Keeper did, with the result that on 22 June the Emperor summoned the Supreme War Council and commanded them to lose no time in taking steps to restore peace, and to disregard the decision of 8 June. This, despite some protest from Umezu, they agreed to do.[6]

There was need for haste. Reports of a coming 'Big Three' Conference at Potsdam had reached Tokyo. Further, the Chinese Foreign Minister, T. V. Soong, was in Moscow and had been received by Stalin. This news, coupled with intelligence of Soviet troop movements from Europe to the Far East, was of ominous import. The Kwantung Army was in no shape to face a Russian assault. Its best divisions had, during 1944, been withdrawn for service on the battle fronts and in defence of the homeland. They were being replaced by reserve divisions of indifferent quality and poorly equipped.[7] Its operational plan was now a defensive one, which provided for a retreat from northern and central Manchuria and a last stand in the south-east and along the Korean border.[8]

---

[1] Kase, *Eclipse of the Rising Sun*, pp. 172–3. See also USSBS, *Japan's Struggle to End the War*, p. 6 and pp. 16–21.

[2] The Army plans took shape in the Wartime Emergency Measure and the National Volunteer Fighting Corps Bill, which were both passed by the Diet on 22 June. The first gave the Government practically despotic power over capital and labour, the second provided for a *levée en masse* of the entire population.

[3] On 22 June the Americans announced the end of fighting on the island. The Japanese Government admitted its loss in an 'Instruction to the Nation' of 26 June (Kase, *Eclipse of the Rising Sun*, p. 186).

[4] ibid. p. 184; evidence of Kido (IMTFE, *Record*, p. 31159).

[5] Kase, *Eclipse of the Rising Sun*, p. 185.

[6] ibid. pp. 185–6; also evidence of Kido (IMTFE, *Record*, pp. 31160–3).

[7] Evidence of General Yukio Kasahara, Chief of Staff of the Kwantung Army, August 1942–April 1945. He said that by the end of 1944 there were no highly trained divisions left, few tanks and aircraft, and limited stocks of munitions and fuel (IMTFE, *Record*, p. 23201).

[8] ibid. This evidence was borne out by that of General Matsumura, chief of the Operations Section of the Kwantung Army Staff, 1943–5 (ibid. pp. 8138–50).

But there was small hope of stemming a Russian invasion for long, and the loss of Manchuria and Korea would entail the complete blockade of Japan and her severance from all supplies from the Continent of Asia.

So, on 7 July, prompted by Kido, the Emperor sent for Suzuki and urged that no more time be lost in seeking Soviet good offices for the restoration of peace. For this purpose a special envoy with a message from the Emperor should be sent to Moscow.[1] On 10 July the Supreme War Council agreed to this, and two days later the Emperor sent for Konoye, who from the first had been designated for the task, and entrusted him with the mission.[2] Konoye was eager to go, for he believed that only a swift end to hostilities could save the dynasty.[3]

On 12 July Togo telegraphed instructions to Sato to inform Molotov of the Emperor's desire for peace, provided it were not unconditional surrender, and to ask for permission to dispatch the Konoye mission.[4] Sato replied the next day that Molotov, about to leave for Potsdam, had been unable to see him, but that he had delivered the message to the Vice-Foreign Minister, Lozovsky, together with a letter from himself to explain that the purpose of the proposed Konoye mission was quite different from that of the projected missions of 1943-4. Lozovsky had replied that it was impossible to make any reply before Molotov left for Berlin, though he agreed to transmit the communications to Molotov and arrange for consultation with him while at the German capital.[5]

This was apparently done, for on 18 July Lozovsky informed Sato that, by order of the Soviet Government, he was to state that since the Emperor's message contained no concrete proposals, and since it was uncertain what was the object of the proposed Konoye mission, the Soviet Government were unable to give any definite reply, either to the message, or to the request to be allowed to dispatch the mission.[6] Sato on 19 July reported this to Togo. Apparently at about the same time he advised the Foreign Minister that Japan would have to state her intentions definitely and also be prepared to accept unconditional surrender.[7] Togo in reply sent two instructions on 21 July. The first, for transmission to the Soviet Government, said that Konoye would come to seek Soviet

---

[1] Kase, *Eclipse of the Rising Sun*, p. 188.   [2] ibid. pp. 188-9.
[3] Evidence of Kido (IMTFE, *Record*, pp. 31170-1).
[4] IMTFE, *Exhibit* 2696.   [5] *Exhibit* 2697.   [6] *Exhibit* 2699.
[7] Kase (*Eclipse of the Rising Sun*, p. 204) says Sato repeatedly gave this advice.

good offices to end the war and would also make clear that Japan desired to pursue a co-operative policy towards the Soviet Union, both during and after the war. That did not take matters much further.[1]

In the second instruction Togo declared that 'we cannot accept unconditional surrender in any circumstances.' The Japanese people, he said, would rise as one man against the enemy if he persisted in this demand. But Japan wanted peace, so long as it was not complete surrender. He went on:

> We cannot ask the Soviet Union to use its good offices without attaching any conditions; at the same time it would be impossible as well as disadvantageous in view of the domestic situation as well as external relations to set forth concrete terms of peace immediately now. In such delicate circumstances Prince Konoye shall convey to the Soviet Government the concrete intention of Japan based upon the Imperial wishes and, after giving full consideration to the Russian demands in East Asia, he shall request the Soviet Government after consultation to negotiate with Britain and the United States.[2]

Konoye, then, was coming to ask the Soviet Government to get the best terms they could for Japan, and he was prepared to pay a good price for them. Togo's instructions of 21 July were delayed in reaching Sato, so that he was not able to carry them out until 25 July.[3] He then assured Lozovsky that Konoye *would* bring definite proposals and that they would cover both the ending of the war and the improvement of Soviet-Japanese relations—i.e. he would have something to offer the USSR.[4]

Meanwhile Truman and Stalin had discussed the question of Soviet participation in the war against Japan at their first meeting in Potsdam on 17 July.[5] Stalin said he had not yet arrived at an agreement with the Chinese, especially in regard to the administration of Dairen. The Russians were asking for somewhat more than had been promised them at Yalta and the new American Secretary of State, Mr. Byrnes, supported the Chinese in resistance to this.[6] At a subsequent meeting Stalin told Truman and Byrnes of the Japanese appeal for Soviet mediation, and of the proposed Konoye mission. He said that the Japanese had been told that their communication was too general in tone to be given a definite reply.[7]

[1] IMTFE, *Exhibit* 2700.   [2] *Exhibit* 2701.
[3] Kase, *Eclipse of the Rising Sun*, p. 205.   [4] IMTFE, *Exhibit* 2703.
[5] J. F. Byrnes, *Speaking Frankly* (London, Heinemann, 1947), p. 205.
[6] ibid.   [7] ibid.

This was what a loyal associate should have done; on the other hand it could be construed as a hint that Stalin had another string to his bow if his demands on China were not fully met.

On 2 July the United States Secretary of War, Mr. Stimson, had submitted to the President the outline of a proposed declaration to Japan, calling upon her to surrender and giving her some inkling of the treatment in store for her.[1] It had been agreed in Washington that such an appeal should be made to the Japanese before the atomic bomb was used against them. That terrible weapon was successfully tested on 16 July in New Mexico. The Stimson proposals were revised by Truman and Byrnes and shown to Churchill, who had some suggestions to make.[2] The document was then sent to Chiang Kai-shek for his approval. That came on the evening of 26 July and the Potsdam Declaration was at once released for publication, while a copy was sent by special messenger to Molotov.[3] He telephoned to ask that the Declaration should be held up for two or three days. When he was told that it had already been released, Molotov was perturbed, and complained that he should first have been consulted.[4] On the same day, the 26th, a meeting of the Chiefs of Staff had been held, at which the Soviet member said that the Red Army would attack Japan in the latter half of August, with the exact date dependent on the conclusion of negotiations then being held with the Chinese.[5] Then on 29 July Molotov, at Stalin's behest, called on Truman and Byrnes to discuss what cause should be given for Soviet entry into war with Japan. He suggested that the Allies should formally request the Soviet Union to do so. This, he added, was on the assumption that the Soviet-Chinese agreement would have been concluded before the USSR entered the war.[6]

Truman and Byrnes did not want to be put in the position of formally asking the Russians to violate their Pact with Japan. Byrnes, indeed, has said that he would have been satisfied had the Russians decided after all to stay out, as otherwise he feared what would happen in Manchuria.[7] The situation had changed since Yalta. The Americans were coming to realize that Japan was at her

[1] H. L. Stimson and M. Bundy, *On Active Service in Peace and War* (London, Hutchinson, 1948), pp. 366–9.   [2] ibid. p. 206.
[3] ibid. pp. 206–7. This document is usually referred to as the Potsdam Declaration, but was in fact entitled 'Proclamation to the Japanese People'. For text see pp. 471–2 below.
[4] ibid. p. 207.   [5] Deane, *Strange Alliance*, pp. 270–1.
[6] Byrnes, *Speaking Frankly*, p. 207.   [7] ibid. p. 208.

last gasp and now they had the atomic bomb ready. After some cogitation a way out was found by appealing to Soviet obligations under the Moscow Declaration of 30 October 1943, and under Article 103 of the (still unratified) Charter of the United Nations.[1] Thus was morality reconciled with expediency and tender consciences salved. The belated hesitations and qualms evinced by the Russians may not unreasonably be ascribed to doubts on their part whether Truman really intended to see that they got the booty promised them by Roosevelt at Yalta. If not, they now knew that they could extract it, and perhaps more, from Japan, as the price of their keeping the peace with her. They probably never seriously considered mediating for her, much less assisting her in any way, because they wanted to see her crushed. Nor, at this time, did they desire any open conflict with the United States, which, in their enfeebled state, might jeopardize their gains in Europe. To be able to take what they were after in the Far East with American approval was therefore the better of the two courses. Hence Stalin's gratification when Truman and Byrnes obligingly presented him with a moral and legal sanction for the treacherous attack which he proposed to make upon Japan, now a crippled Power pleading for peace on any terms, short of complete capitulation.[2] Had Hitler decisively defeated the Soviet Union in 1942 Tojo would no doubt have attacked her in the Far East, but he would not have been so sanctimonious about it.

On 30 July Sato again saw Lozovsky and told him that, with

[1] The Moscow Declaration provided that the four signatories 'for the purpose of maintaining international peace and security pending the re-establishment of law and order and the inauguration of a system of general security . . . will consult with one another and as occasion requires with other members of the United Nations with a view to joint action on behalf of the community of nations.' Article 103 of the UN Charter provided that 'in the event of a conflict between the obligations of the Members of the United Nations under the present Charter and their obligations under any other international agreement, their obligations under the present Charter shall prevail.' The idea of utilizing this article originated with Ben Cohen, who is described by Byrnes as having 'had a hand in important issues ever since the early days of the Roosevelt administration.' He was present at Potsdam as Counsellor and one of Byrnes's trio of advisers (Byrnes, *Speaking Frankly*, pp. 67, 208). Truman's letter to Stalin, which was drafted by Byrnes on the basis of Cohen's suggestion, concluded: 'It seems to me that under the terms of the Moscow Declaration and the provisions of the Charter, above referred to, it would be proper for the Soviet Union to indicate its willingness to consult and co-operate with other great powers now at war with Japan with a view to joint action on behalf of the community of nations to maintain peace and security' (ibid. p. 208).

[2] 'The President later told me that Generalissimo Stalin expressed great appreciation of the communication' (ibid. p. 209).

reference to the Potsdam Declaration, unconditional surrender was out of the question for Japan, but that she was ready to end the war 'on broad terms of compromise', provided that her honour and existence were guaranteed.[1] He also declared even more plainly that Japan was ready to pay a high price for Soviet mediation.[2] But Lozovsky merely replied that Stalin and Molotov were still in Berlin and that no reply could yet be given.[3] Sato warned his Government that the issuance of the Potsdam Declaration had probably ended all chances of Soviet mediation.[4]

The Potsdam Declaration was regarded with relief by the peace group in Japan, since it indicated that there would after all be terms of peace, after the surrender, and that Japan would not be treated with complete ruthlessness.[5] At a meeting of the Supreme War Council on 27 July Togo said that the Declaration did in effect offer a peace on terms and that serious consequences would ensue were it not accepted.[6] The Emperor, too, declared that he considered it acceptable in principle. But the representatives of the armed services, which were singled out for surrender and disarmament, took a different view. They reluctantly agreed to its publication, subject to excision of the more lenient portions of it, but they wanted the Government to reject it in no uncertain terms.[7] In this situation the Supreme War Council decided to wait and see what came of their appeal to the USSR, and in the meantime to make no reply and to instruct the press not to make overmuch of the Declaration.[8] This decision did not satisfy the Army and either on account of their remonstrances or through inadvertence Admiral Suzuki on 30 July told a press conference that the Government intended to ignore the Declaration entirely.[9] He was reported as saying that it was nothing more than a rehash of the Cairo Declaration and that it would make no difference to Japan's fixed policy to fight to the end.[10]

The veteran Premier's statement as reported, and possibly coloured, by the Japanese press and radio, was taken to mean that

---

[1] IMTFE, *Exhibit* 2704.
[2] 'It is expected that the Soviet Government may have various requests and directions to make with regard to its services and I understand that Prince Konoye will be invested with broad authority in negotiating with the Soviet Government' (ibid.).   [3] ibid.
[4] ibid.   [5] Kase, *Eclipse of the Rising Sun*, p. 210.
[6] Evidence of Togo (IMTFE, *Record*, p. 35785).
[7] Kase, *Eclipse of the Rising Sun*, p. 210.   [8] Evidence of Togo.
[9] ibid.; also Kase, *Eclipse of the Rising Sun*, p. 211.
[10] *Syonan Sinbun*, 30 July 1945.

Japan had definitely rejected the appeal made to her. That had not been at all the intention of the Supreme War Council, which was still clinging to the straw of Soviet mediation. But Suzuki's unhappy remark let loose a new horror on Japan and the world, for the decision was now taken to use the atomic bomb.

On 2 August Togo instructed Sato to impress upon the Soviet Government the urgency of the situation. Sato was also told that he could negotiate on the basis of the Potsdam Declaration.[1] Sato did this, but when Molotov and Stalin returned to Moscow on 6 August they made no immediate effort to see Sato, while they did see T. V. Soong. When this news reached Tokyo, Togo agreed with Kase that nothing good was to be expected from Moscow.[2]

On the morning of 6 August the first atomic bomb fell on Hiroshima, virtually obliterating that city. When President Truman's announcement, on 7 August, of what kind of weapon this was reached Japan through a broadcast from San Francisco, Togo went to the Palace and was told by the Emperor that peace had better be made at once without arguing about terms. But the Army leaders remained opposed to this. They issued a communiqué referring to 'a new type of bomb' which had caused 'considerable damage' to Hiroshima. Despite the American broadcasts to Japan and the second bomb on Nagasaki on 9 August, it took time for the people in general to realize what Hiroshima really meant.[3] It was otherwise with the next blow to fall upon Japan.

On 7 August Molotov told Sato that he would see him at 8 p.m. the next day. Later the time was advanced to 5 p.m. When the Japanese Ambassador arrived, Molotov cut short his formal congratulations on his safe return from Berlin, and read him the Soviet declaration of war upon Japan, to be effective on the morning of 9 August.[4] This meant almost at once, as 6 p.m. 8 August Moscow time was 12 p.m. 8 August Tokyo and Hsinking time, and the first attacks began in Manchuria soon after that.[5] Sato expressed regret but remained calm in face of an event which he had been expecting. He asked how he could communicate this news to his Government,

[1] Evidence of Togo (IMTFE, *Record*, p. 35785); Kase, *Eclipse of the Rising Sun*, p. 222.
[2] Kase, *Eclipse of the Rising Sun*, pp. 222–3.
[3] ibid. pp. 212–13.
[4] Sato's report to Yoshida, 15 June 1946. This was made after Sato's repatriation, when Yoshida had become Foreign Minister (IMTFE, *Document* (reject)).
[5] Evidence (offered) of Ryuji Takeuchi, Chief Third (Russian) Section, JFM, 1944–5 (ibid.).

to which Molotov replied that he could send a telegram to Tokyo, in code if he liked. So Sato handed in the telegram to the Russian authorities, but it never reached Tokyo.[1]

Tokyo got its first news of war from a foreign broadcast picked up by Domei in the early morning of 9 August and from a report from Hsinking of the outbreak of hostilities.[2] Malik asked Togo for an interview on the morning of 9 August, but Togo put him off and did not see him until 11.15 a.m. on 10 August.[3] Then Malik gave him the formal Soviet declaration of war.[4]

It has often been said that the Soviet declaration of war was hastened by the dropping of the first atomic bomb. This may be so, yet there is no available evidence or proof that Moscow had not fixed the striking date prior to this occurrence.[5] At Potsdam General Antonov had said that the attack, subject to Sino-Soviet agreement on Manchuria and related topics, would be in the latter part of August. But it may well have been that when Stalin and Molotov got back to Moscow and heard from Lozovsky of the desperate urgency of Japanese appeals for mediation, they thought that any further delay in reply, or a simple refusal to mediate, might equally result in a Japanese surrender. When Molotov advanced by three hours his appointment with Sato this was evidently because he was warned that otherwise Sato would not get the declaration of war until after the Soviet forces had started

---

[1] Sato's report; also Kase, *Eclipse of the Rising Sun*, pp. 223-4, citing Sato's, *The Two Russias*.

[2] Kase, *Eclipse of the Rising Sun*, p. 224; evidence of Togo (IMTFE, *Record*, p. 35785). [3] Evidence of Togo.

[4] This was as follows: 'After the defeat and surrender of Hitlerite Germany, Japan became the only great power that still stood for the continuation of the war. The demand of the three powers, the United States, Great Britain and China, on July 26 for the unconditional surrender of the Japanese armed forces was rejected by Japan, and thus the proposal of the Japanese Government to the Soviet Union on mediation in the war in the Far East loses all basis. Taking into consideration the refusal of Japan to capitulate, the Allies submitted to the Soviet Government a proposal to join the war against Japanese aggression and thus shorten the duration of the war, reduce the number of victims and facilitate the speedy restoration of universal peace. Loyal to its Allied duty, the Soviet Government accepted the proposal of the Allies and has joined in the declaration of the Allied Powers of July 26. The Soviet Government considers that this policy is the only means able to bring peace nearer, free the people from further sacrifice and suffering and give the Japanese people the possibility of avoiding those dangers and destruction suffered by Germany after her refusal to capitulate unconditionally. In view of the above, the Soviet Government declares that from tomorrow, that is August 9, the Soviet Government will consider itself to be at war with Japan' (Kase, *Eclipse of the Rising Sun*, pp. 225-6).

[5] In May 1945 Stalin had told Harry Hopkins that the Soviet Army would be fully deployed on the Manchurian border by 8 August (Sherwood, *White House Papers*, ii. 891).

hostilities. But that does not prove that the decision to start them was not fixed till then; if anything it tends to show the opposite.

The news of war with the Soviet Union, though not by now entirely unforeseen, nevertheless came as a shattering blow to Tokyo. At the same time it greatly strengthened the hand of those who wished to accept the Potsdam Declaration. Kido saw the Emperor on the morning of 9 August and assured him that this must now be done. The Emperor agreed and told Kido to impress this on Suzuki. Suzuki and Togo also saw the Emperor.[1] Then at 10 a.m. the Supreme War Council of six members met. Here Togo proposed to accept the Potsdam Declaration 'in principle'. All were agreed upon that and all also agreed on making an Allied pledge that the Imperial House should be preserved a *sine qua non* of acceptance. But the War Minister and the two Chiefs of Staff insisted on three further conditions. These were: that there should be no Allied occupation of the Japanese homeland; that Japan should voluntarily withdraw her armed forces from occupied territories and herself disarm and demobilize them; and that the Japanese Government should themselves try Japanese accused of war crimes. On this issue the Council remained divided.[2] So did an emergency meeting of the Cabinet, which was summoned in the afternoon of 9 August. Togo explained the situation to the Ministers who, except for the four 'Inner Cabinet' members, had not previously known about the overtures to the USSR. But when the point at issue was put to them, no agreement could be reached. Anami opposed Yonai on the question of the absolute necessity to surrender, subject to the one indispensable condition. The Home Minister declared that he could not guarantee internal peace and order if this were done. He recalled the February 1936 affair, and no doubt sent a chill down the spines of his audience. Several Ministers were obviously 'sitting on the fence' and would not commit themselves. So again no decision could be reached.[3]

Then, as a last resort, a full Imperial Conference was summoned. It included the Emperor himself, the six regular members of the Supreme War Council, the heads of the General Affairs (political)

---

[1] Evidence of Kido (IMTFE, *Record*, p. 31172).

[2] Kase, *Eclipse of the Rising Sun*, pp. 231–2; USSBS, *Japan's Struggle to End the War*, p. 7.

[3] ibid. pp. 232–3; evidence of Togo (IMTFE, *Record*, pp. 35786–7). Nine Ministers agreed with Togo, three with Anami, and three were undecided (USSBS, *Japan's Struggle to End the War*, p. 8).

Bureaux of the Army and the Navy, the chief secretary to the Cabinet, the director of the Combined Planning Board, and the President of the Privy Council, Baron Hiranuma.[1] They all crowded into the air-raid shelter in the Palace at 11.30 p.m. on 9 August. But yet again no agreement could be reached. Togo, Yonai, and Hiranuma were ranged against Anami, Toyoda, and Umezu. After several hours of inconclusive debate Suzuki, who had hitherto kept silent, announced his intention of asking the Emperor to decide.[2] The peace party, foreseeing the deadlock, had, through Kido, prepared the Emperor for this move, which took their opponents by surprise.[3] There were precedents for it in the reign of the Meiji Emperor (1868–1912), though normally by what had become an unwritten, but none the less powerful, convention of the Constitution, the Emperor never participated in debate, but accepted the decisions of his advisers.

Now the Emperor spoke and said that he agreed with Togo—that the Potsdam Declaration should be accepted, with the sole condition regarding the Imperial House. He added, according to Kido, that while he could not bear the sight of his loyal troops being disarmed, or those responsible for the war being punished since they had been unswerving in their devotion to him, 'I think that now is the time to bear the unbearable. Recalling the Emperor Meiji's feelings when he was confronted with the Triple Intervention, I repress my tears and approve the draft plan.'[4] So the decision was made.

It was, of course, endorsed at another Cabinet meeting, and then the Foreign Ministry drafted a Note in English, of which copies went to Berne for transmittal through the Swiss Government to those of the United States and China and also to Stockholm to be sent via the Swedish Government to the British Government and to that of the USSR.[5] In addition, when Togo saw Malik on the morning of 10 August he gave the Soviet envoy the Note as well. It was also broadcast by Domei.[6]

The original draft of the Potsdam Declaration had included a

---

[1] ibid.; Kase, *Eclipse of the Rising Sun*, p. 233.
[2] ibid. Kase says that this was at 2 a.m. on 10 August. Sakomizu (who was present) says 3 a.m. (USSBS, *Japan's Struggle to End the War*, p. 8).
[3] Kase, *Eclipse of the Rising Sun*, p. 236.
[4] Evidence of Kido (IMTFE, *Record*, pp. 31178–9). The reference was to the Dreibund of Russia, Germany, and France which in 1895 had compelled Japan to modify the Treaty of Shimonoseki and retrocede the Liaotung Peninsula to China.   [5] Kase, *Eclipse of the Rising Sun*, pp. 238–9.
[6] ibid.; evidence of Togo (IMTFE, *Record*, p. 35786). For text of the Japanese reply see below, pp. 472–3.

clause intimating that the Japanese monarchy would be preserved, if Japan made peace.[1] But Byrnes, just prior to leaving for Potsdam, had asked Cordell Hull's opinion on this, saying that it was approved by high officials of the State, War, and Navy Departments. Hull had disapproved and had cabled his reasons to Byrnes on 16 July.[2] Hull did not want positively to overthrow the Japanese monarchy, but neither did he want a commitment to preserve it. He wanted to wait and see what happened in Japan, and while he was willing to utilize the imperial authority, he wanted to make it clearly subordinate to that of the Allied Supreme Commander.[3] This view, not necessarily because of Hull's objections only, prevailed; hence the Declaration as issued said nothing of the monarchy.[4] Indeed, paragraphs six and ten might imply that its overthrow was in fact intended.

When the Japanese Note was received in Washington, on the morning of 10 August (Washington time), the President held a conference with the Secretaries of State, War, and of the Navy. Here Byrnes objected to any retreat from unconditional surrender. The President agreed and Byrnes drafted a reply which Truman (and Stimson) approved.[5]

A San Francisco broadcast of the American reply was picked up in Japan on the morning of 12 August (Japanese time).[6] It precipitated another crisis. The Emperor held that the reply was satisfactory, but the service chiefs were of a contrary opinion, and so now was Hiranuma, who held—with more justification than Kase allows—that it was subversive of the imperial prerogatives.[7] Suzuki was inclined to agree with him, but Togo and Kido were firm in their contention that the reply must be accepted.[8] The

---

[1] Hull, *Memoirs*, ii. 1593; Stimson and Bundy, *On Active Service*, p. 368.
[2] Hull, *Memoirs*, ii. 1593–4.   [3] ibid. pp. 1591–3.
[4] ibid. p. 1594; Byrnes, *Speaking Frankly*, p. 206.
[5] ibid. p. 209. For text of reply see below p. 473.
[6] Kase, *Eclipse of the Rising Sun*, pp. 240–1; USSBS, *Japan's Struggle to End the War*, p. 8. The official Note was received at 7 a.m. on 13 August (ibid.).
[7] Kase, *Eclipse of the Rising Sun*, pp. 242–3. Kase remarks: 'the cynical Hiranuma read between the lines (of paragraph 5 of the American reply) a sinister encouragement to subversive activities calculated to overthrow monarchical government.' But Hiranuma was not without cause for his 'cynicism'. A Department of State memorandum of 9 May 1944, on policy towards the Japanese monarchy, included the comment that 'if a substantial movement developed among the Japanese people to abolish the imperial institution, the Allied military authorities should take no action against that movement, except to maintain law and order, and should cease to utilize the Emperor as a political instrument' (Hull, *Memoirs*, ii. 1592).
[8] Kase, *Eclipse of the Rising Sun*, pp. 243–4; evidence of Togo (IMTFE, *Record*, pp. 35788–9); and of Kido (ibid. pp. 31185–6).

Supreme War Council met on 13 August and produced the usual division. Suzuki, who had been talked over again by Kido and Togo, advised, along with Yonai and Togo, that the American reply met Japan's condition and surrender should now be undertaken.[1] Anami, Umezu, and Toyoda were outwardly firm against this course. Behind their apparently intransigent attitude lay their fear of an upheaval by the 'younger officer' groups in the Army and Navy. These now knew what was going on and many of them were endeavouring to organize a revolt. Luckily there was no unanimity among the junior officer grades; some of them had long realized the hopelessness of Japan's position and were prepared to accept the inevitable. These kept the peace group informed of the mutterings and plans of revolt.[2] So far as they could the pro-surrender group had taken steps to deprive their opponents of any effective leadership. The Jushin had been informed of the situation and had all, including Tojo, acquiesced in the imperial decision of 10 August.[3] On 12 August the princes of the blood were called together and agreed to support the Emperor.[4] This was of vital importance, for if any one of them had come out in support of the war party, a Palace coup d'état would thereby have been greatly facilitated.

A meeting of the full Cabinet on the afternoon of 13 August also produced no agreement.[5] So the only remedy was again to have recourse to another Imperial Conference. But at first the service chiefs objected to this; no doubt they foresaw what would occur. They wanted another Note sent to the Allies to request that it should be specified that the Emperor personally should be exempt from the control of the Allied Supreme Commander, and that the ultimate form of the Japanese government should be entirely a matter for the Japanese people to decide.[6] But Togo and his associates stood firm against this.[7] On the morning of 14 August the Emperor summoned the full Cabinet to meet him and at the

[1] Togo (ibid.). Kido says there was no meeting of the Supreme War Council on 13 August, but probably he meant Imperial Conference (ibid. pp. 31185–6).
[2] Kase, *Eclipse of the Rising Sun*, pp. 245–6.
[3] The Jushin meeting was on 10 August (ibid. p. 240).
[4] Kase (ibid.) says this was on 11 August. Kido (loc. cit. p. 31186) said it was on the evening of 12 August. This seems more likely as it puts the meeting after the American reply had been received and the military had opposed its acceptance.
[5] USSBS, *Japan's Struggle to End the War*, p. 9.
[6] ibid. The Chiefs of Staff refused to sign the request for an Imperial Conference. [7] Kase, *Eclipse of the Rising Sun*, p. 251.

same time called in the Chiefs of Staff and the President of the Privy Council. Thus, unexpectedly, except to those who had counselled this, an Imperial Conference was organized.[1] After two hours of discussion and disagreement the Emperor spoke and commanded that the Allied reply be accepted.[2] So ended the great debate, amid scenes of grief and emotion.[3] Anami went home and shortly afterwards committed suicide.[4]

A further Cabinet meeting accepted the decision of the Imperial Conference and an imperial edict to the nation was prepared.[5] On the night of 14 August a recording of this was made in the Imperial Palace for transmission the next day.[6] News of this must have got out, for part of the Imperial Guard, suborned by a group of officers employed in the War Office, revolted, and broke into the palace on the night of 14–15 August in an endeavour to find and destroy the phonograph record of the edict. But in this they failed and were eventually overborne by loyal troops hastily summoned to the rescue.[7] On this and succeeding days sporadic revolts in the capital and elsewhere were also overcome.[8]

On the morning of 15 August the Foreign Ministry dispatched the Note of acceptance to the Swiss Government for transmission to the Allies.[9] At midday the imperial edict was broadcast to a stunned people.[10] On the same day Suzuki resigned, and the Emperor, on Kido's recommendation, summoned Prince Higashikuni, who was his uncle-in-law and a general on the active list, to head a new Cabinet.[11] This took office two days later when the Emperor issued another edict to the Army and Navy bidding them obey the order to surrender.[12] Prince Kanin was sent to Singapore,

[1] ibid. pp. 251–2. Kido and Suzuki had agreed upon this, but Sakomizu was afraid that Anami might counter it by resigning and bringing down the Cabinet (ibid.).

[2] He said, *inter alia*: '. . . I concur in the views of the foreign minister and think the reply is acceptable. You will all please agree to my views. If we do not terminate the war at this juncture, our unique national structure will be destroyed and our nation will suffer extermination. If we save anything, be it ever so little, we could yet hope to rebuild the nation in the future' (ibid. p. 253).

[3] ibid.   [4] ibid. p. 260.

[5] ibid. p. 254; evidence of Kido (IMTFE, *Record*, p. 31191).

[6] Evidence of Kido.

[7] ibid. pp. 31194–7; also Kato, *The Lost War*, pp. 241–3. Kido and Ishiwata, the Household Minister, narrowly escaped discovery and death.

[8] ibid.; Kase, *Eclipse of the Rising Sun*, pp. 260–2.

[9] Evidence of Togo (IMTFE, *Record*, p. 38789). This was the evening of 14 August, Swiss time. For text of the Note see below pp. 473–4.

[10] Evidence of Kido (ibid. p. 31197). For text of the edict see below pp. 474–5.

[11] Evidence of Kido (ibid. p. 31198); Kase, *Eclipse of the Rising Sun*, pp. 262–3.

[12] For text see below pp. 475–6.

Prince Asaka to China, and Prince Takeda to Manchukuo to exhort the forces there to submit.[1] At home Prince Takamatsu successfully used his influence to prevent the Special Attack Corps from resisting the American landing.[2] Thus, narrowly enough, a general military revolt was averted, and Japan saved from invasion and complete destruction.

Meanwhile General MacArthur had been appointed as Supreme Commander for the Allied Powers, not without a difference of opinion between the American Ambassador in Moscow and Molotov, who had at first suggested that there should be two such commanders, MacArthur and the Soviet General Vasilevsky. But this suggestion was dropped by Stalin, who on 12 August agreed to the sole appointment of MacArthur.[3] Stalin also acquiesced in an American refusal to allow Soviet troops to occupy the Hokkaido.[4] Nor did he make any serious difficulties about MacArthur's General Order No. 1, which *inter alia* laid down to whom the various Japanese forces were to surrender.[5] On 2 September, the Instrument of Surrender was formally signed by the Allied and the Japanese representatives on board the United States battleship *Missouri* lying in Tokyo Bay.[6] 'Japan awaited the will of her new masters.'[7]

---

[1] ibid. p. 254.   [2] ibid. p. 264.

[3] Deane, *Strange Alliance*, pp. 278–9.

[4] ibid. p. 281. On 14 August the Secretary of State informed the Japanese Government of the appointment of General MacArthur and instructed them to send emissaries to him to receive his orders (*Surrender of Italy, Germany and Japan*, pp. 79–80). MacArthur on 23 August issued general instructions on disarmament and surrender to the Japanese Government (ibid. pp. 84–89). The first American troops were due to arrive in Japan on 26 August but were delayed for two days by a typhoon (Kato, *Lost War*, p. 255).

[5] This was drafted by the US War Department on 11 August, discussed by the State-War-Navy Co-ordinating Committee on 11 and 12 August, and reviewed by the US Joint Chiefs of Staff. After approval by the President it was communicated to the British and to the Soviet Governments. Stalin replied on 16 August suggesting certain amendments which the American Government accepted. These did not refer to Korea (Statement by Mr. J. C. Webb, US Under-Secretary of State, 16 June 1949, *Korean Aid Hearings*, p. 118. General Order No. 1 was issued by General MacArthur on 2 September 1945. For the principal provisions of the text see below pp. 476–7).

[6] It was signed for Japan by Shigemitsu and Umezu. See Kase (*Eclipse of the Rising Sun*, pp. 4–10) and Kato (*Lost War*, pp. 260–2) for a description of the ceremony from the Japanese side. For text of the Instrument of Surrender see below pp. 477–8). The US Navy had wanted to have Admiral Nimitz as signatory for the United States. The Secretary of the Navy, J. V. Forrestal, managed this by suggesting that the ceremony take place on the *Missouri*, named after Truman's home state (Byrnes, *Speaking Frankly*, pp. 212–13).

[7] Kato, *Lost War*, p. 264.

CHAPTER XIV

Summary and Conclusions

THE tragic history of Eastern Asia since 1937 provokes the ironic reflection that had all the Powers concerned been consciously working to promote the triumph of Communism in that region, they could hardly have been more successful in largely achieving this result. Of recent years much has been said and written in condemnation of the policy of the Democracies, in particular of that of the United States, as having furthered that end. But it must not be forgotten that the principal contributor to the victory of Communism in China and to the heightened menace of Communism elsewhere in the Far East was none other than Japan herself. If it be true, as Oliver Cromwell declared, that none goes so far as he who knows not whither he is going, it also often happens that the destination reached is apt to be vastly different from the intended and desired one. So it was with Japan.

The foreign policy of Japan during 1937–41 did not represent the steady unfolding of a master-plan, aimed at securing the hegemony of Eastern Asia and devised by a coolly calculating and united band of conspirators. It is true that Japanese predominance in East Asia was desired by her military, political, and industrial leaders, but they were at odds among themselves over the form which this should take and the means by which it should be accomplished. Still less was there any preconcerted and continuous co-operation between Japan and the Axis Powers in Europe; on the contrary she was frequently at cross-purposes with them and they with her. It is, indeed, a comparatively rare occurrence in history that a nation's external objectives are clearly defined and pursued with unremitting skill and calculation. When this does happen, it is usually the work of some master of statecraft—a Richelieu, a Cavour, a Bismarck. No such figure appeared upon the Japanese stage during this epoch. More often does it happen that foreign policy becomes the shuttlecock of domestic politics, and a mixture of opportunism and blundering. When short-sighted mediocrities are in charge of affairs they are apt to find too late that they have got themselves into a position in which they must choose either humiliation and disgrace, or else embark upon the dread gamble of war. This was the experience of Japan's rulers in the years which followed the Lukouchiao affair.

Japan in 1936–7 had embarked upon two great undertakings which together were bound to absorb a large proportion of her capital resources. One of these was rearmament, for which, in view of the technical obsolescence of much of her military equipment and of the darkening international scene, there was a good deal of justification. The other was the exploitation of the agrarian and industrial resources of Manchuria, which initially meant a drain upon Japan, but which ultimately promised at all events a partial solution of the problems which had been worrying her soldiers, statesmen, and economists—the paucity of strategic raw materials under her own control, the precariousness of foreign markets, and the pressure of rural overpopulation. It was not an ideal solution, but, given the circumstances in which Japan found herself in the nineteen-thirties, it was one which most other countries in a like position would have been impelled to take.

The Western Powers had protested, but had in fact acquiesced in Japan's seizure of Manchuria and erection of the so-called independent State of Manchukuo. China, although bitterly humiliated at the loss of what she had always held to be an integral part of her territory, had perforce to accept it. It would seem, therefore, that after the Tangku Truce of 1933 it would have been sound policy on the part of Japan to have avoided any further penetration of China, south of the Great Wall, and to have concentrated her efforts upon the consolidation of the political and economic position which she had secured in Manchuria. This, indeed, is what the Kodoha group in the Army appears to have desired.

There were, it is true, considerations on the other side. The resources of North China, especially in coking coal, were complementary to the iron-ore reserves of Manchuria. Most of the inhabitants of Manchuria were mainly of Northern Chinese origin; the task of reconciling them to Japanese rule and of controlling movement between the two regions would be facilitated if a Japanese-sponsored buffer State could be erected in North China. Similar considerations applied in the case of the Mongols of Manchuria and those of Inner and of Outer Mongolia. Empire-builders are frequently tempted to take the further step, in search of the secure strategic frontier which is ever apt to elude them.

But to do this is to court the danger of over-extension and of actuating the very adverse forces which are a source of fear. The Japanese divined that the Soviet Union, while outwardly acquiescing in their seizure of North Manchuria and withdrawing from that region, was not permanently reconciled to this and might some day seek to reverse the balance. They knew also that China would harbour thoughts of revenge. But neither the Soviet Union nor China were strong enough in the Far East, or likely to be in the foreseeable future, to overthrow Japan in Manchuria, especially with the enhanced strength which the successful exploitation of Manchurian resources would give her.

This remained true in 1937, even after Japanese efforts to detach North China from the control of the Central Government at Nanking had strengthened Chinese national feeling to the degree which compelled Chiang Kai-shek to abandon his anti-Communist campaigns and to acquiesce in the formation of a united front to resist any further Japanese penetration. This, in turn, induced Tojo, and those who were of his viewpoint, to urge that the power of Nanking be struck down in North China before it grew too strong. But, as the course of the Sino-Japanese conflict was to show, China was too backward in industrial development, too inchoate politically, and too ineffective in her military organization to have any hope of overthrowing Japan in pitched battle. The Soviet Union, although increasing in strength, was in no shape to fight a major war in the Far East, confronted as it was with internal difficulties and with the growing menace of Nazi Germany. Japan, then, needed only to build and to wait.

Two things prevented her from doing this. One was the feeling among the Army officers that, as they had gained—or regained—political power at home through their successes abroad, they must provide fresh triumphs to retain and consolidate that power. The other was the local particularism and jealousy between different Japanese armies, which evidently impelled the Japanese Army in North China to seek to emulate what the Kwantung Army had achieved in Manchuria. Thus, after the Lukouchiao affair, the Cabinet and the General Staff in Tokyo were unable to control their forces in North China and some of them were dubious about the need to do so.

Chiang Kai-shek in Nanking was in a somewhat similar position. He did not want an all-out war with Japan; on the other hand he could not afford to accept yet another humiliation at her hands. He knew from experience that the demand for resistance to Japan could easily be turned into political and military disaffection to himself. Consequently he could not accept the relatively moderate peace terms which the Japanese at first put forward. By the time he felt himself able to respond to Japanese overtures, the fall of Shanghai and the imminent loss of Nanking itself had produced a wave of chauvinism in Japan which swept away the advocates of a peace of moderation and impelled Konoye to the proclamation of the New Order. So Tokyo and Nanking were plunged into a general conflict which neither had initially desired and which was to prove ultimately fatal to both.

For Japan found herself unable either to impose her will upon China by force of arms or to bring about the collapse of the Kuomintang by political manœuvre and propaganda. She was thus condemned to a long-drawn-out and largely profitless struggle which had serious disadvantages. It was not, indeed, the fatal drain upon her resources which it was widely supposed to be in the West. It provided some training ground for her armies and it enabled the military to exact huge sums from a submissive Diet and so to further the general rearmament programme. But it caused a diversion of money and materials from the huge task of industrialization which Japan had set herself in Manchuria and it ended whatever possibility might otherwise have existed of obtaining foreign loans for that project. Thus development in Manchuria was hampered, while the Army, especially after Nomonhan, became uncomfortably conscious of the growth of Soviet industrial and military power in the Far East at a time when Japan was squandering part of her human and material resources in the endless China conflict. At home Japan's economy was strained and her people condemned to an increasingly austere livelihood, while they were deprived of the glamour of further great victories in the field. This was a menace to the continued popularity and prestige of the Army.

While the outbreak of war in Europe relieved Japanese fears of any immediate third-Power intervention, it accentuated long-term anxieties in Tokyo. Whoever emerged victorious from the European conflict might be in a position to make their will felt in Eastern Asia, especially were Japan still entangled in China. Furthermore the German victories in Europe in 1940 stimulated the southern expansionist school in Japan and engendered increased impatience with the 'chain on her feet'—her involvement in China. It was this impatience which prompted her to take another long step on the road to disaster.

Hitherto, thanks largely to her domestic political divisions, Japan had avoided any formal association with the Axis Powers. She had, indeed, been alienated from Germany by the conclusion of the German-Soviet Pact. With the fall of France the pressure grew for Japan to conclude some sort of accord with Germany if only to assure that, in the anticipated redivision of the world, the spoils of South East Asia should be reserved for the Japanese. This played its part in the making of the Tripartite Pact, but the main motive which induced a doubtful Cabinet and Privy Council to listen to Matsuoka's disastrous counsel was the belief that thereby the Soviet Union could be induced to abandon diplomatic support of free China and that Chiang Kai-shek, confronted by what in effect would be a quadruple association, would be constrained to seek peace.

There could have been no more fatal miscalculation. Even had the Soviet-German rift over the Balkans not occurred, it is doubtful whether the Soviet Union would ever have assisted Japan to escape from the morass into which she had blundered in China, except at a far higher price than Japan was then willing to pay. Of this there is some hint in Matsuoka's conversations in Berlin with Ribbentrop and Hitler. As it was the Japanese got no effective support from either Berlin or Moscow in their efforts to dispose of the China Incident which remained as far as ever from such disposition.

If the Tripartite Pact thus failed to bring Japan the positive benefits which Matsuoka had predicted, it soon produced the evils which the Emperor, Konoye, and—if he may be credited—Kido had all feared. Since the outbreak of war in Europe the United States had, by virtue of circumstances, become the principal opponent among the Democracies of Japanese ambitions in Eastern Asia. At the same time Japan's economic dependence upon the United States had increased since trade with Germany was sharply curtailed by the war. The conclusion of the Tripartite Pact was intended to cow the United States into abandoning support for Great Britain in Europe and for China in the Far East. It had the opposite effect of markedly increasing the antagonism of the

Roosevelt administration towards Japan, which appeared gratuitously to be interfering with the primary purpose of Washington—to sustain Great Britain and to prevent German domination of Europe. Japan was henceforth regarded as a declared enemy who was merely awaiting an opportune time to strike. Consequently the economic sanctions which had been held over her head since the abrogation of the Commercial Treaty of 1911 now progressively descended upon Japan, thinly disguised as necessary measures for America's own defence.

This ominous development in turn drove Japan to take steps from which she had previously refrained despite urgings on the part of Berlin and of the more ebullient elements in Tokyo. Hitherto Japan had made no military move against the Netherlands East Indies or Malaya. As Matsuoka freely confessed to Hitler, the dominant mood in Tokyo was one of caution and, as the Germans divined, Japan wanted to see the invasion and defeat of Great Britain before taking any irretrievable action. But in the early summer of 1941 it did not need any great prescience for the Japanese Government to foresee that in the near future Japanese funds in America might be frozen and supplies of oil to Japan cut off. At the same time their attempts to secure by negotiation what would have amounted to control of the oil supplies and resources of the Netherlands East Indies had been baulked by the stubborn refusal of the Dutch authorities, backed by diplomatic support from Washington and London, to countenance any of the more sweeping demands of the Kobayashi and Yoshizawa missions. Therefore the decision was taken in Tokyo—and taken before the outbreak of the German-Soviet War—to move into southern Indo-China in preparation for a descent upon the East Indies.

The German assault upon the USSR, which Japan neither anticipated nor desired, presented her with fresh alternatives of policy. She might, as Ribbentrop urged and Matsuoka advocated, have scrapped the Soviet-Japanese Neutrality Pact of the previous April and joined with Germany against the Russians. Whether, had she done so, the joint assault would have brought about the downfall of the Soviet Union in the crucial second half of 1941 cannot be asserted with absolute confidence, though it might well have achieved this end. Or, conversely, as Konoye seems to have suggested, Japan might have declared that the German action, taken without any consultation with their Oriental ally, had nullified the Tripartite Pact. She could then have sought to separate her cause from that of the Axis Powers, to rehabilitate herself with the United States, and to further the conversations with that country which had been proceeding since the previous February.

But divided counsels in Tokyo prevented either of these definite courses from being followed. The flurry of Liaison Conferences produced the usual compromise decision which gave Japan the worst of both worlds. No immediate war was to be waged against the Soviet Union, but preparations were made looking to intervention in the event of a decisive German victory. These did not escape the notice of either Moscow or Washington. On the other hand the decision to advance southwards was reiterated, and the occupation of southern Indo-China duly followed.

This move, which Washington and London correctly interpreted as foreshadowing a stroke against the East Indies, was answered by the financial and economic measures which virtually severed all commercial relations with Japan. These measures could not be immediately decisive, since Japan had accumulated considerable stock-piles of strategic materials and was now in a position to augment these by supplies from Manchuria and from occupied China. But she could not prevent the steady diminution of her oil stocks—the idea that the expansion of synthetic oil production would solve this problem was in fact a pipe-dream. Japan must either reach a settlement with the United States—which would entail accord with her other adversaries—or she must fight. Hideki Tojo, who was a man of narrow vision, but who saw clearly what he did see, from the first had no doubt of this. Konoye, on the contrary, pushed into a situation which appalled him, was to the last inclined to cling to straws.

The prospect of war with the United States—and the Japanese High Command never appear to have considered falling upon the British and Dutch possessions and leaving the Philippines untouched upon their flank and rear—was not lightly envisaged by any of the contending groups in Japanese governing circles. They were all aware, in varying degree, of the immense latent resources of their gigantic antagonist. On the other hand, they also perceived, perhaps more clearly than did Washington, that what would count in the initial stages of the conflict was the force which each side could bring to bear upon the battlefield and the advantage which Japan possessed in this respect. Consequently the Army leaders, and ultimately those of the Navy also, were ready to fight if they must, a determination which was better understood by the diplomatic representatives of Great Britain and the United States in Tokyo than it was by their Governments in London and Washington.

The Japanese, then, felt that they held good cards and that the terms they proposed for a settlement were reasonable ones in the light of the general world military and political situation. But Japan's hand would decline in value if it were not played soon— hence the insistence of the Supreme Command that a term be set to the duration of the American-Japanese conversations and that war be embarked upon should no agreement be reached during the specified period. Indeed, what is surprising is not that Japan went to war, but that the peace party proved strong enough to secure an extension of the original deadline set for the latter part of October and even a second brief extension in late November.

Whether, if the projected Roosevelt–Konoye meeting had taken place, a settlement could have been reached is a very moot point. The odds are that it would not have been, since neither Roosevelt nor Konoye possessed a free hand and neither could have agreed to terms which the public opinion of his home country would have repudiated. Of the three main issues at stake, two could probably have been resolved. There seems no doubt that the Japanese Government were ready in fact to nullify, even if not formally to repudiate, the Tripartite Pact, if they could get satisfaction on other matters. On this there was no decisive rift between the Cabinet and the High Command. Konoye, accompanied as he would have been by influential spokesmen of the Army and Navy, might well have got this across to Roosevelt whose perceptions were sharper than those of Hull and who was less insistent upon formalism.

Nor does it appear that the question of Indo-China would have proved at all insoluble. The Japanese had been taken aback by the strength of the Anglo-American reaction to their occupation of southern Indo-China, and, as their later proposals showed, they were ready to reverse this and to withdraw their forces beyond striking distance of Malaya and the East Indies, if the economic sanctions were lifted and accord reached on China.

But the Chinese question was the major and most intractable

issue and the real cause of the war. Konoye, whatever his own personal predilections may have been, could not agree to abandon the policy of the New Order though he might have been authorized to modify it in some degree. Not only the Japanese Army, but the Japanese people in general, would have turned and rent a Government which had agreed to anything like a *status quo ante* settlement with China after four years of costly and dreary conflict. The minimum terms of peace which Konoye could have agreed upon were the recognition by China of Manchukuo, some sort of Sino-Japanese political agreement in the guise of an Anti-Comintern Pact, the stationing, for a term of years, of Japanese garrisons in Inner Mongolia and part of North China, and the preservation, at any rate in those areas, of the Japanese special companies. That would have meant a large degree of Japanese political and economic domination of China.

But it is impossible to suppose that Roosevelt could or would have agreed to sponsor a peace on these terms. Apart from his own personal inclination towards China and exaggerated idea of her importance and strength in the immediate future, the President would have wrecked his position at home and impaired his whole policy had he lent himself to any such proposals. He would have outraged the generally pro-Chinese and anti-Japanese feelings among the American people and he would have been accused of bowing to Japanese menaces and of lowering American prestige. Moreover all the opponents of his European policy would have denounced him for selling China to Japan in order to free his hands for intervention against Hitler in Europe, and they would have got a ready hearing. They might well have asked why, if one aggressor could be bought off in Asia, it was so necessary to go on opposing the other in Europe and sustaining his opponents. *Realpolitik* in Asia would have undermined the whole basis of Rooseveltian policy. The disillusionment and bitterness which events in China since the close of the Second World War have provoked have prompted the suggestion that American policy with regard to the Open Door was too legalistic and unrealistic, that the Open Door, if not closed by a Japanese hand, was fated to be closed by a Chinese one—whether Nationalist or Communist —and that the day of the foreign merchant in China, as distinct from foreign trade with China, was done. But even had Roosevelt clearly foreseen all this and had been personally willing to compromise with Japan at the expense of China and to reverse the whole direction of American policy in the Far East, he could not have done it. He was no Hitler or Stalin, backed by a terrorist régime and a regimented press, to turn friend into foe or foe into friend overnight amid a chorus of sycophantic praise.

It is likely, therefore, that no more agreement over China would have been reached at Juneau or Honolulu than was in fact reached in Washington. Yet, it does not follow from this that a Roosevelt–Konoye meeting would have been devoid of all result or benefit. If there could be no American-Japanese agreement about China there did not necessarily have to be war over the matter. The economic sanctions had been imposed upon Japan because of her threatening move towards the East Indies. They might have been raised, or at least relaxed, in return for a reversal of that move, and the Chinese question left in abeyance. A personal meeting with Konoye might have convinced the President that Japan *would* fight and fight soon unless something of the sort were done. Konoye might, also, have been able to indicate that there was a real conflict of policy in Japan and that if a collision between Japan and America could be averted until the Axis Powers received a decisive check in Europe, much could then be changed in Japan which could not at the moment be altered. Such a limited agreement would not have involved any abandonment of principle on either side. Konoye could still outwardly maintain the principles of the New Order and Roosevelt his refusal to accept them. But America and her associates would have been freed from the immediate menace of a Japanese assault upon the East Indies and Japan from that of the depletion of her oil stocks and consequent hamstringing of her economy. All would then have depended upon the issue of the struggle in Europe. If Germany prevailed, then the United States would be in no position to oppose Japanese ambitions in Asia; if Germany were defeated, Japan would be in no position to persist in those ambitions in face of the United States, the USSR, and the British Commonwealth. Konoye and the Court party did not want to persist in them because their achievement would have meant the consolidation of the political predominance of the Army in Japan, to which the Court party were opposed, but which they dared not yet openly attack.

Yet they were strong enough to frustrate the immediate purposes of Tojo. When the projected Roosevelt–Konoye meeting failed to materialize and the set time-limit drew near, Tojo demanded the ending of the Washington conversations and the implementing of the decision for war, taken in the Imperial Conference of 6 September. But he could not get it; instead, although he got rid of the Konoye Cabinet, he found himself manœuvred into becoming the new Premier, and into agreeing that a last effort should be made at a diplomatic settlement. Hence the final Japanese proposals, including Proposal B, on the acceptance of which at any rate as a basis of discussion lay the last faint hope of peace.

It was here that British diplomacy might have played a greater part, as the Japanese Foreign Ministry had hoped and had asked that it would. That it did not was no fault of the British representative in Tokyo, who, like his American colleague, knew what the outcome would be if Washington maintained its inflexible stand. But Cordell Hull, who regarded the Japanese simply as a bandit nation to be brought to book, and who apparently considered Kurusu to be the architect of the Tripartite Pact because he had been its formal signatory, was not the man to avert the impending disaster. It is true that he, no more than Roosevelt, could have accepted the main Japanese propositions about China. Yet, especially in view of the fact that the Joint Chiefs of Staff were pleading with him to gain more time, it is difficult to see why he had to reject the Japanese interim Proposal B out of hand. It was not wholly acceptable as it stood, but it was a not unreasonable basis of agreement.

Had British diplomacy not been shackled by the belief of Churchill and Eden that Japan would give way before a stern and unyielding front—including an advance commitment of Great Britain to war with Japan, should there be a Japanese-American conflict—it is just possible that the crisis might have been tided over. Great Britain, after all, had a right to participation in the discussions since her possessions and interests in the Pacific were at stake, and were, indeed, to suffer cruelly when war came. Furthermore, in view of Washington's opposition to imperial preference and the general anti-colonial bias exhibited by Roosevelt and Hull, it was unwise of the British Government to leave discussions for a Far Eastern settlement entirely to America and Japan, even had the prospects of success been greater than in fact they were. The unduly subordinate role to which the British

Government confined themselves is illustrated by the fact that, as is revealed in Churchill's memoirs, no advance information was given to Britain of the terms of the American Note of 26 November. If it had been, there should have been someone with enough imagination and knowledge of Japanese psychology to realize what the presentation of such a Note at such a time would infallibly mean, and to have urged that, if it could not be modified, it should at least be kept in reserve. Churchill himself has said that, had the British Government known of the Note, they would not have been stirred, presumably by Chinese agitation, to query the proposed *modus vivendi* which Hull had intended to accompany it, and thereby to contribute to his abandonment of that offer. It is unlikely that the meagre concessions which it contained would have done much to offset the Japanese reaction to the main Note, although this is just within the bounds of possibility, in view of the last-ditch efforts of the peace party to prevent war from being launched even though the conversations were broken off. Had a *modus vivendi* with Japan been reached, and it could have been reached, with less concessions at the expense of China than were later to be made to Stalin at Yalta, almost certainly the Pacific War would thereby have been averted, in view of the German reverses in Russia in the winter of 1941–2 and the growing conviction in Japanese military circles that Germany was bleeding herself to death in her war with the USSR.

The opportunity was lost because Roosevelt and Churchill were still not convinced that Japan, for all the warnings she had given, and the import of the intercepted Japanese messages, would throw down the gage of battle to the United States and the British Commonwealth. This was because they were thinking in terms of their own latent resources, they overestimated those which they had available in the actual theatre of war, and they badly underestimated the initial striking power of Japan. The whole episode is illustrative of the folly of supposing that the rulers of a powerful nation, having committed themselves to an expansionist policy, will abandon or reverse that policy when confronted by the threat of war. So long as they see, or think they see, any possibility of success, they will elect to fight rather than face the humiliation and probable internal revolt which submission to the demands of their opponents would entail.

For Japan the war was one of a limited objective. Her initial victories placed her in possession of territories with the raw materials which she had always coveted and which, could she but retain them, would free her from that economic dependence upon the United States and the British Commonwealth which her military leaders had always regarded as dangerous. Having gained them, she hoped, aided by the remoteness of the main centres of strength of her adversaries, to hold them against any counter-attack. In this she in her turn underrated both the determination and the ingenuity of her enemies—particularly of the United States. She had decided upon war without reference to Germany and she elected to fight it with the minimum of co-ordination with the strategy of that Power, with whom indeed she remained at cross-purposes over the question of the Soviet Union. Thus she failed either to join hands with her Axis partners in the Middle East, or to combine with Germany against the Soviet Union. This parochialism of her war leaders doomed her to defeat, for her one chance of victory lay in co-operating with her European allies to hamstring their enemies at sea, which there was a possibility of doing in 1942. In the event it was she herself who found her mercantile marine decimated and her communications hamstrung, and what had begun as a war for empire turned into one for survival.

This was so because, in their fear and hatred of Japan, the American and British Governments came to overrate her as much as they had previously underrated her and to make her complete destruction as a Power their primary aim. In this there appears to have been no disagreement between Roosevelt and Churchill. The latter's memoirs show that they discussed the unconditional surrender formula at Casablanca, and that Churchill wanted to exclude Italy.[1] This was put up to the British War Cabinet, which disliked the idea of omitting Italy. Churchill, who evidently still wanted her excluded, then dropped the matter of unconditional surrender, which was not included in the official agreed communiqué.[2] There then followed Roosevelt's calculated indiscretion at the press conference of 24 January 1943, in which Churchill, surprised and disconcerted though he was, could not but concur.[3] Churchill was upset, however, simply because he was now committed to

---

[1] Churchill, *Second World War*, iv. 613.
[2] ibid. pp. 614–15.
[3] ibid. p. 615.

include Italy, not because he disapproved of the unconditional surrender formula in the case of either Germany or Japan.

But, if the exclusion of Italy could be considered, why could not also that of Japan? Japan's record was no worse than that of Italy, who in 1940 had fallen upon Great Britain and France simply to ensure herself a share in the spoils of a German victory which Mussolini supposed was already ensured. Japan had not done this; she had fought only when she was driven into a corner, as was well known to both Roosevelt and Churchill. Furthermore Japan was not a totalitarian dictatorship in the sense that Germany and Italy were; something, if not as yet the full story, was known of the internal divisions with which she had been afflicted, and which the victory of the war party in December 1941 had by no means obliterated. The unconditional surrender formula ensured the continued dominance of the Army in Japan, even after the fall of Tojo and of Koiso, because, despite Allied statements that the destruction of the Japanese nation was not intended, it was not clear, until the Potsdam Declaration and the subsequent exchanges of Notes between Japan and the Allies, just what *was* intended. Until then, the advocates of peace in Japan could always be met with the reply that it was useless to talk of peace when the Allies insisted that Japan must first lay down her arms and put herself at their mercy. In the end, the formula had in fact, if not in name, to be modified, since the Potsdam Declaration and the American Note of 10 August 1945 did in fact constitute terms to which the Allies were publicly committed. As Cordell Hull, who was at heart opposed to the formula, puts it, 'Japan surrendered ... when she perceived that the principle of unconditional surrender could be applied conditionally.'[1]

The terms were such that no Japanese Government—or any other Government—would have accepted until it was clear that the alternative was invasion and utter destruction. Even then the military leaders, who still believed that a prolonged resistance would secure less arduous conditions, gave way only upon the personal intervention of the Emperor. By this he saved his throne and his people, for had the projected invasions of the main Japanese islands in 1945 and 1946 actually been launched, there seems no doubt that they would, albeit at great cost, have been successful. All Japan would then have been laid in ruins and the

[1] Hull, *Memoirs*, ii. 1582.

greater part of her people might well have perished in battle, or by famine and disease.

The Potsdam Declaration, which referred to the previous Cairo Declaration of December 1943, provided that Japan should be stripped of all her overseas possessions, should be and should remain disarmed, and, to ensure this, temporarily occupied. The Cairo Declaration had declared that all the territories that Japan had 'stolen' from the Chinese, such as Manchuria, Formosa, and the Pescadores, should be restored to the Chinese, and that she should be expelled from all other territories which she had taken 'by violence and greed'. But this made no distinction between territories which Japan had overrun, but to which she had no legal title, and those such as Korea, Formosa, or Karafuto (southern Sakhalin), which she had acquired by treaty at the end of a victorious war, and had retained with the acquiescence of the Powers in general. If that constituted acquisition by 'violence and greed', the same was true of most of the territories held by Western Powers in the Far East and Pacific, to say nothing of other regions. Such a principle had dangerous implications, especially for Great Britain, with her numerous dependencies. That was something which might have been apprehended at the time, as also might the consequences of depriving Japan of all her colonies. The decision meant that her crowded population must either live on charity, or else enter into more bitter competition for markets than had been the case before the war. This, again, should have been a matter of concern to Great Britain.

Moreover, the complete demilitarization of Japan, combined with the political disunity and industrial backwardness of China, meant that there would be no power in the Far East capable of preventing its domination by the USSR. For the sea and air power of the United States and the British Commonwealth, which was decisive against the island empire of Japan, could not be so effectually exercised against the Eurasian land mass. This, also, was something which might have been foreseen, for it had in the past been the policy of both Washington and London, while opposing Japanese aspirations to the hegemony of the Far East, to regard Japan as a check upon similar Russian designs, and to aim at the preservation of an equilibrium of power in that region.

Had these considerations weighed with Allied statesmen, peace terms could have been offered Japan which would have ensured the attainment of the pre-war objectives of American and of British diplomacy. These were: the abandonment of Japanese plans for political and economic control in China and the removal of the Japanese threat to South East Asia. By the end of 1943 Japan had been constrained by her reverses to cancel her 'basic treaty' of November 1940 with the Wang Ching-wei régime, and to concede, theoretically, the independence of Burma and the Philippines. These were, indeed, mere paper promises while her armies remained in occupation of those countries, and, whatever the intentions of Shigemitsu, were meant by Tojo to rally Asiatic opinion against the West. But in the summer of 1944 the crippling of the Japanese naval air arm in the Battle of the Philippine Sea, the breaching of her inner defence line at Saipan, and the progressive destruction of her mercantile marine, made it clear that she had lost the Greater East Asia War. At the same time the success of the Normandy landings spelled doom for her German ally, who had refused to heed her repeated advice to cut his losses in the East and to come to terms with the Soviet Union. The fall of the Tojo Cabinet was the outward sign of Japanese reaction to these events. Had the Allies then been in a position to offer Japan terms of peace based on the territorial *status quo ante*, but providing for the return of Manchuria to China, with safeguards for Japanese industrial enterprises there, and also for the progressive concession of self-government to the people of Korea and of Formosa, the odds are that she would have been glad to take them.

But it must be fairly recognized that they were not in such a position. The humiliating defeats which Japan had inflicted upon American and British arms in the initial stages of the conflict had aroused public opinion, especially in America, against her to such a degree that nothing short of her complete downfall would have satisfied it. This mood, too, was hardened by the increasing knowledge of the savagery which her soldiers had displayed towards military and civilian captives. Thus a settlement which reason and expediency might have recommended was ruled out of court by the bitter opposition which any suggestion of it would have infallibly produced, especially, though not exclusively, in the United States and in the British Pacific Dominions.

In any case, such considerations were far from the minds of Roosevelt and Churchill. Their concept of the post-war world was one in which a decisive preponderance of armed strength was to be vested in the three great 'satiated' Powers—the United States, the USSR, and the British Commonwealth. These, working in co-ordination, were to be the 'policemen' of the world.[1] The dissatisfied and expansionist peoples were to be rendered impotent through being disarmed, as well as through political division (in the case of Germany) and losses of territory which would make it impossible for them again to threaten the peace. In this matter the only divergence between Roosevelt and Churchill was that the former would have added a fourth 'policeman'— China, whereas Churchill was completely sceptical of China's ability to play any such role. But, apart from his determination to recover all British territory and his opposition to Roosevelt's anti-colonialism, Churchill's interest in Far Eastern political questions was relatively slight, and he went along with Roosevelt in these matters.[2]

The idea that the Soviet Union could be regarded as a national State, with limited territorial ambitions, of which the satisfaction would content her, proved to be a fundamental misconception. The USSR was, and had never ceased to be, the citadel of the Communist revolutionary movement, which was world-embracing in its aspirations, in contrast to the relatively limited objectives of the Axis Powers and of Japan. Yet, during 1941–5, the soft-pedalling of Communist ideological theory, the stress on Russian nationalist themes in Moscow's war propaganda, and the apparent abolition of the Comintern, all combined to give the impression that the fanatical and proselytizing epoch of the Russian Communist movement was beginning to give way to a mellower era in which the permanent coexistence of other ideologies and Powers might be accepted. Stalin not unnaturally sought to foster this impression; hard-bitten, suspicious, and exacting as he often

[1] 'I answered [to Stalin at Teheran] that I wished to meet the Russian grievance [the lack of warm water ports], because the government of the world must be entrusted to satisfied nations, who wished nothing more for themselves than what they had. If the world-government were in the hands of hungry nations there would always be danger. But none of us had any reason to seek for anything more. The peace would be kept by peoples who lived in their own way and were not ambitious. Our power placed us above the rest. We were like rich men dwelling at peace within their habitations' (Churchill, *Second World War*, v. 337).

[2] 'What we had apprehended from Chiang Kai-shek's presence [at Cairo] now in fact occurred. The talks of the British and American Staffs were sadly distracted by the Chinese story, which was lengthy, complicated, and minor' (ibid. p. 289). Churchill makes no reference to the territorial decisions embodied in the Cairo Declaration.

showed himself, it was as the leader of the Russian people, rather than as the successor of Marx and Lenin, that he conferred with his Western Allies. The demands that he made of them, considerable though these were, he put forward on a basis of Russian national security. It is, therefore, understandable that whatever the theoretical tenets of Communism, whether formulated by Marx, Lenin, or in subsequent years by Stalin himself, might contain about the incompatibility between Communism and all other creeds, it was believed that in fact the USSR might live with its neighbours, if not in perfect accord, at all events without mortal hostility.

There had, in recent years, been nothing in Soviet Far Eastern policy to weaken this belief. The Soviet Union, while upholding the Kuomintang-Communist united front in China and deprecating the rifts that appeared in it, had in 1937 concluded a Pact of Non-Aggression with the Chinese National Government, and during 1937–41 had rendered a measure of economic and even military assistance to that Government. The Soviet-Japanese Neutrality Pact of 1941 had been a blow to China, but had not been followed by any general deal with Japan at the expense of China, or withdrawal of diplomatic recognition from Chungking. The Pact with Japan was understandable in view of the German menace and it was equally comprehensible that, after that menace materialized in June, 1941, the USSR should be extremely circumspect in its attitude towards the Pacific War and should carefully avoid any association with Washington and London in matters which concerned that conflict. Japan, for her part, was equally circumspect in her attitude to the USSR, and, especially after the outbreak of the Pacific War, desired with increasing keenness, not to join Germany against that Power, but to mediate peace between them. This desire the Soviet Government were careful to make known to the United States.

The decision of the two Western Powers to bring about the utter defeat of Japan carried with it as a logical consequence their determination to utilize all available means to that end. One of these was Soviet intervention against Japan, and for this they were ready to pay a price, even if not so high a one as Stalin eventually exacted at Yalta. At the same time the concessions made to him at Yalta, which it was hoped represented the sum of his desiderata in the Far East, were not excessive in the light of the obligations which Stalin assumed in return—intervention against Japan and non-interference in Chinese internal affairs. It should furthermore be borne in mind that, had Stalin's demands been refused, he could have obtained them, and perhaps more, from Japan herself, as the price of non-intervention against her, or of sustaining her resistance by some form of economic aid. Furthermore, the Soviet declaration of war against Japan was an important factor in overcoming the determination of the Japanese military chiefs to stage a last-ditch resistance, because it destroyed the illusion of mediation or even aid from the USSR in which some of them had indulged.

At the time of her surrender in 1945 Japan might well have seemed to be permanently eclipsed as a Power of consequence. But the Imperial House, the symbol of unity, had been saved, the Japanese State had not been dissolved, while the cohesive and tenacious character of her people was bound in time to facilitate recovery from the numbing shock of defeat. Added to this was the fact that her industries, though severely damaged and dilapidated, were still the most developed in Asia, and that her people retained the advantage of eighty years of educational and technical training on Western patterns. Nevertheless, had the economic programme outlined in the Potsdam Declaration been fully implemented, Japan would have suffered permanent injury. But, as in the case of Germany, economic considerations combined with social and political ones to bring about a fairly rapid abandonment of that programme. So, in a few years after her defeat and surrender, it became clear that Japan was destined again to play an important role in Asia and that her eventual re-emergence as a Great Power was by no means an impossibility.

APPENDIX

Principal Documents

1. *The Tripartite Pact*[1]

THREE-POWER PACT BETWEEN GERMANY, ITALY, AND JAPAN SIGNED AT BERLIN, 27 SEPTEMBER 1940

THE Governments of Germany, Italy, and Japan consider it the prerequisite of a lasting peace that every nation in the world shall receive the space to which it is entitled. They have, therefore, decided to stand by and co-operate with one another in their efforts in Greater East Asia and the regions of Europe respectively. In doing this it is their prime purpose to establish and maintain a new order of things, calculated to promote the mutual prosperity and welfare of the peoples concerned. It is furthermore the desire of the three Governments to extend co-operation to nations in other spheres of the world who are inclined to direct their efforts along lines similar to their own for the purpose of realizing their ultimate object, world peace. Accordingly, the Governments of Germany, Italy, and Japan have agreed as follows:

Article 1. Japan recognizes and respects the leadership of Germany and Italy in the establishment of a new order in Europe.

Article 2. Germany and Italy recognize and respect the leadership of Japan in the establishment of a new order in Greater East Asia.

Article 3. Germany, Italy, and Japan agree to co-operate in their efforts on aforesaid lines. They further undertake to assist one another with all political, economic, and military means, if one of the three Contracting Powers is attacked by a Power at present not involved in the European War or in the Chinese-Japanese conflict.

Article 4. With a view to implementing the present pact, joint technical commissions, to be appointed by the respective Governments of Germany, Italy, and Japan, will meet without delay.

Article 5. Germany, Italy, and Japan affirm that the above agreement affects in no way the political status existing at present between each of the three Contracting Parties and Soviet Russia.

Article 6. The present pact shall become valid immediately upon signature and shall remain in force for ten years from the date on which

[1] World Peace Foundation, *Documents on American Foreign Relations*, vol. 3, July 1940–June 1941, ed. S. S. Jones and D. P. Myers (Boston, 1941), pp. 304–5, where it is stated that the authorized English translation there given, which differs from other English translations in the grammatical construction of the preamble, is from the German text.

it becomes effective. In due time, before the expiration of the said term, the High Contracting Parties shall, at the request of any one of them, enter into negotiations for its renewal.

In recognition thereof, the undersigned, duly authorized by their respective Governments, have signed this pact and affixed their seals thereto.

Done in triplicate at Berlin on the 27th day of September, 1940, in the eighteenth year of the Fascist era, corresponding to the 27th day of the ninth month of the fifteenth year of Showa.

2. *Joint Declaration of the Assembly of Greater East Asiatic Nations, Tokyo, 5 November* 1943[1]

IT is the basic principle for the establishment of world peace that the nations of the world have each its proper place and enjoy prosperity in common through mutual aid and assistance. The U.S.A. and the British Empire have in seeking their own prosperity oppressed other nations and peoples. Especially in East Asia they indulged in insatiable aggression and exploitation and sought to satisfy their inordinate ambition of enslaving the entire region, and finally they came to menace seriously the stability of East Asia. Herein lies the cause of the present war.

The countries of Greater East Asia, with a view to contributing to the cause of world peace, undertake to co-operate towards prosecuting the War of Greater East Asia to a successful conclusion, liberating their region from the yoke of British-American domination and assuring their self-existence and self-defence and in constructing a Greater East Asia in accordance with the following principles:—

  I. The countries of Greater East Asia, through mutual co-operation will ensure the stability of their region and construct an order of common prosperity and well-being based upon justice.

 II. The countries of Greater East Asia will ensure the fraternity of nations in their region, by respecting one another's sovereignty and independence and practising mutual assistance and amity.

III. The countries of Greater East Asia, by respecting one another's traditions and developing the creative faculties of each race, will enhance the culture and civilization of Greater East Asia.

 IV. The countries of Greater East Asia will endeavour to accelerate their economic development through close co-operation upon a basis of reciprocity and to promote thereby the general reciprocity of their region.

  V. The countries of Greater East Asia will cultivate friendly relations

[1] Ministry of Greater East Asiatic Nations, *Addresses before the Assembly of Greater East Asiatic Nations* (Tokyo, Nov. 1943), pp. 63–65.

with all the countries of the world and work for the abolition of racial discrimination, the promotion of cultural intercourse, and the opening of resources throughout the world and contribute thereby to the progress of mankind.

3. *Three-Power Proclamation to the People of Japan, Potsdam, 26 July 1945 (Potsdam Declaration)*[1]

(1) WE, the President of the United States, the President of the National Government of the Republic of China, and the Prime Minister of Great Britain, representing the hundreds of millions of our countrymen, have conferred and agree that Japan shall be given an opportunity to end this war.

(2) The prodigious land, sea and air forces of the United States, the British Empire and of China, many times reinforced by their armies and air fleets from the west, are poised to strike the final blows upon Japan. This military power is sustained and inspired by the determination of all the Allied Nations to prosecute the war against Japan until she ceases to resist.

(3) The result of the futile and senseless German resistance to the might of the aroused free peoples of the world stands forth in awful clarity as an example to the people of Japan. The might that now converges on Japan is immeasurably greater than that which, when applied to the resisting Nazis, necessarily laid waste to the lands, the industry and the method of life of the whole German people. The full application of our military power, backed by our resolve, *will* mean the inevitable and complete destruction of the Japanese armed forces and just as inevitably the utter devastation of the Japanese homeland.

(4) The time has come for Japan to decide whether she will continue to be controlled by those self-willed militaristic advisers whose unintelligent calculations have brought the Empire of Japan to the threshold of annihilation, or whether she will follow the path of reason.

(5) Following are our terms. We will not deviate from them. There are no alternatives. We shall brook no delay.

(6) There must be eliminated for all time the authority and influence of those who have deceived and misled the people of Japan into embarking on world conquest, for we insist that a new order of peace, security and justice will be impossible until irresponsible militarism is driven from the world.

(7) Until such a new order is established *and* until there is convincing proof that Japan's war-making power is destroyed, points in Japanese

[1] New Zealand, Dept. of External Affairs, *Select Documents on International Affairs, 1945* (Wellington, 1945).

territory to be designated by the Allies shall be occupied to secure the achievement of the basic objectives we are here setting forth.

(8) The terms of the Cairo Declaration shall be carried out and Japanese sovereignty shall be limited to the islands of Honshu, Hokkaido, Kyushu, Shikoku and such minor islands as we determine.

(9) The Japanese military forces, after being completely disarmed, shall be permitted to return to their homes with the opportunity to lead peaceful and productive lives.

(10) We do not intend that the Japanese shall be enslaved as a race or destroyed as a nation, but stern justice shall be meted out to all war criminals, including those who have visited cruelties upon our prisoners. The Japanese Government shall remove all obstacles to the revival and strengthening of democratic tendencies among the Japanese people. Freedom of speech, of religion, and of thought, as well as respect for the fundamental human rights shall be established.

(11) Japan shall be permitted to maintain such industries as will sustain her economy and permit the exaction of just reparations in kind, but not those which would enable her to re-arm for war. To this end, access to, as distinguished from control of, raw materials shall be permitted. Eventual Japanese participation in world trade relations shall be permitted.

(12) The occupying forces of the Allies shall be withdrawn from Japan as soon as these objectives have been accomplished and there has been established in accordance with the freely expressed will of the Japanese people a peacefully inclined and responsible Government.

(13) We call upon the Government of Japan to proclaim now the unconditional surrender of all Japanese armed forces, and to provide proper and adequate assurances of their good faith in such action. The alternative for Japan is prompt and utter destruction.

4. *Japanese Qualified Acceptance of the Potsdam Declaration, 10 August 1945*[1]

... In obedience to the gracious command of His Majesty the Emperor who, ever anxious to enhance the cause of world peace, desires earnestly to bring about a speedy termination of hostilities with a view to saving mankind from the calamities to be imposed upon them by further continuation of the war, the Japanese Government several weeks ago asked the Soviet Government, with which neutral relations then prevailed, to render good offices in restoring peace vis-à-vis the enemy powers. Unfortunately, these efforts in the interest of peace having failed, the Japanese Government in conformity with the august wish of

[1] SCAP, *Political Reorientation of Japan*, Appendixes, p. 414.

His Majesty to restore the general peace and desiring to put an end to the untold sufferings entailed by war as quickly as possible, have decided upon the following.

The Japanese Government are ready to accept the terms enumerated in the joint declaration which was issued at Potsdam on July 26th, 1945, by the heads of the Governments of the United States, Great Britain, and China, and later subscribed by the Soviet Government, with the understanding that the said declaration does not comprise any demand which prejudices the prerogatives of His Majesty as a Sovereign Ruler.

The Japanese Government sincerely hope that this understanding is warranted and desire keenly that an explicit indication to that effect will be speedily forthcoming'.

5. *Reply by the United States Secretary of State to the Japanese Qualified Acceptance*, 11 *August* 1945[1]

... FROM the moment of surrender the authority of the Emperor and the Japanese Government to rule the state shall be subject to the Supreme Commander of the Allied Powers who will take such steps as he deems proper to effectuate the surrender terms.

The Emperor will be required to authorize and ensure the signature by the Government of Japan and the Japanese Imperial General Headquarters of the surrender terms necessary to carry out the provisions of the Potsdam Declaration, and shall issue his commands to all the Japanese military, naval and air authorities, and to all the forces under their control wherever located to cease active operations and to surrender their arms, and to issue such other orders as the Supreme Commander may require to give effect to the surrender terms.

Immediately upon the surrender the Japanese Government shall transport prisoners of war and civilian internees to places of safety, as directed, where they can quickly be placed aboard Allied transports.

The ultimate form of government of Japan shall, in accordance with the Potsdam declaration, be established by the freely expressed will of the Japanese people.

The armed forces of the Allied Powers will remain in Japan until the purposes set forth in the Potsdam declaration are achieved.

6. *Final Japanese Acceptance*, 14 *August* 1945[2]

WITH reference to the Japanese Government's note of August 10 regarding their acceptance of the provisions of the Potsdam Declaration

[1] ibid. p. 415.   [2] ibid. p. 417.

and the reply of the Governments of the United States, Great Britain, the Soviet Union, and China sent by American Secretary of State Byrnes under the date of August 11, the Japanese Government have the honor to communicate to the Governments of the four powers as follows:—

1. His Majesty the Emperor has issued an Imperial rescript regarding Japan's acceptance of the provisions of the Potsdam Declaration.

2. His Majesty the Emperor is prepared to authorize and ensure the signature by his Government and the Imperial General Headquarters of the necessary terms for carrying out the provisions of the Potsdam Declaration. His Majesty is also prepared to issue his commands to all military, naval, and air authorities of Japan and all the forces under their control wherever located to cease active operations, to surrender arms and to issue such other orders as may be required by the Supreme Commander of the Allied Forces for the execution of the above-mentioned terms.

7. *Japanese Imperial Rescript on Surrender*[1]

To our good and loyal subjects:

After pondering deeply the general trends of the world and the actual conditions obtaining in our empire today, we have decided to effect a settlement of the present situation by resorting to an extraordinary measure.

We have ordered our Government to communicate to the Governments of the United States, Great Britain, China and the Soviet Union that our empire accepts the provisions of their joint declaration.

To strive for the common prosperity and happiness of all nations as well as the security and well-being of our subjects is the solemn obligation which has been handed down by Our Imperial Ancestors and we lay it close to the heart.

Indeed, we declared war on America and Britain out of our sincere desire to ensure Japan's self-preservation and the stabilization of East Asia, it being far from our thought either to infringe upon the sovereignty of other nations or to embark upon territorial aggrandizement.

But now the war has lasted for nearly four years. Despite the best that has been done by everyone—the gallant fighting of the military and naval forces, the diligence and assiduity of our servants of the State and the devoted service of our one hundred million people—the war situation has developed not necessarily to Japan's advantage, while general trends of the world have all turned against her interest.

[1] *Syonan Sinbun*, 20 Aug. 1945. Kase (*Eclipse of the Rising Sun*, p. 256) says that the original draft read 'the war situation went daily from bad to worse'. This was modified at the insistence of the War Minister.

Moreover, the enemy has begun to employ a new and most cruel bomb, the power of which to do damage is, indeed, incalculable, taking the toll of many innocent lives. Should we continue to fight, it would not only result in an ultimate collapse and obliteration of the Japanese nation, but also it would lead to the total extinction of human civilization.

Such being the case, how are we to save the millions of our subjects, or to atone ourselves before the hallowed spirits of our imperial ancestors? This is the reason why we have ordered the acceptance of the provisions of the joint declaration of the powers.

We cannot but express the deepest sense of regret to our allied nations of East Asia, who have consistently co-operated with the Empire towards the emancipation of East Asia.

The thoughts of those officers and men as well as others who have fallen in the fields of battle, those who died at their posts of duty, and those who met with death and all their bereaved families, pains our heart night and day.

The welfare of the wounded and the war sufferers, and of those who have lost their home and livelihood is the object of our profound solicitude. The hardships and sufferings to which our nation is to be subjected hereafter will be certainly great.

We are keenly aware of the inmost feelings of all you, our subjects. However, it is according to the dictates of time and fate that we have resolved to pave the way for a grand peace for all the generations to come by enduring the unendurable and suffering what is unsufferable. Having been able to save and maintain the structure of the Imperial State, we are always with you, our good and loyal subjects, relying upon your sincerity and integrity.

Beware most strictly of any outbursts of emotion that may engender needless complications, and of any fraternal contention and strife that may create confusion, lead you astray and cause you to lose the confidence of the world.

Let the entire nation continue as one family from generation to generation, ever firm in its faith in the imperishableness of its divine land, and mindful of its heavy burden of responsibilities, and the long road before it. Unite your total strength to be devoted to the construction for the future. Cultivate the ways of rectitude, nobility of spirit, and work with resolution so that you may enhance the innate glory of the Imperial State and keep pace with the progress of the world.

8. *Japanese Imperial Rescript to the Armed Forces*[1]

SINCE we declared war on America and Britain already three years and eight months have elapsed and during this period our Army and Navy

[1] *Syonan Sinbun,* 21 Aug. 1945.

forces have fought gallantly on fields wild and full of plague and on the raging seas. We are deeply pleased with this. With the Soviet Russia entering the war arena and perceiving that situations at home and abroad would make continuance of war only result in added horrors of war, eventually endangering the very existence of the Empire and notwithstanding that our Imperial Army and Navy forces are still burning with undying fighting spirit, We intend concluding peace with America, Britain, Soviet Russia, and Chungking in order to secure our glorious national polity. We are deeply grieved when we remember our dutiful and gallant officers and men who have died in action as well as of illness and we firmly believe that ye soldiers' faith and gallantry is the gem of our nation true to the tradition of thousands of years. Ye soldiers, We command that ye endeavour to consolidate the foundation of our State for many years to come, by acting in accordance with our wishes, standing in solidarity, and by bearing and overcoming what may seem impossible.

9. *MacArthur's General Order No. 1, September* 1945[1] (*Principal Provisions*)

THE Imperial General Headquarters by direction of the Emperor, and pursuant to the surrender to the Supreme Commander for the Allied powers of all Japanese armed forces by the Emperor, hereby orders all of its commanders in Japan and abroad to cause the Japanese armed forces and Japanese-controlled forces under their command to cease hostilities at once, to lay down their arms, to remain in their present locations and to surrender unconditionally to commanders acting on behalf of the United States, the Republic of China, the United Kingdom and the British Empire, and the Union of Soviet Socialist Republics, as indicated hereafter or as may be further directed by the Supreme Commander for the Allied Powers.

Immediate contact will be made with the indicated commanders, or their designated representatives, subject to any changes in detail prescribed by the Supreme Commander for the Allied Powers, and their instructions will be completely and immediately carried out.

(*a*) The senior Japanese commanders and all ground, sea, air and auxiliary forces within China (excluding Manchuria), Formosa, and French Indo-china north of 16 degrees north latitude shall surrender to Generalissimo Chiang Kai-shek.

(*b*) The senior Japanese commanders and all ground, sea, air and auxiliary forces within Manchuria, Korea north of 38 degrees north latitude and Karafuto shall surrender to the Commander in Chief of Soviet forces in the Far East.

[1] SCAP, *Political Reorientation of Japan*, Appendix, p. 442.

(*c*) The senior Japanese commanders and all ground, sea, air and auxiliary forces within the Andamans, Nicobars, Burma, Thailand, French Indo-China south of 16 degrees north latitude, Malaya, Borneo, Netherlands Indies, New Guinea, Bismarcks, and the Solomons, shall surrender to the Supreme Allied Commander, South East Asia Command or the commanding general, Australians, to be arranged between them, and the details of this paragraph then prepared by the Supreme Commander for the Allied Powers.

(*d*) The senior Japanese commanders and all ground, sea, air and auxiliary forces in the Japanese-mandated islands, Ryukyus, Bonins and other Pacific islands shall surrender to the Commander in Chief, United States Pacific Fleet.

(*e*) The Imperial General Headquarters, its senior commanders, and all ground, sea, air and auxiliary forces in the main islands of Japan, minor islands adjacent thereto, Korea south of 38 degrees north latitude, and the Philippines shall surrender to the Commander in Chief, United States Army Forces in the Pacific.

(*f*) The above indicated commanders are the only representatives of the Allied Powers empowered to accept surrender, and all surrenders of Japanese forces shall be made only to them or to their representatives.

10. *Instrument of Surrender, 2 September* 1945[1]

We, acting by command of and in behalf of the Emperor of Japan, the Japanese Government, and the Japanese Imperial General Headquarters, hereby accept the provisions set forth in the declaration issued by the heads of the Governments of the United States, China and Great Britain 26 July 1945, at Potsdam, and subsequently adhered to by the Union of Soviet Socialist Republics, which four powers are hereafter referred to as the Allied Powers.

We hereby proclaim the unconditional surrender to the Allied Powers of the Japanese Imperial General Headquarters and of all Japanese armed forces and all armed forces under Japanese control wherever situated.

We hereby command all Japanese forces, wherever situated, and the Japanese people to cease hostilities forthwith, to preserve and save from damage all ships, aircraft, and military and civil property and to comply with all requirements which may be imposed by the Supreme Commander for the Allied Powers or by agencies of the Japanese Government at his direction.

We hereby command the Japanese Imperial General Headquarters

[1] US Dept. of State, *Surrender by Japan: Terms between the United States of America and the other Allied Powers and Japan, signed at Tokyo Bay September 2, 1945* (Washington, 1946: US Executive Agreement Series 493).

to issue at once orders to the Commanders of all Japanese forces and all forces under Japanese control, wherever situated to surrender unconditionally themselves and all forces under their control.

We hereby command all civil, military and naval officials to obey and enforce all proclamations, orders, and directives, deemed by the Supreme Commander for the Allied Powers to be proper to effectuate this surrender and issued by him or under his authority and we direct all such officials to remain at their posts and to continue to perform their noncombatant duties unless specifically relieved by him or under his authority.

We hereby undertake for the Emperor, the Japanese Government and their successors to carry out the provisions of the Potsdam Declaration in good faith, and to issue whatever orders and take whatever action may be required by the Supreme Commander for the Allied Powers or by any other designated representative of the Allied Powers for the purpose of giving effect to that declaration.

We hereby command the Japanese Imperial Government and the Japanese Imperial General Headquarters at once to liberate all allied prisoners of war and civilian internees now under Japanese control and to provide for their protection, care, maintenance, and immediate transportation to places as directed.

The authority of the Emperor and the Japanese Government to rule the state shall be subject to the Supreme Commander for the Allied Powers who will take such steps as he deems proper to effectuate these terms of surrender.

11. *Agreement Concerning the Entry of the Soviet Union into the War against Japan, signed at Yalta February 11, 1945, released simultaneously in London, Moscow and Washington, February 11, 1946*[1]

THE leaders of the three Great Powers—the Soviet Union, the United States of America and Great Britain—have agreed that in two or three months after Germany has surrendered and the war in Europe has terminated, the Soviet Union shall enter into the war against Japan on the side of the Allies on condition that:

(1) The *status quo* in Outer-Mongolia (The Mongolian People's Republic) shall be preserved;

(2) The former rights of Russia violated by the treacherous attack of Japan in 1904 shall be restored, viz:

(a) the southern part of Sakhalin as well as all the islands adjacent to it shall be returned to the Soviet Union,

[1] Cmd. 6735.

(*b*) the commercial port of Dairen shall be internationalized, the pre-eminent interests of the Soviet Union in this port being safeguarded, and the lease of Port Arthur as a naval base of the USSR restored,

(*c*) the Chinese-Eastern Railroad and the South-Manchurian Railroad, which provides an outlet to Dairen, shall be jointly operated by the establishment of a joint Soviet-Chinese Company, it being understood that the pre-eminent interests of the Soviet Union shall be safeguarded and that China shall retain full sovereignty in Manchuria.

(3) The Kurile Islands shall be handed over to the Soviet Union.

It is understood that the agreement concerning Outer Mongolia and the ports and railroads referred to above will require concurrence of Generalissimo Chiang Kai-shek. The President will take measures in order to obtain this concurrence on advice from Marshal Stalin.

The Heads of the three Great Powers have agreed that these claims of the Soviet Union shall be unquestionably fulfilled after Japan has been defeated.

For its part the Soviet Union expresses its readiness to conclude with the National Government of China a pact of friendship and alliance between the USSR and China in order to render assistance to China with its armed forces for the purpose of liberating China from the Japanese yoke.

J. V. STALIN. FRANKLIN D. ROOSEVELT. WINSTON S. CHURCHILL.

Bibliography

1. Proceedings of International Tribunals and Government Publications

GERMANY, Auswärtiges Amt. *Documents on German Foreign Policy, 1918–45, from the Archives of the German Foreign Ministry*, published jointly by the US Dept. of State and the British Foreign Office, Series D (1937–45). Washington, USGPO, and London, HMSO, 1949– .

GREAT BRITAIN, Foreign Office. *Documents on British Foreign Policy, 1919–39*, ed. E. L. Woodward and R. Butler, 3rd series, vols. i–iv, 1938–9. London, HMSO, 1949–51.

INTERNATIONAL MILITARY TRIBUNAL, Far East, Tokyo, 1946–8. *Record of Proceedings, Exhibits, Judgment, Dissenting Judgments, Preliminary Interrogations, Miscellaneous Documents* (mimeographed).

INTERNATIONAL MILITARY TRIBUNAL, Nuremberg. *Nazi Conspiracy and Aggression (A collection of documentary evidence and guide materials prepared by the American and British prosecuting staffs for . . . the International Military Tribunal at Nürnberg)*. Washington, USGPO, 1946. 8 vols. with 'Opinion and Judgment' and supplements A and B.

—— *Trial of the Major War Criminals before the International Military Tribunal, 1945–6: Proceedings and documents in evidence*. Nuremberg, 1947–9. 42 vols.

Japan No. 1, 1940, Cmd. 6156. London, HMSO, 1940.

Surrender of Italy, Germany and Japan, World War II: instruments of surrender, public papers and addresses of the President and of the Supreme Commanders . . . October 4, 1945. Washington, USGPO, 1946. (79th Congress, 1st session, Senate document no. 93.)

US Congress, Joint Committee on the Investigation of the Pearl Harbor Attack. *Hearings before the Joint Committee on the Investigation of the Pearl Harbor Attack*. Washington, 1946. 39 pts.

—— *Report of Joint Committee on the Investigation of the Pearl Harbor Attack*. Washington, 1946.

US DEPT. OF STATE. *Foreign Relations of the United States: Japan, 1931–41*. Washington, USGPO, 1946. 2 vols.

—— *Nazi-Soviet Relations, 1939–41: Documents from the Archives of the German Foreign Office*, ed. R. J. Sontag and J. S. Beddie. Washington, USGPO, 1948.

US HOUSE OF REPRESENTATIVES, Committee on Foreign Affairs. *Korean Aid Hearings*, 81st Congress, 1st session, June 8–23, 1949. Washington, USGPO, 1949.

US STRATEGIC BOMBING SURVEY, Naval Analysis Division. *The Campaigns of the Pacific War*. Washington, USGPO, 1946.

—— *Interrogations of Japanese Officials*. Vol. ii. Washington, USGPO, 1946.

—— *Japan's Struggle to End the War*. Washington, USGPO, 1946.

US OFFICE OF STRATEGIC SERVICES, Research and Analysis Branch (all published Washington, USGPO, 1944):
Japanese Administration of Burma.
Japanese Administration of Malaya.
Japanese Domination of Thailand.

2. *Other Documentary Collections*

ROYAL INSTITUTE OF INTERNATIONAL AFFAIRS (published London, Oxford University Press for RIIA):
Documents on International Affairs (for the years 1936; 1937; 1938: vol. i; 1939–46).
Survey of International Affairs (for the years 1937: vol. i; 1938: vol. i).

JAPAN, Ministry of Greater East Asia Affairs. *Addresses before the Assembly of Greater East Asiatic Nations.* Tokyo, 1943.

—— *Official Journal of the Japanese Military Administration, Nichi-nichi Shimbun Sha.* Manila, 1942–3.

SCAP, Government Section, *The Political Reorientation of Japan, September 1945 to September 1948.* Washington, 1950. (Appendixes bound separately.)

PHILIPPINE ISLANDS, Ministry of Foreign Affairs, *Bulletin.* Manila, 1944.

3. *Memoirs*[1]

BYRNES, J. F. *Speaking Frankly.* London, Heinemann; New York, Harper, 1947.

CHENNAULT, C. L. *The Way of a Fighter.* New York, Putnam, 1949.

CHURCHILL, W. S. *The Second World War.* Vols. i–v. London, Cassell, 1948–52; Boston, Houghton Mifflin, 1948–51.

CIANO, GALEAZZO. *Ciano's Diary, 1939–43*, ed. Malcolm Muggeridge. London, Heinemann, 1947.

—— *L'Europa verso la Catastrofe.* Milan, Mondadori, 1948.

CRAIGIE, SIR R. *Behind the Japanese Mask.* London, Hutchinson, 1946.

CROSBY, SIR J. *Siam: the Crossroads.* London, Hollis & Carter, 1945.

DEANE, J. R. *The Strange Alliance.* London, Murray; New York, Viking Press, 1947.

DECOUX, J. *A la barre de l'Indochine.* Paris, Plon, 1949.

DIRKSEN, H. VON. *Moscow, Tokyo, London.* London, Hutchinson, 1951.

GOEBBELS, J. *The Goebbels Diaries*, ed. Louis P. Lochner. London, Hamilton, 1948.

GREW, J. C. *Ten Years in Japan.* London, Hammond; New York, Simon & Schuster, 1944.

HASSELL, ULRICH VON. *The Von Hassell Diaries, 1938–1944.* London, Hamilton, 1948.

[1] Where English and American editions exist, the edition used in this book is given first.

HULL, CORDELL. *The Memoirs of Cordell Hull.* London, Hodder & Stoughton; New York, Macmillan, 1948. 2 vols.

KASE, T. *Eclipse of the Rising Sun.* London, Cape, 1951. American ed. *Journey to the Missouri.* New Haven, Yale University Press, 1950.

KORDT, E. *Nicht aus den Akten.* Stuttgart, Union Deutsche Verlagsgesellschaft, 1950.

MOOK, H. J. VAN. *The Netherlands Indies and Japan; Their Relations, 1940–1.* London, Allen & Unwin; New York, Norton, 1944.

PIGGOTT, F. S. G. *Broken Thread; an Autobiography.* Aldershot, Gale & Polden, 1950.

RECTO, C. M. *Three Years of Enemy Occupation: the Issue of Political Collaboration in the Philippines.* Manila, People's Publishers, 1946.

SABATTIER, G. *Le Destin de l'Indochine.* Paris, Plon, 1952.

SHERWOOD, R. E. *The White House Papers of Harry L. Hopkins.* London, Eyre & Spottiswoode, 1949. 2 vols. American ed. *Roosevelt and Hopkins; an Intimate History.* New York, Harper, 1948.

STIMSON, H. L. and M. BUNDY. *On Active Service in Peace and War.* London, Hutchinson; New York, Harper, 1948.

WEIZSÄCKER, E. VON. *The Memoirs of Ernst von Weizsäcker,* trans. J. Andrews. London, Gollancz, 1951.

WELLES, SUMNER. *Seven Decisions that Shaped History.* New York, Harper, 1950. Eng. ed. *Seven Major Decisions.* London, Hamilton, 1951.

4. Secondary Authorities

BELOFF, M. *The Foreign Policy of Soviet Russia.* London, Oxford University Press for RIIA, 1947–9.

BUSTOS, F. *And Now Comes Roxas.* Manila, Bustos, 1946.

Cambridge History of India. Vol. vi. Cambridge University Press, 1932.

CARLSON, E. F. *The Chinese Army: its Organization and Military Efficiency.* New York, IPR, 1940.

CHAPMAN, F. S. *The Jungle is Neutral.* London, Chatto & Windus, 1949.

CHIT, KHIN KYO. *Three Years under the Japanese.* Rangoon, 1945.

COHEN, J. B. *Japan's Economy in War and Reconstruction.* University of Minnesota Press for IPR, 1949.

DALLIN, D. J. *Soviet Russia's Foreign Policy, 1939–42.* New Haven, Yale University Press, 1942.

—— *The Rise of Russia in Asia.* London, World Affairs Book Club, 1950; New Haven, Yale University Press, 1949.

DE MENDELSSOHN, PETER. *Japan's Political Warfare.* London, Allen & Unwin, 1944.

FEILING, K. *The Life of Neville Chamberlain.* London, Macmillan, 1946.

FEIS, H. *The Road to Pearl Harbor.* Princeton University Press, 1950.

GAFENCU, G. *Prelude to the Russian Campaign.* London, Muller, 1945.

GILMOUR, O. W. *With Freedom to Singapore.* London, Benn, 1950.

GRENFELL, R. *Main Fleet to Singapore.* London, Faber, 1951.

HASHIMOTO, T. *Untold Story of Japanese-American Negotiations.* Tokyo, Shiunso Press, 1946.

HASTAIN, R. *White Coolie.* London, Hodder & Stoughton, 1947.

JONES, F. C. *Manchuria Since 1931.* London, RIIA, 1949.

—— *Shanghai and Tientsin, with Special Reference to Foreign Interests.* London, Oxford University Press for IPR, 1940.

KATO, M. *The Lost War.* New York, Knopf, 1946.

KENNEDY, M. D. *The Problem of Japan.* London, Nisbet, 1935.

KRYLOV, I. *Soviet Staff Officer,* trans. E. Fitzgerald. London, Falcon Press, 1951.

MARTIENSSEN, A. *Hitler and his Admirals.* London, Secker & Warburg, 1948.

MEDLICOTT, W. N. *The Economic Blockade.* Vol. i. London, HMSO and Longmans, Green, 1952. (UK Civil Series, *History of the Second World War,* ed. W. K. Hancock.)

MOORE, F. *With Japan's Leaders; an Intimate Record of Fourteen Years as Councillor to the Japanese Government, ending December 7, 1941.* New York, Scribners, 1942; London, Chapman & Hall, 1943.

MORISON, S. E. *History of US Naval Operations in World War II.* Vol. iii: *The Rising Sun in the Pacific.* London, Oxford University Press, 1948; Boston, Little, Brown, 1947 and 1950.

MOURIN, M. *Les Tentatives de paix dans la Seconde Guerre Mondiale, 1939–45.* Paris, Payot, 1949.

PE, U TUN. *Sun Over Burma.* Rangoon, Rasika Ranjani Press, 1949.

PRATT, SIR J. T. *War and Politics in China.* London, Cape, 1943.

REEL, F. *The Case of General Yamashita.* University of Chicago Press, 1949.

REISCHAUER, E. O. *The United States and Japan.* Cambridge, Mass., Harvard University Press, 1950.

TAKEUCHI, T. *War and Diplomacy in the Japanese Empire.* New York, Doubleday, Doran, 1935; London, Allen & Unwin, 1936.

TEICHMAN, SIR E. *Journey to Turkistan.* London, Hodder & Stoughton, 1937.

TIPTON, L. *Chinese Escapade.* London, Macmillan, 1949.

TOSCANO, M. *Le Origini del patto d'acciaio.* Florence, Sansoni, 1948.

WEEDON, M. *Guest of an Emperor.* London, Barker, 1948.

WILLOUGHBY, C. A. *Sorge, Soviet Master Spy.* London, Kimber, 1952.

WU, A. K. *China and the Soviet Union; a Study in Sino-Soviet Relations.* London, Methuen, 1950.

YANAGA, C. *Japan Since Perry.* New York, McGraw-Hill, 1949.

5. *Newspapers, Pamphlets and Periodicals*

Chicago Daily News.

CHINA ASSOCIATION, London. *Annual Report,* 1939–40 and 1940–41.

CHINA, Ministry of Information. *China Handbook, 1937–43.* New York, Macmillan, 1943.

—— *China Newsweek.* London, 1942–9.

Christian Science Monitor.

Daily Telegraph.

Far Eastern Quarterly. Pennsylvania, Lancaster.

Far Eastern Survey. New York, IPR.

Foreign Affairs. New York, Council on Foreign Relations.

History of the Indonesian National Movement. New York, Republic of Indonesia Office, 1949.

India and Pakistan Year Book, 1949. Bombay and Calcutta, Bennett, Coleman & Co., *Times of India Offices.*

International Affairs. London, RIIA.

Japan Chronicle. Tokyo.

Manchester Guardian.

New York Herald Tribune.

New York Times.

Pacific Affairs. New York, IPR.

Peking and Tientsin Times. Tientsin.

Shonan Times ⎫
Syonan Times ⎬ Shonan (Singapore) 1942–5.
Syonan Sinbun ⎭

The Times.

Tokyo Gazette.

Trans-Pacific. Tokyo.

Vietnam's Fight against Fascism. Paris, Vietnam Delegation Information Service, 1948.

INDEX

PRINTED IN
GREAT BRITAIN
AT THE
UNIVERSITY PRESS
OXFORD
BY
CHARLES BATEY
PRINTER
TO THE
UNIVERSITY